ΥΣΤΕΡΟΝΗΜΑΣΕΚΑΙΚΑΛΛΙΟΝΠΕΡ
ΟΥΔΕΠΟΤΕΜΕΝΤΟΝΕΛΕΟΝ
ΧΡΗΜΩΝΑΦΙΣΤΗ ΟΙΝΠΑΙ
ΔΕΥΩΝΔΕΜΕΤΑΣΥΜΦΟΡΑΣ
ΟΥΚΕΝΚΑΤΑΛΕΙΠΕΙΤΟΝΕΑΥΤ
ΛΑΟΝ ΠΛΗΝΕΩΣΟΥΣΟΦ
ΤΑΥΤΗΜΕΙΝΕΙΠ
ΔΕΕΛΕΓΟΤΕΟΝΕΠΙΤΗΝΠΛΗΓΗ
ΣΙΝ ΕΛΕΑΖΑΡΟΣΤΙΣΤΩΝΠΡΩ
ΤΕΥΟΝΤΩΝΓΡΑΜΜΑΤΑΙΩΝ
ΑΝΗΡΗΔΗΤΙΠΡΟΒΕΒΗΚΩΣΤΗΝ
ΗΛΙΚΙΑΝΚΑΙΤΗΝΠΡΟΣΟΨΙΝΠ
ΠΡΟΣΩΠΟΥΚΑΛΛΙΣΤΟΣΑΝΑΧΕ
ΝΩΝΗΝΑΓΚΑΖΕΤΟΦΑΓΕΙΝΥ
ΚΡΕΑΣΟΔΕΤΟΝΜΕΤΕΥΚΑΙΧΟ
ΘΑΝΑΤΟΝΜΑΛΛΟΝ ΗΤΟΝΜΕΤΑ
ΜΥΣΟΥΣΒΙΟΝΑΝΑΛΕΞΑΜΕΝΟΣ
ΑΥΘΕΡΕΤΩΣΕΠΙΤΟΤΥΜΠΑΝΟΝ
ΠΡΟΣΗΓΕΝ ΠΡΟΠΤΥΣΑΣΔΕΚΑ
ΕΔΕΙΤΡΟΠΟΝΠΡΟΣΕΡΧΕΣΟΛ
ΤΟΥΣΥΠΟΜΕΝΟΝΤΑΣΔΙΥΝΑΣΟ
ΩΝΟΥΘΕΜΕΙΣΓΕΥΣΑΣΟΛΙΠΡΟΣ
ΤΟΖΗΝΦΙΛΟΣΤΟΡΓΙΑΝ ΟΙΔΕ
ΠΡΟΣΤΟΠΑΡΑΝΟΜΩΣΠΛΑΓΧΝΙ
ΣΜΩΤΕΤΑΓΜΕΝΟΙΔΙΑΤΗΝΕΚ
ΠΑΛΑΙΩΝΧΡΟΝΩΝΠΡΟΣΤΟΝ
ΑΝΔΡΑΓΝΩΣΙΝΑΠΟΛΑΜΒΑΝΟΝ
ΤΕΣΑΥΤΟΝΚΑΤΙΔΙΑΝΕΝΕΚΑΛΟΥ
ΘΕΝΕΣΚΟΝΤΑΚΡΕΑΘΙΣΟΚΑΘΗΚΟ
ΑΥΤΩΧΡΑΣΘΑΙΑΥΤΟΥΠΑΡΑ
ΣΚΕΥΑΣΘΕΝΤΑ ΥΠΟΚΡΙΝΑΣ
ΦΩΣΕΣΘΙΟΝΤΑΤΑΧΥΠΟΤΟΥΒΑΣΙ
ΛΕΩΣΤΕΤΑΓΜΕΝΑΤΩΝΑΠΟΤΗΣ
ΘΥΣΙΑΣΚΡΕΩΝ
ΝΑΤΟΥΤΟΠΡΑΞΑΣΑΠΟΛΥΘΗΤΟΥ
ΘΑΝΑΤΟΥ ΚΑΙΔΙΑΤΗΝΑΡΧΑΙΑΝ
ΠΡΟΣΑΥΤΟΥΣΦΙΛΙΑΝΤΥΧΟΙΦΙΛ
ΘΡΩΠΙΑΣ ΟΔΕΛΟΓΙΣΜΟΝΑΣΤ
ΑΝΑΛΑΒΩΝ ΚΑΙΑΞΙΟΝΤΗΣΗΛΙ
ΚΙΑΣ ΚΑΙΤΗΣΤΟΥΓΗΡΟΥΣΥΠΕΡ
ΧΗΣ ΚΑΙΤΗΣΕΠΙΚΤΗΤΟΥΣΚΑΙ
ΕΠΙΦΑΝΟΥΣΠΟΛΙΤΕΙΑΣ ΚΑΙΤΡΟ
ΕΚΠΑΙΔΑΟΣΚΑΛΛΑΣΤΗΣΑΝΑΣΤΡ
ΦΗΣ ΜΑΛΛΟΝΑΛΕΤΗΣΑΓΙΑΣΚΑΙ
ΘΕΟΚΤΙΣΤΟΥΝΟΜΟΘΕΣΙΑΣ
ΑΚΟΛΟΥΘΩΣΑΠΕΦΗΝΑΤΟΤΑ
ΧΕΩΣΛΕΓΩΝΠΡΟΠΕΜΠΕΙΝΕΙΣ
ΤΟΝΑΔΗΝ ΟΥΓΑΡΤΗΣΗΜΕΤΕΡΑΣ
ΗΛΙΚΙΑΣΑΞΙΟΝΕΣΤΙΝΥΠΟΚΡΙΘΗΝ

ΙΝΑΠΟΛΛΟΙΣΤΩΝΝΝΕΣ
ΥΠΟΛΑΒΟΝΤΕΣΕΛΕΑΖΑΡΟΝΤΟ
ΕΝΕΝΗΚΟΝΤΑΣΤΗΜΕΤΑΒΕ
ΒΗΝΑΙΣΑΛΛΟΦΥΛΙΣΜΟΝ
ΚΑΙΑΥΤΟΙΔΙΑΤΗΝΕΜΠΗΥΠΟ
ΚΡΙΣΙΝ ΚΑΙΔΙΑΤΟΜΙΚΡΟΝΚΑΙ
ΑΚΑΙΡΕΟΝΖΗΤΗΔΙΑΛΗΝΘΩΣΙ
ΛΙΣΜΟ ΚΑΙΜΥΣΟΣΚΑΙΚΗΛΙΔΑ
ΤΟΥΤΙΠΡΟΣΚΑΤΑΚΤΗΣΩΜΑΙ
ΕΙΓΑΡΚΑΙΣΙΠΤΟΥΠΑΡΟΝΤΟΣΕΞΕ
ΛΟΥΜΑΙΤΗΝΕΞΑΝΘΡΩΠΩΝΤΙ
ΜΩΡΙΑΝ ΑΛΛΑΤΑΣΤΟΥΠΑΝΤΟ
ΚΡΑΤΟΡΟΣΧΕΙΡΑΣ ΟΥΤΕΖΩΝ
ΟΥΤΕΑΠΟΘΑΝΩΝΕΚΦΕΥΞΟΜΑΙ
ΔΙΟΠΕΡΑΝΑΡΙΘΜΕΝΝΥΝΔΙΑΛΑ
ΛΛΑΣΤΟΝΚΙΟΝ ΤΟΥΜΕΝΓΙΡΩΣ
ΑΞΙΟΟΦΑΝΗΣΟΜΑΙ ΤΟΙΣΔΕΝΑΙ
ΟΙΣΟΥΠΟΛΙΓΜΑΙ ΓΝΝΑΙΟΝΚΑ
ΤΑΔΑΟΗΠΟΣ ΕΙΣΤΟΠΡΟΘΥΜΩΣ
ΚΑΙΓΕΝΝΑΙΩΣΥΠΕΡΤΩΝΣΕΜΝ
ΚΑΙΑΓΙΩΝΝΟΜΩΝ ΑΠΕΥΘΑΝΙ
ΤΙΧΕΠΙΤΟΣΑΥΤΑΛΑΣΕΙΠΩΣ
ΕΠΙΤΟΤΥΜΠΑΝΟΝΕΥΘΕΩΣΕΙΛ
ΘΕΝ ΤΩΝΔΑΣΑΓΟΝΤΩΝΠΡΟΣ
ΑΥΤΟΤΗΝΜΙΚΡΟΠΡΟΤΕΡΟΝ
ΕΥΜΕΝΕΙΑΝΗΑΥΣΕΜΕΝΕΙΑΝ
ΔΙΑΤΩΝΠΡΟΣΕΙΡΗΜΕΝΩΝΛΟ
ΓΩΝ ΩΣΑΥΤΟΙΥΠΕΛΑΜΒΑΝΟΝ
ΑΠΟΝΟΙΑΝΕΙΝΑΙ ΜΕΛΛΩΝΔΕ
ΤΑΙΣΠΛΗΓΑΙΣΤΕΛΕΥΤΑΝ ΑΝΑΣΤ
ΝΑΖΑΣΕΠΕΙΠΓΩΚΩΤΩΤΗΝΑΓΙ
ΓΝΩΣΙΝΕΧΟΝΤΙ ΦΑΝΕΡΟΝΕΣΤΙ
ΟΤΙΔΥΝΑΜΕΝΟΣ ΑΠΟΛΥΘΗΝΑΙ
ΤΟΥΘΑΝΑΤΟΥΣΚΛΗΡΑΣΥΠΟΦΕΡΩ
ΚΑΤΑΣΩΜΑΑΛΓΗΔΟΝΑΣΜΑΣΤΙ
ΓΟΥΜΕΝΟΣ ΚΑΤΑΨΥΧΗΝΑΒΗΔΑΣ
ΘΩΔΙΑΤΟΝΑΥΤΟΥΦΟΚΟΝΤΑΥΠ
ΗΙΑΣΧΩ ΚΑΙΟΥΤΟΣΟΥΝΤΟΥΤΟΝ
ΤΟΝΤΡΟΠΟΝΜΕΤΗΛΛΑΞΕΝ ΟΥ
ΜΟΝΟΝΤΟΙΣΑΝΘΡΩΠΟΙΣΑΛΛΑΚΑΙΤΟΙΣ
ΠΛΙΣΤΟΙΣΤΟΥΘΕΟΝΟΥΣΤΟΝΕΑΥΤΗΝ
ΘΑΝΑΤΟΝΥΠΟΔΑΓΜΑΓΕΝΝΕΟΤΗ
ΤΟΣ ΚΑΙΜΝΗΜΟΣΥΝΟΝΑΡΕΤΗΣ
ΚΑΤΑΛΕΙΠΩΝ

7 ΟΥΝΕΒΗΔΑΟΚΑΙΕΠΤΑΑΔΕΛΦΟΥΣ
ΜΕΤΑΤΗΣΜΗΤΡΟΣΣΥΛΛΗΦΘΕΝΤΑΣ
ΑΝΑΓΚΑΖΕΣΘΑΙΥΠΟΤΟΥΒΑΣΙΛΕΩΣ
ΔΙΟΤΩΝ ΑΘΕΜΙΤΩΝΥΙΩΝΚΡΕ
ΩΝΕΦΑΠΤΕΣΘΑΙ ΜΑΣΤΙΞΙΝΚΑΙ ΝΕ

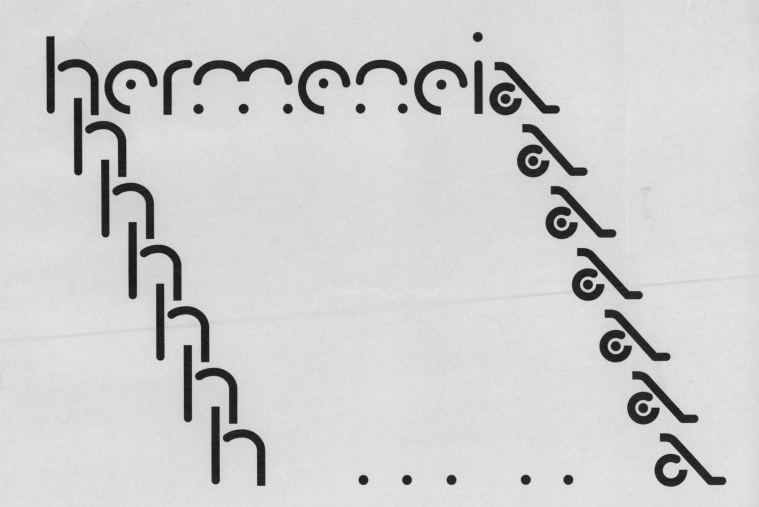

**Hermeneia
—A Critical
and Historical
Commentary
on the Bible**

2 Maccabees

A Critical Commentary

by
Robert Doran

Edited by
Harold W. Attridge

Fortress Press   Minneapolis

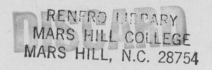
2 Maccabees
A Critical Commentary

Copyright © 2012 Fortress Press, an imprint of Augsburg Fortress

Cover and interior design by Kenneth Hiebert
Typesetting and page composition by
The HK Scriptorium

Library of Congress cataloging-in-publication data is available

The paper used in this publication meets the minimum requirements of American National Standard for Information Sciences—Permanence of paper for Printed Library Materials, ANSI Z329.48–1984.

Manufactured in the U.S.A.

16 15 14 13 12 1 2 3 4 5 6 7 8 9 10

■ *To my three graces*
Susan, Rebecca, and Elizabeth

In memory of my beloved brother,
Richard Doran
(August 17, 1932–June 16, 2011)

The Author

ROBERT DORAN, born in 1940 in Brisbane, Australia, first studied at Blackfriars Studium Generale in Canberra, Australia, before obtaining his Licentiate in Sacred Scripture at the Pontifical Biblical Institute, Rome, in 1971. He then spent a year at the École biblique, Jerusalem, before moving to Harvard Divinity School, where he wrote his doctoral dissertation under John Strugnell. Since 1978 he has been a member of the Religion Department at Amherst College, Amherst, Massachusetts. He is the author of *The Lives of Simeon Stylites* (Kalamazoo, Mich.: Cistercian, 1992); *Birth of a Worldview: Early Christianity in Its Jewish and Pagan Context* (Boulder, Colo.: Westview, 1995); and *Stewards of the Poor: The Man of God, Rabbula, and Hiba in Fifth-Century Edessa* (Kalamazoo, Mich.: Cistercian, 2006).

Contents

2 Maccabees

Foreword — ix
Editor's Note — xi
Preface and Acknowledgments — xiii
Reference Codes
    1. Sources and Abbreviations — xv
    2. Short Titles of Commentaries, Studies and Articles Often Cited — xix
Endpapers — xxvi

■ **Introduction**

The Letters and the Narrative — 1
The Narrative — 3
The Goals of the Author — 13
The Date and Place of Composition — 14
A Suggested Time Line from 2 Maccabees — 17
The Text — 19

■ **Commentary**

1:1-10a	The First Prefixed Letter	23
1:10b-17	The Second Prefixed Letter: Greetings and Well Wishes	39
1:18-36	The Second Prefixed Letter: The Body of the Letter 1	46
2:1-18	The Second Prefixed Letter: The Body of the Letter 2	54
2:19-32	Prologue	65
3:1-39	Heliodorus Comes to the Temple	75
3:40—4:6	Transition to Chaos	91
4:7-22	Jason as High Priest	94
4:23-50	The Death of Onias	112
5:1—6:9a	Antiochus Assaults the Temple	122
6:9b—7:42	Righteous Martyrs	143
8:1-36	Judas Maccabeus Leads a Revolt	167
9:1-29	The End of Antiochus IV Epiphanes	183
10:1-8	The Purification of the Temple	199
10:9-38	Events under Antiochus V Eupator	203
11:1-38	Relations with Lysias	213
Excursus	The Letters in 2 Maccabees 11:16-38	227
12:1-45	Battles with Local Commanders	231
13:1-26	Struggles with Antiochus and Lysias	250
14:1-25	Final Assault on the Temple: The Approach of Nikanor and His Treaty	263
14:26-46	Final Assault on the Temple: The Persecution	276
15:1-36	The Defeat of Nikanor	286
15:37-39	Epilogue	300

■ **Back Matter**

Bibliography — 303
Index — 329
    1. Passages — 329
    2. Names — 350
    3. Greek Words — 352
    4. Subjects — 358
Designer's Notes — 361

The name *Hermeneia,* Greek ἑρμηνεία, has been chosen as the title of the commentary series to which this volume belongs. The word *Hermeneia* has a rich background in the history of biblical interpretation as a term used in the ancient Greek-speaking world for the detailed, systematic exposition of a scriptural work. It is hoped that the series, like its name, will carry forward this old and venerable tradition. A second, entirely practical reason for selecting the name lies in the desire to avoid a long descriptive title and its inevitable acronym, or worse, an unpronounceable abbreviation.

The series is designed to be a critical and historical commentary to the Bible without arbitrary limits in size or scope. It will utilize the full range of philological and historical tools, including textual criticism (often slighted in modern commentaries), the methods of the history of tradition (including genre and prosodic analysis), and the history of religion.

Hermeneia is designed for the serious student of the Bible. It will make full use of ancient Semitic and classical languages; at the same time, English translations of all comparative materials—Greek, Latin, Canaanite, or Akkadian—will be supplied alongside the citation of the source in its original language. Insofar as possible, the aim is to provide the student or scholar with full critical discussion of each problem of interpretation and with the primary data upon which the discussion is based.

Hermeneia is designed to be international and interconfessional in the selection of authors; its editorial boards were formed with this end in view. Occasionally the series will offer translations of distinguished commentaries which originally appeared in languages other than English. Published volumes of the series will be revised continually, and eventually, new commentaries will replace older works in order to preserve the currency of the series. Commentaries are also being assigned for important literary works in the categories of apocryphal and pseudepigraphical works relating to the Old and New Testaments, including some of Essene or Gnostic authorship.

The editors of *Hermeneia* impose no systematic-theological perspective upon the series (directly, or indirectly by selection of authors). It is expected that authors will struggle to lay bare the ancient meaning of a biblical work or pericope. In this way the text's human relevance should become transparent, as is always the case in competent historical discourse. However, the series eschews for itself homiletical translation of the Bible.

The editors are heavily indebted to Fortress Press for its energy and courage in taking up an expensive, long-term project, the rewards of which will accrue chiefly to the field of biblical scholarship.

The editor responsible for this volume is Klaus Baltzer, Emeritus Professor of Old Testament in the Protestant Faculty at the University of Munich.

Peter Machinist   *Helmut Koester*
For the Old Testament   For the New Testament
Editorial Board   Editorial Board

The commentary by Robert Doran contains a fresh translation of the text of 2 Maccabees. Translations from the rest of the New and Old Testaments are usually from the NRSV. Quotations of Latin and Greek authors, except where noted, follow the texts and translations of the Loeb Classical Library, as indicated.

When I had wandered into the seductive fields of late antiquity and Syriac hagiography, the invitation from Professor Cross to return to the war-torn Maccabean times was a challenge I could not resist. Since I had worked on 2 Maccabees in the 1970s, much of the terrain had changed. New inscriptional material from Asia Minor had transformed what we knew of how Seleucid monarchs interacted with their subjects, and the Tyriaion inscription showed how the status of *polis* could be obtained. The Heliodorus inscription made one rethink the events of 2 Maccabees 3. I am indebted to the work of John Ma and Nigel Kennell on these topics. The role of the gymnasium in civic life has been illuminated by the work of Andrzej Chankowski and Angelos Chaniotis. I thank all these scholars, as well as Christopher P. Jones, for patiently enduring my questions via e-mail on all these topics. In addition, I have benefited from many fruitful interactions with Jan Willem van Henten and Daniel R. Schwartz. The generous support of Amherst College and Deans Lisa Raskin and Gregory Call, as well as the inimitable expertise of reference librarians Margaret Groesbeck and Michael Kasper, is most appreciated. I was extremely lucky to have had such an insightful and helpful editor as Harry Attridge. Of course, no words can express my indebtedness to my wife, Susan Niditch, whose incisive sense of the larger tradition of Judaism and her humor kept me sane and in balance.

Finally, I must mention the two giants who inspired me in this work, Frank Moore Cross and John Strugnell (1930–2007). Both scholars and gentlemen, they modeled historical research.

Amherst, Massachusetts
November, 2011

Reference Codes

1. Sources and Abbreviations

AB	Anchor Bible
ABD	*The Anchor Bible Dictionary* (ed. David Noel Freedman; 6 vols.; New York: Doubleday, 1991).
ABRL	Anchor Bible Reference Library
Act. Thom.	*Acts of Thomas*
Aelian	
Var. hist.	*Varia historia*
Aeschylus	
Ag.	*Agamemnon*
Cho.	*Choephori*
Eum.	*Eumenides*
Pers.	*Persae*
Sept.	*Septem contra Thebas*
AGJU	Arbeiten zur Geschichte des antiken Judentums und des Urchristentums
AnBib	Analecta biblica
ANET	*Ancient Near Eastern Texts Relating to the Old Testament* (ed. J. B. Pritchard; 3rd ed.; Princeton: Princeton University Press, 1969)
ANRW	*Aufstieg und Niedergang der römischen Welt* (ed. Hildegard Temporini and Wolfgang Haase; Berlin/New York: de Gruyter, 1972–).
Ap. Const.	*Apostolic Constitutions*
APOT	*The Apocrypha and Pseudepigrapha of the Old Testament* (ed. R. H. Charles; 2 vols.; Oxford: Clarendon, 1913).
Appian	
Bell. civ.	*Bella civilia*
Hisp.	*Hispanica*
Mith.	*Mithridatia*
Syr.	*Syriaca*
Aristophanes	
Ach.	*Acharnenses*
Lys.	*Lysistrata*
Pl.	*Plutus*
Aristotle	
Ath. Pol.	*Constitution of Athens*
Cael.	*De caelo*
Eth. Nic.	*Ethica Nicomachea*
Gen. an.	*De generatione animalium*
Mund.	*De mundo*
Oec.	*Oeconomica*
Poet.	*Poetica*
Pol.	*Politica*
Rhet.	*Rhetorica*
Arrian	
Anab.	*Anabasis*
Artemidorus	
Oneirocr.	*Oneirocritica*
ARW	*Archiv für Religionswissenschaft*
As. Mos.	*Assumption of Moses*
Athenaeus	
Deipn.	*Deipnosophistae*
Athenagoras	
Suppl.	*Supplicatio pro Christianis*
b.	*See Rabbinic Writings*
BA	*Biblical Archaeologist*
BAR	*Biblical Archaeology Review*
BCH	*Bulletin de correspondance hellénique*
Ber.	*See Rabbinic Writings*
BEThL	Bibliotheca ephemeridum theologicarum lovaniensium
BGU	*Ägyptische Urkunden aus den Königlichen Museen zu Berlin, Griechische Urkunden* (15 vols.; Berlin: Weidmann, 1895–1983).
Bib	*Biblica*
BJS	Brown Judaic Studies
BZ	*Biblische Zeitschrift*
BZAW	Beihefte zur Zeitschrift für die alttestamentliche Wissenschaft
CA	*Classical Antiquity*
Caesar	
Bell. civ.	*Civil War*
Callimachus	
Epigr.	*Epigrammata*
CBC	Cambridge Bible Commentary
CBQ	*Catholic Biblical Quarterly*
CBQMS	Catholic Biblical Quarterly Monograph Series
CD	Cairo *Damascus Document*
Chariton	
Chaer.	*De Chaerea et Callirhoe*
CIA	*Corpus inscriptionum atticarum* (= *IG*, vols. 1–4)
Cicero	
Div.	*De divinatione*
De or.	*De oratore*
Dom.	*De domo suo*
Fam.	*Epistolae ad familiares*
Phil.	*Phillipicae*
Pis.	*In Pisonem*
Verr.	*Actio in Verrem*
CIJ	*Corpus inscriptionum judaicarum* (ed. Jean Baptiste Frey; Vatican City: Pontificio istituto di archeologia cristiana, 1936).
CJZC	Gerd Lüderitz, *Corpus jüdischer Zeugnisse aus der Cyrenaika* (Wiesbaden: Reichert, 1983).
Clement of Alexandria	
Strom.	*Stromateis*

ConBNT	Coniectanea biblica: New Testament
CP	*Classical Philology*
CPJ	*Corpus papyrorum judaicarum* (ed. V. Tcherikover and A. Fuks; 3 vols.; Cambridge, Mass.: Harvard University Press, 1957–64).
Demosthenes	
Cor.	*De corona*
Dio Chrysostom	
Or.	*Orations*
Dionysius of Halicarnassus	
Ant. Rom.	*Antiquitates romanae*
Comp.	*De compositione verborum*
Pomp.	*Epistola ad Pompeium*
Thuc.	*De Thucydide*
Dioscorides	
Mat. Med.	*De materia medica*
DJD	Discoveries in the Judaean Desert
DSD	*Dead Sea Discoveries*
EA	Amarna letters
EA	*Epigraphica Anatolica*
Ep. Arist.	*Epistle* (or *Letter*) *of Aristeas*
EtB	Études bibliques
Euripides	
Bacch.	*Bacchae*
Frag.	*Fragments*
Herc. fur.	*Hercules Furens*
Iph. Aul.	*Iphigenia Aulidensis*
Phoen.	*Phoenissae*
Rhes.	*Rhesus*
Suppl.	*Supplices*
Eusebius	
Hist. eccl.	*Historia ecclesiastica*
Praep. ev.	*Praeparatione evangelica*
FB	Forschung zur Bibel
FF	Foundations and Facets
FGH	*Die Fragmente der griechischen Historiker* (ed. Felix Jacoby; 3 vols.; Berlin: Weidmann, 1923–58; reprinted, Leiden: Brill, 1954–64).
Frag.	*Fragment(s)*
Frontinus	
Strat.	*Strategematica*
GRBS	*Greek, Roman and Byzantine Studies*
HA	Handbuch der Altertums-Wissenschaft
Hesiod	
Theog.	*Theogonia*
Homer	
Il.	*Iliad*
Od.	*Odyssey*
HSCP	*Harvard Studies in Classical Philology*
HSM	Harvard Semitic Monographs
HTR	*Harvard Theological Review*
HUCA	*Hebrew Union College Annual*
HZ	*Historische Zeitschrift*
IEJ	*Israel Exploration Journal*
IG	*Inscriptiones Graecae* (Berlin: G. Reimer, 1924–).
I. Delos	*Inscriptions de Delos* (Paris: H. Champion, 1926–).
I. Priene	*Inschriften von Priene* (ed. F. Hiller von Gärtringen; Berlin: Reimer, 1906).
I. Sultan Daği	Lloyd Jonnes, *The Inscriptions of the Sultan Daği*, vol. 1 (Inschriften griechischer Städte aus Kleinasien 62; Bonn: Habelt, 2002).
Isocrates	
Ad Dem.	*Epistola ad Demosthenem*
Ad Nic.	*Ad Nicoclem*
Paneg.	*Panegyricus*
Phil.	*Philippus*
JANESCU	*Journal of the Ancient Near Eastern Society of Columbia University*
JAOS	*Journal of the American Oriental Society*
JBL	*Journal of Biblical Literature*
JH	*Jewish History*
JHS	*Journal of Hellenic Studies*
JJS	*Journal of Jewish Studies*
JNES	*Journal of Near Eastern Studies*
JNSL	*Journal of Northwest Semitic Languages*
Josephus	
Ant.	*Antiquitates judaicae*
Ap.	*Contra Apionem*
Bell.	*Bellum judaicum*
Vita	*Vita*
JQR	*Jewish Quarterly Review*
JRA	*Journal of Roman Archaeology*
JRS	*Journal of Roman Studies*
JSHRZ	Jüdische Schriften aus hellenistisch-römischer Zeit
JSJ	*Journal for the Study of Judaism*
JSJSup	Journal for the Study of Judaism, Supplements
JSNT	*Journal for the Study of the New Testament*
JSOTSup	Journal for the Study of the Old Testament, Supplements
JSP	*Journal for the Study of the Pseudepigrapha*
JSS	*Journal of Semitic Studies*
Lactantius	
Mort.	*De morte persecutorum*
LSJ	H. G. Liddell, R. Scott, and H. S. Jones, *A Greek–English Lexicon* (9th ed., with revised supplement; Oxford: Clarendon, 1996).
Lucian	
Alex.	*Alexander*
Anach.	*Anacharsis*
Encom. Demosth.	*In Praise of Demosthenes*
Hist. conscr.	*Quomodo historia conscribenda sit*
Macr.	*Macrobii*

Nigr.	*Nigrinus*		(ed. A. S. Hunt; London:
Pisc.	*Piscator*		Quaritch, 1911–52).
Tyr.	*Tyrannicida*	*P. Tebt.*	*Tebtunis Papyri* (ed. E. Grenfell,
Zeux.	*Zeuxis*		A. S. Hunt, and J. G. Smyly;
Lycurgus			London: Frowde, 1902–).
Leoc.	*Oration against Leocrates*	PEQ	*Palestine Exploration Quarterly*
m.	*See* Rabbinic Writings	PG	*Patrologia cursus completus: Series*
Mart. Isa.	*Martyrdom of Isaiah*		*graeca* (ed. J.-P. Migne; 162 vols.;
Mart. Pol.	*Martyrdom of Polycarp*		Paris: J.-P. Migne, 1857–86).
NEAEHL	*The New Encyclopedia of*	Philo	
	Archaeological Excavations in	*Abr.*	*De Abrahamo*
	the Holy Land (ed. Ephraim	*Cher.*	*De cherubim*
	Stern; 4 vols.; Jerusalem: Israel	*Decal.*	*De decalogo*
	Exploration Society and Carta,	*Deus imm.*	*Quod Deus sit immutabilis*
	1993).	*Flacc.*	*In Flaccum*
NEchtB	Die neue Echter Bibel	*Gig.*	*De gigantibus*
NovTSup	Supplements to Novum	*Leg. Gaj.*	*Legatio ad Gajum*
	Testamentum	*Mut. Nom.*	*De mutatione nominum*
NTOA	Novum Testamentum et orbis	*Praem. poen.*	*De praemiis et poenis*
	antiquus	*Spec. leg.*	*De specialibus legibus*
OGIS	*Orientis graeci inscriptiones selectae*	*Virt.*	*De virtutibus*
	(ed. W. Dittenberger; 2 vols.;	*Vit. Mos.*	*De vita Mosis*
	Leipzig: Hirzel, 1903–5).	Pindar	
OLA	Orientalia lovaniensia analecta	*Isthm.*	*Isthmian Odes*
OTP	*The Old Testament Pseudepigrapha*	*Nem.*	*Nemean Odes*
	(ed. James H. Charlesworth;	*Olymp.*	*Olympian Odes*
	2 vols.; Garden City, N.Y.:	*Pyth.*	*Pythian Odes*
	Doubleday, 1983, 1985).	PL	*Patrologia cursus completus: Series*
Papyri			*latina* (ed. J.-P. Migne; 217 vols.;
P. Amh.	*Amherst Papyri* (ed. B. Grenfell,		Paris: J.-P. Migne, 1844–64).
	A. Hunt, et al.; London: Frowde,	Plato	
	1900–1901).	*Alc.*	*Alcibiades*
P. Hibeh	*The Hibeh Papyri* (ed. B. Grenfell	*Hipp.*	*Hipparchus*
	and A. Hunt; London, Boston:	*Leg.*	*Leges*
	Egypt Exploration Fund, 1906).	*Phaed.*	*Phaedo*
P. Leid.	Rijksmuseum van Oudheden	*Phaedr.*	*Phaedrus*
	te Leiden, *Papyri graeci Musei*	*Prot.*	*Protagoras*
	antiquarii publici Lugduni-Batavi	*Resp.*	*Republic*
	(Lugduni Batavorum: In Museo	*Tim.*	*Timaeus*
	antiquarie and H. W. Hazenberg,	Pliny	
	1843–1885).	*Hist. nat.*	*Historia naturalis*
P. Lond.	*Greek Papyri in the British Museum*	Plutarch	
	(ed. F. G. Kenyon, H. I. Bell, and	*Aem.*	*Life of Aemelius Paulus*
	W. E. Crum; London: British	*Ag. Cleom.*	*Agis et Cleomenes*
	Museum, 1893).	*Amat.*	*Amatorius*
P. Oxy.	*Oxyrhynchus papyri* (ed. B.	*An seni*	*An seni republica gerenda sit*
	Grenfell, A. Hunt, et al.; London:	*Ant.*	*Life of Marcus Antonius*
	Egypt Exploration Fund, 1898–).	*Apoph. lac.*	*Apophthegmata laconica*
P. Petr.	*The Flinders Petrie Papyri* (ed.	*Caes.*	*Life of Julius Caesar*
	J. P. Mahaffy and W. M. Flinders	*Cat. Maj.*	*Cato Major*
	Petrie; Dublin: University	*Cic.*	*Life of Cicero*
	College, Dublin, 1891–1905).	*Cleom.*	*Life of Cleomenes*
P. Polit. Jud.	*Urkunden des Politeuma der Juden*	*Cohib. ira*	*On Controlling Anger*
	von Herakleopolis (144/3–133/2	*Comp. Ag. Cleom.*	*Comparatio Agidis et Cleomenis*
	v. Chr. (P. Polit. Jud.) (ed. James	*cum Ti. Gracch.*	*cum Tiberio et Gaio Graccho*
	Cowhey and Klaus Maresch;	*Dem.*	*Life of Demosthenes*
	Wiesbaden: Westdeutscher	*Demetr.*	*Life of Demetrius*
	Verlag, 2001).	*Flam.*	*Life of Flamininus*
P. Ryl.	*Catalogue of the Greek Papyri in the*	*Glor. Ath.*	*De gloria Athenensium*
	John Rylands Library, Manchester	*Luc.*	*Life of Lucullus*

Lyc.	Life of Lycurgus
Marc.	Life of Marcellus
Mor.	Moralia
Mulier. virt.	Mulierum virtutes
Nic.	Life of Nicias
Per.	Life of Pericles
Phil.	Life of Philopoemen
Pomp.	Life of Pompey
Praec. ger. reip.	Praecepta gerendae reipublicae
Pyrrh.	Life of Pyrrhus
Quaest. conv.	Quaestiones convivales
Quaest. graec.	Quaestiones graecae
Reg. imp. apophth.	Regum et imperatorum apophtheg-mata
Sera	De sera numinis vindicta
Sull.	Sulla
Superst.	De superstitione
Them.	Life of Themistocles
Thes.	Theseus

Ps.-Philo

| L.A.B. | Liber antiquitatum biblicarum |
| Ps. Sol. | Psalms of Solomon |

Ptolemy

| Geog. | Geographia (ed. Alfred Stückelberger and Gred Graßhoff; Basel: Schwabe, 2006). |
| PW | A. F. Pauly, Paulys Realencyclopädie der classischen Altertumswissenschaft (new ed. by G. Wissowa; 49 vols.; Munich: A. Druckenmüller, 1980). |

Qumran Writings

CD	Cairo Damascus Document
1QH	Hodayoth (Thanksgiving Hymns) from Cave 1
1QM	Milḥamah (War Scroll) from Cave 1
1QS	Community Rule from Cave 1
4Q177	Catena A from Cave 4
4Q248	Acts of Greek King from Cave 4
4Q385	Pseudo Ezekiel from Cave 4
4Q402	Songs of the Sabbath Sacrifice from Cave 4
4Q417	Instruction from Cave 4
11Q13	Melchizedek from Cave 11
11Q19	Temple Scroll from Cave 11
11QT	Temple Scroll from Cave 11

Rabbinic Writings

b.	Babylonian Talmud
m.	Mishnah
t.	Tosefta
y.	Jerusalem Talmud

Tractates

Ber.	Berakot
Meg.	Megillah
Pesaḥ.	Pesahim
Šabb.	Šabbat
Šeqal.	Šeqalim
Taʿan.	Taʿanit

Gen. Rab.	Genesis Rabbah
Pesiq. R.	Pesiqta Rabbati
RArch	Revue archéologique
RB	Revue biblique
REA	Revue des études anciennes
REG	Revue des études greques
REJ	Revue des études juives
RHPhR	Revue d'histoire et de philosophie religieuses
RivB	Rivista biblica italiana
RQ	Revue de Qumran
RSR	Recherches de science religieuse
SB	Sources bibliques
SBLDS	Society of Biblical Literature Dissertation Series
SBLSCS	Society of Biblical Literature Septuagint and Cognate Studies
SBLTT	Society of Biblical Literature Texts and Translations
SBS	Stuttgarter Bibelstudien
SCI	Scripta Classica Israelica
S.E.	Seleucid Era
SEG	Supplementum epigraphicum graecum (Amsterdam: Bieben, 1923–).

Seneca the Elder

| Suas. | Suasoriae |

Sextus Empiricus

Adv. gramm.	Adversus grammaticos
SHR	Studies in the History of Religion
Sib. Or.	Sibylline Oracles
SIG	Sylloge inscriptionum graecarum (ed. Wilhelm Dittenberger; 4 vols.; 3rd ed.; Leipzig: Hirzel, 1915–24).
SJLA	Studies in Judaism in Late Antiquity
SNR	Schweizerische numismatische Rundschau

Sophocles

Ai.	Ajax
Ant.	Antigone
El.	Electra
Oed. Col.	Oedipus Coloneus
Oed. Tyr.	Oedipus Tyrannus
Trach.	Trachiniae
SPB	Studia Post-Biblica
SR	Studies in Religion/Sciences religieuses

Strabo

| Geogr. | Geography |
| StTh | Studia Theologica |

Suetonius

Vesp.	Life of Vespasian
SVTP	Studia in Veteris Testamenti pseudepigrapha
t.	See Rabbinic Writings

Tacitus

| Ann. | Annals |

Hist.	*History*
T. Job	*Testament of Job*
TDNT	*Theological Dictionary of the New Testament* (ed. G. Kittel and G. Friedrich; trans. and ed. Geoffrey W. Bromiley; 10 vols.; Grand Rapids: Eerdmans, 1964–76).
Theophilus	
Autol.	*Ad Autolycum*
TLG	Thesaurus Linguae Graecae
TRev	*Theologische Revue*
TSAJ	Texte und Studien zum antiken Judentum
TU	Texte und Untersuchungen
TUGAL	Texte und Untersuchungen zur Geschichte der altchristlichen Literatur
VCSup	Supplements to Vigiliae Christianae
Vergil	
Aen.	*Aeneid*
Georg.	*Georgics*
VT	*Vetus Testamentum*
VTSup	Supplements to Vetus Testamentum
WAW	Writings from the Ancient World
Xenophon	
Anab.	*Anabasis*
Eq.	*De equitandi ratione*
Cyrop.	*Cyropaedia*
Hell.	*Hellenica*
Hier.	*Hiero*
Hist. Graec.	*Historia Graeca*
Mem.	*Memorabilia*
Sym.	*Symposium*
ZAW	*Zeitschrift für die alttestamentliche Wissenschaft*
ZDMG	*Zeitschrift der deutschen morgenländischen Gesellschaft*
ZDPV	*Zeitschrift des deutschen Palästina-Vereins*
ZNW	*Zeitschrift für die neutestamentliche Wissenschaft*
ZPE	*Zeitschrift für Papyrologie und Epigraphik*

2. Short Titles

Abel, *Les livres*
Felix-Marie Abel, *Les livres des Maccabées* (EtB; Paris: Gabalda, 1949).

Adler and Tuffin, *Chronography*
William Adler and Paul Tuffin, *The Chronography of George Synkellos: A Byzantine Chronicle of Universal History from the Creation* (Oxford: Oxford University Press, 2002).

Aneziri and Damaskos, "Städtische Kulte"
Sophia Aneziri and Dimitris Damaskos,
"Städtische Kulte im hellenistischen Gymnasion," in Kah and Scholz, *Das hellenistische Gymnasion*, 247–71.

Arenhoevel, *Theokratie*
Diego Arenhoevel, *Die Theokratie nach dem 1. und 2. Makkabäerbuch* (Walberger Studien der Albertus-Magnus-Akademie, Theologische Reihe 3; Mainz: Matthias Gruenwald, 1967).

Avi-Yonah, *Holy Land*
Michael Avi-Yonah, *The Holy Land: A Historical Geography from the Persian to the Arab Conquest (536 B.C. to A.D. 640)* (Jerusalem: Carta, 2002).

Barclay, *Jews in the Mediterranean Diaspora*
John M. G. Barclay, *Jews in the Mediterranean Diapora: From Alexander to Trajan (323 BCE–117 CE)* (Edinburgh: T&T Clark, 1996).

Bar-Kochva, *Judas Maccabaeus*
Bezalel Bar-Kochva, *Judas Maccabaeus: The Jewish Struggle against the Seleucids* (Cambridge: Cambridge University Press, 1989).

Bar-Kochva, *Seleucid Army*
Bezalel Bar-Kochva, *The Seleucid Army: Organization and Tactics in the Great Campaigns* (Cambridge: Cambridge University Press, 1976).

Bengtson, *Strategie*
Hermann Bengtson, *Die Strategie in der hellenistischen Zeit: Ein Beitrag zum antiken Staatsrecht* (3 vols.; Munich: Beck, 1964–67).

Bergren, "Nehemiah"
Theodore A. Bergren, "Nehemiah in 2 Maccabees 1:10–2:18," *JSJ* 28 (1997) 249–70.

Bévenot, *Die beiden Makkabäerbücher*
Hugo Bévenot, *Die beiden Makkabäerbücher* (Die Heilige Schrift des Alten Testamentes; Bonn: Peter Hanstein, 1931).

Bickermann, "Beiträge zur antiken Urkundengeschichte"
Elias J. Bickermann, "Beiträge zur antiken Urkundengeschichte, I: Der Heimatsvermerk und die staatsrechtliche Stellung der Hellenen im ptolemäischen Ägypten," *Archiv für Papyrusforschung und verwandte Gebiete* 8 (1927) 216–39.

Bickermann, *Der Gott der Makkabäer*
Der Gott der Makkabäer: Untersuchung über Sinn und Ursprung der makkabäischen Erhebung (Berlin: Schocken, 1937).

Bickermann, *God of the Maccabees*
Elias J. Bickermann, *The God of the Maccabees: Studies in the Meaning and Origin of the Maccabean Revolt* (SJLA 32; Leiden: Brill, 1979).

Bickerman, "Héliodore"
Elias J. Bickerman, "Héliodore au Temple de Jérusalem," *Annuaire de l'Institut de Philologie et d'Histoire Orientales et Slaves* 7 (1939–44) 5–40. Reprinted in idem, *Studies,* 2:159–91.

Bickermann, *Institutions*
Elias J. Bickermann, *Institutions des Séleucides* (Bibliothèque archéologique et historique 26; Paris: Geuthner, 1938).

Bickermann, "Ein jüdischer Festbrief"
Elias Bickermann, "Ein jüdischer Festbrief vom
Jahre 124 v. Chr. (II Macc. 1:1-9)," *ZNW* 32 (1933)
233–54.

Bickermann, "Makkabäerbücher"
Elias Bickermann, "Makkabäerbücher (I. und
II.)" *PW* 14:779–97.

Bickerman, *Studies*
Elias J. Bickerman, *Studies in Jewish and Christian
History* (3 vols.; AGJU 9; Leiden: Brill, 1976–86).

Brill's New Pauly
Hubert Cancik and Helmuth Schneider, eds.,
Brill's New Pauly: Encyclopedia of the Ancient World
(16 vols.; Leiden: Brill, 2002–10).

Bringmann, *Hellenistische Reform*
Klaus Bringmann, *Hellenistische Reform und
Religionsverfolgung in Judäa: Eine Untersuchung
zur jüdisch-hellenistischen Geschichte (175–163
v. Chr.)* (Abhandlungen der Akademie der
Wissenschaften in Göttingen, Philologisch-
Historische Klasse 3/132; Göttingen:
Vandenhoeck & Ruprecht, 1983).

Bunge, "'Theos Epiphanes'"
Jochen Gabriel Bunge, "'Theos Epiphanes': Zu
den ersten fünf Regierungsjahren Antiochos IV.
Epiphanes," *Historia* 23 (1974) 57–85.

Bunge, *Untersuchungen*
Jochen Gabriel Bunge, *Untersuchungen zum zweiten
Makkabäerbuch: Quellenkritische, literarische,
chronologische und historische Untersuchungen
zum zweiten Makkabäerbuch als Quelle syrisch-
palästinensischer Geschichte im 2. Jh. v. Chr.* (Bonn:
Rheinische Friedrich-Wilhelms-Universität,
1971).

Bunge, "Zur Geschichte und Chronologie"
Jochen Gabriel Bunge, "Zur Geschichte und
Chronologie des Untergangs der Oniaden und
des Aufstiegs der Hasmonäer," *JSJ* 6 (1975) 1–46.

Chaniotis, *War*
Angelos Chaniotis, *War in the Hellenistic World:
A Social and Cultural History* (Oxford: Blackwell,
2005).

Chankowski, "Les souverains héllenistiques"
Andrzej S. Chankowski, "Les souverains
héllenistiques et l'institution du gymnase:
politiques royales et modèles culturels," in Curty,
L'huile et l'argent, 95–114.

Cohen, "Ἰουδαῖος τὸ γένος"
Shaye J. D. Cohen, "Ἰουδαῖος τὸ γένος and
Related Expressions in Josephus," in Fausto
Parente and Joseph Sievers, eds., *Josephus and the
History of the Greco-Roman Period: Essays in Memory
of Morton Smith* (SPB 41; Leiden: Brill, 1994)
23–38.

Cohen, "Ioudaios"
Shaye J. D. Cohen, "Ioudaios: 'Judaean' and
'Jew' in Susanna, First Maccabees, and Second
Maccabees," in Peter Schäfer, ed., *Geschichte–
Tradition–Reflexion: Festschrift für Martin Hengel
zum 70. Geburtstag*, vol. 1: *Judentum* (Tübingen:
Mohr, 1996) 211–20.

Cohen, "Religion, Ethnicity"
Shaye J. D. Cohen, "Religion, Ethnicity and
'Hellenism' in the Emergence of Jewish Identity
in Maccabean Palestine," in Per Bilde et al.,
eds., *Religion and Religious Practice in the Seleucid
Kingdom* (Studies in Hellenistic Civilization 1;
Aarhus: Aarhus University Press, 1990).

Corsten, *Die Inschriften*
Thomas Corsten, *Die Inschriften von Prusa ad
Olympum* (2 vols.; Inschriften griechischer Städte
aus Kleinasien 39, 40; Bonn: Habelt, 1991, 1993).

Cotton and Wörrle, "Seleukos IV"
Hannah M. Cotton and Michael Wörrle,
"Seleukos IV to Heliodorus: A New Dossier of
Royal Correspondence from Israel," *ZPE* 159
(2007) 191–205.

Couvenhes and Fernoux, *Les cités grecques*
Jean-Christophe Couvenhes and Henri-Louis
Fernoux, eds., *Les cités grecques et la guerre en
Asie Mineure à l'époque hellénistique* (Tours:
Universitaires François-Rabelais, 2004).

Cross, "Divine Warrior"
Frank Moore Cross, "The Divine Warrior in
Israel's Early Cult," in Alexander Altman, ed.,
Biblical Motifs: Origins and Transformations
(Philip W. Lown Institute of Advanced Judaic
Studies, Brandeis University, Studies and Texts
3; Cambridge, Mass.: Harvard University Press,
1966) 11–30.

Curty, *L'huile et l'argent*
Olivier Curty, ed., *L'huile et l'argent: Gymnasiarchie
et évergétisme dans la Grèce hellénistique. Actes du
colloque tenu à Fribourg du 13 au 15 octobre 2005,
publiés en l'honneur du Professeur Marcel Piérart
à l'occasion de son 60ème anniversaire* (Paris:
Boccard, 2009).

Danker, *Benefactor*
Frederick W. Danker, *Benefactor: Epigraphic Study
of a Graeco-Roman and New Testament Semantic
Field* (St. Louis: Clayton, 1982).

Daux, *Delphes*
Georges Daux, *Delphes au IIe et au Ier siècle depuis
l'abaissement de l'Etolie jusqu'à la paix romaine
191-31 av. J.-C.* (Paris: Boccard, 1936).

de Bruyne, *Les anciennes traductions*
Donatien de Bruyne, *Les anciennes traductions
latines des Machabées* (Anecdota Maredsolana 4;
Maredsous: Abbaye de Maredsous, 1932).

Delorme, *Gymnasion*
Jean Delorme, *Gymnasion: Étude sur les monuments
consacrés à l'éducation en Grèce (des origines à
l'Empire romain)* (Paris: Boccard, 1960).

Denniston, *Greek Prose Style*
J. D. Denniston, *Greek Prose Style* (Oxford:
Clarendon, 1965).

Diels and Schramm, *Exzerpte*
Hermann Diels and Erwin Schramm, *Exzerpte
aus Philons Mechanik B.VII und VIII* (Berlin:
Akademie der Wissenschaften, 1920).

Dimant, "Apocryphon of Jeremiah"
Devorah Dimant, "An Apocryphon of Jeremiah from Cave 4 (4Q385^B = 4Q385 16)," in George J. Brooke, ed., *New Qumran Texts and Studies: Proceedings of the First Meeting of the International Organization for Qumran Studies, Paris, 1992* (STDJ 15; Leiden: Brill, 1994) 11–30.

Dommerhausen, *1. Makkabäer 2. Makkabäer*
Werner Dommerhausen, *1. Makkabäer. 2. Makkabäer* (NEchtB 12; Würzburg: Echter Verlag, 1985).

Doran, "Jason's Gymnasion"
"Jason's Gymnasion," in Harold W. Attridge, John J. Collins, Thomas H. Tobin, eds., *Of Scribes and Scrolls: Studies on the Hebrew Bible, Intertestamental Judaism, and Christian Origins Presented to John Strugnell on the Occasion of His Sixtieth Birthday* (College Theology Society Resources in Religion 5; Lanham, Md.: University Press of America, 1990) 99–109.

Doran, *Temple Propaganda*
Robert Doran, *Temple Propaganda: The Purpose and Character of 2 Maccabees* (CBQMS 12; Washington, D.C.: Catholic Biblical Association, 1981).

Enermalm-Ogawa, *Un langage de prière*
Agneta Enermalm-Ogawa, *Un langage de prière juif en grec: Le témoinage des deux premiers livres des Maccabées* (ConBNT 17; Stockholm: Almqvist & Wiksell, 1987).

Exler, *Form*
Francis Xavier J. Exler, *The Form of the Ancient Greek Letter: A Study in Greek Epistolography* (Washington, D.C.: Catholic University of America Press, 1923).

Fischer, *Seleukiden und Makkabäer*
Thomas Fischer, *Seleukiden und Makkabäer: Beiträge zur Seleukidengeschichte und zu den politischen Ereignissen in Judäa während der 1. Hälfte des 2. Jahrhunderts v. Chr.* (Bochum: Brockmeyer, 1980).

Fitzmyer, "Some Notes"
Joseph A. Fitzmyer, "Some Notes on Aramaic Epistolography," *JBL* 93 (1974) 201–25.

Foucault, *Recherches*
Jules A. de Foucault, *Recherches sur la langue et le style de Polybe* (Collection d'études anciennes; Paris: Belles Lettres, 1972).

Frye, *History*
Richard N. Frye, *The History of Ancient Iran* (HA 3.7; Munich: Beck, 1983).

Gauthier, "Bulletin épigraphique"
Philippe Gauthier, "Bulletin épigraphique," *REG* 105 (1992) 435–47.

Gera, "Credibility"
Dov Gera, "On the Credibility of the History of the Tobiads (Josephus, *Antiquities* 12, 156–222, 228–236)," in A. Kasher, U. Rappaport, and G. Fuks, eds., *Greece and Rome in Eretz Israel: Collected Essays* (Jerusalem: Yad Ben-Zvi, 1990) 29–30.

Gera, *Judaea*
Dov Gera, *Judaea and Mediterranean Politics 219 to 161 B.C.E.* (Jewish Studies 8; Leiden: Brill, 1998).

Gera, "Olympiodoros"
Dov Gera, "Olympiodoros, Heliodoros and the Temples of Koilê Syria and Phoinikê," *ZPE* 169 (2009) 125–55.

Gera and Horowitz, "Antiochus IV,"
Dov Gera and Wayne Horowitz, "Antiochus IV in Life and Death: Evidence from the Babylonian Astronomical Diaries," *JAOS* 117 (1997) 240–52.

Ginzberg, *Legends of the Jews*
Louis Ginzberg, *Legends of the Jews* (trans. Henrietta Szold; 7 vols.; Philadelphia: Jewish Publication Society, 1925).

Goldstein, *I Maccabees*
Jonathan A. Goldstein, *I Maccabees: A New Translation with Introduction and Commentary* (AB 41; Garden City, N.Y.: Doubleday, 1976).

Goldstein, *II Maccabees*
Jonathan A. Goldstein, *II Maccabees: A New Translation with Introduction and Commentary* (AB 41A; Garden City, N.Y.: Doubleday, 1983).

Goodman and Holladay, "Religious Scruples"
Martin Goodman and A. J. Holladay, "Religious Scruples in Ancient Warfare," *Classical Quarterly* 36 (1986) 151–71.

Grabbe, "Maccabean Chronology"
Lester Grabbe, "Maccabean Chronology: 167–164 or 168–165 BCE?" *JBL* 110 (1991) 59–74.

Grimm, *Das zweite, dritte und vierte Buch*
Carl L. W. Grimm, *Das zweite, dritte und vierte Buch der Makkabäer* (Leipzig: Hirzel, 1857).

Gruen, *Hellenistic World*
Erich S. Gruen, *The Hellenistic World and the Coming of Rome* (2 vols.; Berkeley: University of California Press, 1984).

Gruen, *Heritage*
Erich S. Gruen, *Heritage and Hellenism: The Reinvention of Jewish Tradition* (Hellenistic Culture and Society 30; Berkeley: University of California Press, 1998).

Habicht, *2. Makkabäerbuch*
Christian Habicht, *2. Makkabäerbuch* (JSHRZ 1; Historische und legendarische Erzählungen 3; Gütersloh: G. Mohn, 1976).

Habicht, "Royal Documents"
Christian Habicht, "Royal Documents in Maccabees II," *HSCP* 80 (1976) 1–18.

Hanhart, *Maccabaeorum liber II*
Robert Hanhart, *Maccabaeorum liber II, copiis usus quas reliquit Werner Kappler* (Septuaginta 9.2; 2nd ed.; Göttingen: Vandenhoeck & Ruprecht, 1976).

Hanhart, *Zum Text*
Robert Hanhart, *Zum Text des 2. und 3. Makkabäerbuches: Probleme der Überlieferung, der Auslegung und der Ausgabe* (Nachrichten der Akademie der Wissenschaften in Göttingen, Philologisch-historische Klasse, 1961, 13; Göttingen: Vandenhoeck & Ruprecht, 1961).

Haran, "Archives"
Menahem Haran, "Archives, Libraries, and the Order of the Biblical Books," *JANESCU* 22 (1993) 51–61.

Hengel, *Judaism and Hellenism*
Martin Hengel, *Judaism and Hellenism: Studies in Their Encounter in Palestine during the Early Hellenistic Period* (2 vols.; London: SCM, 1974).

van Henten, *Maccabean Martyrs*
Jan Willem van Henten, *The Maccabean Martyrs as Saviours of the Jewish People: A Study of 2 and 4 Maccabees* (JSJSup 57; Leiden: Brill, 1997).

Holladay, *Fragments*
Carl R. Holladay, *Fragments from Hellenistic Jewish Authors* (4 vols.; SBLTT 20, 30, 39, 40; Chico, Calif., and Atlanta: Scholars Press, 1983–96).

Holleaux, *Études*
Maurice Holleaux, *Études d'épigraphie et d'histoire grecques* (ed. Louis Robert; 6 vols.; Paris: E. de Boccard, 1952–68).

Honigman, "Jewish Politeuma"
Sylvie Honigman, "The Jewish Politeuma at Heracleopolis," *SCI* 21 (2002) 251–66.

Honigman, "*Politeumata*"
Sylvie Honigman, "*Politeumata* and Ethnicity in Ptolemaic and Roman Egypt," *Ancient Society* 33 (2003) 61–102.

Houtman, *Empsychoi Logoi*
Alberdina Houtman, Albert de Jong, Magda Misset-van de Weg, *Empsychoi Logoi–Religious Innovations in Antiquity* (Leiden: Brill, 2008) 385–401.

Ilan, *Lexicon*
Tal Ilan, *Lexicon of Jewish Names in Late Antiquity* (Tübingen: Mohr, 1995), vol. 1 of Tal Ilan, Thomas Ziem, and Kerstin Hünefeld, *Lexicon of Jewish Names in Late Antiquity* (4 vols.; TSAJ 91; Tübingen: Mohr Siebeck, 2002–).

Inscriptions de Délos
Inscriptions de Délos (Paris: H. Champion, 1926–).

Isaac, "Seleucid Inscription"
Benjamin Isaac, "A Seleucid Inscription from Jamnia-on-the-Sea: Antiochus V Eupator and the Sidonians,"*IEJ* 41 (1991) 132–44.

Jones, "Inscription"
Christopher P. Jones, "The Inscription from Tel Maresha for Olympiodoros," *ZPE* 171 (2009) 100–104.

Jonnes and Rici, "New Royal Inscription"
Lloyd Jonnes and Marijana Rici, "A New Royal Inscription from Phrygia Paroreios: Eumenes II Grants Tyriaion the Status of a *Polis*," *Epigraphica Anatolica* 29 (1997) 1–30.

Kah and Scholz, *Das hellenistische Gymnasion*
Daniel Kah and Peter Scholz, eds., *Das hellenistisch Gymnasion* (Wissenskultur und gesellschaftlicher Wandel 8; Berlin: Akademie, 2004).

Kamerbeek, "Conception"
Jan Coenraad Kamerbeek, "On the Conception of ΘΕΟΜΑΧΟΣ in Relation with Greek Tragedy," *Mnemosyne*, 4th series, 1 (1948) 271–83.

Katz, "Text of 2 Maccabees"
Peter Katz, "The Text of 2 Maccabees Reconsidered," *ZNW* 51 (1960) 10–30.

Kellermann, *Auferstanden*
Ulrich Kellermann, *Auferstanden in den Himmel: 2 Makkabäer 7 und die Auferstehung der Märtyrer* (SBS 95; Stuttgart: Katholisches Bibelwerk, 1979).

Kennell, "New Light"
Nigel M. Kennell, "New Light on 2 Maccabees 4:7-15," *JJS* 56 (2005) 10–24.

Kern, *Die Inschriften*
Otto Kern, *Die Inschriften von Magnesia am Maeander* (Berlin: W. Spemann, 1900).

Kolbe, *Beiträge*
Walter Kolbe, *Beiträge zur syrischen und jüdischen Geschichte: Kritische Untersuchungen zur Seleukidenliste und zu den beiden ersten Makkabäerbüchern* (Stuttgart: Kohlhammer, 1926).

Lange, "2 Maccabees 2:13-15"
Armin Lange, "2 Maccabees 2:13-15: Library or Canon?" in Xeravits and Zsengellér, *Books of the Maccabees,* 155–67.

Launey, *Recherches*
Marcel Launey, *Recherches sur les armées héllenistiques* (2 vols.; Paris: Boccard, 1949, 1950).

Laurentin, "Weʿattah"
André Laurentin, "*Weʿattah – Kai nun:* Formule caractéristique des textes juridiques et liturgiques (à propos de Jean 17,5)," *Bib* 45 (1964) 168–95.

Lenger, *Corpus*
Marie-Thérèse Lenger, *Corpus des ordonnances des Ptolémées (C. Ord. Ptol.): bilan des additions et corrections (1964–1988), compléments à la bibliographie* (Bruxelles: Fondation égyptologique Reine Elisabeth: E. van Balberghe, 1990).

Le Rider, *Suse*
Georges Le Rider, *Suse sous les Séleucides et les Parthes: Les trouvailles monétaires et l'histoire de la ville* (Mémoires de la Mission archéologique en Iran 38; Paris: Geuthner, 1965).

Lindenberger, *Ancient Aramaic and Hebrew Letters*
James M. Lindenderger, *Ancient Aramaic and Hebrew Letters* (ed. Kent Harold Richards; 2nd ed.; WAW 14; Atlanta: Society of Biblical Literature, 2003).

Lüderitz, "What Is the Politeuma?"
Gert Lüderitz, "What Is the Politeuma?" in Jan Willem van Henten and Pieter Willem van der Horst, eds., *Studies in Early Jewish Epigraphy* (AGJU 21; Leiden: Brill, 1994) 183–225.

Ma, *Antiochus III*
John Ma, *Antiochus III and the Cities of Western Asia Minor* (Oxford: Oxford University Press, 1999).

Mason, "Jews, Judaeans"
Steve Mason, "Jews, Judaeans, Judaizing, Judaism: Problems of Categorization in Ancient History," *JSJ* 38 (2007) 457–512.

Milik, *Dédicaces*
Josef T. Milik, "Dédicaces faites par des dieux (Palmyre, Hatra, Tyr) et des thiases sémitiques à l'époque romaine," in *Recherches d'Épigraphie Proche-Orientale,* vol. 1 (Paris: Geuthner, 1972).

Miller, *Divine Warrior*
Patrick D. Miller, *The Divine Warrior in Early Israel* (HSM 5; Cambridge, Mass.: Harvard University Press, 1973).

Mittag, *Antiochus IV. Epiphanes*
Peter Franz Mittag, *Antiochos IV. Epiphanes: Eine politische Biographie* (Klio: Beiträge zur Alten Geschichte n.F. 11; Berlin: Akademie, 2006).

Moffatt, "Second Book"
James Moffatt, "The Second Book of Maccabees," in *APOT* 1:125–54.

Mölleken, "Geschichtsklitterung"
Wolfgang Mölleken, "Geschichtsklitterung im I Makkabäerbuch (Wann wurde Alkimus Hoherpriester?)," *ZAW* 65 (1953) 205–28.

Momigliano, *Prime linee*
Arnaldo Momigliano, *Prime linee di storia della maccabaica* (Turin, 1931; reprinted, Amsterdam: Hakkert, 1968).

Momigliano, "Second Book of Maccabees"
Arnaldo Momigliano, "The Second Book of Maccabees," *CP* 70 (1975) 81–88.

Mørkholm, "Accession"
Otto Mørkholm, "The Accession of Antiochus IV of Syria: A Numismatic Comment," *American Numismatic Society Museum Notes* 11 (1964) 63–76.

Mørkholm, *Antiochus IV*
Otto Mørkholm, *Antiochus IV of Syria* (Classica et mediaevalia, dissertationes 8; Copenhagen: Gyldendal, 1966).

Mørkholm, *Studies*
Otto Mørkholm, *Studies in the Coinage of Antiochus IV of Syria* (Copenhagen: Munksgaard, 1963).

Morrison, "Composition"
Gary Morrison, "The Composition of II Maccabees: Insights Provided by a Literary *topos,*" *Bib* 90 (2009) 564–72.

Moulton and Turner, *Grammar of New Testament Greek*
James H. Moulton and Nigel Turner, *A Grammar of New Testament Greek* (4 vols.; Edinburgh: T&T Clark, 1901–76).

Nickelsburg, *1 Enoch 1*
George W. E. Nickelsburg, *1 Enoch 1: A Commentary on the Book of 1 Enoch, Chapters 1–36; 81–108* (Hermeneia; Minneapolis: Fortress Press, 2001).

Nickelsburg, *Resurrection*
George W. E. Nickelsburg, *Resurrection, Immortality, and Eternal Life in Intertestamental Judaism* (Cambridge, Mass.: Harvard University Press, 1972).

Nicklas, "Der Historiker"
Tobias Nicklas, "Der Historiker als Erzähler: Zur Zeichnung des Seleukidenkönigs Antiochus in 2 Makk. IX," *VT* 52 (2002) 80–92.

Niese, "Kritik"
Benedikt Niese, "Kritik der beiden Makkabäerbücher nebst Beiträgen zur Geschichte der makkabäischen Erhebung," *Hermes* 35 (1900) 268–307, 453–527 = *Kritik der beiden Makkabäerbücher* (Berlin: Weidmann, 1900).

Otto, *Zur Geschichte*
Walter Otto, *Zur Geschichte der Zeit des 6. Ptolemäers: Ein Beitrag zur Politik und zum Staatsrecht des Hellenismus* (Munich: Bayerischen Akademie der Wissenschaften, 1934).

Parker, "Letters"
Victor L. Parker, "The Letters in II Maccabees: Reflections on the Book's Composition," *ZAW* 119 (2007) 386–402.

Parker and Dubberstein, *Babylonian Chronology*
Richard A. Parker and Waldo H. Dubberstein, *Babylonian Chronology 626 B.C.–A.D. 75* (Brown University Studies 19; Providence, R.I.: Brown University Press, 1956).

Préaux, "Les Étrangers"
Claire Préaux, "Les Étrangers à l'époque hellénistique (Egypte-Delos-Rhodes)," *L'Étranger/ Foreigner* (Recueils de la Société Jean Bodin pour l'histoire comparative des institutions 9; Paris: Dessain et Tolra, 1984) 141–93.

Preisigke, *Wörterbuch*
Friedrich Preisigke, *Wörterbuch der griechischen Papyrusurkunden mit Einschluss der griechischen Inschriften, Aufschriften, Ostraka, Mummienschilder usw. aus Ägypten* (ed. E. Kiessling; 4 vols.; Berlin: Selbstverlag der Erben; Wiesbaden: Harrassowitz, 1925).

Pritchett, *Greek State at War*
William Kendrick Pritchett, *The Greek State at War* (4 vols.; Berkeley: University of California Press, 1971–91).

Rajak, *Jewish Dialogue*
Tessa Rajak, *The Jewish Dialogue with Greece and Rome: Studies in Cultural and Social Interaction* (AGJU 48; Leiden: Brill, 2001).

Ray, *Archive of Ḥor*
John D. Ray, *The Archive of Ḥor* (Excavations at North Saqqâra Documentary Series 1; London: Egypt Exploration Society, 1976).

Richnow, "Untersuchung zu Sprache"
Wolfgang Richnow, "Untersuchung zu Sprache und Stil des 2. Makkabäerbuches: Ein Beitrag zur hellenistischen Historiographie" (Ph.D. diss., Göttingen, 1967).

Rigsby, *Asylia*
    Kent J. Rigsby, *Asylia: Territorial Inviolability in the Hellenistic World* (Hellenistic Culture and Society 22; Berkeley: University of California Press, 1996).

Risberg, "Textkritische und exegetische Anmerkungen"
    Bernhard Risberg, "Textkritische und exegetische Anmerkungen zu den Makkabäerbüchern," *Beiträge zur Religionswissenschaft* 27 (1918) 6–31.

Robert, "Un corpus des inscriptions"
    Louis Robert, "Un corpus des inscriptions juives," *REJ* 101 (1937) 73–86.

Robert, *Hellenica*
    Louis Robert, *Hellenica: recueil d'épigraphie de numismatique et d'antiquités grecques II–III* (Paris: Maisonneuve, 1947).

Rothschild, *Luke-Acts*
    Clare K. Rothschild, *Luke-Acts and the Rhetoric of History: An Investigation of Early Christian Historiography* (WUNT 175; Tübingen: Mohr Siebeck, 2004).

Roussel, "Le miracle"
    Pierre Roussel, "Le miracle de Zeus Panamaaros," *BCH* 55 (1931) 70–116.

Runia, "Philonic Nomenclature"
    David T. Runia, "Philonic Nomenclature," *Studia Philonica Annual* 6 (1994) 1–27.

Sachs and Wiseman, "Babylonian King List"
    Abraham J. Sachs and Donald J. Wiseman, "A Babylonian King List of the Hellenistic Period," *Iraq* 16 (1954) 202–12.

Scaer, *Lukan Passion*
    Peter J. Scaer, *The Lukan Passion and the Praiseworthy Death* (New Testament Monographs 10; Sheffield: Sheffield Phoenix, 2005).

Schlatter, *Jason von Kyrene*
    Adolf von Schlatter, *Jason von Kyrene: Ein Beitrag zu seiner Wiederherstellung* (Munich: Beck, 1891).

Schmitz, "Geschaffen aus dem Nichts?"
    Barbara Schmitz, "Geschaffen aus dem Nichts? Die Funktion der Rede von der Schöpfung im Zweiten Makkabäerbuch," *Sacra Scripta* 9 (2009) 199–215.

Scholz, "Elementarunterricht"
    Peter Scholz, "Elementarunterricht und intellektuelle Bildung im hellenistischen Gymnasion," in Kah and Scholz, *Das hellenistische Gymnasion*, 103–28.

Schubart, "Königsideal"
    Wilhelm Schubart, "I. Aufsäze. Das hellenistische Königsideal nach Inschriften und Papyri," *Archiv für Papyrusforschung und verwandte Gebiete* 12 (1937) 1–26.

Schürer, *History*
    Emil Schürer, *The History of the Jewish People in the Age of Jesus Christ (175 B.C.–A.D. 135)* (rev. and ed. Geza Vermes and Fergus Millar; 3 vols.; Edinburgh: T&T Clark, 1973–87).

Schwartz, *2 Maccabees*
    Daniel R. Schwartz, *2 Maccabees* (Commentaries on Early Jewish Literature; Berlin and New York: de Gruyter, 2008).

Sherwin-White and Kuhrt, *From Samarkhand to Sardis*
    Susan Sherwin-White and Amélie Kuhrt, *From Samarkhand to Sardis: A New Approach to the Seleucid Empire* (Hellenistic Culture and Society 13; Berkeley: University of California Press, 1993).

Sievers, "Jerusalem"
    Joseph Sievers, "Jerusalem, the Akra, and Josephus," in Fausto Parente and Joseph Sievers, eds., *Josephus and the History of the Greco-Roman Period: Essays in Memory of Morton Smith* (SPB 41; Leiden: Brill, 1994) 195–209.

Smith, *From Symposium to Eucharist*
    Dennis Edwin Smith, *From Symposium to Eucharist: The Banquet in the Early Christian World* (Minneapolis: Fortress Press, 2003).

Smith, *Palestinian Parties*
    Morton Smith, *Palestinian Parties and Politics That Shaped the Old Testament* (2nd ed.; London: SCM, 1987).

Smyth, *Greek Grammar*
    Herbert Weir Smyth, *Greek Grammar* (Cambridge, Mass.: Harvard University Press, 1920).

Stern, *Greek and Latin Authors*
    Menahem Stern, *Greek and Latin Authors on Jews and Judaism* (3 vols.; Fontes ad res Judaicas spectantes; Jerusalem: Israel Academy of Arts and Sciences, 1974–84).

Tcherikover, *Hellenistic Civilization*
    Victor Tcherikover, *Hellenistic Civilization and the Jews* (Philadelphia: Jewish Publication Society, 1959).

Tcherikover, *Jews in the Greco-Roman World*
    Victor Tcherikover, *The Jews in the Greco-Roman World* (in Hebrew; Tel Aviv: Neumann, 1960–61).

Thompson, *Motif-Index*
    Stith Thompson, *Motif-Index of Folk Literature* (rev. ed.; 6 vols.; Bloomington: Indiana University Press, 1955–58).

Torrey, "Letters"
    Charles C. Torrey, "The Letters Prefixed to Second Maccabees," *JAOS* 60 (1940) 119–50.

Urman and Flesher, *Ancient Synagogues*
    Dan Urman and Paul V. M. Flesher, *Ancient Synagogues: Historical Analysis and Archeological Discovery* (2 vols.; SPB 47; Leiden: Brill, 1995).

VanderKam, "2 Maccabees 6,7a"
    James C. VanderKam, "2 Maccabees 6,7a and Calendrical Change in Jerusalem," *JSJ* 12 (1981) 52–74.

VanderKam, *From Joshua to Caiaphas*
    James C. VanderKam, *From Joshua to Caiaphas: High Priests after the Exile* (Minneapolis: Fortress Press, 2004).

Van Hook, *Metaphorical Terminology*
Larue Van Hook, *The Metaphorical Terminology of Greek Rhetoric and Literary Criticism* (Chicago: University of Chicago Press, 1905).

Verdin, Schepens, and de Keyser, *Purposes of History*
Herman Verdin, Guido Schepens, and Els de Keyser, eds., *Purposes of History: Studies in Greek Historiography from the 4th to the 2nd Centuries B.C. Proceedings of the International Colloquium, Leuven, 24-26 May 1988* (Studia Hellenistica 30; Louvain: n.p., 1990).

Wacholder, "Letter from Judah Maccabee"
Ben-Zion Wacholder, "The Letter from Judah Maccabee to Aristobulus: Is 2 Maccabees 1:10b–2:18 Authentic?" *HUCA* 49 (1978) 89–133.

Walbank, "Polybian Experiment"
Frank W. Walbank, "*ΦΙΛΙΠΠΟΣ ΤΡΑΓΩΙΔΟΥ-ΜΕΝΟΣ*: A Polybian Experiment," *JHS* 58 (1938) 55–68.

Walbank, *Polybius*
Frank W. Walbank, *A Historical Commentary on Polybius* (3 vols.; Oxford: Clarendon, 1957–79).

Welles, *Royal Correspondence*
C. Bradford Welles, *Royal Correspondence in the Hellenistic Period: A Study in Greek Epigraphy* (New Haven: Yale University Press, 1934).

White, *Light from Ancient Letters*
John L. White, *Light from Ancient Letters* (FF; Philadelphia: Fortress Press, 1986).

Wilhelm, "Zu einigen Stellen"
Adolf Wilhelm, "Zu einigen Stellen der Bücher der Makkabäer," *Akademie der Wissenschaften in Wien, Philosophisch-historische Klasse: Anzeiger* 74 (1937) 15–30.

Will, *Histoire politique*
Édouard Will, *Histoire politique du monde hellénistique: 323–30 av. J.-C.* (2 vols.; 2nd ed.; Annales de l'Est. Mémoire 30, 32; Nancy: Presses universitaires de Nancy, 1979, 1982).

Witkowski, *Epistulae privatae*
Stanislaw Witkowski, *Epistulae privatae graecae quae in papyris aetatis Lagidarum servantur* (Leipzig: Teubner, 1906).

Wolff, *Das Recht*
Hans Julius Wolff, *Das Recht der griechischen Papyri Ägyptens in der Zeit der Ptolemäer und des Prinzipats* (2 vols.; HA 10.5; Munich: Beck, 1978).

Xeravits and Zsengellér, *Books of the Maccabees*
Géza G. Xeravits and József Zsengellér, eds., *The Books of the Maccabees: History, Theology, Ideology* (JSJSup 118; Leiden: Brill, 2007).

Zambelli, "La composizione"
Marcello Zambelli, "La composizione del secondo libro di Maccabei e la nuova cronologia di Antioco IV Epifane," in *Miscellanea Greca e Romana* (Studi pubblicati dall'Istituto di Storia Antica 16; Rome: n.p., 1965) 195–299.

Zeitlin, *First Book*
Solomon Zeitlin, *The First Book of Maccabees: An English Translation* (Eng. trans. Sidney Tedesche; New York: Harper, 1950).

Zeitlin, *Second Book*
Solomon Zeitlin, *The Second Book of Maccabees* (Eng. trans. Sidney Tedesche; New York: Harper, 1954).

Zollschan, "Earliest Jewish Embassy"
Linda T. Zollschan, "The Earliest Jewish Embassy to the Romans: 2 Macc. 4:11?" *JJS* 55 (2004) 37–44.

Zwick, "Unterhaltung und Nutzen"
Reinhold Zwick, "Unterhaltung und Nutzen: Zum literarischen Profil des 2. Buches der Makkabäer," in Johannes Frühwald-König, Ferdinand R. Prostmeier, and Reinhold Zwick, eds., *Steht nicht geschrieben? Studien zur Bibel und ihrer Wirkungsgeschichte: Festschrift für Georg Schmuttermayr* (Regensburg: Pustet, 2001) 125–49.

Front and back endpapers show folios 212 (verso)
through 214 (recto) of the fifth-century Codex
Alexandrinus, one of the oldest Bibles in existence,
containing 2 Maccabees 5:24—8:1 (the defilement of the
Temple by Antiochus, the martyrdoms of Eleazar and
seven brothers and their mother, and the appearance of
Judas Maccabeus). Photographs courtesy of the British
Library.

The work entitled 2 Maccabees presents a host of challenges to conventional assumptions. First of all, the title itself is misleading. Second Maccabees is not a continuation of 1 Maccabees: its narrative component contains an account quite different in both style and content from that in 1 Maccabees. Second, this work is not a history of the Maccabees' revolt against their Seleucid overlords in the modern sense of the word "history." It is a highly rhetorical narrative that sets out not to give a blow-by-blow description of events but to move its audience to commit to faithfully following the ancestral traditions of Judaism. The narrative itself is paradoxical in that its author is the first we know to speak of Judaism and to contrast it with Hellenism, and yet he displays considerable awareness of Greek rhetorical style in his presentation. Finally, 2 Maccabees, a complex work, is not a single document. It has three components: the first two are letters and the third, which is the largest, is a narrative. What is the relationship between these letters and the narrative? Were the former meant to introduce the narrative or are they there haphazardly, simply because they mention some characters in the narrative? We begin our introduction with a treatment of these letters.

The Letters and the Narrative

Clement of Alexandria wrote that Aristobulos, one of the recipients of the second prefixed letter, is mentioned by "the composer of the epitome of the Maccabees [ὁ συνταξάμενος τὴν τῶν μακκαβαιῶν]" (*Strom.* 5.14.97.7).[1] Clement, writing at the end of the second century C.E., chose the participle of the verb whose root the author of the narrative had used in his prologue and epilogue to describe his work (2:23: δι᾽ ἑνὸς συντάγματος ἐπιτεμεῖν; 15:38-39: τῇ συντάξει). Such a word choice

underscores that Clement saw the letters and the narrative as linked, but there has been considerable debate over what constitutes that link.

The number of letters before the prologue to the narrative has often been debated. Jochen Gabriel Bunge conveniently catalogued the opinions: one letter: Grätz, Niese, Kolbe; two letters: Grimm, Knabenhauer, Torrey, Winckler, Herkenne, Kugler, Abel, Penna, Zeitlin; three letters: Bruston, Willrich, Büchler, Laqueur, Kahrstedt, Bévenot, Buchers, Rinaldi.[2] Since the brilliant analysis of Elias Bickermann, a basic consensus has emerged that there were two letters.[3] But what is the relationship between these letters and the narrative? Benedikt Niese and Bunge were the strongest supporters of the notion that the same author wrote the letters and the narrative.[4] Bunge in particular pointed to the presence of the particle δέ in 2:19, which suggested that the letter led into the narrative. However, the different descriptions of Antiochus IV's death in the second letter and in the narrative in 2 Maccabees 9 spoke decisively against this position. So too did the hope expressed in the second letter that God's mercy would be shown in the end of the dispersion of Israel (1:27-29; 2:7, 18), an idea that is not at all present in the narrative, where the hope of those killed for the sake of the ancestral laws is for a renewal in resurrection. The major problems for the connection of the letters and the narrative were thus found in the second letter. This led to the suggestion by both Arnaldo Momigliano and Christian Habicht that the second letter had somehow been appended to the first.[5] Jonathan Goldstein suggested that since "the practice of Hellenistic scribes was to place at the end of a document earlier documents which were evidence or provided motivation," the author of the second letter had attached it to the first.[6] However, there are even problems with

1   Clement of Alexandria *Strom.* 5.14.97.7. See also Eusebius *Praep. Ev.* 8.9.38.

2   Jochen Gabriel Bunge, *Untersuchungen zum zweiten Makkabäerbuch. Quellenkritische, literarische, chronologische und historische Untersuchungen zum zweiten Makkabäerbuch als Quelle syrisch-palästinischer Geschichte im 2. Jh. v. Chr.* (Bonn: Rheinische Friedrich-Wilhelms-Universität, 1971) 34 n. 7.

3   Elias Bickermann, "Ein jüdischer Festbrief vom Jahre 124 v. Chr. (II Macc. 1: 1-9)," *ZNW* 32 (1933) 233-53.

4   Benedikt Niese, "Kritik der beiden Makkabäer-

bücher nebst Beiträgen zur Geschichte der makkabäischen Erhebung," *Hermes* 35 (1900) 268-307, here 278; Bunge, *Untersuchungen*, 203-4.

5   Arnaldo Momigliano, "The Second Book of Maccabees," *CP* 70 (1975) 81-88, here 82-83; Christian Habicht, *2. Makkabäerbuch* (JSHRZ 1; Historische und legendarische Erzählungen 3; Gütersloh: G. Mohn, 1976) 174-75.

6   Jonathan A. Goldstein, *II Maccabees: A New Translation with Introduction and Commentary* (AB 41A; Garden City, N.Y.: Doubleday, 1983) 167.

connecting the first letter to the narrative: no mention is made of Antiochus IV's persecution; no mention is made of the Day of Nikanor. The linguistic argument based on the presence of καταλλάσσειν in 1:5b and in the narrative in 7:33 and 8:29, with καταλλαγή in 5:20, is not conclusive. The verb καταλλάσσειν is used in Paul to designate reconciliation with God and is also found with this meaning in Josephus *Ant.* 6.143, in which work it is also used to signify reconciliation between enemies and within families.[7] Philo, too, speaks of how transgressors have "three intercessors . . . to plead for their reconciliation with the Father" (τῶν πρὸς τὸν πατέρα καταλλαγῶν) (*Praem. peon.* 166). Since the verb and noun are used by three very different Jewish authors of the first century C.E., one cannot argue that the presence of the verb in the first letter and in the narrative proves satisfactorily that they were written by the same author.[8] While the use of this term as well as the technical term for the feast of Tabernacles, σκηνοπηγία, evidences a knowledge of Greek and LXX usage, the convoluted greeting formula suggests someone more at home writing in Aramaic or Hebrew.

The common opinion is that the two letters were originally independent works that were later joined together.[9] Because the three works, the two letters and the narrative, have been side by side since before the time of Clement of Alexandria, the tendency has been to try to find some rationale for this arrangement. Jan Willem van Henten argued that the narrative was connected to the letters to provide an explanation for why the feast of Hanukkah should be celebrated.[10] However,

as noted in the commentary, the first letter contains no mention of either Antiochus IV or the martyrdoms. The rhetoric seems to be at odds with van Henten's explanation. Daniel Schwartz attempted to show that the author of the letters knew the narrative and, in fact, rearranged it. Schwartz removed the contradiction generated by the account of Antiochus IV's death in 1:13-16 in comparison with that of chap. 9 by claiming that the letter's account is a later interpolation, but he did not suggest who the interpolator might be.[11] He also claimed that "the Hasmonean authorities in Jerusalem . . . added a section on the [Hanukkah] festival's origins into the book at 10:1-8 and attached two accompanying letters at the book's outset."[12] I shall argue against both these positions in the commentary, but it is important to note how important Schwartz sees the role of the later "authorities" in settling the composition of the narrative.

All three works in 2 Maccabees hold that God's temple is holy and that God defends it against its attackers, and all call for the celebration of the rededication of the temple. However, these common elements remain very general connections. Bertram Herr, supporting his case on the presence of καταλλάσσειν in both the first letter and the narrative, stated that the epitomator connected the two works. Herr emphasized the importance of the martyrdoms in the narrative and argued that the letter had the same orientation. As a pastorally oriented theologian, the epitomator stressed the need to stand fast in belief precisely when in difficulties.[13] However, once one does not accept the linguistic basis

7   Within families: Josephus *Ant.* 5.138; 7.184, 196; 11.195; between enemies: *Ant.* 6.353; 14.278.

8   I earlier argued that the use of the verb pointed "to purposeful connections being made between the first letter and the epitome" (Robert Doran, *Temple Propaganda: The Purpose and Character of 2 Maccabees* [CBQMS 12; Washington, D.C.: Catholic Biblical Association, 1981] 12).

9   Carl L. W. Grimm, *Das zweite, dritte und vierte Buch der Maccabäer* (Leipzig: S. Hirzel, 1857) 22–25; Richard Laqueur, *Kritische Untersuchungen zum zweiten Makkabäerbuch* (Strassburg: K. J. Trübner, 1904) 52–71; Elias Bickermann, "Makkabäerbücher (I. und II.)," *PW* 14:779–97, here 791; Hugo Bévenot, *Die beiden Makkabäerbücher* (Die Heilige Schrift des Alten Testaments; Bonn: Peter Hanstein, 1931) 11; Diego Arenhoevel, *Die Theo-*

kratie nach dem 1. und 2. Makkabäerbuch (Walberger Studien der Albertus-Magnus-Akademie, Theologische Reihe 3; Mainz: Matthias Gruenwald, 1967) 110–11; Victor Parker, "The Letters in II Maccabees: Reflections on the Book's Composition," *ZAW* 119 (2007) 386–402, here 386–89.

10   Jan Willem van Henten, *The Maccabean Martyrs as Saviours of the Jewish People: A Study of 2 and 4 Maccabees* (JSJSup 57; Leiden: Brill, 1997) 57.

11   Daniel R. Schwartz, *2 Maccabees* (Commentaries on Early Jewish Literature; Berlin/New York: de Gruyter, 2008) 133, 146–47.

12   Ibid., 37.

13   Bertram Herr, "Der Standpunkt des Epitomators: Perspektivenwechsel in der Forschung am Zweiten Makkabäerbuch," *Bib* 90 (2009) 1–31, here 28–31.

for his connecting the two pieces, one is left with two pieces exhorting steadfastness in the face of persecution. Rather than speculate on who put these three works together and for what reason, a better approach is to examine each piece in itself and see what insights it provides.

The Narrative

The narrative of the events in Judea from 175 B.C.E. to 164 B.C.E. has been explored primarily for what it can tell about the Hasmonean revolt. As Schwartz has noted, there is very little evidence that the work was known by Philo, Josephus, or the rabbinic tradition.[14] What was interesting were the martyrdom stories, mentioned probably in Heb 11:35-38 and in the Apostolic Fathers.[15] John Chrysostom devoted three sermons to the topic "On the Maccabean Martyrs and Their Mother."[16]

Until the work of Benedikt Niese,[17] the narrative of 1 Maccabees was preferred to that of 2 Maccabees in terms of reliability as a historical source. Niese's analysis of the problems in the account of 1 Maccabees has brought about a greater sense of the literary and theological qualities in that work.[18] The explosion of inscriptional and papyrological evidence further emphasized

that the narrative in 2 Maccabees reliably reflects the language and institutions of the second century B.C.E.[19] But what kind of narrative is it?

The Genre of the Narrative

When approaching the narrative of 2 Maccabees, scholars have tried to fit it into Hellenistic historiography. Niese set the stage by identifying it as "tragic," part of the predominant genre of Hellenistic historiography. As I discussed thirty years ago,[20] this categorization is not sufficient. We have to be reminded that all Hellenistic historians were trained in rhetoric. As Thomas Wiedemann succinctly remarked, "Rhetoric may be used properly or not."[21] As Frank Walbank has shown, Polybius himself could use emotional and vivid description.[22] The connection between tragedy and history "is in fact a fundamental affinity going back to the earliest days of both history and tragedy."[23] Polybius's attack on "tragic" historiography should therefore be seen as an attack on the inappropriate use of emotional rhetoric.

Rhetoric had to be tailored to one's audience, purpose, and subject. If, as we will suggest, the author intended to move his audience both to follow the ancestral traditions of the Jews by narrating how the ancestral God of the Jews had defended his temple in Jerusalem

---

14 Schwartz, *2 Maccabees*, 85–90.

15 See Jan Willem van Henten, "Zum Einfluß jüdischer Martyrien auf die Literatur des frühen Christentums, II: Die Apostolischen Väter," *ANRW* 2.27.1 (1993) 700–723. See also Marie-Françoise Baslez, "The Origin of the Martyrdom Images: From the Book of Maccabees to the First Christians," in Géza G. Xeravits and József Zsengellér, eds., *The Books of the Maccabees: History, Theology, Ideology* (JSJSup 118; Leiden: Brill, 2007) 113–30.

16 *PG* 50:617–28. On the later history, see Daniel Joslyn-Siemiatkoski, *Christian Memories of the Maccabean Martyrs* (New York: Palgrave Macmillan, 2009); Raphaëlle Ziadé, *Les martyrs Maccabées: de l'histoire juive au culte chrétien. Les homélies de Grégoire de Nazianze et de Jean Chrysostome* (VCSup 80; Leiden: Brill, 2007).

17 Niese, "Kritik," 268–307.

18 See the work of Nils Martola, *Capture and Liberation: A Study in the Composition of the First Book of Maccabees* (Acta Academiae Aboensis: Humaniora 63.1; Åbo: Åbo Akademie, 1984); David S. Williams, *The Structure of 1 Maccabees* (CBQMS 31; Washington, D.C.: Catholic Biblical Association, 1999).

19 Details are given throughout the commentary, but the work of Charles Bradford Welles on royal letters, Elias Bickermann on Seleucid institutions, and Victor Tcherikover on Jews in the ancient world stand out for the early twentieth century, as does the recent work by John Ma and Dov Gera.

20 Doran, *Temple Propaganda*, 84–94.

21 Thomas Wiedemann, "Rhetoric in Polybius," in Herman Verdin, Guido Schepens, and Els de Keyser, eds., *Purposes of History: Studies in Greek Historiography from the 4th to the 2nd Centuries B.C. Proceedings of the International Colloquium, Leuven, 24–26 May 1988* (Studia Hellenistica 30; Louvain: [s.n.], 1990) 300.

22 Frank W. Walbank, "ΦΙΛΙΠΠΟΣ ΤΡΑΓΩΙΔΟΥΜΕΝΟΣ: A Polybian Experiment," *JHS* 58 (1938) 55–68.

23 Frank W. Walbank, "History and Tragedy," *Historia* 9 (1960) 216–34, here 233.

against attackers and also to celebrate the new festivals inaugurated in honor of this defense, then he would have needed to use highly emotional and dramatic rhetoric. I will therefore explore the style and organization of the narrative to see how he tried to achieve these results.

The Style of the Narrative

The narrative of 2 Maccabees is known for its unusual words and its use of rhetorical figures. For example, the author uses adverbs like λεοντηδόν (11:11), κρουνηδόν (14:45), ἀγεληδόν (3:18; 14:14); poetic words such as ῥωμαλέοι (12:27), οἰωνοβρώτους (9:15), ἀενάου (7:36); and many words that are now extant only in this work, such as δυσπέτημα (5:20) and συμμισοπονηρεῖν (4:36).[24] In his syntax and attempt to avoid hiatus, the author can stand comparison with contemporary Greek writers.[25] He varies his word usage as in 5:16: ταῖς μιεραῖς χερσὶ . . . ταῖς βεβήλοις χερσί and as is particularly shown in his many ways of expressing "die"—χειρώσασθαι (4:34, 42), παρέκλεισεν (4:34), ἀπεκόσμησε (4:38), προπέμπειν εἰς τὸν ᾄδην (6:23), προωθοῦσιν εἰς ὄλεθρον (13:6)—as well as the many epithets for "God."

The author also uses many rhetorical figures:

1. litotes, for example, οὐκ ὀλιγούς (8:6; 10:24; 14:30), οὐ μικρά, οὐ μικρῶς (3:14; 14:8), and οὐ ῥᾴδιον (2:26; 4:17)
2. hendiadys, for example, 15:26, 29: μετ᾽ ἐπικλήσεως καὶ εὐχῶν; κραυγῆς καὶ ταραχῆς
3. chiasm, for example, 5:19 (οὐ διὰ τὸν τόπον τὸ ἔθνος, ἀλλὰ διὰ τὸ ἔθνος τὸν τόπον)
4. homoioteleuton, for example, 2:25 (ἐφρον-τίσαμεν . . . ψυχαγωγίαν, . . . εὐκοπίαν, . . . ὠφέλειαν)
5. hypallage, 7:9 (αἰώνιον ἀναβίωσιν ζωῆς)
6. parachesis, 4:27 (ἐκράτει . . . εὐτάκτει)

Frequently, the author shows his fondness for paronomasia: 3:24 (αὐτόθι δὲ αὐτοῦ) and 15:37 (αὐτὸς αὐτόθι); 5:3 (βελῶν βολάς); the contrast between words beginning with the prefixes ευ- and δυσ- (5:6; 6:29); and the examples in 3:22 (τὰ πεπιστευμένα τοῖς πεπιστευ-κόσι), 4:26 (ὑπονοθεύσας ὑπονοθευθείς), 5:9 (ἀπο-ξενώσας ἐπὶ ξένης), 6:18 (πρόσοψιν τοῦ προσώπου), 10:20-21 (φιλαργυρήσαντες . . . ἀργυρίου), 12:22 (ἐπιφανείσης . . . ἐπιφανείας), 12:42 (ἁμάρτημα . . . ἀναμαρτήτους . . . ἁμαρτίαν), 14:28 (δυσφόρως ἔφερεν), and 14:36 (ἅγιε παντὸς ἁγιασμοῦ). The paronomasia in 10:26 (ἐχθρεῦσαι τοῖς ἐχθροῖς αὐτῶν καὶ ἀντικεῖσθαι τοῖς ἀντικειμένοις) stems from Exod 23:22.[26]

This enjoyment of words by the author is found also in the use of double entendre. When the king asks the mother to speak to her last son for his physical salva-tion (7:25: ἐπὶ σωτηρίᾳ), she speaks to him about what will bring about his death so that he may be resurrected (7:29). The same verbal delight is true of the author's use of the term εὐημερηκώς in 8:35: while Judas had been described at the beginning of the incident as having been successful in his military endeavors (8:8: ἐν ταῖς εὐημερίαις προβαίνοντα), Nikanor is sarcastically described as being successful in the destruction of his army. Tobias Nicklas notes well how in 9:4 the action of the defenders of the temple at Persepolis is described as "evil" or "injury" (κακία), whereas "the context makes it absolutely clear that the acts of the inhabitants of Persepolis are perfectly comprehensible. Although the narrator does not say any *direct* negative word about Antiochus, with just one word he manages to point to the Seleucid's spiritual blindness."[27]

One of the more important features of the author's style is his use of asyndeton. This stylistic feature has often been seen simply as a method of shortening the narrative. This may be true in some cases, as, for exam-ple, at 14:21b-23a, where the author's main concern is the confrontation between Seleucids and Jews and so he skips over a peace meeting. At other times, however, the author appears to use asyndeton skillfully, particularly

---

24 For a full listing, see Wolfgang Richnow, "Untersu-chung zu Sprache und Stil des 2. Makkabäerbuches. Ein Beitrag zur hellenistischen Historiographie" (Ph.D. diss., Göttingen, 1967) 48–58; Schwartz, *2 Maccabees*, 67 n. 69.

25 See Doran, *Temple Propaganda*, 24–42.

26 Frank Shaw has given a thorough discussion of

paronomasia in 2 Maccabees in an unpublished essay, "Paronomasia in 2 Maccabees."

27 Tobias Nicklas, "Irony in 2 Maccabees?" in Géza G. Xeravits and József Zsengellér, eds., *The Books of the Maccabees: History, Theology, Ideology* (JSJSup 118; Leiden: Brill, 2007) 101–11, here 106.

with participles, to show how events are closely interconnected: for example, in 11:13, Lysias's not being stupid is closely connected with his analysis of what had happened to him (οὐκ ἄνους δὲ ὑπάρχων πρὸς ἑαυτὸν ἀντιβάλλων) and in 10:35, the young men burn with courage and so storm the wall (πυρωθέντες τοῖς θυμοῖς διὰ τὰς βλασφημίας προσβαλόντες τῷ τείχει). The use of asyndeton is particularly noticeable in the contrast between 13:10, where law, fatherland, and holy temple are syndetically connected, and 13:14, where laws, temple, city, fatherland, and constitution are asyndetically linked. Why the change? One cannot really ascribe it to the desire for a shortened narrative. Rather, I suggest that in 13:10 Judas asks the people to pray, while in 13:14 Judas addresses his troops and tries to arouse their emotions by the tight grouping of all that they are fighting for. Similarly, the asyndeton in 14:25 emphasizes how quickly Judas accepts Nikanor's proposal to bring order back to affairs.

Words and Narrative Structure
The author's concern for words leads him to use words to structure his narrative. We noted above, for example, how the root εὐημερ- is found at both the beginning (8:8) and end (8:35) of the first battle against Nikanor. Alcimus and Rhazis are both connected, but differently, with the time of ἀμιξία or "separation" (14:3, 38). Both the pious high priest Rhazis and the traitorous high priest Alcimus claim to be speaking for their citizens and seeking peace for the kingdom (4:6: ἀδύνατον εἶναι τυχεῖν εἰρήνης ἔτι τὰ πράγματα; 14:10: ἀδύνατον εἰρήνης τυχεῖν τὰ πράγματα), but they have contrasting notions of what such peace would entail. The author chooses to emphasize that the leader of the first conflict against Judas is named Nikanor and is called τρισαλιτήριος (8:34), and then the final opponent in the narrative also has the name Nikanor and is also called τρισαλιτήριος (15:3).
    Repetition is also used to help structure the narrative.

The most glaring repetition is that found at the end of the institution of the feasts of Hanukkah and the Day of Nikanor:

10:8: ἐδογμάτισαν δὲ μετὰ κοινοῦ προστάγματος καὶ ψηφίσματος.
15:36: ἐδογμάτισαν δὲ πάντες μετὰ κοινοῦ ψηφίσματος.

The author by this repetition intends to organize his narrative around the events leading up to these two feasts. The author also uses markers in tracing out the narrative:

3:40: καὶ τὰ μὲν κατὰ Ἡλιόδωρον καὶ τὴν τοῦ γαζοφυλακίου τήρησιν οὕτως ἐχώρησεν
7:42: Τὰ μὲν οὖν περὶ τοὺς υπλαγχνισμοὺς καὶ τὰς ὑπερβαλλούσας αἰκίας ἐπὶ τοσοῦτον δεδηλώσθω
10:9: Καὶ τὰ μὲν τῆς Ἀντιόχου τοῦ προσαγορευθέντος Ἐπιφανοῦς τελευτῆς οὕτως εἶχεν
13:26: οὕτως τὰ τοῦ βασιλέως τῆς ἐφόδου καὶ τῆς ἀναζυγῆς ἐχώρησεν
15:37: Τῶν οὖν κατὰ Νικάνορα χωρησάντων οὕτως.

These concluding rubrics were noticed by Adolf Büchler and Diego Arenhoevel,[28] but Bunge went further and suggested that these rubrics reflected the hand of the supposed original author, Jason of Cyrene, and helped uncover the structure of his five-volume work. This suggestion is not convincing,[29] particularly as the last example, 15:37, betrays the hand of the author of the condensed narrative, for the main clause following the genitive absolute has the verb in the first person singular. The first three rubrics are in a μέν . . . δέ construction and so lead on to the following events, while the fourth wraps up the events under Antiochus V and leads the narrative over to the reign of Demetrius. It is important to note here, as Reinhold Zwick has emphasized,[30] that

---

28 Adolf Büchler, *Die Tobiaden und die Oniaden im II. Makkabäerbuch und in der verwandten jüdisch-hellenistischen Literatur* (Vienna: Verlag der Israel.-theol. Lehranstalt, 1899) 325; Arenhoevel, *Theokratie*, 108 n. 28.
29 See Doran, *Temple Propaganda*, 13–17, 76 n. 82.
30 Reinhold Zwick, "Unterhaltung und Nutzen: Zum literarischen Profil des 2. Buches der Makkabäer," in Johannes Frühwald-König, Ferdinand R. Prostmeier, and Reinhold Zwick, eds., *Steht nicht geschrieben? Studien zur Bibel und ihrer Wirkungsgeschichte: Festschrift für Georg Schmuttermayr* (Regensburg: Pustet, 2001) 125–49, here 137–42.

the hand of the author of the condensed narrative runs throughout the narrative. In the prologue and particularly in the epilogue, the author, using the first person singular, makes claim to the work as a whole. Within the narrative, not only in the explicit reflection found in 6:12-17 but also peppered throughout the work, the author unfolds for his audience the significance of what is happening and what will happen: for example, what will happen to those who hold ancestral traditions in contempt (4:16-17), what will happen to Jason (5:8), what caused the persecution and how it will end (5:18-20), the prophecy by the last brother of what will happen to Antiochus IV (7:35-38). Particularly interesting is the way he uses speeches—for example, the speeches of the brothers and Eleazar as well as the threat of Nikanor—as he seeks to engage and move his audience. Second Maccabees is thus a well-crafted work, not a simple, shortened version. This analysis does not entail, of course, that there was no work by Jason of Cyrene, as Zwick is tempted to conclude, in agreement with Wolfgang Richnow.[31] What the literary analysis does mean is that one has to take the narrative as a whole.

A Subgenre of Local History

The narrative is thus not a universal history like the work of Polybius on the rise of Rome, but a local history, not of events of a mythic time, but of recent events concerning a particular city. As such, it is comparable to the works of local historians like Syriskos, who wrote the history of Chersonesus, or Eudemus, Myron, and Timocritus, who wrote the history of Rhodes.[32] These works also would have included epiphanies of the patron god/goddess in defense of the city. There also exists the narrative of the defense of Delphi by Apollo against attacking Persians (Herodotus *Hist.* 8.35–39), but such epiphanic deliverances are attested also in inscriptions. From Panamaros is an inscription that tells how Zeus Panamaros defended the city,[33] and the Lindos Chronicle describes how Athena delivered the citizens from a siege by the Persians.[34] An account of how the Gauls were driven back from Delphi by Apollo in 279 B.C.E. is found in Pausanias (10.23.1–12) and also in an inscription from Cos in which cities are invited to celebrate this event.[35] I have termed this account a topos in which a general shared pattern is found: "The attackers approach, the defenders ask help of the deity, the deity responds, the attackers are repulsed, and the defenders rejoice."[36] Justin's comment after his discussion of the repulse of the Gauls is interesting: "Hence it happened that, of so great an army, which a little before, presuming on its strength, contended even against the gods, not a man was left to be a memorial of its destruction" (*Hist.* 24.8). Here the notion of a theomachy is present.[37]

This sense of a theomachy is pronounced in the narrative of 2 Maccabees. While at first Antiochus IV is portrayed somewhat benignly as he punishes the murderer of Onias (4:37-38), he soon is described as "haughty in spirit" (5:17), arrogantly supposing that "he could make the land navigable and the sea walkable" (5:21; see, similarly, 9:8), and "able to grasp the stars of heaven" (9:10). He thought himself to be godlike (9:12). In fact, Antiochus is accused of fighting against God (7:19: $\theta\epsilon o\mu\alpha\chi\epsilon\hat{\imath}\nu$).[38] Similarly, Nikanor is at first seen as reasonable and fair-minded (14:18-25) but is soon por-

31 Ibid., 143–45; Richnow, "Untersuchung zu Sprache," 41–42. See also Doran, *Temple Propaganda*, 81–83. Charles Mugler ("Remarques sur le second livre des Macchabées: La statistique des mots et la question de l'auteur," *RHPhR* 11 [1931] 419–23) made a strong argument from the abundant use of participles by the author that the work was a condensation.

32 Syriskos at *FGH* 807; Eudemus at *FGH* 524; Myron at *FGH* 106 F 5; and Timocritus at *FGH* 522. See Doran, *Temple Propaganda*, 103–4.

33 Pierre Roussel, "Le miracle de Zeus Panamaros," *BCH* 55 (1931) 70–116.

34 *FGH* 532.

35 Justin (Junianus Justinus, Latin historian) *Hist.* 24.7–8; Diodorus Siculus 24.9.1–3. See Georges Nach-

tergael, *Les Galates en Grèce et les Sôtéria de Delphes: Recherches d'histoire et d'épigraphie hellénistiques* (Mémoires de l'Académie royale de Belgique 63; Brussels: Palais des Académies, 1977).

36 Doran, *Temple Propaganda* 47; see also 104.

37 See Jan Coenraad Kamerbeek, "On the Conception of *ΘΕΟΜΑΧΟΣ* in Relation with Greek Tragedy," *Mnemosyne*, 4th series, 1 (1948) 271–83.

38 A confrontation between God and Antiochus would seem to be at the heart of the story of the mother and her seven sons (2 Maccabees 7). See comment thereon.

trayed as arraying himself against God as he threatens to tear down the temple of God (14:33) and claims to be master on earth (15:5), who can override the demands of God. He, too, is arrogant (15:6). Both of these men are killed, and in each case a festival is inaugurated in honor of the victory of God. This pattern—challenge to the deity, battle, victory of the deity, celebration concerning the temple—has a peculiar resonance in biblical literature. The work of Frank Moore Cross, Patrick Miller, and Paul Hanson has shown how pervasive this pattern is in the exodus story as well as elsewhere.[39] In using this particular pattern twice in the narrative, the author was deploying a powerful rhetorical tool from his audience's traditional literature to engage and move them. Once this traditional narrative pattern is recognized, one does not have to speculate as to why or by whom the rededication of the temple has been "inserted" between 9:29 and 10:9. The phrase "the events at the end of Antiochus" (10:9) includes by reason of the rhetorical pattern the celebration at his death.

Reorganization of the Narrative

To use this rhetorical pattern most effectively, with the death of the challenger against God, Antiochus IV, coming before the rededication of the temple, the author chose to rearrange the events of the narrative. To see what the author has done, it is necessary to provide some suggestions for the sequence of events from 165 B.C.E. to the arrival of Demetrius I.

The starting point is provided in the third letter in the collection of letters in 2 Maccabees 11. I take this letter (11:27-33) to be a genuine letter of Antiochus IV, although the date given at the end of the letter is unlikely. Antiochus IV responds to the request of Menelaus that the Jews be allowed to live by their ancestral customs, and the date of the thirtieth of Xanthikos is given. This month would fall in late March or early April. I suggest that Menelaus had approached Antiochus IV after the king's spectacular showcasing of his forces at

Daphne in 166 B.C.E., but before the king left on his eastern campaign in 165 B.C.E. I do not think that Menelaus would have traipsed after the king as he was campaigning. By this reckoning, the persecution would have lasted not quite a year and a half, but resistance was already under way and Menelaus was seeking to stop it early in its tracks. Antiochus IV agreed and allowed the return to ancestral traditions in March/April 165 B.C.E. Antiochus IV appointed his son, Antiochus V, as co-regent when he left to campaign. However, Judas did not desist from his insurgency, which led to the sending of troops by Ptolemy, governor of Coele-Syria and Phoenicia (8:8), in late 165 B.C.E. to quell the resistance. When this was unsuccessful and the insurgents began to gain a foothold even in Jerusalem (8:31), in response neighboring communities began to harass the Jews, as in 10:14-38. When these efforts failed, Lysias, as guardian of Antiochus V and in charge of affairs, came in person in 164 B.C.E. He recognized the extent of Judas's forces and his support and sought to come to terms with Judas, as in 11:16-21. Lysias wrote to the king, but in late 164 B.C.E. Antiochus IV died, before an answer had been received. The response to the peace negotiations is given by the letter of 11:22-26, on the inauguration of Antiochus V as sole ruler. In response to attacks on Jews outside the borders of Judea, Judas and his forces began to engage in battles outside their own territory. These military excursions led to the second invasion, by Lysias and Antiochus V, in 163/162 B.C.E.

My brief chronology shows that the events narrated in 10:14—11:15 took place while Antiochus IV was still alive and Antiochus V was co-regent. The author of the narrative in 2 Maccabees wanted Antiochus IV to be an arch-villain, a blasphemer who fought against God and was suitably punished. He did not want to have Antiochus repeal the harsh measures against the ancestral traditions of Judea or have Menelaus in any way try to ameliorate the situation. In conformity with the tradition of the victory enthronement pattern of the divine war-

39   Frank Moore Cross, "The Divine Warrior in Israel's Early Cult," in Alexander Altman, ed., *Biblical Motifs: Origins and Transformations* (Philip W. Lown Institute of Advanced Judaic Studies, Brandeis University: Studies and Texts 3; Cambridge, Mass.: Harvard University Press, 1966) 11–30; Patrick D. Miller, *The Divine Warrior in Early Israel* (HSM 5; Cambridge, Mass.: Harvard University Press, 1973); Paul D. Hanson, "Jewish Apocalyptic against Its Near Eastern Environment," *RB* 78 (1971) 31–58; idem, *The Dawn of Apocalyptic: The Historical and Sociological Roots of Jewish Apocalyptic Eschatology* (rev. ed.; Philadelphia: Fortress Press, 1979).

rior, Antiochus IV had to die fighting against God. The author thus rearranged the narrative so that events that took place while Antiochus IV was alive but were instigated by Lysias as guardian of Antiochus V were placed after the death of Antiochus IV. These events took place while Antiochus V was ruling, but only as co-regent. Rhetoric has shaped the structure of the narrative.

Such a rhetorical reorganization would mean that the sequence of the events in the narrative of 2 Maccabees is basically the same as that in 1 Maccabees, with two expeditions of Lysias, one while Antiochus V was co-regent and the second after the death of Antiochus IV.

The Scope of the Narrative: Beginnings and Endings
The ability to control how one's history is told is a great boon not only for groups but also for individuals. Here the criticism of Thucydides by Dionysius of Halicarnassus is interesting. Thucydides should not have started where he did, but, as becomes a patriot ($\varphi\iota\lambda\acute{o}\pi o\lambda\iota\varsigma$), he should have begun when Athens was flourishing and then noted how the Spartans started the Peloponnesian War through envy and fear. He should have then narrated the setbacks of the Athenians.

> But Thucydides made his beginning at the point where Greek affairs started to decline. This should not have been done by a Greek and an Athenian, especially an Athenian who was not one of the outcasts, but one whom his fellow citizens counted among their foremost men in appointing to commands and other offices of state. And such is his malice, that he actually attributes the overt causes of the war to his own city, though he could have attributed them to many other sources. He might have begun his narrative not with the events at Corcyra, but with his country's splendid achievements immediately after the Persian War (achievements which he mentions later at an inappropriate point and in a rather grudging and cursory way). After he had described these events with all the goodwill of a patriot, he might then have added that it was through a growing feeling of envy and fear that the Lacedaemonians came to engage in the war, although they alleged motives of a different kind. . . . The concluding portion of his narrative is dominated by an even more serious fault. Although he states that he was an eyewitness of the whole war and has prom-
ised to describe everything that occurred, yet he ends with the sea-battle which took place off Cynossema between the Athenians and the Peloponnesians in the twenty-second year of the war. It would have been better, after describing all the events of the war, to end his history with a climax, and one that was most remarkable and especially gratifying to his audience, the return of the exiles from Phyle, which marked the beginning of the city's recovery of freedom. (Dionysius of Halicarnassus *Pomp.* 3)

For Dionysius, Herodotus knew how to tell history properly—he started with the problem of the barbarians injuring the Greeks and ended when punishment and retribution overtook the barbarians. One has to know when to start and when to end, and for Dionysius that meant choosing the most favorable beginning and ending. Cicero has basically the same advice for writing about individuals. The writing of history is to put forward one's hero, or one's native city to the best advantage. It is to construct an identity.

> Not that I am unconscious of the effrontery of what I am about, first in laying such a burden upon you (pressure of work may refuse me), and secondly in asking you to write about me eulogistically. . . . If I prevail upon you to undertake the task, I persuade myself that the material will be worthy of your ready and skilful pen. I fancy a work of moderate length could be made up, from the beginning of the plot down to my return from exile. . . . Moreover, my experiences will give plenty of variety to your narrative, full of a certain kind of delectation to enthrall the minds of those who read, when you are the writer. . . . So I shall be especially delighted if you find it best to set my story apart from the main stream of your work, in which you embrace events in their historical sequence—this drama, one may call it, of what I did and experienced; for it contains various "acts," and many changes of plan and circumstance. (Cicero *Ad Lucceium* [*Fam.* 5.12.2–4, 6])[40]

Dionysius of Halicarnassus might have been pleased with the structure of the condensed work, although hardly with its content or style. The opening shows

Jerusalem prosperous and at peace; a problem is brought in through envy. After various disasters, the Hebrews once again gain control of the city where "Hebrew" is the traditional, honorable name. Not everyone has been pleased with this ending, as it raises questions for inquiring minds: Nikanor is beaten, but what will be the reaction of the king who sent him? If the Akra remains unconquered, is the city really in the hands of the Hebrews? Is not Alcimus still high priest? In the light of what really happened, the author would seem to have been at the very least misleading. In response to Nikanor's defeat, Demetrius I sent Bacchides, who retook Jerusalem, defeated Judas's army in an engagement in which Judas himself was killed, and reinstalled Alcimus as high priest. Various answers have been proposed to explain why the work ends where it does:

1. Jason of Cyrene's work, the author's source, stopped at this point, even though the author knew of events that occurred later, for example, the embassy of Eupolemos and Jason to Rome. Niels Hyldahl even suggests that the diplomat Jason be identified with Jason of Cyrene, as this would explain why 2 Maccabees ends just before the diplomat's mission to Rome.[41]
2. The *author* chose to end at this point, in contrast to Jason of Cyrene. Jonathan Goldstein stresses the "I" of 15:37. Such a suggestion maintains the reliability of Jason as a historian and blames the author for misleading his readers.[42] This explanation would appear to be the opinion also of Daniel Schwartz, for whom the author "should want to leave them with the impression that the ideal situation continues until his and their own day."[43]

3. Goldstein also supplies a theological motif: from the end of the narrative on, "believing" Jews are in charge of the temple. Goldstein admits that this interpretation would implicitly include Alcimus among the "believers," as opposed to the "renegades," Jason and Menelaus.[44]
4. Hermann Lichtenberger suggests that the author could not have continued the narrative and have Judas die in battle soon after the victory over Nikanor. Lichtenberger noted that according to the narrative in 12:39-46, "death on the battlefield is the consequence of sin; or, even more precisely, of idolatry. Judas had nothing to do with all that."[45]

The first two suggestions do not touch the question of why Jason or the author ended at this juncture. As for Goldstein's suggestion, Alcimus is not presented as a sterling character in 2 Maccabees. Lichtenberger's proposal is seductive but neglects the central role that the defense of the temple plays in the narrative and the establishment of the festivals. The success of Judas comes because he fights for God, who is defending his temple. Judas, in this sense, is secondary to the main protagonist, God.

The first part of the sentence at 15:37, "As the actions at the time of Nikanor turned out this way," is very similar to the phrase in 13:26, "So turned out the events of the king's advance and return," which ends events under Antiochus V Eupator. The author maintains that after the death of Antiochus IV, the city and temple remained in danger under Antiochus V and Demetrius I. Lysias came to make the city a home for Greeks and to levy tribute on the temple as he had done on the sacred places of other nations (11:2-3). His repulse forces him to allow the Jews to enjoy their ancestral laws (11:24-31).

40 Translation is from D. R. Shackleton Bailey, *Cicero's Letters to His Friends* (Classical Resources Series 1; Atlanta: Scholars Press, 1996) 59–61.
41 Niels Hyldahl, "The Maccabean Rebellion and the Question of 'Hellenization,'" in Per Bilde et al., eds., *Religion and Religious Practice in the Seleucid Kingdom* (Studies in Hellenistic Civilization 1; Aarhus: Aarhus University Press, 1990) 201.
42 Goldstein, *II Maccabees*, 505.
43 Schwartz, *2 Maccabees*, 556.
44 Goldstein, *II Maccabees*, 504.
45 Hermann Lichtenberger, "The Untold End: 2 Maccabees and Acts," in Alberdina Houtman, Albert de Jong, and Magda Misset-van de Weg, eds., *Empsychoi Logoi — Religious Innovations in Antiquity: Studies in Honour of Pieter Willem van der Horst* (Leiden: Brill, 2008) 402.

Antiochus V comes with barbarous arrogance "to show forth to the Jews worse things than those committed at the time of his father" (13:9), but ends up honoring the temple and being generous to the place (13:23). Nikanor, too, threatens that he will "make this precinct of God into a plain and the altar I will raze to the ground and I will raise up a prominent temple there to Dionysos" (14:33). With God's help, the place remains undefiled (15:34), the final reprieve from attempts to destroy the ancestral religion. At 15:37, then, the author is claiming not independence for the Jews but the cessation of attempts to dismantle their ancestral laws.

What I would suggest about the endpoint of the narrative goes back to Arnaldo Momigliano's stress on the festal character of the epitome.[46] The author does not end because the sequence of events has reached its conclusion; he ends because the feast of Nikanor has been inaugurated. For the author, a central tenet of being a Judean is the ability to observe the ancestral feasts and customs of the Jews. After the defeat of Nikanor, that ability was no more in doubt. One might recall that later on, Antiochus VII Sidetes, while besieging Jerusalem, will accede to a request from John Hyrcanus for a truce during the festival of Tabernacles and will even send a sacrifice (Josephus *Ant.* 13.242–44). The epitome thus begins with the honor given to the temple (3:1-2) and ends with the festival of the deliverance of the temple. The observance of the festivals is central to the identity of the Jews. As regards the scope of the narrative, the author is governed by the rules of rhetoric.[47]

Conundra

How many Timothys are there? In 1 Maccabees 5, a Timothy takes part in a battle near Jazer (5:6) and then reemerges in upper Gilead at Dathema, on the eastern side of the Jordan, to fight again (5:11, 34, 37, 40); these events take place after the cleansing of the temple. In 2 Maccabees, a Timothy fights against Judas around the time of the attack of Nikanor (8:30, 32; 9:3) and then fights against Judas with cavalry near Gazara. This Timothy is at the head of a tremendous force (10:24) and is killed when he retreats to Gazara. Then later in 2 Maccabees, a Timothy is mentioned leading forces in Gilead (12:2, 10, 18-21, 24). Should one attempt to reconcile the accounts in 1 and 2 Maccabees and state either that the author of 2 Maccabees is hopelessly confused or that the author has deliberately changed Jazer to Gazara? Or were there two Timothys? The author of the narrative in 2 Maccabees certainly portrays them as two different commanders.

And how many Philips are there? In 1 Maccabees there is one: Antiochus IV, on his deathbed, appointed this Philip as ruler over all his kingdom and as guardian of his son (6:14). On his return to Antioch, this Philip took control of the city. When Lysias heard of this development (6:55-56), he withdrew from the assault on Jerusalem, returned to Antioch, and regained the city (6:63). In contrast, in 2 Maccabees Philip was simply one of Antiochus IV's courtiers. He took the king's body back to Antioch and then fled to Egypt because he feared Antiochus V (9:29). Later in 2 Maccabees, Lysias and Antiochus V break off their campaign when they hear that the Philip who had been left in charge of the government has lost his senses (13:23). The narrative here suggests that this Philip had been left in charge of the government by Antiochus V and Lysias. Are there two Philips?

Schwartz noted that there are problems in the account of 1 Maccabees. It dates the second campaign of Lysias to 150 s.e. [Seleucid Era] (1 Macc 6:20), either autumn 163/162 B.C.E. or 162/161 B.C.E. Bezalel Bar-Kochva argued that this campaign took place in 162 B.C.E.[48] However, since Antiochus IV's funeral procession was in Babylonia in January 163 B.C.E.,[49] Philip would likely have arrived in Antioch in February of that year. That the campaign of Antiochus V and Lysias would have been mounted after the return of Philip seems unlikely. Schwartz, holding that the return of Philip caused the end of the siege of Jerusalem, redated the campaign of

---

46   Momigliano, "Second Book of Maccabees," 81–88.
47   See also Eckhard Plümacher, "Cicero und Lukas: Bemerkungen zu Stil und Zweck der historischen Monographie," in Jens Schröter and Ralph Brucker, eds., *Geschichte und Geschichten: Aufsätze zur Apostelgeschichte und zu den Johannesakten* (WUNT 170; Tübingen: Mohr Siebeck, 2004).
48   Bezalel Bar-Kochva, *Judas Maccabaeus: The Jewish Struggle against the Seleucids* (Cambridge: Cambridge University Press, 1989) 543–51.
49   Dov Gera and Wayne Horowitz, "Antiochus IV in Life and Death: Evidence from the Babylonian Diaries," *JAOS* 117 (1997) 240–52, here 249–52.

Lysias and Antiochus V to late 164 or early 163 B.C.E. and eventually was led to suggest that there was only one campaign of Lysias and Antiochus V.[50] The simplest suggestion would seem to be that 1 Maccabees is indeed wrong, but not about the date. Rather, the author of 1 Maccabees was misled as to who forced Antiochus V and Lysias to cut off their campaign.[51]

The author of the condensed narrative seems to enjoy having people of the same name in important positions—note the Nikanor of 2 Maccabees 8 and the Nikanor of 2 Maccabees 13–15. First and Second Maccabees seem to mention two Bacchides as well, one who was present in Judea early on (2 Macc 8:30) and one who is governor of the province Beyond the River during the reign of Demetrius I (1 Macc 7:8).

The Work of Jason of Cyrene
Attempts to reconstruct the work of Jason of Cyrene have been many.

The Excision Route
Scholars have excised the prologue and epilogue, the reflections of the author (4:17; 5:17-20; 6:12-17), as well as the deaths of the mother and her seven sons and the references to resurrection.[52] Marcello Zambelli suggested that one should also exclude from Jason's work the last four chapters, as the prologue mentions only events from the reigns of Antiochus IV and Antiochus V, and only in 13:1 do we find dates given.[53] However, this excision would mean that neither Judas's triumph over Nikanor and the feast of Nikanor nor the second invasion of Antiochus V would be mentioned by Jason. Zambelli also suggested that the description of the death of Antiochus IV (9:18-27) was added later to Jason's work.[54]

The Addition Route
Other scholars have suggested that Jason's work extended to the death of Judas, noting the reference to the work of Eupolemos in 4:11 and identifying the Bacchides of 8:30 with the general at the time of Demetrius I.[55] However, Bacchides is not an unusual name in Seleucid prosopography, and the reference to Eupolemos would seem, as Schwartz noted,[56] to come from the author of the condensed narrative.

Given the above arguments for the rhetorical style and structure of the condensed narrative as well as the author's express aim to embellish the work of Jason of Cyrene (2:25-31), one should recognize that there was a Jason of Cyrene, but that attempts to reconstruct his work or to date it are like Don Quixote's tilting at windmills.

The Structure of the Narrative
There have been numerous suggestions as to how one should see the structure of the work. George W. E. Nickelsburg proposed a Deuteronomic pattern:[57]

50 Schwartz, 2 Maccabees, 30, 32.

51 Schwartz (2 Maccabees, 25-37) argued that the "original" work behind the author's condensation did not contain the material in the present 2 Maccabees 10–11, but after the death of Antiochus IV in 2 Maccabees 9 had the sequence 2 Maccabees 13; 12; 14–15. Driving his argument are the two conundra mentioned above, as well as a sense that the "original" document reflects what actually happened. The linguistic features that he isolates to back up his argument are, as he himself acknowledges, not probative. For example, he notes that only in 2 Maccabees 10–11 are the Jews called ἀδελφούς, not πολῖται as in the rest of the narrative. However, in 10:21, "brethren" is used in a case of betrayal where the term "brethren" highlights strongly the sense of outraged community. In 11:7, Judas is encouraging his forces to go to the aid of their "brethren." Again, the term is used effectively where connections to those attacked are being noted. One can easily isolate terms that are found in 2 Maccabees 10–11 and in the rest of the narrative, e.g., κράτος in 11:4;

12:28; ὀχύρος in 10:18; 12:13, 18, 27; ὀχύρωμα is used five times in 2 Maccabees 10–11 and also in 12:19. The syntax of these chapters remains uniform.

52 For discussion and references, see Habicht, 2. Makkabäerbuch, 171.

53 Marcello Zambelli, "La composizione del secondo libro di Maccabei e la nuova cronologia di Antioco IV Epifane," in Miscellanea Greca e Romana (Studi pubblicati dall'Istituto di Storia Antica 16; Rome: [s.n.], 1965) 286–87.

54 Zambelli, "La composizione," 287–99. Parts of 2 Maccabees 3 were excised in Elias Bickermann, "Héliodore au Temple de Jérusalem," Annuaire de l'Institut de Philologie et d'Histoire Orientales et Slaves 7 (1939–44) 5–40, here 18–40.

55 See especially Bunge, Untersuchungen, 207.

56 Schwartz, 2 Maccabees, 14–15, 221.

57 George W. E. Nickelsburg, Jewish Literature between the Bible and the Mishnah (Philadelphia: Fortress Press, 1981) 118.

1. Blessing: the priesthood of Onias (3:1-40)
2. Sin: the innovations of Jason and Menelaus (4:1—5:10)
3. Punishment: the persecution of Antiochus IV (5:11—6:17)
4. Tipping point: the deaths of the martyrs and the people's prayers (6:18—8:4)
5. Judgment and salvation: God brings about victory for his people (8:5—15:36).

Such a neat theological scheme, however, provides a very unbalanced structure, with the first four sections covering five chapters of the narrative and the fifth section covering eight.

John Bartlett argued for two main parts with two main climaxes: the defeat of Nikanor and the cleansing of the temple (8:1—10:8) and the defeat of Nikanor and the inauguration of the festival of the Day of Nikanor (15:6-36).[58] Jan Willem van Henten posited a fourfold structure: 3:1—4:6; 4:7—10:9; 10:10—13:26; 14:1—15:36.[59] David S. Williams has also proposed a fourfold structure:[60]

A. God defends the temple because the people observe the laws (3:1—4:6).
B. God punishes the people because of their sinfulness, but a turning point changes God's wrath to mercy and God destroys the enemy, Antiochus IV; subsequently God's people restore the temple and institute a festival (4:7—10:9).
A′. God defends the people because they observe the laws (10:10—13:26).
B′. God destroys the enemy, Nikanor, leaving the temple in the hands of the Jews, who celebrate by instituting a festival (14:1—15:37a).

Reinhold Zwick maintains a basic twofold structure (4:1—10:8; 10:9—15:36) introduced by an overture (3:1-40).[61]
History is always messy and cannot be fitted into a neat, logical structure. The reason one is tempted to do so with the narrative in 2 Maccabees is that the author has skillfully repeated patterns throughout the work—for example, the Divine Warrior in 9:1—10:8 and 14:26—15:36, the martyrs in 6:18—7:42 and Rhazis in 14:37-46, the appearance of Onias in 15:12, and the individual Judean villains like Simon (3:4) and Alcimus (14:3), who arrive on the scene to upset the applecart. So, while all the attempts at finding the structure of 2 Maccabees are instructive and enlightening, I find it interesting that the proposals of both van Henten and Williams follow the reigns of Seleucid kings: Seleucus IV in 3:1—4:6; Antiochus IV in 4:7—10:9; Antiochus V in 10:10—13:26; Demetrius I in 14:1—15:36. Although van Henten and Williams characterize each block of their fourfold structure differently, the underlying frame of the narrative would seem to be given by the reigns of the kings. Ulrike Mittmann-Richert noted this pattern as well and proposed a concentric structure for the narrative. The central turning point would be when the narrative begins to recount the deaths of those persecuted; on one side of this point would be the attack on the temple and ancestral constitution, while on the other side the narrative relates the deaths of the persecuted, the first victory of Judas, the death of Antiochus IV, and the rededication of the temple. Further out would fall the successful repulse of Heliodorus, which is mirrored by the defeat of Nikanor at the end of the narrative.[62] Such a concentric ordering would underscore the theatrical quality of the narrative, but there are so many differences in detail between the corresponding elements of the structure that it seems difficult to embrace.

The structure that I would therefore advocate follows the reigns of the four kings:

Prologue, 2:19-32
A. Events in the reign of Seleucus IV and the high priest Onias IV (3:1—4:6)
B. Events in the reign of Antiochus IV (4:7—10:8)

---

58 John R. Bartlett, *The First and Second Books of the Maccabees* (CBC; Cambridge: Cambridge University Press, 1973) 47.
59 Van Henten, *Maccabean Martyrs*, 25–26.
60 David S. Williams, "Recent Research in 2 Maccabees," *Currents in Biblical Research* 2.1 (2003) 69–83, here 77–78.
61 Zwick, "Unterhaltung und Nutzen," 149.
62 Ulrike Mittmann-Richert, *Historische und legendarische Erzählungen* (JSHRZ 6; Gütersloh: Gütersloher Verlagshaus, 2000) 41–43.

i. Events under Jason and Menelaus as high priests (4:7-50)

ii. The "revolt" of Jerusalem and its consequences (5:1–7:42)

iii. The deaths of the persecuted move God to support Judas (chap. 8)

iv. The death of the God-fighter, Antiochus IV (chap. 9)

v. The restoration of the temple (10:1-8)

C. Events in the reign of Antiochus V (10:9–13:26)

    i. The defense of Judea against external threats and a treaty with the king (10:9–11:38)

    ii. The defense of Jews living outside Judea and a second treaty with the king (chaps. 12–13)

D. Events in the reign of Demetrius I and the high priest Alcimus (14:1–15:37)

    i. First attack on Judas peacefully resolved (14:1-25)

    ii. The attack of the God-fighter Nikanor defeated (14:26–15:37)

Epilogue (15:37-39)

The Goals of the Author

The rhetorical permeation of 2 Maccabees raises the question of the aims of the author. To what end did he use this rhetoric? What behavior did he want to persuade his audience to adopt?

First, the choice of the subgenre of a deity defending his/her temple from attackers and the inauguration of new festivals shows that the author wanted to impress on his audience the high honor in which the God of the Jews was to be held and the need to participate in the festivals inaugurated to commemorate these events. The audience is also moved to hold in high regard the ancestral traditions of the Jews and to follow them. How the author emphasizes this sense of "ancestral" is interesting. Jason and those who follow him in frequenting the gymnasium are despising "ancestral honors" (πατρῴους τιμάς) in favor of Hellenic honors (4:15). But it is after Antiochus IV has inaugurated his new policy toward Judea that one finds the stress on "ancestral traditions." The king is shown throughout the narrative of 2 Maccabees to have the power to allow ancestral laws or to change them (4:11 [cf. Josephus *Ant.* 12.142]; 11:24, 31).

Antiochus IV compels the Jews "to change from their ancestral laws and not to be governed by the laws of God" (6:1: μεταβαίνειν ἀπὸ τῶν πατρίων νόμων καὶ τοῖς τοῦ θεοῦ νόμοις μὴ πολιτεύεσθαι). From then on, the Jews could not observe the ancestral festivals (6:6), and the seven brothers prefer to die rather than transgress ancestral laws (7:2, 24, 37) and express their refusal using their ancestral voice (7:8, 27). The ancestral voice is raised in triumph at the defeat of Nikanor (15:29), while Jason (4:13) and Menelaus (5:15) are depicted as traitors to the fatherland (5:15). By describing the insurgency as a defense of ancestral laws, the author was appealing to the strong civic patriotism of local communities. Erich Gruen has said that ancestral law, like freedom, was a slogan that carried great emotional appeal and that opposing parties would both assert that they were the champions of the ancestral laws.[63] By using this emotion-laden phrase, the author strives to engage his audience and move them to maintain and follow ancestral traditions. Recognition of this motif also clarifies why the author expounds so much on the building of a gymnasium in Jerusalem. The gymnasium was the symbol of Greek education par excellence. The author warns his audience against full acceptance of Hellenistic culture and stresses instead the need for the traditional educational goals of a Judean community.

Second, the theme of the Jews as good citizens surfaces. Individual Jews like Simon, Jason, Menelaus, and Alcimus upset the smooth functioning of affairs through their desire for power; Jews who follow their ancestral laws can live in harmony with their Gentile neighbors. In my early analysis of 2 Maccabees, I noted and stressed this theme. I was struck by the opening greeting of Antiochus IV's final letter to the Jews, which begins at 9:19: "to the well-deserving Jews, the citizens, much greeting, good health and prosperity" (Τοῖς χρηστοῖς Ἰουδαίοις τοῖς πολίταις πολλὰ χαίρειν καὶ ὑγιαίνειν). Its message is revealing. This high estimation of the Jews continues throughout the letter. The king recalls with affection their esteem and goodwill. In the transfer of power to his son, Antiochus IV trusts that the Jews will

---

63 Erich Gruen, in a private communication. I have discussed this subject in "The Persecution of Judeans by Antiochus IV: The Significance of 'Ancestral Laws,'" in Daniel C. Harlow et al., eds., *The "Other" in Second Temple Judaism: Essays in Honor of John J. Collins* (Grand Rapids: Eerdmans, 2011), 423–33.

make sure everything goes smoothly. He asks the Jews to continue their goodwill toward himself and his son. While it is true that in its present location the content of this letter jars with the king's earlier treatment of the Jews, which was certainly not "with mildness and benevolence" (9:27), the very fact that the author can present the Jews as esteemed citizens of a king underscores his desire to so portray them.

In 2 Maccabees, it is subverters of the peace such as Simon (3:4; 4:1), Jason (5:5), Antiochus himself (5:11, 22), Gorgias (10:14), the surrounding commanders (12:2), and Alcimus (14:3-10, 26) who start conflict, not the Jews, who are not allowed to live in peace (12:1-2). Scythopolis is not harmed by Judas, as it had treated its Jewish inhabitants favorably (12:29-31). Non-Jews show their respect for the Judean victims of unjust outrages (4:35, 49). This theme resonates particularly with what one finds also in the Greek Additions to Esther and in *3 Maccabees*. The accusation by Alcimus is the same as that found in the letter of Artaxerxes inserted in the Greek Esther at 3:13 (Addition B). This latter accusation, brought forward by Haman to the king in Esther, is proved false, and so too is the accusation of Alcimus. In *3 Maccabees,* King Ptolemy uses the same language of Jewish malice toward Greek citizens to plot his campaign against the Jews (*3 Macc* 3:26), but he is later forced to repent of his folly and admit that it is the Jews who brought stability and glory to his kingdom (*3 Macc* 6:28). He claims that evil friends had persuaded him that the Jews would not allow his state to be stable because of the ill will they bear all nations (*3 Macc* 7:4). In the text of 2 Macc 14:25, with its string of verbs, $\dot{\epsilon}\gamma\dot{\alpha}\mu\eta\sigma\epsilon\nu, \epsilon\dot{\nu}\sigma\tau\dot{\alpha}\vartheta\eta\sigma\epsilon\nu, \dot{\epsilon}\kappa\sigma\iota\nu\dot{\omega}\nu\eta\sigma\epsilon\ \beta\dot{\iota}\sigma\upsilon$, Judas Maccabeus is shown as quite content to live under the governorship of Nikanor. Ethnic identity can be maintained within the framework of an imperial power that can restrain, not unleash, anti-Judean sentiment.

The author thus has a twofold aim: he seeks to engage his audience in maintaining their ancestral traditions, and, at the same time, he insists that Jews can live in peace with local Gentile communities and with an imperial power.

The Date and Place of Composition

Both date and place of composition have been hugely debated, complicated further by the fact that the narrative is a condensed version of an account by Jason of Cyrene. As noted above, the scope of Jason's work cannot be reclaimed, and therefore that work cannot be placed or dated with certainty, except to say that it came before the condensed narrative.

Date of the Narrative

If one connects the narrative to the prefixed letters, then one will be inclined to date the narrative in line with the date given to the prefixed letters, particularly to the first. F.-M. Abel and Christian Habicht saw the narrative as attached to the first letter and therefore dated the former to 124 B.C.E., in conformity with the date at the end of the latter (1:10a).[64] Only later, they suggested, was the second prefixed letter added by someone, who also, according to Habicht, inserted material into the narrative.[65] Momigliano saw the narrative as accompanying the first letter: when the Jerusalem council was writing to the Egyptian Jews encouraging them to celebrate the feast of Hanukkah, it had someone make a summary of Jason's work, which he appended.[66] Schwartz, however, dated the first prefixed letter to 143 B.C.E. and so dated the narrative before that date.[67]

If, however, the narrative is uncoupled from the prefixed letters, it can be dated, as Bartlett suggested, "almost anywhere in the last 150 years B.C."[68] Bickermann placed the work of Jason around 100 B.C.E. and

---

64   Felix-Marie Abel, *Les livres des Maccabées* (EtB; Paris: Gabalda, 1949) XLII–XLIII; Habicht, *2. Makkabäerbuch*, 174–75.

65   Habicht, *2. Makkabäerbuch*, 174–75.

66   Momigliano, "Second Book of Maccabees," 83. See also van Henten, *Maccabean Martyrs*, 50; idem, "2 Maccabees as a History of Liberation," in Menahem Mor et al., eds., *Jews and Gentiles in the Holy Land in the Days of the Second Temple, the Mishnah,*

and the Talmud (Jerusalem: Yad Ben-Zvi, 2003) 68–86, here 83.

67   Schwartz, *2 Maccabees*, 14–15.

68   Bartlett, *First and Second Books*, 215. Stephanie von Dobbeler (*Die Bücher 1/2 Makkabäer* [Neue Stuttgarter Kommentar: Altes Testament 11; Stuttgart: Katholisches Bibelwerk, 1997]) also dates the condensed narrative before 12 B.C.E.

the condensed narrative at 60 B.C.E.[69] Arenhoevel placed Jason's work earlier than the debate over the legitimacy over the Hasmoneans, so around 100 B.C.E. or even earlier,[70] while Hugo Bévenot placed it between 124 B.C.E. and 70 C.E., that is, before the fall of Jerusalem, and van Henten had it between 124 and 63 B.C.E., that is, before the capture of Jerusalem by Pompey the Great.[71] Solomon Zeitlin dated it to the time of Agrippa I (41–44 C.E.) and Werner Dommerhausen to the late first century B.C.E.[72] If the letters are detached, the condensed narrative must be dated from internal hints. The goals of the author as outlined above could apply to any time in the Hellenistic period. However, the tossed-off reference to the diplomatic activity of Eupolemos in 4:11 as something well known to the audience suggests, as Schwartz rightly noted, something about the date. According to 1 Macc 8:17, Judas Maccabeus chose Eupolemos as one of his envoys to Rome to establish friendship and alliance (φιλίαν καὶ συμμαχίαν), the very same terms found in 4:11. This event occurred after the defeat of Nikanor, which is the last incident in the condensed narrative of 2 Maccabees. Eupolemos, a diplomat from a distinguished Jewish family, can likely be identified with the author of a work in Greek, fragments of which have been preserved in Eusebius of Caesarea's *Praeparatio evangelica*.[73] In the final fragment, Eupolemos gives the number of years from the time of Adam to the fifth year of the reign of Demetrius, while Ptolemy was in his twelfth year as king of Egypt. Despite problems with correlating the dates of both kings, the date would appear to be 158/157 B.C.E., the fifth year of Demetrius I. Eupolemos uses both the LXX and the Hebrew text, and since he dates his work by reference to Seleucid rulers,

he appears to be located in Jerusalem.[74] He would thus be writing in Jerusalem around the same time as an envoy named Eupolemos was sent to Rome on a diplomatic mission. It seems probable that the author of the fragments and the envoy are the same man. One does not know how long Eupolemos lived. His writing activity and his breakthrough diplomatic activity in making connection with Rome, however tenuous, would probably have made him well known to the audience for whom the author of the condensed narrative was writing, those who get involved in history's narratives and like to read (2:24-25). The history by Eupolemos, written in Greek, would have been ideal for educating young Jews who read Greek in their ancestral traditions. This assessment of Eupolemos unfortunately does not provide us with a hard time frame, as Eupolemos's work was still around to be excerpted by Alexander Polyhistor around 50 B.C.E. However, it does point again to the circles for whom the author of the condensed narrative was writing.

Place of Composition

The earlier scholarly consensus had been that the narrative stemmed from the Diaspora, most likely from Alexandria, although Zeitlin argued for Antioch.[75] Bévenot and Arenhoevel suggested that Jason came from Cyrene or Alexandria but went to Jerusalem, where he gathered information about the Hasmonean revolt.[76] Bévenot had the condensed narrative written in Alexandria.[77] The origin in Jerusalem has recently come into favor.[78] John M. G. Barclay does not include it in his list of works that definitely originated in the Diaspora;[79] for van Henten, "it is obvious that 2 Maccabees is of Judean origin."[80] Lee I. Levine holds that it was created "very likely in

---

69 Bickermann, "Makkabäerbücher," 791; idem, "Ein jüdischer Festbrief," 234.

70 Arenhoevel, *Theokratie*, 117.

71 Bévenot, *Die beiden Makkabäerbücher*, 11; van Henten, *Maccabean Martyrs*, 51–53.

72 Solomon Zeitlin, *The Second Book of Maccabees* (trans. Sidney Tedesche; New York: Harper & Brothers, 1954) 27–30; Werner Dommerhausen, *1 Makkabäer 2 Makkabäer* (NEchtB 12; Würzburg: Echter Verlag, 1985) 9.

73 For a critical edition and commentary on the fragments, see Carl R. Holladay, *Fragments from Hellenistic Jewish Authors*, vol. 1: *Historians* (SBLTT 20; Chico, Calif.: Scholars Press, 1983) 93–156.

74 Francis Fallon, "Eupolemus," *OTP* 2:861–72, here 862–63.

75 Zeitlin, *Second Book*, 20–21.

76 Bévenot, *Die beiden Makkabäerbücher*, 9 (Jason came from Cyrene); Arenhoevel, *Theokratie*, 115–16 (Jason possibly brought up in Alexandria).

77 Bévenot, *Die beiden Makkabäerbücher*, 9.

78 An exception is Dommerhausen, *1. Makkabäer 2. Makkabäer*, 8.

79 John M. G. Barclay, *Jews in the Mediterranean Diaspora: From Alexander to Trajan (323 B.C.E.–117 C.E.)* (Edinburgh: T&T Clark, 1996) 12.

80 Van Henten, *Maccabean Martyrs*, 50.

Jerusalem."[81] Originally, I held that there was no reason why a work of this quality of Greek could not have been written in Jerusalem.[82] Schwartz has, however, strongly argued that 2 Maccabees is a "diasporan book."[83] I too place the author in the Diaspora, and the question of education provides the main grounds for this placing of 2 Maccabees.

Second Maccabees has been mined for its more intensive narration of the events leading up to the Maccabean revolt. The one-line account in 1 Macc 1:14 of the building of a gymnasium cannot compare with the extended account in 2 Maccabees 4. In an earlier work[84] I stressed the relationship between gymnasium education and citizenship (πολιτεία) and drew particular attention to Plutarch's description of how Philopoemen treated Sparta:

Now, glutting his anger at the Lacedaemonians and unworthily trampling upon them in their misery, he treated their constitution [τὴν πολιτείαν] in the most cruel and lawless [παρανομώτατον] fashion. For he took away and abolished the system of training which Lycurgus had instituted [τὴν Λυκουργεῖον ἀγωγήν] and compelled their boys and their young men [τοὺς ἐφήβους] to adopt the Achaean in place of their ancestral discipline [τῆς πατρίου παιδείας μεταλαβεῖν] being convinced that while they were under the laws of Lycurgus [ἐν τοῖς Λυκούργου νόμοις] they would never be humble.

For the time being, then, owing to their calamities. the Spartans suffered Philopoemen to eat away, as

it were, the sinews of their city, and became tractable and submissive; but a while afterwards, having obtained permission from the Romans, they abandoned the Achaean polity [τὴν Ἀχαικὴν πολιτείαν] and resumed and reestablished that which had come down from their fathers [τὴν πάτριον], so far as was possible after their many misfortunes and ruin. (Plutarch Phil. 16.5–6)

The language of this passage resonates with the language of 2 Macc 4:10-17. The author deals with the setting up of the gymnasium in half a verse (4:9b) but spends eight verses (4:10-17) commenting on Jews' going to the gymnasium as dissolving the Judean constitution/ way of life. This subject appears very dear to his heart. Here is a writer well trained in the writing of Greek, who knows the technical terms of Greek historiographical writing, and who yet insists that Jews should not go to the gymnasium. I can only conclude from the author's passionate dissent from the practice that some Jews were in fact going to gymnasia. While there is mention of a xystus in Jerusalem at the time of the Jewish revolt in 67 C.E., I do not think this reference means that there was a full-blown gymnasium in the city. Rather, the concern expressed by the author of the narrative would seem most at home with Jews going to gymnasia in Hellenistic cities. Inscriptional evidence for such participation surfaces at the beginning of the first century C.E. in Cyrene, where a catalogue of ephebes contains a few clearly Jewish names.[85] Later, Jewish names are found in lists of ephebes in Iasos, in Caria, and Korone, in Messenia.[86] At Hypaipa, near Sardis, a group of young men called them-

---

81 Lee I. Levine, *Judaism & Hellenism in Antiquity: Conflict or Confluence?* (Seattle: University of Washington Press, 1998) 79.

82 Doran, *Temple Propaganda*, 112–13.

83 Schwartz, *2 Maccabees*, 45–55; quotation from 45. I do not find some of Schwartz's arguments probative. For example, he contrasts 1 Macc 5:54, where Judas's men bring sacrifices, and 2 Macc 12:31-32, where they simply celebrate Pentecost. However, the sacrifices in 1 Macc 5:54 are mentioned specifically to contrast *Judas's* men, who were unscathed, with the followers of Joseph and Azariah in the next incident, who are routed and of whom two thousand die, thus showing that they do not belong to the family through whom deliverance was given to Israel

(1 Macc 5:60-62). Schwartz notices many important elements, but they need not be diasporan.

84 Robert Doran, "Jason's Gymnasion," in Harold W. Attridge, John J. Collins, and Thomas H. Tobin, eds., *Of Scribes and Scrolls: Studies on the Hebrew Bible, Intertestamental Judaism, and Christian Origins Presented to John Strugnell on the Occasion of His Sixtieth Birthday* (College Theology Society Resources in Religion 5; Lanham, Md.: University Press of America, 1990) 99–109.

85 Gert Lüderitz, *Corpus jüdischer Zeugnisse aus der Cyrenaika* (Wiesbaden: Reichert, 1983) nos. 6 and 7.

86 Louis Robert, "Un corpus des inscriptions juives," *REJ* 101 (1937) 73–86, here 85; *IG* 5.1:1398. See Louis Robert, *Hellenica: recueil d'épigraphie de numis-*

16

selves "younger Jewish," Ἰουδαῖοι νεώτεροι, according to the usual division of Greek ephebes.[87] Barclay has argued that the privilege mentioned in Josephus (*Ant.* 12.120) whereby Jews in the gymnasia could buy their own non-Gentile oil most probably refers to Jews training in the gymnasium.[88] I would suggest that Jewish participation in the gymnasium had been going on before this date, and that the author of the narrative in 2 Maccabees holds that it destroys Jewish identity. Such a theme would be most at home in the Diaspora.

But where in the Diaspora? Suggestions have centered mainly on Alexandria and Antioch. As we noted, however, Jews in Asia Minor also participated in the gymnasium, and in 8:20 there is mention of an otherwise unknown battle against Galatians. However, for an audience who enjoyed history's narrative (2:20), this could have been known elsewhere. The main reason for preferring Alexandria lies in the abundance of Jewish-Hellenistic literature located there and particularly in the correspondences between the Greek Additions to Esther and *3 Maccabees*. Furthermore, I have argued that some of this Jewish-Hellenistic material would find its home in a system of Greek education. The work of Demetrius and his rival Philo evidences a close reading of the biblical narrative and a concentration on the characters and the time frame of the events, features that parallel the basic curriculum of the Greek educational system, which focused on the Greek classics. Aristobulos concentrates on explaining the deeper significance behind the text of the Bible. Ezekiel the Tragedian writes a play on the encounter of Moses with God that shows the influence of Aeschylus and Euripides.[89] The author of the narrative in 2 Maccabees might thus be arguing that young Jews

should participate in this "traditional" education system, perhaps as he had when learning Greek, rather than in the civic gymnasium. One might also note the author's emphasis on the value of the ancestral traditions of the Jews, particularly on observance of the Sabbath (6:6, 11; 8:26-28). Of special note is 5:25, where Apollonius deceitfully uses the day of the Sabbath to attack Jews. This view of the sanctity of the Sabbath stands in stark contrast to that of the Hellenistic historian Agatharchides, who was writing in Alexandria in mid-second century B.C.E. Agatharchides characterized the observance of the Sabbath as folly (ἄνοια) (Josephus *Ap.* 1.208-12). The narrative, with its emphasis on how God defends those who follow his laws, could be a response to such attacks on Judean traditions.

Conclusions about the dating and location of the work are therefore difficult to arrive at.

A Suggested Time Line from 2 Maccabees

Few dates are given in the narrative of 2 Maccabees. Often the author is content with "around this time" (5:1; 9:1), "after not much time" (6:1), "after an extremely short interval" (11:1), or "after three years" (4:23; 14:1). At the end of the letters in 11:21, 33, 38 is found the date 148 S.E. [Seleucid Era]; in 13:1, year 149 S.E. is given for the invasion of Lysias and Antiochus V; year 151 S.E. is given for the approach of Alcimus to Demetrius I (14:4). These dates are according to the Seleucid Macedonian system, where year 1 = autumn 312 B.C.E. to autumn 311 B.C.E., so 148 S.E. = autumn 165 B.C.E. to autumn 164 B.C.E.[90]

---

matique et d'antiquités grecques XI–XII (Paris: Maisonneuve, 1960) 3:100–101.

87 *CPJ* 1:30 n. 99.

88 Barclay, *Jews in the Mediterranean Diaspora*, 256 n. 63.

89 Robert Doran, "The High Cost of a Good Education," in John J. Collins and Gregory E. Sterling, eds., *Hellenism in the Land of Israel* (Christianity and Judaism in Antiquity 13; Notre Dame, Ind.: University of Notre Dame Press, 2001) 94–115, here 103–5. The texts of Demetrius have been critically edited in Holladay, *Fragments*, 1:51–91; Ezekiel in Holladay, *Fragments*, 2:301–529; Aristobulos in Holladay, *Fragments*, vol. 3.

90 The main problems arise in the dating of events in

1 Maccabees, and various proposals have been raised to determine how events should be dated.
(1) There is one system of dating in 1 Maccabees that begins in autumn 312 B.C.E.; see Klaus Bringmann, *Hellenistische Reform und Religionsverfolgung in Judäa: Eine Untersuchung zur jüdisch-hellenistischen Geschichte (175–163 v. Chr.)* (Abhandlungen der Akademie der Wissenschaften in Göttingen, Philologisch-historische Klasse 3/132; Göttingen: Vandenhoeck & Ruprecht, 1983) 15–40. There would thus be no overlap between the date in 1 Maccabees (150 = spring 162 to spring 161) and that of 2 Maccabees (149 = autumn 164 to autumn 163), and one would have to decide which was most reliable.

What timetable of events would be found if one looked only at the data that can be gleaned from 2 Maccabees, without trying to gauge whether 1 or 2 Maccabees is more correct? My starting point for constructing the chronology is the information contained in the letter in 11:27-33, dated to March 165 B.C.E. = Xanthikos 148 S.E., which records that an amnesty was granted by Antiochus IV to the Jews at the instigation of Menelaus. This letter would have been written just before Antiochus IV left on his eastern campaign and appointed Antiochus V as co-regent under the guardianship of Lysias.

Seleucus IV Philopator (187–175)

187–75	Heliodorus is chancellor of the empire. At some point there is a failed attempt to confiscate money from the temple in Jerusalem. In 178 Olympiodorus is appointed to regulate the temples of Coele-Syria and Phoenica.

Antiochus IV Epiphanes (175–164)

	Jason becomes high priest.
173/172	Antiochus travels through Coele-Syria and Phoenica.
February 169	First Invasion of Egypt by Antiochus.
Spring 168	Second Invasion of Egypt.
July 168	Withdrawal from Egypt forced by the Romans. On his return, Antiochus plunders Jerusalem and its temple, as he thinks it is in rebellion.
Fall 167	Geron in Jerusalem to change the political structure.
December 167	Profanation of the temple.

166	The celebration of the festival at Daphne.
February/March 165	Menelaus intervenes to ask for the restoration of ancestral laws in Judea (11:27-33).

Antiochus V Eupator co-regent

Spring 165	Antiochus IV sets off to Armenia and then on to his eastern campaign. He leaves Antiochus V as co-regent under the guardianship of Lysias.
	The amnesty does not work. Continued insurgency under Judas Maccabeus.
	Ptolemy, son of Dorymenes, sends Nikanor to quell the uprising. Nikanor is defeated. Judas has some entry into Jerusalem (8:30-33).
164	Lysias makes his first expedition into Judea. Having noted the size of the insurgency, he proposes sending to Antiochus IV to suggest a further settlement.
November/December 164	News in Babylonia that Antiochus IV has died. The Jews purify the temple.

Antiochus V Eupator

164	On his accession, Antiochus V agrees to a settlement, and the Jews are to live according to their ancestral laws.

---

(2) There are two systems of dating in 1 Maccabees, one for internal Jewish events, which would follow the Seleucid Babylonian system and begin in spring 311 B.C.E., and one for external events like Seleucid expeditions, which would begin in autumn 312 B.C.E.; see Elias Bickerman, *The God of the Maccabees: Studies in the Meaning and Origin of the Maccabean Revolt* (trans. Horst R. Moehring; SJLA 32; Leiden: Brill, 1979) 155–58. In 1 Macc 10:21, for example, the feast of Booths is said to occur in Tishri, the sev-

enth month. This presupposes a calendar beginning in spring.
(3) There are two systems of dating in 1 Maccabees, where the calendar for dating internal Jewish events would have begun in spring 312 B.C.E., while external events would be dated beginning with autumn 312 B.C.E.; see Lester Grabbe, "Maccabean Chronology: 167–164 or 168–165 B.C.E.?" *JBL* 110 (1991) 59–74.

| 163 | Harassment of the Jews living outside Judea drives Judas and his forces to fight outside the territorial limits of Judea (2 Maccabees 12). |

These outside forays lead to the second expedition of Lysias and Antiochus V Eupator (2 Maccabees 13), which ends in a settlement between the two sides.

Demetrius I

late 162	Demetrius becomes king.
	Nikanor sent to Jerusalem to install Alcimus. Peaceful relationship with Judas.
March 161	Nikanor defeated.

What is fascinating in this outline of events is the number of attempts to settle the uprising. Within two years of the decrees of Antiochus IV that changed the polity of Jerusalem, Menelaus succeeds in showing the king that this action has antagonized part of the population and that he should change back to the older ways. Lysias then recognizes that Judas's forces are capable of forging order, and so he sets out to make a settlement. Antiochus V agrees with this approach. Lysias and Antiochus V have to intervene when Judas's forces range outside Judea, but another settlement is reached. Finally, Judas and Nikanor make an agreement. This time line reinforces the motif that the Jews are a peaceful people if left alone to follow their ancestral laws.

The Text

The text of 2 Maccabees is found in the two uncial manuscripts, Alexandrinus from the fifth century C.E. and Venetus from the eighth century C.E., but not in Sinaiticus. It is also in more than thirty minuscules that are divided according to whether they are seen as having undergone "improvements" (attributed to Lucian of Samosata). There are translations into Latin, of which the most important is the Vetus Latina, edited by Donatien de Bruyne,[91] and into Syriac, Armenian, and Coptic. The critical edition of the text is by Robert Hanhart, who built on work begun by his predecessor, Werner Kappler.[92] The revised second edition of Hanhart's work is the basis for my translation.[93] The first edition of 1959 was roundly criticized, particularly by Peter Katz, and some of Katz's criticisms still remain valid,[94] even after the response by Hanhart.[95] Where I have departed from the edition by Hanhart is noted in the text-critical apparatus.

---

91 Donatien de Bruyne, *Les anciennes traductions Latines des Machabées* (Anecdota Maredsolana 4; Maredsous: Abbaye de Maredsous, 1932).

92 Werner Kappler, "De memoria alterius libri Maccabaeorum" (Ph.D. diss., Göttingen, 1929).

93 Robert Hanhart, *Maccabaeorum liber II, copiis usus quas reliquit Werner Kappler* (Septuaginta 9.2; 2nd ed.; Göttingen: Vandenhoeck & Ruprecht, 1976).

94 Peter Katz, "The Text of 2 Maccabees Reconsidered," *ZNW* 51 (1960) 10–30.

95 Robert Hanhart, *Zum Text des 2. und 3. Makkabäerbuches: Probleme der Überlieferung, der Auslegung und der Ausgabe* (Nachrichten der Akademie der Wissenschaften in Göttingen, Philologisch-historische Klasse, 1961, 13; Göttingen: Vandenhoeck & Ruprecht, 1961).

Commentary

1   **1:1-10a**

1/	To the brothers, the Jews throughout Egypt, greetings from the brothers, the Jews in Jerusalem and those in the territory of Judea. 2/ Best wishes, and may God treat you well and recall his covenant in the presence of Abraham, Isaac, and Jacob, his faithful servants. 3/ May he give you all a heart to reverence him, and to do what he wants with a full heart and a willing spirit. 4/ May he open up your heart in his law and in his statutes. May he make peace 5/ and may he hearken to your entreaties and may he be reconciled to you and may he not abandon you at a bad time. 6/ And now we are praying for you.	a	Codices 62 and 55 read 148, the year of the dedication of the altar (1 Macc 4:52).
7/	When Demetrius was king, in the year 169, we Jews wrote to you: "In the extreme oppression that came upon us during those years, from the time that Jason and his companions left the holy land and the kingdom 8/ and they burnt the gate and shed innocent blood, we besought the Lord and we were heard. We offered sacrifices and choice flour and we kindled the lamps and we set out the breads."		
9/	So now celebrate the days of Booths in the month of Kislev.		
10a/	In the year 188.[a]		

Commentary by Verse

■ **1** The initial address follows the pattern "To B χαίρειν A," where A (nominative case) sends greetings to B. This pattern is found in letters from the Ptolemaic period,[1] and differs from the customary opening, "A to B, greeting." The pattern "To B, A" is frequently found in Aramaic letters.[2]

"brothers." In Aramaic letters, familial language is sometimes used in an honorific sense, as in "To my brother Pir-amurri from your brother Bel-etir" in a letter between two military officers,[3] even though no family connection is attested. Sometimes the relationship of "brother" is used in the address even if not correct—for example, a father addresses a letter, "To my son Sheloman from your brother Oshea."[4] The use of fraternal

---

1   Francis X. Exler, *The Form of the Ancient Greek Letter: A Study in Greek Epistolography* (Washington, D.C.: Catholic University of America Press, 1923) 42–44, 65–66; John L. White, *Light from Ancient Letters* (FF; Philadelphia: Fortress Press, 1986) 194–96.

2   Joseph A. Fitzmyer, "Some Notes on Aramaic Epistolography," *JBL* 93 (1974) 201–25, here 211–14.

3   Ashur ostracon in James M. Lindenberger, *Ancient Aramaic and Hebrew Letters* (ed. Kent Harold Richards; 2nd ed.; WAW 14; Atlanta: Society of Biblical Literature, 2003) §1.

4   Lindenberger, *Ancient Aramaic and Hebrew Letters*, no. 9.

language emphasizes the close bonds between sender and recipient. Familial language was used also by various associations to stress group identity.[5]

Ἰουδαῖοι. This word has the connotation of one from the land of Judea. Elias Bickermann and Claire Préaux held that such a designation reflects the Ptolemaic practice of identifying noncitizens by their point of origin, be it Macedonian, Lycian, Athenian, or Judean, even if sometimes the original city-state no longer existed and if those so designated had lived in Egypt for generations.[6] But the situation is not quite so clear cut. Csaba La'da has shown that "ethnic designations in demotic (and Greek) official documents from Hellenistic Egypt are generally not trustworthy indicators of real ethnicity" and some ethnic designations "became occupational-status designations."[7] A Ἰουδαῖος could be labeled ethnically as Πέρσης τῆς ἐπιγονῆς, a Ἰουδαία is referred to by the civic label Γαργάρισσα (P. Polit. Jud. 8.11–15). Later, one of two brothers, Ἰουδαῖοι, is labeled Μακεδών.[8] A Ἰουδαῖος, therefore, could have several ethnic designations. As Sylvie Honigman shows, "there was in Alexandria a Jewish community whose members had diverging legal statuses: . . . we met Jews who were Ἀλεξανδρεῖς, Μακεδόνες or perhaps Ἕλληνες, Ἰουδαῖοι members of the politeuma, Ἰουδαῖοι from Egypt or

Syria."[9] Even if the ethnic designation Ἰουδαῖος signified point of origin, point of origin involves much more than geography. In the felicitous phrase of Paula Fredriksen, "gods run in the blood,"[10] and so geography, ethnicity, and cultural practices—including religious ones—are intimately connected. A preferable translation is "Jews." In modern English, "Judean" has much too narrow a geographic connotation, as Daniel Schwartz has noted.[11] Therefore, I have translated the term Ἰουδαῖοι throughout this commentary as "Jews," and speak of Jews rather than Judeans.

"Best wishes" is literally "good peace." Scholars have puzzled over the presence both of the initial greeting usual in Greek, χαίρειν, and of the phrase in the accusative, εἰρήνην ἀγαθήν, which seems to reflect the initial greeting found in Aramaic or Hebrew, שְׁלָם, שָׁלוֹם ("greetings," literally "peace"). Most scholars have taken the wording to be duplication, perhaps caused by a redactor. Christian Habicht suggests either eliding one of the greetings or adding the conjunction καί ("and") before εἰρήνην ἀγαθήν.[12] Jonathan Goldstein has the most radical solution. Noting that εἰρήνην ἀγαθήν is in the accusative and is not an initial greeting formula, he suggests taking it as the object of the succeeding verb. He then reads this verb not as ἀγαθοποιῆσαι ("treat

---

5   Philip A. Harland, "Familial Dimensions of Group Identity: 'Brothers' (Ἀδελφοί) in Associations of the Greek East," *JBL* 124 (2005) 491–513.

6   Elias Bickermann, "Beiträge zur antiken Urkundengeschichte, I: Der Heimatsvermerk und die staatsrechtliche Stellung der Hellenen im ptolemäischen Ägypten," *Archiv für Papyrusforschung und verwandte Gebiete* 8 (1927) 223–25; Claire Préaux, "Les Étrangers à l'époque hellénistique (Egypte-Delos-Rhodes)," in *L'Étranger/Foreigner* (Recueils de la Société Jean Bodin pour l'histoire comparative des institutions 9; Paris: Dessain et Tolra, 1984) 141–93, esp. 189–93. See further Koen Goudriaan, *Ethnicity in Ptolemaic Egypt* (Dutch Monographs on Ancient History and Archaeology 5; Amsterdam: Gieben, 1988); Per Bilde, Troels Engberg-Pedersen, Lise Hannestad, and Jan Zahle, eds., *Ethnicity in Hellenistic Egypt* (Studies in Hellenistic Civilization 3; Aarhus: Aarhus University Press, 1992); Margaret H. Williams, "The Meaning and Function of *Ioudaios* in Graeco-Roman Inscriptions," *ZPE* 116 (1997) 249–62; Shaye J. D. Cohen, *The Beginnings of Jewishness: Boundaries, Varieties, Uncertainties* (Hellenistic Culture and Society 31; Berkeley: University of California Press, 1999); Steve Mason, "Jews, Judaeans,

Judaizing, Judaism: Problems of Categorization in Ancient History," *JSJ* 38 (2007) 457–512.

7   Csaba A. La'da, "Ethnicity, Occupation and Tax-status in Ptolemaic Egypt," in *Acta demotica: Acts of the Fifth International Conference for Demotists, Pisa, 4th–8th September 1993* (Pisa: Giardini, 1994) 189.

8   *CPJ* 2, nos. 142–143. See the discussion in Sylvie Honigman, "*Politeumata* and Ethnicity in Ptolemaic and Roman Egypt," *Ancient Society* 33 (2003) 61–102, here 80.

9   Honigman, "*Politeumata*," 90.

10   Paula Fredriksen, "Mandatory Retirement: Ideas in the Study of Christian Origins Whose Time to Go Has Come," *SR* 35 (2006) 231–46, here 232.

11   Daniel R. Schwartz, "'Judean' or 'Jew'? How Should We Translate Ἰουδαῖο in Josephus?" in Jörg Frey, Daniel R. Schwartz, and S. Gripentrog, eds., *Jewish Identity in the Greco-Roman World/Jüdische Identität in der griechisch-römischen Welt* (Ancient Judaism and Early Christianity 71; Leiden: Brill, 2007) 3–27.

12   Habicht, *2. Makkabäerbuch*, 43.

you well") but, following q, as ἀγαθά ποιήσαι. His translation reads, "A good peace may God make for you." Since Goldstein thought that this prayer for peace would then duplicate the prayer at 1:4, εἰρήνην ποιήσαι ("may he make peace"), he argued that the clause in 1:4 was a marginal note that was later incorporated into the main text.[13] Such a complex reconstruction of the text and its transmission history seems unwarranted.

When the form of the greeting is "To A, peace," the nominative form is used, εἰρήνη, as at Ezra 5:7 (= 2 Esdr 5:7) and Dan 4:1 (Theodotion) and 6:26. Here, however, the sender is placed in the nominative and so one could not have the nominative εἰρήνη. Double formulas are found in the greeting of letters, as at Lachish 3 ישמע יהוה את אדני שמעת שלם ושמעת טב ("May Yahweh hear my lord, may you hear peace and may you hear good"); Hermopolis 3 שלם וחן שלחת לך ("I send you peace and life"); Lachish 5.9 ישמע יהוה את אדני שמעת שלם וטב ("May Yahweh hear my lord, may you hear peace and good").[14] Double formulas are therefore to be found, although not usually as far apart from each other as here and without a connective.

I therefore suggest that the accusative εἰρήνην ἀγαθήν, literally "good peace," is similar to the wish formula found in the Lachish letters: שלם וטב, literally "peace and good." Since the first part of 1:1 follows the initial greeting pattern of letters of petition, To A χαίρειν B, I have separated εἰρήνην ἀγαθήν from this initial greeting and placed it, as does Goldstein, among the wishes for well-being. One should presuppose a verb such as "we send," שלחנו in Hebrew.

■ **2-5** These verses contain a series of eight expressions of wish in the optative mood arranged paratactically with the conjunction καί. The series appears to be divided into two parts: the first four expressions (vv. 2-4a) begin with the optative ἀγαθοποιήσαι, which picks up on ἀγαθήν in the first wish for well-being at the end of v. 1; the second four begin with εἰρήνην ποιήσαι, which picks up on εἰρήνην, which is the other component of the first wish for well-being at the end of v. 1.

■ **2** The preposition πρός here governs the indeclin-

able names Abraham, Isaac, and Jacob and the genitive of "his faithful servants." Since, in the construction "a covenant πρός . . ." πρός is usually followed by the accusative,[15] one finds in the manuscripts either that πρός is changed to περί (19-62) or the genitive is changed to the accusative (46-52, 55). Carl L. W. Grimm suggested that the writer either was thinking that the verb μιμνήσκω ("to remember") takes the genitive and so put the appositive "his faithful servants" as the object of the verb or followed a pattern like διαθήκη τῶν πατέρων (1 Macc 2:20, 50; 4:10). Πρός can govern the genitive[16] both with a local sense, as is found in the LXX Josh 15:8 (πρὸς θαλάσσης, "toward the sea"); Ruth 3:4, 7, 8, 14 (πρὸς ποδῶν, "near his feet"); and 1 Sam 19:13; 26:7 (πρὸς κεφαλῆς αὐτοῦ, "near its head"), and with other relations, as is found in Gen 29:34 (πρὸς ἐμοῦ ἔσται ὁ ἀνήρ μου, "my husband will be on my side") and Gen 31:5 (ὅτι οὐκ ἔστιν πρὸς ἐμοῦ, "he is not on my side"). Πρός + genitive also has the sense of "in the presence of, in the sight of" as in 4 Macc 6:20 (καταγελώμενοι πρὸς ἁπάντων ἐπὶ δειλίᾳ, "being mocked in the sight of all for cowardice"); Homer Il. 1.339 (μάρτυροι ἔστων πρός τε θεῶν μακάρων πρός τε θνητῶν ἀνθρώπων, "let them be witnesses in the sight of the blessed gods, in the sight of mortal men"). If one takes the text as in the majority of manuscripts, one need not assume a mistake on the part of the writer, but translate "his covenant in the sight of Abraham," rather than "his covenant with Abraham." In this sense, Abraham, Isaac, and Jacob were witnesses to the compact that God established with his people.

In 1 Macc 4:10, Judas Maccabeus prays that God will remember the ancestral covenant (μνησθήσεται διαθήκη πατέρων), since Mattathias had decided to follow the ancestral covenant (1 Macc 2:20, 50), but no specification of the "fathers" is given as it is here. God promised, if the Israelites were punished and then repented, to remember his covenant with Jacob, his covenant with Isaac, and his covenant with Abraham (Lev 26:42; see also Ps 105:8-10 and Deut 4:31). When God heard the groaning of the Israelites in Egypt, he remembered his

---

13   Goldstein, *II Maccabees*, 141.

14   Lindenberger, *Ancient Aramaic and Hebrew Letters*, §§62, 4.5 (see also 9); 66–67.

15   E.g., Gen 6:18; 9:11; 17:19, 21; Exod 2:14; 6:4; Lev

26:44; Deut 5:2; 7:2; Josh 9:154-16; 24:25; Neh 9:8; Isa 33:8; 1 Macc 11:9.

16   Herbert Weir Smyth, *Greek Grammar* (Cambridge, Mass.: Harvard University Press, 1920) §1695.

covenant with Abraham, Isaac, and Jacob (Exod 2:24: καὶ ἐμνήσθη ὁ θεὸς τῆς διαθήκης αὐτοῦ τῆς πρὸς Ἀβρααμ καὶ Ἰσαακ καὶ Ἰακωβ; see also Exod 6:5-8). The Jews in Egypt would probably have picked up the allusion to the exodus event. When Hezekiah urged all the people to celebrate the Passover, his letter began, "O people of Israel, return to the Lord, the God of Abraham, Isaac and Jacob, so that he may turn again" (2 Chr 30:6).

Abraham is said to be faithful in Neh 9:8 and Sir 44:20; Moses is said to be "faithful" in Num 12:7; Nathan prophesies that David will be faithful in my house" (1 Chr 17:14: καὶ πιστώσω αὐτὸν ἐν οἴκῳ μου); it is prophesied that a faithful priest will arise to replace the house of Eli (1 Kgdms 2:35). Only here, however, are the three patriarchs called "faithful servants."

■ **3-4** In the third and fourth wishes, the term καρδία ("heart") is found three times. The two wishes are therefore bound together: the heart given to reverence God and do what he wants (τὰ θελήματα, which literally means "wills, desires") is a heart open to perceive God's will expressed in the law and statutes. The general term τὰ θελήματα is specified as being in the law and the statutes. Psalm 102:7 LXX states: "[The Lord] made known his ways to Moses, to the children of Israel what he wanted [τὰ θελήματα αὐτοῦ]." The idea recalls the promise in Ezek 11:19-20: "I will give them one heart [δώσω αὐτοῖς καρδίαν ἑτέραν] . . . so that they may follow my statutes [ὅπως ἐν τοῖς προστάγμασίν μου πορεύωνται]."[17]

■ **3** In 1 Chr 29:19, David prays that God will give a heart to Solomon to do God's commands; in 2 Chr 17:6, of King Jehoshaphat it is said that "his heart was exalted [ὑψώθη] in the way of the Lord."

In 1 Chr 28:9, David prays that Solomon serve God with a whole heart and a willing mind (בלב שלם ובנפש חפצה, ἐν καρδίᾳ τελείᾳ καὶ ψυχῇ θελούσῃ). The phrase לב שלם is found at Qumran (CD 1.10; 1QHᵃ

8.15, 25), as is its variant לב טוב (4QpsEzekᵃ frg. 5 line 2 [4Q385]).[18] Qohelet (9:7) advises his readers to drink their wine "with a contented heart" (בלב טוב). For a "contented heart", see also Sir 13:26.[19] The phrase בנפש חפצה has been reconstructed in 4QpsEzekᵃ frg. 5 line 2 (4Q385) by the editor, Devorah Dimant, and is also found at 4Q302 3 ii 5, but, as Dimant rightly notes, the phrase here probably should be read negatively, as in Isa 66:3. Willingness of heart is expressed also by the combination נדיב לב, as in Exod 35:22, 2 Chr 29:31, and 1QM 10.5. The combination of whole heart and willing mind resonates with Deut 6:5 and is reflected in CD 15.9-10 and 1QH 6.26-27. See also the prayer in *Ap. Const.* 8.6.15, ἐν καρδίᾳ πλήρει καὶ ψυχῇ θελούσῃ.

■ **4** In the Qumran *Hodayot*, the hymnist declares that "my heart opens to an everlasting spring" (1QH 18.31), that God has "opened a broad space in my heart" (1QH 13.32-33), and that he has "opened my heart to your knowledge" (1QH 22 [frg. 4].12). In the concluding hymn in 1QS 11.15-16, the poet says, "Blessed be you, my God, who opens the heart of your servant to knowledge" (הפותח לדעה לב עבדכה). The phrase "to open the heart/mind" is also found in Acts 16:14 and Luke 24:45.

"in his law." To some the preposition ἐν appeared superfluous, as it does not seem to have the meaning of instrument, means, or manner by which the heart is opened. If the sense is that the heart be opened to accept into it the law and statutes, a simple dative would suffice. C. C. Torrey inserted a verb to account for the preposition.[20] Grimm suggested that the phrase refers to the area in which the opening of the heart ought to take place. However, as noted above on vv. 3-4, the phrase seems to specify what God wants of his followers. Schwartz has pointed to a phrase in the prayer of Mar, the son of Rabina: "May you open my heart in your law, and may my soul pursue your commandments" (תהיהפתח לבי בתורתך ובמצותיך תרדוף נפשי) (*b. Ber.* 17a). Similarly, in the prayer in *Ap. Const.* 8.6.5 is found: "May

---

17 See also Ezek 36:26-27; Jer 31:31-34 (= LXX 38:31-34).

18 See Devorah Dimant, ed., *Qumran Cave 4.XXI: Parabiblical Texts, Part 4: Pseudo-Prophetic Texts* (DJD 30; Oxford: Clarendon, 2001) 42-44.

19 Yochanan Muffs (*Studies in the Aramaic Legal Papyri from Elephantine* [Handbook of Oriental Studies, Section 1: The Near and Middle East 66; Brill:

Leiden, 2003]) has investigated the history and meaning of the Aramaic phrase "my heart is satisfied" in the legal papyri from Elephantine, where it signifies the satisfaction of a seller on receipt of payment and relinquishment of the title to a property.

20 Charles C. Torrey, "The Letters Prefixed to Second Maccabees," *JAOS* 60 (1940) 119–50, here 141 n. 14.

he open the ears of their hearts to engage in his law" (διανοίξη τὰ ὦτα τῶν καρδιῶν αὐτῶν πρὸς τὸ ἐν τῷ νόμῳ αὐτοῦ καταγίνεσθαι).

Law and statutes are found in tandem in Exod 18:16, 20; 2 Chr 31:21; Isa 24:5; Amos 2:4; Bar 4:1; and Tob 14:9 (AB).

"may he make peace." Here begins the second part of the expression of wish. This phrase is usually connected with the previous phrase about opening the heart. However, the peace sought is a covenantal peace, similar to the peace treaty that Demetrius seeks to make between himself and the Jews in 1 Macc 13:40, whereby God will act as covenantal ally toward the Jews. As the succeeding three phrases in 1:5 are all concerned with such covenantal issues, I have connected the phrase with them.

■ 5 The meaning of καταλλάσσω, "to reconcile," is common in Greek,[21] but as Stanley Porter has pointed out, its use in speaking about reconciliation with the gods is rare before its appearance in 2 Maccabees in 5:20; 7:33; 8:29. It is found in Sophocles *Ai* 744: "Well, [Ajax] has gone, intent on the purpose best for him, to be reconciled to the gods after his anger [θεοῖσιν ὡς καταλλαχθῇ χόλου]."[22]

As in any treaty, when infringements occur, the parties are to patch up differences, and when one party is attacked, the covenant partner is to help. So God, as a covenant partner, is to listen to his people when they call on him. He is not to be angry with them but is to show his mercy and not desert his covenant partners when they are in trouble. Toward the end of his prayer at the dedication of the temple, Solomon asks that, if the people go out to battle and pray to the Lord, the Lord "hear from heaven their petition" (εἰσακούει ἐκ τοῦ οὐρανοῦ τῆς δεήσεως αὐτῶν) and their prayer and do the right thing by them. Solomon prays that if the people sin and repent, God will hear their plea and be merciful to them (ἵλεως ἔση) and listen to them because of what God spoke through Moses (1 Kgs 8:44-52). In Deut

4:29-31, Moses advises the people that, when dispersed among the nations they turn to the Lord and seek the Lord in their distress (ἐν τῇ θλίψει), the merciful God will not abandon (ἐγκαταλείψει) them, nor forget the covenant with their ancestors. In Judg 10:10-16, when the Israelites sin against the Lord and he is angry with them, he tells them that they had abandoned (ἐγκατελίπετε) him and so now they should cry to those other gods in the time of their distress (ἐν καιρῷ θλίψεως). Nevertheless, the Israelites put away those other gods and the Lord is merciful to them. See also Neh 9:26-27, where Nehemiah tells God that the people are in great distress (ἐν θλίψει μεγάλη). In some sense, the covenant is summed up in 2 Chr 15:2: "If you seek him, he will be found by you, but if you abandon him, he will abandon you [ἐὰν ἐγκαταλίπητε αὐτόν, ἐγκαταλείψει ὑμᾶς]." See the similar sentiment in 2 Chr 24:20. As the psalmist states in Ps 94:12-14 (LXX 93:12-14), God will give those whom the Lord teaches by his law respite from days of trouble (ἀφ' ἡμερῶν πονερῶν), for the Lord will not abandon (ἐγκαταλείψει) his heritage. Sirach recalls how he prayed to the Lord not to forsake him in the days of his trouble (μὴ με ἐγκαταλιπεῖν ἐν ἡμέραις θλίψεως) and how God rescued him in time of trouble (ἐκ καιροῦ πονηροῦ) (Sir 51:10-12). See also Pss 9:10 and 102:2 (LXX 101:3).

"at a bad time." This phrase, found also in Ps 36:19 LXX; Mic 2:3; Qoh 9:12, has been seen by some scholars as having a specific historical reference, the hostility of Ptolemy VIII Euergetes II (Physcon) against the Jews of Egypt. The references in the previous paragraph suggest rather that "at a bad time" should be understood in a general sense, as part of a covenant partner's responsibility. Moreover, as will be discussed below, it is by no means sure that Physcon was always hostile to the Jews.[23]

---

21 The active voice is found in Herodotus 5.29.1; 6.108.5; Aristotle *Oec.* 1348b9; the middle voice in Herodotus 1.61.2; 7.145.1; the passive in Euripides *Iph. Aul.* 1157; Xenophon *An.* 1.6.1; Thucydides 4.59.4. An interesting use of the verb is found in *P. Oxy.* 104.25–27. It discusses the case of whenever a woman is estranged from her husband (ἐὰν ἀπαλλαγῇ τοῦ ἀνδρός) until she is reconciled to him (μέχρι οὕ . . . καταλλαγῇ).

22 See Stanley E. Porter, Καταλλάσσω *in Ancient Greek Literature, with Reference to the Pauline Writings* (Estudios de filología Neotestamentaria 5; Cordoba: El Almendro de Cordoba, 1994).

23 See Victor Tcherikover, *CPJ* 1:21–24.

■ **6** Περί begins to encroach on the meaning of ὑπέρ in the Hellenistic period,[24] and so I have translated "praying for you."

The formula "and now" is found both in the Hebrew Scriptures and in the corpus of Aramaic letters and occurs in various spellings: כען, וכען, כעת, וכעת, כענת. In the corpus of Aramaic letters, it can introduce the body of the letter or can be a message divider;[25] here, however, the formula does not introduce the body of the letter but is part of the initial greeting. Nor does the formula fit easily into any of the situations that André Laurentin has found for the phrase in legal and liturgical contexts.[26] Rather, the sense is that of a continuation whereby the spirit of community set in 1:1-5 is maintained and evidenced in the prayers of the Jews for their Egyptian kinsfolk.

■ **7** This verse has given rise to many difficulties. Is γεγράφαμεν, the perfect tense of the verb "to write," to be taken as an epistolary perfect[27] and the verse translated, "In the year 169 with Demetrius as king, we Jews write to you in the extreme oppression . . ."? Or is the verb to be read as a perfect tense, "we Jews wrote to you"? The perfect tense of γράφειν is used in letters to refer to previous correspondence.[28] If one takes the former meaning, then two problems arise. (1) What does one do with the date given in 1:10a? Is it to be placed in the second letter? Dates are usually given at the end of

letters, not at the beginning.[29] (2) The extreme distress for the Jews in Jerusalem in 144/143 B.C.E. would surely have been the capture and execution of their leader Jonathan. However, no mention is made of this event; rather, the treachery of Jason over twenty years previously is highlighted. That the commonly used noun θλῖψις ("distress," "oppression") is found both here and in the speech given by Simon Maccabeus after Jonathan Maccabeus had been captured and Jerusalem threatened (1 Macc 13:5) is not enough to establish that the letter was written in 143 B.C.E.

Since Bickermann's brilliant analysis,[30] most scholars have been convinced that the authors are quoting here from a letter written in the year 169 of the Seleucid era. Bickermann provides examples where no hint is given that a quotation is being introduced. There has been considerable discussion over the precise reference of "when Demetrius was king, in the year 169." According to the Seleucid Macedonian calendar, year 1 fell between fall 312 and fall 311, while a Seleucid Babylonian calendar has been posited in which year 1 ran from spring 311 to spring 310.[31] Following the Seleucid Macedonian reckoning, year 169 would be fall 144/fall 143, while in the Seleucid Babylonian counting, year 169 would be spring 143/spring 142. Which reckoning should one choose?

The Demetrius of this letter is Demetrius II Nicator, who became king in year 165 of the Seleucid era (1 Macc

---

24 Maximilian Zerwick, *Graecitas Biblica* (3rd ed.; Rome: Pontifical Biblical Institute, 1955) no. 69; James H. Moulton and Nigel Turner, *A Grammar of New Testament Greek* (4 vols.; Edinburgh: T&T Clark, 1963) 3:269–70.

25 Fitzmyer, "Some Notes," 201–25.

26 André Laurentin, "Weʿattah–Kai nun: Formule caractéristique des textes juridiques et liturgiques," *Bib* 45 (1964) 168–95.

27 Smyth, *Greek Grammar*, §1942.

28 *SEG* 39 (1989) no. 1133; C. Bradford Welles, *Royal Correspondence in the Hellenistic Period: A Study in Greek Epigraphy* (New Haven: Yale University Press, 1934) no. 19.16.

29 Schwartz (*2 Maccabees*, 522) states that, since "the first epistle is plainly a Semitic document, to interpret it according to the standards of Greek letters, and to translate it according to what is usual in Greek and without regard for the fact that they render a Hebrew or Aramaic text, would seem to be a mistake." However, Bickermann's argument ("Ein

jüdischer Festbrief," 233–54) is based on the form of a letter. As Lindenberger (*Ancient Aramaic and Hebrew Letters*, 8) noted, the date in ancient Aramaic and Hebrew letters, where one is found, is placed at the end of the letter. In one case the date is given after the initial greeting: the Passover letter from Elephantine; see Lindenberger, *Ancient Aramaic and Hebrew Letters*, no. 30. However, in this case the specific date is given because it refers to the date of Passover for that year (וכעת שנתא זא). So the evidence we have from letters in Aramaic and Hebrew shows that they follow the same form as Greek letters with the date at the end of the letter.

30 Bickermann, "Ein jüdischer Festbrief," 233–54.

31 See Bickermann, *Der Gott der Makkabäer,* 101–11.

28

11:19).[32] However, his position was attacked by one of the previous ruler's generals, Diodotus Tryphon, in the name of that ruler's son, Antiochus VI. Demetrius II had to flee Antioch in the summer of 144 B.C.E. but maintained control of Cilicia, Mesopotamia, and Babylonia. The Jews under Jonathan switched allegiance from Demetrius II to Antiochus VI but then later switched back to Demetrius II. The reference to Demetrius as king must be dated after the Jews had left Antiochus VI and Tryphon. The sequence of events that led to this turnabout is described in 1 Maccabees: Tryphon feared that Jonathan would thwart his attempt to usurp the position of Antiochus VI and so treacherously captured him (1 Macc 12:39-48); Simon was elected leader in Jonathan's place (13:1-10); Simon paid ransom to Tryphon (13:12-20); Tryphon invaded Judea anyway but was foiled by an unexpected snowstorm (13:20-22); Jonathan was executed (13:23); later Antiochus VI was murdered (13:31); Simon strengthened fortifications and stored food to resist a siege (13:33); then he reconciled with Demetrius (13:34); as a consequence, in 170 the Jews start their own calendar reckoning (13:41-42).

In the attempt to fix an absolute time frame for this relative chronology, three elements have taken center stage. First, coins of Antiochus VI were minted dated 170, which, according to the official Seleucid Macedonian reckoning, would be fall 143/fall 142[33] and dated 171, fall 142/fall 141.[34] Bickermann did not know of these coins from 171 and so argued that the many coins of Antiochus VI from 170 signified that he had been murdered most likely in spring 142 B.C.E. As a consequence, Tryphon would have invaded Judea in late fall 143, and after this date the Jews would have gone over to Demetrius. The letter would therefore come from the end of the year 143 B.C.E.[35] Goldstein knew of the coins but argued that some local cities, out of partisanship, may have kept on issuing coins even though Antiochus VI was dead.[36] The existence of these coins does, however, cast doubt on the "absolute" date of Antiochus VI's death in 142 B.C.E. Livy places that event in 138/137 B.C.E.[37] Henri Seyrig suggests that Tryphon first ousted Antiochus VI, in 142/141 B.C.E., but did not kill him until later.[38] Here Seyrig is trying to make sense of the confused account of the boy's death in Josephus *Ant.* 13.187, 218.

The second historical peg is the unexpected snowfall that stopped Tryphon's march on Jerusalem (1 Macc 13:22). In Bickermann and Goldstein's chronology, this snowfall would have taken place in late fall. Klaus Bringmann rightly points out that snow usually falls in Judea in January/February.[39]

Bringmann also brings into play the third historical peg: fall 143/fall 142 B.C.E. was a sabbatical year. He bases this calculation on the mention of a sabbatical year in 1 Macc 6:49. Bringmann argues that a shortfall of food would occur at the end of the sabbatical year, and so the invasion of Lysias recounted in 1 Macc 6:28-54 took place in the summer of 163 B.C.E., that is, at the end of the sabbatical year that ran from fall 164 to fall 163 B.C.E.[40] This would entail that a sabbatical year fell in fall 143/fall 142. Bringmann concludes that Simon would not have been able to store provisions in strongholds (1 Macc 13:33) during this sabbatical year and must therefore have stocked up before the sabbatical

32 The year is known from Demotic Papyrus Strassburg 21 (*PW* 23.2, col. 1717).

33 Ernest Babelon, *Les Rois de Syrie, d'Arménie et de Commagène* (Paris: Rollin & Feuardent, 1890) cxxxiv–cxxxv.

34 S. Ben-Dor, "Some New Seleucid Coins," *PEQ* 78 (1946) 43–48; Georges Le Rider, *Suse sous les Séleucides et les Parthes: Les trouvailles monétaires et l'histoire de la ville* (Mémoires de la Mission archéologique en Iran 38; Paris: Geuthner, 1965) 370 n. 2.

35 Bickermann, "Ein jüdischer Festbrief," 143–44.

36 Jonathan A. Goldstein, *I Maccabees: A New Translation with Introduction and Commentary* (AB 41; Garden City, N.Y.: Doubleday, 1976) 478–79.

37 Livy *periocha* 55; see Justin 36.1.7; Appian *Syr.* 67.

38 Henri Seyrig, *Notes on Syrian Coins* (Numismatic Notes and Monographs 119; New York: American Numismatic Society, 1950) 16.

39 Bringmann, *Hellenistische Reform*, 22.

40 Ibid., 20, 22 n. 29. Lester L. Grabbe ("Maccabean Chronology: 167–164 or 168–165 B.C.E.?" *JBL* 110 [1991] 59–74, here 63 n. 21) also holds that a sabbatical year fell on 164/163. See also Bar-Kochva, *Judas Maccabaeus*, 543–45.

year began; in other words, he was already preparing to defend himself against Tryphon well before the fall of 143 B.C.E., and his overtures to Demetrius II probably took place before the beginning of the sabbatical year, that is, in year 169 according to the Seleucid Macedonian reckoning. This reconstruction would thus not follow the sequence of events as recounted in 1 Macc 13:31-34, where Antiochus VI's death precedes the buildup of Simon and the sending of emissaries to Demetrius. This sequence has difficulties. The author of 1 Maccabees likes to group events together, and one can see how he has skillfully tied the events under Tryphon and Antiochus VI together. First Maccabees 13:31-32 ("Tryphon dealt treacherously with the young king Antiochus; he killed him and became king in his place, putting on the crown of Asia" [ἐβασίλευσεν ἀντ' αὐτοῦ καὶ περιέθετο τὸ διάδημα τῆς Ἀσίας]) forms an *inclusio* with 1 Macc 12:39 ("Then Tryphon attempted to become king in Asia and put on the crown" [Βασιλεῦσαι τῆς Ἀσίας καὶ περιθέσθαι τὸ διάδημα]). The clustering of these events also highlights the treachery of Tryphon and works to justify the switching of allegiance to Demetrius II. This sequence should not therefore be accorded absolute stability, and Antiochus VI could have been murdered after the rapprochement with Demetrius II. The main sticking point for Bringmann's hypothesis remains the uncertainty surrounding the dating of the sabbatical year.[41]

There are thus numerous problems in ascertaining the precise date for the letter. Bringmann's scenario remains the most probable: Tryphon captured Jonathan, and in response Simon strengthened the strongholds and may have made overtures to Demetrius. Tryphon then invaded Judea in the winter of 143 B.C.E., was foiled by a snowfall, and executed Jonathan. Simon was elected leader, and negotiations with Demetrius were finalized. The date 169 thus should be located according to the Seleucid Babylonian reckoning, that is, from 5 April 143 to 26 March 142 B.C.E.[42] The letter would have been written when the Jews were subjects of Demetrius II, before the yoke of the Gentiles was lifted in 170 S.E. (1 Macc 13:41). It must have been composed while negotiations were continuing with Demetrius II and before documents were dated according to the years of Simon (1 Macc 13:42); these negotiations could have begun as soon as Simon was aware of Tryphon's intention to invade Judea.

"in[43] the extreme oppression." The Greek phrase ἐν τῇ θλίψει καὶ ἐν τῇ ἀκμῇ is best seen, following Grimm, as a hendiadys, where ἀκμή would have the sense, frequent in medical works, of "critical point." Ms 58 uses another word found in combination with θλίψις—ἀνάγκη ("constraint")—as in Job 15:24; Zeph 1:15; and Ps LXX 106:6, 13, 19, 28. The Syriac uses the frequent formula ܐ‎ ܘܐ‎ ("in distress and oppression"). These appear to be attempts to make sense of the more unusual ἀκμή rather than to preserve the most likely reading. Ἀκμή has the meaning of "high point" in 4:13. Habicht understands the extreme distress to refer to the time after Jonathan's execution by Tryphon, but the phrase refers to the following temporal clause, that is, to the time of Jason.

"left the holy land and the kingdom." The verb

---

41 See Ben Zion Wacholder, "The Calendar of Sabbatical Cycles during the Second Temple and the Early Rabbinic Period," *HUCA* 44 (1973) 153–96. His study was critiqued by Don Blosser, "The Sabbath Year Cycle in Josephus," *HUCA* 52 (1981) 129–39, to which Wacholder replied in "The Calendar of Sabbath Years during the Second Temple Era: A Response," *HUCA* 54 (1983) 123–33. Goldstein (*I Maccabees*, 315–18) also criticized Wacholder. See also Robert North, "Maccabean Sabbath Years," *Bib* 34 (1953) 501–15; and Bar-Kochva, *Judas Maccabaeus*, 544–45.

42 See Richard A. Parker and Waldo H. Dubberstein, *Babylonian Chronology 626 B.C.–A.D. 75* (Brown University Studies 19; Providence, R.I.: Brown University Press, 1956) 41.

43 As he sees this prepositional phrase joined to the previous γεγράφαμεν, Schwartz translates ἐν as "concerning" and refers to Deut 6:7, where the Hebrew, ודברת בם, is translated in the LXX as καὶ λαλήσεις ἐν αὐτοῖς. While the Hebrew preposition ב can have the meaning of "about," this meaning is usually found only with verbs of speaking, considering, remembering: דבר, חלל, הגה, שיח, ידע, זכר. Sometimes ב appears simply to mark the object. For example, in Deut 3:26, the LXX simply ignores the preposition. "Write concerning" would seem to be כתב על as in 2 Kgs 22:13; 2 Chr 9:29; Esth 8:8: ואתם כתבו על היהודים, "and you shall write concerning the Jews"; 4Q177 frg. 2, line 3: כא[שר עליהם כתוב, "as it is written concerning them"; 11Q13 frg. 2, line 23: כאשר כתוב עליו, "as it is written concerning him."

ἀπέστη has usually been taken to mean "rebel, revolt."[44] Goldstein senses that there are problems in talking about a revolt against a land rather than against a person and suggests only that "the differences probably reflect the historical facts confronting the senders."[45] In 5:8, Jason is called an ἀποστάτης, but the meaning of "apostate, rebel" is given by the qualifier "against the laws," and also by the context—Antiochus IV hears the Jews are rebelling (5:11). F.-M. Abel suggested, with David Sluys,[46] that ἀπέστη be understood in an absolute sense, with no reference to the holy land. The prepositional phrase "from the holy land and the kingdom" would qualify rather "his companions." This suggestion is difficult to accept, however, for with whom would the Jews be contrasted? With partisans from outside the Seleucid realm? Further, ἀφίστημι ἀπό + place-name is common. The position taken by Abel does focus the problem on the issues surrounding the translation of the verb as "rebelled." The most normal way of translating ἀφίστημι ἀπό + place is "to leave from such and such a place": in Josh 8:15-16, "Joshua and Israel retreated from their face, and they pursued after the sons of Israel and they themselves left the city" (ἀπέστησαν ἀπὸ τῆς πόλεως); in 1 Esdr 1:28, "Take me from the battle" (ἀποστήσατέ με ἀπὸ τῆς μάχης); in Sir 47:24, "Jeroboam, son of Nabal, who led Israel into sin and gave to Ephraim the way of sin, and their sins increased greatly so that they left their land" (ἀποστῆσαι αὐτοὺς ἀπὸ τῆς γῆς αὐτῶν). For further examples see Num 12:10; 16:27; and Job 31:22. The same meaning of moving from a place is found also in phrases where someone is removed from someone's face (1 Sam 19:10; 2 Kgs 17:18; 23:27; 24:3; 2 Chr 35:19) or sleep leaves from one's eyes (Dan 4:15). The locative meaning found in LXX 3 Kgdms 11:29, to lead someone off the way, is evident also in the phrases found at Ezek 33:8A and Jdt 5:18 ("When they departed from the way which he had laid down for them" [ὅτε δὲ ἀπέστησαν ἀπὸ τῆς ὁδοῦ ἧς διέθετο αὐτοῖς]). One exception may seem to be Tob

1:4: "All the tribe of Naphtali my ancestor left the house of Jerusalem" (ἀπέστη ἀπὸ τοῦ οἴκου Ἱεροσολύμων); even here, however, a physical removal is basic, as the northern tribes returned to their tents.

The simplest translation, therefore, is that Jason and his companions left the holy land and the kingdom. The phrase "the holy land" undergoes change over time. In Zech 2:16 it refers to an area larger than Judea; in Wis 12:3 and Ps.-Philo L.A.B. 19:10 it refers to the land to be given to Israel; it is used in 2 Bar. 63:10 to refer to the kingdom at the time of Hezekiah. In 4 Ezra 13:48 the phrase refers to a special place where those who are within in its borders will be saved at the coming of the Lord. In T. Job 33:5 the holy land refers to the unchangeable world.

"the kingdom." What is the relation of "holy land" to "kingdom"? Habicht held that "kingdom" here refers to the kingdom of God and therefore implies that "holy land" and "kingdom" are in some sense identical, as does Schwartz. Habicht cited Bickermann,[47] but Bickermann had previously shown that the official name of the Seleucid Empire was "the kingdom."[48] One should also note that, in v. 7, Demetrius is said to be king (βασιλεύοντος Δημητρίου). Isaac Heinemann, Abel, and Goldstein see "kingdom" here as referring to the Seleucid kingdom, so that "holy land" would fall within the confines of the Seleucid realm. If one accepts that ἀποστῆναι has here a locative meaning, 1:7 would refer to Jason's withdrawal from Judea and from the Seleucid kingdom.

■ 8 "burnt the gate and shed innocent blood." Second Maccabees 5:5 does not state that when Jason and his followers stormed Jerusalem, they burned the gate; 8:33 records this act as the work of Callisthenes. According to 1 Macc 1:31, the chief collector of tribute (5:24: Apollonius, captain of the Mysians) burned the city with fire and tore down its houses and surrounding walls. As for shedding innocent blood, Jason is said to have slaughtered fellow citizens mercilessly (5:6) but to have done so in the context of besieging a city. In 1 Macc

44 Abel; Bickermann (Der Gott der Makkabäer, 34), Habicht, Goldstein, Schwartz.
45 Goldstein, II Maccabees, 148.
46 David M. Sluys, De Maccabaeorum libris I et II [i.e. primo et secundo] quaestiones, (Amsterdam: J. Clausen, 1904).
47 Bickermann, Der Gott der Makkabäer, 34.
48 Elias Bickermann, Institutions des Séleucides (Bibliothèque archéologique et historique 26; Paris: Geuthner, 1938) 3.

1:38, those stationed in the Akra are said to have shed innocent blood in a treacherous attack, a more appropriate narrative setting for the phrase. Rather than looking for precise instances where the gates of Jerusalem were burned or innocent blood shed, one might recall that these are stock phrases. Burned gates evoke the image of a defenseless city, as the city's enemies can no longer be closed out (Jer 17:27; Isa 45:1 on open gates). Wicked men pour out innocent blood (Isa 59:7; Jer 7:6; 22:3, 17; Ps 106:38 [LXX 105:38]; Prov 6:17), and those wicked men who did so, Manasseh and Jehoiakim (2 Kgs 21:16; 24:4; 2 Chr 36:5 LXX), brought about the destruction and capture of Jerusalem. The perpetrators in 1:8 are thus shown to be wicked traitors and to bring about the destruction of Jerusalem. Since Jason is not said elsewhere to have burned the gates, I once argued that one might take the third person plural verbs "they burned" (ἐπύρισαν) and "they shed" (ἐξέχεαν), as passive. [49] However, there is no sound grammatical reason for such a reading: the verb "he left" (ἀπέστη) is singular, as Jason is the more important subject, [50] but both he and his followers combine to burn the gate and here the verb is in the plural. The leaving of the land and the treacherous destruction of the city are seen as occurring together. One can find examples in the LXX, following closely the MT, where "and" (καί) introduces an anterior action, for example, Jer 43:20 LXX (= MT 36:20): "And they went in to the king into the court, and they gave the scroll to keep in the house of Elishama." The scroll must have been left in the house of Elishama before the officials went in to report to the king, but this action is placed after the entry into the court. See also Num 17:15. [51] The Syriac translator made sense of the verse by translating: "After Jason and his companions were sent from the kingdom to the holy land and they burnt the gate." In this translation, Jason is seen as coming into the holy land, as did the collector of tribute in 1 Macc 1:29-49; he is not leaving the land.

"we besought." This verb is connected to "they burnt the gate and shed innocent blood" by the connective καί. Should it be connected to the temporal clause "from the time that Jason," or does it signal the beginning of the main clause? The most appropriate place for a change from a dependent to a main clause is where the subject of the verbs changes. Here the third person changes to the first person. Καί before "we besought" reflects the use of the Hebrew conjunction waw. [52] The Jerusalem Jews' response to the crisis was prayer, and they were heard as Solomon had asked (1 Kgs 8:29-30). "We besought . . . and we were heard" (ἐδεήθημεν . . . καὶ εἰσηκούσθημεν). The action of the Jews and its result reflect linguistically what the Jerusalem Jews asked for their Egyptian kin in v. 5: "hearken to your entreaties" (ἐπακοῦσαι ὑμῶν τῶν δεήσεων).

The list of rituals here is often taken to refer to the daily ritual offerings and those made weekly. The daily offering consisted of the morning sacrifice of one lamb with "one-tenth of a measure of choice flour mixed with one-fourth of a hin of beaten oil and one-fourth of a hin of wine for a drink offering" and a similar evening sacrifice (Exod 29:38-42; Num 28:3-8). The lamps were to be kept lit before the Lord continually (Exod 27:20-21; Lev 24:1-4). The bread of the Presence was to be set out every Sabbath (Lev 24:5-9; Exod 25:30). Goldstein properly asks why there is no mention of incense, as in Exod 30:7-8, in the summary of ritual activity in 2 Chr 13:11, and in the description of what Judas Maccabeus and his followers did when they purified the temple (1 Macc 4:50-53; 2 Macc 10:3). However, the authors of this letter are not putting forward a complete picture of ritual activity—why no mention of the drink offering or of the consecration of the new altar?—but rather are showing how normal ritual activity has been resumed. One might also note that this list of activities seems close to the outline of Leviticus where first a burnt offering is mentioned ("sacrifice" [θυσία] punctuates the verses in 1:9, 13, 17) and then a grain offering, where the offering shall be of fine flour (σεμίδαλις, in Lev 2:1, 2, 4, 5, 7).

49   Robert Doran, "The Second Book of Maccabees," *The New Interpreter's Bible* (13 vols.; Nashville: Abingdon, 1994–2004) 4:190.

50   Smyth, *Greek Grammar*, §966.

51   Paul Joüon, *A Grammar of Biblical Hebrew* (trans. and rev. Takamitsu Muraoka; Rome: Pontificio Istituto Biblico, 1996) no. 166j.

52   See Anneli Aejmelaeus, *Parataxis in the Septuagint: A Study of the Renderings of the Hebrew Coordinate Clauses in the Greek Pentateuch* (Annales Academiae Scientiarum Fennicae: Dissertationes humanarum litterarum 31; Helsinki: Suomalainen, 1982) 126–47.

After a description of the sacrificial system and the system of purity come a list of appointed festivals (Leviticus 23) and then the lighting of the lamps and the bread of the Presence (Lev 24:1-9). In Leviticus, the references to incense are sparse. Leviticus 4:7, 18; 10:1 are concerned with the sprinkling of blood on the altar of incense during a purification ceremony; 16:12-13 focuses on the ritual of the Day of Atonement. The four ritual activities mentioned in 2 Macc 1:8 seem to encapsulate the description of ritual activity in Leviticus.

■ **9** "So now" ($\kappa\alpha\grave{\iota}\ \nu\hat{\upsilon}\nu$) is best understood here not in terms of a transitional formula (see comment on 1:6) but rather, as used frequently in the Hebrew Scriptures, to introduce an imperative, a decision to be taken after the description of a situation (Gen 50:16-17; 1 Sam 9:6, 13).[53] Here the authors of the letter have provided the historical background, and now they call for a decision by the Egyptian community.

Imperatival $\H{\iota}\nu\alpha$ is found in Hellenistic Greek. However, Nigel Turner suggests that, given the "wealth [of LXX examples] and the secular poverty of examples, we may claim the imperatival $\H{\iota}\nu\alpha$ as virtually a Semitism."[54]

The festival of Booths is celebrated in the seventh Hebrew month, Tishri. Kislev is the ninth month of the Hebrew calendar.

■ **10** "in the year 188." Bickermann, Abel, and Schwartz connect the genitive of the year to the preceding "month of Kislev." Schwartz argued that normally the date of a letter gives the day in the dative with the month and year in the genitive, as in 11:21, 33. Since he had previously argued in his comment on 1:7 that the letter was written in 169 s.e., he concluded that the year date given here could not be 188 s.e. but must be 148 s.e., which is found in some manuscripts. The Jews in Egypt are therefore being asked to celebrate "the days of Booths of the month Kislev of the year 148 s.e." Schwartz provides no Hellenistic parallel to this way of referring to a festival.[55] Just as I argued above on formal grounds that 1:7 could not provide the date of the letter, so too here, in agreement with Goldstein, I propose that the date placed at the end of a letter is meant to be the date of the letter. When the date of a letter is given, normally the year in the genitive comes first, followed by the month and then the day, as in 11:21, 33. I suggest that in transmission the year was kept but not the day and month. On formal grounds, since the letter is quoting a letter from 169 s.e., the date must be 188 s.e.[56]

The year 188 of the Seleucid Macedonian era would run from 9 October 125 to 27 September 124, of the Seleucid Babylonian era from 5 April 124 to 25 March 123.[57] As the letter calls upon the Egyptian Jews to celebrate in the month of Kislev (Nov.–Dec.), according to the Seleucid Macedonian era it could have been written in 125 or 124, whereas according to the Seleucid Babylonian era it would have to have been written in 124. As I have argued above that the date in 1:7 is according to Seleucid Babylonian reckoning, I would hold that here too the date is according to Seleucid Babylonian reckoning.

No farewell formula is found at the end of this letter, but this absence is not unusual.[58]

General Commentary

Several basic questions need to be answered about this letter: What kind of a letter is it? Who wrote it and why? To whom was it written?

(1) What kind of a letter is the first prefixed letter?
Scholars have dubbed this a festal letter and pointed to parallels in the Hebrew Scriptures (2 Chr 30:1-9; Esth 9:20-32), in the Elephantine corpus (the "Passover" letter),[59] and in the rabbinic corpus (*t. Sanh.* 2:5-6; *b. Sanh.* 11a-b), where letters were sent out to celebrate a festival. While recognizing that these texts all point to a literary topos, one should also be alert to the differences between them. Some letters are commands from officials. The incident reported in 2 Chr 30:1-9 is found

---

53 See Laurentin, "We‘attah."

54 Moulton and Turner, *Grammar of New Testament Greek*, 3:95.

55 Schwartz's reference to United States commemorations of the Fourth of July and 9/11 is unpersuasive.

56 The fact that 188 s.e. is a less-important year for the history of Israel than 148 s.e., the year of the rededication of the temple (1 Macc 4:52), is also a *lectio difficilior* argument for accepting it.

57 Parker and Dubberstein, *Babylonian Chronology*, 42.

58 See Fitzmyer, "Some Notes," 217.

59 Lindenberger, *Ancient Aramaic and Hebrew Letters*, 30.

in a description of the reinvigoration of the worship of Yahweh (2 Chr 29:3–31:21) that is not paralleled in the account of the reign of Hezekiah in 2 Kgs 18:4-8. The proper celebration of Passover is ascribed to King Josiah in 2 Kgs 23:21-23 (2 Chr 35:1-19), where Josiah commands all the people, "Keep the Passover to the Lord." Such a command from a king to celebrate a festival may be evidenced also in the fragmentary Passover letter from the Elephantine corpus, dated 419 B.C.E. From an otherwise unknown Jew Hananyah to the garrison of Jews at Elephantine, this letter conveys news of a command from King Darius sent to Arshama, the Persian satrap of Egypt, about the celebration of Passover. Such a letter reinforces the sense of the literary topos in 2 Chr 30:1, where King Hezekiah is said to have written letters to Ephraim and Manasseh. The topos has been used rhetorically to show the division between Israel and Judea, as most of the cities in Ephraim and Manasseh mock and scorn the couriers with their letters, while the cities in Judea have one heart to do what the king and his officials command (2 Chr 30:10-12).

In Esth 9:20-21, Mordechai, now second in command to the Persian king, is said to have written scrolls to all the Jews in the Persian provinces enjoining them to celebrate the festival of Purim. It is a letter of full written authority (Esth 9:29). Yet, as it introduces a new feast, the letter contains a summary of important recent events (9:24-26); the Jews accept the proposal (9:23, 27: וקבלו, προσεδέξαντο, προσεδέχοντο). The Greek verb is the same as that found in inscriptions from Magnesia on Maeander calling on other cities to celebrate a festival. The pattern remains one of a high official enjoining a festival.

Some letters do not enforce or command. The pattern in the rabbinic passages is different. They are not precisely about the celebration of a festival but about ritual and calendar events. In this they may be similar to the Passover letter from Elephantine. Rabbi Gamaliel is said to have written letters, but they simply state what the proper time for observing the festival is. These letters, said to exemplify the humility of Rabbi Gamaliel, contain a prayer for well-being ("May your peace increase,"

שלומכון יסנא). The body of the letters to Upper and Lower Galilee and to the south does not contain any imperative to collect, in this case, the tithe, but says, "We make known to you that the time of 'removal' has arrived." To those in Babylon and Media, the rabbi wrote that "the doves are still tender and the lambs still too young and the crops not yet ripe and the affair was pleasing in my sight and in the sight of my colleagues and I added to this year thirty days" (*b. Sanh.* 11b). Here the tone is not that of an order but rather that of a respectful statement of facts.

Outside Jewish tradition, one finds several examples of Greek cities inviting other cities to participate in a festival to commemorate the rescue of a temple or the liberation of a city-state. One of the best examples of this process is evidenced by more than seventy inscriptions found at Magnesia on Maeander. A festival had been established in 220/219 B.C.E. in honor of Artemis Leucophryene ("White-browed"), for her epiphany to save the city during an incursion of the Gauls, who remained a menace even after their defeat by Attalus I around 237 B.C.E. After a temple to Artemis had been built, the Magnesians sent envoys in 206 B.C.E. to invite numerous Greek cities to participate in a festival for the goddess. The inscriptions at Magnesia include letters from kings and votes from cities that recognized the festival as ranking with the Pythian games and promised to send envoys and participants for the athletic and musical festivals. The envoys, according to the decree from the city of Epidamnos, in Illyria,

delivered the decree and they discoursed with great distinction as they set forth, through the oracles of the god, through the poets and through the historians writing the acts of the Magnesians, the epiphany of Artemis, the help given by their ancestors to the temple in Delphi when they conquered in battle the barbarians who were marching to seize and plunder the property of the god, and the good service they did to the Cretan community by putting an end to the civil war. They also set forth the good services done to the other Greeks.[60]

---

60 Otto Kern, *Die Inschriften von Magnesia am Maeander* (Berlin: W. Spemann, 1900) no. 46, lines 7–14, p. 36.

Here we see that the envoys have marshaled all their facts, providing elaborate footnotes to their discourse before the assembly of Epidamnos. One should imagine that the bearers of this first letter in 2 Maccabees would have orally communicated and expanded upon its theme to the major Jewish communities in Egypt. They, too, would have stressed the epiphany of Yahweh, and their exposition could have referred to historians of the events, like Jason of Cyrene. But one should note that the rhetoric of the letter in 1:1-10a leads the audience in a direction other than that of the epitome of Jason's work and if the envoys were true to the letter's rhetoric, their exposition would have sounded different from that of the epitome, for there is no mention of Antiochus IV or of any Seleucid threat, no mention of an epiphanic deliverance. The disaster came upon the Jews in Jerusalem solely because of Jason the high priest. We will explore later why this letter may have taken this approach.

This letter therefore falls within a range of letters written to bring about participation in a festival. In the Elephantine Passover letter and those of Mordechai, the festival has to be celebrated by the recipients of the letter; the letters of Hezekiah call the Israelites to celebrate the festival in Jerusalem (2 Chr 30:1); in the Greek tradition, envoys were sent from various cities to represent their city at the celebration in the city of the senders. The Elephantine Passover letter and those of Hezekiah and Mordechai are orders to celebrate; the letters from Magnesia on Maeander are requests to participate. In Esther, both elements are combined: Mordechai enjoins the celebration, and the recipients accept the proposal to celebrate Purim in their own cities. The festival at Magnesia, the festival of Purim, and the feast of Sukkoth in Kislev are all recently established festivals, whereas the others are traditional festivals. Since the letter in 1:1-10a is a request to celebrate a recently established festival, it appears closer to the Magnesian correspondence. However, as the letter wants the recipients to celebrate the festival in their own community, it also diverges from the Magnesian tradition. It is also not an invitation to celebrate a new festival, for at the time of the letter's composition Hanukkah had been celebrated for over

twenty years. It is interesting to note that three of the inscriptions at Magnesia from cities in Pergamon are dated fifty years after the inauguration of the festival.[61]

(2) Who wrote the first prefixed letter?

Although John Hyrcanus had assumed the high priesthood on the death of his father, Simon, in February 135 or 134 B.C.E. (1 Macc 16:24), no mention is made of either John Hyrcanus or the council of the Jews in this letter of 125/124 B.C.E. Later rabbinic statements are sometimes adduced to show that the king and the high priest were not involved in liturgical decisions (*t. Sanh.* 2:15; *m. Roš Haš.* 2:7).[62] Even if these statements could be reliably retrojected to the Hasmonean era, however, they concern only the question of determining whether a year should be intercalated. One would expect the head of a community to be involved in the writing of a letter requesting another community to celebrate a recently established festival. There is no indication that John Hyrcanus forwent any of his privileges as high priest. Rather, here all marks of hierarchy within the community are effaced to emphasize the solidarity among all Jews.

But why was the letter written in 124 B.C.E.? The historical details of this period are scanty, so any suggestions must be extremely tentative. What information we have about these years is political, concerning either internal politics or international relations. Given the state of our knowledge, one is tempted to place the first letter within this political framework and ask what political motivations may have lain behind its composition. This is a proper question, but it should not blind us to the possibility of other motivations of which we have no knowledge—personal and religious—which could have prompted the writing.

(3) To whom was the first prefixed letter written?

The question of the historical situation of the senders cannot be divorced from the historical situation of the recipients.[63] The replacing of Jerusalem under Seleucid control by Antiochus VII Sidetes in 131/130 B.C.E. had driven home to John Hyrcanus that his desired independence depended on a weak Seleucid power. When

---

61   Ibid., nos. 85–87.
62   See Elias Bickerman, *Studies in Jewish and Christian History* (AGJU 9; Leiden: Brill, 1976–86) 2:147–48; Goldstein, *II Maccabees*, 139.
63   For a fuller account of the events summarized here, see Édouard Will, *Histoire politique du monde hellénistique (323–30 av. J.-C.)* (2 vols.; Annales de l'Est. Mémoire 30, 32; Nancy: Berger-Levrault, 1966,

Antiochus VII Sidetes was killed, the Egyptian ruler Ptolemy VIII Euergetes II Physcon supported Alexander Balas against the returned Demetrius II, who was put to death in 126/125 B.C.E. When Alexander showed signs of independence, Ptolemy supported Antiochus VIII Grypos, and in 123 B.C.E. Alexander was put to death. After the death of Antiochus VII, Hyrcanus is said to have extended his control north, south, and east (Josephus *Ant.* 13.254–58) and to have faced no threat from the Seleucids (Josephus *Ant.* 13.267, 13.270–74). However, he no doubt realized that with Demetrius II dead, the power of Alexander Balas could be curtailed only through the Ptolemies.

Unfortunately, we know little about the Jews in Egypt during the turbulent time of Ptolemy VIII. We know from papyri that Jews were spread throughout Egypt in all kinds of occupations—as soldiers, farmers, police, tax gatherers (*CPJ* 1:11–19)—so one must always be cautious and not assert that there was a single attitude toward this disparate group. Josephus (*Ap.* 2.49-56) mentions the importance of the Jewish generals under Ptolemy Philometor and Cleopatra II, Onias and Dositheos, and of their support of Cleopatra II against Ptolemy VIII Euergetes II Physcon in 145 B.C.E. He embellishes this report with a story of a miraculous deliverance of the Jews in Alexandria, an event also known from *3 Maccabees* but there placed in the time of Ptolemy IV Philopator. For the rest of the reign of Ptolemy VIII down to 116 B.C.E., we possess two inscriptions that dedicate synagogues to Ptolemy VII and to both of his queens.[64] Later, under Cleopatra III, the Jews Chelkias

and Ananias were held in high favor (Josephus *Ant.* 13.284-87, 353-54). There is no evidence that the Jews in Egypt or Alexandria supported Cleopatra II in her break with Ptolemy VIII, nor that Ptolemy VIII took vengeance on them when he retook Alexandria in 127 B.C.E. Scholars like Walter Otto have presupposed that the Jews in Egypt were a monolithic group and that the Jewish generals would have remained loyal to Cleopatra II through thick and thin, even though it is known that later they supported her rival, Cleopatra III.[65] The Jewish soldiers were based outside Alexandria, and their loyalty probably reflected their own best interests. There is no evidence to support the assumption about the loyalty of the Jewish generals to Cleopatra II and every reason to question the assumption about the monolithic nature of the Jews in Egypt.

Given the diffusion of Jews throughout the whole of Egypt,[66] the greeting in the letter in 1:1-10a presupposes some system of communication among the various communities "from the slope into Libya to the boundaries of Ethiopia" (Philo *Flacc.* 43). Presumably, messengers would have been sent out to announce the request from Jerusalem. Although the dispersion of Jews throughout Egypt is well known, scholars still often interpret the addressees of the letter in 1:1-10a as dominated by the Jews settled in the Heliopolite nome at Leontopolis and as being chided for their "sin" in building a temple at Leontopolis.[67] However, there is no indication that the Jews in Egypt lost their attachment to the temple in Jeru-

---

64 *SB* 1, §5862; 4, §7454; possibly also *OGIS* 1:96 and 129, though doubted by Walter Otto (*Zur Geschichte der Zeit des 6. Ptolemäers: Ein Beitrag zur Politik und zum Staatsrecht des Hellenismus* [Munich: Bayerischen Akademie der Wissenschaften, 1934] 66 n. 3) but accepted by Leo Fuchs (*Die Juden Ägyptens in ptolemäischer und römischer Zeit* [Vienna: Rath, 1924] 14–15).

65 See Walter Otto, *Zur Geschichte der Zeit des 6. Ptolemäers: Ein Beitrag zur Politik und zum Staatsrecht des Hellenismus* (Munich: Bayerische Akademie der Wissenschaften, 1934).

66 *CPJ* 1:3–4; appendix 1.

67 We know little about this temple at Leontopolis. Josephus, our main source, provides two divergent accounts of its founding. He gives five motivations for the building of a temple at Heliopolis: (1) to fulfill the prophecy of Isa 19:19 (*Ant.* 13.64; *Bell.* 7.432); (2) to make the Jews allies of the Ptolemies and hostile to the Seleucids (*Bell.* 7.423-25); (3) to unite the Jews in Egypt (*Ant.* 13.65-66); (4) for Onias IV to gain glory for himself (*Ant.* 13.63); and (5) to set up a rival temple to the one in Jerusalem (*Bell.* 7.431). In his discussion of the temple at Leontopolis as modeled on the one in Jerusalem, Josephus evidences his dislike of it. Apart from the first motivation, the other four seem supplied by Josephus. In *Bell.* 7.432, he grudgingly admits the Isaian prophecy, but accepts it more fully in *Ant.* 13.64. One suspects that this verse of Isaiah may

The reference markers 1967) 306, 356–66; Peter Green, *From Alexander to Actium: The Historical Evolution of the Hellenistic Age* (Hellenistic Culture and Society 1; Berkeley: University of California Press, 1990) 533–44.

salem because of the temple at Leontopolis,[68] and they continued to go on pilgrimage to Jerusalem. Ananias, a descendant of Onias IV, advised Cleopatra III not to launch an attack on Jerusalem (Josephus *Ant.* 13.352–55). Whatever the position of the temple at Leontopolis among Jews in Egypt, it was the military base of the Oniads, who were active in Ptolemaic politics. Any letter sent from Judea in 124 B.C.E. to the Jews throughout Egypt would have come to their attention.

Herein lies the answer, I think, to the form and content of the letter. The form, a letter of petition, implies recognition of the higher status of the group petitioned. The Jews in Jerusalem recognized that whoever sat on the Seleucid throne depended on Egyptian support or neglect, and so they wrote to their brethren in Egypt, some of whom were powerful players on the Egyptian scene. As noted before, there is no evidence either that the Oniads were curtailed in any way or that Jews throughout Egypt were persecuted on the return of Ptolemy Physcon in 127 B.C.E. That the content of the letter blames Jason the high priest for all the troubles in Judea is put in a new light if we recall that the same Jason ousted Onias III from the high priesthood (4:7-10). Jason had also gone to Egypt after his abortive attack on Jerusalem to regain power (5:5-8). The highly colored and condensed account of this incident in 5:7-10 specifies neither when Jason arrived in Egypt (probably after the repulse of Antiochus IV from Egypt by the Romans in July 168 B.C.E.) nor how long he stayed. We cannot reconstruct the reception he was given in Egypt, but as a former high priest exiled by the enemy of the Ptolemies and with an openness to Greek culture, Jason may have found a friendly reception, if not among the Oniads in Heliopolis. The letter of 124 B.C.E. would thus be a pro-Oniad, anti-Jason document appealing to the powerful

base of the Oniads in Egypt to celebrate the feast of Sukkoth in Kislev. Such motivation could lie behind both the letter of 143 B.C.E. and that of 124 B.C.E.

As noted above, the letter of 124 B.C.E. would have been written as John Hyrcanus was extending his control over territories on the borders of Judea and as the Seleucid ruler was dependent on Ptolemaic support. The letter would have been appropriate, as John Hyrcanus sought political support for his independence. The rhetoric of the letter is most interesting. First, the letter has the respectful form of a letter of petition. Second, neither high priest nor senate is mentioned, unlike another letter said to have been sent under Jonathan (1 Macc 12:6). Rather, all signs of hierarchy and status are missing, as is any reference to the territories captured by Jonathan. The emphasis remains squarely on the homeland of Judea with its capital, Jerusalem. Third, the letter is top-heavy, with over half given to the prayer for the well-being of the Jews in Egypt. Within this prayer, the mention of God's remembering his covenant in the presence of Abraham, Isaac, and Jacob conjures up the exodus tale, the foundation narrative of the Israelite nation and worshiping community, a story inextricably bound to Egypt. The description of the cultic practices of the Jews is metonymic, the part standing for the whole. It reinforces this sense of shared community, as in the exodus narrative Yahweh had led the Israelites out of Egypt to worship on his holy mountain. Finally, the letter makes no reference to the persecution by Antiochus IV and the tumultuous surrounding events but mentions only actions of Jason the high priest. The rhetoric strongly appeals to the bonds of kinship as well as emphasizes the rejection of Jason.

As for the letter of 143 B.C.E., it would have been written as Simon was building up the strongholds of Judea

---

have been used by the proponents of the Heliopolis temple. However, since the temple had a history of around two hundred years, one cannot be sure it was part of the motivation of Onias IV for building. The introductory formula in Isa 19:19, "on that day," with its eschatological overtones and the prediction of cooperation between Egypt and Assyria in Isa 19:23 might be associated with the expectations found in *Sib. Or.* 3:652-56. If the Isaianic text was used at the time of Onias IV, it might well fit with Ptolemy VI Philometor's designs on Syria, almost realized in 145 B.C.E. (1 Macc 11:13).

68   *Letter of Aristeas; 3 Maccabees; Sib. Or.* 3:286–94, 564–67, 657–731, 767–80.

(1 Macc 13:33), when Demetrius II and Tryphon were struggling against each other for the Seleucid throne, and as the Jews prepared to claim independence (1 Macc 13:41-42). This would have been an excellent time to write to Egypt to ask their brethren to celebrate the festival marking the beginning of their freedom. The letter's emphasis on Jason as the bad guy would have helped squelch any hint that the Jews in Jerusalem were promoting independence movements outside Judea. Since we have only this snippet from the letter of 143 B.C.E., little more can be said of it.

1

1:10b-17

Greetings and Well Wishes

10b/ Those in Jerusalem and those in Judea and the senate and Judas[a] to Aristobulos, teacher of Ptolemy the king and one from the stock of anointed priests, and to the Jews in Egypt, greetings and good health.

11/ Saved by God from great dangers, we greatly thank him as one who draws himself up[b] against a king.[c] 12/ For he repulsed those drawn up against the holy city. 13/ For, when the commander and the seemingly unstoppable force around him came into Persia, they were cut down in the temple of Nanaia as the priests serving Nanaia used a trick. 14/ For on the pretext of wedding her, Antiochus and his friends came to the place to take most of the temple treasure for the reckoning of the dowry. 15/ When the priests of that temple of Nanaia set these out on display and he came forward with a small retinue to the enclosure of the precinct, [the priests] closed the temple when Antiochus entered, 16/ opened the hidden door of the ceiling, threw down rocks, struck the commander like a thunderbolt. They dismembered [them], cut off their heads,[d] and threw them to those outside. 17/ In every way, blessed be our God who handed over[e] those acting impiously.

a The Syriac reads "the senate of Judea." The Syriac, misled by the date of the previous letter, tried to avoid the problem of having Judas live until 188 s.e.

b The manuscripts read the nominative plural, παρατασσόμενοι ("as those who array themselves against a king"). Grimm and Goldstein accept it, but it is hard to see how this clause describing the battle readiness of the people explains why they thank God. The danger involved in fighting kings is not a reason for thanksgiving. With Abel and Habicht, I accept the emendation of Charles Bruston ("Trois lettres des Juifs de Palestine," *ZAW* 10 [1890] 115), who reads the dative singular, παρατασσαμένῳ, a change from the majuscule *OI* to *ΩI*; the clause describes God as one who fights for his people. Goldstein rejected this emendation, as he held that it would make the following sentence redundant. However, v. 12 specifies the general description of God as fighter by pointing to a demonstration of his power. A secondary reason for accepting the emendation lies in the author's use of repetition—great dangers, greatly thank. In v. 12, God throws out τοὺς παραταξαμένους ("those drawn up"), and the repetition of the verb παρατάσσω suggests that God is the subject of the verb as it occurs in v. 11—God arrays himself against a king and throws out those who array themselves against the holy city. The Syriac reads, "We very greatly give thanks to God who helped us and delivered us from all the afflictions which came upon us," and so also holds that God is the fighter.

c Classical authors generally did not use the article when referring to the Persian king. Therefore, here "king" without the article could refer specifically to the Seleucid king as successor to the Persians and not just to any king.

d Several manuscripts, Syriac, 55, La[p], read the singular, but presumably the priests mistreated everyone who entered the temple precinct.

e The Lucianic manuscript tradition, L'-62 58, as well as the Latin and Syriac translations read παρέδωκε(ν). One frequently finds this variation between ἔδωκε and παρέδωκε in the Greek manuscripts of the Bible, and so I see no need to follow the Lucianic reading. Δίδωμι has the sense of "give up, surrender."

Commentary by Verse

■ **1:10b** The "letter" of 1:10b–2:18 has the normal form of the opening address: "A (sender) to B (recipient) greeting." John White has stated how "by the mid-second century b.c.e., and into the late first or early second centuries c.e., letter writers began to combine the health wish with the address/salutation in the form: . . . χαίρειν καὶ ἐρρῶσθαι (or ὑγιαίνειν) i.e., . . . greeting and health."[1] Elias Bickermann had earlier suggested that, since the combination of χαίρειν καὶ ὑγιαίνειν is not attested until the middle of the first century b.c.e., its

---

1 White, *Light from Ancient Letters*, 200.

use in this letter purporting to derive from the time of Judas Maccabeus shows the letter to be a forgery.[2] Since the survival of ancient letters depends on chance, scholars such as White are now agreed that such an address could have occurred in the second century B.C.E. There survives one example from the first half of the fourth century B.C.E.,[3] and Goldstein has provided a list of ten examples from the mid-60s B.C.E. to 42 C.E.[4]

The senders of the letter are identified more specifically than those in the first letter. Their self-presentation is interesting. Not only are the people of Jerusalem and Judea mentioned, but also the *gerousia* and Judas. A *gerousia* ("senate") of the Jews is mentioned in a letter of Antiochus III granting the Jews the right to live according to their ancestral customs, as well as in a letter of Antiochus IV and one of Jonathan, brother of Judas Maccabeus (Josephus *Ant.* 12.138–44; 2 Macc 11:27; 1 Macc 12:6). The role of the senate here is similar to that in Judith, where the high priest and the senate in Jerusalem send orders to the rest of the Jews (Jdt 4:8; 11:14; see also 15:8). This usage echoes that of Deut 27:1 LXX, where Moses and the senate (*gerousia;* זִקְנֵי) of Israel command the people to keep the commandments.

Grimm listed earlier scholars who questioned whether this Judas referred to Judas Maccabeus. Some suggested Aristobulos, son of John Hyrcanus, also called Judas (Josephus *Ant.* 20.240), or Judas the Essene, who flourished at the time of Aristobulos (Josephus *Bell.* 1.78; *Ant.* 13.311). David M. Sluys suggested a radical emendation so that the letter was from Aristobulos to Onias IV in Egypt: Ἰουδας Ἀριστοβουλος Ὀνίᾳ ἀπὸ τοῦ τῶν χριστῶν ἱερέων γένους.[5] Both suggestions arose from dating the letter to 188 S.E., as in 1:10a. Since this date belongs to the previous letter, there is no reason to seek another Judas besides Judas Maccabeus. See the general commentary for a discussion of Aristobulos.

■ **11-12** The phrase "saved from great dangers" is found often in inscriptions. For example, Apollonius, son of Sosibios, made a dedication to the great gods of Samothrace σωθεὶς ἐγ μεγάλων κινδύνων.[6]

The particle ὡς ἄν is used here to express the reason for thanks. It is frequently used by Polybius.[7]

The phrase παρατάσσειν ἐν often has the meaning in the LXX of "array/fight against," translating ב נלחם.[8] The ἐν here contrasts with the ἐκ- in the verb earlier in the sentence, ἐκβράζω. The twofold use of παρατάσσειν, as noted in textual comment b, underscores that God is the ally of the Jews against adversaries.

Schwartz has pointed to the presence of ἐκβράζειν both here and in 5:8, where it is used to describe Jason's flight. He argued that this correspondence shows that the writer of the second letter knew the epitome. However, Schwartz neglected to look at the way each verb is used. In 5:8, the verb is used as often in Greek: Jason is thrown up onto Egypt as ships or people are washed ashore, thrown onto land from the sea.[9] The sense is that Jason is thrown up on shore like flotsam and jetsam, not a very flattering picture. Here in 1:12, the meaning is quite different. The verb is used in the sense of "to drive out, expel." One can find this meaning metaphorically, as when temper casts forth intemperate words (Plutarch *Cohib. ira* 456C), but the sense "to drive someone away, to make someone flee" is found in Neh 13:28 LXX, where it translates the *hiphil* of חרב. This Hebrew verb, as well as the Aramaic *ʾaphel* of ברח, has the meaning of "to make flee," as in 1 Chr 8:13; 12:16; and Prov 19:26. Since there are indications of Semitisms in this verse, as noted above, it would appear that either this letter was written in Hebrew/Aramaic and translated into Greek, or the writer's Greek is influenced here by Semitic verb usage. The two uses of the verb thus show no comparison.

■ **13** The term "unstoppable" is used to describe the army of Philip V of Macedon and that of Antiochus III when speaking of their attacks on temples (Diodorus Siculus 28.3).

2 Bickermann, "Ein jüdischer Festbrief," 233–34.
3 Wilhelm Crönert, "Die beiden ältesten griechischen Briefe," *Rheinisches Museum* 65 (1910) 157.
4 Goldstein, *II Maccabees*, 164–65.
5 David M. Sluys, *De Maccabaeorum libris I et II [i.e. primo et secundo] quaestiones* (Amsterdam: J. Clausen, 1904) 66–68.
6 *OGIS* 1:69. See also Strabo 16.4.7.
7 See Jules A. de Foucault, *Recherches sur la langue et le style de Polybe* (Collection d'études anciennes; Paris: Belles Lettres, 1972) 175–76.
8 Judges 8:1; 9:45; 11:9, 27; 12:3; Neh 4:8; Zech 14:3.
9 Herodotus 7.188, 190; Diodorus Siculus 14.68.7;

The author of the condensed version has Antiochus IV attempt to pillage the temple in Persepolis (9:2), but 1 Macc 6:1-4 and Josephus *Ant.* 12.354 have Antiochus IV menace the temple in Elymais. However, these latter authors speak of a city called Elymais, whereas Elymais is the Greek name of a region, today in southwest Iran, which lay in the ancient empire of Elam. This mountainous region east of the prosperous plains around Susa was described by Strabo as a "nursery for soldiers" (Strabo 16.1.18: ἡ δ᾽ ὀρεινὴ στρατιώτας τρέφει), and central Seleucid control was most likely not strong.[10] In the middle of the second century B.C.E. a local independent dynasty flourished for a time. The title "king of Elymais," mentioned in Plutarch (*Pomp.* 36) and Tacitus (*Ann.* 6.44), indicates their independence from Parthia.[11] The region seems to be characterized by several large sanctuaries: to gain resources, Antiochus III attempted to pillage the temple of Bel in Elymais, while later Mithridates I carried away treasure from both the temple of Athena and that of Aphrodite (Strabo 16.1.18).[12]

Nanaia, or Nanâ, is a goddess of Mesopotamian origin. In the Hellenistic period, she was often named Artemis. A dedicatory inscription found at Piraeus from the Roman period names her Artemis Nanai.[13] Polybius (31.9) and Josephus (*Ant.* 12.354) both name the temple that Antiochus IV attacked a temple of Artemis. Appian (*Syr.* 66) says that it was a temple of Aphrodite. A temple of Artemis Nanaia, built in Roman times, was found at Dura-Europos, and a dedicatory inscription named Nanaia as the city's chief goddess. The temple contained statues of Aphrodite, Nike, and Tyche.[14] Nanaia thus was associated with several Greek goddesses. Nanaia was also the chief goddess of Susa, as her depiction on coinage shows:

the rayed halo and polos crown of Artemis represented on coins of Mithridates II, issued around 110

B.C. at Susa . . . transferred Nanâ's functions to the syncretic cult of Artemis-Nanâ. . . . Bronze coins of the kings of Elymais, probably issued at Susa after the establishment of Parthian rule at Elymais and at Susa, depict Artemis-Nanâ as a frontal or profile head with a radiate halo or polos, or as a complete figure dressed in the fashion of a Greek huntress with or without the radiate halo, and occasionally with a crescent by her side.[15]

Nanaia was thus a major goddess figure in the region, and her temple was rich.

■ **14** The claim to a sacred marriage,[16] or to kinship with a goddess, was a ruse often used to gain money. The second-century C.E. author Granius Licinianus (28) states that Antiochus IV had pretended to marry Diana/Artemis at Hierapolis. While the banquet was being set up, Antiochus IV took off with all the vessels of the temple as a dowry and left only one ring for the goddess. Earlier, in 304 B.C.E., Demetrius Poliorketes had set up residence in the Parthenon at Athens on the grounds that he claimed to be the younger brother of Athena (Plutarch *Demetr.* 23–24). A story about Mark Antony had the Athenians entreating him, as Dionysos, to marry Athena; Mark Antony agreed, but for a dowry of one thousand talents (Seneca the Elder *Suas.* 1.6).

■ **15-16** The priests trick the one who thinks he is tricking them. Reconstruction of maneuvers and setting is difficult. As Abel rightly observes, the terms περίβολος, τέμενος, and ἱερός should not be taken in the strictest sense. The king is lured into the sanctuary of the goddess, not just into the enclosure. The image of the sanctuary with a door in the ceiling that could be opened is intriguing. Some Egyptian temples had windows in their inner

21.16.3; Plutarch *Quaest. Graec.* 294F; Josephus *Bell.* 3.427.

10   Richard N. Frye, *The History of Ancient Iran* (HA 3.7; Munich: C. H. Beck, 1983) 158.

11   See Frye, *History,* 273–75; Josef Wiesehöfer, "Elymais," in Hubert Cancik and Helmuth Schneider, eds., *Brill's New Pauly: Encyclopedia of the Ancient World* (16 vols.; Leiden and Boston: Brill, 2004) 4:931.

12   In Diodorus Siculus 28.3, the temple of Bel is called the temple of Zeus.

13   *IG*³ 3.131 (= *CIA* 3.1.131): Αξιος κ[α]ὶ Κ[λε]ὼ Ἀρτέμιδι Νάνᾳ εὐξάμενοι ἀνέθηκαν.

14   Franz Cumont, *Fouilles de Doura-Europos (1922–1923)* (Paris: Geuthner, 1926) 196–99.

15   G. Azarpay, "Nanâ, the Sumero-Akkadian Goddess of Transoxiana," *JAOS* 96 (1976) 536–42, here 537–38.

16   On sacred marriage, see Samuel N. Kramer, *The Sacred Marriage Rite: Aspects of Faith, Myth and Ritual in Ancient Sumer* (Bloomington, Ind.: Indiana University Press, 1969).

sanctuary, but rarely,[17] and there seems to be no archaeological evidence of doors in temple roofs from the Mesopotamian region. Grimm suggested that the letter may be referring to the form of an open-air, or hypaethral, temple described in Vitruvius 3.2.8. However, there is no mention of a secret door/window in the roof of these types of temples, as there simply is no roof. A. Trevor Hodge has shown how in many Greek temples there exist remains of stone stairways that must have led to the attic between the ceiling of the cella and the roof. He speculates that in some temples the attic could have been used "as some kind of shrine and for storage."[18] The spaces between the beams of the cella ceiling could perhaps have allowed the priests to construct "doors" through which to hurl down stones. If one were to consider that this window/door had symbolic meaning, it would be interesting that in the *Baal* cycle, Baal eventually allows Kothar to build a window in his house/temple.

> I will make (one), Kothar, this day;
> Kothar, this very hour.
> A casement shall be opened in the house,
> A window within the palace.
> Yea, *I'll open rifts in* the clouds
> At thy word, O Kothar wa-Khasis.[19]

The use of the term "door" may reflect descriptions of the heavens such as found in *1 Enoch*, where the sun, moon, and stars come out of the doors in the heavens.[20] The term, therefore, might suggest that the architecture of the temple was modeled on views of the universe.

That priests were tricky is a motif found in the story of *Bel and the Dragon*, in which the priests have secret passageways for entering the temple. One might also note the way Lucian of Samosata describes the trickery of Alexander the False Prophet in seducing his customers (*Alex.* 8–22).

The verb used to describe the effect of the priests' stone throwing is συνεκεραύνωσαν and reflects the word for "thunderbolt," κεραυνός, the weapon of Zeus. I suggest that the author wittily plays on this resemblance

to have the ruler of the gods punish the arrogance of Antiochus. The focus of the action is thus Antiochus, not his followers, and I do not see the necessity of adding, as Habicht does, "and those with him."

The phrase for "dismember," μέλη ποιήσαντες, is literally "making members" and is reminiscent of the threats uttered by Nebuchadnezzar in Dan 2:5 (הַדָּמִין תִּתְעַבְדוּן) and 3:29: "you will be made limbs."

■ **17** This benediction recalls the thanksgiving of 1:11-12 and so rounds off the section of well wishes. The death of Antiochus IV is followed by a call to celebrate the festival, which suggests that the death preceded the deliverance of the temple. In 1 Macc 6:5-17, the deliverance of the temple precedes the death of Antiochus IV.

General Commentary

The letter that starts in 1:10b can be viewed as following the usual form of a letter: initial address (1:10b); assurance of the senders' well-being (1:11-17); body of the letter (1:18–2:18). The date of the letter is not given.

The Initial Address
The initial address follows the customary pattern in letters, "A to B, greeting." Here the greeting is enlarged with a wish for the well-being of the addressees. The senders of the letter are quite specific: besides the Jerusalemites, those in the land of Judea are also mentioned, so as to cover all the inhabitants. The senders then specify the *gerousia* (= senate). Aristotle had spoken of a *gerousia* of Sparta and of one at Carthage (*Pol.* 1270b24; 1272b37). Polybius echoed Aristotle's words in his treatment of the legislation of Lycurgus for Sparta, which, Polybius held, united "all the distinctive excellences of the best governments" (6.10.6). In Lycurgus's legislation, kingship was restrained by the populace, and the populace by the elders (ἀπὸ τῶν γερόντων), and so the legislation united monarchy, aristocracy, and democracy. Polybius finds the same mixture of the three forms

---

17   Rolf Gundlach, "Temples," in Donald B. Redford, ed., *The Oxford Encyclopedia of Egypt* (3 vols.; Oxford: Oxford University Press, 2001) 3:363–79, here 365.

18   A. Trevor Hodge, *The Woodwork of Greek Roofs* (Cambridge Classical Studies; Cambridge: Cambridge University Press, 1960) 36–38; quotation from 37.

19   James B. Pritchard, ed., *The Ancient Near East*, vol. 1: *An Anthology of Texts and Pictures* (Princeton: Princeton University Press, 1958) 106.

20   *1 Enoch* 33:2; 34:2-3; 35:1; 36:1-3; 72:2-3. In the extant Greek text in 101:2 and 104:2, the term used is θυρίδας ("small doors, windows").

of government in the Roman constitution, in which the Roman senate takes the place of the elders at Sparta (6.11.12). Interestingly, Plutarch later calls the senate the *gerousia* (*Praec. ger. reip.* 789E). The senders of this letter in 1:10b, in presenting themselves as a group made up of the populace, a senate, and one leader, would thus identify the Jews as possessing an ideal form of government. This group can be compared with the form of government said by Hecataeus of Abdera to have been bestowed by Moses on the Jews—the most accomplished were selected to be priests and judges, and of these men, the most outstanding in practical wisdom and excellence was to rule as high priest (as in Diodorus Siculus 40.3.4–5). Here a different constitutional model is in play, one more along Platonic lines.[21] The letter senders therefore portray themselves as belonging to an ideal society.

The letter is addressed to Aristobulos and the Jews in Egypt. Aristobulos is chiastically paired with Judas, almost as his counterpart. Aristobulos is further characterized as a teacher of King Ptolemy and from the tribe of the anointed priests. Fragments by a Jewish writer named Aristobulos were preserved by the Christian writer Clement of Alexandria (d. ca. 215 C.E.), Anatolius (d. ca. 282 C.E.), and Eusebius of Caesarea (d. ca. 339 C.E.). After editing the fragments and *testimonia* concerning this latter Aristobulos and reviewing all the debates about Aristobulos and his work, Carl Holladay concluded that Aristobulos's work should be dated to the reign of Ptolemy VI Philometer (180–145 B.C.E.).[22] The work was written in the form of a dialogue between Ptolemy and Aristobulos wherein Aristobulos answers the king's questions about the Torah, somewhat like the symposium found in *Ep. Arist.* 187–294. Aristobulos would have adopted this literary form and could have addressed his work to the king without ever expecting that the king would read it.[23] His purpose was to show that the Torah, if read properly, could be explained to educated Greeks, and his method of reading included allegorical interpretation.[24] One important element of this strategy was to claim that Greek philosophers and poets like Pythagoras and Plato had taken parts of their teaching from the Torah (Clement of Alexandria *Strom.* 1.22.150.1–3; Eusebius *Praep. ev.* 13.12.1; 8.10.4). One should understand the description of Aristobulos as the teacher of Ptolemy in the light of the fragments, as a Jewish scholar interpreting the wisdom of the Torah to Gentiles.

This teacher of Ptolemy is also described as from the tribe of anointed priests. Aaron was anointed by Moses (Lev 8:12), and his successor in the high priesthood was also to be anointed (MT Lev 6:15; LXX Lev 6:22). The phrase "anointed priest" is found in Lev 4:3, 5, 16. One should note the increasing importance of the figure of Levi in the writings of the second century B.C.E. Levi is set apart for the priesthood (*Jub.* 32:1-3; 4Q213b [4QLevi^c ar]).[25] This Levi tradition also emphasizes the value of wisdom, which Levi stresses to his sons as he dies (4Q213 [4QLevi^a ar]).[26] The term γένος has a wide range of meaning, from race to tribe to clan to family. Does Aristobulos belong to the tribe of Levi or, more specifically, to the house of Zadok[27] or the family of the Oniads (Sir 50:1)? The very imprecision of the lineage details underscores the connection being made between the ancient traditions of Judaism and the Hellenistic world as represented by the Ptolemaic king. In this letter, then, the representatives of the best constitutional form of government address a group headed by someone at home in his ancestral tradition and open to the wider Hellenistic world.

21 Doron Mendels, "Hecataeus of Abdera and a Jewish 'Patrios Politeia' of the Persian Period," *ZAW* 95 (1983) 96–110.
22 Holladay, *Fragments*, 3:74–75.
23 Ibid., 75.
24 See also Nikolaus Walter, *Der Thoraausleger Aristobulos: Untersuchungen zu seinen Fragmenten und zu pseudepigraphischen Resten der jüdisch-hellenistischen Literatur* (TUGAL 86; Berlin: Akademie, 1964) 27–28.
25 As reconstructed by Michael E. Stone and Jonas C. Greenfield in G. J. Brooke et al., in consultation with J. VanderKam, *Qumran Cave 4.XVII: Parabiblical Texts, Part 3* (DJD 22; Oxford: Clarendon, 1996) 40–41. See also Jonas C. Greenfield, Michael E. Stone, and Esther Eshel, *The Aramaic Levi Document: Edition, Translation, Commentary* (SVTP 19; Leiden: Brill, 2004) 70–71, 90–91.
26 As reconstructed by Stone and Greenfield in DJD 22, 8–11. See also Greenfield et al., *Aramaic Levi Document*, 102–5.
27 2 Samuel 20:25; 1 Kgs 1:32-45; Ezek 40:46; 43:19; 44:15; 48:11.

The Well-being of the Senders

Following the formulaic concern about the recipient's welfare comes an assurance of the senders' well-being. This assurance consists of a thanksgiving to God because of their rescue from danger, obliquely informing the recipients of the present well-being of the senders. An example of such a thanksgiving is found in the letter of Apion, where the young recruit Apion, after praying for the welfare of his father, sister, and cousin, continues: "I give thanks to the Lord Sarapis because, when I was endangered at sea, he rescued me immediately. When I arrived at Misenum, I received three gold pieces from Caesar for traveling expenses and I am well."[28] Then follows a request for a return letter.

The oblique reference to the senders' well-being consists of a fascinating account of the death of Antiochus IV. At first blush, this narrative would seem to have little to do with the retaking of the temple: there is no mention of the battle at Emmaus (1 Macc 4:1-25; 2 Maccabees 8) or of the withdrawal of Lysias (1 Macc 4:26-35), events much more specific to expelling those lined up against the holy city. Nor is any mention made of the Seleucid garrison stationed in the Akra (1 Macc 4:41-60). The senders do not discuss these events because they have framed the whole narrative in a highly mythological fashion wherein a challenge to God's authority by a ruler is met with a response. The action of the divine warrior is classically portrayed in the hymn in Exodus 15 and in the reaction to the boasting of the king of Assyria (Isa 10:5-32; 2 Kings 18–19). In this worldview, the death of Antiochus IV means the defeat of his attack on the temple. So God is described as a king-fighter, and his destruction of Antiochus IV is how he expels the besiegers of Jerusalem. Note too how this description is inaccurate. Contrary to the implication of the letter, Jerusalem is in no way under attack by the Seleucid army in the first battles before the cleansing of the temple.

The narrative of the death of Antiochus IV[29] given here differs from those given in Polybius 31.9, Appian *Syr.* 66, 1 Macc 6:1-16, and even the epitome in 2 Maccabees 9. Common to all accounts is an attempt on a temple in Persia. Polybius, Appian, and 1 Maccabees specify this temple as the temple of Artemis in Elymais; 2 Maccabees 9 situates the narrative in Persepolis. Except for Appian, all hold that the attempt to pillage was unsuccessful, but only this account in the second prefixed letter has the king die in the attempt. The other accounts all have the king retreat and later die of illness; however, all have his death linked to divine outrage. First and Second Maccabees link his illness and despair to his attack on the Jerusalem temple, as does also Josephus *Ant.* 12.354-59; Polybius reports stories of Antiochus being smitten by madness. Such divine outrage is frequently found in stories where temples are pillaged. For example, the army and navy of King Prusias of Bithynia are destroyed because they pillaged temples and shrines, and the Cretans are punished for sacking the temple at Siphnos (Diodorus Siculus 31.35, 45). After attempting to pillage the sanctuary of Zeus in Elymais, Antiochus III received punishment from the gods (Diodorus Siculus 28.3; 20.15).

The second prefixed letter has the punishment occur immediately. The whole narrative is full of wit. The arrogance of the king is highlighted by an image of unstoppableness that would be used of the arrogant Philip V of Macedon and Antiochus III (Diodorus Siculus 28.3). The leader and his army are cut to pieces, an image that is gruesomely realized in the dismemberment of Antiochus.[30] In the story of Antiochus, the priests gradually separate him from his army, seducing him by laying out the money to be seen. Once inside the temple, they "zeus" (συνεκεραύνωσαν) him by throwing stones as Zeus threw thunderbolts. Antiochus's arrogance at wanting to mate with a goddess is rewarded by the priests' imitating the gods; his desire for union results in his being made less than human, without head or arms.

---

28   *BGU* 2:423; White, *Light from Ancient Letters*, 103A.

29   Attempts to show that here is narrated the death of Antiochus III or Antiochus VII Sidetes are unsuccessful. The argument of Charles C. Torrey ("Die Briefe 2 Makk. 1,1–2,18," *ZAW* 20 [1900] 225–42) for Antiochus VII presupposes, among other things, that the letter was written in 124 B.C.E. Against Antiochus III, see Maurice Holleaux, *Études* *d'épigraphie et d'histoire grecques* (6 vols.; Paris: E. de Boccard, 1952–68) 3:255–79.

30   Rather than highlighting the inconsistency between the whole army being destroyed in v. 13 and only Antiochus and a few friends being slaughtered in v. 16, as Grimm does, I would see the former verse as a hyperbolic description of the stopping of the army.

What happens to the army of Antiochus is not spelled out, but the sudden dismembering of their leader would have left them headless, and their recognition of divine vengeance on their commander would have led them to disperse.

The story is skillfully told, but there are two further points worthy of notice. First, this is not a usual story of divine deliverance. The goddess does not appear to chase away her attempted despoiler as Apollo chased away the Gauls at Delphi (Herodotus 8.36). Rather, the priests do the dirty work in much less miraculous fashion, although one can imagine how their own spruced-up version of events might have sounded. Second, all these events take place in a far-off temple of a pagan goddess yet are ascribed to the activity of Yahweh. No derogatory epithets are used either of the goddess or of her priests—they are the agents of Yahweh. Does the concluding blessing of God, who hands over those who act impiously, refer only to the attack on the holy city, or is the attack on the temple of Nanaia also included in this impiety? This account of Antiochus IV's death does not have the goddess acting but does suggest that her temple should not be pillaged. The theme of openness to the Gentiles that we noted in the opening address of this letter surfaces again. The author is not against forging respectful relationships with Gentiles.

1

1:18-36

The Body of the Letter 1

18/ About to celebrate on the twenty-fifth Kislev the purification of the temple, we thought it necessary, so that you yourselves might celebrate, to make a clear statement to you about Sukkoth and the fire[a] when Nehemiah offered sacrifices after building the temple and the altar. 19/ For in fact, when our forefathers were led into the land of Persia, the devout priests at that time took some of the fire from the altar and secretly hid it in a hollow of a waterless cistern,[b] which[c] they secured so that the spot would be unknown to all. 20/ After a suitable number of years had elapsed, when it was decreed by God, Nehemiah, commissioned by the king of the land of Persia, sent the descendants of the priests who had been involved in the concealment to retrieve the fire. When they explained that truly[d] they did not find fire but a viscous liquid, he commanded them to draw [some] and bring [it]. 21/ When [the liquid] was brought,[e] Nehemiah commanded the priests to sprinkle the materials of the sacrifices, both the pieces of wood and what was set thereon. 22/ When this was done and time passed and the sun, earlier clouded, shone forth, a great fire was lit so that everyone marveled. 23/ As the sacrifice was being consumed, the priests prayed, both the priests and everyone—Jonathan led off and the rest responded as Nehemiah [did]. 24/ The prayer was like this:
Lord, Lord God, the founder of all things, the fearsome, powerful, just and merciful one, the only king who is also benevolent, 25/ the only leader of the dance, the only just, almighty and eternal one, the one who preserves Israel from all evil, the one who chose our forefathers and sanctified them, 26/ accept the sacrifice on behalf of all your people Israel, guard carefully and sanctify completely your portion. 27/ Gather us together, we who have been scattered,

a The text here has caused difficulty. In most manuscripts, A′ V 62 46–53 55, no article is read before σκηνοπηγίας, while some, L′ q 58 347 771, read τῆς σκηνοπηγίας and 106 reads τὰς σκηνοπηγίας. The major Greek manuscripts, A′ V 62 46–52 55 311, omit ὡς, but Hanhart follows q l[-62] 58 and the Latin, Syriac, and Armenian translations in adding it. Often it has been suggested that the text is missing key words. Grimm, for example, suggested that one follow the Syriac and read ἄγετε αὐτόν, "celebrate it [the purification]." Grimm would also insert τὰς ἡμέρας before τῆς σκηνοπηγίας, and so the phrase would read "celebrate it as the days of Sukkoth," analogously to 1:9. Most scholars (Grimm, Abel, Bunge [*Untersuchungen*, 95–105], Habicht) are agreed that to make sense, τὰς ἡμέρας should be inserted, and so the text would read: ἵνα καὶ αὐτοὶ ἄγητε [αὐτὸν] ὡς [τὰς ἡμέρας τῆς] σκηνοπηγίας, "so that you yourselves celebrate [it] as [the days] of Sukkoth."
I myself have resisted such interpolations. I have read the text as in the major Greek manuscripts: ἵνα καὶ αὐτοὶ ἄγητε σκηνοπηγίας καὶ τοῦ πυρός. The verb "you may celebrate" does not require an object, as it can be presupposed from the previous participial phrase. The genitive "Sukkoth and the fire" is governed by the verb διασαφέω. The close connection between the verb and the matter that is to be clarified explains the use of the genitive; see Smyth, *Greek Grammar*, §1380. Bunge (*Untersuchungen*, 99) suggested that the preposition περί had dropped out of the manuscript tradition, in which suggestion he is close to a proposal of Torrey ("Letters," 133, 143 n. 27). However, it is not necessary. If the writers of the letter are making clear to their addressees the facts about the celebration of Sukkoth by Nehemiah, then this interpretation also explains why the article is used before "fire." The article shows that the authors have in mind that particular fire which occurred when Nehemiah celebrated Sukkoth. One does not then need to posit some unknown Festival of Fire, as Ben Zion Wacholder has done ("The Letter from Judah Maccabee to Aristobulus: Is 2 Maccabees 1:10b–2:18 Authentic?" *HUCA* 49 [1978] 89–133, here 112–17).

b The text reads ἐν κοιλώματι φρέατος τάξιν ἔχοντος ἄνυδρον, "in the hollow of a cistern having a waterless disposition." The text has generated much discussion as a result of its circumlocution. Is it the hollow of a waterless cistern, or is the hollow like a waterless cistern? Adolf Wilhelm followed the latter view and suggested emending ἔχοντος to ἔχοντι in apposition to κοιλώματι and, with L′-62 311, reading ἄνυδρου in apposition to φρέατος. His translation would thus be, "in a hollow like a waterless cistern" ("Zu einigen Stellen der Bücher der Makkabäer," *Akademie der Wissenschaften in Wien, Philosophisch-*

free those enslaved among the nations, look upon the contemned and loathed, and let the nations know that you are our God. 28/ Torment those acting with oppression and arrogant violence. 29/ Plant your people into your holy place, just as Moses said.

30/ Now the priests were singing the hymns, 31/ but, just as the elements of the sacrifice were consumed, Nehemiah commanded [them] to pour the leftover liquid [upon]^f rather large stones. 32/ When this was done, a flame was lit up, for when the light from the altar shone opposite, [the liquid] was used up.

33/ When the affair became public, it was announced to the king of the Persians that in the very spot where the priests who had been transferred had hidden the fire, had appeared the liquid from which those accompanying Nehemiah had purified the elements of the sacrifice. 34/ The king, after examining the affair, enclosed [the spot] and made it sacred. 35/ Those on whom the king was bestowing much money, used to accept and share [it].^{g} 36/ Those around Nehemiah named this [liquid] nephthar, which is interpreted "purification." It is commonly called nephthai.

historische Klasse. Anzeiger 74 [1937] 15–30, here 16–17). However, I see no reason not to accept the text as is: the priests put the fire in the hollow where there had previously been a cistern, but which had dried up. Wilhelm's reconstruction is a more normal Greek construction, as it uses the phrase τάξιν ἔχειν + genitive to express a similarity, which is often found in Greek. The text as it stands in the manuscript would be less usual, suggesting perhaps a writer who is not completely sure how to use the word τάξις.

c The relative pronoun has been attracted into the dative case.

d Reading ἦ μὴν instead of ἡμῖν; see Bernhard Risberg, "Konjekturer till några ställen i de apokryfiska böckerna," *Eranos* 15 (1915) 33–35. One does not need to see here a slip of the pen whereby the writer evidences that he is quoting from an allegedly eyewitness source.

e Wilhelm ("Zu einigen Stellen," 19–20) has rightly argued that the general description τὰ τῶν θυσιῶν ("the elements of the sacrifices") is not to be connected to the verb ἀνηνέχθη and so translated "when the elements of the sacrifices were brought/placed," but that this general description is specified by the mention of wood and other things necessary for the sacrifice and is governed by the verb ἐκέλευσεν. The subject of "was brought" is the liquid of the previous verse that Nehemiah had commanded be brought (φέρειν).

f The verb καταχέω normally has its object in the dative or genitive case, not in the accusative as here, or it uses the prepositions εἰς or ἐπί. Katz ("Text of 2 Maccabees," 13) restored ἐπί, maintaining that the corruption was due to haplography: ἐκελευσ–<Ε>ΕΠΙΛΙθους. He also said that the absence of ἐπί in a translated Greek text would be a Hebraism. I agree that ἐπί should be added. The Syriac and part of the Lucianic tradition interpret the text so that Nehemiah commands that the place be covered with large stones, which does not fit the context. See the comment on the verse.

g The text here is very difficult. The singular verb, with the king as subject, does not make much sense. The NRSV translates: "[the king] exchanged many gifts with those whom he favored." However, this account does not fit the context of the king's action toward the holy spot he had set up and suggests a random distribution to his courtiers. Bernhard Risberg ("Textkritische und exegetische Anmerkungen zu den Makkabäerbüchern," *Beiträge zur Religionswissenschaft* 27 [1918] 6–31, here 17–18), followed by Schwartz, proposed a more radical solution and read ἐξηρύσαντο ("who had drawn out for themselves") instead of ἐχαρίζετο. While this fits the context, the main clause remains a problem. How is one to translate μετέδιδου? Does the king take in lots of money and share it with those who had drawn out the liquid? Schwartz translates the verb as "bestowed," but the verb is not simply the same as "gave." Moreover, this translation does not explain the use of the imperfects in the main clause, which suggests an ongoing distribution, and the context suggests that the king was paying the expenses for the upkeep of the spot and that the people so favored shared his benefactions. Benedetto Marzullo ("Vetus Latina II Macc. 1,33-35 [Rec.P]," *Quaderni dell'Istituto di filologia greca* 3 [1968] 62–67) also suggested that one read the aorist ἐχαρίσατο rather than the imperfect ἐχαρίζετο, which would mean a onetime gift of the king, but this reading is not necessary. If one reads the third person plural verbs, ἐλάμβανον καὶ μετεδίδουν, with L$^{·534\ 19\ 62}$ 311 and the Syriac, one could translate, "Those on whom the king was bestowing much money used to accept and share it."

Commentary by Verse

■ **18** Three Nehemiahs are mentioned in the Bible: (1) Nehemiah, one of the leaders of the Jewish community who returned with Jeshua and Zerubbabel to Judea around 538 B.C.E., after the exile in Babylonia (Ezra 2:2; Neh 7:7; 1 Esdr 5:8); (2) Nehemiah, son of Azbuk, a ruler around Beth-Zur who participated in the rebuilding of the walls of Jerusalem (Neh 3:16); (3) Nehemiah, son of Hacaliah, the central figure of the book of Nehemiah, who began his activity in Jerusalem around 445 B.C.E. (Neh 1:1; 2:1-11). As 2 Macc 1:20 refers to Nehemiah being commissioned by the king of Persia, the reference must be to the third of these figures. However, this is the only place where Nehemiah is said to build the temple and the altar. Other texts have the high priest Jeshua and the governor Zerubbabel build the altar and offer sacrifice,[1] while in Ezra 3:7-11 they begin work on the temple. Ezra 5:16 and 1 Esdr 6:20 state that Sheshbazzar laid the foundations of the temple. Nehemiah is said to have rebuilt the city walls of Jerusalem (Neh 2:17–7:3; 12:27-43; Sir 49:13). Goldstein attempted to explain this discrepancy between the biblical accounts and that in 1:18b by seeing this text as the first evidence for the identification of Nehemiah and Zerubbabel, an identification found in *b. Sanh.* 38a. Theodore Bergren pointed out the implausibility of Goldstein's arguments.[2] What we have here is simply an alternative telling of the events of the return from exile that highlights the role of Nehemiah. Given the fluidity of the biblical books and the extraordinary creativity reflected in the writings found at Qumran, one should not be surprised at such a rewriting.

One could recall that the story of Abraham and Sarah as told by Josephus (*Bell.* 5.379–81), by his own account an accurate interpreter of the Bible, varied quite markedly from the version in Genesis 12.

■ **19** The exile to Babylon took place under Nebuchadnezzar in 587 B.C.E. Persia here refers not to the eastern province of Persia but to the territory of the later Persian/Achaemenid Empire, which included Babylon. As Goldstein notes, Cicero called the Parthians Persians, so the term Persia could have a wide significance.[3]

When we read this story, it is well to put aside some assumptions we might have about the physics of the universe. For us, heat and fire are the motion of bodies, but for the ancients fire was a material substance. There were corpuscles of fire as of the other elements of air, earth, and water. Plato spent a great deal of effort to show how these small bodies could interchange.[4] Plato also spoke of different types of fire (*Tim.* 45B–D; 58C–D). I am not suggesting that the writers of this letter had read Plato or the Greek cosmologists—though Aristobulos might have—but that fire was considered a bodily substance that could be stored.

■ **20** After Cyrus captured Babylon in 539 B.C.E., he issued a decree in 538 B.C.E. that allowed exiles to return home. The senders of the letter in 2 Maccabees skip over the complex story of the return from exile to Judea: the role of Zerubbabel, the governor, and Jeshua, the high priest; the enthusiasm of the prophets Haggai and Zechariah; the building of the temple in 520–515 B.C.E.; and the much later mission of Ezra, whenever dated. Rather, the senders concentrate on Nehemiah, who was governor of Judea from 458 B.C.E.

1   Ezra 3:2-6, 1 Esdr 5:49–6:2, Hag 1:1-15, Zech 4:9; 6:11-13, Sir 49:11-12.
2   Theodore A. Bergren, "Nehemiah in 2 Maccabees 1:10–2:18," *JSJ* 28 (1997) 249–70, here 254–57.
3   Goldstein, *II Maccabees*, 349, quoting Cicero *Dom.* 23.60.
4   See Gregory Vlastos, *Plato's Universe* (Seattle: University of Washington Press, 1976) 66–97.

■ **21** Given that fire was considered a bodily substance, it is no wonder that the priests are astonished when they find not the deposited fire but its opposite—water that is solidifying. The opposition of fire and water had been used in the miracle Elijah wrought against the priests of Baal to heighten the effect (1 Kgs 18:34-35), but here another point is being made.

■ **22** This viscous liquid derived from fire is later, in 1:36, called by the senders nephthar, although it is usually called naphtha elsewhere. Other authors who discuss naphtha mention its rapacious appetite for fire (δύναμιν ἁρπακτικήν) (Dioscorides *Mat. Med.* 1.73.2), which naphtha snatches from a distance (Strabo 16.1.15; Dioscorides *Mat. Med.* 1.73.2). Plutarch held that in bodies that are either dry and porous or possess an ample amount of oily moisture, the rays and streams of fire collect and burst into fire (*Alex.* 35.6). The image is of particles of fire being caught out of the air. Plutarch goes on to explore what kind of material the naphtha is, but unfortunately, the full discussion is missing from the manuscripts. For these Greek and Latin writers, naphtha is a natural material that responds to ordinary flames. By contrast, the author of the letter in 2 Maccabees insists that the naphtha they are discussing at first only responds to the sun and that the naphtha on the stones flares up in response to the fire on the altar. The naphtha Nehemiah has uncovered is thus a special kind, not just regular naphtha: it is ignited when the sun shines on it; it catches rays of fire from the sun. Such a view of igniting the naphtha is in line with the way solar language is used of Yahweh in the Hebrew Scriptures, classically expressed in Ps 84:12: "for a sun and shield is Yahweh." This use of solar imagery for Yahweh is found also in postbiblical times.[5] As Karel van der Toorn notes, "Although the God of Israel never came to be regarded as immanent in the sun, he did take over the role of sun god."[6] That it is the fire from the sun that the naphtha catches expresses the naphtha's

sacred character and underlines that the fire in the newly built temple is divinely sanctioned and in continuity with the former temple.[7]

■ **23-29** The igniting of the naphtha is appropriately followed by a prayer, which consists of six verses (vv. 24-29), surrounded by introductory (v. 23) and closing statements (v. 30). This long prayer is thus a major component of the story. It begins with a string of divine epithets (vv. 24-25) before stating the actual requests (vv. 26-29).

■ **23** Several priests called Jonathan are mentioned in Nehemiah[8] and Ezra (8:6; 10:15), but one should not expect exactitude in this letter. Note how the high priest is responded to by Nehemiah and the community, with the high priest leading and the rest of the community responding. A similar situation is envisioned in Jdt 15:14, and the prayer itself resembles in some ways the opening portion of the prayer of Ezra in Neh 9:6.

■ **24-25** The twofold "Lord, Lord" resonates with the self-disclosure of Yahweh in Exod 34:6: "The Lord, the Lord, a God merciful and gracious," although the LXX does not have the double title. This duplication is found also in LXX Esth 13:9; *3 Macc* 2:2; and *Jub.* 14:2, 8. After this introductory naming and the mention of God come seven phrases governed by the article. The first five concern cosmology, the last two God's actions in history.

The epithets used to describe God as ruler of the universe are, in the main, frequently found in the Hebrew Scriptures. God is described as κτίστης in LXX 2 Kgdms 22:32; Sir 24:8; *4 Macc* 11:5. On παντοκράτωρ (= almighty), Jan Willem van Henten has shown that the opposition between Jews and non-Jews specifies the meaning of this term and must be placed alongside passages in the condensed narrative that imply a tolerant view of other gods and religions. Therefore, "the idea of the omnipotence of the Lord in 2 Macc is not fully developed and remains ambiguous."[9] More unusual is the term χορηγός. The χορηγός was the leader of a chorus

---

5 Mark S. Smith, "The Near Eastern Background of Solar Language for Yahweh," *JBL* 109 (1990) 29–39; Morton Smith, "Helios in Palestine," *Eretz Israel* 16 (1982) 199–214.

6 Karel van der Toorn, "Sun," *ABD* 6:238.

7 This story, then, is of a quite different character from stories where sacrificial offerings are consumed automatically by fire. For example, Pausanias relates a story about Alexander the Great's general Seleucus. Seleucus was about to leave Macedonia

with Alexander, and as he was sacrificing at Pella to Zeus, "the wood that lay on the altar advanced of its own accord to the image and was set on fire without fire" (Pausanias 1.16.1).

8 Nehemiah 12:11 (called Johanan in Neh 12:22; Josephus *Ant.* 11.297), 14, 18.

9 Jan Willem van Henten, "ΠΑΝΤΟΚΡΑΤΩΡ ΘΕΟΣ in 2 Maccabees," in Karel A. Deurloo and Bernd J. Diebner, eds., *YHWH-Kyrios: Antitheism or the Power of the Word; Festschrift für Rochus Zuurmond* (Heidel-

in the Greek classical theater, and the term was also used for one who defrayed the costs for producing a chorus. The verb χορηγεῖν is used in Sir 39:33 to state that God, all of whose works are good, "will supply [χορηγήσει] every need in its time." In Sir 1:10, 26, God is said to bestow (ἐχορήγησεν, χορηγήσει) wisdom on those who love him and keep his commandments. According to *Ep. Arist.* 259, God supplies (χορηγῶν) health and mental capacity and all other gifts to humans. Influenced by Pythagoras's sense of the music of the spheres, Plato speaks of Apollo, the Muses, and Dionysos as fellow choristers and choir leaders (συγχορευτάς τε καὶ χορηγούς) to humans (*Leg.* 665A; 653D–E). Dio Chrysostom also speaks of the immortal gods initiating mortals and, "night and day, both in the sunlight and under the stars, are—if it is lawful so to speak—really dancing around them [περιχορευόντων] eternally" (*Or.* 12.34).[10] When Dionysos speaks of his entrance to Athens, he states that he has set Asia dancing (χορεύσας) and has established his rituals there so that he might be a manifest god to humans (Euripides *Bacch.* 20–22). I have therefore translated the word as "the leader of the dance," which I hope preserves the nuances of involvement as well as bestowal, so that God not only is the creator of the cosmos but also governs it. Philo, in interpreting allegorically the visit of God to Abraham in Genesis 18, distinguishes between the two terms God (θεός) and Lord (κύριος): "The title of the [the creative potency] is God, since it made and ordered the All; the title of the [kingly potency] is Lord, since it is the fundamental right of the maker to rule and control what he has brought into being" (*Abr.* 121).

After the description of God as founder comes a series of four adjectives governed by one article; after the description of God as leader of the dance comes a series of three adjectives governed by one article. Both groups show a desire for balance—the fearsome and powerful one is also just and merciful, his eternal power

is tempered by his justice[11]—and both qualify the description of God as creator and governor. The central epithet in this group of five also reflects this balance: the only king is also benevolent. With this description of God's kingship begins an emphasis on the uniqueness of God, where the term μόνος ("only") occurs three times.

The last two descriptions of God state God's protection of Israel and then his bestowal of special privileges. The second is in a sense the reason for the first—the election of Israel's ancestors ensures God's protection.[12] The continuous action of God's preserving Israel is indicated by the use of the present participle, while the aorist participle reflects God's particular choice of Israel's ancestors. Abraham is called by God in Gen 12:1-2, but neither he nor Isaac is called ἐκλεκτός ("chosen") in the LXX. However, in Neh 9:7, God is said to have chosen Abraham. Philo uses the term of Abraham in several places.[13] The term is more frequently used of Jacob as standing for the people (Isa 41:8; 44:1; Ps 105:6) and its reference to the people as a whole is increasingly attested, as in Deut 7:6-7; Ps 106:5. In the apocalyptic literature, it comes to represent the remnant of Israel who followed God's covenant faithfully (*1 Enoch* 1:5),[14] but this is not the case here. Rather, the reference to the choice of the ancestors and their holiness suggests perhaps that the priests are reminding God of the זכות אבות ("the merits of the fathers"). Their separation from other peoples by God's choice means that the people are to be holy: "You will be holy to me, for I the Lord am holy, and I have separated you from the other peoples to be mine" (Lev 20:26; cf. Deut 7:6).

■ 26-29 The body of the prayer consists of nine imperatives that are concerned with the sanctification and ingathering of Israel. The first three imperatives, linked paratactically, are joined by the ambivalence surrounding the term μερίς ("portion")—is it God's portion of the sacrifice, or is it the people itself? In accepting the sacri-

---

berg: Selbstverlag der Dielheimer Blätter zum Alten Testament, 1996) 117–26; quotation from 126.

10 Later in the sentence, he uses a synonym for χορηγός, κορυφαίος, to say how the leader of the choir is in charge of the whole affair and directs the entire heaven and universe.

11 For the later development of the juxtaposition of justice and mercy in rabbinic literature, see Ephraim E. Urbach, *The Sages: Their Concepts and Beliefs* (2 vols.; Jerusalem: Magnes, 1979) 1:451.

12 Agneta Enermalm-Ogawa saw in the first of these phrases a principle of individualization at work to dilute the historical aspect of God's action (*Un langage de prière juif en grec: Le témoignage des deux premiers livres des Maccabées* [ConBNT 17; Stockholm: Almquist & Wiksell, 1987] 80).

13 Philo *Abr.* 82, 83; *Cher.* 7; *Gig.* 64; *Mut. nom.* 66, 69, 71.

14 See G. Shrenk, "ἐκλεκτός," *TDNT* 4 (1967) 181–92.

fice, does God take on the task of protecting the whole people? In Deut 32:9; Sir 17:17; and LXX Esth 4:17g, Israel is God's portion, and it is where Wisdom roots herself (Sir 24:12). The call to sanctify ($\kappa\alpha\vartheta\alpha\gamma\acute{\iota}\alpha\sigma o\nu$) God's portion links back to God's sanctification ($\dot{\alpha}\gamma\iota\acute{\alpha}\sigma\alpha\varsigma$) of the ancestors. The reference to the whole people leads to the next request, to gather what is dispersed.[15] The next two requests are linked chiastically—literally, "free those enslaved among the nations the contemned and loathed look upon." Here, "among the nations" belongs to both cola. The verb $\ddot{\epsilon}\pi\iota\delta\epsilon$ ("look upon") resonates with Exod 2:25, when God heard the groans of the people in Egypt: "God looked upon [$\dot{\epsilon}\pi\epsilon\acute{\iota}\delta\epsilon\nu$] the Israelites, and he recognized them." The marvel of the ingathering of the people will show the nations that God protects Israel. The return of the dispersed people to their homeland was a sign of God's favor.[16] The recognition formula that God acts for his people is similar to what is said in 2 Kgs 19:19 (= Isa 37:20); Ezek 35:15; 36:38. It is also said by Elijah as he asks God to send down fire to consume the offerings and outperform the priests of Baal (1 Kgs 18:36-39).

■ **28** The theme of just deserts, or repayment in kind, surfaces here. The language of "torment" ($\beta\alpha\sigma\alpha\nu\acute{\iota}\zeta\epsilon\iota\nu$) and "oppression" ($\kappa\alpha\tau\alpha\delta\upsilon\nu\alpha\sigma\tau\epsilon\acute{\upsilon}\epsilon\iota\nu$) is found in the retelling of the exodus story in Wisdom of Solomon.[17] This term for oppression occurs in connection with the oppression of the Israelites in Egypt (Exod 1:13) and the Babylonian exile (Jer 50:33 [LXX 27:33]). The term thus conjures up paradigmatic oppressions.

■ **29** The prayer concludes with a further nod to the exodus narrative. The language is closest to Exod 15:17, with its terminology of "planting" ($\kappa\alpha\tau\alpha\varphi\acute{\upsilon}\tau\epsilon\upsilon\sigma o\nu$) and "holy place" ($\tau\grave{o}\nu\ \tau\acute{o}\pi o\nu\ \tau\grave{o}\nu\ \ddot{\alpha}\gamma\iota\acute{o}\nu\ \sigma o\upsilon$).[18] However, Moses' promise of return from Diaspora, on the condition of repentance, is found in Deut 30:1-5.

■ **31-32** Now that the fire on the altar is alight, and the sacrifices are consumed, there is no need any longer for the sacred liquid, as it has served its purpose. Nehemiah therefore does not store it away in a cave but pours it out in the open on rocks. According to its nature, it flames up as soon as it catches the particles of fire from the altar flame and is used up.

■ **33-35** The senders emphasize that the affair was fully investigated by the Persian king as to its truthfulness, and use the verb $\dot{\alpha}\gamma\nu\acute{\iota}\zeta\epsilon\iota\nu$, which can mean both "purify" and "offer, burn as sacrifice," to emphasize the sacredness of the spot. The Zoroastrian reverence for fire among the Persians was well known. Where the holy spot was located is not known. The description in 1:19 suggests that the priests took the fire with them to Persia, but as the story of Nehemiah unfolds, it almost seems as if the fire was available in Jerusalem near the temple. However, it would seem to make sense for the Persian king to have made an area in Persia sacred.

In v. 33, the use of $\kappa\alpha\acute{\iota}$ to introduce the main clause after a temporal clause could be an Aramaism.

In my translation, 1:35 is linked to the previous story so that the Persian king donates money to the priests in Jerusalem to continue their liturgy, rather than to his favorites. Such donations would be in line with what the author of the condensed version describes in 3:1-3.

■ **36** Greek writers such as Dioscorides and Plutarch use the term $\nu\acute{\alpha}\varphi\vartheta\alpha$ when describing this substance. All kinds of suggestions have been made to explain the form found in the manuscripts for this verse, $\nu\epsilon\varphi\vartheta\alpha\iota$ or $\nu\epsilon\varphi\vartheta\alpha\rho$. In *m. Šabb.* 2:2, the Hebrew reads נפט, which Jastrow vocalizes as *nepht*; in Persian the word is *naft*, in Akkadian *naptu*.[19] Goldstein notes that the loss of final *r* was common in Hebrew and Aramaic, and in Greek transcriptions from Aramaic.[20] However, this explanation

---

15 For a full discussion of this motif, see Esther G. Chazon, "'Gather the Dispersed of Judah': Seeking a Return to the Land as a Factor in Jewish Identity of Late Antiquity," in Lynn LiDonnici and Andrea Lieber, eds., *Heavenly Tablets: Interpretation, Identity and Tradition in Ancient Judaism* (JSJSup 119; Leiden: Brill, 2007) 159–75.

16 Deuteronomy 30:3-5; LXX Ps 146:2; Neh 1:9; *Ps. Sol.* 8:34.

17 $\beta\alpha\sigma\alpha\nu\acute{\iota}\zeta\epsilon\iota\nu$: Wis 11:9; 12:23; 16:1, 4; $\kappa\alpha\tau\alpha\delta\upsilon\nu\alpha\sigma\tau\epsilon\acute{\upsilon}\epsilon\iota\nu$: Wis 15:14; 17:2.

18 See Shozo Fujita, "The Metaphor of Plant in Jewish

Literature of the Intertestamental Period," *JSJ* 7 (1976) 30–45; Patrick A. Tiller, "The 'Eternal Planting' in the Dead Sea Scrolls," *DSD* 4 (1997) 312–35.

19 Marcus Jastrow, *A Dictionary of the Targumim, the Talmud Babli and Yerushalmi, and the Midrashic Literature* (2 vols.; New York: Pardes, 1950) 2:923; Robert J. Forbes, *Studies in Ancient Technology* (9 vols.; 2nd ed.; Leiden: Brill, 1955-) 1:12–13.

20 Goldstein, *II Maccabees*, 181.

does not account for the final *i*. No satisfactory answer has been given for the translation of νεφθαρ to καθα-ρισμός ("purification"). Abel suggested that νεφθαρ was short for νεφαθαρ, a combination of nephta and the Persian word for fire, *atar*; fire for the Persians was purification par excellence. Goldstein suggested a derivation from פטר, but this really means "to set fire." Others have proposed some resonance with Hebrew טהר ("purification"). Such suggestions possibly credit the author with too much erudition. Perhaps he simply is connecting the testing and purifying quality of fire[21] with the naphtha. As the element most liable to catch fire, naphtha is given the quality of purifying. Such a connection by the authors enables them to talk of Nehemiah's festival as the purification of the Sukkoth.

General Commentary

After the initial greeting and well wishes, the body of the letter begins. It is a call for the Jews in Egypt to celebrate the cleansing of the temple, and it provides a clarification about the feast. This clarification consists of three parts: (1) the continuity between the First Temple and that of Nehemiah (1:18b-36); (2) the discontinuity between the First Temple and that of Nehemiah (2:1-12); (3) the comparison between Nehemiah and Judas (2:13-15). The festival of cleansing is linked to the activity of Nehemiah from the start and suggests that a connection is being made between the two figures of Nehemiah and Judas, one the former governor of Judea and the other the present leader of the *gerousia* in Judea. This implicit comparison is made explicit in 2:13-15, where both Nehemiah and Judas found libraries and collect books. Bergren, following Menaham Haran, noted how the functions and attributes of Nehemiah—leader, builder, pious one, founder of a library—were those of enlightened Hellenistic rulers.[22] Judas is being cast in this mold.

The material about Nehemiah frames quotations from a work about Jeremiah's activity. The prophet warned those being led away to captivity not to be seduced by pagan idols. However, the narrative also insists that some of the elements of the First Temple will not be in Nehemiah's temple but will appear only when God ingathers his people (2:7). The priest Jonathan in the presence of Nehemiah prays for such an ingathering (1:27), and the senders of the letter hope that God will accomplish it soon (2:18). Addressed to Jews in Egypt, the letter thus stresses the holiness of the Second Temple and its continuity with earlier traditions, and yet recognizes that the whole people of God is still not reunited around the temple. This argument fits well with a call to be united in observing the festival of purification.

The Continuity between the First and Second Temples (1:18b-36)

The letter is an attempt to get the receivers to celebrate a festival honoring the purification of the present temple in Jerusalem. As the first part of this endeavor, the senders set out to show the importance of the present temple and its divine stamp of approval. Their persuasion consists of a story about the first celebration in the temple, and how it was divinely brought about. The narrative skips over details of the return from Babylon and the rebuilding of the walls of Jerusalem and of the temple itself; it is hazy as well on points of chronology and geography. Is the fire hidden by the priests in Babylonia, and, if so, do the priests have to return to Babylonia to retrieve it? Or is it hidden in Judea, and the Persian king declares a spot in Judea sacred? Whatever the answers to these detailed questions, the story itself starts off as if it is going to be a story about finding hidden treasure. The spot chosen by the priests is unknown to all. Will it be able to be found? In the next story told in the letter, the hiding place is not found. Is the story going to be like so many traditional stories where treasure is discovered through a dream or a magic object or through the return of someone from the dead?[23] Quickly the hearer learns that this is not the case. The whereabouts of the hiding place have been handed down from generation to generation among the priests. The story is one not of find-

---

21   For example, LXX Ps 11:6, "silver fired [πεπυρω-μένον] and tested on the ground, purified [κεκαθα-ρισμένον] seven times."

22   Bergren, "Nehemiah," 249–70; Menaham Haran, "Archives, Libraries, and the Order of the Biblical Books," *JANESCU* 22 (1993) 51–61. See the earlier discussion of Nehemiah as tyrant in Morton Smith, *Palestinian Parties and Politics That Shaped the Old Testament* (2nd ed.; London: SCM, 1987) 107–9.

23   Stith Thompson, *Motif-Index of Folk Literature* (rev.

ing hidden treasure but of God's action, by means of the sun, in reigniting the sacred fire from the First Temple. The Second Temple is thus the place where God still meets his people, and the festival celebrates that fact.

The emphasis on the continuity of worship is underscored also by the response prayer. Several scholars have noted that nothing in the prayer is tightly tied to the present context.[24] However, the prayer uses much traditional language—"portion," "look upon," "oppression"—as well as an explicit reference to Moses to close the prayer as part of a rhetorical strategy that underlines

the continuity of worship between the First and the Second Temples.

This section of the letter also continues the theme of respectful relations between Jews and Gentiles. Granted, the description of life in exile is not pretty—servitude, loathing, arrogant overlords—but the continuation of the story shows the Persian king as acting benevolently toward the exiles. He cordons off the spot where the priests had hidden the fire and recognizes its sacredness. He distributes gifts for the functioning of the temple service.

---

ed.; 6 vols.; Bloomington: Indiana University Press, 1955–58), N 530–49 Discovery of treasure; E 371 Return from death to reveal hidden treasure.

24   For example, Abel; Bunge (*Untersuchungen*, 120) suggested that it suited the context of the actual

purification under Judas better and that it was a prayer of Judas.

2

2:1-18

The Body of the Letter 2

1/ Now, it is found in the written records that Jeremiah the prophet[a] ordered those being carried away[b] to take some of the fire, as was signified above, 2/ and that the prophet commanded those being carried away[b] tendering them the law, not to forget the ordinances of the Lord and not to be led astray in their thoughts when they saw golden and silver images and the ornamentation on them. 3/ Telling other such things, he was exhorting them not to remove this law from their heart.

4/ Now there was in the document how the prophet, once an oracle had been made, commanded that the tent and the ark accompany him, how he went out to where Moses went up and saw the inheritance of God. 5/ When Jeremiah arrived, he found a cave-like chamber; he brought in there the tent and the ark and the incense altar and blocked up the entrance. 6/ Now some of those accompanying him came forward so as to mark the way, but they were not able even to find it. 7/ When Jeremiah perceived [this], he faulted them and said, "This place be altogether unknown until God effects the gathering of the people, and mercy[c] occurs. 8/ Then the Lord will show forth these things, and the glory of the Lord will be seen and the cloud, both as it used to be shown at the time of Moses and as Solomon prayed so that the place might be greatly sanctified."

9/ Now it was also being explained how, as he was wise, he offered a sacrifice of dedication and of the completion of the temple. 10/ Just as Moses prayed to the Lord and fire came down from heaven and consumed the sacrifice, so Solomon prayed and the fire which came down consumed the burnt offerings. 11/ Now Moses said, "It was consumed because the sin offering had not been eaten." 12/ Likewise, Solomon also celebrated eight days.

a By prolepsis, "Jeremiah the prophet" is found in the main clause rather than in the subordinate clause, where it belongs. The Vulgate reads *in descriptionibus Hieremiae prophetae* ("in the writings of Jeremiah the prophet").

b Reading $\mu\epsilon\tau\alpha\gamma o\mu\acute{\epsilon}\nu o\upsilon\varsigma$, as in V 29-71-107-130-370 62 46-52 311[mg] 771 La[VBM], rather than $\mu\epsilon\tau\alpha\gamma\epsilon\nu o\mu\acute{\epsilon}\nu o\upsilon\varsigma$, as in La[L] Sy Arm, or $\mu\epsilon\tau\alpha\gamma\iota\nu o\mu\acute{\epsilon}\nu o\upsilon\varsigma$, as in L'[-62 542]. $M\epsilon\tau\alpha\gamma\acute{\iota}\gamma\nu o\mu\alpha\iota$ has the meaning "happen later," which would be inappropriate here, not "go away, transfer." In 1:33, one finds $\mu\epsilon\tau\acute{\alpha}\gamma\epsilon\iota\nu$ used in the phrase $o\acute{\iota}\ \mu\epsilon\tau\alpha\chi\vartheta\acute{\epsilon}\nu\tau\epsilon\varsigma\ \acute{\iota}\epsilon\rho\epsilon\hat{\iota}\varsigma$. $M\epsilon\tau\acute{\alpha}\gamma\epsilon\iota\nu$ is also the term used in the prayer of Solomon at the dedication of the temple in 3 Kgdms 8:47-48 and LXX 2 Chr 6:37; 36:3 to describe deportation.

c Grimm, Abel, and Habicht all read $\acute{\iota}\lambda\epsilon\omega\varsigma$ ("be gracious, propitious"). Habicht bases his choice on the occurrence of $\acute{\iota}\lambda\epsilon\omega\varsigma$ in 2:22 and 7:37, but both of these occurrences are in the epitome and may not be decisive for the use of the letter senders. Hanhart and Goldstein read $\acute{\epsilon}\lambda\epsilon o\varsigma$. I have chosen to follow them, as the verb $\acute{\epsilon}\lambda\epsilon\acute{\epsilon}\omega$ occurs later in the letter in 2:18 in conjunction with the verb for "ingathering," and this combination of "ingathering" and "mercy" reflects Deut 30:3.

13/ Now the same things are related also in the records and in the memoranda according to Nehemiah: how he established a library and gathered the materials[d] about the kings and prophets, those of David, and letters of kings about votive offerings. 14/ Likewise, Judas also gathered together for us[e] all the documents that had been missing because of the past war, and we have them. 15/ So, if you need them, send those who will carry them back to you.

16/ Therefore, as we are about to celebrate the purification, we are writing to you. So you will act well if you celebrate these days. 17/ Now, God [is] the one who saved the whole people and assigned to all the inheritance, the crown, the priesthood, and the sanctification, 18/ just as he announced through the law. For we hope in this God that he soon will have mercy on us and gather us from everywhere under the sky to his holy place. For he has delivered us from great evils and has purified the place.

d   I follow q and omit βιβλία and so read τὰ περὶ τῶν βασιλέων καὶ προφητῶν. The present position of βιβλία breaks up the connection, formed by the single article, between "kings and prophets" as well as the parallel with the following τὰ τοῦ Δαυιδ. Rather than speaking of specific works, the writer talks of collecting all the materials pertaining to the kings and the prophets.

e   With Habicht and Goldstein, I connect ἡμῖν with the main verb, not, as does Abel, with the participial description of the past war.

Commentary by Verse

■ **2:1** Ἀπογραφή has the meaning of "a list, register," although it is used to translate כְּתָב in Dan 10:21. Here, and in the use of ἀναγραφή in 2:13, the emphasis seems to be on the public character of the document. The second and third parts of the body of this second letter are clearly introduced with a reference to other writings (2:1: ἐν ταῖς ἀπογραφαῖς; 2:13: ἐν ταῖς ἀναγραφαῖς καὶ ἐν τοῖς ὑπομνηματισμοῖς). Fragments about Jeremiah have been discovered in cave 4 at Qumran (4Q383; 4Q384 [?]; 4Q385[B]; 4Q387[B]; 4Q389[A]). Devorah Dimant states that they are written in a late Hasmonean or early Herodian book hand (ca. 50–25 B.C.E.) and attest "to the existence of one or more compositions about the prophet, circulating in Eretz Israel during the Second Temple Period (note also the reference in CD 8.20 to the words of Jeremiah)."[1] These fragments evidence widespread traditions about the prophet found in works such as the Epistula Jeremiae, *Paralipomena Jeremiou* (*4 Baruch*), *2 Baruch*, *Pesiqta Rabbati* 131b, and also Eupolemus (Eusebius *Praep. ev.* 9.39.5).

■ **2:1-3** In *2 Bar.* 10:1-5 and *Paralip. Jer.* 3:15, Jeremiah goes to Babylon with the captives. Epistula Jeremiae is a letter addressed to the captives in Babylon. Both 4Q385 and 2 Macc 2:2 have Jeremiah talking directly

---

1   Devorah Dimant, "An Apocryphon of Jeremiah from Cave 4 (4Q385[B] = 4Q385 16)," in George J. Brooke, ed., *New Qumran Texts and Studies: Proceedings of the First Meeting of the International Organiza-* *tion for Qumran Studies, Paris, 1992* (STDJ 15; Leiden: Brill, 1994) 29. The information about dating is on p. 13. See also her publication of the text in DJD 30:91-260.

to the captives and telling them how to behave in the land of their captivity. 4Q385, like *Pesiq. R.* 131b, may have Jeremiah accompany the captives to the Euphrates. *Epistula Jeremiae*, as well as 2 Macc 2:2, warns against idol worship, and *Paralip. Jer.* 7:29-31a has Jeremiah lament over the people calling out to a foreign god. 4Q385 has Jeremiah in the land of Egypt warning against idolatry, as in Jeremiah 44. Dimant notes how the phrase in 4Q385 "concerning the words which God had commanded him" (4Q385ᴮ i 8), whereby the people are to listen to the voice of Jeremiah, is so similar to the phrase used about Moses in Exod 19:7, and also how Jeremiah gives commands near a river as Moses did near the Jordan. Dimant sees the commands given to Jeremiah as intended for the conditions in exile, just as the commands given to Moses were intended for life in the Israelites' land.[2] God gave Moses the stone tablets, that is, the law and the commandments (Exod 24:12; Neh 9:13; Sir 45:5); Moses gave the law before the people (Deut 4:8; 31:9); and Joshua made statutes and ordinances as he was about to die (Josh 24:25). Moses warned against going after idols and letting their hearts stray (Deut 29:17-19, particularly v. 18: ἐν τῇ ἀποπλανήσει τῆς καρδίας). The phrase, "I will give my laws" (δώσω νόμους μου), is found in Jer 31:33 (LXX 38:33) with reference to a new covenant. So, at a threshold of new conditions, Jeremiah is said to give the law to the priests going into exile. Yet, in 2 Macc 2:2, as with 4Q385ᴮ, the emphasis is on continuity in keeping the covenant.

The one element peculiar to 2:1-3 is that Jeremiah gives the departing priests the fire from the altar. Here Jeremiah is explicitly tied to the preceding story of continuity between the First and Second Temples.

■ **4-5** 4Q385ᴮ reports only that the vessels of the house of God were taken to Babylon, repeating what is found in 2 Chr 36:18 and 1 Esdr 1:54. The inventories of articles taken from the temple that are given in 2 Kgdms 25:13-17; 2 Chr 36:18; and Jer 52:17-23 do not mention the ark, the tent, and the tablets of the law. According to *4 Ezra* 10:22, the ark was plundered, the holy things polluted. Eupolemus has Jeremiah withhold the ark and the tablets within it (Eusebius *Praep. ev.* 9.39.5); the *Paralipomena* of Jeremiah has Jeremiah and Baruch hand over the vessels of the temple service to the earth, which swallows them (*Paralip. Jer.* 3:9-11, 18-19), and Jeremiah also throws away the keys of the temple to the sun (*Paralip. Jer.* 4:4). In *2 Bar* 6:7-9, an angel assigns to the earth the veil, the holy ephod, the mercy seat, the two tablets, the holy raiment of the priests, the altar of incense, the forty-eight precious stones of the priests, and all the holy vessels of the tabernacles.[3] All these stories maintain the hope of renewal in the future. Second Maccabees 2:4 is the only place where the tent and the ark are said to be hidden by Jeremiah. Since 2 Chr 36:18 had stated that all the vessels of the temple were taken to Babylon, whereas 1 Kgdms 8:4 and 2 Chr 5:5 had stated that besides the holy vessels, the priests also took the ark and the tent of witness and placed them in the temple of Solomon, the author may be implying that the tent and the ark were not taken to Babylon. By so doing, the author links what Jeremiah is doing to the actions of Solomon and Moses. In v. 5, Jeremiah is said to have brought also the altar of incense. This altar was to stand before the curtain over the ark (Exod 30:1-8) and was most holy. According to Exod 30:10, it was to be part of the ritual of atonement, and this may explain why it is mentioned, even though, as Goldstein noted, this altar was overlaid with gold (Exod 30:3) and all the gold was said to have been taken away by the Babylonians (2 Kgdms 25:15). According to Lev 4:7, the altar of incense was within the tent. The author thus has Jeremiah take the appurtenances within the tent, except for the cherubim and the mercy seat (Exod 25:17-22), which are so holy that no human could touch them (Lev 16:13). Taking the materials located in the tent suggests a return to life outside the promised land. One finds elsewhere the image of inanimate objects

---

2   Dimant, "Apocryphon of Jeremiah," 26.

3   For the lists in rabbinic sources, see Ben Zion Wacholder, *Eupolemus: A Study of Judaeo-Greek Literature* (Monographs of the Hebrew Union College 3; Cincinnati: Hebrew Union College–Jewish Institute of Religion, 1975) 242 n. 74. The late *Lives of the Prophets* has Jeremiah take the ark and what is in it. See also George W. E. Nickelsburg, "Narrative Traditions in the Paralipomena of Jeremiah and 2 Baruch," *CBQ* 35 (1973) 60–68.

following someone, where it means that they were brought. See Aelian *Varia Historia* 12.40: "The other supplies, filled with luxury and pretension, followed [εἵπετο] Xerxes, and even water from the Choaspes followed [ἠκολούθει] him."

"inheritance." In Num 34:2 and Deut 12:9-10, the land of Israel is described as the inheritance given to the Israelites. The story of Moses seeing the promised land is found in Deut 34:1-5.

■ **6-8** The condensed summary of a larger narrative is suggested by the way v. 6 is tagged onto the previous narration by a participle. The verb used to describe the companions, "those accompanying" (τῶν συνακολουθούντων), was used in v. 4, where Jeremiah commanded the tent and the ark to accompany him. These companions presumably had carried these rather heavy and bulky objects all the way from Jerusalem to Mount Nebo, and not Jeremiah by himself. There is no hint how Jeremiah by himself could have carried the tent, the ark, and the altar of incense into the cave without the knowledge of his companions, nor is there mention that Jeremiah had forbidden them to try to know the way to the cave. Yet these objects belong to the holy of holies, and the way toward them should not be available to all. Here emerges the motif of the punishment of curiosity or inquisitiveness, a motif found in much folk narrative.[4] Whereas the narrative up to this point has been brief, one now has a long speech by Jeremiah (vv. 7-8) in response to his companions' meddling. Jeremiah faults them (μέμφομαι). The verb is not frequently used in the LXX, except for Sir 11:7; 41:7. A better parallel for its use here is found in the New Testament in Heb 8:8, where God is said to find fault with the previous priests; and the text goes on to predict a new covenant, quoting Jer 31:31-34. The pattern of finding fault followed by a punishment is familiar from the Hebrew Scriptures: the Eden story and the expulsion of Adam and Eve (Genesis 2–3); the episode of the tower of Babel (Gen 11:1-11); the refusal to go into the promised land and the subsequent wandering in the desert (Num 14:26-34); Saul's disobedience followed by the prediction of his losing the kingship (1 Sam 15:10-11). Here the fault of Jeremiah's companions brings punishment—the things hidden will not be found until the Lord decrees. The implication is that if the compan-

ions had not tried to mark out the way to the cave, the tent, the ark, and the altar of incense would have been available before the ingathering of the people. A cognate accusative is used (συναγάγῃ . . . ἐπισυναγωγήν) to describe the ingathering. That they are not in the Second Temple is thus no fault of the returnees under Cyrus, but of the priests of the First Temple. Now the appearance of these holy objects is to be delayed until an event like that in the wilderness and that of the founding of the First Temple. Here the significance of Jeremiah's journey to Mount Nebo becomes clear. He is to cross outside the promised land. There Moses had been buried in a place that no one knew. So now the appurtenances of the tent are buried there. Such a grouping links with the sense of a dispersal from the land of inheritance and looks forward to a regrouping of Israel, a new exodus.

Other traditions linked Moses, the holy vessels, and the story of the entrance into the promised land. Josephus recounts how, in the time of Pontius Pilate, an unnamed Samaritan led people to Mount Gerizim, where he promised to show them the sacred vessels that Moses had deposited there (*Ant.* 18.86–87). In this story, the finding of the holy vessels is connected with Moses and the mountain from which the priests, after crossing the Jordan, were to bless the people (Deut 27:12). Hopes for restoration are couched in new exodus terms: Jeremiah leaves Jerusalem to go out of the land and points to when the holy objects will be brought back to the land (Moses) and to a temple (Solomon).

"the glory of the Lord . . . the cloud." Exodus 40:34 describes how the cloud, which had been with the Israelites since they began their journey (Exod 13:21), "covered the tent of meeting, and the glory of the Lord filled the tent." After the priests deposited the ark of the covenant in the temple that Solomon had just built, "a cloud filled the house of the Lord, so that the priests could not stand to minister because of the cloud; for the glory of the Lord filled the house" (1 Kgdms 8:10-11). There is thus an explicit connection made between the covenant with Moses, the tent of meeting in the wilderness, and the temple of Solomon.

■ **9** "being explained." This refers presumably to the document just quoted. The last section of Jeremiah's prayer had referred to incidents in the careers of Moses

4   Thompson, *Motif-Index*, Q 341–42.

57

and Solomon, and so the author develops this further. While Solomon had requested and been granted wisdom in 1 Kgdms 3 and 2 Chr 1:7-12, the reference here may be to the description of the fame of Solomon's wisdom found in 1 Kgdms 6:29-34, which immediately precedes the preparations for the building of the temple. Sirach also stresses Solomon's early wisdom and his widespread fame for knowledge (Sir 47:12-19), as does Josephus (*Ant.* 8.42–49). The language of this verse reflects that of the LXX.

"sacrifice of dedication" (θυσίαν ἐγκαινισμοῦ). Cf. 1 Kgdms 8:63: "King Solomon sacrificed the sacrifices of peace offerings [ἔθυσεν . . . θυσίας τῶν εἰρηνικῶν] . . . and he dedicated [ἐνεκαίνισεν] the house of the Lord, and all Israel [with him]." (See also 2 Chr 7:5, where sacrifices and dedication are linked).

"of the completion" (τῆς τελειώσεως). Second Chronicles 8:12-16 describes how Solomon offered sacrifices to the Lord, appointing priests and following all that the Lord commanded, and concludes that all this activity was done after the foundation of the temple and before "Solomon completed [ἐτελείωσεν] the house of the Lord" (2 Chr 8:16). The verb συντελέω ("to complete, finish") is found in 1 Kgdms 9:1 and 2 Chr 7:11 to describe the end of the building of the temple.

The author has neatly chosen to have depend on a single substantive two genitives, one of which has the sense of "newness, beginning" and the other the sense of "end, completion, perfection."

■ **10-12** The referent of v. 10 is not immediately clear. The specific verb προσεύχομαι ("to pray") is not used of Moses in the LXX, whereas it is used of Solomon when he finishes his long prayer at the dedication of the temple (1 Kgdms 8:54). Moses usually prays (εὔχομαι) to stop some disaster. When Moses does pray (ηὔξατο) to the Lord in Num 11:2, fire does not come down. He prays to stop the serpents in Num 21:7 and the anger of the Lord in Deut 9:26. Fire comes forth from the Lord when Moses and Aaron come out of the tent of meeting and bless the Lord (Lev 9:23-24).

After Solomon finished praying, fire came down from heaven and devoured the burnt offerings and the sacrifices (2 Chr 7:1, but not in 1 Kings 8). During Moses' lifetime, the only time fire consumes sacrifices is in Lev 9:24, on the eighth day at the end of the priestly ordination. This incident also seems to be behind the saying attributed to Moses in 2:11, in which the articular infinitive is found in the perfect tense, βεβρῶσθαι ("to have been eaten"), as its action, or non-action, occurs before the time of the main verb in the aorist, ἀνη-λώθη ("was consumed"). In Lev 6:30, the regulation is given that "no sin offering [τὰ περὶ τῆς ἁμαρτίας] from which any blood is brought into the tent of meeting to make atonement in the holy place shall be eaten [οὐ βρωθήσεται]." But to what event does the saying of Moses refer, where the sin offering was burned because it had not been eaten? At the first act of the priesting of Aaron and his sons, a sin offering is slaughtered, but no part of it is eaten (Lev 8:16-17). Rather, the bull—its skin, flesh, and dung—is burned. The saying attributed to Moses in 2:11 thus would be an explanation of why the sin offering at the ordination was not burned. In Lev 8:31-33, Moses instructs Aaron to stay at the entrance of the tent of meeting for seven days and to eat the flesh of the ram of ordination and the bread; what is left over is to be burned. This instruction is similar to the regulation about the Passover in Exod 12:10, where any leftovers of the Passover sacrifice are to be burned. In discussing when to burn the Passover sacrifice if its owners died, Rabbi Yohanan b. Beroqa decided it should be burned immediately "because it lacks eaters" (לפי שאין לו אוכלין) (*m. Pesaḥ.* 7:9; cf. *y. Pesaḥ.* 7:9).

The referent of both v. 10 and v. 11 would therefore be the eight-day ordination ritual of Leviticus 8–9, which inaugurates the sacrificial worship of the Israelites. This referent would be an appropriate one for the reinstitution of worship under Nehemiah. That the inauguration of general sacrifices takes place on the eighth day (Leviticus 9) also links to the inauguration of the temple of Solomon (2 Chr 7:9) and to the festival of Sukkoth, which lasts for seven days until on the eighth day a holy convocation is held and an offering by fire is presented to the Lord (Lev 23:36). Such a referent seems more appropriate than the events of Lev 10:16-20, where Aaron's sons Eleazar and Ithamar do not eat (οὐκ ἐφάγετε) the goat of the sin offering, but instead it is burned. Aaron explains that they did not eat the goat because of the mourning for his two dead sons, Nadab and Abihu, killed by fire coming forth from the Lord. Moses accepts this explanation. However, in this story the sin offering was burned and so could not be eaten, whereas the saying in 2:11 states that the sin offering was not eaten and so it was burned. Grimm suggested that the Syriac translation supported a reference to Lev 10:16 as it translated "sin offering" of 2:11 by "goat of the sin offering" (ܟܡܐܕܐ ܕܚܛܝܐ). However, this phrase is also found for the sin offering on the eighth day of the ordination ritual in Lev 9:3. The narrative in Leviticus 10 also does not seem to carry as much liturgical resonance for the story of Nehemiah as the narrative of the inauguration of the sacrificial system. One does not need, therefore, to emend the text as Goldstein does, to bring it in line with Lev 10:16-17. He would read: "For what reason did you not eat the sin offering but it was consumed by fire" ($\Delta\iota\grave{\alpha}$ $\tau\grave{\iota}$ $\mu\grave{\eta}$ $\beta\epsilon\beta\rho\tilde{\omega}\sigma\vartheta\eta$ $\tau\grave{o}$ $\pi\epsilon\rho\grave{\iota}$ $\tau\tilde{\eta}\varsigma$ $\dot{\alpha}\mu\alpha\rho\tau\acute{\iota}\alpha\varsigma$ $\dot{\alpha}\lambda\lambda\grave{\alpha}$ $\dot{\alpha}\nu\eta\lambda\acute{\omega}\vartheta\eta$). Goldstein does not explain why, in this emendation, $\mu\acute{\eta}$ is used with indicative, nor does he note that the emendation brings about a strong hiatus of $\dot{\alpha}\lambda\lambda\grave{\alpha}$ $\dot{\alpha}\nu\eta\lambda\acute{\omega}\vartheta\eta$. Goldstein also refers to Exod 29:33 to explain 2:11, as Exod 29:33 is "the only text in the Torah which explicitly requires a priest to eat the meat of a sin-offering."[5] However, Exod 29:33-34 refers not to a sin offering (חטאת; $\tau\grave{o}$ $\pi\epsilon\rho\grave{\iota}$ $\tau\tilde{\eta}\varsigma$ $\dot{\alpha}\mu\alpha\rho\tau\acute{\iota}\alpha\varsigma$) but to the ram of ordination as in Exod 29:22 (איל מלאים; $\tau\epsilon\lambda\epsilon\acute{\iota}\omega\sigma\iota\varsigma$). Exodus 29:34 explicitly refers to the remaining flesh of ordination (יותר מבשר המלאים; $\dot{\alpha}\pi\grave{o}$ $\tau\tilde{\omega}\nu$ $\kappa\rho\epsilon\tilde{\omega}\nu$ $\tau\tilde{\eta}\varsigma$ $\vartheta\upsilon\sigma\acute{\iota}\alpha\varsigma$ $\tau\tilde{\eta}\varsigma$ $\tau\epsilon\lambda\epsilon\iota\acute{\omega}\sigma\epsilon\omega\varsigma$). The word used just before, in 2:9, to talk of the sacrifice of completion ($\tau\epsilon\lambda\epsilon\acute{\iota}\omega\sigma\iota\varsigma$) is the same Greek word as that used for the ordination of

Aaron (Exod 29:26), perhaps a further indication that the reference is to Leviticus 8-9.

■ **13** Records and the memoranda of Nehemiah form the second group of documents quoted in this letter. There is no need to see the second phrase as epexegetic, that is, as stating specifically what records are meant. The over eight hundred manuscripts discovered in the caves near Qumran evidence an abundant writing activity in Second Temple Judaism. As noted above, stories similar to what is said about Jeremiah in the letter have been found in the Qumran corpus, but not stories similar to what is said about Nehemiah and his fire.

The three-item list of what was in Nehemiah's library[6] has sparked interest in the precise identity of these items, primarily in regard to the canonical Hebrew Scriptures.[7] If the list refers to the canon, the materials about the kings and prophets would most probably include 1-2 Samuel, 1-2 Kings, 1-2 Chronicles, and possibly Ezra and Nehemiah, while the prophets would include the canonical prophets (excepting Daniel) as well as the "former prophets" Joshua and Judges; "those of David" would refer to the Psalms, while "letters of kings" would refer to letters such as those found in Ezra, 1 and 2 Maccabees, and also Josephus *Ant.* 12.134-44. However, one should avoid neat solutions. The finds at Qumran have brought forth noncanonical psalms ascribed to David (11QPs[a]),[8] and the Jewish writer Eupolemus wrote a

5 Goldstein, *II Maccabees*, 185.
6 Stefan Schorch ("The Libraries in 2 Macc 2:13-15, and the Torah as a Public Document in Second Century Judaism," in Géza Xeravits and József Zsengellér, *The Books of the Maccabees: History, Theology, Ideology* [JSJSup 118; Leiden: Brill, 2007] 173) tried to insist on a distinction between a library and an archive and that what was intended here was an archive, not a library. However, in the same volume, Armin Lange ("2 Maccabees 2:13-15: Library or Canon?" 155-64) showed quite clearly that this distinction does not hold. See also Arie van der Kooij, *Die alten Textzeugen des Jesajabuches: Ein Beitrag zur Textgeschichte des Alten Testaments* (OBO 35; Freiburg: Universitätsverlag; Göttingen: Vandenhoeck & Ruprecht, 1981) 332-35.
7 Shnayer Z. Leiman, *The Canonization of Hebrew Scripture: The Talmudic and Midrashic Evidence* (Transactions 47; Hamden, Conn.: Archon Books, 1976) 51-124; Roger T. Beckwith, *The Old Testament Canon of the New Testament Church and Its Background in Early Judaism* (London: SPCK, 1985); Arie van

der Kooij, "The Canonization of Ancient Books Kept in the Library of Jerusalem," in Arie van der Kooij and Karel van der Torn, eds., *Canonization and Decanonization: Papers Presented to the International Conference of the Leiden Institute for the Study of Religions, Held at Leiden 9-10 January 1997* (SHR 82; Leiden: Brill, 1998) 17-40; idem, "Canonization of Ancient Hebrew Books and Hasmonean Politics," in Jean-Marie Auwers and Henk Jan de Jonge, eds., *The Biblical Canons* (BEThL 163; Leuven: Leuven University Press, 2003) 27-38; Lange, "2 Maccabees 2:13-15," 155-67; Schorch, "Libraries in 2 Macc 2:13-15," 169-80.
8 George J. Brooke refers to the exclusively Davidic character of 11QPs and to the letter of Patriarch Timotheus I, which speaks of more than two hundred psalms of David ("The Explicit Presentation of Scripture in 4QMMT," in Moshe Bernstein et al., eds., *Legal Texts and Legal Issues: Proceedings of the Second Meeting of the International Organization for Qumran Studies, Cambridge, 1995·* Published in Honour

work entitled "On the Kings in Judea" ($\pi\epsilon\rho\grave{\iota}\ \tau\hat{\omega}\nu\ \grave{\epsilon}\nu$ $\tau\hat{\eta}\ \text{'}Iου\delta\alpha\acute{\iota}\alpha\ \beta\alpha\sigma\iota\lambda\acute{\epsilon}\omega\nu$) (Clement of Alexandria *Strom.* 1.23.153.4), which tells us that Moses and Joshua were prophets, shows interest in the activity of Elijah and Jeremiah, and provides letters exchanged between Solomon and the kings of Egypt and Tyre (Eusebius *Praep. ev.* 9.30.1; 9.39.1–5; 9.31.1–34.3). The threefold list is often related to that in the prologue of Sirach: "through the law and the prophets and the others following after them," to that in Luke 24:44: "the law of Moses, the prophets, and the psalms," and to that in 4QMMT: "the book of Moses [and the words of the pro]phets and of David [and the annals of eac]h generation."[9] Significantly, in *4 Ezra* 144:37-48, Ezra dictates ninety-four books, of which twenty-four are to be public, but the other seventy are for the wise.

The distribution of the writings is noteworthy. Ezra's collection emphasizes his role as teacher. The list in the prologue of Sirach is geared toward learning the tradition and its heroes. Luke and 4QMMT speak first of the law, and then 4QMMT adds to the list in Luke the reference to the annals of each generation, which, from the context, seems to imply a moral evaluation of each generation. In this letter in 2 Maccabees, however, the emphasis is on kings and cult, where possibly the prophets are seen as anointers and counselors of kings (2 Kgdms 9:1-3) and as protectors of true worship (e.g., 1 Kingdoms 18–19; 20:35-43). If the reference is to King David's psalms, cult and kingship are again combined. The letters of foreign kings about votive offerings also concern worship. The emphasis in this letter is thus on the proper cultic activity of Judea and its recognition by outside monarchs. Such stress recalls both the recognition of the sacredness of the holy fire by the Persian monarch (1:34) and the opening lines of the condensed version (3:1).

■ **14-15** Judas is portrayed as carrying on the work of Nehemiah in maintaining the ancestral traditions. First

Maccabees 1:56 describes how the Seleucids tore to pieces and burned any books of the law that they found. Grimm surmises that v. 15 refers to noncanonical books that are not in the possession of the Egyptian Jews. Apart from the fact that the notion of a canon is anachronistic, the verse could refer to the need for the transcription of copies. There is no hint that the Egyptian Jews possess inferior copies, as mentioned in *Ep. Arist.* 29–31. In fact, Josephus noted how in the days of Ptolemy Philometor, Alexandrian Jews debated with Samaritans and proved from the law and the succession of the high priests the honor that the temple had been shown by all the kings of Asia (*Ant.* 13.74–79). Here an openhanded, generous offer reinforces the sense of community between the Jews of Judea and those of Egypt, while at the same time implying that the library in Jerusalem is superior to what can be found in Alexandria.[10] The verb for collecting the scrolls, $\grave{\epsilon}\pi\iota\sigma\upsilon\nu\acute{\alpha}\gamma\omega$, is the same as that for the ingathering of the people (1:27; 2:18) and so a resonance is set up between the two actions.

■ **16** The phrase of 1:18 is repeated, and by this repetition the reason for the letter is again brought to the fore. The epistolary aorist tense is used here. The formula "you will act well" ($\kappa\alpha\lambda\hat{\omega}\varsigma\ \pi\text{o}\iota\epsilon\hat{\iota}\nu$) is found frequently as a polite way of making a request at the conclusion of the body of a letter.[11] Usually it is used by those in authority, not by a petitioner (see, e.g., 1 Macc 11:43; 2 Macc 11:26).

■ **17-18** That God is a savior was stated in 1:11, but now he is said to be savior of all the people. The grammar of vv. 17-18 is difficult. The $\delta\acute{\epsilon}$ at the beginning of v. 17 is connective, not adversative. Verses 17-18a have no verb and no main clause, but v. 18b has as conjunction the particle $\gamma\acute{\alpha}\rho$ ("for"), which normally gives the reason for a previous statement and presupposes that the statement is complete. Scholars have suggested an ellipsis, that the phrase "we hope in God that . . ." was an afterthought (Abel and Grimm), or that something has been omitted

of Joseph M. Baumgarten [STDJ 23; Leiden: Brill, 1997] 67–88, here 87).

9 4QMMT 95-96–4Q397 frgs. 7 and 8, lines 10–11. G. Brin (in his review of DJD 10 in *JSS* 40 [1995] 334–42) proposed a four-part restoration (pp. 341-42). See also Timothy H. Lim, "The Alleged Reference to the Tripartite Division of the Hebrew Bible,"

RQ 20 (2001–2) 23–37; and Eugene Ulrich, "The Non-attestation of a Tripartite Canon in 4QMMT," *CBQ* 65 (2003) 202–14.

10 Lange, "2 Maccabees 2:13-15," 166–67.

11 White, *Light from Ancient Letters*, 204.

(Goldstein). I suggest that the sentence "For we hope in this God . . ." gives the reason why the Egyptian Jews should celebrate the purification (v. 16), and that what is found in vv. 17-18a is an appositive defining in what God one hopes.

The term "all"—"all the people" ($\tau\grave{o}\nu$ $\pi\acute{a}\nu\tau\alpha$ $\lambda\alpha\acute{o}\nu$) and "the inheritance to all" ($\tau\grave{\eta}\nu$ $\kappa\lambda\eta\rho o\nu o\mu\acute{\iota}\alpha\nu$ $\pi\hat{\alpha}\sigma\iota$)— is repeated in a short space. In the first instance, the adjective in the attributive position denotes the whole as the sum of all its parts, the collective body. The repetition stresses the notion of God's action to the people of Israel in its entirety. As such, vv. 17-18a do not seem to refer to God's action in the war with the Seleucids since, as Goldstein recognizes, "God had restored only a part of the 'heritage,' none of the 'kingdom,' and little of anything of the 'sanctification.'"[12] Rather, vv. 17-18a refer back to the founding of God's entire people, when God saved them by leading them out of Egypt and into the promised land. The notion of promised inheritance is expressed strongly throughout Deuteronomy: "Enter, take possession/inherit [$\kappa\lambda\eta\rho o\nu o\mu\acute{\eta}\sigma\alpha\tau\epsilon$] the land that I swore to your ancestors, to Abraham, to Isaac, and to Jacob, to give to them and to their descendants after them" (Deut 1:8-9). Scholars such as Goldstein have been reluctant to see a reference to the past because of the aorist participle $\grave{a}\pi o\delta o\acute{u}\varsigma$, which they translate as "restoring, handing back." But the verb $\grave{a}\pi o\delta\acute{\iota}\delta\omega\mu\iota$ can simply mean "assign." Abel noted that the Greek verb often translates the Hebrew verb נתן ("to give") and contains a sense of fulfilling previous pledges. For example, "the Lord commanded my lord to give [לתת; $\grave{a}\pi o\delta o\hat{u}\nu\alpha\iota$] the land for inheritance by lot to the Israelites" (Num 36:2).

The mention of "kingdom, priesthood, and sanctification" echoes LXX Exod 19:6: "you shall be to me a kingly priesthood and a holy nation [$\beta\alpha\sigma\acute{\iota}\lambda\epsilon\iota o\nu$ $\grave{\iota}\epsilon\rho\acute{a}\tau\epsilon\upsilon\mu\alpha$ $\kappa\alpha\grave{\iota}$ $\acute{\epsilon}\vartheta\nu o\varsigma$ $\acute{a}\gamma\iota o\nu$]." The same phrase is inserted in LXX Exod 23:22, where God promises the Israelites that they will conquer Canaan and that he will bring them to the land he prepared for them. Second Maccabees 2:17 sepa-

rates the terms, as does the Syriac translation of Exod 19:6: "kingdom and priests and a holy people." Revelation 1:6 reads, "He made us a kingdom, priests to God his father." This separation should not be seen as suggesting "the concept of a diarchic constitution, a form of government with two individuals (or institutions) sharing leadership, king and priest, or, if the priest is regarded as the superior one, priest and king."[13] The author, by using the abstract terms "kingdom" and "priesthood," is not claiming that one individual could not be both priest and king but simply stating the existence of both institutions in Judaism. That is, this rephrasing of Exod 19:6 should not be seen as part of an anti-Hasmonean, specifically anti–Alexander Jannaeus movement, such as John Collins has seen in the Qumran distinction between the Messiahs of Aaron and Judah.[14] By recalling the exodus tradition, where the whole people was brought into the promised land, the author bases his call for a common celebration of the festival on the hope that God will again unite his people. The author repeats the theme already expressed in 1:27-29 and 2:7. The call to celebrate is a call to return to the Lord and, as such, recalls Deut 30:1-5, where Moses told the people that if they turned to the Lord with all their heart among the nations where the Lord had driven them, the Lord would have mercy ($\grave{\epsilon}\lambda\epsilon\acute{\eta}\sigma\epsilon\iota$) on them and again gather ($\sigma\upsilon\nu\acute{a}\xi\epsilon\iota$) them back to the land, even if they were in the outermost parts of heaven ($\grave{a}\pi$ $\acute{a}\kappa\rho o\upsilon$ $\tau o\hat{u}$ $o\grave{u}\rho\alpha\nu o\hat{u}$ $\acute{\epsilon}\omega\varsigma$ $\acute{a}\kappa\rho o\upsilon$ $\tau o\hat{u}$ $o\grave{u}\rho\alpha\nu o\hat{u}$), which their ancestors possessed/inherited ($\grave{\epsilon}\kappa\lambda\eta\rho o\nu\acute{o}\mu\eta\sigma\alpha\nu$) and they would inherit ($\kappa\lambda\eta\rho o\nu o\mu\acute{\eta}\sigma\epsilon\iota\varsigma$) (see also LXX Ps 105:47). "Under the sky" is literally "the [land] under the sky." This ellipse of $\gamma\hat{\eta}\varsigma$ is found also in Prov 8:28 and Bar 5:3.

The final sentence of v. 18 grounds the hope expressed in the previous sentence: God has acted; he has purified the temple; and this purification could be the first step toward the ingathering of the people. The use of the article $\grave{\epsilon}\pi\grave{\iota}$ $\tau\hat{\omega}$ $\vartheta\epsilon\hat{\omega}$ specifies that it is the God of the previous sentence in whom the writers hope.

12 Goldstein, *II Maccabees*, 187.

13 Arie van der Kooij, "The Use of the Greek Bible in II Maccabees," *JNSL* 25 (1999) 127–38, here 130.

14 John J. Collins, *The Scepter and the Star: The Messiahs of the Dead Sea Scrolls and Other Ancient Literature* (ABRL; New York: Doubleday, 1995) 74–95. This distinction may also be present in 4Q245; see

Michael O. Wise, "4Q245 (psDanᶜ ar) and the High Priesthood of Judas Maccabaeus," *DSD* 12 (2005) 313–62.

Envisaged is not an end-time ingathering but rather the reversal of the process begun in the time of Jeremiah (2:1-2) and the fulfillment of the return begun under Nehemiah (1:20). The verb "to deliver" ($\dot{\epsilon}\xi\alpha\iota\rho\epsilon\hat{\iota}\nu$), which is found frequently in the LXX, is particularly interesting where it is used in the scene of the burning bush. God tells Moses he has come down "to deliver [$\dot{\epsilon}\xi\epsilon\lambda\acute{\epsilon}\sigma\vartheta\alpha\iota$] [the Israelites] from the hand of the Egyptians and to lead them out of that land and bring them into a good land" (Exod 3:8). The phrase "from many evils" resonates with the phrase "from many dangers" at the beginning of the letter (1:11) and so brings the letter to a close.

General Commentary

The body of the letter (1:18—2:15) is followed by a conclusion (2:16-18). The body is a call for Jews in Egypt to celebrate the cleansing of the temple and its purification and provides a clarification about this feast. This clarification consists of three parts: (1) the fiery Sukkoth celebrated by Nehemiah (1:18b-36), (2) quotations from a work about Jeremiah's activity (2:1-12), and (3) the library activity of Nehemiah and Judas (2:13-15). The second and third segments are clearly introduced with a reference to other writings. Throughout the body of the letter, two themes emerge: the comparison between Nehemiah and Judas, and the reinstitution of traditional worship at the temple, even if it is not fully complete.

Authenticity

Whether Judas Maccabeus and the senate in Jerusalem wrote the letter has been hotly debated. Most have deemed it inauthentic, though some, for example, Arnaldo Momigliano and Bunge, have held that 1:10b-18a + 2:16-18 is an authentic letter, while 1:18b—2:15 is an interpolation.[15] Opponents of authenticity have noted the similarities between the accounts of the death of Antiochus III and that of Antiochus IV and have argued

that the letter's account is anachronistic and false, while defenders of authenticity have countered by saying that the narrative emphasizes the disgraceful manner of Antiochus IV's death.[16] Opponents of authenticity have argued that there was no time for such a letter to have been sent between the receipt of the news of the king's death in Jerusalem, at least ten days after his death between 20 November and 18 December 164 B.C.E., and the sending of a courier from Jerusalem to Alexandria, a journey that would have taken at least two weeks.[17] There was not enough time before 25 Kislev 148 S.E. Wacholder countered such an argument by holding that the letter was for the festival celebrated on the 25 Kislev 149 S.E.,[18] but Goldstein argued that on 25 Kislev 149 S.E. Jerusalem was under siege (13:1-26).[19] Bickermann argued that the salutation of the letter was anachronistic, but in this he has not been followed.[20]

The discussion about authenticity has so far been limited to issues external to the letter itself. Could the letter have been delivered by a certain date? Is the salutation possible in mid-second century B.C.E.? Little attention has been focused on the worldview present in the letter. Judea is presented as independent and governed by a senate ($\gamma\epsilon\rho o \upsilon\sigma\acute{\iota}\alpha$). Any external threat to security has been dealt with; its national institutions of temple and library have been restored. Its leading personage, Judas, can be compared to a former restorer of national fortune, Nehemiah. It does not possess all that it had had before the Babylonian exile, but that is no fault of the present generation but rather of the exilic generation. The repeated longing for an ingathering of the people (1:27; 2:7, 18) suggests a state that wants to increase its population. A worldview of a stable state seeking to enlarge its population does not fit well with the worldview of Judas immediately after the retaking of the temple. According to 14:25, Judas had no ambitions for independence but was quite content to live under Seleucid rule. A better time frame for the letter would seem to be after the independence of Judea was gained (1 Macc 13:41-42) and Simon

15 Arnaldo Momigliano, *Prime linee di storia della tradizione maccabaica* (Turin, 1931; repr., Amsterdam: Hakkert, 1968) 84–94; Bunge, *Untersuchungen*, 32–152.

16 Wacholder, "Letter from Judah Maccabee," 100.

17 Goldstein, *II Maccabees*, 157–58.

18 Wacholder, "Letter from Judah Maccabee," 92.

19 Elias Bickermann, "Ein jüdischer Festbrief von Jahre 124 v. Chr (II Macc 1:1-9," *ZNW* 32 (1933) 234.

20 Ibid., 164–65.

began expanding Judea's borders to include Joppa and Gazara (1 Macc 13:11, 43-48), a movement continued by his successors (Josephus *Ant.* 13.254-58, 275-81). The policy of evicting those who did not undergo circumcision (1 Macc 13:48; Josephus *Ant.* 13.254-58, 397; 15.254) and the extent of Alexander Jannaeus's kingdom (Josephus *Ant.* 13.395-97) suggest a need for a larger Jewish population. It makes sense, then, to regard the letter as inauthentic. The stability of the state as envisaged by the letter would seem to make it fit better in the time of John Hyrcanus or Alexander Jannaeus.

The Use of Traditions

The author of the letter presents himself as an upholder of tradition. The letter mentions liturgical actions and antiphonal prayer and refers in prayer to the exodus and the choice by God of Israel as his holy portion. The author also explicitly refers to the great figures of Moses, Solomon, David, and Nehemiah as well as to the prophet Jeremiah. The author clearly reveres the tradition and respects its practices and rituals. Yet, as discussed in the notes on 2:10-11, the author does not always make it easy to determine to which part of the Hebrew Scriptures he is referring. He expects his readers to know the tradition. He is also very creative in his use of traditional material. That stories about Jeremiah were alive and well in the Second Temple period is well attested, but the author has creatively tied such traditional material to his overall purpose. The hiding of the ark, the tent, and the altar of incense resonates with the hiding of the temple fire. However, although the hidden fire is recovered and the temple sacrifices can be reinstituted, these temple vessels are not found. The emphasis of the author is clearly seen in the way the condensed and brief narrative of 2:4-6 is suddenly followed by a long speech of Jeremiah (2:7-8) in response to the meddling priests. Their overinquisitiveness brings the punishment that the temple vessels will not be found until the Lord arrives. The implication is that if the prophet's companions had not tried to mark out the way to the cave, then the tent, the ark, and the altar of incense would have been available for use in the Second Temple. That they are not is the fault not of the returnees under Cyrus but of the priests of the First Temple. The author is concerned to explain why the Second Temple is not as complete as the First.

Several themes of a new exodus are woven together here: Jeremiah leaves Jerusalem to go out of the land to the mountain that Moses went up and where he saw the inheritance of God. Only when God shows his mercy will the people be gathered together as they were in Moses' time, and they will enter the promised land and set up the full temple as in the time of Solomon. Here is the hope for a full national restoration of Jews.

Supporter of the State

The most interesting figure referred to by the author is Nehemiah. Nowhere else is Nehemiah said to build the temple and the altar; the contrast with Ezra 3:2-11; 5:16 is strong. Rather than search for possible ways to explain away the discrepancy—for example, the author is identifying Nehemiah with Zerubbabel—I suggest that the author is providing an alternative telling of the story. Bergren, following Haran, noted how the functions attributed to Nehemiah in this letter—pious leader, builder, founder of a library—were the traits of enlightened Hellenistic rulers.[21] Nehemiah, the former governor of Judea, is thus a model for Judas, the leader of the senate in Judea, and Judas is shown as inaugurating a stable society. In this context, the list of three components of Nehemiah's library is extremely interesting, for, as noted in the commentary on 2:13, the list emphasizes kings and cult, and thus underlines that Nehemiah and Judas are leaders.

A Stable Society

The senders of the letter present themselves as a group made up of the populace, the senate, and Judas. This self-identification resonates with the way Polybius argues that Lycurgus's legislation united all the distinctive excellencies of the best governments: kingship was restrained by the populace, and the populace by the elders. The legislation united monarchy, aristocracy, and democracy (6.10). Polybius finds the same mixture in the Roman constitution, where the Roman senate takes the place of the elders in Sparta (6.11.12), and it is interesting that Plutarch calls the Roman senate by the name γερουσία (*An seni* 789E).

---

21   Bergren, "Nehemiah," 261–64; Haran, "Archives,"
      51–61; Smith, *Palestinian Parties*, 96–112.

The wittily told story of the death of Antiochus IV in the extended assurance of the senders' well-being is interesting in this regard. To make such fun of powerful monarchs requires that one feel secure. Jokes are a favorite tool of underdogs who cannot overtly attack their overlords, as a means of gaining some sense of self-worth, some sense of superiority over their lords.

In this case I think that the joke is told by an underdog who does not expect to be crushed immediately.

Conclusion

This letter presents Judea as a stable society in need of more Jewish returnees. It is a society respectful of its traditions and in which the temple, if not completely the same as the First Temple, is functioning properly.

2 2:19-32

19/ The events concerning Judas the Maccabee and his brothers, the purification of the greatest^a temple and the dedication of the altar, 20/ as well as the wars against Antiochus Epiphanes and his son Eupator 21/ and the heavenly manifestations to those who acted strenuously and eagerly on behalf of Judaism so that, though few in number, they took the entire region as a prize and drove off the barbarian hordes, 22/ they recovered the temple renowned throughout the world, they freed the city and restored the laws about to be abrogated, as the Lord in full fairness dealt propitiously with them: 23/ [these events], set forth by Jason of Cyrene in five scrolls, we will attempt to treat concisely in one composition. 24/ For, as we considered the profusion of lines and, because of the mass of the material, the difficulty present to those wanting to involve themselves in the history's stories, 25/ we devised persuasiveness for those who like to read, ease for those who work hard^b so as to recollect from memory, and usefulness for all who read (it).

26/ Now, it was not a light matter for us as we undertook the wearisome task of this concise version, but one of sweat and sleeplessness, 27/ just as it is no easy [matter] to one preparing a drinking party and seeking what sets others at ease. Nevertheless, we will endure with pleasure this wearisome task for the sake of the gratitude^c of the many. 28/ We concede to the historian the minute presentation concerning every particular, but we work hard at proceeding by means of the general descriptions [appropriate to] a concise version. 29/ For, just as the construction chief of a new building must pay attention to the entire structure but the one endeavoring to paint in encaustic and to paint living figures must examine carefully the things suitable for adornment,

a   q reads μεγάλου rather than μεγίστου.

b   With Habicht I accept the emendation suggested by Risberg ("Textkritische und exegetische Anmerkungen," 18–19) to read φιλοπονοῦσιν rather than φιλοφρονοῦσιν ("those who enjoy, embrace"). The middle voice φιλοφρονέομαι is attested; where the active φιλοφρονέω is found, it is a scribal mistake for φίλα φρονέω ("greet friendly," as in Homer *Od.* 16.17). The active has been restored by its editor on a broken inscription, *SIG* 1268 ii 2. Goldstein suggests that one should understand the active form analogously to φιλοσοφέω ("to pursue wisdom") and so φιλοφρονέω would mean "pursue φρόνησις" ("prudence/practical wisdom"). Since the author of 2 Maccabees enjoys contrasts, as discussed above in the Introduction, I think it more likely that he is contrasting φιλοπονέω ("love to work hard") with εὐκοπία ("ease").

c   Reading, with Hanhart and Habicht, εὐχαριστίαν as in La^V rather than, with Abel and Goldstein, εὐχρηστίαν ("utility"), as in L' 58 311 La^{VBM}. Verse 25 had already mentioned usefulness, and in verse 27, λυσιτέλεια has the sense of "advantage, profit."

so I think also about us. 30/ The first constructor of the history is bound to enter in and make a place for narratives and inquire closely into particulars, 31/ but one who makes its paraphrase must be allowed to pursue conciseness of diction and to avoid the complete treatment of the historical treatise. 32/ Consequently, let us begin the narrative, enclosing so much of what is said by way of preface. For [it would be] silly to be expansive before the narrative, but to treat concisely the narrative.

Commentary by Verse

■ **19** The presence of the particle δέ as the second word of the sentence is particularly intriguing. Δέ marks off something as different from what precedes.[1] Its presence here thus suggests that the epitome is connected to the preceding letters, and scholars such as Torrey[2] and Abel argue that the letters were placed there by the author of the epitome. Goldstein rightly suggests that the particle δέ was added when the prefixed letters were placed before the condensed version.[3]

With v. 19 begins a long sentence that runs through v. 23 and of which vv. 19-23a contain the object of the sentence.

The coupling of Judas and his brothers is more common in 1 Maccabees (3:25, 42; 4:36, 59; 5:10), but at the crucial first battle in 2 Maccabees against the Seleucid general Nikanor, Judas installs his brothers as leaders of the three divisions of the army (8:22-23).

"the purification of the greatest temple." The purification occurs in 10:3-5. The festival was called thus in the second letter (1:18; 2:16), and the second letter ends with the statement that God purified the place. Purification is present also at Nehemiah's festival, as the naptha is called "purification" (1:36) and the priests and all the people are purified at the dedication of the wall in Jerusalem (Neh 12:27-45).

"dedication." The term is used earlier in the second letter of Solomon's dedication of the temple (2:9). It describes both Solomon's dedication of the altar in 2 Chr 7:9 and Ezra's dedication of the temple (Ezra 6:16 = LXX 1 Esdr 7:17), and the verbal form is found in 3 Kgdms 8:63 and 2 Chr 7:5; 15:8.

"altar." Here βωμός is used rather than θυσιαστή-ριον. Βωμός is often used of idolatrous altars in the LXX, but in Sir 50:12-14, the two words are used interchangeably. Josephus (*Ant.* 9.223) uses βωμός where the corresponding section in the LXX has θυσιαστήριον. Perhaps the short-syllabled βωμοῦ was chosen to resonate with ἱεροῦ.

"the greatest temple." Habicht takes the adjective as substantivized and translates "des Tempels des Höchsten." Μέγιστος is used as an adjective of God in 3:36 (τοῦ μεγίστου θεοῦ) and also as an adjective of ἱερός in 14:13, 31. Here the use of the article and the attributive adjective places emphasis on the noun, "*the* temple," and so the adjective does not need to be read as substantivized.

■ **20** The events under Demetrius I, which occupy chaps. 14–15, are not mentioned explicitly, as the focus remains on the desecration of the temple under Antiochus IV and the events surrounding its restoration.

■ **21** τὰς ἐξ οὐρανοῦ . . . ἐπιφανείας ("the heavenly manifestations"). The author is fond of epiphanies: see

---

1 Smyth, *Greek Grammar*, §§2834–36.
2 Torrey, "Letters," 139.
3 Goldstein, *II Maccabees*, 190.

3:24; 5:2-4; 11:8; 12:22; 15:27 and also the prayer for an epiphany in 14:15. God is called τὸν ἐπιφανῆ κύριον (15:24), which is a clear contrast to Antiochus IV, who is called τὸν Ἐπιφανῆ (2:20), and to the threat of Nikanor (14:33) to make the temple "a prominent temple [ἱερὸν . . . ἐπιφανές] to Dionysos." In David's prayer for the continuity of his dynasty in 2 Kgdms 7:23, God is praised as the one who "does greatness and divine manifestation" (μεγαλωσύνην καὶ ἐπιφάνειαν). The verbal form describes God's appearing to Jacob (Gen 35:7); also important is its use in the priestly prayer in LXX Num 6:25: "The Lord make his face to shine [ἐπιφάναι Κύριος τὸ πρόσωπον αὐτοῦ] upon you and be gracious to you" and likewise, in the prophecy in LXX Zeph 2:11: "The Lord will manifest himself [ἐπιφανήσεται] against them, and will destroy all the gods of the nations of the earth."

Traditional stories and cult often said that the Greek gods manifested their divine power and that this divine power had been experienced by human recipients,[4] and the late Hellenistic word ἐπιφάνεια ("manifestation, appearance, epiphany") becomes frequent in lists of healing miracles and of stories of salvation from danger.[5] Istros (ca. 250 B.C.E.) is said to have written two lost works, "The Epiphanies of Apollo" and "The Epiphanies of Herakles,"[6] while an inscription honors the third-century B.C.E. historian Syriskos because he recorded the

epiphanies of Athena.[7] Note also how poets and history writers told of the epiphanic help of Artemis.[8]

ἀνδραγαθεῖν ("act strenuously") is found in 1 Macc 5:61, 67; 16:23; 2 Macc 14:18 speaks of the ἀνδραγαθία ("bravery") of Judas's men.

φιλοτίμως ("eagerly"). The basic root meaning is "loving honor," and so one gets the sense of "ambition, rivalry." However, here the sense seems to stress not rivalry or vying with one another but eagerness or zealousness to fight on behalf of Judaism. It is used this way by Xenophon (Cyrop. 1.6.26). In Wis 18:3, φιλότιμος has the sense of "glorious."

Ἰουδαϊσμός, found also in 8:1 and 14:38, is here coined in opposition to "foreign ways" (ἀλλοφυλισμός) (4:13; 6:24). Ἑλληνισμός ("Hellenism") is paired with ἀλλοφυλισμόν in 4:13, but the author prefers the adjective Ἑλληνικός ("Hellenic"; 4:10, 15; 6:9; 11:24; 13:2). While it is true that "Judaism" is never explicitly contrasted with the term "Hellenism,"[9] in 4:15 "ancestral honors" are contrasted with "Hellenic distinctions." This is the first known occurrence of the term Ἰουδαϊσμός. Goldstein, in his comment on 4:13, nicely suggests that the word Ἑλληνισμός, which originally meant "use of a pure Greek style or idiom," during the Persian wars of the sixth and fifth centuries B.C.E. came to mean "loyal to the Greek cause" in opposition to "Medism," Μηδισμός, "loyalty to the Persian cause."[10] Here the author contrasts

---

4 For the use of divine appearances in Greek tradition, see E. Pax, "Epiphanie," *Reallexicon für Antike und Christentum: Sachwörterbuch zur Auseinandersetzung des Christentums mit der antiken Welt* (ed. Theodor Klauser; 23 vols.; Stuttgart: Hiersemann, 1950–) 5:834–35; Martin P. Nilsson, *Geschichte der griechischen Religion* (2 vols.; Munich: Beck, 1950) 2:214–16; W. Kendrick Pritchett, *The Greek State at War*, part 3: *Religion* (Berkeley: University of California Press, 1979) 6–46; Dieter Lührmann, "Epiphaneia: Zur Bedeutungsgeschichte eines griechischen Wortes," in Gert Jeremias et al., eds., *Tradition und Glaube: Das frühe Christentum in seiner Umwelt. Festgabe für Karl Georg Kuhn zum 65. Geburtstag* (Göttingen: Vandenhoeck & Ruprecht, 1971) 185–99.

5 The pledge of thanksgiving offerings after Apollo saved Delphi from the Gauls (SIG³ 398.16–21); the catalogue of epiphanies of Athena found in the Lindian Temple Chronicle from 99 B.C.E. (*FGH* 532, section D). I am indebted to Albert Henrichs for these references and for the whole discussion of

epiphany in a lecture he delivered at Smith College, 17 Oct. 2005, "Epiphany, Miracle, Mystery: The Dynamics of Divine Self-Revelation in the *Homeric Hymn to Demeter* and Euripides' *Bacchae*."

6 *FGH* 334 F 50–54.
7 *FGH* 807.
8 Kern, *Die Inschriften*, §46, line 10.
9 Erich S. Gruen, *Heritage and Hellenism: The Reinvention of Jewish Tradition* (Hellenistic Culture and Society 30; Berkeley: University of California Press, 1998) 3–4.
10 See Mason, "Jews, Judaeans," 460–70.

those loyal to the Jewish cause with their opponents, the barbarian hordes.

"barbarian." In 4:25; 5:22; 15:2, the word has the connotation of "wild, untamed, savage"; in 10:4 it is paired with "blasphemous." βάρβαρος was the word used of all non-Greeks. Of particular interest is the way it turns up in the epiphanic accounts of Herodotus and the Lindos Chronicle, where, respectively, the Gauls in their attacks on Delphi and the Persians in their attack on the temple at Lindos are called barbarians (Herodotus 8.36).[11] The author here has neatly reversed customary speech and contrasts Judaism with Greek Seleucid lack of culture. Philo seems to place the Jews among the βάρβαροι (Vit. Mos. 2.27).[12]

"few in number." The overcoming of the many by the few through the help of God is a theme that is sounded in Deut 7:17-18 and Judges 7, and also appears in the narrative where huge numbers are attributed to the enemy (2 Macc 8:20; 11:4; 12:19-20; 15:24-27). The emphasis on fewness in number stands at the beginning of the result clause, and the genitive absolute describing God's graciousness at the end of this clause qualifies the action of the few. What starts out as praise of the heroic actions of the few ends with an emphasis on dependence on God.

λεηλατεῖν. The usual meaning is "to plunder," whereby the army of one country attacks another and carries off livestock and food. It seems strange to say that Judas plundered his own country, unless one sees it as Judas wresting control away from the Seleucids with the country itself as a prize.

■ 22 "renowned." Josephus (Ant. 12.137) reports that Polybius spoke of the splendid[13] appearance of the temple.[14]

"freed." The author has the dying Antiochus IV promise to make the city free (9:14). As Gruen has convincingly shown, Hellenistic dynasts' practice of declaring Greek communities free "served as a convenient instrument for rival dynasts to use against one another. . . . It legitimized wars, the overthrow of regimes, and the exercise of suzerainty."[15] In Israel's worldview as celebrated in cult at Passover each year—founded as a nation from slavery in Egypt to freedom in the promised land—such language had enormous resonances.

"abrogated." The same term appears in 4:11 to describe what the high priest Jason attempted to do. Antiochus V in 11:24 speaks rather of "the change toward the Hellenic lifestyle initiated by my father." "Restore" is found also in 5:20.

"with full fairness" (μετὰ πάσης ἐπιεικείας). The Greek prepositional phrase, μετὰ πάσης + substantive, is a favorite of the author and can be found in 3:1; 5:20; 15:6-7. Ἐπιείκεια has the sense of "equity" and is found in 10:4, where God is said equitably or fairly to discipline the people if they sin. Such action gives "human interests priority over personal rights or legal privilege."[16] Here God equitably rewards those who act eagerly on behalf of Judaism.

"propitiously." The seventh martyred brother prays that God deal propitiously with his people (ἵλεως . . . γενέσθαι; 7:37), and God's wrath does turn to mercy (8:5: ἔλεος).

■ 23 On Jason of Cyrene and the concise version, see the Introduction.

■ 24 A similar sentiment is found in Dionysius of Halicarnassus (1.3.5) where he promises the readers that he will be of least trouble to them.

συνορῶντες. See the similar language used by Diodorus Siculus 1.3.1: Διὸ καὶ θεωροῦντες; 1.4.1: Διόπερ ἡμεῖς ὁρῶντες. The author uses the authorial first person plural throughout the prologue and also in 14:34, except in the curious mixture in 2:29: "so I think about us [δοκῶ καὶ ἐπὶ ἡμῶν]." In the epilogue, the author will consistently use the first person singular.

---

11   FGH 532 D.

12   See Hans Windisch, "βάρβαρος," TDNT 1 (1964) 546–52.

13   The word ἐπιφάνεια is used in this verse not of a divine manifestation but of the striking appearance of the temple.

14   See also Josephus Ant. 13.77; Philo Leg. Gaj. 191, 198.

15   Erich S. Gruen, The Hellenistic World and the Coming of Rome (2 vols.; Berkeley: University of California Press, 1984) 1:142; see the entire discussion on pp. 132–42.

16   Frederick W. Danker, Benefactor: Epigraphic Study of a Graeco-Roman and New Testament Semantic Field (St. Louis: Clayton, 1982) 351. On ἐπιείκεια, see Aristotle Eth. Nic. V.10 (1138a2–3).

"profusion of lines." I have previously argued for this meaning, rather than "mass of numbers."[17] As Larue Van Hook observed, "χεῖν and its derivatives furnish a number of words designating speech and style, from the idea of water continuously flowing."[18] See, for example, Longinus *Subl.* 12.4, where χύσις means "copiousness of speech." Goldstein's comment that "'number' was a unit of about sixteen syllables of writing, the standard measure of length in Greek books" would support this understanding of ἀριθμός as meaning "line."

"involve themselves." I have taken εἰσκυκλεῖσθαι as a middle voice. Ἐισκυκλέω is a term taken from the theater and means "to turn things inward by machinery." It is especially appropriate here, as the author is going to present vivid descriptions of events such as the martyrdom of the seven brothers. The article before "history" refers back to the work of Jason of Cyrene, which the author is going to enliven by shortening and by means of deletions.

"material." ὕλη describes the content of a historical source in Polybius 12.25c.1, where one of the tasks of a historian is the comparison of the content (τῆς . . . ὕλης) of different memoirs (ὑπομνήματα). Polybius also speaks of certain tales as "matter for tragedy" (2.16.14: τὴν τραγικὴν . . . ὕλην). The use of the term suggests something unformed, needing to be given shape by the author. Van Hook noted the various meanings of "ὕλη: literally it referred, for example, to material like timber used in building; then it came to refer to any raw material; finally, it came to mean in rhetoric, the subject-matter of the discussion."[19] Tacitus rebuked writers who fear that an abundance of material may make their students bored (*Ann.* 6.7: ne pari taedio lecturos adficeret).

■ 25 The author gives three aims of his writing, using a μέν . . . δέ . . . δέ construction with the aim placed at the end of each clause. He uses homoioteleuton in his description of the aims.

φροντίζω + accusative has the sense of "devise, contrive," rather than the meaning with the genitive of "take thought of, care about."

"persuasiveness for those who like to read." ψυχαγωγία is literally "the leading of souls," and ψυχαγωγός is an epithet of Hermes as he leads the dead to the underworld. Plato sees rhetoric as ψυχαγωγία : "Is [rhetoric] not in its entire nature an art which leads the soul (ψυχαγωγία) by means of words?" and "it is the function of speech to lead souls by persuasion (ψυχαγωγία)" (*Phaedr.* 261A; 271C; see also Plutarch *Per.* 15.4).

The root sense of "leading the soul" could also connote "diversion, distraction": Josephus stated: "[Herod] would also devise everything possible for distraction [εἰς ψυχαγωγίαν], arranging banquets and parties, and yet none could help" (*Ant.* 15.241). Lucian too linked with diversions: "Sitting as in a theatre . . . I observe what happens, some of which supply much diversion and laughter [ψυχαγωγίαν καὶ γέλωτα], and some of which put to the proof a person's true steadfastness" (*Nigr.* 18). Note how the NRSV translates the word with the verb "to please." This latter sense sometimes leads to ψυχαγωγία being relegated to the incidental, as in "What Eratosthenes says is not true, that every poet aims at winning of souls/distraction, not teaching [ψυχαγωγίας, οὐ διδασκαλίας]" (Strabo 1.1.10; see also Livy 5.21.8-9). Polybius too distinguishes between what catches one's attention and what is useful: "For the mere statement of a fact wins one's attention [ψυχαγωγεῖ] but is not useful [ὠφελεῖ δ' οὐδέν]" (12.25b.2; see also Dionysius of Halicarnassus *Pomp.* 6). Polybius sometimes contrasts usefulness (ὠφέλεια, χρήσιμος) and pleasure (τέρψις, ἡδεῖα), but also states that both can be derived from history (15.36.3; 1.4.11; 7.7.8; 31.31.1). Polybius always stresses usefulness, profit (ὠφέλεια) to be gained from hearing histories, and even when he speaks of pleasure, he seems more concerned with the content of the stories rather than the way the stories are told (7.7.8; 15.36.1-9; 31.30.1-3). Dionysius of Halicarnassus speaks of how people engaged in civic government take "pleasure in a comprehensive survey of all the circumstances that accompany events" and that their knowledge of such events helps them, in difficult times, to lead through their speech (ἄγειν . . . διὰ τοῦ λόγου), to make their fellow citizens follow them willingly (*Ant. rom.* 11.1.4).

As noted above, ψυχαγωγία is intimately connected with rhetoric; it is therefore interesting that our author

17 Doran, *Temple Propaganda*, 77–78.
18 Larue Van Hook, *The Metaphorical Terminology of Greek Rhetoric and Literary Criticism* (Chicago: University of Chicago Press, 1905) 13.
19 Ibid., 41.

has chosen this term to describe one of his aims. For Cicero, history was a branch of oratory (*De or.* 2.9.36), and Clare Rothschild has shown well how history was always connected with rhetoric in ancient Greek and Hellenistic historiography.[20] Important here is the way Duris of Samos discusses history: "Ephoros and Theopompos fall short of most of the events that happened; because in their account they give no space to any imitation [of the historical reality], nor to the pleasure [which results from it], but they care only about style."[21] When one recalls that to read in antiquity was to read aloud,[22] the use of ψυχαγωγία in 2:25 suggests the rhetorical persuasion that comes from vibrant presentation. Such good rhetoric captures people's souls and leads them on to follow and agree with the argument. This attempt at "winning the soul" is particularly evident in the author's vividly sketched scenes of distress (3:15-22) and persecution (6:18–7:42; 14:37-46), as well as in the stark contrasts between the Jews and their enemies (e.g., 15:6-11, 25-27). Here the author sets out to depict a spectacle[23] before the eyes of his listeners so as to move their emotions. As Aristotle had argued, reversals were one of the most important parts of the plot by which a tragedy "draws the soul" (ψυχαγωγεῖ) (*Poet.* 6.17 [1450a33]), and we shall see several reversals in 2 Maccabees.

"ease." The term εὐκοπία is used to describe the easy attainment of food without much labor (Diodorus Siculus 1.36.4; 3.17.1), and Diodorus Siculus also stated that he wanted to write a history that would both benefit his hearers and trouble them the least (ἐλάχιστα . . . ἐνοχλήσουσαν) (1.3.5). Here the author uses the term to

speak of ease in recollecting from memory. This concern for remembering in itself suggests a concern for educating his readers. Diodorus Siculus had the same concern: "In all systematic historical treatises, it behooves the historian to include in his books actions of states or of kings which are complete in themselves from beginning to end; for so I conceive history to become most easy to remember and most intelligible to its readers [εὐμνημόνευτον καὶ σαφῆ γενέσθαι τοῖς ἀναγινώσκουσιν]" (16.1.1). Here the emphasis on making the work a unified whole as the basis for easy memorization is important. While other Greek historians did not expressly speak of memory, they were concerned about the unity of their work. Polybius insisted that his universal history had only one theme (1.4.1), while Cicero was sure his part in the civil wars would make a nice monograph as the work would center on one person and one self-contained event (*Fam.* 5.12).[24] For Aristotle, plots in tragedy must not begin and end at random: "As then creatures and other organic structures must have a certain magnitude and yet be easily taken in by the eye [εὐσύνοπτον], so too with plots: they must have a length but must be easily taken in by the memory [εὐμνημόνευτον]" (*Poet.* 7.10 [1451a]).

"all who read [it]." ἐντυγχάνω has often, from the context, the sense of "readers," as at 6:12 and 15:39 (e.g., Polybius 1.3.10; 1.4.2). One should not, however, forget the broader meaning of "come into contact with," as we often think of reading as a solitary affair, not as being publicly spoken.

"usefulness." That history should be useful/profitable was a rhetorical commonplace. Isocrates had distin-

---

20   Cicero *De Orat.* 207. Clare Rothschild, *Luke-Acts and the Rhetoric of History: An Investigation of Early Christian Historiography* (WUNT 175; Tübingen: Mohr Siebeck, 2004) 1–23.

21   FGH 76, F 1: Ἔφορος δὲ καὶ Θεόπομπος τῶν γενομένων πλεῖστον ἀπελείφθησαν· οὔτε γὰρ μιμήσεως μετέλαβον οὐδεμιᾶς οὔτε ἡδονῆς ἐν τῷ φράσαι, αὐτοῦ δὲ τοῦ γράφειν μόνον ἐπεμελήθησαν. I have followed the interpretation and translation of Karl Meister, *Historische Kritik bei Polybios* (Wiesbaden: Steiner, 1975) 109–22.

22   See, for example, Polybius 15.36. There were, of course, exceptions. See B. M. W. Knox, "Silent Reading in Antiquity," *GRBS* 9 (1968) 421–35.

23   Note how for Aristotle scenic display draws the soul (ψυχαγωγικὸν) but has nothing to do with the

content of a play (*Poet.* 6.28). As Paul Pédech writes of Duris of Samos: "L'histoire est donc avant tout une peinture. Par suite elle a recours à des moyens de nature descriptive, à une narration qui fait une place à des tableaux et à des scènes de façon à captiver et à flatter la sensibilité et l'imagination" (Pédech, *Trois historiens méconnus: Théopompe–Duris–Phylarque* [Collection d'études anciennes 119; Paris: Belles Lettres, 1989] 372).

24   For a full discussion, see Gert Avenarius, *Lukians Schrift zur Geschichtsschreibung* (Meisenheim am Glan: Hain, 1956) 105–13.

guished for orators those discourses that gave useful advice and teaching and those that abounded in crowd-tickling stories of contests and battles and games among the demigods (*Ad Nic.* 48–49). Thucydides had set the standard for historians when he wrote, "And it may be that the absence of the fabulous from my narrative will seem less pleasing to the ear; but whoever shall wish to have a clear view, both of the events which happened, and of those which some day, in all probability, shall happen again in the same or a similar way—for these to adjudge my history profitable will be enough for me" (1.22.4).[25]

In this verse the author has spoken of his concern to provide a memorable presentation that will inspire his audience to act in the same manner as his heroes in similar circumstances.

■ **26** After the emphatic position of ἡμῖν as the second word in the sentence, the particle μέν is here answered by the adversative particle ὅμως ("nevertheless") in v. 27 so that the difficulty of the work contrasts with the author's willingness to do it. Note how the term κακοπάθειαν ("wearisome task") is repeated in the contrastive sentence in v. 27. Polybius (12.27.4–5) stressed the need for hardship (κακοπάθεια) in the personal investigation of historical events and the interrogation of living witnesses as opposed to the mere reading of books. Diodorus Siculus (1.4.1), too, emphasized the great amount of labor and time—thirty years—his project had required. Callimachus spoke of the sleeplessness of an author.[26] The author uses two negatives—οὐ ῥάδιον and οὐ εὐχερές—to highlight the difficulty of the task. In 2:24 he had spoken of the difficulty (δυσχέρειαν) for readers; now he speaks of the difficulty/no easy matter (οὐ εὐχερές) of his own task.

■ **27** Grimm rightly noted that the reference here is not to the host of the party, but to the president of the drinking party, the συμποσίαρχος. In Herodotus 9.82, "to prepare the meal" (παρασκευάζειν τὸ δεῖπνον) refers to what the servants are commanded to do, but that is not the issue here. As in Sir 32:1-2, the one chosen to

preside at a dinner has to take care of the others first and to see to all their needs (πᾶσαν τὴν χρείαν) before he sits down. Plutarch, in question 4 of book 1 of his *Quaestiones convivales*, discussed the role of the president (συμποσίαρχος) at a meal (1.4, 620A–622B). One of the president's duties was to give commands that have in view both the pleasure and the profit (πρὸς ἡδονὴν καὶ ὠφέλειαν) of the participants (622A). Part of the role of the president was also to know how to mix the wine for the different guests (620E–F), an image that returns at the end of 2 Maccabees, in 15:39, and hints at the unity of the work.

"sets others at ease" (τὴν ἑτέρων λυσιτέλειαν). The word λυσιτέλεια has the sense of profit as it relates to economics (Diodorus Siculus 1.36.4; 16.55.3). Diodorus Siculus speaks of the advantages to farmers from the flooding of the Nile: "in general, the Nile contributes such ease to the lands [τοῖς μὲν ἔργοις εὐκοπίαν], such profit to the people [τοῖς δ' ἀνθρώποις λυσιτέλειαν] . . . they gather great heaps of grain without much expense or exertion [χωρὶς δαπάνης πολλῆς καὶ κακοπαθείας]" (1.36.4). Here the concatenation of words used also by the author of 2 Maccabees (λυσιτέλεια and κακοπάθεια) is intriguing. The term λυσιτέλεια is also linked with the notion of luxurious ease, for Alexander the Great is said to have upbraided the Persian king Darius for despising glory and choosing "profit and the luxuriousness that comes from a life of ease [τὴν λυσιτέλειαν καὶ τὴν ἐκ τῆς ῥᾳστώνης τρυφήν]" (Diodorus Siculus 17.54.6). Λυσιτέλειαν may be used here to resonate stylistically with the similar sounding εὐχαριστίαν and κακοπάθειαν.

■ **28** This nicely balanced clause consisting of two participial phrases, each beginning with an articular infinitive and ending with a participle, ends the long sentence that began in v. 26. The μέν . . . δέ construction begins a series of contrasts between larger works and the way this author conceives of his own presentation. A similar contrast is found in Strabo as he contrasts his physical description of a country with descriptions by surveyors:

---

25 See also Paul Scheller, *De hellenistica historiae conscribendae arte* (Leipzig: R. Noske, 1911) 72–78.

26 Callimachus (*Epigr.* 27) uses the term to describe the vigilance of Aratos. Selina Stewart ("Emending Aratus' Insomnia: Callimachus Epigr. 27," *Mnemosyne* 61 [2008] 586–600) has suggested that

Callimachus is here reflecting the use of this term in Aristophanes *Lys.* 27.

"We, however, do not have to take the same care [φρον-τιστέον] as is necessary for those measuring a country, but only to describe generally [ὑπογραπτέον] such as our predecessors have" (13.4.12).

"proceeding by means of the general descriptions [appropriate to] a concise version" (ἐπιπορεύεσθαι . . . τοῖς ὑπογραμμοῖς τῆς ἐπιτομῆς). The dative here is a dative of manner, describing how the author tends to proceed. I have taken the genitive here as a genitive of possession, that is, an epitome possesses the characteristic of providing general descriptions, rather than detailed ones. This phrase has given rise to various interpretations—Grimm: "wandeln auf dem Boden der Regeln [des Epitome]"; Abel: "suivre les contours d'un simple précis"; Habicht: "nach den Grundlinien der Epitome . . . hindurchzumarschieren"; Goldstein: "proceed . . . along the lines of an abridgement." It is hard to envision exactly what these translations intend. The principal challenge is how to understand ὑπογραμμός. The main argument for its translation as "rules," "contours," or "lines" seems to derive from the way children in Greece were taught to write letters: "just as writing-masters first draw letters in faint outline [ὑπογράψαντες γραμμάς] with the pen for their less advanced pupils, and then give them the copy-book and make them write according to the guidance of their lines, so the city sketches out for them the laws [νόμους ὑπογράψασα] devised by good lawgivers of yore, and constrains them to govern and be governed according to these" (Plato *Prot.* 326D).[27] However, while the appearance of letters was standardized, were there standardized rules for the appearance of an epitome?

I have translated the term as "general descriptions." Often the verb ὑπογράφω is used in the sense of giving a general description in contrast to a detailed exposition. Plato wrote, "given the fact that we are only outlining [ὑπογράψαντα] a regime's figure in speech and not working out its details precisely [μὴ ἀκριβῶς ἀπερ-γάσασθαι]." (*Resp.* 8.548D). Isocrates wrote, "If I fall short in some way and cannot write in the same manner as I did before, I still think I will sketch out [ὑπογρά-φειν] pleasantly for those who can fill in the details and complete it [τοῖς ἐξεργάζεσθαι καὶ διαπονεῖν δυναμένοις]" (*Phil.* 5.85).[28] And Strabo wrote: "I assume that such changes to the lower areas which took place generally describe [ὑπογράφειν] the differences of modes of life and forms of government, but one must examine these things elsewhere" (13.1.25).

The opposition in this verse suggests that ὑπογραμ-μός should be understood as a general description as opposed to specific details, rather than as a general description that follows already provided outlines or rules.

■ **29** The comparison begins with two contrasting clauses, each ending with a verbal adjective, that form a homoioteleuton.

It is unusual for καταβολή to signify the whole building, rather than the foundation.

Encaustic is a painting technique in which colors are mixed with heated wax, a technique well-known in antiquity (see Pliny *Hist. nat.* 35, 122–24, 149). It stresses color whereas ζωγραφεῖν ("to paint living animals") stresses the figural quality. Since γράφειν means both "to write" and "to paint," the comparison between the two was a familiar one. As Plutarch wrote:

Simonides, however, calls painting [ζωγραφίαν] inarticulate poetry [ποίησιν] and poetry articulate painting: for the actions which painters portray as taking place at the moment, literature [οἱ λόγοι] narrates and records after they have taken place. Even though artists with color and design, and writers with words and phrases, represent [δηλοῦσιν] the same subjects, they differ in the material and the manner of their imitation; and yet, the underlying end and aim of both is one and the same; the most effective historian is he who, by a vivid representation of emotions and

---

27   See also H.-I. Marrou, *A History of Education in Antiquity* (New York: Sheed & Ward, 1956) 152: "The master would draw one of the letters, probably very lightly—like the lines written with dotted lines in writing books—and then, before he let the child try it by himself, take his hand and make him go over it, so as to give him the 'feel' of the letter." Note how Aristotle uses the image of painters: "Painters, as we know, first of all sketch in [ὑπογράψαντες] the figure of the animal in outline, and after that go on to apply the colors" (*Gen. an.* 743b24). See also Plato *Leg.* 11.934C.

28   In the translation by Terry L. Papillon, *Isocrates II* (Austin: University of Texas Press, 2004) 93.

characters, makes his narration like a painting. (*Glor. Ath.* 346F–347A).[29]

Polybius pokes fun at Timaeus with such a comparison: "if he ever comes near the truth, he resembles those painters [ζωγράφοις] who make sketches from stuffed bags. For in their case, the outlines are sometimes preserved but we miss that vividness and animation of the real figures which the graphic art [τῆς ζωγραφικῆς τέχνης] is especially capable of rendering" (12.25ʰ.2-3; see also 12.25ᵉ.7).

The contrast in this verse is thus between the person in charge of the building's construction—"architect" does not have this connotation—and the person who paints the walls. The historian Timaeus does not make the same contrast when he claims that the difference between history and epideictic oratory is like the difference between real buildings and paintings of real buildings (Polybius 12.28ᵃ.1). Rather, the contrast here suggests that the author thinks of himself as making the narrative come alive, rather than remain drab and dull.

■ **30-31** The final contrast is between detailed narratives and condensed versions.

"first constructor." The author had used ἀρχιτέκτονι in the previous contrast to describe the construction chief, and in this contrast he uses a similar term, ἀρχηγέτης, which has the sense of "founder." Here the author imagines that a history narrative is written by one person and subsequently paraphrased by a second. The article before μετάφρασιν refers to the larger narrative.

"make a place for narratives" is literally "to make a walk of narratives/speeches" (περίπατον ποιεῖσθαι λόγων). The image seems to be one of entering onto a property (ἐμβατεύειν) and taking a stroll while talking. When Josephus and Plutarch speak of giving summaries of material, they use the verb ἐπιτρέχω ("to run over"). Referring to events that occurred before the revolt against Rome, Josephus says he will "run over them concisely" (ἐπιδραμῶ συντόμως) (*Bell.* 1.18). Plutarch, in his life of Nicias, says he will summarize what previous historians have written, "running over quickly" (ἐπιδραμῶν βραχέως) (*Nic.* 1.1.5).

"Inquire closely" (πολυπραγμονεῖν) and its substantive πολυπραγμοσύνη are frequently used by Polybius (12.25ⁱ.2; 12.26ᶜ.3; 12.27.4-6; 12.28ᵃ.3-4).

Polybius frequently uses πραγματεία to describe the work of a historian (1.1.4; 1.3.1; 2.56.3; 5.33.8; 8.11.1), as does Dionysius of Halicarnassus (*Ant. rom.* 1.1.1).

Μετάφρασις and the verb μεταφράζω mean "change of expression," as in Dionysius of Halicarnassus *Thuc.* 45 and Plutarch *Dem.* 8.2, and "translate," as at Plutarch *Cat. Maj.* 19.3 and *Cic.* 40.2. Unlike "paraphrase" in English, μετάφρασις thus has no connotation of length. Since the context demands shortness, has the author deliberately chosen a general term in order to underscore that his work is on a par with that of Jason?

■ **32** The last word of the prologue, ἐπιτέμνειν ("to cut short"), is the same as the last word of the introductory sentence of the prologue in v. 23, and the substantive ἐπιτομή is found in vv. 26 and 28 to describe the author's work. Lucian of Samosata had ridiculed those whose prefaces are brilliant or quite long and whose work pales in comparison (*Hist. conscr.* 23).

General Commentary

Lucian writes that the prologue to a work should engage readers, informing them that it concerns a noble and lofty subject, that the author has done his homework, and that it will be useful to them (Dionysius of Halicarnassus *Ant. rom.* 1.1.2; Lucian *Hist. conscr.* 53–54). Our author sets out to follow this advice: his story is about the restoration of a temple renowned throughout the world. It is a story of the little guy beating the big guy. He couches the narrative as one against barbarians (2 Macc 2:21), alluding to Herodotus's description of Greek victories and barbarian defeats, particularly the defeat of the barbarians when they attacked the temple at Delphi (Herodotus 1.4; 8.37). The author puts forth Antiochus IV Epiphanes as the main protagonist in the attack against the temple, a figure well known to Egyptians on account of his invasions and to others on account of his benefactions. Our author also emphasizes his own industriousness and the trustworthiness of his source, the *five*-volume work of Jason of Cyrene. In comparing his concise version with that of the historian, he brings

---

29 It is interesting that Plutarch takes Thucydides as his model for such vividness.

to the reader's attention that the historian, that is, Jason, provided a minute presentation about every particular, paid attention to the whole structure, and took time in going over particulars. The author's work is trustworthy, for his source is trustworthy.[30] Is perhaps Polybius's use of Aratos as his source comparable to our author's use of Jason of Cyrene? (Polybius 2.37–71; books 4–5). As noted above, the author uses an abundance of terms that are frequently found in discussions by Hellenistic historians and so stakes a claim to be considered a Hellenistic historian.

Our author is in no way apologetic for his concise version. Zwick has noted that the prologue divides into two parts: first, a description of Jason's work (2:19-23a) and then, the author's description of his own work (2:23b-32).[31] In the author's eyes, this work is no CliffsNotes for Jason of Cyrene, no summary that makes reading the original unnecessary. Rather, the author insists that he is providing a vivid, memorable presentation just like a painter, one that the reader will be able to recall easily and imitate if ever he or she finds himself or herself in a similar situation. His use of rhetorical features in the prologue, for example, homoioteleuton, and the way in which he balances his sentences evidence his concern for style and its effect. Zwick reads both the description of Jason's work as full of lines with a mass of material (2:24) and the analogies that portray this work as a vivid presentation of the material as the author criticizing the work of Jason.[32]

Our author says that he is writing for all those who like to involve themselves in the stories of this history, which may hint at his history being part of a wider competitive debate over the Jews and their temple, as discussed in the Introduction. Posidonius and Apollonius Molon had written, or were writing, disparaging stories about the temple in Jerusalem and about what Antiochus IV had found inside it, and other historians like Polybius and Strabo the Cappadocian (Josephus *Ap.* 2.79, 84)[33] had written of the plundering of the temple in Jerusalem by Antiochus IV. The author is out to redress these accounts. And if, as suggested here, the narrative is written primarily along the lines of a defense by a deity of her or his temple, the intent of the author would be also to glorify the God of the Jews and the Jews' way of life.

---

30   Clare Rothschild (*Luke-Acts*, 231–40) speaks of an epitomizing rhetoric but focuses on an angle different to that adopted here.
31   Zwick, "Unterhaltung und Nutzen," 132.
32   Ibid., 132–37.

33   See also Diodorus Siculus 34.1.1–5, where Antiochus VII Sidetes is told by his advisors that Antiochus IV had found in the temple the statue of a bearded man sitting on an ass.

3

1/ When the holy city dwelt amid complete peace and the laws were maintained most admirably through the piety of Onias the high priest and his hatred of evil, 2/ the kings themselves were honoring the place and they were glorifying the temple with excellent gifts 3/ so that, for his part, Seleucus the king of Asia supplied from his own income all the expenses that were falling due for the sacrificial victims.

4/ Now Simon, of the tribe of Balgea,[a] who had become administrator of the temple, quarreled with the high priest about market regulation throughout the city. 5/ When he could not prevail over Onias, he went to Apollonius, son of Thraseas, at that time the governor of Coele-Syria and Phoenicia, 6/ and declared that the temple in Jerusalem was full of immense funds so that the excess amount could not be counted. This [excess] had no connection[b] with the account for sacrifices, but could fall under the authority of the king. 7/ In a conversation with the king, Apollonius disclosed the funds revealed to him. [The king] selected Heliodorus, the chancellor of the realm, and sent him with orders to effect the removal of the aforesaid funds. 8/ Immediately Heliodorus was on the march, in outward appearance as if to visit the cities throughout Coele-Syria and Phoenicia but in reality to accomplish the purpose of the king.

9/ When he came into Jerusalem and was welcomed by the high priest and[c] the city, he made reference to the disclosure that had been made and made clear why he was present. He was inquiring whether these things were truly like this. 10/ The high priest was pointing out that there were deposits of widows and orphans 11/ as well as some things of Hyrcanus, son of Tobias, very much a man placed in authority, [that it was] not as the impious Simon was

a   I have followed the Latin and Armenian tradition, La$^{L(X)BD}$ Arm^{txt}. The Greek manuscripts La^V Sy read *beniam(e)in*.

b   Hanhart, with q, reads προσήκειν . . . πρός; VL: προσήκειν . . . εἰς; A: προσένεγκειν . . . πρός; Latin: *pertinet ad*. The looser Syriac tradition presupposes προσήκειν as it uses "it is right, appropriate" (ܪܓ‍ܒ). I have followed the VL reading, as q seems a stylistic change to follow the normal pattern προσήκειν . . . πρός. Προσένεγκειν ("to add, to bring to") does not seem appropriate, as the subject is not expressed. While προσήκειν . . . εἰς is unusual, the preposition nicely captures the sense of the money being included in the amount.

c   "And" (καί) is found in V L′ 55 311 Latin, Syriac, and Armenian. Without it, "of the city" (τῆς πόλεως) is redundant, as Onias is by definition the high priest of the city. Its separate mention, however, underscores the widespread reception of Heliodorus. The same combination, "by Jason and the city," is found in 4:22.

accusing, and the whole total was four hundred talents of silver and two hundred of gold. 12/ [He pointed out] that it was utterly inconceivable that those who had trusted in the holiness of the place and in the majesty and inviolability of the temple honored throughout the whole world should be wronged. 13/ But the other one, because of the kingly orders he held, was saying that these things must in any event be assumed into the royal treasury. 14/ Having determined a day, he was about to enter to direct the inspection of these [funds]. There was immense anguish throughout the city. 15/ The priests threw themselves down in front of the altar in their priestly robes and were appealing heavenward that he who had legislated about deposits would preserve these [funds] intact for the depositors. 16/ Now whoever was seeing the appearance of the high priest was pierced in mind. For his face and its change of color were disclosing his anguish of soul. 17/ For a frightening bodily shudder was spread over the man by which the pain lodged in his heart became clear to all who beheld it. 18/ The men stampeded out of their houses [to take part in]^d a supplication by the whole people because the place was about to come into contempt. 19/ The married women wrapped themselves below their breasts with sackcloth and were growing in numbers throughout the streets. As for the enclosed unmarried girls, some were gathering on gate towers, others on the walls, some were looking out through the windows, 20/ and all were stretching forth their hands toward heaven and making entreaty. 21/ Pitiable were the obeisance of the diverse multitude and the anticipation of the greatly anguishing high priest. 22/ These then were appealing to the all-powerful Lord to preserve intact with total security

d Literally "toward." I have thought it necessary to supply "take part in" to give a better English meaning.

what had been entrusted for those who had trusted, 23/ but Heliodorus was intending to accomplish what had been determined.

24/ However, just as he with his bodyguards was already near the treasury, the ruler of the spirits and of every authority made a great epiphany, so that all those who had insolently come along, panic-stricken at the power of God, were changed to weak-kneed cowardice. 25/ For there appeared to them a horse adorned with gorgeous harness and a frightening rider. With a rush it shook its front hooves incessantly at Heliodorus, and the cavalier was seen to wear a golden suit of armor. 26/ There appeared to him another group of two men, remarkably strong, splendidly beautiful, and magnificently arrayed. Standing beside [him], they whipped him from each side unceasingly, inflicting many blows on him. 27/ As he suddenly fell to the ground surrounded by much darkness, they seized him and put him on a litter 28/ and carried him, who just now was entering the treasury with a large company and an entire bodyguard, helpless amid his arms, as he had learnt[e] the lordship of God. 29/ Now he through the divine activity lay prostrate, unable to speak and stripped of all hope and well-being, 30/ but they were praising the Lord who had marvelously distinguished his own place. The temple, which a short time before was full of fear and tumult, was full of joy and festivity, for the Almighty had manifested himself.

31/ Shortly, some of Heliodorus's friends were requesting Onias to appeal to the Most High and to bestow life to one utterly at his last breath. 32/ The high priest, worried that the king might judge that some villainy had been perpetrated by the Jews in the affair of Heliodorus, offered a sacrifice for the well-being of the man. 33/ As the high priest was performing the

e Reading, with Hanhart, the singular ἐπεγνωκότα, not the plural ἐπεγνωκότες, as L' 311 La[BFP].

atonement, the same young men, dressed in the same garments, appeared again to Heliodorus. They stood and said, "Be very grateful to Onias the high priest, for on his account the Lord has bestowed on you life. 34/ Now, you who were whipped by heaven, proclaim to all the majestic power of God." When they had said this, they disappeared.

35/ Heliodorus offered sacrifice and vowed large votive offerings to the one who had preserved his life; he welcomed Onias and decamped toward the king. 36/ He was bearing witness to everyone to what works of the greatest God he had been eyewitness. 37/ When the king asked Heliodorus what kind of person would be suitable to be sent once again to Jerusalem, he said, 38/ "If you have an adversary or a betrayer of the state, send him there. You will get him back whipped, if indeed he comes through safe, because a power of God is truly around the place. 39/ For the same one who possesses a heavenly domicile is overseer and helper of that place and destroys with blows those who are there intending oppression."

Commentary by Verse

■ **1** As in so many traditional stories, the narrative begins with an initial situation where everything is as it should be, everything is ideally ordered. Particularly noteworthy is the author's statement that the keeping of the laws depends on the righteousness of the high priest. Onias III, son of Simon, is the third high priest of the name Onias.[1] The author has nicely balanced the positively phrased "piety" ($\epsilon\dot{v}\sigma\acute{\epsilon}\beta\epsilon\iota\alpha\nu$) and the negatively phrased "hatred of evil" ($\mu\iota\sigma\sigma\pi\sigma\nu\eta\rho\acute{\iota}\alpha\nu$). Piety is "the beginning of all the virtues" (Philo *Decal.* 52), while "hatred of evil" is a virtue expected in officeholders from kings

down. "Hatred of evil" and the related verb, adjective, and adverb, stem from the Attic orators and become frequent in Hellenistic authors and inscriptions.[2] The author holds to the principle, stated forcefully in 5:19-20, that the inviolability of the place is secured through the holiness of the people, not the other way around, and he also emphasizes here that the holiness of the people results from good leaders. Such an idea is present also in the warning given by God to King Solomon to follow his statutes or Israel would be cast off and the temple demolished (1 Kgs 9:1-9). The history of 1 Samuel through 2 Kings reflects this ideology, for kings are classified as good or bad according to whether they follow

---

1 Josephus *Ant.* 12.156–57, 223–25; cf. 20.236–37; Sir 50:1. See the discussion in Erich S. Gruen, "The Origins and Objectives of Onias' Temple," *SCI* 16 (1997) 48–57.

2 See Louis Robert, "Sur des inscriptions d'Éphèse: fêtes, athletes, empereurs, épigrammes," *Revue de Philologie* 41 (1967) 7–84, here 12 n. 7.

God's commandments. The idyllic picture painted here in 3:1 contrasts with other descriptions of this period. While one has to be cautious about reading social history from a wisdom work such as Sirach, nevertheless Sirach's repeated emphasis on almsgiving as atoning for sin (3:30) and the frequent discussion of relationships between rich and poor (e.g., 13:15-23) suggest an imbalance in society. The pre-Maccabean writing of *1 Enoch* 1–11 also points to tensions within Judean society. The symbolic tellings of history in the Animal Apocalypse (*1 Enoch* 83–91) and in the *Damascus Document* (CD 1) suggest a time of crisis and blindness throughout Judean society, a society divided between the elect and the ungodly.

■ **2-3** συμβαίνω used impersonally can mean "to come to pass, happen," and also of consequences, "to result, follow." The author seems to suggest that the proper following of the laws results in the kings honoring the temple. The impersonal construction is frequently used by Greek historians, as by our author.[3] The construction in Greek places more emphasis on the action that follows, unlike the construction in English.

Using a nice chiastic structure (τιμᾶν τὸν τόπον καὶ τὸ ἱερὸν . . . δοξάζειν) the author enhances the idyllic quality of Judea as he describes the gifts sent by the kings for the upkeep of the temple. "Place" as a term for temples is known from the biblical period.[4] The word ἀποστολή is literally "a sending forth" and therefore gives the meaning of "something sent, a gift," as in 1 Macc 2:18 and LXX 1 Esdr 9:51, 54.

Both the Persian and the Seleucid kings had supported centers of worship, for example, at Babylon. Ezra 6:9-10 and 7:20-24 show Persian kings providing for the sacrificial cult in Jerusalem, and the Ptolemies and Seleucids had followed in this practice (Josephus *Ap.* 2.48; *Ant.* 12.50, 58, 138–44; 13.78). Given the development of the

narrative in 2 Maccabees 3, Seleucus IV Philopator must be the Seleucus envisioned here. The Heliodorus stele, which will be discussed more fully in the general commentary, certainly shows Seleucus IV taking an interest in the temples in his kingdom: "observing that nothing can obtain its appropriate good fortune without the favor of the gods."[5] Asia was commonly used to denote the stretch of the Seleucid Empire, as in 1 Macc 8:6.[6] What is particularly interesting about this initial description is that no desire for independence is voiced, nor any complaint about the Seleucid donations.

■ **4-6 Initial Problem**

The harmonious scene described in the initial verses is disturbed by a troublemaker and so begin the events of the Maccabean resistance. The disturber of the peace is a member of Judean society, of the priestly clan of Bilgah (Neh 12:5; 1 Chr 24:14).[7] The reading of the Greek manuscripts, "of the tribe of Benjamin," probably arose because "tribe" (φυλή) is most often used in the LXX of one of the twelve tribes of Israel.

The author is not concerned to go into details about the origins of the strife, and so one has only the cryptic reference to Simon's position and to the debate. That the strife was fierce is shown by the language of v. 5—Simon could not prevail, literally "conquer"—and the quarrels noted in 4:3. The term for "administrator" (προστάτης) is a general term for someone in charge of some work or group. In the LXX, there is one case that speaks of a προστάτης of the high priest (2 Chr 24:11). There this official and the king's scribe collect the taxes to repair the temple. This role in collecting funds for the temple is similar to one in Hellenistic Egypt, where the official is normally a priest. A priest of Isis, ὁ προστάτης θεοῦ, gives a receipt for taxes paid to the temple.[8] From

---

3 See 2 Macc 4:30; 5:2, 18; 7:1; 9:2, 7; 10:5; 12:24, 34; 13:7.
4 David Vanderhooft, "Dwelling Beneath the Sacred Place: A Proposal for Reading 2 Samuel 7:10," *JBL* 118 (1999) 628–30.
5 Lines 18–20 of the text as published by Hannah M. Cotton and Michael Wörrle, "Seleukos IV to Heliodorus: A New Dossier of Royal Correspondence from Israel," *ZPE* 159 (2007) 191–205, here 192. Additional fragments of the stele were then published by Dov Gera, "Olympiodoros, Heliodoros and the Temples of Koilê Syria and Phoinikê," *ZPE*

169 (2009) 125–55. Christopher P. Jones then made some helpful comments to improve the text and its interpretation: "The Inscription from Tel Maresha for Olympiodoros," *ZPE* 171 (2009) 100–104.
6 *OGIS* 54, 8; 253.
7 Schwartz (*2 Maccabees*, 95) prefers the reading of the Greek manuscripts, though with hesitation.
8 Ulrich Wilcken, *Griechische Ostraka aus Ägypten und Nubien: ein Beitrag zur antiken Wirtschaftsgeschichte* (2 vols.; Leipzig and Berlin: Giesecke & Devrient, 1899) 1:253–55.

Tebtunis in Egypt comes a petition of a προστάτης that mentions the plunder committed by Antiochus IV's soldiers (*P. Tebt.* 781). At Delphi, an office of a προστάτης τοῦ ἱεροῦ is found.[9] Simon would thus have been an important person in Judean society and one well positioned to know the finances of the temple. It is not said who appointed Simon to his position.[10] That Simon's function was connected with the collection of taxes led Gerassimos Aperghis to conclude that Simon was the king's representative.[11]

"market regulation" (ἀγορανομία). The markets in Greek cities were regulated by ἀγορανόμοι (market stewards), whose duties varied according to the city. Aristotle states that for fourth-century B.C.E. Athens, these market regulators were elected by lot and controlled the quality and genuineness of goods, as well as supervising other business associated with the market (*Ath. Pol.* 51.1). They had the power to punish and fine (Plato *Leg.* 6.764B). In Ptolemaic Egypt, the ἀγορανόμοι were also notaries and were responsible for archiving deeds and business transactions.[12] Regulation of the market was an important source of revenue for a city. The ἀγορανόμος kept the market in repair, collected the rents from leasing stalls, fixed opening and closing hours, inspected the goods for sale, and verified that the weights and measures were correct. He had to make sure enough provisions were available at a fair price, and in some cities he could fix prices.[13] In a temple city such as Jerusalem, particularly at the major festivals, regulation of the market would have been extremely important, especially when one considers purity requirements for animals. Disagreement

about such matters appears, for example, between the different requirements found in the *Temple Scroll* from Qumran and the decree of Antiochus III. The decree forbade in Jerusalem the skins only of unclean animals (Josephus *Ant.* 12.146), whereas the *Temple Scroll* demanded that the only animal hides allowed in Jerusalem be those from animals sacrificed in Jerusalem (11QT 47.7–18). Restrictions on the supply of skins would raise their price. The exact cause of the friction between Onias and Simon is unknown, but market prices and the income derived therefrom could always generate factions.

■ **5** Otherwise unknown, this Apollonius was some relation, possibly a brother, of the Ptolemy, son of Thraseas, who was originally in the service of the Ptolemies (Polybius 5.65.3) but later became governor of Coele-Syria and Phoenicia for the Seleucids. Frank Walbank suggested that the reference here is to Ptolemy, son of Thraseas, and that the name has been confused with that of Ptolemy's successor, Apollonius, son of Menestheus.[14] The Heliodorus stele enabled Dov Gera to provide a list of the governors of Coele-Syria and Phoenicia: Ptolemy, son of Thraseas, was governor in 195 B.C.E., and Gera surmises that he was succeeded by his brother, Apollonius, son of Thraseas; in 178 B.C.E. Dorymenes was governor of this satrapy, and he was succeeded by Apollonius, son of Menestheus; in 167 B.C.E., Ptolemy, son of Menestheus, presumably was governor (6:8) and certainly was in 165 B.C.E. (8:8; 1 Macc 3:38).[15] Accordingly, Gera holds that the author of 2 Maccabees deliberately specified which Apollonius "in order to defame a certain Apollonius son of Thraseas."[16] However, the

9   Georges Daux, *Delphes au IIe et au Ier siècle depuis l'abaissement de l'Etolie jusqu'à la paix romaine 191–31 av. J.-C.* (Paris: Boccard, 1936) 433.

10 On the use of καθίστημι for appointing, see the comment in Hannah Cotton, "The Guardianship of Jesus Son of Babatha: Roman and Local Law in the Province of Arabia," *JRS* 83 (1993) 94–108, here 95. See also *OGIS* 56, 73–74.

11 Gerassimos G. Aperghis, *The Seleukid Royal Economy: The Finances and Financial Administration of the Seleukid Empire* (Cambridge: Cambridge University Press, 2004) 285, 287.

12 Hans Julius Wolff, *Das Recht der griechischen Papyri Ägyptens in der Zeit der Ptolemäer und des Prinzipats* (2 vols.; HA 10.5; Munich: Beck, 1978) 2:8–27.

13 For this job description, I have drawn on A. H. M. Jones, *The Greek City from Alexander to Justinian*

(Oxford: Clarendon, 1940) 215–17. For an example of its importance for the economic condition of a city, see William H. Buckler, "Labour Disputes in the Province of Asia," in William H. Buckler and William M. Calder, eds., *Anatolian Studies Presented to Sir William Mitchell Ramsay* (Manchester: Manchester University Press, 1923) 27–50. Also Daniel Sperber, "On the Office of the Agoranomos in Roman Palestine," *ZDMG* 127 (1977) 227–43.

14 Frank W. Walbank, *A Historical Commentary on Polybius* (3 vols.; Oxford: Clarendon, 1957–79) 1:592.

15 Gera, "Olympiodoros," 141–44. See also Dov Gera, "Philonides the Epicurean at Court: Early Connections," *ZPE* 125 (1999) 77–83.

16 Gera, "Olympiodoros," 142.

motivation for such defamation is unstated and, given that the narrative has been condensed, it is unlikely to be uncovered. Gera appears to assume that the events described on the Heliodorus stele (see below) were the cause of whatever happened in 2 Maccabees 3. As the text explicitly says that Apollonius, son of Thraseas, was governor at that time, it is possible that an attempt to confiscate some of the temple treasury took place before Dorymenes became governor of the satrapy. Heliodorus, after all, was chancellor from 187 to 175 B.C.E. At this time, the king still needed money to pay the indemnity owed to Rome. The reorganization of the satrapy could be in response to a first, failed attempt at getting money out of the temple. The structure of the narrative of 2 Maccabees suggests that the events of 2 Maccabees 3 took place not long before the death of Seleucus V (4:7), but the text does not give a timeline for the growing tensions in Jerusalem narrated in 4:1-6. Simon's accusation of Onias III in 4:1 would have some basis if the appointment of Olympiodorus was the result of an earlier failed attempt to get money from the temples in Coele-Syria and Phoenicia.

Originally, Coele-Syria referred to the long depression that ran southward from between the Lebanon and Anti-Lebanon along the Jordan valley to Aqaba and the Red Sea, but it came to cover, with Phoenicia, the area between Egypt and Cilicia.

■ **6** προσαγγελίαι were criminal denunciations.[17] Excess amount is literally "amount of differences." Τὸ διάφορον ("difference") came to mean "amount over, balance" and could mean simply "ready money." In this context, it signifies the excess beyond what was required for the sacrifices.

In an extremely influential article, Elias Bickerman proposed that Simon was appointed to his position by the Seleucid government and that his report to the Seleucid governor concerned the fact that Seleucus IV had sent money to Jerusalem to pay for the sacrificial services (3:3), but that the priests had not spent all of it and the balance would have belonged to the king.[18]

Bickerman was right to point to the interpretation of τῶν διαφορῶν as "excess amount," but this reading is too narrowly focused. His statement that καθεσταμένος does not simply mean "appointed" but indicates that Simon was a Seleucid appointee claims too much. The context must determine who appoints. While in Egypt the ἀγορανόμος was a Ptolemaic appointee,[19] in Jerusalem he may not have been a Seleucid appointee. No context is given in 3:4. Further, Bickerman implies that a superintendent (ἐπιστάτης) of a temple is the same as a προστάτης of a temple, and he imports the Ptolemaic bureaucratic system, where an ἐπιστάτης was a paid official. However, the ἐπιστάτης could also be the high priest (ἀρχιερεύς) of a temple.[20] The use of the participle καθεσταμένος indicates that the position was not hereditary and that Simon obtained it,[21] not that Simon was a Seleucid official. One might even argue from the context of inner-city rivalry—the use of "to prevail, conquer" (νικῆσαι) in 3:5 and "contentiousness" (φιλονεικία) in 4:4—that Simon was not a Seleucid official but a leader of a faction against the high priest.

As for the second part of Bickermann's argument, on the money sent to the temple, the text distinguishes between what pertains to the account for sacrifices and the rest of the money in the temple, not between the amount Seleucus IV gave and the amount the priests spent. As Goldstein noted, the rest of the story concerns Heliodorus's attempt to confiscate any monies deposited in the temple, not just the extra amount Seleucus might have given. The ironic twist of Simon's story is that Seleucus IV is paying for the sacrifices when there is plenty of money available in the temple. Simon appeals to Seleucus IV not as a tight-fisted auditor but as someone who wants to lay his hands on as much money as possible. His father, Antiochus III, died pillaging a temple, and Seleucus's brother Antiochus IV would play the same game.

■ **7-8** The author enlarges the importance of the event by having the king send the royal chancellor, Heliodorus; most probably the high priest of the satrapy, Olympiodo-

---

17 Ulrich Wilcken and Ludwig Mitteis, *Grundzüge und Chrestomathie der Papyrusurkunde* (2 vols.; Leipzig: Teubner, 1912) 2:21.
18 Bickerman, "Héliodore," 159–91.
19 Wolff, *Das Recht*, 2:14.
20 *OGIS* 56, 73. See Walter Otto, *Priester und Tempel im hellenistischen Ägypten* (2 vols.; Leipzig: Teubner, 1908) 2:72, 243–44, 312–13.
21 At Delphi, the position of προστάτης τοῦ ἱεροῦ seems to have been annual; see Daux, *Delphes*, 433.

ros, would have been sent.[22] Heliodorus is known from an inscription as the son of Aeschylos from Antioch. He was brought up with Seleucus and placed as chancellor of the realm (σύντροφος βασιλέως Σελεύκου τεταγμένος δὲ καὶ ἐπὶ τῶν πραγμάτων).[23] Heliodorus himself dedicated some valuable vases to Apollo at Delos.[24] He is reported to have assassinated Seleucus IV in September 175 and may have attempted to gain the throne (Appian *Syr.* 45). However, Édouard Will has argued that the speed of Antiochus IV's change from being a hostage in Rome to regaining the throne with help from Pergamon indicates a carefully laid-out plot by Rome and Pergamon to replace Seleucus with Heliodorus, an unsuspecting dupe.[25]

The verb for "on the march" (ἐφοδεύειν) has the sense in the Tebtunis papyri of inspecting various areas or of a police officer patrolling fields near his village.[26] The μὲν ... δέ construction emphasizes the duplicity of Heliodorus.

■ 9-13 First Confrontation

The author emphasizes the gracious welcome[27] afforded to the chancellor by the high priest and the city and so underscores the cordial relations noted in 3:3. To this he juxtaposes the brusque declaration of the real purpose of the visit. The noun "disclosure" (ἐμφανισμός) refers back to the verb in v. 7, where the governor discloses (ἐμφαίνειν) the matter to the king. The noun also sounds similar to the term for "outward appearance" (ἔμφασις)

in v. 8. At first, however, Heliodorus asks simply for a verbal clarification and response to the accusation. These the high priest provides.

■ **10** The first part of the high priest's answer is that part of the money in the temple consists of deposits of widows and orphans—money was placed in a temple for safekeeping. For Heliodorus to abscond with such a temple deposit would be a serious affront to Jewish tradition (Philo *Spec. leg.* 4.30–32; Josephus *Ant.* 4.285).[28] Since widows and orphans are frequently portrayed as the neediest in society[29] and most in need of protection,[30] it is surprising that they have deposits in the temple large enough to be noticed. There are at least three possible interpretations. If the genitive is objective, these are deposits on behalf of widows and orphans that the temple authorities can dispense when needed. If the genitive is subjective, that is, widows and orphans deposit the money, this could be either a rhetorical ploy to suggest how heinous taking the money would be and that it will be avenged (Exod 22:22-24; Deut 10:18; Ps 68:5) or evidence of widows inheriting their husband's wealth as, for example, had Judith, who had been left gold and silver, male and female slaves, livestock, and fields (Jdt 8:7; Sir 22:4).[31] Job 24:3 presupposes that an orphan could own a donkey, and a widow an ox.

■ **11** Scholars have latched onto the reference to Hyrcanus's having left money in the temple. From Josephus we know of one Hyrcanus, son of Joseph, son of Tobias (*Ant.* 12.186–222, 228–236), one of the characters in the

22 Gera, "Olympiodoros," 149.

23 *IG* XI 4 (1914), nos. 1112–14; *OGIS* 247.

24 Félix Dürrbach, *Choix d'inscriptions de Délos* (Paris: E. Leroux, 1921–22) 95–96.

25 Will, *Histoire politique*, 2:256–57.

26 *P. Tebt.* 703.40-411 (a steward sent out to inspect various departments of the royal revenues); 788.15 (an official sent to the nome by the sovereigns); 730.1 (police officer). Polybius 6.35.9–36.1 speaks of troops being sent out to check up on the sentinels. See also Pierre Roussel, "Un reglement militaire de l'époque macédonienne," *RArch* series 6, 3 (1934) 39–47.

27 In a letter of 182 b.c.e. from Eumenes II to a Carian city, the king asks the city to receive his envoys kindly (φιλοφρόνως). Welles, *Royal Correspondence*, no. 49.6. See also the discussion at Welles, *Royal Correspondence*, 316.

28 See Jerzy Linderski, "Sacrilegium," in *Brills New Pauly* (2008) 12:855; Wilhelm Schubart,

"Παρακατατίθεσθαι in der hellenistischen Amtssprache," *Philologische Wochenschrift* 52:1077–84.

29 See 2 Macc 8:28; Deut 14:29; 24:17; Job 24:3; Tob 1:8.

30 See Deut 27:19; Isa 1:17, 23; Jer 7:6; 22:3; Ezek 22:7; Zech 7:10; Ps 94:6.

31 See Bickerman, "Héliodore," 169–70; Tal Ilan, *Jewish Women in Greco-Roman Palestine: An Inquiry into Image and Status* (TSAJ 44; Tübingen: Mohr, 1995) 167–74; Hannah Cotton, "The Law of Succession in the Documents from the Judaean Desert Again," *SCI* 17 (1998) 115–23.

larger story of the Tobiads (*Ant.* 12.154–222, 228–36). The story, replete with folktale motifs,[32] tells of the rise to power of a clever young man, Joseph, son of Tobias, in opposition to a niggardly older relation, the high priest Onias, of the unusual birth of Joseph's son Hyrcanus, and of the replacement of Joseph by this clever son. It ends with the suicide of Hyrcanus, when faced with the might of Antiochus IV. Joseph became rich as collector of taxes for the Ptolemies, and in this he was followed by Hyrcanus, who is thus a client of the Ptolemies. There is bad blood between Hyrcanus and his brothers, who try to kill him and succeed in ousting him from Jerusalem to the Transjordan at the site now called ʿArāq el-Emīr. A second story involving the Tobiads has them battling for power with the high priest Onias (Josephus *Bell.* 1.31–33). Expelled from Jerusalem, they went to Antiochus IV and persuaded him to invade Jerusalem. The framing of this second story in terms of rival Ptolemaic and Seleucid groups has colored much of the discussion of 3:11. Josephus's dating of the Tobiad story is hopelessly muddled, but scholars have tried to find a kernel of history within it. One can say that Josephus portrays the small city-state of Jerusalem as riven by factions and at least in the second story sees these factions as pro-Ptolemaic and pro-Seleucid. Scholars have imported Josephus's categories into the narrative of 2 Maccabees 3, so that the presence in the temple of deposits from Hyrcanus, son of Joseph, evidences a pro-Ptolemaic bias on the part of the high priest.[33] Such a reading of 2 Maccabees through the mention of Hyrcanus distorts the whole chapter. This text is not a reliable report of an actual conversation between Heliodorus and Onias. It is embedded in a story that belongs to stories that tell of an epiphanic deliverance of a city by its tutelary deity. One has to be very cautious about attempting to reconstruct a whole political debate from this type of material. Second Maccabees 3 is concerned to show the unity of the Jerusalemite community, apart from the wicked Simon (δυσσεβής ["impious"], as opposed to the εὐσέβεια ["piety"] of Onias in

3:1), and stresses the cordial relations with the Seleucid government. As the high priest attempts to convince Heliodorus that Simon is wrong, it would be a grave rhetorical mistake to say that the money of a notorious anti-Seleucid, pro-Ptolemaic rebel is in the temple and to characterize that rebel as a man of very high position in Jewish society. Goldstein recognizes how these circumstances would weaken Onias's case but argues that the reference to Hyrcanus must have been inserted into the telling by the later Onias IV, an admirer of Hyrcanus and pro-Ptolemaic. Rather than resort to this solution, I suggest that either the name of Hyrcanus the Tobiad carried a certain aura of richness and power even if the details of his history were not known, like the name of Midas for gold, or this Tobiad Hyrcanus is not Hyrcanus, son of Joseph. Scholars have consistently read "Hyrcanus, son of Tobias," as referring not to the name of the actual father of Hyrcanus but to his family name,[34] or have emended the text so that Tobias becomes an alternate name for Hyrcanus: Ὑρκανοῦ τοῦ καὶ Τωβίου.[35] The most obvious reading is that the actual father of Hyrcanus was someone called Tobias. To identify the Hyrcanus of 3:11 with the Hyrcanus of Josephus's story is to jump to conclusions based on the slimmest prosopographical evidence and evidences a desire to synthesize what little evidence we have.

Onias also refutes Simon by showing that the money is not so immense that it cannot be counted but is rather a precise, if not small, amount. If one takes the ratio of gold to silver to be roughly 1:10 (see Livy 38.11.8), the value of the gold and silver in the treasury would be equivalent to twenty-four hundred talents of silver. The Seleucid annual tribute to Rome after the treaty of Apamea was one thousand talents of silver (Polybius 21.42.9), which suggests that the Jerusalem amount was not insignificant. There is no recorded grant of asylum by the Seleucids to the temple in Jerusalem, although Philo later uses the term (Philo *Leg Gaj.* 43). Kent Rigsby

32 Susan Niditch, "Father–Son Folktale Patterns and Tyrant Typologies in Josephus' *Ant.* 12:160–222," *JJS* 32 (1981) 47–55.

33 Martin Hengel, *Judaism and Hellenism: Studies in Their Encounter in Palestine During the Early Hellenistic Period* (2 vols.; Philadelphia: Fortress, 1974) 1:272–77; Victor Tcherikover, *Hellenistic Civilization and the Jews* (Philadelphia: Jewish Publication Society, 1959) 138–39.

34 See Eduard Meyer, *Ursprung und Anfänge des Christentums* (2 vols.; Stuttgart: J. G. Cotta, 1925) 2:134 n. 1.

35 Tcherikover, *Hellenistic Civilization*, 461 n. 49.

argues that no specific grant of immunity is in play here, only a general sense that temples should be immune.[36]

The appeal of the high priest runs from v. 10 through v. 12 and is a genitive absolute construction. In v. 12 the parallelism between τόπος and ἱερόν is kept as in 3:1: there the place is honored (τιμᾶν) whereas here the temple is honored (τετιμημένου). The response of the chancellor is the main clause of the sentence, and the particle δέ underlines the contrast between the position of Onias and that of Heliodorus. The argument of the high priest is brushed aside, and the author makes clear the realpolitik of the situation—the king wanted the money. Τὸ βασιλικόν is a technical term for the royal treasury.[37]

■ **14-23 Second Confrontation**

The whole scene is carefully contrived. Heliodorus starts out on his mission, where the imperfect tense of the verb denotes the beginning of an action.[38] In the LXX, ἐπίσκεψις also means "numbering" (Num 1:21; 1 Chr 21:5; 23:34). C. Bradford Welles suggests also "audit."[39] "Immense" is literally "not small." The understatement of the litotes, οὐ μικρά, intensifies the emotion. Reference is made to the anguish of the whole city (v. 14b), which is then broken down into groups—priests and high priest (vv. 15-17), men (v. 18), married women (v. 19a), unmarried women (vv. 19b-20). The language of v. 15 is picked up again in v. 21 (v. 15: ἦν . . . ἀγωνία; v. 21: ἐλεεῖν δ' ἦν . . . ἀγωνιῶντος ἀρχιερέως) before the final summation of the events by a μέν . . . δέ construction in vv. 22-23. The language of the first part of this summation, the μέν section, resonates with that of v. 15. Both v. 15 and v. 22 have the verb "were appealing" (ἐπεκαλοῦντο); both have forms of the verb διαφυλάσσειν; and both contain wordplays: v. 15 "deposits . . .

depositors" (παρακαταθήκης . . . παρακαταθεμένοις) and v. 22 "entrusted . . . trusted" (πεπιστευμένα τοῖς πεπιστευκόσι), where the same perfect participial construction is used as in the refutation of Simon's charge in v. 12 (τοὺς πεπιστευκότας).[40] The corresponding δέ in v. 23 uses the imperfect as in v. 14 to describe Heliodorus attempting to accomplish his purpose. Throughout, the unity of the city against Heliodorus is emphasized, a unity based on following the laws laid down by God, the legislator (τὸν . . . νομοθετήσαντα) as in 3:1. The emotional description of the people's anguish might be compared with Philo's description of the anguish at the news that Gaius Caligula was to set up a statue in the temple (Philo *Leg. Gaj.* 223–44).[41] This section clearly demonstrates the author's intention to involve the audience in the action, as he highlights the tragic emotions. In v. 18, "stampeded" is literally "rushed out like a herd." "To rush out" (ἐκπηδάω) is used in Esth 4:1 to describe Mordechai's rushing into the streets when he hears of the decree Haman has drawn up against the Jews. Note how the omission of the article before ὁρῶντα in v. 16 would include the author's audience.[42] Polybius rails against Phylarchus for his description of the plight of the Mantineans when their city was taken by the Macedonians and the Achaeans: "In [Phylarchus's] eagerness to arouse the pity [ἔλεον] and attention of his readers, he treats us to a picture of clinging women with their hair disheveled and their breasts bare, or again of crowds of both sexes together with their children and their aged parents weeping and lamenting as they are led away into captivity" (2.56.7).[43]

The classification of roles in the description of the population is interesting. The priests in their formal attire form a distinct group with the most attention, two verses, given to describing the grief of the high

---

36   Kent J. Rigsby, *Asylia: Territorial Inviolability in the Hellenistic World* (Hellenistic Culture and Society 22; Berkeley: University of California Press, 1996) 527–31. See also Henri Seyrig, "Antiquités syriennes. 24: Les rois séleucides et la concession de l'asylie," *Syria* 20 (1939) 35–39.

37   See Welles, *Royal Correspondence,* 321.

38   Smyth, *Greek Grammar,* §1900.

39   Welles, *Royal Correspondence,* 335.

40   The same play on forms of πιστεύειν is found in Xenophon *Sym.* 8:18; Isocrates *Ad Dem.* 30.

41   See also the mourning in Joel 2:16-17.

42   The same verb, ἐμφαίνειν ("disclose"), is used in v. 16 and in the disclosure of the funds by Apollonius (v. 7) and Heliodorus's reporting of his mission (v. 9).

43   See also the description of piteous crowds at the funeral of Demetrius, attributed to Duris of Samis, and found in Plutarch *Demetr.* 53.

priest, which is comparable to the description that Josephus gives of the high priest Jaddus as he learns of the approach of Alexander (Josephus *Ant.* 11.326: ἐν ἀγωνίᾳ καὶ δέει, "in an agony of fear"). The males participate in the public (πάνδημον) supplication (v. 18), while the married women express their grief with bared breasts and sackcloth around their waists, symbolizing their role as childbearers. The contrast between the two groups of women in v. 19 narrows the meaning of γυναῖκες to "married women." In the Hebrew Bible, men frequently gird themselves with sackcloth (Gen 37:34; Jonah 3:6; Isa 15:3; Esth 4:1), but here the signs of mourning are kept for the women (see Jer 9:17-22).[44] This gendered distinction reflects the author's view that men played a public role but the role of women was in the private sphere. The implication is that women should throng the streets only when there is public mourning (cf. Philo *Spec. leg.* 3.169–77).[45] The use in v. 20 of the indirect middle voice of ποιεῖσθαι after the previous three active verbs underscores the action of the women.

Does the distinction reflect a view, found so frequently in Philo and elsewhere in male-centered Greek literature, that men are more rational, women more emotional? The role of the final group, the unmarried but nubile women, also reflects the author's sense that the unmarried women should not be present in public. That the unmarried women gather at the doorways and peek through the windows shows their desire to be part of the communal lamentation. One should note that these notions of public and private spheres have been challenged by recent work on the lives of women in antiquity,[46] but the author of 2 Maccabees presents a male-centered ordering of reality.

■ **20** Hands outstretched is the classic stance for prayer, as in 1 Tim 2:8 and in the figures of the orant in late antique and early Christian art.[47]

■ **21** I have taken the phrase τὴν τοῦ πλήθους παμμιγῆ πρόπτωσιν to be an example of hypallage, where the adjective παμμιγῆ should really agree with the genitive πλήθους rather than the accusative πρόπτωσιν, with which it grammatically agrees. The sentence nicely balances the multitude with the high priest.

■ **23** The imperfect is a conative imperfect, emphasizing the attempted action.[48]

■ **24-31 Defense of the Temple**

The first epiphany in the narrative contains expected motifs—the golden armor and the handsome young men, the stupor of the one to whom the epiphany occurs (v. 25), and the thanksgiving (v. 30). Bickerman has noted well the statuesque image of the reared horse with flashing hooves and its place in Greek art.[49] Xenophon observed how such an image transfixes and how the gods and the heroes were depicted on rearing horses (*Eq.* 11.8). As for the young men, there are often two in this kind of epiphany (Justin 20.3.8; Dionysius of Halicarnassus *Ant. rom.* 6.13). In the *Genesis Apocryphon*, Pharaoh is whipped by an angel when he approaches Sarah (1QapGen 20.10–18; see also *Gen. Rab.* 40.2). Whipping by angels is found in later Christian literature (Eusebius *Hist. eccl.* 5.28.12).[50] To be whipped was humiliating (Prov

44 In Joel 1:8, a young girl is girded with sackcloth at the death of her husband.

45 The intransitive use of πληθύνω, which I have translated as "growing in numbers," instead of the usual intransitive use of πληθύω, seems to have increased in the Hellenistic period.

46 Sarah B. Pomeroy, *Goddesses, Whores, Wives, and Slaves: Women in Classical Antiquity* (New York: Schocken, 1975); eadem, *Women in Hellenistic Egypt: From Alexander to Cleopatra* (New York: Schocken, 1984); Mary R. Lefkowitz and Maureen B. Fant, *Women's Life in Greece and Rome* (Baltimore: Johns Hopkins University Press, 1982); Ross Shepard Kraemer, *Maenads, Martyrs, Matrons, Monastics: A Sourcebook on Women's Religions in the Greco-Roman World* (Philadelphia: Fortress Press, 1988); eadem, *Her Share of the Blessings: Women's Religions among Pagans, Jews, and Christians in the Greco-Roman World* (New York: Oxford University Press, 1992).

47 According to Robin Margaret Jensen, "The orant is a universal and popular figure of late antique art, almost always shown as a veiled woman, standing, facing front, gazing heavenward, with her hands outstretched and slightly lifted" (*Understanding Early Christian Art* [New York: Routledge, 2000] 35).

48 See Smyth, *Greek Grammar*, §1895.

49 Bickerman, "Héliodore," 178–79.

50 Also in the Syriac *Life of Simeon Stylites*: see Robert Doran, *The Lives of Simeon Stylites* (Cistercian Studies Series 112; Kalamazoo: Cistercian, 1992) 147.

26:3). In classical Greece, only slaves were whipped, although there were exceptions (Pausanias 6.2.2; Aristophanes *Ach.* 723).[51] In the Hellenistic period, citizens were flogged (Polybius 15.28.1).[52] The Hebrew Scriptures stipulated that no more than forty lashes were to be given, as otherwise the person would be degraded (Deut 25:1-3; see also Josephus *Ant.* 4.238). The unceasing flogging of Heliodorus until he fainted suggests complete degradation. Heliodorus is punished on the spot rather than being driven away to receive his punishment later.

Scholars have suggested that this scene does not hang together. The horse and his rider are not mentioned again; the action is carried only by the two young men. On the grounds that this verse is missing in part of the Latin manuscript tradition, Peter Katz suggested that it was an interpolation,[53] but as the verse is found in the rest of the manuscript tradition, this proposal seems a last resort to solve a problem. A source-critical solution was elaborated by Bickerman[54] who, followed by Goldstein, suggested that there were two sources behind the account, one in which the god/goddess appears to all and defeats the adversary and the faithful praise the deity, and one in which the person to whom the god/goddess appears recognizes the power of the god/goddess. Of particular importance to Bickerman was that there are two times when Heliodorus is said to have fallen, in v. 27 and in v. 29. In v. 28, the followers of Heliodorus carry him off the scene, and yet in v. 29 he is still said to be lying prostrate. For Bickerman and Goldstein, v. 28 is incompatible with v. 29. Having noticed this duality, Bickerman then assigned the verses of the narrative to one of two sources: vv. 24-25, 27-28, and 30 are attributed to source A and vv. 26, 29, and 31-34 to source B. The difficulty with this reconstruction is that in the present form of the text, vv. 29-30 are welded together by a μὲν . . . δέ construction. Goldstein recognized this, and so his source A consists of vv. 24-25 and 29-30, and his source B of vv. 26-28 and 31-36. Goldstein did not address the reasons that led Bickerman to place vv. 27-28 in his first source. Bickerman saw a close linguistic connection between v. 24 and v. 28: v. 24, δορυφόροις and v. 28, δορυφορίας; v. 24, γαζοφυλάκιον and v. 28, τὸ προειρημένον . . . γαζοφυλάκιον; v. 24, δυνάστης and v. 28, δυναστείαν. In fact, the whole section from v. 24 through v. 30 is tightly connected. For Bickerman and Goldstein, the one exception is the contrast between the imperfect "they carried" (ἔφερον) in v. 28 and the pluperfect "lay prostrate" (ἔρριπτο) of v. 29. I suggest that this contrast is not there. Bickerman and Goldstein both assume that v. 29 is speaking of Heliodorus lying prostrate in the very same spot. But Heliodorus, stretched out on a litter, is still prostrate. He cannot stand up or move around by himself. The effects of his being thrown down are still felt. In v. 31, Heliodorus is reported to be lying absolutely on the point of his last breath. There thus seems no contradiction between the action of Heliodorus's attendants, who carry him off stretched out on a litter, and the resumptive pluperfect description of him in v. 29 as lying prostrate. If there is no linguistic basis for source analysis, one is left with the attempt by Bickerman and Goldstein to argue that there are two types or forms of an epiphany that cannot be together. But pure forms do not exist and that an author cannot combine elements from different types of stories to create his own more striking version seems too restrictive. The attack on Heliodorus is such a unified account, wherein both the fearsome power of the god/goddess is shown and the punishment inflicted on the attacker recounted. As for the fact that the horse and rider are not mentioned again after v. 25, this would seem to be another touch to

---

51 Plato suggested that neglect of parents deserved whipping (*Leg.* 932B).

52 Actors who do not act the part of the gods worthily were to be whipped (Lucian *Pisc.* 33). See the examples of the whipping of slaves in Franciszek Sokolowski, *Lois sacrées des cités grecques* (Travaux et mémoires 18; Paris: Boccard, 1969) nos. 37, lines 9–10; 84, line 16; 115, line 6; 149, line 6. Of particular interest is no. 65, lines 39–43, an inscription from Andania from 92 B.C.E. on the regulation of the mysteries: "Whenever the sacrifices and the mysteries are being celebrated, all [are] to keep reverent silence [εὐφαμεῖν] and to listen to the instructions [τῶν παραγγελλομένων]; but whoever refuses compliance or behaves toward the divinity in an unseemly manner, let the priests whip him and keep him away from the mysteries."

53 Katz, "Text of 2 Maccabees," 19.

54 Bickerman, "Héliodore," 172–87.

heighten the divine character of the repulse. When the Persians are repulsed by Apollo in their attack on Delphi (Herodotus 8.36–38), weapons mysteriously appear before the temple of Apollo, but no use is made of them later. One should not suppose another account in which Apollo puts on these arms to rout the Persians. So here, the horse and rider should be seen as part of the vivid spectacle the author is creating.

■ **24** "the ruler of the spirits and of every authority." LXX Num 16:22 and 27:16 have the title "God of the spirits and of all flesh" ($\vartheta\epsilon\grave{o}\varsigma$ $\tau\hat{\omega}\nu$ $\pi\nu\epsilon\nu\mu\acute{a}\tau\omega\nu$ $\kappa\alpha\grave{i}$ $\pi\acute{a}\sigma\eta\varsigma$ $\sigma\alpha\rho\kappa\acute{o}\varsigma$). The title "Lord of the spirits" is found altogether 104 times in *1 Enoch*, for example, in *1 Enoch* 37:2-4; 38:4; 39:2, 7. In Heb 12:9, the title is "Father of spirits."

"Ruler" ($\delta\upsilon\nu\acute{a}\sigma\tau\eta\varsigma$) is a favorite term of the author for God, found in 12:25, 28; 15:3, 4, 29. It is also found in *3 Macc* 2:3; 5:51; 6:59. In the LXX, the term is found in Gen 49:24; Job 36:22; Sir 16:11; 46:5-6, 16. God is also called the sole ruler in *Sib. Or.* 3.719, and the term is found in 1 Tim 6:15.

"every authority." The phrase is found in 1 Cor 15:24: "after he has destroyed every rule and every authority [$\pi\hat{a}\sigma\alpha\nu$ $\dot{\epsilon}\xi\upsilon\sigma\acute{i}\alpha\nu$] and power." See also Eph 1:21; Col 1:16; 2:10, 15; 1 Pet 3:22. The term may also be present in *1 Enoch* 41:9 and perhaps in *1 Enoch* 61:10.

"great epiphany." The author promised to speak of the epiphanies of God (2:21). A decree from Olymos speaks of the $\mu\epsilon\gamma\acute{a}\lambda\alpha\varsigma$ $\dot{\epsilon}\pi\iota\varphi\alpha\nu\epsilon\acute{i}\alpha\varsigma$ connected with Leto, Apollo, and Artemis.[55]

"insolently come" ($\tau\upsilon\grave{v}\varsigma$ $\kappa\alpha\tau\alpha\tau\upsilon\lambda\mu\acute{\eta}\sigma\alpha\nu\tau\epsilon\varsigma$). The same verb is used in 5:15 to describe Antiochus IV's entrance into the temple.

"Weak-kneed cowardice" is a hendiadys and is literally "to weakness and cowardice."

■ **25** "Incessantly" is literally "fluidly, abundantly."

■ **26** It is not clear whether only Heliodorus sees the two young men. His attendants have run away, and only he is left.

■ **27-28** Rather than see the word "suddenly" ($\ddot{a}\varphi\nu\omega$) as inappropriate because the horse and rider have already appeared, one should see it as referring to Heliodorus's keeling over all of a sudden after being whipped. See, for example, Acts 28:6, where, after Paul has been bitten by a snake, the onlookers want to see if he will swell up or fall down dead all of a sudden.

"To be surrounded by darkness" poetically captures the closeness of death. See 2 Kgdms 1:9 and also Euripides *Phoen.* 1453.

There is no change of subject between v. 26 and v. 27, and so one must see the two young men as carrying Heliodorus away from the treasury.

Those punished by a god learned to recognize his power. See, for example, Sophocles *Ant.* 960. The second participle, $\dot{\epsilon}\pi\epsilon\gamma\nu\omega\kappa\acute{o}\tau\alpha$, which is asyndetic, expresses the reason for the preceding helplessness of Heliodorus.

■ **29-30** Another $\mu\grave{\epsilon}\nu$ ... $\delta\acute{\epsilon}$ construction contrasts Heliodorus with the citizens. "Activity" ($\dot{\epsilon}\nu\acute{\epsilon}\rho\gamma\epsilon\iota\alpha$) is used of God by Aristobulos (Eusebius *Praep. ev.* 8.10.12), and in the Wisdom of Solomon, Wisdom is the unspotted mirror of the $\dot{\epsilon}\nu\acute{\epsilon}\rho\gamma\epsilon\iota\alpha$ of God (Wis 7:26).[56]

"marvelously distinguished" ($\pi\alpha\rho\alpha\delta\upsilon\xi\acute{a}\zeta\upsilon\nu\tau\alpha$). The term is used of God acting marvelously on Israel's behalf (Exod 8:22; 9:4; 11:7; Wis 19:5) and against them (Deut 28:59; Sir 10:13). God also works marvelously on behalf of the righteous (Wis 5:2). The participle $\dot{\epsilon}\pi\iota\varphi\alpha\nu\acute{\epsilon}\nu\tau\upsilon\varsigma$ ("manifested, epiphanizing") resonates with $\dot{\epsilon}\pi\iota\varphi\acute{a}\nu\epsilon\iota\alpha$ of v. 24. The Almighty ($\pi\alpha\nu\tau\upsilon\kappa\rho\acute{a}\tau\omega\rho$) harks back to the adjective $\pi\alpha\gamma\kappa\rho\alpha\tau\acute{\eta}\varsigma$ in v. 22.

■ **31-36 The Healing of Heliodorus**
The narrative continues with another appearance of the two young men, a healing miracle during the cult, and the recognition by Heliodorus of the power of the god in Jerusalem. As noted in the general commentary, such recognition of divine power is found in Greek narratives of epiphanies, as, for example, in the Lindos Chronicle. In the Hebrew Scriptures, Nebuchadnezzar and Darius proclaim the God of Israel after miracles (Dan 2:47; 3:28-29; 4:37; 6:25-27), and the motif is also found in the Additions to Daniel (Bel 41-42). Naaman the Syrian confessed God after being healed by Elisha (2 Kgs 5:1-19). All these stories of important officials recognizing the God of Israel evidence a desire of the Israelites, particularly those in exile, to have non-Israelites respect their religion.

---

55   *SEG* 39 (1988) no. 1135, line 5.
56   For a monistic use of the term, see Pseudo-Philolaus in Hermann Diels, *Die Fragmente der Vorsokratiker:* *Griechisch und Deutsch* (3 vols.; Berlin: Weidmann, 1922) 1:248, lines 7–8 [B no. 21].

■ **31** As with most miracle stories, the healer has to be approached. In this case, the high priest as mediator with the God of Israel is approached. "Most High" (ὕψιστος) as a title for God is found in Hellenistic Jewish literature: in Ezekiel the tragic poet (Eusebius *Praep. ev.* 9.29.14); in Philo the epic poet (Eusebius *Praep. ev.* 9.24); in Wis 5:15; 6:3, in *3 Macc* 6:2; 7:9, and frequently in the LXX;[57] and also in Josephus (*Ant.* 16.163). It was widely used as a title by both Jews and Gentiles.[58]

The same verb, ἐπικάλειν, is used here, when Onias is asked to pray for Heliodorus, and at vv. 15 and 22, when the priests and people prayed for the protection of the temple.

■ **32** The tricks of priests were often pointed out. In the second prefixed letter to 2 Maccabees, their machinations in the death of Antiochus IV were noted (1:15-16). The story of Bel and the Dragon shows priests being caught in their attempt to deceive, and Lucian of Samosata mocks the false god and the tricks set up by Alexander of Abonuteichos (*Alex.* 6–17). Philo speaks of those who did not believe the biblical marvels (*Vit. Mos.* 1.212; see also Dionysius of Halicarnassus *Ant. rom.* 2.68.1–2). Our author notes here the possibility of construing the event as priestly trickery not only as an authentication that a miracle did occur but also to prepare for the conversation between Heliodorus and Seleucus (vv. 37-39) and, more importantly, to set the stage for the further machinations of Simon (v. 32: "villainy" [κακουργίαν]; 4:1: "speaking evilly" [ἐκακολόγει]). Here one begins to note the breakdown of the trust between the Seleucid emperor and the Jews (3:2-3).

The sacrifice that Onias offered for Heliodorus is not specified. Brazen, high-handed affronts were punishable by death (Num 15:30-31), and deliberate sins had to be confessed (Lev 5:5). The request by the friends of Heliodorus, who cannot speak, must be seen as such an acknowledgement of guilt. The high priest would have offered an expiatory sacrifice, but whether it was a whole burnt offering (Leviticus 1) or the more specific reparation offering for deposits (Lev 6:1-7; Num 5:5-10) is not specified. In Num 5:8, the offering is called a ram of atonement (τοῦ κριοῦ τοῦ ἱλασμοῦ δι᾽ οὗ ἐξιλάσεται) and Onias performs an atonement (v. 33: τὸν ἱλασμόν). It does not seem to have been a purificatory offering, for the sanctuary had not been defiled.

■ **33-35** Heliodorus probably offered a sacrifice of thanksgiving (Lev 7:12-14; 22:29) and promised future offerings. An interesting case of a mediator praying on behalf of others is found in Exod 32:10-14. There God threatened to destroy Israel, but Moses interceded, using as an argument the worry that the Egyptians spread false stories about God (Exod 32:12). So God was propitiated (ἱλάσθη) to preserve (περιποιήσαντι) his people, just as God here preserves the life of Heliodorus.

The author uses paronomasia in v. 33 (χάριτας . . . κεχάρισται) and v. 35 (εὐχὰς . . . εὐξάμενος).

When Heliodorus had been warmly welcomed (ἀποδεχθείς) to Jerusalem by the high priest (3:9), he had brusquely responded with the purpose for his visit. Now he welcomes (ἀποδεξάμενος) Onias before returning to the king.

■ **36** The reality of the epiphany is underscored—Heliodorus had been an eyewitness (ὑπ᾽ ὄψιν). God is called "the greatest" (ὁ μέγιστος) in the Greek Addition at Esther 8:13, in Eupolemos (Eusebius, *Praep. ev.* 9.31), in *Ep. Arist.* 19, 37, and in *3 Macc* 3:11; 5:25.

■ **37-39** With the question to Heliodorus, the author hints that Seleucus still wants to get hold of the money. Heliodorus warns that a second inspector might not get off as he had done. As in 3:1, the term τόπος (place) is used. Given that the king's question was whom he should send to Jerusalem (3:37), the term appears to embrace the city and not just the temple.

"With blows" is literally "striking, smiting."

God is called "overseer" (ἐπόπτης) also in 7:35 and "all-overseeing" (παντεπόπτης) in 9:5.[59] The word reso-

---

57   Genesis 14:18-19; Num 24:16; Deut 32:8; 2 Kgdms 22:14; Pss 7:17; 12:6; Isa 14:14; Dan 3:26; 4:14; 5:18, 29; 1 Esdr 2:3; Jdt 13:18; Sir 4:10.

58   See G. Bertram, "ὕψιστος," *TDNT* 8 (1972) 614–20; Arthur Darby Nock, "The Guild of Zeus Hypsistos," in idem, *Essays on Religion and the Ancient World* (ed. Zeph Stewart; 2 vols.; Cambridge, Mass.: Harvard University Press, 1972) 1:414–43; A. Thomas Kraa-bel, "*Hypsistos* and the Synagogue at Sardis," *GRBS* 10 (1969) 87–93; Herbert Niehr, *Der höchste Gott: Alttestamentlicher JHWH-Glaube im Kontext syrisch-kanaanäischer Religion des 1. Jahrtausends v. Chr.* (BZAW 190; Berlin: de Gruyter, 1990).

59   See also LXX Esth 5:1; *Ep. Arist.* 16; *3 Macc* 2:21; *4 Macc* 5:13.

nates with Exod 2:25, where God saw the sons of Israel. The image of the all-seeing eyes of the Lord is common in biblical tradition.[60] God as the helper ($\beta o \eta \vartheta \acute{o} \varsigma$) of Israel had earlier rendered Heliodorus helpless (v. 28: $\dot{\alpha}\beta o \acute{\eta}\vartheta\eta\tau o\varsigma$). As noted earlier, given that Heliodorus later assassinated Seleucus (Appian *Syr.* 45), the author seems to be making a sly joke about the interaction between the two when Heliodorus says that Seleucus should send an enemy to Jerusalem.

General Commentary

This first event in the condensed version evidences the author's stylistic traits. There is evidence of shortening: the reader is not told exactly who Hyrcanus and Tobias are, and v. 35 ends with a cryptic reference to Heliodorus welcoming Onias before decamping. The narrative itself is full of stylistic devices. There is paronomasia, repetition of the same root to make connections, in v. 15, $\pi\alpha\rho\alpha\kappa\alpha\tau\alpha\vartheta\acute{\eta}\kappa\eta\varsigma \ldots \pi\alpha\rho\alpha\kappa\alpha\tau\alpha\vartheta\epsilon\mu\acute{\epsilon}\nu o\iota\varsigma$; in v. 22, $\tau\grave{\alpha}\ \pi\epsilon\pi\iota\sigma\tau\epsilon\upsilon\mu\acute{\epsilon}\nu\alpha\ \tau o\hat{\iota}\varsigma\ \pi\epsilon\pi\iota\sigma\tau\epsilon\upsilon\kappa\acute{o}\sigma\iota$; and in vv. 33 ($\chi\acute{\alpha}\rho\iota\tau\alpha\varsigma \ldots \kappa\epsilon\chi\acute{\alpha}\rho\iota\sigma\tau\alpha\iota$) and 35 ($\epsilon\grave{\upsilon}\chi\grave{\alpha}\varsigma\ \mu\epsilon\gamma\acute{\iota}\sigma\tau\alpha\varsigma\ \epsilon\grave{\upsilon}\xi\acute{\alpha}\mu\epsilon\nu o\varsigma$). He uses unusual words: $\varphi\rho\iota\kappa\alpha\sigma\mu\acute{o}\varsigma$ (v. 17); $\dot{\alpha}\gamma\epsilon\lambda\eta\delta\acute{o}\nu$ (v. 18). He maintains the unity of the narrative by the repetition of the same root throughout, using, for example, variations on the verb "to appear" ($\varphi\alpha\acute{\iota}\nu\epsilon\iota\nu$): v. 9, $\dot{\epsilon}\mu\varphi\alpha\nu\iota\sigma\mu\acute{o}\varsigma$; v. 16, $\dot{\epsilon}\nu\acute{\epsilon}\varphi\alpha\iota\nu\epsilon$; v. 24, $\dot{\epsilon}\pi\iota\varphi\acute{\alpha}\nu\epsilon\iota\alpha\nu$; v. 25, $\dot{\epsilon}\varphi\alpha\acute{\iota}\nu\epsilon\tau o$; v. 26, $\pi\rho o\epsilon\varphi\acute{\alpha}\nu\eta\sigma\alpha\nu$; v. 28, $\varphi\alpha\nu\epsilon\rho\hat{\omega}\varsigma$; v. 30, $\dot{\epsilon}\pi\iota\varphi\alpha\nu\acute{\epsilon}\nu\tau o\varsigma$; v. 33, $\dot{\epsilon}\varphi\acute{\alpha}\nu\eta\sigma\alpha\nu$; and v. 34, $\dot{\alpha}\varphi\alpha\nu\epsilon\hat{\iota}\varsigma$. By this repetition, he intensifies the sense of providing a spectacle. He also stresses the power of God through repetition of the root for "power" ($\kappa\rho\acute{\alpha}\tau o\varsigma$): v. 22, $\pi\alpha\gamma\kappa\rho\alpha\tau\hat{\eta}$; v. 34, $\kappa\rho\acute{\alpha}\tau o\varsigma$; and v. 30, $\pi\alpha\nu\tau o\kappa\rho\acute{\alpha}\tau\omega\rho$. Of particular interest is the way he binds the narrative together through the use of the root "to maintain, preserve" ($\tau\eta\rho\acute{\epsilon}\omega$): in 3:1, $\sigma\upsilon\nu\tau\eta\rho o\upsilon\mu\acute{\epsilon}\nu\omega\nu$; and in 3:40, $\tau\acute{\eta}\rho\eta\sigma\iota\nu$.[61] The author enjoys contrasts. Of the five uses of the $\mu\grave{\epsilon}\nu \ldots \delta\acute{\epsilon}$ construction, three are contrastive (vv. 8, 22, and 29) while the other two are associative (vv. 19 and 26). The author also interweaves scenes. For example, Heliodorus begins to enter the treasury in v. 14 and this action is picked up again in v. 23, after a long description of the emotional reaction to Heliodorus's movement to the treasury. Here one sees how the author concentrates on the emotional struggle of Heliodorus with Onias and the inhabitants of Jerusalem. The reader is not given any detail about the precise cause of the quarrel between Simon and Onias. The dispute between Onias and the Seleucid minister is over money, and the author exploits that element in stressing that the money mainly belongs to orphans and widows, those whom society should most help. The author is not interested in detailing Heliodorus's journey to Jerusalem (v. 8) or his departure (v. 35b). He does not inform the reader about Seleucus's reaction to Heliodorus's advice. All is concentrated on the emotional confrontation between Onias and Heliodorus and the sudden reversal of fortune for Heliodorus. His concern is to "win the souls" (2:25: $\psi\upsilon\chi\alpha\gamma\omega\gamma\acute{\iota}\alpha$) of his audience. He also seeks to persuade his audience that they should observe the law. The author stresses in the opening line of the narrative that the temple was secure because the laws were maintained through the piety of the high priest. The temple is protected because of that piety and that observance of the laws.

The unified narrative conforms to the general pattern of a deity's defense of his/her temple: the attackers approach, the defenders ask the deity for help, the deity responds, the attackers are repulsed, and the defenders rejoice. There are many examples of this type of narrative, such as the story told on a Babylonian clay tablet from around the second half of the sixth century B.C.E. of the repulse of Kuturnaḫḫunte, king of Elam, by Enlil and the other gods when the king and his official tried to take a diadem from the temple at Nippur.[62] The defense of Delphi by Apollo against marauding Persians in 480 B.C.E. (Herodotus 8.35–39) and against the Gauls in 279 B.C.E. (Pausanias 10.23.2; Justin 24.8.3; Diodorus Siculus

---

60 See 2 Chr 16:9; Job 34:21; Ps 14:2; 66:7; Prov 15:3; Zech 4:10; 9:1 LXX.

61 See also the use of the verb $\pi\epsilon\rho\iota\chi\acute{\epsilon}\omega$ in vv. 17 and 27; $\dot{\epsilon}\pi\iota\kappa\alpha\lambda\acute{\epsilon}\omega$ in vv. 15, 22, and 31; $\mu\alpha\sigma\tau\iota\gamma\acute{o}\omega$ in vv. 26, 34, and 38.

62 Niels Stockholm, "Zur Überlieferung von Heliodor (2 Makk. 3), Kuturhaḫḫunte, und anderen missglückten Tempelraübern," *StTh* 22 (1968) 1–22.

22.9) are further cases, as is the defense of Panamaros by Zeus Panamaros.[63] The citizens of Chersonesus honored a local historian, Syriskos, for his history, in which he placed particular emphasis on how Athena had helped the city.[64] Within the biblical tradition is found the repulse of Sennacherib from Jerusalem at the time of King Hezekiah, when the Lord sent an angel to destroy the Assyrians (2 Chr 32:1-22; 2 Kgs 18:17–19:36).

The narrative does not end with the repulse of the attackers but continues on to tell of the recognition of God's power by Heliodorus. There are other instances of such witness in 2 Maccabees: in 8:36, Nikanor proclaims God's sovereignty, and in 9:17, Antiochus IV promises to do so if he lives. The account of Heliodorus is similar in this respect to the Lindos Chronicle,[65] in which the citizens are said to have been delivered by a miraculous intervention of Athena from a siege led by the Persian naval commander Datis. The Lindos Chronicle has the Persian fleet stymied and their leader proclaim the greatness of Athena before sailing on. Datis and his fleet later took part in the battle at Marathon; Heliodorus later assassinated Seleucus IV.

Does the telling of the survival of Heliodorus intimate that the author knew the later story of the assassination of Seleucus IV by Heliodorus? If so, this would suggest that the author indulges in sly humor in the conversation between Seleucus and Heliodorus that ends this narrative. Heliodorus advises the king that if he has an enemy, he should send him to Jerusalem to be whipped, if not worse. Heliodorus, as the future assassin of Seleucus, had just had such a whipping. He will indeed be an enemy of and traitor to Seleucus.

The Heliodorus stele has now thrown new light on this episode. In 178 B.C.E., Seleucus IV appointed Olympiodorus to take responsibility for the sanctuar-ies (ἱερά) in Coele-Syria and Phoenicia. On the basis of the parallels with the letters of Antiochus III concerning the choice of Nikanor as high priest and the king's appointment of high priestesses for the cult of Laodike, the king's wife, Gera argued that Olympiodorus was appointed high priest of the satrapy of Coele-Syria and Phoenicia,[66] a position with which Christopher Jones agrees.[67] This reform was intended to make this satrapy similar to the rest of the Seleucid Empire. As Hannah Cotton and Gera both emphasize, this new administrative structure may have been seen by the Jerusalem temple authorities as a threat, but also by some, perhaps Simon, as an opportunity for advancement.[68] As Gera notes, it "is likely that the Seleukid official who confronted the Jerusalem authorities was in fact Olympiodoros, and not Heliodoros. . . . Onias III should not be given orders by a pagan high priest."[69] The author of 2 Maccabees, however, did not pursue this confrontation. Olympiodorus was middle-level management, and the author preferred to intensify the situation by having the chancellor of the empire confront God. As noted in the comment on v. 5, Gera's position presupposes that the event of 2 Maccabees 3 is a replacement for a visit by Olympiodorus to gain money after his appointment in 178 B.C.E., in which case the author of 2 Maccabees 3 was wrong in stating explicitly that the governor at the time was Apollonius, son of Thraseas. As we do not know the exact time line of the events surrounding Seleucus IV's attempts to obtain money from temple treasuries in Coele-Syria and Phoenicia, one should be cautious. If Gera's assumption is correct, this could be a fascinating example of how an economic issue can, when transposed into narrative form, morph into a full-blown story of how the deity defends his/her temple.

---

63 "Roussel, "Le miracle," 70–116. For a fuller list, see Jan N. Bremmer, "Close Encounters of the Third Kind: Heliodorus in the Temple and Paul on the Road to Damascus," in *Empsychoi Logoi: Religious Innovations in Antiquity. Studies in Honour of Pieter Willem van der Horst* (Leiden: Brill, 2008) 367–84, here 375.

64 *FGH* 807 T1.

65 *FGH* 532.

66 Gera, "Olympiodoros," 139.

67 Jones, "Inscription," 104.

68 Cotton and Wörrle, "Seleukos IV," 203; Gera, "Olympiodoros," 148–49.

69 Gera, "Olympiodoros," 148–49.

3   3:40—4:6

40/ **In this way the events relating to Heliodorus and the preservation of the treasury turned out, 4:1/ but the previously mentioned Simon, an informer about the money and against his homeland, was speaking evilly about Onias, how he had both stirred up Heliodorus and been the author of evils. 2/ He was daring to say that the benefactor of the city, the protector of his kindred and zealous follower of the laws, was a plotter against the state. 3/ The enmity grew to such an extent that murders were perpetrated by one of those approved by Simon. 4/ When Onias saw the severity of the contentiousness and that Apollonius, son of Menestheus, the governor of Coele-Syria and Phoenicia, was helping increase the evil that Simon did, 5/ he crossed over to the king. He was not becoming an accuser of the citizens, but was keeping in mind the public and private interests of the entire group. 6/ For he saw that, without the king's provision, it would be impossible for the state still to obtain peace and Simon to cease his folly.**

Commentary by Verse

■ **3:40** This verse begins a $\mu\grave{\epsilon}\nu$ ... $\delta\acute{\epsilon}$ construction that binds the repulse of Heliodorus to the further developments of the narrative. The author is fond of using this means of connecting events, as in 7:42–8:1 and 10:9-10. He also likes to end narratives with the construction "so ... to turn out" ($o\check{\upsilon}\tau\omega\varsigma$ ... $\chi\omega\rho\acute{\epsilon}\omega$) as in 13:26 and 15:37. In 7:42 and 10:9, he uses a different verb with the adverb.

"treasury." This word links back to the opening claim by Simon (3:6) as well as to Heliodorus's attempt to enter the treasury (3:24, 28).

"preservation." The verbal root of this noun ($\tau\acute{\eta}\rho\eta$-$\sigma\iota\nu$) was used in 3:1 to describe how the laws were maintained ($\sigma\upsilon\nu\tau\eta\rho\acute{\epsilon}\omega$) under Onias.

■ **4:1** The action of Simon is depicted as not only concerned with money but also a betrayal of the fatherland. Here begins the theme of the defense of the fatherland ($\pi\alpha\tau\rho\acute{\iota}\varsigma$)[1] and of the ancestral laws ($\pi\acute{\alpha}\tau\rho\iota o\iota\ \nu\acute{o}\mu o\iota$; see 6:1; 7:2, 37). Defeated by Onias, Simon tries another tactic. In this verse, the presence of the root "evil" ($\kappa\alpha\kappa\acute{o}\varsigma$) in the verb "speak evilly" ($\kappa\alpha\kappa o\lambda o\gamma\acute{\epsilon}\omega$) and in the description of Onias as the author of evils, $\tau\hat{\omega}\nu\ \kappa\alpha\kappa\hat{\omega}\nu\ \delta\eta\mu\iota o\upsilon\rho\gamma\acute{o}\varsigma$,[2] resonates with the worry of Onias in 3:32 that the king might think the Jews had perpetrated some villainy ($\kappa\alpha\kappa o\upsilon\rho\gamma\acute{\iota}\alpha\nu$) against Heliodorus. The verb used here, $\grave{\epsilon}\pi\iota\sigma\epsilon\sigma\epsilon\iota\kappa\acute{\omega}\varsigma$, which I have translated "stirred up,"

---

1   See 5:8, 9, 15; 8:21, 33; 13:3, 11, 14; 14:18.
2   Euripides *Frag.* 1059, line 7, describes woman as "author of evils" ($\delta\eta\mu\iota o\upsilon\rho\gamma\grave{o}\varsigma\ ...\ \kappa\alpha\kappa\hat{\omega}\nu$).

literally means "to shake at," as one brandishes a weapon against someone to frighten that person. Usually the one threatened is in the dative, whereas here Heliodorus is in the accusative. Goldstein rightly noted that the verb with the accusative usually means "to incite, to stir up" as in Judg 1:14; 1 Kgdms 26:19; 2 Kgdms 24:1; and 1 Chr 21:1. Schwartz attempted to avoid this difficulty by suggesting that one emend the text so that the verb ἐνσείω be used rather than ἐπισείω, and he points to the frequent use of ἐνσείω in 2 Maccabees: 3:25; 12:15, 37; 14:46. However, Schwartz does not evade the difficulty, for in all these cases, the person attacked is in the dative case.

Goldstein concluded that Simon is accusing Onias before the citizens of Jerusalem of having provoked Heliodorus to rob the temple treasury, much as the former high priest Onias had been undiplomatic in his dealings with the Ptolemies about paying taxes and had been replaced by Joseph the Tobiad (Josephus *Ant.* 12.172). Goldstein is right to see the slander as inner-Jerusalem factional fighting, as the enmity in 4:3-4 shows, rather than as another accusation made to the Seleucid government. Rather than tying the accusation to a time before Heliodorus tried to enter the treasury,[3] I suggest that Simon is raising concern about what Heliodorus will do once he returns to Antioch. The reader knows that Heliodorus proclaims God's sovereignty and that another attempt should not be made on the treasury (3:36-39), but this fact would not have been known to Simon's audience. Simon, as a clever politician, thus plays on the fears of his audience. Is the use of the verb ἐπισείειν ("to stir up"), which resonates with the verb used in 3:25, ἐνέσεισε, to describe the shaking of the horse's hooves at Heliodorus, even a snide attack on the epiphany? Simon is arguing that Heliodorus might have been rebuffed once, but that he will return. Such an argument downplays the power of God to defend his temple. As noted in the general comment on 3:5, we do not have a specific time line for these events. If a failed attempt to gain the temple treasury led to the reorganization of the satrapy and the appointment of Olympiodorus as high priest of the temples of Coele-Syria and Phoenicia in 178 B.C.E.,

Simon could have claimed that the actions of Onias III had prompted such a reorganization.

■ **2** The titles "benefactor" and "protector" are often found in honorific inscriptions for rulers of cities: for example, a famous doctor is called "the benefactor of the fatherland" (εὐεργέτην τῆς πατρί[δ]ος),[4] and in a popular demonstration in honor of the ruler of a city, the ruler is called "the protector for the city" (κηδεμόνα τῇ πόλι) (*P. Oxy.* 41.13, 26). Tarkondimotus is honored in Cilicia as τὸν εὐεργέτη[ν] καὶ κηδεμόνα τοῦ δήμου ("the benefactor and protector of the people").[5] Onias's zeal for the law had been noted in 3:1. In 1 Macc 2:26-27, Mattathias is said to be zealous for the law, and he calls on all those zealous for the law to follow him. In Acts 21:20, James tells Paul that the Jews who have become followers of Jesus are all zealous for the law. The use of the plural "the laws" here echoes the plural use in 3:1. In 4:16, the priests are said to emulate/be zealous for (ἐζήλουν) the training of the Greeks.

"plotter against the state." This description is also used of the kind of person Heliodorus suggests to the king be sent to Jerusalem where he will be humiliated (3:38). The high priest Alcimus also accuses Judas Maccabeus of being a plotter against the kingdom (14:26).

■ **3** In 3:4-6, Simon seemed to work alone. Here he is pictured as head of a faction. The unity of the city, so dramatically depicted in 2 Maccabees 3, has broken down, and the violence of factional strife has emerged. We do not know how long this factional violence lasted. "The evil that Simon did" is literally "the evil of Simon." The genitive is a genitive of origin.

■ **4** "saw." The verb συνορᾶν is frequently used by the author (2:24; 5:17; 7:4, 20; 8:8).

"Apollonius, son of Menestheus." In 3:5, Simon was able to gain access to the governor of Coele-Syria, but here he is openly supported by his successor. According to 4:4, 21, this Apollonius served under both Seleucus IV and Antiochus IV. He is most likely the ambassador of Antiochus IV to Rome in 173 B.C.E. (Livy 42.6.6). Polybius reports that an Apollonius who had been in high favor with Seleucus IV had removed to Miletus; that is,

---

3   Such a position is tied to the view that the mention of Hyrcanus, son of Tobias, in 3:11 would have been an affront to the Seleucid minister. See comment on 3:11.

4   *SIG*³ 804.14.

5   *OGIS* 752. See Danker, *Benefactor;* and Tessa Rajak, *The Jewish Dialogue with Greece and Rome: Studies in Cultural and Social Interaction* (AGJU 48; Leiden: Brill, 2001) 373–91.

he had left the service of Antiochus IV when Antiochus IV acceded to the throne (31.13.3).[6] Otto Mørkholm suggested that "succession" here refers to the murder of Seleucus IV's son, co-regent with Antiochus IV from 175 to 170 B.C.E. and that Apollonius's break with Antiochus IV therefore came after the events of 4:4, 21.[7] Apollonius's sons later became adherents of Demetrius I, the brother of the murdered son of Seleucus IV (Polybius 31.13.2). Goldstein cautioned that the family mentioned in Polybius may be a branch of a large influential family and that one need not necessarily identify the Apollonius of 4:4, 21 with the one mentioned by Polybius.

The audience is not told why Apollonius, son of Menestheus, has a different view from that of the previous governor of Coele-Syria. The Heliodorus stele shows that Seleucus V had instigated a new policy toward the sanctuaries in Coele-Syria and Phoenicia.

■ **5-6** "crossed over." In the passive voice, διακομίζω means "to cross over." This sense is found in 9:29 and *3 Macc* 1:9. It has the connotation of moving into foreign territory. The use of ὡς as a preposition is unusual.[8]

The author uses all the devices he can to show Onias as devoted and high-minded, concerned only about the welfare of his fellow citizens and not at all ambitious for his own position. The terminology for "public and private" is well known from inscriptions. John Ma has noted how it is a trope "used in civic decrees to describe past εὐεργεσίαι, or by royal letters in future promises: benefaction extends both to the public sphere and to individuals, each of whom ideally benefits from the benefactions."[9] Onias holds that the state will not be at peace while Simon is around, just as Alcimus holds that the state will not be at peace while Judas Maccabeus is around (14:10). Alcimus also appeals to the providential care of the king (14:9), for the king is seen as the guarantor of law and order.[10] The "provision" (πρόνοια)[11] of the king is contrasted aurally with Simon's folly (ἄνοια). The idea of futurity is stressed when talking of Onias's appeal about Simon, and so the future participle is used.

Literally the text reads "not receiving an end of his folly." Onias's appeal to the king suggests that Onias was well aware of how to play hardball politics and of how to get rid of Simon. One hears nothing of how his attempt to gain an audience went. He would have had a formidable opponent in the courtier Apollonius. When next seen, Onias is in Antioch, the royal seat. Perhaps he had resided there since leaving Jerusalem.

General Commentary

This section is transitional in that it has many verbal links to 2 Maccabees 3 but also to later events in 2 Maccabees 4. Simon is prominent in 3:4-7 and in this section but disappears, never to be heard of again in the narrative except as the brother of Menelaus (4:23). The visit of Heliodorus is mentioned in this section, and the "peace" of 3:1 is now still to be sought in 4:6. "Betrayer of the state" in this section both continues its use in 3:38 and looks forward to the description of Menelaus in 4:50 as betrayer. The description of Onias in 4:2 as caring only for the citizens resonates with the desire of the envoys unjustly killed in 4:48 to stand up for the city and the commons. The evil of Simon in 4:4 is legalized in Menelaus in 4:50 as citizens are killed. The envoys speak justly (δικαιολογίαν) against Menelaus in 4:44 but are unjustly condemned to death, whereas the evil-speaking Simon (4:1: ἐκακολόγει) is not punished.

The section is full of contrasts: the informer Simon remains in the city with the backing of the Seleucid governor; the pious protector of his people is called the author of the city's evils and leaves the city. Onias will not return to Judea until he comes in a dream to Judas Maccabeus, and he is depicted as praying for the whole army of the Jews (15:12). When Onias leaves the city, the city loses peace and from now on will be wracked with war until, in the author's opinion, Onias's prayers are answered with Judas's victory over the Seleucid general Nikanor (15:37).

---

6 For detailed references, see Walbank, *Polybius*, 3:323–24, 481.

7 Otto Mørkholm, *Antiochus IV of Syria* (Classica et mediaevalia, dissertationes 8; Copenhagen: Gyldendal, 1966) 38–50.

8 Smyth, *Greek Grammar*, §§1702, 3003. It is found also in *4 Macc* 4:5 and Josephus *Ant.* 18.273.

9 John Ma, *Antiochus III and the Cities of Western Asia Minor* (Oxford: Oxford University Press, 1999) 188.

10 Wilhelm Schubart, "I. Aufsätze. Das hellenistische Königsideal nach Inschriften und Papyri," *Archiv für Papyrusforschung und verwandte Gebiete* 12 (1937) 8.

11 On "provision/forethought" in benefactor inscriptions, see Danker, *Benefactor*, 359–60.

4

4:7/ **When Seleucus died and Antiochus called Epiphanes succeeded to the kingdom, Jason
the brother of Onias obtained
the high priesthood fraudulently 8/ as he offered to the
king through a petition 360
talents of silver and 80 talents of some other revenue.
9/ Besides these [amounts],
he was promising to pay also
another 150 talents, if he were
allowed**ᵃ **by [the king's] authority to establish a gymnasium
and ephebic training for [the
king] and to inscribe the Antiochenes in Jerusalem. 10/ When
the king assented and [Jason]
gained possession of the office,
he immediately changed his
kinsfolk toward the Hellenic
type. 11/ He was despoiling the
royal privileges established for
the Jews through John, father
of Eupolemos, who served on
the embassy for friendship and
alliance toward the Romans. He
was annulling legitimate citizen
practices and introducing new,
unlawful usages. 12/ For he
gladly laid out a gymnasium
under the very acropolis. He
put the strongest of the young
men under the broad-brimmed
hat and trained [them]. 13/ Such
was the so-called flowering of
Hellenism and the growth of
foreign ways because of the
excessive impurity of the impious and fake high priest Jason
14/ that the priests were no
longer eagerly engaged in the
services of the altar. Slighting
the temple and neglecting the
sacrifices, they were hasten-
ing to take part in the unlawful
practices of the wrestling area
after the summons of the gong.
15/ They held the ancestral
honors of no account but reck-
oned the Hellenic distinctions
the most noble. 16/ Because of
these [opinions], a painful cir-
cumstance encompassed them:
those whose training they were
emulating and were wanting
to assimilate completely, they
ended up having as enemies
and avengers. 17/ For it is no
light matter to be impious
toward the divine laws, but the**

a   The major difficulty occurs with the verb ἐπιχορηγηθῇ. q and L′ mainly read ἐπιχωρηθῇ,
συγχωρηθῇ with the meaning "he was allowed,"
the more usual verb for a king granting permission.
See, for example, the correspondence between
Eumenes II and the Tyriaions wherein he is asked
to grant (ἐπιχωρηθῆναι) them a city constitution
(πολιτείαν) and the use of their own laws as well
as a gymnasium (Lloyd Jonnes and Marijana Rici,
"A New Royal Inscription from Phrygia Paroreios:
Eumenes II Grants Tyriaion the Status of a *Polis*,"
Epigraphica Anatolica 29 [1997] 1–30, here 3–4). The
more difficult reading, which Hanhart accepts, is
ἐπιχορηγηθῇ as ἐπιχορηγέω does not mean "to
allow, grant, concede, etc." but "to supply, furnish."
The root form is χορηγέω, "to lead a chorus" and,
eventually, "to defray the cost of bringing out the
chorus." The χορηγός was the person who defrayed
the costs. The context here is not a question of
Antiochus IV paying for the construction of the
gymnasium, and so I judge that the form usually
found in such requests, ἐπιχωρηθῇ, be read.

18/ period of time about to follow will make these things clear. When the quinquennial games were held in Tyre and the king was present, 19/ Jason the polluted sent envoys as Antiochenes[b] from Jerusalem to convey 300 drachmas of silver toward the sacrifice to Herakles. However, even the conveyers thought fit not to use the money for a sacrifice because it was not appropriate, but to employ it toward another expense. 20/ These [monies] were paid, as far as the sender was concerned, toward the sacrifice to Herakles, but, because of the conveyers, toward the fitting out of the triremes.

21/ After Apollonius, son of Menestheus, was sent to Egypt for the inaugural festival[c] of King Ptolemy Philometor,[d] Antiochus, realizing that [Ptolemy][e] had become unfavorably disposed toward his empire, was taking heed for his own security. So he came to Joppa and went down to Jerusalem. 22/ Lavishly welcomed by Jason and the city, he was admitted with a pageant of torches and acclamations. So then he took up quarters in Phoenicia.

b   Hanhart follows q in reading Ἀντιοχέας, the older classical form of the accusative plural, rather than Ἀντιοχεῖς with V L' 55 311.

c   The Greek manuscripts read both πρωτοκλήσια and πρωτοκλίσια, which Abel accepts and which Habicht prefers because of its appearance in an inscription from Delos. See Félix Dürrbach, Pierre Roussel and Marcel Launey, *Inscriptions de Délos* (7 vols.; Paris: H. Champion, 1925–) vol. 4, §1520, lines 32–34. See the commentary on the verse.

d   Most manuscripts have only the epithet "Philometor," while the Armenian translation has only the name "Ptolemy." However, L 311 La^LVP read Ptolemy Philometor. As Habicht notes, the fuller reading is most likely, as, except at 10:13, 2 Maccabees has both the individual name and the epithet. However, both kings had been fully named just prior to this verse (9:29; 10:10), while Ptolemy Philometor is first mentioned in 4:21.

e   By using the pronoun "him," the grammar could suggest that Apollonius is meant, but clearly Ptolemy is understood.

Commentary by Verse

■ **7-8** "Died" is literally "exchanging life." The phrase was originally used of heroes who as immortals did not die but changed their states. By the second century B.C.E., it was simply a euphemism for "die."[1]

The author does not concern himself with the details of Seleucus IV's death and the rise to power of his brother Antiochus IV Epiphanes. Seleucus IV died on 2/3 September 175 B.C.E.[2] According to Appian *Syr.* 45,

he was assassinated by his minister Heliodorus. Scholars have seen the assassination as part of a plot by Rome and Eumenes II of Pergamon to rid themselves of an opponent.[3] Eumenes II certainly sent Pergamene forces to escort Antiochus IV and was thanked officially by the Athenians for helping Antiochus gain power.[4] Part of the conspiracy was seen in the replacement of Antiochus as a hostage in Rome by Seleucus's son Demetrius, but this event took place before 178/177 B.C.E., when Antiochus was in Athens,[5] and so the plot would have

1   See Welles, *Royal Correspondence*, 348.

2   Abraham J. Sachs and Donald J. Wiseman, "A Babylonian King List of the Hellenistic Period," *Iraq* 16 (1954) 202–12, here 204, 208.

3   See Will, *Histoire politique*, 256–57; Walbank, *Polybius*, 3:284–85.

4   *OGIS* 248; see Maurice Holleaux, "Un prétendu

décret d'Antioche sur l'Orient," in idem, *Études d'épigraphie et d'histoire grecques* (ed. Louis Robert; 6 vols.; reprinted, Paris: Boccard, 1952–68) 2:127–47.

5   Stephen V. Tracy, "Greek Inscriptions from the Athenian Agora Third to First Centuries BC," *Hesperia* 51 (1982) 57–64, here 61–62.

had to be long in gestation. Rather, Heliodorus seems to have acted on his own motives and placed himself as guardian of the young son of Seleucus IV, a boy named Antiochus.[6] Eumenes acted on Antiochus IV's behalf to end the tensions between the Seleucid and Attalid kingdoms.[7] Antiochus IV ascended the throne before 22/23 September 175 B.C.E.[8] It seems that Antiochus, son of Seleucus IV, was on the throne before Antiochus IV's arrival and remained co-regent until his execution in October 170 B.C.E.[9] The title "Epiphanes" appears on the second series of tetradrachm coins issued by Antiochus IV, which Otto Mørkholm dates to 173/172 B.C.E.; he emphasizes that the title means little more than "illustrious."[10] Jochen G. Bunge dates the coins earlier and sees the title as a cult title.[11]

At his accession, a new king would appoint or confirm rulers in their positions (see 1 Macc 11:24-27, 57-58). Onias's brother seizes the opportunity to outbid his brother. The verb ὑπονοθεύω, which I have translated "obtain fraudulently," literally means "to seduce." Josephus reports that Jason's name was Joshua (Ἰησοῦς) (*Ant.* 12.238), but the author of 2 Maccabees uses only the Greek name.[12]

■ **8** Josephus recounts, in contradiction to this verse and to 4:34, that Jason was given the high priesthood by Antiochus IV when Onias died and that it was Menelaus and the Tobiads who sought to build a gymnasium in Jerusalem (*Ant.* 12.238–41).

The author likes to form numbers by giving one number + πρός with another number in the dative. Sometimes he places the smaller number first with the larger in the dative, as here and in 4:9; 5:21; 11:11, and sometimes the larger number first, as in 5:24; 8:22; 10:31; 11:11; 12:20.

Bickermann argued that the taxes were ordinarily 300 talents of silver, but this position is far from certain.[13] The 360 talents presumably came from regular taxation sources in Judea, but where the extra talents were to come from is unknown. Did Jason promise to pay 440 talents per year, or 360 as regular tribute and the 80 as a onetime event? The former would seem to be a heavy increase in taxation for the tiny province of Judea. According to *4 Macc* 4:17, Jason promised 3,660 talents.

"petition." Similar to this request of Jason was the request of the people of Teos in 205–201 B.C.E. that their city and its land be recognized as sacred, inviolable, and tax free, a request that the kings of Athamania granted.[14]

■ **9** The author shows that he is not primarily interested in the details so important to modern historians but rather in driving home his negative image of what Jason did. He spends eight verses (4:10-17) attacking the results of Jason's action and only one convoluted verse saying what Jason actually did. This one verse has given rise to much speculation.

This extremely complicated conditional clause has been translated in various ways:

Abel: "si on lui accordait d'établir de sa propre autorité un gymnase et une éphébie et de dresser une liste des Antiochéens de Jérusalem."

Habicht: "wenn ihm zusätzlich gewährt würde, in eigener Kompetenz ein Gymnasion und eine Ephebie zu gründen und die Liste derer aufzustellen, die in Jerusalem Bürger von Antiocheia sein sollten."

Goldstein: "if he should be granted by virtue of his office the power to establish a gymnasium and an ephebic organization and to draw up the list of the Antiochenes in Jerusalem."

---

6   Otto Mørkholm, "The Accession of Antiochus IV of Syria: A Numismatic Comment," *American Numismatic Society Museum Notes* 11 (1964) 63–76.

7   Gruen, *Hellenistic World*, 2:646–47.

8   Sachs and Wiseman, "Babylonian King List," 208.

9   See Mørkholm, "Accession," 72–74.

10   Mørkholm, *Antiochus IV*, 48, 132–33.

11   Jochen Gabriel Bunge, "'Theos Epiphanes': Zu den ersten fünf Regierungsjahren des Antiochus IV Epiphanes," *Historia* 23 (1974) 57–85.

12   On double names, see Susan Sherwin-White, "Aristeas Ardibeltaios: Some Aspects of the Use of Double Names in Seleucid Babylonia," *ZPE* 50 (1983) 209–21.

13   Bickermann, *Institutions*, 108. See the critique in Tcherikover, *Hellenistic Civilization*, 459 n. 39.

14   Welles, *Royal Correspondence*, no. 35. See Friedrich Preisigke, *Wörterbuch der griechischen Papyrusurkunden mit Einschluss der griechischen Inschriften, Aufschriften, Ostraka, Mummienschilder usw. aus Ägypten* (ed. E. Kiessling; 4 vols.; Berlin: Selbstverlag der Erben; Wiesbaden: Harrassowitz, 1925) 1:499, s.v. ἐντευχις; Octave Guéraud, *ENTEUXEIS: Requêtes et plaintes adressées au roi d'Égypte au IIIe siècle avant*

NRSV: "if permission were given to establish by his authority a gymnasium and a body of youth for it, and to enroll the people of Jerusalem as citizens of Antioch."

Kennell: "if it be granted to him through his authority to establish a gymnasium and ephebate and to inscribe those in Jerusalem as Antiochenes."[15]

I have taken both pronouns αὐτοῦ and αὐτῷ to refer to the king, as it is not a reflexive pronoun. I have taken the genitive to refer to the king, rather than to Jason. If Jason, the subject of the clause, were intended, the reflexive pronoun ἑαυτοῦ would be required. Grimm argued that a reflexive pronoun was not necessarily required, as 1 Macc 5:39 provided an instance of the pronoun αὐτός being used reflexively, but in that sentence in 1 Maccabees, the subject need not necessarily be the same as the referent of the pronoun. In addition, this example is not the case of an indirect reflexive pronoun, for which the oblique cases of αὐτός may be used,[16] as Jason is the subject of the dependent clause. Here, Jason is asking for permission. The king's authority allows Jason to establish the gymnasium. Most commentators take the genitive pronoun as reflexive and as referring to Jason, so that he is able by virtue of his own power/authority to set up the gymnasium and ephebic training.[17] If the authority was Jason's, is a distinction being made between Jason and the *gerousia*? I would argue that the very act of building a gymnasium required the king's authority, as is shown in the inscription from Tyriaion, where Eumenes II gives permission for the settlement to become a *polis* and to have a gymnasium: ". . . that there be awarded [ἐπιχωρηθῆναι] to you a constitution, your own laws, a gymnasium, and all that these entail . . . Certainly, any concession from me to you at the present time would be permanent, as I am vested with full authority [ἐκτη-

μένου κυρ[ί]ως] through receipt from the Romans . . . Nevertheless . . . I grant . . ."[18]

I have also translated the dative pronoun αὐτῷ as a dative of interest on two grounds. First, although most often it is translated as though it were a dative following ἐπιχορηγεῖν/συγχωρεῖν, that is, "if it were furnished/granted to him," the passive need not be translated as an impersonal verb but can be translated with Jason as the subject. Second, the position of the dative is so far from the verb and belongs to the accusative and infinitive construction. It would be possible, given that the verb is a compound verb formed with the preposition "with" (σύν) to translate "to constitute . . . with him [i.e., the king]."

A dative of interest could mean in a general fashion that having a gymnasium in Jerusalem would be in the king's best interests, but it could also have a more specific meaning. It could refer to the dedication of the gymnasium to Antiochus IV. Gymnasia were named after individuals: in Halicarnassus there was the Philippeion, in Iasos the Ptolemaieion and the Antiocheion,[19] in Miletus *to Kapitonos*.[20] Of particular interest is a formula in which the king's name is given in the dative: Βασιλεῖ Πτολεμαίωι Ἀπολλόδωρ[ο]ς τὸ γυμνάσιον ("to King Ptolemy, Apollodoros [dedicates] this gymnasium").[21] This example would seem to be analogous to the intention of Jason to build a gymnasium in honor of Antiochus IV.

"the Antiochenes in Jerusalem" (Τοὺς ἐν Ἱεροσολύμοις Ἀντιοχεῖς). NRSV takes Antiochenes as an appositive and translates "the people of Jerusalem as Antiochenes," while Abel ("des Antiochéens de Jérusalem") and Habicht ("derer aufzustellen, die in Jerusalem Bürger von Antiocheia sein sollten") appear to restrict

J.-C. (Cairo: Institut français d'archéologie orientale, 1931).

15   Nigel M. Kennell, "New Light on 2 Maccabees 4:7-15," *JJS* 56 (2005) 10–24, here 10.

16   Smyth, *Greek Grammar*, §1228a.

17   The term ἐφηβία here has the same meaning as in Artemidorus *Oneirocr.* 1.54 and is equivalent to ἐφηβεία. See LSJ, s.v. ἐφηβεία, 2.

18   *I. Sultan Daği* 393, 9–26. Jonnes and Rici, "New Royal Inscription," 4. The translation is that of Kennell, "New Light," 13.

19   Louis Robert, *Études anatoliennes: Recherches sur les*

inscriptions grecques de l'Asie mineure (Études orientales 5; Paris: Boccard, 1937) 452.

20   Erich Ziebarth, *Aus dem griechischen Schulwesen* (Leipzig: Teubner, 1914) 49–52. For other examples, see Jean Delorme, *Gymnasion: Étude sur les monuments consacrés à l'éducation en Grèce* (Bibliothèque des écoles françaises d'Athènes et de Rome 196; Paris: Boccard, 1960) 257–60.

21   Pierre Jouguet, "Une nouvelle requête de Magdola," in *Raccolta di Scritti in onore di Felice Ramorino* (Milan: Vita e Pensiero, 1927) 382.

the number on the list Jason was drawing up. At issue is how to read the article.

A. "The Antiochenes in Jerusalem"

At first blush the article would seem to be the definite article for the noun Ἀντιοχεῖς. Here ἐν Ἱεροσολύμοις would specify the place, as in 14:23. In 2 Maccabees, the article is often separated from the word it qualifies, as, for example, in 4:14: τὰς τοῦ θυσιαστηρίου λειτουργίας, "the services of the altar." In the present case, the phrase would be translated as "the Antiochenes in Jerusalem." As such, the phrase would specify where this group called the Antiochenes is located, as opposed to Antiochenes in other cities and would seem to limit the extent of the group—the Antiochenes in Jerusalem as opposed, say, to the Pharisees in Jerusalem. This view of the phrase has given rise to three political models to explain to whom this phrase refers:

1. Goldstein suggested that Antiochus IV set up an Antiochene republic within his kingdom on the model of the Roman republic. Jason and other rich people in Jerusalem wanted to become members of this republic and enjoy the privileges of such a citizenship.[22] However, studies of Antiochus IV's attitudes toward the various elements of his enormous empire suggest that he followed previous Seleucid practice in maintaining, if not indeed fostering, local diversity.[23]

2. Bickerman used the model of a corporation (πολίτευμα).[24] This corporation would be similar to the situation at Apamea-Silhu in Babylonia and Seleucia-Eulaeus at Susa, for in both places a Greek colony with the status of a *polis* existed alongside the local population.[25] One must be wary of using the term πολίτευμα in this sense, as the recent discussion over its meaning has shown.[26] As Sylvie Honigman noted, "all the *politeumata* of the Ptolemaic period for which we have evidence have military connections."[27] In Apamea-Silhu and Seleucia-Eulaeu in the third century B.C.E., the

22 Goldstein, *I Maccabees*, 112–21; idem, *II Maccabees*, 227.

23 After analyzing the diversity of municipal coinage in the reign of Antiochus IV, Mørkholm (*Antiochus IV*, 114–30) concludes that Antiochus fostered local diversity. On the Seleucid policy in general, see Susan Sherwin-White and Amélie Kuhrt, *From Samarkhand to Sardis: A New Approach to the Seleucid Empire* (Hellenistic Culture and Society 13; Berkeley: University of California Press, 1993).

24 Bickerman, *God of the Maccabees*, 38–42.

25 Sherwin-White and Kuhrt, *From Samarkhand to Sardis*, 20. Arguments were raised against Bickermann on linguistic grounds: "the name of members of a corporation normally terminated with *-stai* or *-ioi*" (Tcherikover, *Hellenistic Civilization*, 538–39 n. 51), and the place suffix *-eus* would normally make Ἀντιοχεύς mean "citizen of Antioch." However, an inscription from Cos from the third century B.C.E. speaks of Charmylos, who is the hero "of the Charmylenes" (τῶν χαρμυλεῶν) (Charles Michel, *Recueil d'inscriptions grecques* [Brussels: H. Lamertin, 1900] 641 no. 748). Here the cult association of Charmylos has a collective name based on a personal name that ends in *-eus*. However, we do not have any evidence of a cult organization named Ἀντιοχεῖς, as opposed to the more usual name for such an association, Ἀντιοχίσται, and the normal meaning of Ἀντιοχεῖς would seem to prevail, that is, "citizen of Antioch."

26 See the analysis of the term in Gert Lüderitz, "What Is the Politeuma?" in Jan Willem van Henten and Pieter Willem van der Horst, eds., *Studies in Early Jewish Epigraphy* (AGJU 21; Leiden: Brill, 1994) 183–225. Lüderitz responds to the previous work by Constantine Zuckerman, "Hellenistic *politeumata* and the Jews: A Reconsideration," *Scripta Classica Israelica* 8–9 (1985–88) 171–85. The discussion continues since the publication of the archive from the *politeuma* of Heracleopolis by James M. S. Cowey and Klaus Maresch (*Urkunden des Politeuma der Juden von Herakleopolis [144/3–133/2 v. Chr] [P. Polit. Jud.]* [Abhandlungen der Nordrhein-Westfälischen Akademie der Wissenschaften, Papyrologica Coloniensia 29; Wiesbaden: Westdeutscher Verlag, 2001]). The publication has already led to a lively discussion: Sylvie Honigman, "The Jewish Politeuma at Heracleopolis," *Scripta Classica Israelica* 21 (2002) 251–66; eadem, "*Politeumata*"; Klaus Maresch and James M. S. Cowey, "'A Recurrent Inclination to Isolate the Jews from their Ptolemaic Environment?' Eine Antwort auf Sylvie Honigman," *Scripta Classica Israelica* 22 (2003) 307–10; Aryeh Kasher "Review Essay," *JQR* 93 (2002) 257–68.

27 Honigman, "Jewish Politeuma," 263, with references. See also Kasher, "Review Essay," 263, with references.

poleis founded alongside native populations were Greek colonies set up to support Seleucid power by the foundation of Greek cities and colonies.[28] In 2 Maccabees, the high priest is not contemplating a colony of Antiochenes alongside Jerusalem whose members he would register.

3. Victor Tcherikover insisted that Jason had requested and received permission to change Jerusalem into a *polis* named Antioch-at-Jerusalem because he saw Jason and his supporters as enacting a constitutional change in Jerusalem: *de iure*, even if in fact it did not happen, the citizens of this new *polis* could abrogate the Mosaic laws and enact new legislation.[29] Since Tcherikover also assumed that citizenship in this new *polis* could be obtained only through attendance at the ephebate, Jason would effectively control who became a citizen, and the list would be restricted to his elite supporters.[30] Both assumptions will be discussed below.

B. "Those in Jerusalem as Antiochenes"
This translation interprets the article as a substantive-making article similar to 12:8: τοὺς ἐν Ἰαμνείᾳ ("those in Jamnia") and 13:22: τοῖς ἐν Βαιθσούροις ("to those in Beth-Zur"). If one takes the article as substantive making, then Antiochenes is a predicate accusative. However, in 12:8 and 13:22, no noun such as Antiochenes is present that could be qualified by the definite article. The article can make other parts of speech substantival, for example, adjectives, participles, adverbs, infinitives, genitives, and prepositions with case,[31] but here there already is a substantive. Nigel Kennell has adduced parallels for a predicative accusative with ἀναγράψαι, but the examples he adduces all refer to specific individuals and

groups, for example, to inscribe Conon as a benefactor.[32] The advantage of this interpretation is that it does not restrict who in Jerusalem is an Antiochene.

On the basis of these grammatical considerations, the most straightforward translation would seem to be "the Antiochenes in Jerusalem," which I have chosen. How is one to understand this phrase? Where does it put the emphasis? The *Antiochenes* in Jerusalem, as opposed to some other group in Jerusalem? Or the Antiochenes *in Jerusalem*, as opposed to those in Antioch? For the first suggestion, Jason would have asked permission to establish a gymnasium named after and dedicated to Antiochus IV. Would the registered members of the gymnasium be called Antiochenes? In this scenario, "to inscribe" (ἀναγράψαι) would be used as on numerous inscriptions to introduce lists of ephebes.[33] Members of the gymnasium, a voluntary association, would have been called Antiochenes after the name of the gymnasium, the Antiocheion. The major objection to this interpretation is that there are ephebes and Jason sends θεωροί ("envoys") to the games at Tyre (4:19)—ephebes and envoys normally belonged to a *polis*,[34] although not always.[35]

Most scholars accept the model whereby Jerusalem became a *polis* and the city was given a new name. There are numerous examples of such a change,[36] and the name of Jerusalem would, under this model, have been changed to Antioch-at-Jerusalem. They were the Antiochenes *in Jerusalem*. Given the presence of ephebes and envoys, this appears the most logical choice. In this view, the phrase "to inscribe the Antiochenes in Jerusalem"

---

28   Sherwin-White and Kuhrt, *From Samarkhand to Sardis*, 20–21.
29   Tcherikover, *Hellenistic Civilization*, 166.
30   Ibid., 161.
31   Smyth, *Greek Grammar*, §1153.
32   Kennell, "New Light," 15. He quotes from *SIG*³ 108, 29–30; 126, 3–4; 193, 21–22.
33   For example, *IG* iii 1197, 1121–22, 1125, 1127–28.
34   For a recent discussion on envoys, see Nora M. Dimitrova, *Theoroi and Initiates in Samothrace: The Epigraphical Evidence* (Princeton: American School of Classical Studies at Athens, 2008) 9–20.
35   Nigel Kennell, in a private communication, noted that there are examples of ephebes not in a *polis*. Ian Rutherford, also in a private communication, noted

that there were some exceptions where θεωροί may be associated with non-*poleis*; in particular, he mentioned Astypalaia/Isthmos on Kos, which sent a *theoria* to Delos even after the Koan *sympoliteia* and within Attica Marathon might have sent independent *theoriai*.
36   A fairly complete list is in Victor Tcherikover, *Die hellenistischen Städtegründungen von Alexander dem Grossen bis auf die Römerzeit* (Philologus Supplementband 19.1; Leipzig: Dieterich, 1927) 1–111, although one might make changes as to which king founded which city. See Sherwin-White and Kuhrt, *From Samarkhand to Sardis*, 20–21, 142–44. For cities with the name Antiocheia, see *OGIS* 2:588, and Le Rider, *Suse*, 410–11.

would refer to the recording of the citizens' names on a stele. This practice is known from Priene.[37]

There are, however, some nagging questions. The first is that the author is so unconcerned about a change of name. He knows how to describe and deplore a name change, as in 6:2-7, and one would have thought that he would have exploited the opportunity to berate Jason for such a step. Perhaps, however, the name change did not alter traditional usage and locals continued to call the city Jerusalem. The second difficulty is that Antiochus IV would be acceding to the request of a newly appointed high priest on an important symbolic issue. A senate ($\gamma\epsilon\rho o\upsilon\sigma i\alpha$) was still in place in Jerusalem (4:44), as it had been in the time of Antiochus III (Josephus *Ant.* 12.142). When Antiochus IV offered an amnesty to the Jews and a return to their previous way of life, he wrote to the $\gamma\epsilon\rho o\upsilon\sigma i\alpha$ ("senate") and the other Jews (11:27). Little is known about the process by which a city changed its name. One case is provided by Sicyon, where Demetrius defeated a Ptolemaic garrison, helped the people fortify the city, and restored free government. The citizens voted to grant Demetrius divine honors and to call the city Demetrias (Diodorus Siculus 20.102.2–3). In this example, the citizens voted for the name change. The same process was at work at Tyriaion in Phrygia, where the settlers sent men[38] to ask Eumenes II to change this military colony to a *polis*.[39] Once again, a large group was involved in the request, and the settlers and the locals living with them were united into one citizen body. Would

not one expect that Antiochus IV would also require a request from the ruling body in Jerusalem? Or does the author want to place all possible blame on Jason?

The evidence is scanty, yet nevertheless the simplest explanation, given the parallels, is to interpret "to inscribe the Antiochenes in Jerusalem" as an offhand and oblique way of referring to naming the city Antioch-at-Jerusalem, and only Jason, not the entire community and its leaders, appears to be the instigator of this change. Does this reading require that a constitutional change took place in Jerusalem, and that, *de iure*, the citizens of the new *polis* could abrogate the Mosaic laws and enact new legislation, as Tcherikover held?[40] Such a view assumes that *polis* in the Hellenistic period always meant an independent city-state with a Greek type of government and institutions, which, as Roger van der Spek has shown, was not the case.[41] Becoming a *polis* did mean that the city-state had a recognized legal status vis-à-vis the Seleucid government that was different from those of non-*poleis*.[42] Since the evidence for name change comes primarily from coinage, we do not know what the change signified. Sometimes the name changed again within one or two generations as, for example, at Antioch in Ptolemais. Would constitutional change have occurred every time? The retention of indigenous titles for officials at Laodicea on the Sea, Seleuceia on the Tigris, and Sidon suggests that after their change to *poleis*, these cities retained their original civic structure.[43] In his account of the transformation of the village of Bethsaida into a

---

37   *I. Priene* 47.22. See Adolf Wilhelm, *Beiträge zur griechischen Inschriftenkunde* (Sonderschriften des österreichischen archäologischen Institutes in Wien 7; Vienna: Hölder, 1909) 234–35.

38   Note ἄνδρες (*I. Sultan Daği* 3) not θεωρούς.

39   Jonnes and Rici, "New Royal Inscription," 3–5. Although not πόλις but πολίτευμα is used in the inscription, this would seem to correspond to other cases where the latter term is used to mean "state" or "government," as in Polybius 21.17.12. See Lüderitz, "What Is the Polituema?" 206.

40   Tcherikover, *Hellenistic Civilization*, 166.

41   Roger van der Spek, "The Babylonian City," in Susan Sherwin-White and Amelie Kuhrt, eds., *Hellenism in the East: The Interaction of Greek and Non-Greek Civilizations from Syria to Central Asia after Alexander* (Berkeley: University of California Press, 1987) 57–74, here 58.

42   See Arthur H. M. Jones, *The Greek City from Alexan-*

der *to Justinian* (Oxford: Clarendon, 1940) 95–112; Susanne Carlsson, *Hellenistic Democracies: Freedom, Independence, and Political Procedure in Some East Greek City-States* (Historia, Einzelschriften 206; Stuttgart: Franz Steiner, 2010).

43   Getzel M. Cohen, *The Seleucid Colonies: Studies in Founding, Administration and Organization* (Historia, Einzelschriften 30; Wiesbaden: Franz Steiner, 1978) 80; Elias Bickermann, "Sur une inscription grecque de Sidon," in *Mélanges syriens offerts à Monsieur René Dussaud* (2 vols.; Paris: P. Geuthner, 1939) 1:91–99, here 99.

polis named after Julia by Philip the Tetrarch, Josephus does not note any change in civic structure (*Ant.* 18.28). Although Eumenes II granted the citizens of the new *polis* at Tyriaion in Phrygia the right to use their own laws, he retained the right to abrogate laws that would be detrimental to his own interests, as every king did. But the new *polis* maintained its own civic structure.[44] Thus, if Jerusalem's name was changed to Antioch-at-Jerusalem, no constitutional change necessarily accompanied the alternation, which would not have meant a huge increase in status for Jerusalem.[45]

One major question still has to be faced in interpreting this verse: What did setting up a gymnasium and ephebic training mean in the first half of the second century B.C.E.? What took place in such an institution? Who would have taken part?

The Gymnasium

No self-respecting city could be without a gymnasium (Strabo 5.4.7; Pausanias 10.4). While discussing the new inscription from Tyriaion, Lloyd Jonnes and Marijana Rici observe that the gymnasium "was reserved for *ephebes* (18–20 years) and *neoi* (20–30 years), while *paides* (12–18 years) were allowed to enter only on special occasions, such as festivals."[46] The gymnasium was a public building, usually municipally owned, and the man in charge, often called a gymnasiarch, was a public official.[47]

Privately owned gymnasia came under the purview of the city, as education remained very much a state concern.

What took place in such an institution? The gymnasium and ephebic status had originally been designed for physical exercises and training, particularly military training. Although the tactics of military warfare had changed with the advent of the phalanx, the emphasis on military training and preparedness remained central to the institution. An inscription from Babylon of 109–108 B.C.E. records the winners in contests with the bow, javelin, curved and oblong shield, and in the sprints and the long race.[48] The correspondence of this list with others from, for example, Athens, Samos, and Tralles suggests that similar exercises would have taken place in Jerusalem. Other exercises in Hellenistic gymnasiums were the discharging of catapults, stone hurling, and the study of tactics.[49] While these exercises were not primarily geared toward fighting in the phalanx, they would be of use in defending cities from siege, and the ephebes were sent out to patrol the borders of the city. The primary function of the gymnasium in Hellenistic times remained the maintenance of military preparedness to defend the city.[50]

The author of 2 Maccabees provides little information about the activities of the gymnasium in Jerusalem, neither about its architectural complex nor about the activities that it housed. Some men from Jerusalem may have participated in the games at Tyre (4:19) and so would

---

44 Jonnes and Rici, "New Royal Inscription," 3–5.

45 See the important article by Andrzej S. Chankowski, "Les souverains héllenistiques et l'institution du gymnase: politiques royales et modèles culturels," in Olivier Curty, ed., *L'huile et l'argent: Gymnasiarchie et évergétisme dans la Grèce hellénistique. Actes du colloque tenu à Fribourg du 13 au 15 octobre 2005, publiés en l'honneur du Profeseur Marcel Piérart à l'occasion de son 60ème anniversaire* (Fribourg: Séminaire d'histoire ancienne de l'Université de Fribourg, 2009) 95–114; idem, "Date et circonstances de l'institution de l'éphébie à Érétrie," *Dialogues d'histoire ancienne* 19 (1993) 17–44. See also Klaus Bringmann, "Gymnasion und griechische Bildung im Nahen Osten," in Daniel Kah and Peter Scholz, eds., *Das hellenistische Gymnasion* (Wissenskultur und gesellschaftlicher Wandel 8; Berlin: Akademie, 2004) 323–33.

46 Jonnes and Rici, "New Royal Inscription," 15.

47 Delorme, *Gymnasion*, 254–55.

48 Bernard Haussolier, "Inscriptions grecques de Babylone," *Klio* 9 (1909) 352–63, here 353.

49 See the full discussion in Daniel Kah, "Militärische Ausbildung im hellenistischen Gymnasion," in Kah and Scholz, *Das hellenistische Gymnasion*, 47–90, followed by the response by Miltiades B. Hatzopoulos, "La formation militaire dans les gymnases hellénistiques," 91–96.

50 Andrzej S. Chankowski, "L'entraînement militaire des éphèbes dans les cités grecques d'Asie Mineure à l'époque hellénistique: nécessité pratique ou tradition atrophiée?" in Jean-Christophe Couvenhes and Henri-Louis Fernoux, eds., *Les cités grecques et la guerre en Asie Mineure à l'époque hellénistique* (Tours: Universitaires François-Rabelais, 2004) 55–75; idem, "L'éphébie, une institution d'éducation civique," in Jean-Marie Pailler and Pascal Payen, eds., *Que reste-t-il de l'éducation classique? Relire "le Marrou,"* Histoire de l'éducation dans l'antiquité (Toulouse: Presses Universitaires du Mirail, 2004) 271–79; John Ma, "Une culture militaire en Asie Mineure hellénistique," in Couvenhes and Fernoux, *Les cités grecques,* 199–219.

have been trained to compete in them. Josephus mentions that at the time of Agrippa, there existed in Jerusalem a xystus (ξυστός), which in a gymnasium would have been a covered colonnade for training during bad weather (*Bell.* 2.344).[51] However, it is not certain that this structure would have been part of Jason's gymnasium.

In 4:14, a *palaistra*, a wrestling yard, is mentioned. The *palaistra* in the Hellenistic period shows the complexity of what went on in a gymnasium. The *palaistra* was usually a court surrounded by a colonnaded porch with rooms leading off it;[52] it was thus not simply a place for exercise. Over the centuries, the gymnasium became a place where lectures were given, meals were eaten, and honors bestowed.[53] But one must not imagine that the Hellenistic gymnasium was a school in the sense of today's elementary, secondary, and tertiary education. Peter Scholz has convincingly shown how this notion of the role of the Hellenistic gymnasium relies too much on importing into the past modern notions of education.[54] Even when the city ruled that parents should have their children educated, how this rule was satisfied was left up to the parents, and education was not publicly financed. Scholz argues that the four examples where rich private citizens or kings provided for all freeborn children to have an elementary education must be seen as dependent on specific circumstances.[55]

Ephebic Training

Second Maccabees does not specify what took place in the gymnasium, and one can only speculate. But the presence of ephebic training can guide our speculation. As noted above, the instruction that the ephebes received in a city's gymnasium was oriented toward military training, but it also was civic training in that the ephebes took part in each city's religious and cultural events.[56] The ephebes were trained to be good citizens, to take part in their city's religious festivals and traditions. Participation in the ephebate was not necessarily a requirement for citizenship. It had been in Athens from 336/335 to 323/322 B.C.E., where it meant compulsory military service for all citizens, and it remained so in Pellene, although Pausanias noted it as an unusual practice (7.25.5). When the ephebate became a place to which only the rich could afford to send their sons, ephebic training was presumptive proof of citizenship: all ephebes were citizens, but not all citizens went through ephebic training.[57]

■ **10** "assented" (ἐπινεύσαντος). The same verb is used in line 14 in Eumenes II's granting of the status of *polis* to Tyriaion in Phrygia. As Jonnes and Rici note: "ἐπινεῦσαι: this rather poetic verb, ever since Homer used of gods, is rare in inscriptions. We were able to find only one late parallel in the famous petition of the villagers of Skatopara in A.D. 238. In Polybius, it is once used of an Aetolian decision (XXI, 5)."[58] Finally, one must ask what moved Antiochus IV to accede to the request. As Eumenes II said to the inhabitants of Tyriaion, it was no small matter to accede to their request. Jonnes and Rici suggest that Eumenes II, who had recently been granted control of the region by the Romans, wanted by this

---

51   On xystus, see Delorme, *Gymnasion*, 387–90.
52   See Christian Wacker, "Die bauhistorische Entwicklung der Gymnasien: Von der Parkanlage zum 'Idealgymnasion' des Vitruv," in Kah and Scholz, *Das hellenistische Gymnasion*, 349–51; also Delorme, *Gymnasion*, 260–71.
53   Clarence A. Forbes, "Expanded Uses of the Greek Gymnasium," *CP* 40 (1945) 32–42; Elena Mango, "Bankette im hellenistischen Gymnasion," in Kah and Scholz, *Das hellenistische Gymnasion*, 273–311; and, in the same volume, Sophia Aneziri and Dimitris Damakos, "Städtische Kulte im hellenistischen Gymnasion," 247–71.
54   Scholz observes, "Keineswegs nämlich war die intellektuelle Erziehung notwendigerweise an den Besuch einer öffenlichen Institution wie des Gymnasions geknüpft. Gerade im Fall von Jugendlichen vornehmer Abkunft war private Erziehung im familiären Umfeld durch Hauslehrer üblich" ("Elementarunterricht und intellektuelle Bildung im hellenistischen Gymnasion," in Kah and Scholz, *Das hellenistische Gymnasion*, 103).
55   Ibid., 107–8.
56   "Als städtische Bildungsinstitution mit vielfältigen religiösen Funktionen dokumentiert das Gymnasion also am besten das Eindringen der Religion in alle Formen des Lebens der griechischen Polis-Gemeinden und die Verschmelzung von Sakralen und Profanem" (Aneziri and Damaskos, "Städtische Kulte," 247).
57   Doran, "Jason's Gymnasion," 99–109. See also Diana Delia, *Alexandrian Citizenship during the Roman Principate* (American Classical Studies 23; Atlanta: Scholars Press, 1991) 71–88.
58   Jonnes and Rici, "New Royal Inscription," 16.

action to show that he was a benevolent and generous king, eager to promote the interests of his loyal subjects.[59] The author of 2 Maccabees suggests that Antiochus IV was only after the money, and kings are always ready to acquire new funds. As Mørkholm has shown, however, "Antiochus IV tried to maintain the dignity of the Seleucid house by rivalling even the most generous of his fellow kings."[60] Having recently obtained rulership, Antiochus may have wanted to show his generosity toward cities like Jerusalem that had helped Antiochus III when he gained control over Coele-Syria. Antiochus III requited them for their help and allowed them to follow their own laws (Josephus *Ant.* 12.138–44). Antiochus IV may have wanted to follow this example. One may also ask if Antiochus's permission for the gymnasium and ephebic training may not be indicative of his interest in having a city near his southern border with the Ptolemies that would be prepared militarily to defend itself if the Ptolemies decided to invade his territory. According to Jean Delorme's analysis, in the second century B.C.E., the gymnasium at Jerusalem would have been the only one founded between the one in Laodicea on the Sea and possibly one in the Nile delta.[61] Not only would the gymnasium desired by Jason have increased the status of Jerusalem and perhaps been a minor rival to the games held in Tyre and Sidon, but Antiochus IV may also have jumped at the chance to increase military readiness in the southern part of his kingdom.[62]

"changed" ($\mu\epsilon\tau\acute{\epsilon}\sigma\tau\eta\sigma\epsilon\nu$). The verb $\mu\epsilon\vartheta\acute{\iota}\sigma\tau\eta\mu\iota$ is used by classical authors to describe changes in government,[63] and is used this way in the LXX (4 Kgdms 23:33; Dan 2:21; 1 Macc 8:13). It also has covenantal resonances. In Judg 10:16, the people banish ($\mu\epsilon\tau\epsilon\acute{\sigma}\tau\eta\sigma\alpha\nu$) foreign gods from their midst; in 4 Kgdms 17:23, the Lord removes ($\mu\epsilon\tau\acute{\epsilon}\sigma\tau\eta\sigma\epsilon\nu$) Israel from his face; in Isa 54:10, the Lord promises that even though the mountains change ($\mu\epsilon\tau\alpha\sigma\tau\acute{\eta}\sigma\epsilon\sigma\vartheta\alpha\iota$), his covenant

of peace will not change ($\mu\epsilon\tau\alpha\sigma\tau\hat{\eta}$); in Dan 11:31, the Theodotionic version reads that the armed forces of the last king will change ($\mu\epsilon\tau\alpha\sigma\tau\acute{\eta}\sigma\sigma\upsilon\sigma\iota\nu$) the daily offering. The author thus uses this word to bring out the covenant-breaking resonances of what Jason is doing. He says that Jason is changing his kinsfolk ($\acute{o}\mu o\phi\acute{\upsilon}\lambda o\upsilon\varsigma$), an uncommon word in the LXX, but by it the author emphasizes that it is one of their own who does this, not a foreigner ($\grave{\alpha}\lambda\lambda\acute{o}\phi\upsilon\lambda o\varsigma$), as in 10:2, 5.

"Hellenic type." The word $\chi\alpha\rho\alpha\kappa\tau\acute{\eta}\rho$ not only has the general meaning of "type" or "characteristic" but also was used of a seal, a stamp, and a branding iron. It thus brings a suggestion of domination, of being owned.

"takes control." Jason is portrayed throughout as the prime mover. Once he takes control, Jerusalem will be in trouble until the Hebrews take control of the city after the defeat of Nikanor (15:37).

■ 11 "despoiling." The verb $\pi\alpha\rho\acute{o}\omega/\pi\eta\rho\acute{o}\omega$ means "to maim, mutilate, incapacitate."

"royal privileges." $\phi\iota\lambda\acute{\alpha}\nu\vartheta\rho\omega\pi\alpha$ is frequently used to describe the actions of a king towards his subjects.[64] Theoretically, the king could do whatever he liked with a city,[65] as is shown in 4:30, where the citizens of Tarsus and Mallos revolt because they were given to the king's concubine as a grant. Priene is said to have been given its liberty by Antiochus I at the request of a dancer who came from the city (Sextus Empiricus *Adv. gramm.* 1.13). But the Seleucid custom, following that of the Achaemenids, was to respect the customs and usages of the various constituencies they controlled. The league of Ionian cities requested that Antiochus I allow them "to live according to their ancestral customs" ($\pi o\lambda\iota[\tau]\epsilon\acute{\upsilon}\omega\nu\tau\alpha\iota$ $\kappa\alpha\tau\grave{\alpha}$ $\tau o\grave{\upsilon}\varsigma$ $\pi\alpha\tau\rho\acute{\iota}[o\upsilon\varsigma$ $\nu\acute{o}\mu o\upsilon\varsigma$).[66] Eumenes II allowed the Tyriaions to use their own laws.[67] When Antiochus III sent Jewish colonists to Phrygia, he permitted them to use their own laws (Josephus *Ant.* 12.150). When he gained control of Jerusalem, he recognized the inhabit-

59   Ibid., 18.
60   Mørkholm, *Antiochus IV*, 56.
61   Delorme, *Gymnasion*, fig. 63.
62   Chankowski, "Les souverains héllenistiques."
63   As in Xenophon *Hist. Graec.* 4.8.27: "[Thrasybulus] also changed [$\mu\epsilon\tau\acute{\epsilon}\sigma\tau\eta\sigma\epsilon$] the government of the Byzantines from an oligarchy to a democracy [$\epsilon\grave{\iota}\varsigma$ $\tau\grave{o}$ $\delta\eta\mu o\kappa\rho\alpha\tau\epsilon\hat{\iota}\sigma\vartheta\alpha\iota$]." See also 5.4.64; Plato *Resp.* 553C; Aristotle *Pol.* 1301a22; Polybius 2.47.3; 6.9.10.
64   Welles, *Royal Correspondence*, 373; Schubart, "Königsideal," 10–11; and especially Ma, *Antiochus III*, 182–94.
65   Bickermann, *Institutions*, 133–40.
66   *OGIS* 222, line 18; see also 229.
67   Jonnes and Rici, "New Royal Inscription," 3, lines 10, 27–28.

ants' ancestral customs because of the goodwill they had shown on his behalf (Josephus *Ant.* 12.138–44).[68] The role of John, father of Eupolemos, in this recognition by Antiochus III is mentioned only here. Evidently this is a distinguished family with a record of diplomatic service. The role of Eupolemos is mentioned also in 1 Macc 8:17, where we learn that his father was the son of Hakkoz. The family of Hakkoz is said in Ezra 2:61-63 (LXX 1 Esdr 5:38-40) to have been barred from the priesthood after the return from exile because its name could not be found in the genealogical entries. However, the family is present in the list of priestly ancestral houses in 1 Chr 24:10. Its diplomatic activity in the second century B.C.E. attests to its continued prominence. The Eupolemos mentioned here may be the author of a historical work of which only fragments remain.[69] Linda Zollschan tried to construe the sentence as if it was John who made the embassy to the Romans, an otherwise unknown private attempt on the part of John after Jason had introduced the new customs sometime in 174 B.C.E.[70] The argument rests on the fact that the preposition διά governs four genitives: John, "father," Eupolemos, and the participle τοῦ ποιησαμένου. She argues that the participle should be connected with John rather than Eupolemos, so that John would have two appositives attached to it. This seems unlikely, as one would expect a connective particle between two appositives, as in 4:2 (τὸν εὐεργέτην . . . καὶ τὸν κηδεμόνα . . . καὶ ζηλωτήν) and 13:2 (Λυσίαν τὸν ἐπίτροπον καὶ ἐπὶ τῶν πραγμάτων). Since the participial phrase comes immediately after Eupolemos, the normal reading would be that Eupolemos governs the participial phrase. More importantly, Zollschan does not deal with the meaning of ποιεῖσθαι πρεσβείαν. She provides no instance when πρεσβεία refers to an individual's visit to a foreign power.[71] The treaty with

Rome in which Eupolemos participated took place after the defeat of Nikanor, the last event narrated in 2 Maccabees. The author thus knows of events that occurred later than his story, and he seems to presuppose that his audience would know of Eupolemos and his activity. Habicht, following Momigliano, sees this reference as a leftover from Jason of Cyrene, but this would suggest that the author did not know what he was writing. Why does the author mention Eupolemos's embassy to the Romans here? It comes at the beginning of a series of contrasts the author constructs between the new usages that Jason introduces and the traditional way of life. This section ends with a reflection by the author about the peril of abandoning God's laws and how future events will disclose such a peril. The reference to the Romans thus accomplishes two things: first, it recalls to the audience that Antiochus IV was forced by the Romans to leave Egypt; second, it reminds the hearers that the Jews would eventually regain control of their city and laws. Another example of a city, possibly Apollonia on the Rhyndakos, whose own ancestral way of life and laws were taken away by a Seleucid king and then restored by Eumenes II, is found in an inscription discovered in Prusa.[72] An inscription in Athens from 265/264 B.C.E. spoke of those "who attempted to annul the laws and the ancestral polity [τοὺς καταλύειν ἐπιχειροῦντας τούς τε νόμους καὶ τὰς πατρίους πολιτείας]."[73]

On the term "friendship and alliance," see the penetrating study by Gruen.[74] The phrase could imply no more than cordial relations, or it could be combined with detailed treaty elements. The Romans politely received the Jewish envoys but did not take any concrete steps to support the Jews in their struggles with the Seleucids.

The author contrasts legitimate/lawful (νομίμους) with unlawful (παρανόμους). To emphasize the contrast,

---

68 Josephus *Ant.* 12.138–44. Josephus makes no mention of Jewish delegates. See Bickerman, *Studies*, 2:44–104.

69 Eusebius *Praep. ev.* 9.26.1; 9.30.1–9.34.20; 9.39.2–5; Clement of Alexandria *Strom.* 1.141.4.

70 Linda T. Zollschan, "The Earliest Jewish Embassy to the Romans: 2 Macc. 4:11?" *JJS* 55 (2004) 37–44.

71 Zollschan's reasoning ("Earliest Jewish Embassy," 39)—the phrase says not that the embassy went to Rome but that it went to the Romans and so suggests two different embassies—misses the mark, as πρός + the accusative is used in 1 Macc 8:19, where

the ambassadors say they were sent πρὸς ὑμᾶς, and 1 Macc 12:1 reads ἀνανεώσασθαι τὴν πρὸς αὐτοὺς φιλίαν.

72 Thomas Corsten, *Die Inschriften von Prusa ad Olympum* (2 vols.; Inschriften griechischen Städte aus Kleinasien 39, 40; Bonn: Habelt, 1991–93) 2, no. 1001.

73 *SIG*³ 434/35. See *SEG* 25 (1971) 97.

74 Gruen, *Hellenistic World*, 1:54–95 and appendixes 2, 3.

he chose to have νομίμους qualify the feminine noun πολιτείας, as one finds elsewhere.[75] In other contexts, he uses πολιτεία in the sense of city constitution (8:17; 13:14), but here he uses the plural in the sense of the daily life of the citizen, the ways each citizen behaves properly.[76] He may have chosen the plural to balance the normal use of the plural of ἐθισμός ("custom") to refer to the usages or customs of a city (Polybius 1.13.12; 1.17.11). If Jason has just managed to raise Jerusalem to a *polis*, it is interesting how the author talks of the ancestral way of life using a word derived from *polis*. In his letter to the Toriatai, Eumenes II spoke of the settler requesting a πολιτεία (*I. Sultan Daği* 9 and 40). It is also important to recall how, in a traditional culture, the new is always suspect. Socrates was sentenced to death for introducing new gods.

If Jason did succeed in having Jerusalem become a *polis* called Antioch-at-Jerusalem, it is striking that the author stresses the gymnasium and the system of training of the youth. The language of vv. 10-17 interprets the introduction of a new educational system as the introduction of a new political structure. In this connection the author follows Greek ethnographic tradition, where the educational system is viewed as an integral part of each culture's *politeia* or system of polity.[77] When describing what Philopoemen did to Sparta after defeating it in 188 B.C.E., Plutarch speaks of how Philopoemen treated the Spartan *politeia* most cruelly, and the first proof he offers is that Philopoemen abolished the Lycurgan system of education (ἀγωγή) and forced the ephebes to take the Achaean instead of their ancestral discipline (τὴν Ἀχαικὴν ἀντὶ τῆς πατρίου παιδείας μεταλαβεῖν) (Plutarch *Phil.* 16.5-6). To change the ἀγωγή was to change the πολιτεία ("polity"). So the author uses this topos of Greek ethnography to attack Jason's innovations, because there is no evidence that Jason abrogated any of the Mosaic laws.

■ **12** "under the very acropolis." The exact location of the gymnasium is uncertain. The gymnasium would have consisted of a *palaistra* and facilities for field events such as running—a covered running track (*xystos*) and open air tracks (*paradromides*)—and for throwing the discus and javelin. The facilities would thus have required quite a bit of level land and construction. One of the main problems lies in the term "acropolis." In 4:28, the author mentions a Seleucid commander of the acropolis; in 5:5, Menelaus flees to the acropolis. This acropolis of the Seleucid garrison would correspond to the Ptolemaic Akra mentioned in the letter of Antiochus III (Josephus *Ant.* 12.138) and later fortified, at the beginning of Antiochus IV's persecution (1 Macc 1:33). Bezalel Bar-Kochva has persuasively argued that the Akra, including the Ptolemaic Akra, should be located on the southeastern hill of Jerusalem, thus lower than the Temple Mount and the western hill,[78] but there are competing suggestions.[79] Although the author of 2 Maccabees knows the term Akra (15:31, 35), he uses the more grandiose, if geographically inaccurate, term "acropolis." Since the western hill was unpopulated at this time, one should probably locate the gymnasium there.[80] By his language, the author suggests a central location for the gymnasium, almost a studied insult to the city of David.

"The broad-brimmed hat" (πέτασος) was used to protect the athletes' heads from the sun and was the distinctive apparel of the ephebe.[81] Hermes, a favorite god of the gymnasium, was depicted wearing a broad-brimmed hat on his journeys. Kennell emphasizes the military overtones of the verb ὑποτάσσειν ("put under") and suggests that Jason is drawing up an elite force, especially since the term κρατίστοι ("strongest") is used to refer to the strongest young men.[82] One does not have to follow Kennell in seeing this elite force as Jason's enforcers.

■ **13-15** The author keeps up the rhetorical attack with the dismissive τις ("so-called")[83] and by coupling

75 Isocrates *Ad Nic.* 22: τὴν πόλιν πάρεχε . . . νόμιμον; Aristotle *Mund.* 400b24: κατὰ μίαν πρόσταχιν ἢ νόμιμον ἐξουσίαν.
76 See LSJ, s.v., I.2.
77 Doran, "Jason's Gymnasion," 103–6.
78 Bar-Kochva, *Judas Maccabaeus*, 445–65.
79 See the possibilities outlined in Y. Tsafrir, "The Location of the Seleucid Akra in Jerusalem," *RB* 82 (1975) 501–21.
80 See Benjamin Mazar and Hanan Eshel, "Who Built the First Wall of Jerusalem?" *IEJ* 48 (1998) 268. Also Bar-Kochva, *Judas Maccabaeus*, 447 n. 7.
81 E. Schuppe, "Petasos," *PW* (1938) 19:1119–24.
82 Kennell, "New Light," 21–22, citing Diodorus Siculus 13.44.6; 52.1 and Plutarch *Pyrrh.* 24.4.
83 Smyth, *Greek Grammar*, §1268.

Hellenism with ἀλλοφυλισμός, an abstract term for ἀλλόφυλος that is regularly used in LXX to describe foreigners, particularly enemies. Goldstein has rightly noted how the coining of the term Hellenism (Ἑλληνισμός) as well as the use of ἀλλοφυλισμός mirror the term used by the Greeks during the Persian War to characterize traitors to the Greek cause—μηδισμός, the aping of Persian ways. Jason is particularly pilloried as being impure and defiled[84] and therefore technically unable to enter the temple. "Fake high priest" is literally "not high priest." The emphasis is on Jason's impurity; his lack of strict observance of religious duties (ἀναγνεία) leads to the conclusion that Jason is not really a high priest.

The word χορηγία, here translated "practices," usually means performing the office of a χορηγός, a chorus leader who later becomes rather the defrayer of the costs for bringing out a chorus, and χορηγία gains the sense of "expense, supply, abundance." Here, however, the author is contrasting the word χορηγία with λειτουργία. These two words can have a similar meaning of "expenses," but in v. 14 λειτουργία refers to the service and ministry of the priests at the altar. Note how in 3:2, Seleucus is said to have furnished (χορηγεῖν) everything necessary for the services (τὰς λειτουργίας) of the sacrifices. I suggest that the author has used χορηγία here in the general sense of actions or practices that take place in the wrestling area rather than the more specific sense related to chorus activities. These practices most likely, as Kennell notes, refer to the distribution, "commonly called choregiai (χορηγίαι), of oil, sweet wine, meat, or even money . . . a prominent feature of the Hellenistic gymnasium."[85]

In the Greek world, χορηγία was one kind of public service, or λειτουργία. In contrasting the two, the author not only indulges in his usual wordplay but also evidences knowledge of the proper Greek terminology. Those who supplied oil for the gymnasium were seen as benefactors and were frequently honored in inscriptions.[86] In an inscription from Athens in 38 B.C.E., Sosis is honored in part for supplying oil for three days.[87] This honor may be the kind mentioned as Hellenic distinctions in 4:15. Here the author uses τιμή for the ancestral honors and δόξα for Hellenic honors/distinctions. Is the author consciously playing on the other meaning of δόξα, "opinion," to contrast the real value of ancestral honor with the seeming, superficial value of Hellenic estimation?

This practice (χορηγία) is characterized as unlawful. This judgment may simply reflect a general attitude toward the gymnasium as in 4:11, but one also wonders if it indicates a Jewish reluctance to use Gentile oil (Josephus Bell. 2.591; Vita 74; Ant. 12.120). Joseph Baumgarten, in dealing with Qumran attitudes to oil, has noted the special susceptibility of liquids to impurity.[88]

"Summons of the gong" is literally "of the discus." This refers not to the actual exercise of discus throwing but to a signal that the gymnasium was open (Plutarch Per. 6.5; Cicero De or. 2.5.21).[89]

"ancestral honors." M. Yoma 2:2 describes how the use of lots to assign priestly duties came into practice because of competition among the priests.[90] As noted above, these ancestral honors may be in opposition to the Greek honors bestowed on benefactors who contributed the oil to the gymnasium as a χορηγία. In 178 B.C.E., Seleucus IV appointed Olympiodoros as high priest of the sanctuaries of Syria and Phoenicia precisely to ensure that they, like the sanctuaries in the other

---

84 See the description of Oedipus in Sophocles Oed. Tyr. 823.
85 Kennell, "New Light," 18.
86 See ibid., 19.
87 IG II² 1043, lines 61–71; see also IG XII 1.3, 4.
88 Joseph M. Baumgarten, Studies in Qumran Law (SJLA 24; Leiden: Brill, 1977) 88–97. See also Martin Goodman, "Kosher Olive Oil in Antiquity," in Philip R. Davies and Richard T. White, eds., A Tribute to Geza Vermes: Essays on Jewish and Christian Literature and History (JSOTSup 100; Sheffield: JSOT Press, 1990) 227–45.

89 See Adolf Wilhelm, Neue Beiträge zur griechischen Inschriftenkunde: Fünfter Teil (Sitzungsberichte der Akademie der Wissenschaften in Wien 214; Vienna and Leipzig: Hölder-Pichler-Tempsky, 1932) 44–47.
90 Emil Schürer, The History of the Jewish People in the Age of Jesus Christ (175 B.C.–A.D. 135) (rev. and ed. Geza Vermes and Fergus Millar; 3 vols.; Edinburgh: T&T Clark, 1973–87) 2:245–46, 292–308.

satrapies, received the ancestral honors (τὰς πατρίο[υς] κομίζηται τιμάς) with the appropriate maintenance (Heliodorus stele, lines 20–22).[91]

■ **16-17** The author here pauses to reflect on the significance of the events, as he does also in 5:17-20 and 6:12-17. Such digressions were a traditional feature of Greek historiography (Polybius 38.5–6; Diodorus Siculus 20.30.1),[92] and the author uses one here to point out what was for him the theological significance of what Jason and the participants were doing–they were acting against the divine laws. The author uses this break to warn his audience against such gymnasium participation, for it will have dire consequences.

The author uses tense nicely: two aorists (περιέσχεν, ἔσχον) encompass two imperfects (ἐξήλουν, ἤθελον). The aorists are used to survey at a glance the course of a past action from beginning to end, where the aorist ἔσχον is a resultative aorist. The imperfects convey the sense of an action attempted or intended in the past but not completed. The author also uses alliteration (περιέσχον . . . περίστασις) to achieve the sense of being surrounded.

ἀγωγή can mean "policy, conduct" as in 6:8 but often means "way of life." When Esther is married to the king she does not reveal that she is a Jew, but when Mordechai commands her to fear God and do his commandments, she "does not change her behavior/way of life" (οὐ μετήλλαξε τὴν ἀγωγὴν αὐτῆς) (LXX Esth 2:20).[93] The word is also frequently used of education.[94] Sparta's education system was called its ἀγωγή (Plutarch *Phil.* 16.5–6).[95] In the succeeding narrative, the author does not specify how those who attended the gymnasium were punished by the Seleucids, except in the cases of Jason (5:7-9) and Menelaus (13:4-8). He does mention how Antiochus IV made a slaughter in Jerusalem and despoiled the temple (5:12-16), about which event Josephus says that Antiochus IV did not spare those who had

let him in (Josephus *Ant.* 12.249–50). In the narrative of 1 Maccabees, Bacchides is said to have become angry with the "renegades" and killed some of them (1 Macc 9:69), but this event occurs later than the events narrated in 2 Maccabees.

The verb ἀσεβεῖν ("to be impious") resonates with the description of Jason as impious in 4:13.

■ **18-20** Quinquennial games were held after four years, at the beginning of the fifth year. There are several possibilities as to the origin of these games at Tyre, as Goldstein has noted. (1) The games originated in an ancient festival. When Alexander the Great captured Tyre in 332 B.C.E., he found a delegation from Carthage, trapped there during the seven-month siege. Its members had come to participate in an ancient festival for the Phoenician god Melqart (Arrian *Anab.* 2.24.5; Curtius 4.2.10). However, Curtius states that this was an annual event. (2) Alexander celebrated games at Tyre after capturing the city (Arrian *Anab.* 2.24.6; 3.6.1; Diodorus Siculus 17.46.6). (3) The games celebrated the beginning of the Tyrian era in 275/274 B.C.E.[96] Whatever their origin, the games must be placed before the replacement of Jason as high priest by Menelaus "after three years" (4:23). Since Antiochus IV came to power in 175 B.C.E. and Jason's appointment followed after this date, the Tyrian games must fall before 173/172 B.C.E., possibly in 174 B.C.E. Jason thus wasted no time in exhibiting his desire for closer ties with neighboring cities as well as his loyalty to the king. The presence of Antiochus IV at the games is no doubt explained by his desire both to show himself in control of his kingdom after taking it over in an uncertain fashion and to make clear to the Ptolemies, who disputed Seleucid claims to Coele-Syria,[97] that he was master there.

"Polluted" (μιερός) is used three times of Antiochus IV (5:16; 7:34; 9:13) and once of Nikanor (15:32), both of whom attacked the temple. The interpretation of this

---

91 For the text, see Cotton and Wörrle, "Seleukos IV," 192.

92 See Norbert Zegers, *Wesen und Ursprung der tragischen Geschichtsschreibung* (Cologne: Universität zu Köln, 1959) 47–51; Walbank, *Polybius*, 46–47; Doran, *Temple Propaganda*, 95–97.

93 See Welles, *Royal Correspondence*, 309.

94 For example, by Chrysippus, as in Hans Friedrich August von Arnim, *Stoicorum veterum fragmenta* (4 vols.; Leipzig: Teubner, 1921–24) 3:173.

95 See Clarence A. Forbes, *Greek Physical Education* (New York: Century, 1929) 12–43.

96 F. Bölte, "Tyros," *PW* (1948) 7A:1896.

97 Polybius 28.20.9; Appian *Syr.* 5; Josephus *Ant.* 12.154; Porphyry in *FGH* 260 F47.

verse is linked with how the Antiochenes of 4:9b are viewed.

If the Antiochenes are citizens of Antioch-at-Jerusalem, then these envoys are representatives of that *polis*. There is ample evidence of such a nomenclature: for example, an Antiochene from Pyramus (Ἀντιοχεὺς ἀπὸ Πυράμου).[98] Habicht argues further that the word for envoy, θεωροί, meant an official representative of a Greek city-state, and so Jerusalem must have become such a Greek *polis*.[99] Habicht does not discuss that it is Jason who sent the envoys, not the people (δῆμος) or the community (κοινόν) of the city, as is usually found on inscriptions.

If it is the case that the Antiochenes are members of a community in Jerusalem, rather than that the city was renamed Antioch-at-Jerusalem, then the reference to the Antiochenes as qualifying the envoys is explained. The fact, however, that in the vast majority of cases, only Greek city-states could send θεωροί and participate in such games, still stands. Herodotus narrates a story in which a would-be competitor in the Olympic games had to prove his Greek descent (5.22). In this connection, Jason the high priest claimed kinship with the Spartans (5:9). As stated in the letters found in 1 Macc 12:5-23 and attributed to Onias I, the Spartan–Jewish connection goes back to Abraham. A fictive kinship with Herakles, the supposed progenitor of the Spartan kings, is given by another Jewish writer, Cleodemus Malchus (Josephus *Ant.* 1.239–41). Such a connection would have provided entrée to the games.

When envoys were representatives of a city at another city's festival and games, they offered sacrifices in the name of their city. Many examples can be found in the inscriptions from Magnesia on the Maeander.[100] By dubbing Jason polluted and insisting that it was Jason who sent money for a sacrifice to Herakles,[101] the author underscores that, in his eyes, Jason was unfaithful to Judaism and had overstepped an important boundary. He is here taking a stance on what defines a Jew: Jews do not participate in pagan cults. The question of participation in pagan cults was more hotly debated at that time than is often thought. For example, the Jewish historian Eupolemos (with good reason identified with the ambassador of Judas Maccabeus to the Romans[102]) writes that Solomon sent to the king of Tyre "the golden pillar that is now set up in the temple of Zeus at Tyre" (as cited in Eusebius *Praep. ev.* 9.34.18).[103] Eupolemos immediately follows this statement with a quotation from another writer: "Theophilus says that Solomon sent the surplus gold to the king of Tyre, who had a full-length statue of his daughter made and plated it with gold" (Eusebius *Praep. ev.* 9.34.19). Nothing is known of Theophilus beyond this statement. However, the adjective "surplus" connects the report to the building of the temple and thus suggests a Jewish writer.[104] Theophilus here shows a concern to distance Solomon from any contact with a foreign cult and evidences the same qualms that Jason's envoys felt. An inscription from the middle of the second century B.C.E. from Iasos in Asia Minor notes that a resident alien, Nicetas, son of Jason, a Jerusalemite (Νικήτας Ἰάσονος Ἱεροσολυμίτης) contributed one hundred drachmas toward the festival of the Dionysia.[105] Although it is not certain that this Nicetas was Jewish, that he gives his hometown as Jerusalem would seem

---

98 *SIG*[3] 585.286. See also the list in *OGIS* 2:588 and Le Rider, *Suse*, 410.

99 See also Bringmann, *Hellenistische Reform*, 90, but see nn. 34 and 35 above for possible exceptions.

100 Kern, *Die Inschriften*, nos. 31, 36, 48, 57.

101 The genitive here is an objective genitive. See Smyth, *Greek Grammar*, §§1331–32. The god here is Herakles/Melqart. See Corinne Bonnet, *Melqart: cultes et mythes de l'Héraclès tyrien en Méditerranée* (Studia Phoenicia 8; Leuven: Peeters, 1988).

102 See the comment above on 4:11.

103 On the golden pillar at Tyre, Herodotus (2.44) mentions one in the temple of Herakles, while Josephus (*Ap.* 1.118) notes that Menander of Ephesus dedi-

cated the golden pillar in the temple of Zeus. See also the comment on 4:11 above.

104 Contra Menahem Stern (*Greek and Latin Authors on Jews and Judaism* [3 vols.; Fontes ad res Judaicas spectantes; Jerusalem: Israel Academy of Sciences and Humanities, 1974–84] 1:126–27), who links this Theophilus to a non-Jewish writer mentioned by Josephus (*Ap.* 1.215–16).

105 *CIJ* 2, no. 749.

to argue for this identification. From later in Cyrene (60 C.E.), mention is made of an Eleazar, son of Jason, a guardian of the laws (νομοφύλαξ) whose name is found with those of two priests of Apollo on an inscription in honor of a pagan deity.[106] There is no reason to suppose that Eleazar had renounced Judaism. From earlier in Cyrene (3/4 C.E.; 23/24 C.E.), Jews are found in the list of ephebes and participated in the dedication to Hermes and Herakles.[107]

The relationship of Jews to the cults of their neighbors is best brought into focus by noting the LXX translation of Exod 22:28a. The MT reads אלהים לא תקלל, which the LXX renders θεοὺς οὐ κακολογήσεις ("You shall not revile gods"). Is the translator suggesting that one should not revile the gods of other nations? These gods are not the God of the Jews (Exod 20:3), but they should not be treated disrespectfully. The question "How far?" was thus a lively one for Jews living in a multicultural world. Jason the high priest took a more liberal stance; the envoys were more conservative and their position would later be echoed in Philo and Josephus.[108] Could the envoys have made this decision on their own to forgo the ritual action in favor of the more practical fitting out of triremes? Would they have had to request[109] permission from the organizer of the games or from Antiochus IV himself? This decision by the envoys has an interesting parallel in a letter from the emperor Hadrian to Aphrodisias in which Hadrian enthusiastically grants the request of the magistrates and the people that the high priests should fund the building of an aqueduct rather than gladiatorial games, "which were given regularly at civic imperial cult festivals."[110] Angelos Chaniotis also noted how at Tempsianoi, a priest, following the request of the city, used the money for the building of an aqueduct rather than for banquets.[111] On the parallel with Tempsianoi, would Jason have bowed to the wishes of the envoys? In any event, the author has chosen to give the credit to the envoys and to discredit Jason. Note how the author uses two different prepositions, διά + accusative for Jason and ἕνεκα for the envoys, both of which express motive,[112] to underline the difference between the two parties.

The amount of money mentioned, 300 drachmas, seems in line with what we see in the inscriptions for the festival at Magnesia on the Maeander. There, the Archarnians vote to send 150 silver drachmas for the sacrifice, while an unknown Dorian city gives 300 drachmas to the envoys for the visit.[113]

"the fitting out of triremes." At the time of Antiochus III, his navy vessels were provided by the maritime states. Sidon gave the right wing, while Tyre, Arados, and Sidetes gave the left wing (Appian *Syr.* 27; Livy 37.30.9; 35.48.6). After defeating Antiochus III, the Romans reduced the Seleucid navy to ten undecked ships, none of which could be driven by more than thirty oars (Polybius 21.43.13).[114] The stipulation was not rigorously enforced (Polybius 31.2.11).[115] As Chaniotis has noted, many ships were named after gods, but nothing is known about the religious ceremonies conducted at the naming of a ship, although most likely libations and sacrifices would have been performed.[116]

106 *CJZC*, no. 8. See Shimon Applebaum, *Jews and Greeks in Ancient Cyrene* (SJLA 28; Leiden: Brill, 1979) 178, 186.

107 Mario Luni, "Documenti per la storia della istituzione ginnasiasle e dell'attività atletica in Cirenaica, in rapporto a quelle della Grecia" in Pietro Romanelli and Sandro Stucchi, eds., *Cirene e la Grecia* (Quaderni di archeologia della Libia 8; Rome: Bretschneider, 1976) 223–84, 247–49. For Jewish ephebes in Asia Minor in the second century C.E., see Robert, "Un corpus des inscriptions," 85.

108 Peder Borgen, "'Yes,' 'No,' 'How Far?': The Participation of Jews and Christians in Pagan Cults," in idem, *Early Christianity and Hellenistic Judaism* (Edinburgh: T&T Clark, 1996) 15–43.

109 The verb ἀξιόω + only infinitive has the sense of "think fit," and so I have translated it here. With the accusative and infinitive, the verb can mean "request."

110 Joyce M. Reynolds, "New Letters from Hadrian to Aphrodisias: Trials, Taxes, Gladiators, and an Aqueduct," *JRA* 13 (2000) 5–20, here 19.

111 Angelos Chaniotis, "Epigraphic Bulletin for Greek Religion 2001," *Kernos* 17 (2004) 240 no. 152. Prof. Chaniotis graciously brought this reference to my attention.

112 Smyth, *Greek Grammar*, §1679.

113 Kern, *Die Inschriften*, nos. 31 and 57.

114 See the emendation by Walbank, *Polybius*, 3:159.

115 For Antiochus IV's invasion of Cyprus with a fleet in 168 B.C.E., see Livy 44.19.9; 45.11.9; 45.12.7.

116 In a private communication. See also Angelos

■ **21-22** Apollonius, son of Menestheus, was, according to 4:4, the governor of Coele-Syria and Phoenicia under Seleucus IV. He also served as Antiochus IV's ambassador to Rome in 173 B.C.E. (Livy 43.6.6). Polybius states that Apollonius retired to Miletus during the succession of Antiochus to the throne (31.13.3), but most probably this move occurred after Antiochus murdered Seleucus IV's son, who was co-ruler from 175 to 170 B.C.E.[117] It is uncertain exactly what the festival in honor of Ptolemy Philometor was or when it occurred. Hanhart reads πρωτοκλησία ("first calling," perhaps at a coming-of-age banquet), but there is also strong evidence for reading πρωτοκλισία ("couch of honor at a banquet"). The problem is that the article τὰ is a neuter plural accusative, whereas πρωτοκλισία elsewhere is feminine. Habicht preferred πρωτοκλισία because of its occurrence in an inscription at Delos (see text critical note c above), but there also it is feminine. The neuter πρωτοκλησίον is not elsewhere attested. Given its mention before the removal of Jason from the high priesthood, the festival must have occurred before 172 B.C.E. and therefore cannot be identified with the ἀνακλητήρια, the festival for the coming-of-age, that took place in early 169 B.C.E.[118] Bunge suggested that it was a festival in honor of the first anniversary of Ptolemy VI's coronation, which occurred in March/April 175 B.C.E.[119] Mørkholm held that it was a state banquet at which Ptolemy VI presided,[120] whereas for Walter Otto it was the first public appearance of Ptolemy VI after the death of the regent Cleopatra I.[121] However, since Cleopatra I died in 176 B.C.E., Otto's interpretation seems unlikely. The event must have been some official state action to which ambassadors from other nations were invited. Antiochus IV was the uncle of Ptolemy VI and was intent on maintaining formal relations with the Ptolemaic Empire. Apollonius must have noticed some hint of hostile intentions on the part of the Ptolemies. In response, Antiochus IV visited the harbor city of Joppa and also Jerusalem. Gruen has argued well that Apollonius's embassy to Rome on behalf of Antiochus IV to renew friendship (Livy 42.6.10–12) was also part of Antiochus's strategy to checkmate the Ptolemies.[122] We do not know what other cities Antiochus visited, but that he visited Jerusalem is intriguing. Alexander the Great had not bothered to do so, contrary to later accounts. The novel of *3 Maccabees* has Ptolemy IV Philopator visit Jerusalem. But this actual visit of Antiochus IV might suggest a mutual desire to bring Jerusalem firmly into the Seleucid state as well as to provide Antiochus with a chance to see how the gymnasium was progressing. Jason's plan to place Jerusalem squarely in the Seleucid world was working well.

General Commentary

This section on the high priesthood of Jason encapsulates the difficulties of the condensed version. The author teases the reader with some data—but not enough to enable the situation to be fully understood—and spends most of his energy characterizing Jason as wicked and the source of all things bad. The author thus strongly contrasts Jason with Onias, under whose reverent leadership all had gone well. However, the author does let slip that it was not simply Jason who was in favor of the innovations, as the author has other priests eager to be benefactors of the gymnasium.

The data supplied by the author do not allow us to know with certainty exactly what happened. We do not know if Jason requested that Jerusalem become a *polis*, although this is highly possible. We do not know whether becoming an Antiochene in Jerusalem was restricted to an elite class or to followers of Jason, or whether all Jews in Jerusalem could be Antiochenes. Although in my opinion the last seems most likely, the text does not force one to that conclusion. Furthermore, as Joseph Sievers has noted,[123] the role of the Seleucid garrison in the Akra is not mentioned. Surely these soldiers would have taken advantage of the presence of a gymnasium nearby, and they might have supplied some of the instructors in the

---

Chaniotis, *War in the Hellenistic World: A Social and Cultural History* (Oxford: Blackwell, 2005) 145.

117 Mørkholm, *Antiochus IV*, 38–50; Walbank, *Polybius*, 3:481.

118 Walbank, *Polybius*, 3.345; Polybius 28.12.8.

119 Bunge, "'Theos Epiphanes,'" 70–71. Goldstein objects that the first anniversary would have fallen in 175 B.C.E., too early in the high priesthood of Jason.

120 Mørkholm, *Antiochus IV*, 68.

121 Otto, *Zur Geschichte*, 15–18.

122 Gruen, *Hellenistic World*, 649–50.

123 Joseph Sievers, "Jerusalem, the Akra, and Josephus," in Fausto Parente and Joseph Sievers, eds., *Josephus and the History of the Greco-Roman Period: Essays in Memory of Morton Smith* (SPB 41; Leiden: Brill, 1994) 195–209, here 202–3.

use of arms and tactics. As Sievers surmises, the soldiers may have been "among the promoters of the construction project."[124] The participation of the presumably Cypriot soldiers in the gymnasium would be a clear sign of the way Jason wanted Judea to be an integral part of the Seleucid Empire. Contrary to the intentions of the author of 2 Maccabees, however, this innovation should not be seen as a desire on the part of Jason to abrogate the Mosaic Law and constitution. Becoming a *polis* in the Hellenistic world did not mean abandoning ancestral laws, and Jerusalem was, after all, a temple city whose income depended on maintaining the worship of the God of the Jews. Nevertheless, Jason's attempt to change the educational system in Jerusalem is seen by the author of 2 Maccabees as erasing one identity marker of the difference between Jews and Gentiles.

The rhetorical strategy that the author has used to depict the interaction between Jason and the king in 4:9 is worthy of note. He coldly describes their interaction as a monetary arrangement—Jason will give the king a certain amount of money if the king will furnish something in return. Such a description bypasses the complex notion of gift giving in the Hellenistic world. Gifts implied reciprocal obligation (Aristotle *Eth. Nic.* 1119b22–1124b9; *Rhet.* 1361a37–b2), and a larger gift was expected in return from someone of higher standing. Klaus Bringmann has excellently explored how this notion of gift giving could move over into bribery,[125]

as in the case of Eumenes II and the Achaean Federation (Polybius 22.8–9). However, seen in the light of the interactions between cities and kings that Bringmann and Ma[126] have so thoroughly explored, the interaction between Jason and Antiochus IV finds its place. Jason brings a gift to the new king, and the king, in return, furnishes him with what he requested for the city. Although the author of 2 Maccabees does not discuss the financial details, perhaps the king, as so often in the Hellenistic world, helped defray the cost of building a gymnasium. In an inscription from before 167 B.C.E., an official, Eirenias, is praised by the citizens of Miletus for persuading Eumenes II to give as a gift 160,000 medimnoi of wheat (between 160 and 270 talents, depending on the price of wheat) for the building of a gymnasium.[127] What Jason was doing was therefore what any upstanding citizen might have attempted to do within the contours of gift giving. In return, Antiochus IV would have provided facilities for military training not only for the ephebes but also for the Seleucid garrison, and he would perhaps have been honored by having the gymnasium named after him or have received some honor as its founder. Perhaps Antiochus IV would have received an honor comparable to one from Cos, where a sacrifice was offered to the gods for the well-being of Ariarathes IV and Queen Antiochis as well as the citizens of Cos.[128]

124 Ibid., 203.
125 Klaus Bringmann, *Schenkungen hellenistischer Herrscher an griechische Städte und Heiligtümer*, part 2: *Historische und archäologische Auswertung*, vol. 1: *Geben und Nehmen. Monarchische Wohltätigkeit und Selbstdarstellung im Zeitalter des Hellenismus* (Berlin: Akademie, 2000) 127–33.
126 Ma, *Antiochus III*, 179–242.
127 *SEG* 36, no. 1046. Klaus Bringmann, Hans von Steuben, et al., *Schenkungen hellenistischer Herrscher an griechische Städte und Heiligtümer*, part 1: *Zeugnisse und Kommentare* (Berlin: Akademie, 1995) no. 284 [E 1].
128 Ibid., 253 no. 225 [E].

4

4:23/ After three years, Jason sent Menelaus, brother of the afore-mentioned Simon, to convey the money to the king and to bring about royal decisions[a] on matters of necessity. 24/ When [Menelaus] was introduced to the king, he magnified [the king][b] in posing as powerful, and he obtained for himself the high priesthood by outbidding Jason by three hundred talents of silver. 25/ He arrived with the kingly orders in hand, but he bore nothing worthy of the high priesthood and had the appetites of a cruel tyrant and the passions of an untamed beast.

26/ So Jason, having defrauded his own brother, was himself defrauded by another and forced as a fugitive into the region of Ammon. 27/ While Menelaus possessed the office, he was paying nothing of the money promised to the king in an orderly fashion 28/[c] even though Sostratos, commander of the citadel, made a formal demand. For the recovery of the balance was his concern. Because of this, the two were summoned by the king. 29/ Now Menelaus left behind Lysimachos, his own brother, as his stand-in for the high priesthood, while Sostratos left Krates, commander of the Cypriots.

30/ While such things were at issue, it happened that the citizens of Tarsus and Mallos rebelled because they were being given to Antiochis, the king's concubine, as a grant. 31/ So the king went back quickly to set affairs in order, leaving behind as stand-in Andronikos, one of those held in repute. 32/ Believing that he had received a suitable opportunity, Menelaus appropriated golden objects from those belonging to the temple and freely gave some of them to Andronikos, and others he had just then exported for sale to Tyre and the surrounding cities. 33/ When Onias clearly discovered this,[d] he exposed it and retired to a place of refuge at Daphne lying near

a Reading ὑπομνηματισμούς with Hanhart and Abel rather than χρηματισμούς ("negotiations, decrees") with Habicht. As Goldstein noted, ὑπομνηματισμούς refer to the records kept by the king's secretary. See Welles, *Royal Correspondence*, 283–84, no. 70, line 4.

b The Syriac reads the passive tense, "he was magnified," ܐܬܪܒ, and Goldstein took the accusative masculine singular pronoun (αὐτόν) as a reflexive pronoun—he magnified himself. However, in the same sentence the author uses the reflexive pronoun (ἑαυτόν), so why did he not use the correct reflexive form here if he meant it?

c As punctuated by Hanhart, the sentence is ungrammatical, starting off with a genitive absolute construction followed by an interlocution and without a main clause. Katz ("Text of 2 Maccabees," 13) suggested changing the particle δέ to δή, but George Dunbar Kilpatrick, in his review of Hanhart, *2 Maccabees* and Hanhart, *Text* in *Göttingische gelehrte Anzeigen* (215 [1963] 17), rightly objected that this would not correspond to the usual use of δή. Habicht held that one could either follow Katz's suggestion or simply erase δέ. I would change Hanhart's punctuation and connect the genitive absolute clause to the previous sentence and retain δέ, as it provides an adversative nuance.

d Reading ἃ καί with V L' 46-52 58 311. The verb ἐπιγιγνώσκω ("to discover") requires an object. To make the sentence clear, I have translated the relative neuter plural pronoun as "this."

Antioch. 34/ For which reason, Menelaus took Andronikos aside and was encouraging him to subdue Onias. [Andronikos], persuaded toward treachery, went to Onias.[e] When welcomed, he gave his right hand with oaths. Although held in suspicion, he persuaded [Onias] to come out from the place of refuge, and immediately he shut him up without respecting what is just. 35/ For which cause, not only the Jews but many also of other nationalities were horrified and angry over the unjust murder of the man. 36/ When the king returned from the regions throughout Cilicia, the Jews throughout the city, with the Hellenes also hating the wickedness, were petitioning [him] concerning Onias's having been killed without regard for principle. 37/ Then Antiochus, grieved in soul and turned toward compassion, wept because of the moderation and very orderly behavior of the deceased. 38/ Burning with anger, he immediately stripped off Andronikos's purple, tore his tunic, and led him around throughout the whole city to the very spot where he had sinned against Onias. There he removed the murderer from the world, as the Lord assigned to him the appropriate retribution.

39/ Many objects plundered from the temple by Lysimachos in tandem with the purpose of Menelaus were [found] throughout the city. When news [of this] spread abroad, the populace was united against Lysimachos, since many golden objects were already carried away. 40/ With the crowds aroused and absolutely filled with anger, Lysimachos armed about three thousand men and began unjust, violent measures. The one who started it was a certain Auranos,[f] a man advanced in age but no less in folly. 41/ On seeing the attack of Lysimachos, some snatched up rocks, others stout pieces of wood, while others grabbed the dust lying about, and they were

e   This sentence has a troubled textual history. Hanhart provides the best attested reading, but emendations have been suggested. Instead of πεισθείς ("persuaded") Niese preferred πίστεις, an accusative plural noun found in three Lucianic manuscripts. This reading would require further modifications, as a verb would be needed. Habicht thought that the sentence would read better if πεισθείς were placed before Andronicus's coming to Onias, that is, before the participle παραγενό-μενος. However, although I could not reproduce it in English, the sentence as structured shows a chiastic pattern: persuaded (πεισθείς) . . . welcomed (δεξιασθείς) . . . gave right hand (δοὺς δεξιάν) . . . persuaded (ἔπεισεν). The whole is framed by "went to [παραγενόμενος ἐπί] . . . come out from [ἐκ . . . προελθεῖν]." I have therefore kept Hanhart's reading. The sentence opens with five participles before the main clause, followed by a relative clause. I have broken it into three sentences.

f   The Lucianic manuscripts, as well as the Latin and Syriac, give the name as Tyrannos.

hurling themselves at Lysimachos's followers. 42/ For which
cause, they wounded many,
some they struck down, and
they forced them all to flight.
As for the temple robber, they
subdued him by the treasury.
43/ A suit was lodged against Menelaus concerning these events.
44/ When the king came down
to Tyre, the three men sent by
the council pleaded the case
in his presence. 45/ Already
defeated, Menelaus promised
sufficient funds to Ptolemy, son
of Dorymenes, to persuade the
king. 46/ So Ptolemy took the
king aside into one of the colon-
nades as he was taking a break,
and changed his mind. 47/ He
acquitted Menelaus, the one
responsible for the whole evil,
of the accusations, but determined death for those unfortu-
nates who, if they had spoken
even before Scythians, would
have been acquitted uncon-
demned. 48/ Immediately then,
those who spoke on behalf of
the city and the commons[g] and
the holy vessels suffered the
unjust penalty. 49/ For which
cause, also Tyrians, hating the
wickedness, magnificently supplied what was needed for their
funeral. 50/ Menelaus, however,
because of the greediness of
those who held rule, continued
in office, cleaving to evil and
having become a great betrayer
of the citizens.

g   Both δήμων and δῆμου are solidly attested by the
manuscripts. As Habicht noted, the author prefers
for "people" the term λαός to δῆμος (6:16; 8:2;
10:21; 13:11; 14:15; 15:14). Here the plural could
refer, as in the Hebrew Bible, to either the clans
of the tribes of Israel or the tribes of Israel (Neh
4:13; Judg 17:7). See also Jdt 4:8: "the council of
every tribe of Israel" (ἡ γερουσία παντὸς δῆμου
Ἰσραηλ). Here the council (γερουσία) is said to sit
in Jerusalem but to represent every tribe. Δῆμος
can also have the meaning, as in classical Greek, of
villages, and so Abel, Habicht, and Goldstein have
taken it here in opposition to city. I have kept the
translation "commons" to provide a sense of the representative character of the council.

Commentary by Verse

■ **23-25** "after three years," that is, in the third year. The
author does not make clear whether the embassy took
place in the third year after Antiochus IV's accession in
October 175 B.C.E. or after Antiochus's visit to Jerusalem.

For all Jason's attempts to show his loyalty to Antiochus IV, the king does not reciprocate but awards the
high priesthood to another bidder, Menelaus, brother
of Simon. Josephus states that Menelaus, called Onias,
was a brother of Jason, but this is unlikely (*Ant.* 12.238;
20.35). As noted in 3:4, this Simon was probably an
appointee of the Seleucid government and had been on

good terms with the governor of Coele-Syria, Apollonius,
son of Menestheus (4:4), who had just performed well
for Antiochus IV (4:21). These connections may have
helped Menelaus's case and would have provided a good
introduction for him to the king. What one certainly sees
is the factionalism in Jerusalem along family lines—the
Oniads versus the Balgea family.

Did Menelaus present to the king a onetime offering
of 300 talents, or did he offer to increase the annual tax
by raising it either from 440 to 740 talents, by 68 percent, or from 360 to 660 talents, by 80 percent? Such an
increase in annual tax would not have made him friends
at home. In 4:27, Menelaus is said not to have made regu-

lar payments of the money promised, but this statement could refer just as well to the payment over time of 300 talents as to the annual payment of taxes.

■ **24** "In posing as powerful" is literally "in the countenance of power/resources." The term for power can also mean "wealth, resources." In this context, the two meanings seem combined.

■ **25** "kingly orders." The same term is used to describe Heliodorus's mission in 3:13. Such ordinances might include not only Menelaus's appointment as high priest but also the decisions about the matters of necessity mentioned in v. 23. The result is the portrayal of Menelaus as a puppet of the king.

Here begins a series of $\mu\grave{\epsilon}\nu \ldots \delta\acute{\epsilon}$ constructions as the author highlights a number of contrasts. Both parts of the construction here end with a present participle of two syllables, $\varphi\acute{\epsilon}\rho\omega\nu \ldots \acute{\epsilon}\chi\omega\nu$, to set up similar sounding endings. In the $\delta\acute{\epsilon}$ clause here, the author uses a chiasm: the appetites of a cruel tyrant and of a beast untamed the passions, where "appetites" at the beginning of the description balances "passions" at the end with "cruel tyrant" placed next to "beast untamed." Here I have translated $\vartheta\upsilon\mu o\acute{\upsilon}\varsigma$ as "appetites" and $\grave{o}\rho\gamma\acute{\alpha}\varsigma$ as "passions." Both words can have the more specific meaning of "anger, wrath," but the use of the plural suggests the more general connotation of appetites and passions. Antiochus IV is described in 7:27 as a cruel tyrant, and the same adjective $\beta\acute{\alpha}\rho\beta\alpha\rho o\varsigma$ characterizes both Antiochus IV and Philip the Phrygian in 5:22 as untamed, wild, savage, barbarous. "Tyrant" translates $\tau\acute{\upsilon}\rho\alpha\nu\nu o\varsigma$. Polybius had said that the very word alone conveys the height of impiety (2.59.6).[1]

■ **26-28** The author again uses a $\mu\grave{\epsilon}\nu \ldots \delta\acute{\epsilon}$ construction to show the turnover from Jason to Menelaus. The same verb ($\kappa\rho\alpha\tau\epsilon\hat{\imath}\nu$) is used of Menelaus's gaining control as of Jason's (4:10) and the Hebrews' gaining control (15:37). He employs the theme of appropriate retribution to describe what happened to Jason. Part of Menelaus's scheme was to brook no opposition, and so he forced, by what means we are not told, Jason's departure

across the Jordan. The Tobiad Hyrcanus had also been forced out of Jerusalem and had gone to Ammon. People also escaped to the land of Ammon, a traditional enemy of the Israelites (see Amos 1:13-15; Ezek 25:1-5), from Jerusalem.[2]

■ **26** Note the paronomasia $\acute{\upsilon}\pi o\nu o\vartheta\epsilon\acute{\upsilon}\sigma\alpha\varsigma \ \acute{\upsilon}\pi o\nu o\vartheta\epsilon\upsilon\vartheta\epsilon\acute{\iota}\varsigma$ ("defrauding defrauded") where the aorist active participle is placed alongside the aorist passive participle to highlight the notion of just deserts.

■ **27-28** Within the $\mu\grave{\epsilon}\nu \ldots \delta\acute{\epsilon}$ construction connecting vv. 26 and 27 is another $\mu\grave{\epsilon}\nu \ldots \delta\acute{\epsilon}$ construction within v. 27. In this second construction, the author ends each clause with a similar sounding verb, an example of parachesis: $\acute{\epsilon}\kappa\rho\acute{\alpha}\tau\epsilon\iota \ldots \epsilon\grave{\upsilon}\tau\acute{\alpha}\kappa\tau\epsilon\iota$.

Once in power, Menelaus found it easier to promise than to pay. $\Delta\iota\alpha\varphi\acute{o}\rho\omega\nu$ could mean simply "money," but given the contrast to $\chi\rho\eta\mu\acute{\alpha}\tau\omega\nu$ in the previous sentence and the suggestion that Menelaus was not paying in a regular fashion, it would seem here to mean "balance."

Verse 28 betrays the hand of an abridger, as the reader is suddenly told that there is a Seleucid garrison stationed in the citadel. As noted in 4:12, a Ptolemaic garrison was in place before 198 B.C.E. (Josephus *Ant.* 12.138) and was presumably replaced by a Seleucid one. The statement here shows that being the commander of the citadel was not simply a military post but also entailed certain administrative and bureaucratic duties. As the death of Onias occurred in late 170 B.C.E. (see note on 4:38) and Menelaus came to power in 172 B.C.E., the payment for only one year's taxes would have intervened before Sostratos complained. If it were simply a matter of Menelaus not having paid on time, it would seem strange that both Menelaus and Sostratos would be summoned to the king. As the previous high priest Jason had paid through Menelaus (4:23), perhaps Menelaus disputed the interference of Sostratos in collecting the balance.

■ **29** The evidence of abridgment is found in the mention of both Sostratos and Krates, who do not figure again in the narrative. As Cyprus was at this time still

---

1   See also 5.11.6: "a tyrant's role is to do evil that he may make himself the master of men by fear against their will."

2   The assassin of the governor Gedaliah fled to the land of Ammon (Jer 41:11, 15). Also, Hyrcanus the

Tobiad retired "to the country beyond the Jordan" (Josephus *Ant.* 12.222, 229).

115

held by the Ptolemies, "the Cypriots" refers to a group of mercenaries. In 12:2, Nikanor is a leader of Cypriots. Marcel Launey showed that Cypriots are not frequently mentioned in Hellenistic military history,[3] and Bezalel Bar-Kochva surmised that the Cypriots mentioned here were some of the garrison troops who had formerly served the Ptolemies in Cyprus and later defected.[4] However, I see no reason to reject the ethnic designation of the group.

Ma notes that the verb ἀπολείπειν conveys the sense of the provincial office as "the representation of an absent ruler."[5]

■ **30-31** As Menelaus and Sostratos are to be questioned by the king, Antiochus IV has to leave to settle a dispute between two cities in Cilicia, Tarsus and Mallos.[6] Cilicia was the only region in Asia Minor left to the Seleucids after the peace of Apamea in 188 B.C.E. (Polybius 21.42.4–6).[7] Theoretically, the king could dispose of the territory under his control.[8] Herodotus (2.98.1) claimed that a town in Egypt was allocated to provide for a Persian queen's shoes; Xenophon (*Anab.* 1.4.9) stated that he camped in a place given to a Persian queen in order to provide for her girdle-money ("pin-money"); Themistocles, according to Thucydides (1.138.5), was given three cities, each to pay for one part of his meals.[9] Cicero haughtily summed up this data by saying that the barbarian kings of the Persians and the Syrians were accustomed to have many wives and to give them cities as presents (*Verr.* 2.3.76).

Antiochis was also the name of the daughter of Antiochus III (Diodorus Siculus 31.19.7) who was married to Ariarathes IV, king of Cappadocia. She apparently was in Antioch when Antiochus IV died and was murdered by Lysias (Polybius 31.7.2–3).

In 4:38, Andronikos is said to have worn a purple robe, the sign of the group known as Friends of the King.[10] He may be the same as Andronikos the Macedonian, the Seleucid commander who defended the garrison in Ephesus against the Romans in 190 B.C.E. (Livy 37.13.9–10). See comment on 4:38.

■ **32** The wisdom tradition recommended gifts as a way to success (Prov 17:8; 18:16; 21:14) but also recognized how a gift could become a bribe (Prov. 17:23; Exod 23:8; Deut 16:19; 27:25; see also 1 Sam 8:3). The wily Menelaus knew how to seize the moment and thought to influence Andronikos. As Schwartz notes, the "author's arrangement of the material makes it seem as if not only the soon-to-be-reported murder of Onias, but also the robbery in Jerusalem, became possible only due to the king's absence." The author uses two asyndetic participles—νομίσας ("believing") and νοσφισάμενος ("appropriating")— to convey the sense of close connection between the absence and the appropriation. He used temple vessels to influence Andronikos and achieve his purpose. Presumably, the sales in Tyre and elsewhere were to provide ready cash.

Did the high priest have the authority to sell temple vessels? In deciding this issue, one might look to the case of King Hezekiah. When threatened by Sennacherib, king of Assyria, Hezekiah agreed to pay a penalty of three hundred talents of silver and thirty talents of gold. "Hezekiah gave them all the silver found in the house of the Lord and in the treasuries of the house of the king. At that time he broke up the doors of the temple of the Lord and the doorframes that he himself had plated, and gave them to the king of Assyria" (2 Kgdms 18:15-16).[11] This incident is simply not reported when 2 Chronicles narrates the deeds of the good king Hezekiah, and Jose-

3   Marcel Launey, *Recherches sur les armées hellénistiques* (2 vols.; Paris: Boccard, 1949–50) 1:487–89.

4   Bar-Kochva, *Judas Maccabaeus*, 118; also 119 n. 12.

5   Ma, *Antiochus III*, 54 n. 5, where he refers to Hermann Bengtson, *Die Strategie in der hellenistischen Zeit: Ein Beitrag zum antiken Staatsrecht* (reprinted, 3 vols.; Munich: Beck, 1964–67) 2:102.

6   Mørkholm (*Antiochus IV*, 122) raises some doubts about how significant these uprisings were. On Tarsus, see C. Bradford Welles, "Hellenistic Tarsus," *Mélanges de l'Université Saint Joseph* 38 (1962) 41–75. On Mallos, see Arthur Houghton, "The Seleucid Mint of Mallus and the Cult Figure of Athena Magarsia," in Leo Mildenberg and Arthur Hough-

ton, eds., *Festschrift für Leo Mildenberg: Numismatik, Kunstgeschichte, Archäologie–Studies in Honor of Leo Mildenberg: Numismatics, Art History, Archeology* (Wetteren: Editions NR, 1984) 97–102.

7   See A. H. McDonald, "The Peace of Apamea (186 B.C.)," *JRS* 57 (1967) 1–8.

8   Bickermann, *Institutions*, 133–35.

9   See Plato *Alc.* 123b-c.

10   Bickermann, *Institutions*, 42.

11   An inscription of Sennacherib boasts that Hezekiah gave him thirty talents of gold and eight hundred talents of silver (*ANET*, 288).

phus mentions only that the king emptied his treasuries (2 Chronicles 31–32; Josephus *Ant.* 10.4). In the account in 2 Kings, no blame is attached to the good king for so acting. According to 2 Kings, the king had the authority so to act, whereas the silence of 2 Chronicles implies it was better to leave out such information in shaping a thoroughly positive portrait of Hezekiah.

Hezekiah faced a time of national emergency, but can one say the same about Menelaus? Did Menelaus think that the king would exact severer payment if not forestalled? The Seleucids had not shown themselves above looting temples for money, and Menelaus may have considered it better to lose some temple vessels than to lose them all. One cannot know. The stance of the author of 2 Maccabees is clear—he has the pious former high priest Onias condemn what Menelaus is doing.

■ **33** When last heard of, Onias had been on his way to see Seleucus IV (4:5). Over three years have passed, a new king is on the throne, and Onias's brother Jason is now in exile. Onias seems to have spent these years in the Seleucid capital, Antioch. He reappears in the narrative to defend the sanctity of the temple and its treasures one last time. Onias, however, also knows with whom he is dealing and retreats to asylum. His choice is interesting. Daphne, the place of asylum referred to, was a park near Antioch that Seleucus I had dedicated to the royal gods, especially Apollo, the tutelary god of the Seleucids. Most probably he sought the famous temple of Apollo and Artemis, whose precinct was a place of asylum (Strabo *Geogr.* 16.2.6).[12] In Daphne there was a theater, a stadium, and a gymnasium where the kings celebrated games (Polybius 30.25–26). Given the author's earlier abhorrence of the gymnasium in Jerusalem, it is intriguing to see the pious Onias taking advantage of the protection afforded by a pagan temple. Tcherikover was sensitive to the problem and suggested that Onias had retreated to the synagogue at Antioch mentioned by Josephus (*Bell.* 7.44).[13] However, as Habicht notes, one would have expected the author to mention this fact. Moreover, there is no evidence that synagogues in Seleucid Syria had the right of asylum.[14] More significantly, the reaction of non-Jews to the horror of Andronikos's deed

is more likely based on the breaking of the asylum of a pagan temple. Is Onias's refuge a tacit recognition of the power of these pagan gods, or does he cynically take advantage of the pagans' superstition?

■ **34-38** The story of the murder of Onias III by Andronikos brims with pathos. Recounting the dastardly murder and the appropriate punishment of the murderer is the main concern of the author, so that he even neglects to inform the reader why Menelaus had originally been brought before the king (4:27-28). The author leads his audience on with the intimate details of Menelaus's treachery but explains neither how he knows these details nor why Menelaus is not inculpated with Andronikos. The inquiring reader would also like to know why such a high-ranking personage as Andronikos, the deputy of the king, would be so in the power of a petty prince like the Jewish high priest that, even for a bribe, he would violate the laws of asylum and commit such treachery. The author ignores such questions as he focuses on the treacherous deed instigated by Menelaus with the corrupting power of money.

There is no convincing reason to doubt that Onias died in Antioch. There is a basic confusion in Josephus: in the *Jewish War* Onias flees to Egypt (1.33; 7.423), while in the *Antiquities of the Jews* Onias dies before Menelaus becomes high priest (12.237). The account in 2 Maccabees—Onias goes to the king before Jason becomes high priest and ultimately dies in Antioch—appears to hang together.

■ **34** Here begins a series of euphemisms for "kill." See $\pi\alpha\rho\alpha\kappa\lambda\epsilon\acute{\iota}\epsilon\iota\nu$ later in this verse and $\grave{\alpha}\pi\sigma\kappa\sigma\mu\epsilon\widehat{\iota}\nu$ in v. 38. The verb $\chi\epsilon\iota\rho\sigma\widehat{\upsilon}\nu$ has the basic sense of "to make worse, master, subdue." The verb $\chi\epsilon\iota\rho\sigma\widehat{\upsilon}\nu$ is also used in 4:42. For such a use, see Xenophon *Cyrop.* 7.5.30.

"without respecting what is just" ($\tau\grave{\sigma}$ $\delta\acute{\iota}\kappa\alpha\iota\sigma\nu$). That the murder is not just is repeated in v. 35: $\grave{\epsilon}\pi\grave{\iota}$ $\tau\widehat{\omega}$ . . . $\grave{\alpha}\delta\acute{\iota}\kappa\omega$ $\phi\acute{\sigma}\nu\omega$ ("over the unjust murder").

"Shut up" ($\pi\alpha\rho\alpha\kappa\lambda\epsilon\acute{\iota}\omega$) is a euphemism for "kill," as seen in v. 35 and in the use of $\kappa\alpha\tau\alpha\kappa\lambda\epsilon\acute{\iota}\omega$ in 13:21.[15]

---

12   Rigsby, *Asylia*, 496–99.
13   Tcherikover, *Hellenistic Civilization*, 469.
14   Rigsby, *Asylia*, 571–73.

15   See Polybius 5.39.3, although the text is disputed (Walbank, *Polybius*, 1:569).

■ **35-38** The author enjoys pointing out that Jews and non-Jews have the same reaction to unjust behavior (4:49) and that they can live together (12:30-31).[16] It is part of his purpose to portray the Jews as good citizens (9:19) and as not rebellious. The complaint to Antiochus does not mention that Andronikos had broken the law of asylum at a major sanctuary of the Seleucids, but only that Onias's death was παρὰ λόγον—unprincipled, without cause, or perhaps without proper procedure. The pious Onias is described in v. 37 as the very model of a Greek citizen. Polybius states that Scipio Africanus "established a reputation among everyone for good order and moderation [ἐπ' εὐταξία καὶ σωφροσύνη]," especially against a display of wealth and in matters of money (Polybius 31.25.6–9).[17] The complaint and Antiochus IV's reaction are centered on the death of the particular person of Onias rather than connected with the breaking of asylum. Andronikos therefore may have had Onias executed without sensationally tricking him to come out of asylum.

■ **35** The combination of the unusual verb δεινάζειν with δυσφορεῖν is found also at 13:25.

■ **36** "hating the wickedness." The verb συμμισο-πονερεῖν reflects the hatred of evil by Onias (3:1), and God is asked to hate evil in 8:4.

■ **37-38** The depiction of Antiochus IV is striking. This king, who will be so cruel a persecutor of the Jews, is here portrayed as grieving over the virtuous Onias. Even given that the author may be overstating the case, it is fascinating that he can portray the king as so concerned about ethical issues. The phrase πυρωθεὶς τοῖς θυμοῖς (here translated "burning with anger") is used to depict the righteous anger of followers of Judas Maccabeus in response to blasphemies (10:35) and the zeal of Rhazis (14:45). Here the king is portrayed as the instrument of justice, meting out the appropriate punishment. First, Andronikos's high status is taken away; purple was a mark of distinction in the Seleucid Empire.[18] Public humiliation followed, as Andronikos was paraded through the city, like the two women in 6:10.[19] A contrast is found in the public honor given to Jonathan when Alexander Balas clothed him in purple and had him taken into the middle of the city (1 Macc 10:62-63). Following the motif of just deserts, Andronikos is killed where he had had Onias killed. Note how the author interconnects all these actions by the use of asyndeton between the four participles. The first action, burning with anger, πυρωθείς, is linked asyndetically with the action described by the two following parallel participles, περιελόμενος καὶ . . . περιρρήξας. The third action of leading him around the city, περιαγαγών, is linked asyndetically to the second action and repeats the prefix περί. The quick, rapid-fire succession stresses the immediacy of the king's reaction.

"Remove from the world" is another euphemism for "kill." The image may derive from mourning rites where the women would discard their jewelry (see Pausanias 7.26.9).

Andronikos is said to have murdered the son of Seleucus IV on behalf of Antiochus IV but then to have been executed by Antiochus (Diodorus Siculus 30.7.2–3).[20] According to the Babylonian king list, the co-regent of Antiochus IV, also named Antiochus, was executed by Antiochus IV in July/August 170 B.C.E.[21] Walbank suggests that the tradition whereby Andronikos actually killed the boy king "may be the official version, whereas

---

16 Gary Morrison ("The Composition of II Maccabees: Insights Provided by a Literary *topos*," *Bib* 90 [2009] 564–72, here 568) overstates his case when he proposes that the author's suggestion that even Greeks protest over the murder of Onias is unlikely. Rather, the particle καί has here the sense of ascending climax: not only the Jews, but also. . . .

17 Alcibiades is said to have been advised by Plato (*Alc.* 1.122c) to strive after Spartan virtues, among which was εὐταξία.

18 Bickermann, *Institutions*, 42–44; Meyer Reinhold, *History of Purple as a Status Symbol in Antiquity* (Collection Latomus 116; Brussels: Latomus, 1970) 34–35.

19 Polybius (2.60.7) asserts that the traitor Aristomachos of Argos should not have been tortured to death by night, but should have suffered public humiliation by being led around the whole Peloponnesus and tortured as a public spectacle.

20 John of Antioch in Karl Müller and Theodor Müller, eds., *Fragmenta historicorum graecorum* (5 vols.; Paris: Firmin-Didot, 1878–85) 4:558 no. 58.

21 Sachs and Wiseman, "Babylonian King List," 202–3; see also Mørkholm, *Antiochus IV*, 36–50.

the king-list (its date of compilation is unknown) though official-looking, may have given what were later believed (no doubt rightly) to be the facts."[22] Whatever the case, the dating of the king list would seem to place the death of Onias in the second half of 170 B.C.E. Daniel 9:26 may refer to the death of Onias: "after sixty-two weeks an anointed one will be removed."

■ **39-42** While these events were taking place in Antioch, similar retribution was being meted out in Jerusalem. The pericope opens with reference to objects plundered from the temple (ἱεροσυλήματα, v. 39) and ends with the death of the temple plunderer (ἱερόσυλος, v. 42). Here ἱεροσυλήματα refers not to the act of temple robbery but to the objects stolen from the temple. Lysimachos's method seems to have been to take the vessels out of the temple and store them throughout the city prior to their being sent away. News of this activity leaked out. Both Grimm and Goldstein take the adverb "outside" (ἔξω) to mean "outside the city," that is, to the countryside, and so the uprising would start from the less hellenized country folk. But it is more natural to take the adverb as referring simply to the spread of the knowledge of the stealing.

■ **40** Bar-Kochva accepts the reliability of the figure of three thousand, a considerable force.[23] Faced with such an angry mob, Lysimachos and his followers apparently panicked and attacked first. The phrase is literally "began unjust hands." Such an attack, from Homer through Virgil, was always seen as treacherous. The identity of Auranos is not known, but the author derides his folly as precipitating the clash. Auranos is said to be foolish, as was Simon (4:6) and, later, Alcimus (14:5) and Nikanor (15:33). The description of Auranos as an old man but foolish contrasts also with the descriptions of Onias (4:37) and Eleazar (6:23).

■ **41-42** Again the asyndetic grouping of the participles, "seeing . . . snatching . . . hurling" (συνιδόντες . . . συναρπάσαντες . . . δρασσόμενοι), emphasizes the suddenness of the reaction. In vv. 41 and 42 the author again uses the μέν . . . δέ construction—to effect in v. 41 as he links the various "weapons" used by the attack-

ers, but in v. 42 to describe the effect on those attacked. As will be more evident in later battles, the zeal of one side makes up for its opponent's size and armor, and the unarmed group routs the three thousand armed followers of Lysimachos. As Andronikos had been killed at the spot where he had killed Onias (4:38), so here too Lysimachos, the temple robber, is appropriately dispatched by the treasury, part of the temple enclosure (1 Kgdms 7:51; 2 Chr 5:1). The same euphemism for kill, χειροῦν, is used as in 4:34. Earlier, in 3:24, Heliodorus was said to have approached the treasury when he was miraculously attacked.

■ **43-50** These verses discuss the last of the four incidents involving Menelaus prior to Antiochus IV's incursion into Egypt. The scene has shifted from Antioch to Tyre. As noted above, the death of Andronikos occurred in late 170 B.C.E. At this time, war between the Seleucids and the Ptolemies was imminent, and they both sent embassies to Rome in the winter of 170/169 B.C.E. (Polybius 27.19; 28.1),[24] so it is understandable that Antiochus should have come toward his southern border and be at Tyre. It is also understandable that Antiochus would want stability to reign in his kingdom, particularly in the area of Syria. His need for a strong man in control may have been as much a factor in his decision to exonerate Menelaus as any other. The author, however, shows no concern for these larger dynastic issues but focuses once again on Menelaus's use of bribery. It is noteworthy that the author assumes that the king would have acted justly and was deterred only by the bad advice of his bribed counselor. It is difficult to imagine how Menelaus could have bribed Ptolemy during the trial, but there may have been a break in the deliberations.

■ **44** The *gerousia*, or council of elders, is here mentioned for the first time in the narrative. Antiochus III had recognized its position (Josephus *Ant.* 12.138), and it still functioned later during the high priesthood of Menelaus (11:27). The number 3 may reflect the regulation concerning witnesses in Deut 17:6 and 19:15. That the king took no further measures against the "rebels" of vv. 40-42 might be seen as mild.

22 Walbank, *Polybius*, 3:285. See also Dov Gera, *Judaea and Mediterranean Politics 219 to 161 B.C.E.* (Jewish Studies 8; Leiden: Brill, 1998) 129–31.

23 Bar-Kochva, *Judas Maccabaeus*, 57.

24 See Walbank, *Polybius*, 3:321–24; Gruen, *Hellenistic World*, 651–52, 689.

■ **45** Ptolemy, son of Dorymenes, is said in 1 Macc 3:38 to be one of the Friends of the King along with Nikanor and Gorgias. The documents of the Heliodorus stele mention a Dorymenes who was evidently the governor of Coele-Syria and Phoenicia in 178 B.C.E. Hannah Cotton and Michael Wörrle have noted the difficulty in knowing exactly who this Dorymenes is.[25] Whether the Ptolemy, governor of Coele-Syria and Phoenicia, mentioned in 8:8 was Ptolemy son of Dorymenes or Ptolemy Makron, governor of Coele-Syria and Phoenicia in 10:11-13, is debated. Habicht originally identified the Ptolemy in 8:8 as Ptolemy son of Dorymenes but is since reported to have changed his mind and to see the Ptolemy of 8:8 as Ptolemy Makron.[26] Gera has argued that the Ptolemy of 8:8 was Ptolemy son of Dorymenes and has pointed out that even if Ptolemy son of Dorymenes was not already governor of Coele-Syria and Phoenicia at the time of the events in 4:43-50, as son of a former governor of the area he would have been an influential person at court.[27] At the time of the investigation of Menelaus, however, Ptolemy may already have succeeded Apollonius, son of Menestheus (4:4, 21) who may have broken with Antiochus IV after the murder of Seleucus IV's son and retired to Miletus.[28] Apollonius had supported the claims of Simon against the high priest Onias (4:4). There is thus a tradition of support between the governors of Coele-Syria and the family of Simon and Menelaus. In this scenario, Ptolemy the son would have taken the position his father, Dorymenes, had held.

■ **47** The Scythians were a byword in antiquity for cruelty. Their barbarous behavior was described by Herodotus (4.64–73), and Polybius and Cicero use the Scythians as the standard for cruelty (Polybius 9.34.11; Cicero, *Verr.* 2.5.58 no. 150; *Pis.* 8 no. 18). Gary Morrison notes how the author, by the use of this comparison, shows his contempt for Seleucid justice and officials.[29] The councillors receive the punishment that Menelaus should have received (Deut 19:16-19). The conditional clause has the form of a simple past conditional clause, emphasizing the author's belief.

■ **48** The author seems to like threes, as here—city, commons, holy vessels. See 15:17 (city, holy things, temple) and 15:18 (wives and children, family and kin, temple) and also 4:2, where Onias is benefactor, protector, and zealous follower of the laws The article is lacking before Tyrians, and so not the Tyrians as a whole but some Tyrians are meant.

■ **49-50** The Greek phrase δι᾽ ἣν αἰτίαν (here translated "For which cause") occurs once again, as in 4:28, 35, and 42, that is, in each of the four incidents in this chapter involving Menelaus. The author also uses the same Greek phrase in 8:26 and 12:40. Its use here and the reaction of the Tyrians who hate injustice (μισοπονηρήσαντες) echo the reaction of the citizens of Antioch in v. 36 who hate injustice (συμμισοπονηρούντων). The language here contrasts strongly with that used in 4:1-6 of Onias the high priest. Onias was accused of being the cause of the evils (4:1: τῶν κακῶν δημιουργὸς καθεστηκώς), whereas Menelaus is responsible for the whole evil (4:47: τὸν . . . τῆς ὅλης κακίας αἴτιαν Μενέλαον). Onias was accused of being a betrayer of the state (4:2: ἐπίβουλον τῶν πραγμάτων), but Menelaus is a betrayer of the citizens (4:50: μέγας τῶν πολιτῶν ἐπίβουλος καθεστώς). Onias was not an accuser of the citizens (4:5: οὐ γινόμενος τῶν πολιτῶν κατήγορος) and was later murdered, as were the three members of the council who spoke on behalf of the city (4:48: προηγορήσαντες). Onias sought the public and private interests of the whole people (4:5), whereas Menelaus stayed in power because of the greediness of individuals. That the envoys were given a magnificent funeral contrasts with the deaths of Jason (5:10) and, particularly, Menelaus himself (13:5-8).

General Commentary

Affairs go from bad to worse as Menelaus gains power and the high priesthood moves from the priestly family of the Oniads to that of the family of Bilgah. The author does not stress this change, as the office remains in the

---

25 Cotton and Wörrle, "Seleukos IV," 200–201. See also the discussion in Gera, "Olympiodoros," 144.

26 As reported in Cotton and Wörrle, "Seleukos IV," 201 n. 77. Schwartz also holds this opinion (*2 Maccabees,* 331). Cotton and Wörrle leave the question open.

27 Gera, "Olympiodoros," 142–43. For his arguments against identifying the Ptolemy in 8:8 with Ptolemy Makron, see p. 143 n. 89.

28 Walbank, *Polybius,* 3:481, correcting Polybius 31.13.3.

29 Morrison, "Composition," 566.

hands of a priestly family. He concentrates more on the character of Menelaus, but he does show the way power is kept within the family of Bilgah, as Menelaus places his own brother as deputy.

While the interaction between Jason and Antiochus IV could be viewed in the cultural context of gift giving, this approach to the interactions between Menelaus, Andronikos, and Ptolemy is not possible. Here a bribe is in play, and so Menelaus is portrayed as perverting justice and robbing the temple. Whereas the story had opened in 3:2 with the temple being honored and gifts sent to it, now its treasure is being sold to maintain Menelaus's position.

Two themes emerge in this account of the rule of Menelaus. The first is the theme of just deserts, in which the punishment fits the crime. This theme will surface again in 2 Maccabees in the death of Jason (5:9-10), the painful disease that attacks Antiochus IV (9:5-6), the escape of Nikanor (8:34-36), and the death of Nikanor (15:32-35). This theme is present elsewhere in Jewish writings, for example, in the Elijah cycle (1 Kgdms 21:17-19; 2 Kgdms 9:30-37), in Wis 11:5, 15-16; 18:3-4; and in Josephus's description of the death of Apion (*Ap.* 2.143–44). The second theme is the way that a less imposing force can overcome the more imposing, as the unarmed citizens of Jerusalem scatter the armed forces of the garrison. Note the victory against the Gauls, when a small force defeats a greater one (8:20) and also the way the opposing forces of Nikanor and Judas are described (15:20-27). So the episode of Menelaus is strongly contrasted with the peaceful rule of Onias, but within it there are signs of hope and relief.

5

5:1–6:9a

1/ Around this time, Antiochus made his second inroad[a] into Egypt. 2/ Now all over the city for almost forty days there happened to appear racing throughout the sky cavalry in gold-wrought armament, organized in units with spears[b] at the ready; 3/[c] troops of horses ranged in battle order, each side attacking and charging; shields were in motion. There were scores of spear shafts, swords were being drawn, arrows shot. Golden adornment shone brightly and diverse kinds of breastplate armament.

4/ Because of this, everyone was praying that the divine appearance was for the good. 5/ When a false report arose to the effect that Antiochus had died, Jason mustered no fewer than a thousand men and suddenly perpetrated an attack against the city. When those on the wall were being driven away and the city now at last was occupied, Menelaus fled to the acropolis.

6/ Jason was slaughtering mercilessly his own citizens, not acknowledging that good fortune at the expense of one's kinsfolk is the greatest misfortune but imagining that he was setting down monuments of the defeat of enemies, not of those of the same race. 7/ However, he did not gain control of the government, but, in the end, carried off the shame of treachery and again came as a fugitive to the region of Ammon. 8/ Then, at length he suffered a sorry reversal. Accused[d] before Aretas, chief of the Arabs, fleeing from city to city, pursued by all, abhorred as a rebel against the laws, and loathed as a public [enemy] of fatherland and citizens, he was driven to Egypt. 9/ He who estranged many from the fatherland perished in a strange place, as he set sail for the Lacedaemonians with the intention of seeking protection because of kinship ties. 10/ He who cast forth a multitude of unburied people was unlamented and enjoyed no kind of mourning

a A reads "departure" (ἄφοδος), which does not make sense. The middle form with the cognate accusative, ὁδὸν στέλλεσθαι, means "to set out, be on one's way," and the use of "departure" points in the opposite direction.

b Rather than "spears" (λόγχας, as in La^VP and Hanhart), Abel, followed by Habicht, prefers λόχους ("a company, a body of men"), as found in 64*-236-728-19-62-93 La^VP. One also finds in the manuscripts λυχνους, λυχους. I have taken λόγχας as an accusative of respect qualifying the perfect middle participle ἐξωπλισμένους ("fully prepared, all ready").

c With the Lucianic, Latin, Syrian, and Armenian, I have placed "swords were being drawn" (μαχαιρῶν σπασμούν) after "scores of spear shafts." After discussing cavalry movements, the author discusses specific armaments like shield, spears, and swords.

d Reading ἐγκληθείς ("accused") rather than ἐγκλεισθείς ("confined, imprisoned"). The construction of ἐγκλεισθείς with πρός does not make sense.

whatsoever nor had a part in a grave in his fatherland. **11/ When news came to the king of what had happened, he believed that Judea had seceded. Consequently, he withdrew from Egypt in a brutish disposition and took the city captive. 12/ He ordered his soldiers to mow down without mercy those who met them and to slaughter those who had gone into their homes. 13/ Young and old men were slain, women and children exterminated, mothers and infants slaughtered. 14/ In the entire three days, eighty thousand were ruined, forty thousand in the engagement, and no fewer than the number slaughtered were those sent away to be sold. 15/ Not satisfied with these actions, he presumptuously entered into the holiest temple in the whole world with Menelaus as his guide, Menelaus who had become a betrayer of the laws and of the fatherland. 16/ [Antiochus]ᵉ grasped the holy vessels with his polluted hands and swept up into his unholy hands what had been dedicatedᶠ by other kings for the exaltation, glorification, and honor of the place. 17/ Antiochus was haughty in spirit as he did not see that because of the sins of those dwelling in the city, the Master was for the moment angered and therefore the place was neglected. 18/ But if it wereᵍ not that the place was previously involved in many sins, this fellow alsoʰ would have been brought forward, flogged on the spot, and overthrown because of his insolence just as Heliodorus had been when sent by King Seleucus to investigate the treasury. 19/ But the Lord did not single out for himself the nation on account of the place, but the place on account of the nation. 20/ So the place itself participated in the ill fortune of the nation and shared in the later good fortune. Abandoned during the wrath of the Almighty, it was once more**

e Goldstein argues that at the end of this verse, the reading of L′ 311 Sy should be accepted and ἐπεδίδου ("he was giving over") should be kept. He then argues that the subject of this verb should be Menelaus, not Antiochus. However, there is no indication of a change of subject, and the author of 2 Maccabees likes to string together participial phrases. In this case, the parallelism between the two phrases is excellent. One could argue that the verb ἐπεδίδου was added to complement the participle of λαμβάνω ("take, grasp") by providing a verb of giving (see 1:35) and to differentiate between the two appearances of "hands."

f Reading with L′ 46–52 55 58 106 ἀνατεθέντα, as do Grimm, Abel, and Habicht, instead of ἀνασταθέντα ("set up, erected") with Hanhart.

g I have read, with Hanhart, the imperfect συνέβαινε, rather than, with A and Abel, the aorist συνέβη. Both are possible in a simple conditional sentence, but the imperfect captures the sense of continuing action.

h With Habicht and V 58 Laᴮᴰᴸˣᴾⱽ, a καί should be inserted here.

i Risberg ("Textkritische und exegetische Anmerkun-

restored with all glory when the great Master was reconciled.

21/ Antiochus then carried off one thousand eight hundred talents from the temple and quickly went away to Antioch. He arrogantly supposed that he could make the land navigable and, because of his heart's haughtiness, the sea walkable. 22/ He left behind overseers to maltreat the race; in Jerusalem, Philip, by race a Phrygian but in temper more barbarous than his appointer; 23/ in Gerizim, Andronikos; in addition to these, Menelaus, who worse than the others was exalting himself over the citizens. With an extremely[i] hostile disposition toward the Jewish citizens, 24/ [Antiochus] sent Apollonius, a Mysian leader, with a force of twenty-two thousand men and ordered him to slaughter all men of military age and to sell the women and minors. 25/ [Apollonius] came to Jerusalem and played the part of a peaceful person. He refrained until the holy day of the Sabbath. Scanning the Jews at ease, he ordered maneuvers for those under him. 26/ All who came out to the spectacle he immediately stabbed. Then, running into the city with his soldiers, he laid low a considerable multitude.

27/ Judas, also called Maccabeus, being about the tenth, withdrew to the wilderness,[j] and in the hills lived like the untamed animals with his companions. They persevered in eating grasslike forage so that they would not participate in the pollution.

6:1/ After not much time, the king dispatched Geron the Athenian to compel the Jews to change from their ancestral laws and not to conduct the government by the laws of God, 2/ as well as to pollute the temple in Jerusalem and to name it [the temple] of Zeus Olympios and the one in Gerizim [the temple] of Zeus Protector of Hospitality, as are[k] those who dwell in that place. 3/ Grievous and utterly

gen," 20) makes a strong case for reading the intensive particle δή here, rather than δέ.

j Hanhart omits "to the wilderness," but with Abel and Habicht, I have followed V L$^{r\cdot542}$ 55 58 La Sy Arm Lucif. in retaining it.

k The text has often been changed from ἐτύγχανον to ἐνετύγχανον ("requested") since Benedikt Niese ("Kritik," 519 n. 2) commented that the former was meaningless and proposed the second reading. The change is in line with the request of the Sidonians in Shechem reported by Josephus (*Ant.* 12.258–61). However, I will argue below that the first reading is not meaningless. The phrase is an example of brachylogy, where the adjective ξένιοι ("hospitable") is to be supplied from the context: "just as those dwelling in that place were hospitable."

l Several manuscripts read the plural and seem to refer

offensive was the exercise of evil. 4/ For the temple was filled with debauchery and carousals by the Gentiles as they idled away with courtesans and had sex with women in the holy precincts and, moreover, they brought inside what was unseemly. 5/ The altar was filled with lawless things rejected by the laws. 6/ It was forbidden to keep the Sabbath, to observe the ancestral festivals, and, in a nutshell, to acknowledge to be a Jew. 7/ At the monthly birthday [celebration] of the king, they were brought under bitter compulsion to the banquet meal. When the festival of Dionysos occurred, they were compelled, wreathed in ivy, to take part in a procession to Dionysos. 8/ On the suggestion of Ptolemy,^{1} a vote went forth to the neighboring cities that they observe the same conduct toward the Jews and to compel them^m to eat the banquet meal, 9a/ to slaughter those who did not choose to change over to the Hellenic lifestyle.

to the citizens of Ptolemais, a coastal city in Phoenicia mentioned in 1 Macc 5:15 as hostile to the Jews and therefore a possible reading. However, it would seem more likely that this coordinated effort would stem from the governor of Coele-Syria and Phoenicia (8:8) who had already shown hostility toward the Jews (4:46). Ptolemy would not have been able to enjoin a decree on these cities, but his suggestion would have carried great weight.

m Habicht rightly notes that the text as it stands has the Greeks as the subject of "to eat a sacrificial meal" (σπλαγχνίζειν). He therefore suggests that one insert αὐτοὺς ἀνακάσαι, "to compel them."

Commentary by Verse

■ **1** The author usually is not precise in connecting episodes in his narrative; see 6:1, 9:1, and 11:1. However, he is quite precise in stating that the attack of Antiochus IV took place after his second invasion of Egypt. This second invasion took place in the spring of 168 B.C.E. The author gives no details about a first campaign. Attempts to harmonize this verse with the account in 1 Macc 1:20-23, where Antiochus IV attacks Jerusalem after his first invasion of Egypt, are not satisfactory. Abel interpreted "the second inroad" as meaning a second phase in the first invasion of Egypt, a reading that would mean there is conflict between the two accounts. Dov Gera suggests that in the narrative of 2 Maccabees, this reference would be to the second approach to Egypt after the first one in 4:21 and would thus refer to the first invasion of Egypt.^{1} The word ἔφοδος can have a general meaning of "approach" or a more specific meaning of "advance, attack, assault." Elsewhere in 2 Maccabees it usually has the more specific connotation (8:12; 12:21; 13:26; 14:15; 15:8), particularly when paired with the term for "withdrawal" as in 13:26, a term present in 5:11.^{2} However, since there has been no mention of a first attack on Egypt and the only earlier reference to Egypt was when Antiochus IV sent Apollonius there on the occasion of a festival honoring Ptolemy Philometor, I have tried in the translation to use an equally ambivalent term. A similar

---

1   Gera, *Judaea*, 155–56.

2   In 3:8, the verb ἐφοδεῦσαι has the sense of "on the march, make inspection."

problem arises in Xenophon *Anab.* 3.4.41: "From this summit there was a way of approach [ἔφοδον] to the hill where the enemy were." In 1 Maccabees, the term is found both with the meaning of "attack" (9:68) and with the more general meaning of "approach" (11:44, 14:21). Since the term is used in 2 Maccabees only in the sense of "attack" and is linked here with the term "withdrawal" in 5:11, and since ἔφοδος, or its cognates, is not at all present in 4:21, Gera's suggestion lacks support. Rather, one can see here evidence that this is a concise version and also that the author is not concerned with giving details but focuses on the emotional hardships of the Jews and stresses the horrible characters of Jason, Menelaus, and Antiochus IV.

■ **2-3** These two verses are one long sentence in the Greek, a list of phrases connected by "and." To maintain the breathless quality of the Greek, I have omitted the conjunction. Within this series there is paronomasia at βελῶν βολάς ("arrows shot") and the parachesis of χρυσέων κόσμων ("golden adornment").

Forty is a figure well known in the biblical tradition, as in the forty-year wandering in the desert during the exodus from Egypt and Moses' forty-day stay on Mount Horeb (Exod 21:24). This number is combined with traditional accounts of impending events.

The verb φαίνεσθαι ("to appear") is the basic root for the term ἐπιφάνεια, found in v. 4. Epiphanic appearances were promised in 2:21, and the first occurred in 3:24.

"gold-wrought armament." Some of the statues of gods, daemons, and heroes carried in the grand procession at Daphne organized by Antiochus IV are described by Polybius as wearing "gold-wrought armaments" (30.25.13), the same phrase as here. The horseman who attacked Heliodorus earlier wore golden armor (3:25). Golden clothes were a sign of divine presence. The armament of the soldiers parading in the procession at Daphne is described by Polybius as variegated, some soldiers wearing golden crowns, others having golden, bronze, or silver shields. They are said to wear purple surcoats, many embroidered with gold and figural designs (30.25).

"organized in units." The adverb σπειρηδόν reflects the military tactical unit σπεῖρα, which comprised 256 men. Later, Polybius made it equivalent to the Roman *manipulus,* which consisted of about 150 men (5.4.8; 11.23.1; Plutarch *Aem.* 17). The term was later used about a cohort (Josephus *Bell.* 3.42).

The author uses a traditional motif of premonitory signs to signal the beginning of some great event. Pliny records how it was told that

during the wars with the Cimbrians a noise of clanging armor and the sounding of a trumpet were heard from the sky, and that the same thing happened frequently both before then and after. In the third consulship of Marius, the inhabitants of Ameria and Tuder saw the spectacle of heavenly armies advancing from the east and the west to meet in battle, those from the west being routed. (*Hist. nat.* 2.148)

Josephus, in foretelling the future destruction of Jerusalem, says: "For before sunset throughout all parts of the country chariots were seen in the air and armed battalions hurtling through the clouds and encompassing the cities" (*Bell.* 6.298).[3] He chastises those who did not pay attention to the prodigies (*Bell.* 6.288). This description belongs to the wide range of prodigy literature one finds in Greco-Roman histories.[4]

■ **4** What is interesting in this case is that the meaning of the portents is unclear. In the above quotation from Pliny, the west is routed—the reader knows the portended outcome. The author of 2 Maccabees treats the portent like an oracle whose meaning has to be deciphered and so raises interest in what the outcome will be. The ambiguity of portents and oracles was trenchantly stated by Thucydides when he discussed the relevance of the saying, "A Dorian war shall come and with it death."

So a dispute arose as to whether dearth and not death had not been the word in the verse; but at the present juncture, it was of course decided in favor of the latter; for the people made their recollection fit in with their sufferings. I fancy, however, that if another

---

3   For the full list of prodigies, see 6.288–309. See also Tacitus *Hist.* 5.13.

4   See, e.g., Caesar *Bell. civ.* 3.105; Virgil *Georg.* 1.467–88; Lucan *De bello civili* 1.525. On war during the

Dorian war should ever afterwards come upon us, and a dearth should happen to accompany it, the verse will probably be read accordingly (2.54).[5]

■ **5** The author gives us no clear timeline for the events. After the famous confrontation between the Roman legate Popillius Laenas and Antiochus IV in July 168 B.C.E. (Polybius 29.27.1–10; Livy 45.12.3–8),[6] Antiochus quickly withdrew from Egypt. If the report of Antiochus's death refers to his humiliation at that meeting, there would seem to be little time for Jason to hear the report, gather his force, march from Ammon to Jerusalem, and get there before Antiochus. Gwyn Morgan therefore suggested that the report may have arisen while Antiochus went first to Memphis and ravaged the countryside, before he approached Alexandria (Livy 45.12.1–2).[7] The phrase "that Antiochus had died" has the same form as that used for the death of Seleucus V in 4:7.

The author emphasizes the suddenness of Jason's attack, perhaps to make it more credible. No hint is given that Jason received any help from inside sympathizers, although given the unrest in Jerusalem described earlier (4:40-42), Menelaus may not have found much support. In 4:40, Lysimachos is said to have armed three thousand followers, and a sudden, unexpected attack may have been enough to breach the walls. No role is given to the Seleucid garrison, except as a place where Menelaus could find refuge.

The verb "driven away" is the same as that used in 4:26 for Jason's being driven away from the city.

"fled." the precise meaning of φυγαδεύω is "to exile, banish." V and the Lucianic versions read the simpler form ἔφυγεν. However, the verb seems at this time to mean simply "flee," as in 1 Macc 2:43; 2 Macc 9:4; 10:15; 14:14.

■ **6** The evil character of Jason is stressed by the author.

Just as he had formerly been said to be no genuine high priest (4:13) but had wanted to make his kinsmen follow Greek ways (4:10, 13), so now he treats his fellow citizens as if not of the same race. One might note how Plutarch condemns the Gracchi for fighting against their fellow citizens (*Comp. Ag. Cleom. cum Tr. Gracch.* 3.1).

The contrast is also heightened by the wordplay between good fortune and misfortune, εὐημερίαν and δυσημερίαν. "Good fortune" (εὐημερία) is used frequently to describe military success.[8]

The author uses three terms, each a little broader than its predecessor, to describe Jason's opponents—citizens (πολῖται), kinsfolk (συγγενεῖς), same race (ὁμοέθνοι)—and so increase the emotion.

"setting down trophies." Trophies were often erected to signal victory.[9] In Euripides' *Phoenician Women*, when Polynices besieges his fatherland, Thebes, Jocasta asks him how, if he sacks the city, he will set up trophies to Zeus (*Phoen.* 570–77).

■ **7** The term for "government," ἀρχή, also has the meaning of "beginning, first," and so the author makes a play on words in this μὲν . . . δέ construction, as Jason does not obtain the first place but ends up ("in the end" [τὸ τέλος]) defeated. The term "treachery" (ἐπιβουλή) harks back to the accusation by Simon that Onias was a traitor (4:2: ἐπιβούλος) and the depiction of Menelaus as a traitor (4:50). The author proleptically describes the end of Jason, heightening the dramatic sense of reversal. Jason is forced to retreat to the region of Ammon, and the same terms are used as when he fled as a refugee to Ammon in 4:26.

The author does not say who thwarted Jason's plans. Tcherikover, followed in this by Schwartz, deduced from the separation between the statement that Jason did not attain the government (v. 7) and the return of Antiochus IV (v. 11) that Jason must have been forced out of Jerusa-

Hellenistic period as a time of miracles and saviors, see Chaniotis, *War*, 143–65.

5   See also Herodotus 1.53, 74; Diodorus Siculus 17.41.5–6; Cicero *Div.* 2.56.115–16; Suetonius *Vesp.* 4.5.

6   For Egyptian evidence, see John D. Ray, *The Archive of Ḥor* (Excavations at North Saqqâra Documentary Series 1; London: Egypt Exploration Society, 1976) 127–28.

7   Gwyn Morgan (in Gruen, *Hellenistic World*, 265) in his response to Gruen's essay.

8   Louis Robert, "Notes d'épigraphie hellénistique," *BCH* 54 (1930) 322–51, here 339 n. 1.

9   Pritchett, *Greek State at War*, 2:246–75; A. H. Jackson, "Hoplites and the Gods: The Dedication of Captured Arms and Armour," in Victor D. Hanson, ed., *Hoplites: The Classical Greek Battle Experience* (London: Routledge, 1991) 228–49.

lem by a force such as that described in 4:39-41.[10] Since Menelaus was shut up in the citadel and Antiochus was not yet on the scene, some other group must have forced Jason to leave. However, this argument does not take into account the literary character of the description as noted above. If such a third force did arise, one would expect even the author of this condensed version to mention it, as he mentions the uprising against Lysimachos. Rather, the juxtaposition of Jason's departure and Antiochus's attack suggests that the latter was precipitated by the former.[11]

■ **8** With Grimm, I have taken πέρας as adverbial, meaning "at length." Here ἀναστροφή does not have the meaning of "behavior, way of life" as found in 6:23, but its more common sense of "upset, reversal."

The description of Jason's wicked end is told in one long sentence, vv. 8b-10. After five participial phrases, ἐγκληθείς, φεύγων, διωκόμενος, στυγούμενος, and βδελυσσόμενος, follow four main clauses coordinated by καί: ἐξεβράσθη, ἀπώλετο, ἐγενήθη, μετέσχεν. I have read ἐγκληθείς with Grimm, Nestle[12], and Habicht. The verb ἐγκλεισθείς ("confined, imprisoned") does not make sense with the following prepositional phrase, πρὸς Ἀρέταν ("to, towards Aretas"), as the phrase should read something like "imprisoned by Aretas." However, the prepositional phrase makes good sense with the verb "to accuse." Aretas I, king of the Nabateans, is here mentioned for the first time in history.[13] Who accused Jason or of what he was accused is not known. Schwartz suggested that the accusation was "due to a complaint and extradition request—on the part of Antiochus or some Seleucid official."[14]

The asyndetic piling up of participial clauses heightens the sense of urgency and of Jason's constantly being on the run. The first two participial phrases form a chiasm in which the first phrase opens with the participle ἐγκληθείς ("accused") and the second phrase ends with the participle φεύγων ("fleeing"). The last two participles are in parallel: "abhorred as . . . , loathed as . . . ." The parallelism between "rebel against the laws" and "public [enemy] of fatherland and citizens" suggests that "the laws" here should not be construed to refer specifically to the Torah but as a general description of a criminal. Goldstein rightly draws attention to the last days of Hannibal, who first went to Antiochus III, then to Prusias, king of Bithynia, and finally committed suicide rather than be handed over to the Romans (Livy 39.51).[15]

Egypt, just delivered from Antiochus IV by means of the Romans, was a safe place to get away from Antiochus. The use of the verb "driven up" (ἐκβράζω) gives the sense of being washed up on the shore like flotsam and jetsam.

■ **9-10** The author again uses the motif of the punishment fitting the crime (see also 4:38). Jason is not said earlier to have banished or estranged people from Judea, except for Onias. There is use of paronomasia and similarity of sound: ἀποξενώσας ἐπὶ ξένης ἀπώλετο ("estranged . . . perished in a strange place"). The use of kinship to regulate relations between states was a constant factor in the Greek world.[16] The existence of a kinship relationship between Sparta and the Jews is presumed in the correspondence found in 1 Macc 12:6-23; 14:20-23.[17] The Jewish writer Cleodemus Malchus writes that three descendants of Abraham by Keturah (Gen

10   Tcherikover, *Hellenistic Civilization*, 187–88.

11   See James C. VanderKam, "2 Maccabees 6,7a and Calendrical Change in Jerusalem," *JSJ* 12 (1981) 52–74, here 61 n. 29.

12   Eberhard Nestle, "Einiges zum Text des zweiten Makkabäerbuchs," *Septuagintastudien, IV* (Stuttgart: Vereins-Buchdruckerei, 1903) 19–22, here 22.

13   Abraham Negev, "The Nabateans and the Provincia Arabia," *ANRW* 2.8 (1977) 520–686, here 521–46; Robert Wenning, "Eine neuerstellte Liste der nabatäischen Dynastie," *Boreas* 16 (1993) 25–38, here 27–29.

14   Schwartz, *2 Maccabees*, 255. For a discussion on extradition, he refers to the work on 1 Macc 15:21 by Uriel Rappaport, "The Extradition Clause in 1

Maccabees XV, 21," in Karel van Lerberghe and A. Shoors, eds., *Immigration and Emigration within the Ancient Near East: Festschrift E. Lipiński* (OLA 65; Leuven: Peeters, 1995) 271–83.

15   See also the speech of Scipio (Livy 37.45.16), where he shows his undying hatred of Hannibal.

16   Christopher P. Jones, *Kinship Diplomacy in the Ancient World* (Revealing Antiquity 12; Cambridge, Mass.: Harvard University Press, 1999).

17   Erich Gruen, "The Purported Jewish-Spartan Affiliation," in Robert W. Wallace and Edward M. Harris, eds., *Transitions to Empire: Essays in Greco-Roman History, 360–146 B.C., in Honor of E. Badian* (Norman: University of Oklahoma Press, 1996) 254–69.

25:1) campaigned with Herakles in Libya and that Herakles married a daughter of one of Abraham's sons (Josephus *Ant.* 1.240–41).[18] As Herakles was claimed to be the progenitor of the Spartan kings, a kinship relationship was created through this connection. Jason had attacked his kinsfolk (5:6: συγγενεῖς) and now claims kinship ties (συγγένεια) with Sparta. "Protection" (σκέπη) had a legal as well as a technical meaning.[19]

To die unburied in the land of one's fathers was a curse (1 Kgs 13:22). The same motif recurs in the deaths of Antiochus IV (9:28) and Menelaus (13:7-8). In *Ps. Sol.* 2:30-31, Pompey is said to have died in Egypt because of his arrogance toward God. Recall the story of Antigone and her brother as told in Euripides' *Antigone*.

■ **11-16** The author gives no indication of what happened in Egypt so that Antiochus IV was forced to leave by the Romans, nor is the event recorded by the author of 1 Maccabees, although Dan 11:29-30 does mention the intervention of the Romans (Kittim). The author of 2 Maccabees focuses the whole story on Antiochus's dealings with the Jews. Earlier Menelaus had been described as having the passions of an untamed beast (4:25). The characterization of Antiochus in 2 Maccabees is interesting. Previously he had been described as overcome with emotion when he heard of Onias's death (4:37-38), and now he gives vent to beastlike anger. He is thus portrayed not as an ideal king, who controls his emotions, but as under the control of his emotions. In excluding the events of Antiochus's dismissal by the Romans from Egypt, the author would not have the reader think that the cause of Antiochus's attack on Jerusalem was frustration or even the need for funds, but rather that Antiochus felt the city was in rebellion.[20]

■ **11-12** Goldstein rightly stresses the importance of the term δοριάλωτον, which I have translated "captive" and

he translates "as enemy territory captured in war." Literally δοριάλωτος means "taken by the spear." Goldstein notes that "persons or cities captured through combat were completely at the mercy of the conqueror." In a document from the second century B.C.E. (Demosthenes *Cor.* 181–87),[21] it is held that Philip of Macedon had captured cities in war (πόλεις . . . δοριαλώτους) and that

of some Greek cities he overthrows the constitution [τὰς πολιτείας καταλύει] and puts a garrison in them, others he razes to the ground, selling the inhabitants into slavery, others he colonizes with barbarians instead of Greeks, handing over to them the temples and sepulchres. (Demosthenes *Cor.* 182)

Livy records how the town Haliartus was besieged during the Third Macedonian War and captured in 171 B.C.E. The elderly and the young were cut down, and twenty-five hundred Boeotians were sold into slavery; the adornments of the city and any costly booty were taken and the city razed to the ground (42.63.10–11).

"Without mercy" (ἀφειδῶς) is the same term that is used of Jason's attack in 5:6.

■ **13-14** In his description of Antiochus's sacking of Jerusalem, the author spares no pains to emphasize the cruelty and mercilessness of Antiochus with his groupings of those slaughtered, from the oldest to the youngest, including women and infants. The numbers are inflated. Although there is debate about the size of pre-Maccabean Jerusalem, it was certainly not a city of 80,000 people. Josephus gives the number of those taken prisoner as around 10,000 (*Ant.* 12.251). Pseudo-Hecataeus of Abdera stated that the population of pre-Maccabean Jerusalem was around 120,000 (Josephus *Ap.* 1.197), but Bezalel Bar-Kochva has shown that this is a late work,

18 Josephus is here quoting Alexander Polyhistor, a first-century B.C.E. compiler of traditions.

19 See Marta Piatkowska, *La ΣΚΕΠΗ dans l'Égypte ptolémaïque* (Wroclaw: Zaklad Narodowy im Ossolinskich, 1975).

20 Curiously, Porphyry is quoted by Jerome in his commentary on Dan 11:44 as saying that Antiochus IV "would overcome the resistance of the Aradians and lay waste the entire province along the coastline of Phoenicia." This section of Daniel is referring to a time well after the invasion of Egypt in 168 B.C.E. and Antiochus's repulse by the Romans. It does not

seem to have any foundation. Mørkholm (*Antiochus IV*, 122–27) has shown that the coinage of Arados and Phoenicia remained undisturbed throughout the reign of Antiochus IV.

21 On its being a forgery, see Piero Treves, "Les documents apocryphes du 'Pro Corona,'" *Les études classiques* 9 (1940) 138–74.

that these figures are inflated, and that the population would have been no more than 7,500.[22] Nahman Avigad estimates that at this time the population of Jerusalem was no more than a few thousand.[23]

"In the engagement" (ἐν χειρῶν νομαῖς) is literally "in the feedings of the hands." The phrase is found also in a second-century B.C.E. inscription, *SIG* 2, no. 700, 29. The manuscripts A 46–52 58 read ἐν χειρῶν νομοῖς, as Grimm rightly accents, where νομός has the same meaning as νομή. It is similar to the phrase ἐν χειρῶν νόμῳ, known from Herodotus 8.89; 9.48, and found frequently in Polybius and Diodorus Siculus, where one is not sure whether to accent as νόμῳ ("law") or νομῷ ("feeding, pasturage"). In *3 Macc* 1:5 one also finds the phrase ἐν χειρονομίαις, which seems to be a variant of this phrase, ἐν χειρῶν νομαῖς.[24]

■ **15-16** "Presumptuously entered" is literally "dared to enter." The same verb, "to dare" (κατατολμᾶν), was used when Heliodorus tried insolently to enter the temple (3:24). The description as most holy is similar to 2:19. *Third Maccabees* 1:16—2:24 recounts how the Ptolemaic king was prevented from entering the temple by a miraculous event. However, Josephus reports that Antiochus VII Sidetes, Pompey, Licinius Crassus, and Julius Caesar found nothing improper when they entered the temple (Josephus *Ap.* 2.82). Menelaus had already been described as a plotter against his citizens (4:50); now he is described as a betrayer of the fatherland, using language similar to that used of Jason (5:8-9). The role of Menelaus suggests that he had been rescued by the arrival of Antiochus and set free from the citadel. The city and the temple were already completely in the hands of Antiochus IV, so Menelaus could roam where he willed. The author's antagonism toward Menelaus is shown in the description of Menelaus as Antiochus's guide. The author emphasizes that Antiochus IV had

hands polluted (ταῖς μιεραῖς χερσί) and profane (ταῖς βεβήλοις χερσί).[25] Christine Hayes notes that the term here does not mean that Antiochus was impure because he was a Gentile; his was a moral impurity.[26] However, the terms themselves have the undertones of desecration, particularly in the context of entrance into a temple. For example, in Ps 74:7 (LXX Ps 73:7) enemies "desecrated [ἐβεβήλωσαν] the dwelling place of your name"; in Jdt 9:8, Judith prays that God will destroy his enemies "for they intend to defile your sanctuary [βεβηλῶσαι τὰ ἅγιά σου]."

First Maccabees 1:21-23 gives a detailed list of the vessels taken by Antiochus from the temple. None of those there mentioned would have been within the holy of holies. Diodorus Siculus reports that Antiochus Epiphanes is said to have entered the innermost sanctuary of the temple (εἰσῆλθεν εἰς τὸν ἄδυτον τοῦ θεοῦ σηκόν) and found there an image of a man seated on an ass (34.1.3-4).[27] The author of 2 Maccabees insists that this desecration was at odds with the way earlier kings had honored the temple (3:2).

■ **17-20** Here the author inserts another in a series of reflections on what has happened, as in 4:16-17 and 6:12-17.

■ **17** "haughty in spirit." The verb μετεωρίζω is used also in 7:34 and often has the meaning of being buoyed up with false confidence (see Polybius 3.70.1; 25.3.4). The metaphor is caught in Obad 4: "Though you soar aloft [μετεωρισθῇς] as an eagle, . . . from there I will bring you down, says the Lord." An *inclusio* is formed in 5:21, where the haughtiness (μετεωρισμός) of Antiochus's heart is noted.

The sense of the sinfulness of the nation causing the anger of God is clearly expressed by the youngest martyr in 7:33-38. Note how the same language, βραχέως ἐπώργισται, is used in 7:33, but this anger is turned to mercy

22 Bezalel Bar-Kochva, *Pseudo-Hecataeus, On the Jews: Legitimizing the Jewish Diaspora* (Hellenistic Culture and Society 21; Berkeley: University of California Press, 1996) esp. 112.

23 Nahman Avigad, "Jerusalem: The Second Temple Period," in Ephraim Stern, ed., *The New Encyclopedia of Archeological Excavations in the Holy Land* (4 vols.; Jerusalem: The Israel Exploration Society & Carta, 1993) 2:717–25, here 720–21.

24 See also Adolf Wilhelm, "Ἐν χειρῶν νομαῖς und ἐν χειρῶν (χειρὸς) νομῷ," *Glotta* 24 (1936) 133–44.

25 Recall Lam 1:10: "Enemies have stretched out their hands over all her precious things."

26 Christine E. Hayes, *Gentile Impurities and Jewish Identities* (Oxford: Oxford University Press, 2002) 51.

27 See also Apion in Josephus *Ap.* 2.80–81, 92–96.

in 8:5 ($τῆς ὀργῆς \ldots εἰς ἔλεον$). Isaiah said of Assyria that it was the rod of God's anger (Isa 10:5), but that it would be punished because of its arrogant boasting (Isa 10:12).

"The place was neglected" is literally "there was neglect in regard to the place." Isaiah 57:11 LXX, after God complains that the people have neither remembered him nor given him a thought, reads: "So I, seeing you, neglect [$παρορῶ$] you, and you have not feared me." That God is Master ($δεσπότης$) is stressed again with the repetition of the term in 5:20.

■ **18** The reference back to the events of 2 Maccabees 3 shows how far astray Jason and Menelaus have led the people. Note the asyndetic participles $προαχθείς \ldots$ $μαστιγωθείς$ ("brought forward . . . flogged"). This use of asyndeton seems not just to condense the telling but also to point to how God, if not angry with his people, responds immediately to an attack on his temple.

■ **19** This pithy contrast is similar to the statement ascribed to Agesilaus when as a boy he was assigned to an unimportant position by the dance director: "I shall show that it is not the places that make men held in honor, but the men the places" ($οὐχ οἱ τόποι τοὺς$ $ἄνδρας ἐντίμους, ἀλλ᾽ οἱ ἄνδρες τοὺς τόπους ἐπι-$ $δεικνύουσιν$) (Plutarch *Apoph. lac.* 208D–E).[28]

The author continues the call of the prophets that the temple without true moral behavior is no safeguard. As Jeremiah said, "Do not trust in these deceptive words: 'This is the temple of the Lord, the temple of the Lord, the temple of the Lord'" (Jer 7:4; see also ch. 19). At the dedication of the temple, God had put before Solomon a blessing if the people followed God's commandments, a curse if they did not (2 Chr 7:12-22).

The term "Almighty" ($παντοκράτωρ$) emphasizes that all is in God's power. It is interesting how the author uses this term in times of persecution (6:26; 7:35; 8:11, 18; 15:8) and also in times of triumph (8:24; 15:32).

■ **20** The sentence contains two clauses, each well balanced in contrastive parallelism. Note the homoioteleuton of $δυσπετημάτων \ldots εὑρετημάτων$ ("ill fortune . . . good fortune"), as well as the alliteration of $κατα$-$λειφθείς \ldots καταλλαγῇ$ ("abandoned . . . reconciliation"). "Was reconciled" is literally "in the reconciliation of the great Master." In Greek, the phrasing echoes and stands in contrast to the previous phrase, "in the wrath of the Almighty."

The language of the second half of the sentence resonates with the language of the martyrdom of the seven brothers. The fifth brother claims that God has not abandoned his people definitively—the verb is in the perfect tense (7:16)—while the seventh brother claims that God, after being angry, will be reconciled (7:33; see also 8:29). The verb for restoration ($ἐπανορθοῦν$) is the same as that used in the prologue when speaking of the restoration of the laws about to be abrogated (2:22).

■ **21** The narrative is resumed, as is shown by the repetition of the term $μετεωρισμόν$ ("haughtiness").

Eighteen hundred talents was a not inconsiderable sum. Antiochus III had been obliged by the treaty of Apamea to pay the Romans one thousand talents a year for twelve years (Polybius 21.42.19). In 3:6, Simon claimed that there were immense funds in the temple, and Onias countered that the deposits amounted to four hundred talents of silver and two hundred of gold (3:11). Since Menelaus had fallen behind in paying the taxes (4:28) and had sold temple vessels as a short-term solution (4:32), one wonders at the coherence of the numbers. Nevertheless, the large amount emphasizes the importance of the temple.

The author indulges again in parallelism, balancing "arrogantly" ($ἀπὸ τῆς ὑπερηφανίας$) with "because of his heart's haughtiness" ($διὰ τὸν μετεωρισμὸν τῆς$ $καρδίας$) and contrasting land and sea. Similar impossibilities are thought by Antiochus in 9:8, 10. This arrogance of Antiochus would have brought to the audience's minds how Xerxes in his attack on Greece had made a canal at Mount Athos for his ships to cross and had placed a bridge over the Hellespont (Herodotus 7.22-24, 34-37). This action was seen as hubris against the gods (Aeschylus *Pers.* 744-51), and the historian Justin stated that Xerxes acted "as if lord of nature itself" in leveling mountains and paving seas (2.10.24). This resonance

---

28 Recall also the saying attributed to Jesus: "The sabbath was made for humans, not humans for the sabbath" (Mark 2:27).

with Xerxes' actions would have reinforced the rhetorical aim of the author to claim that the Jews are more cultivated than the Seleucids (2:21).

■ **22-23** An overseer, ἐπιστάτης, was a civilian official in charge of a city on behalf of the king.[29] The overseers' job here is to maltreat, κακοῦν, the race, recalling how in Exod 1:11 taskmasters were set over the Israelites to oppress, ἵνα κακώσωσιν, them. Through a μὲν . . . δέ construction, the author here links those in Jerusalem and the Samaritans in Gerizim as belonging to the same race, τὸ γένος, as he does also in 6:2. Josephus preserves a letter from the Sidonians in Shechem to Antiochus IV, dated to 167/166 B.C.E., requesting that they not be molested as they are different from the Jews (*Ant.* 12.258–64).[30] Philip is mentioned again in 6:11 and 8:8. Phyrgians are attested as mercenaries in Hellenistic armies.[31] Again, the Seleucid administrator is lined up alongside barbarians. Andronikos is not otherwise mentioned in the account. Menelaus continues as high priest, but his position as ruler of the city has been curtailed and subordinated to that of Philip.

"was exalting himself." The verb ὑπεραίρω can mean, in the middle voice, "to exalt oneself, to lord over," and this appears to be the only case where the person over whom one exalts oneself is in the dative. In Demosthenes *Cor.* 18.220, the active verb is followed by the dative in what one excels, and perhaps this usage is being followed here.

■ **24** The time between the appointment of Philip and the sending of Apollonius is not specified. Antiochus means to treat this city as captured in war (5:11). Apollonius is to be identified with the personage in 1 Macc 1:29, although the dating is different and he is there called a tax-gathering official. Here Apollonius is called a Mysarch (μυσάρχην), a commander of mercenaries from Mysia in Asia Minor.[32]

■ **25-26** After the onslaughts of Jason (5:6) and Antiochus (5:13-14), one wonders how many were left in Jerusalem to sell or kill and why Apollonius had to resort to a ruse to trick the inhabitants. Apollonius's action is clearly intended to depopulate the city and perhaps leave it open for other settlers. The people of Jerusalem, already under an overseer, would not have been expecting this further harsh measure. The ruse is found also in the corresponding account in 1 Macc 1:30. Apollonius's "playing the part" (ὑποκριθείς) will contrast with Eleazar's refusal to play a part in the next chapter (6:21, 24-25). Taking advantage of the Sabbath rest of the Jews is noted by Agarthachides of Knidos (Josephus *Ap.* 1.209–11; *Ant.* 12.5–6),[33] and the story of the group of Jews who would not defend themselves on the Sabbath is told in 1 Macc 2:29-38.[34]

The use of ἐξοπλισίαν ("maneuvers") resonates with the use of ἐξωπλισμένους ("arranged") in the vision in 5:2. Does this connection suggest that this event is the fulfillment of the vision?

Gera dates the attack of Apollonius in the early summer of 167 B.C.E., whereas Bickermann and Bringmann date it to 168 B.C.E.[35]

■ **27** The author stresses the sorry state of the Jews by the contrast between Apollonius with his twenty-two thousand men and the ten men around Judas. The wilderness, with its abundance of caves, provided ready-made hiding places. It is a traditional place of refuge in the Bible: there Moses flees from Pharaoh (Exod 3:1),

---

29 See Peter Rhodes, "Epistatai," *Brill's New Pauly* 4:1131.

30 Elias Bickermann ("Un document relatif à la persécution d'Antiochos IV Épiphane," in idem, *Studies in Jewish and Christian History* [3 vols.; AGJU 9; Leiden: Brill, 1976–86] 2:105–35) considered it authentic, but this judgment has been strongly questioned by Uriel Rappaport ("The Samaritans in the Hellenistic Period," in Alan D. Crown and Lucy A. Davey, eds., *Essays in Honour of G. D. Sixdenier: New Samaritan Studies of the Société d'Études Samaritaines, III & IV: Proceedings of the Congresses of Oxford 1990, Yarnton Manor and Paris 1992, Collège de France: With lectures given at Hong Kong 1993 as participation in the ICANAS Congress* [Studies in Judaica 5; Sydney:

Mandelbaum, 1995] 283–87). Seth Schwartz ("John Hyrcanus I's Destruction of the Gerizim Temple and Judean-Samaritan Relations," *Jewish History* 7 [1993] 9–25, here 15, 23–24 n. 35) has questioned the argument of Rappaport.

31 Launey, *Recherches*, 1:481–83.

32 Otto Schulthess, "Mysarches," *PW* (1935) 16:2287.

33 See also Frontinus *Strat.* 2.1.17; Plutarch *Mor.* 169C; Dio Cassius 37.16.2–4.

34 On this topic, see Martin Goodman and A. J. Holladay, "Religious Scruples in Ancient Warfare," *Classical Quarterly* 36 (1986) 151–71.

35 Gera, *Judaea*, 223–24; Bickermann, *God of the Maccabees*, 111; Bringmann, *Hellenistische Reform*, 33.

David from Saul (1 Sam 23:14), Elijah from Jezebel (1 Kgs 19:1-9). The wilderness is an ambivalent image, used to denote good or evil. It can be the place where no human dwells, a place of deep darkness (Jer 2:6) where the night hag alights (Isa 34:14), a place of chaos (Deut 32:10) to which one sends the goat of sin offering on Yom Kippur (Lev 16:22), a punishment from God (Zeph 2:13). There the Israelites had continuously murmured against God during the Exodus (Psalm 78; Ezekiel 20). Yet it is also where God showed his unfailing love for Israel and where he covenanted with them (Jer 2:2-3; Hos 2:14-15). Further, time in the wilderness can be seen positively as a time of leaving society with its corrupting mores (Isa 52:11-12), a time of renewal before the entry into the promised land (1QS 9.19–20).[36]

The description of Judas and his companions is also ambivalent. Daniel has a dream in which Nebuchadnezzar is punished by God "so that with the beasts of the earth in the mountains he will eat grass like an ox" ($\mu\epsilon\tau\grave{\alpha}$ $\tau\hat{\omega}\nu$ $\vartheta\eta\rho\acute{\iota}\omega\nu$ $\tau\hat{\eta}\varsigma$ $\gamma\hat{\eta}\varsigma$ $\dot{\epsilon}\nu$ $\tauo\hat{\iota}\varsigma$ $\ddot{o}\rho\epsilon\sigma\iota$ $\chi\acute{o}\rho\tauo\nu$ $\dot{\omega}\varsigma$ $\beta o\hat{\upsilon}\varsigma$ $\nu\acute{\epsilon}\mu\epsilon\tau\alpha\iota$) (Dan 4:12, 24-25; see also 5:21). Yet Judas's escape is pictured not as a punishment but positively, as an escape from pollution. Elijah too had fled to the wilderness, from Jezebel, and then to Mount Horeb (1 Kgs 19:4-8). In *Mart. Isa.* 2:8, Isaiah is said to flee from the great iniquity in Jerusalem and Bethlehem and dwell on a mountain in a desert place. Judas forsakes the impure society for the world of nature. With this word of pollution, $\mu o\lambda\upsilon\sigma\mu\acute{o}\varsigma$, the author sets up what is about to happen in the succeeding sections. The temple is to be polluted (6:2: $\mu o\lambda\hat{\upsilon}\nu\alpha\iota$), and Eleazar refuses to pollute himself (6:19, 25: $\mu\acute{\upsilon}\sigmao\varsigma$). This time of pollution lasts until the temple is cleansed (10:3); Alcimus is described as polluted (14:3). The author thus has Judas and his companions leave Jerusalem before it is embroiled in pollution. The author of 1 Maccabees, however, narrates how Mattathias, the father of Judas, and his sons left Jerusalem after the beginning of the persecution and the building of altars in Jerusalem (1 Macc 2:1). The author of 1 Maccabees uses the imprecise phrase "in those days."

■ **6:1** The author suggests that all these events occurred within a short period. They must have occurred between the time Antiochus IV left Pelusium on 30 July 168[37] and the setting up of the "abomination of desolation" in the temple on 15 Kislev, that is, 6 December 167 B.C.E. (1 Macc 1:54).[38] Habicht points to other Athenians in the service of the Seleucids.[39] The author of the abridged version provides much more detail than the general account in 1 Macc 1:41-54, where the king writes letters to every city in his kingdom and appoints overseers to every people. Such a general decree is highly unlikely.[40] To the contrary, the author of 2 Maccabees stresses how these measures are specific to the Jews.

$\gamma\acute{\epsilon}\rho o\nu\tau\alpha$ $\dot{A}\vartheta\eta\nu\alpha\hat{\iota}o\nu$ (Geron the Athenian). Wilhelm convincingly suggests that a proper name, Geron, $\Gamma\acute{\epsilon}\rho\omega\nu$, be read here, rather than "the old Athenian." Geron is otherwise unknown.[41]

The sense of compulsion ($\dot{\alpha}\nu\alpha\gamma\kappa\acute{\alpha}\zeta\epsilon\iota\nu$, "compel") will recur in 6:7 ($\dot{\alpha}\nu\acute{\alpha}\gamma\kappa\eta$) and in 6:18 and 7:1 ($\dot{\alpha}\nu\alpha\gamma$-$\kappa\acute{\alpha}\zeta\epsilon\sigma\vartheta\alpha\iota$) and tie the martyrdoms to Geron's mission. It is important to note the antithetical parallelism between "change from ancestral laws" and "not to conduct the government [$\mu\grave{\eta}$ $\pi o\lambda\iota\tau\epsilon\acute{\upsilon}\epsilon\sigma\vartheta\alpha\iota$] by the laws of God." The polity of Judea is stated to be the Torah, so that to change the polity is to attack the Torah. The author had already seen Jason's measures as an attack on lawful ways of conduct (4:11: $\tau\grave{\alpha}\varsigma$ . . . $\nu o\mu\acute{\iota}\mu o\upsilon\varsigma$ . . . $\pi o\lambda\iota\tau\epsilon\acute{\iota}\alpha\varsigma$).

"conduct the government." $\Pi o\lambda\iota\tau\epsilon\acute{\upsilon}\epsilon\sigma\vartheta\alpha\iota$ is used in the letter of Antiochus V in which he grants the Jews the right to live according to the ways of their ancestors (11:25).[42]

---

36 Shemaryahu Talmon, "The 'Desert Motif' in the Bible and in Qumran Literature," in Alexander Altmann, ed., *Biblical Motifs: Origins and Transformations* (Philip W. Lown Institute of Advanced Judaic Studies, Brandeis University, Studies and Texts 3; Cambridge, Mass.: Harvard University Press, 1966).

37 Ray, *Archive of Ḥor*, 14–29.

38 See Bar-Kochva, *Judas Maccabaeus*, 562–65.

39 *OGIS* no. 261; *Inscriptions de Délos*, nos. 1544–45.

40 Erich S. Gruen, "Hellenism and Persecution: Antiochus IV and the Jews," in Peter Green, ed., *Hellenistic History and Culture* (Hellenistic Culture and Society 9; Berkeley: University of California Press, 1993) 250–52.

41 Wilhelm, "Zu einigen Stellen," 20–22.

42 See Peter Hermann, "Epigraphische Notizien, 10: $\pi o\lambda\iota\tau\epsilon\acute{\iota}\alpha$–$\pi o\lambda\iota\tau\epsilon\acute{\upsilon}\epsilon\sigma\vartheta\alpha\iota$," *EA* 21 (1993) 70–72.

■ **2** The verb "pollute" picks up on the reason Judas left Jerusalem (5:27). The author here uses the Attic form for temple, $\nu\epsilon\dot{\omega}\varsigma$, as also in 9:16; 10:3, 5; 13:23; 14:33.

Antiochus IV had resumed construction of the temple of Zeus Olympios, unfinished since the days of the Peisistratids (Polybius 26.1.11; Livy 41.20.8; Pausanias 1.18.6), and he presented a noteworthy curtain by Syrian craftsmen to the temple of Zeus in Olympia (Pausanias 5.12.4). As Mørkholm has noted, "It cannot be denied that Antiochus IV took a very special interest in the cult of Zeus, according him a place of preference on his coinages, donating freely to his sanctuaries, and promoting his cult within his kingdom."[43] It is not surprising, then, that Antiochus IV would rename the temple in Jerusalem after this god. However, this is not to say that Antiochus IV identified himself with Zeus Olympios, as E. R. Bevan proposed[44] or rejected the worship of other gods, as the representation of all the gods in the procession at Daphne shows (Polybius 30.25.13–15). There is no doubt that Antiochus IV was a philhellene, as the numerous gifts to Greek cities show (Polybius 26.1.10).[45]

Zeus, protector of hospitality ($Z\epsilon\grave{\upsilon}\varsigma\ \xi\acute{\epsilon}\nu\iota o\varsigma$), was a widely known epithet of Zeus.[46] Temples dedicated to Zeus under this title are found throughout the Greek world.[47] The text has often been emended to bring it into line with the correspondence between a group that called themselves the Sidonians in Shechem and Antiochus IV (Josephus *Ant.* 12.258–61).[48] This group requested that Antiochus IV tell Apollonius, the governor of the district, and Nikanor, the royal agent, not to molest them as they were the Jews, and also that their previously anonymous temple be named Zeus Hellenios ($Z\epsilon\grave{\upsilon}\varsigma\ {}^{{}^{\backprime}}E\lambda\lambda\eta\nu\acute{\iota}o\varsigma$). Antiochus IV is said to have granted their request. Scholars have therefore emended 6:2 to read that the temple was named Zeus, protector of hospitality, just as those who dwelt in that place requested ($\dot{\epsilon}\nu\epsilon\tau\acute{\upsilon}\gamma\chi\alpha\nu o\nu$, rather than $\dot{\epsilon}\tau\acute{\upsilon}\gamma\chi\alpha\nu o\nu$).[49] I have argued elsewhere that one should not harmonize these two narratives.[50] The context in 2 Maccabees is the harsh measures taken by Antiochus IV against the Jews and the Samaritans, and the naming of the temple in Gerizim is to pollute it. In 5:22-23, the overseers are to plague the nation ($\tau\grave{o}\ \gamma\acute{\epsilon}\nu o\varsigma$), which includes both Jerusalem and Gerizim.[51] The Samaritans are depicted as co-sufferers with the Jews in Jerusalem. Further, if a request was being discussed, one would expect the aorist tense,[52] not

43 Mørkholm, *Antiochus IV*, 131.
44 E. R. Bevan, "A Note on Antiochus Epiphanes," *JHS* 20 (1900) 26–30.
45 See the discussion in Mørkholm, *Antiochus IV*, 130–34, and more fully, in his *Studies in the Coinage of Antiochus IV of Syria* (Copenhagen: Munksgaard, 1963) 7–75.
46 Homer *Il.* 13.625; Aeschylus *Ag.* 61–62, 374; Pindar *Olymp.* 8.21; *Nem.* 11.8; Plato *Leg.* 12.953E; Plutarch *Amat.* 20; and the work attributed to Aristotle *Mund.* 7.401a.
47 Hans Schwabl, "Zeus I. Epiklesen. Olympios," *PW* 19:341.
48 See n. 30 for the relevant discussion. One should note that since the redating of the coins from Antioch by Mørkholm (*Studies*, 36–37), Bickermann's dating of the letter by titular usage is no longer valid.
49 See Schwartz, *2 Maccabees*, appendix 4, 537–40.
50 Robert Doran, "2 Maccabees 6:2 and the Samaritan Question," *HTR* 76 (1983) 481–85.
51 Ferdinand Dexinger rejects this interpretation, "da es keinen Beleg für die besondere Gastfreundlichkeit der Sichemiten gibt" ("Der Ursprung der Samaritaner im Spiegel der frühen Quellen," in Ferdinand Dexinger and Reinhard Pummer,

eds., *Die Samaritaner* [Darmstadt: Wissenschaftliche Buchgesellschaft, 1992] 67–140, here 130). However, there are few examples of unfriendly behavior except in the later works of Josephus (*Ant.* 9.256; 11.114–15; 12.156) and Luke (9:53), although this last is offset by the story of the Good Samaritan (Luke 10:33-37). Dexinger neglects the context of 6:2, where clearly the author sees the Samaritans as part of the race (5:22-23), and he does not discuss whether the Eupolemos fragment in Eusebius *Praep. ev.* 9.17.2–9 could be by the Judean follower of Judas. On the lack of hostility between Jews and Samaritans, see Seth Schwartz, "John Hyrcanus I's Destruction of the Gerizim Temple and Judaean–Samaritan Relations," *Jewish History* 7 (1993) 9–25.
52 As in Josephus *Ant.* 12.263, where Antiochus IV states that the Sidonians have submitted ($\dot{\epsilon}\pi\acute{\epsilon}\delta\omega\kappa\alpha\nu$) a memorial. Van Henten (*Maccabean Martyrs*, 88 n. 6) stated that the change to $\dot{\epsilon}\nu\epsilon\tau\acute{\upsilon}\gamma\chi\alpha\nu o\nu$ was unnecessary as "the simplex $\tau\upsilon\gamma\chi\acute{\alpha}\nu\omega$ can mean 'gain one's request,' see *LSJ* 1833 s.v. $\tau\upsilon\gamma\chi\acute{\alpha}\nu\omega$ B 1." However, the text adduced at LSJ 1833 B1 for this meaning, Herodotus 1.213, has $\tau\upsilon\gamma\chi\acute{\alpha}\nu\omega$ linked to the aorist passive participle of the deponent verb $\delta\acute{\epsilon}o\mu\alpha\iota$ ("to beg, request"), $\delta\epsilon\eta\vartheta\epsilon\grave{\iota}\varsigma\ \ldots\ \acute{\epsilon}\tau\upsilon\chi\epsilon$. So

the imperfect that here is an imperfect of description[53] telling the audience what the people in Gerizim are like.[54] The reference to those in Gerizim as hospitable may be an allusion to the story of how Abraham was received by Melchizedek (Gen 14:18-20).[55] As retold by the Jewish author Eupolemos, Abraham was received hospitably ($\xi\epsilon\nu\iota\sigma\vartheta\hat{\eta}\nu\alpha\iota$) by Melchizedek (Eusebius *Praep. ev.* 9.17.2–9). The title Zeus, protector of hospitality, would thus reflect traditional stories about the inhabitants of Gerizim, just as the title Zeus Olympios reflected traditional Jewish stories of God as the lord of thunder (Ps 29:3-10).

In their request, the Sidonians in Shechem portrayed the observance of the Sabbath as a commemoration of the end of a major drought and therefore as an agricultural festival to provide a good harvest. This suits the naming of the temple as that of Zeus Hellenios, as this epithet recalled how Zeus sent rain to the Greeks in time of drought (Pindar *Nem.* 5.12; Pausanias 2.29.8). The reference in the request to the Jews being dealt with according to their wickedness and as guilty of certain charges (Josephus *Ant.* 12.260–61) suggests that this request comes after the initial decision by Antiochus IV recounted in 6:2. The request to be allowed to follow their own customs is thus similar to the later request to Antiochus IV by Menelaus to allow the Jews to follow their ancestral laws (11:29).

■ **3** $X\alpha\lambda\epsilon\pi\eta$ (here translated "grievous") was used in 4:16 (there translated "painful") to foretell the coming disaster. The word $\dot{\epsilon}\pi\acute{\iota}\sigma\tau\alpha\sigma\iota\varsigma$, which I have translated as "exercise," resonates with the appointment of overseers ($\dot{\epsilon}\pi\iota\sigma\tau\acute{\alpha}\tau\alpha\varsigma$) in 5:22. "Offensive" ($\delta\upsilon\sigma\chi\epsilon\rho\acute{\eta}\varsigma$) occurs in the accounts of the torture of Antiochus IV (9:7, there translated "awkward") and Rhazis (14:45, there translated

"hard to endure"), as well as in a more general setting (9:24, there translated "difficulty").

This verse functions as an editorial comment to introduce what is to happen.

■ **4-5** These two verses recount what was done in the temple before the next two verses narrate what the Jews were forced to do. The activities in 6:4 are often said to refer to cultic prostitution. As Tcherikover phrased it, "wanton women were the sacred prostitutes so characteristic of the cults of Syria and so utterly foreign to any Greek cult."[56] Here Tcherikover follows Bickermann.[57] This notion of sacred prostitutes follows from the brilliant suggestion of Bickermann that the cult introduced into Jerusalem at this time was a Syrian cult and from its development by Tcherikover that proposed that the cult was introduced by the Syrian military settlers.[58] These scholars have attempted to reconstruct what actually happened using all the sources at their disposal. They have noted that the "abomination of desolation" (שקוץ משומם) mentioned in Dan 11:31 suggests a play on words with the Syrian deity, Lord of heaven (בעל שמים) (see also 1 Macc 1:54). From this perspective, the scholars then interpret the cult as described in 6:4-5. However, if one looks solely at the account of events in 2 Maccabees, a different picture emerges. Not Syrian, but Mysian soldiers are said to settle the garrison in Jerusalem (5:24). Elsewhere, Cypriot soldiers are said to be in Jerusalem (4:29). An Athenian is sent to enforce the decrees (6:1). None of these notices points to Syrian soldiers. The names given to the temples in Jerusalem and Gerizim are good Greek names. As for the description of carousing with courtesans, it is well to remember that this account is not the report of a disinterested onlooker. The author was aware of the strict separation

$\tau\upsilon\gamma\chi\acute{\alpha}\nu\omega$ on its own does not have the meaning "gain one's request."

53 Smyth, *Greek Grammar*, §1898.

54 Schwartz (*2 Maccabees*, 538–39) does not seem to note that the verb $\tau\upsilon\gamma\chi\acute{\alpha}\nu\epsilon\iota\nu$ can be used like $\epsilon\hat{\iota}\nu\alpha\iota$ (LSJ, s.v. A II.2). Preisigke (*Wörterbuch* 2:624–25) gives an example from *P. Amh.* 81.6: $\ddot{\eta}\nu\iota\kappa\alpha$ $\dot{\epsilon}\tau\acute{\upsilon}\gamma$-$\chi\alpha\nu\epsilon\nu$ $\gamma\rho\alpha\mu\mu\alpha\tau\epsilon\acute{\upsilon}\varsigma$. See also the discussion of W. Gunion Rutherford, *The New Phrynichus, Being a Revised Text of the Ecloga of the Grammarian Phrynichus* (London: MacMillan, 1881) 342–44. Also, Schwartz's further argument (539) that the verse is

thus disappointing stylistically as it is unbalanced does not note the clear unbalance of 5:22-23.

55 See Hengel, *Judaism and Hellenism*, 2:196.

56 Tcherikover, *Hellenistic Civilization*, 195.

57 Bickermann, *God of the Maccabees*, 74–75; Hengel (*Judaism and Hellenism*, 2:194 n. 225) questions whether there was sacral prostitution.

58 Tcherikover, *Hellenistic Civilization*, 194.

within the structure of the temple between the court for Gentiles, that for Jewish women, that for Jewish men, and the area where only the priests could enter. To come to the temple one had to be in a state of purity, and sexual intercourse rendered one unclean and so unable to enter the temple (Lev 15:18).[59] These rules were amplified in the *Temple Scroll* from Qumran so that no man was supposed to have sex with his wife within the whole city (11QT 45.7–12; see also CD 12.1–2). The *Letter of Aristeas* stresses that the temple liturgy was carried out in an orderly manner and in silence (*Ep. Arist.* 92). Given these presuppositions, the author depicts the Gentiles behaving improperly by transgressing these basic rules of Jewish behavior.[60] Also, *pace* Bickermann, banquets (συμπόσια) were celebrated in temples as well as in private homes.[61] At such banquets, most probably the usual entertainment would be in the form of a flute girl. I would suggest, therefore, that the activity in 6:4 reflects the celebration of banquets within the temple area, possibly in the outer rooms, and that the author has put the worst possible spin on what took place at these festive gatherings, just as non-Christians would later accuse Christians of taking part in sexual orgies and Thyestean feasts at their celebrations (Justin Martyr *Dial.* 10; Athenagoras *Suppl.* 32–35).

■ **4** Τὰ μὴ καθήκοντα ("unseemly"). In 4:19, the author had the envoys of Jason outfit triremes rather than pay for a sacrifice to Herakles that was inappropriate (μὴ καθήκειν), and in 6:21, Eleazar is tempted to pretend to eat unlawful food while in fact eating what he could legally use (καθῆκον αὐτῷ). Here the reference seems a general one, that is, there were not only women in the temple area but also other items not found in the description in the Torah of what should be in the temple. Antiochus III had decreed that no foreigner was to enter the enclosure of the temple and that no one could bring into the city certain animals forbidden to the Jews (Josephus *Ant.* 12.145–46).

■ **5** "lawless things." In 7:1 and 10:34, the same term is used, though μὴ θέμις is used in 12:14. The combina-tion of verbs and nouns from the roots of διαστέλλειν and ἀθετεῖν is found also in 13:25 and 14:28. The specific reference to the Torah would indicate breaking the rules for clean and unclean animals, as well as not heeding the emphasis placed in the Torah on the use of unblemished animals (Leviticus 11; 22:20-25; Numbers 28). First Maccabees 1:47 narrates that Antiochus IV ordered that pigs and other unclean animals be sacrificed.

■ **6** When Leviticus 23 lays out the feasts appointed by the Lord, it begins with the celebration of the Sabbath, followed by Passover and the other festivals. Since Antiochus IV no longer allowed the Jews to observe their ancestral laws, the Torah was no longer the law of the land and these ancestral festivals were not to be observed.

"profess to be a Jew." This phrase sums up "in a nutshell" (ἁπλῶς) the previous clauses, where the celebration of the Sabbath and ancestral festivals is forbidden. It is connected to the previous clause by the repetition of the negative οὔτε. In a society where religion, politics, and culture were enmeshed to form identity, to erase one marker was to erase all. To be unable to follow the ancestral laws and celebrate the festivals that embedded the lifestyle, history, and stories of the people was in practical terms to cease to be a Jew. It is thus not that one cannot say, "I am a Jew," but that one cannot behave like a Jew. Note, for example, the connection between profession and action in 1 Esdr 9:8-9, "And now, give profession [ὁμολογίαν], glory to the Lord God of our fathers, and do his will, and separate from the Gentiles of the land, and from the foreign women." Later, Christian martyrs would profess to be Christians and be executed, but the very profession entailed a worldview inimical to that of Rome. Justin Martyr would try to argue that the charge was only about the name "Christian" (Justin Martyr *Apol.* 5), but it was really deeper than that and implied a rejection of the gods who protected Rome's sovereignty.

---

59   See *Ps. Sol.* 8:12 for Gentiles coming into the sanctuary with menstrual blood.
60   See Joann Scurlock, "167 B.C.E.: Hellenism or Reform?" *JSJ* 31 (2000) 125–61.
61   Bickermann, *God of the Maccabees*, 74; see Dennis Edwin Smith, *From Symposium to Eucharist: The* *Banquet in the Early Christian World* (Minneapolis: Fortress, 2003) 23–24.

In a series of articles, Shaye J. D. Cohen has argued that this verse indicates a shift in the meaning of Ἰουδαῖος from an ethnic and geographic designation to one that is more religious.[62] Rather than hold that the resonance of Ἰουδαῖος in 6:6 is different from that in 6:1, I see 6:6 as a summary of what had gone before. In 6:1 the author used "political" language: πολιτεύεσθαι ("to conduct the government"). Here in 6:6 he stresses that if one can no longer live under the government given by God or celebrate the festivals, one can no longer live as a Jew. In a Diaspora setting, this situation would require adjustment, for which a certain level of independence from the surrounding society was necessary. The same is true of the usage of Ἰουδαῖος in 9:17, where the suffering Antiochus IV vows to make Jerusalem a free city, to maintain through his own finances the sacrifices at the temple, and to become a Jew. This is no doubt hyperbole and perhaps sly humor as the persecutor wants to become one of those he persecuted. However, Antiochus IV is promising that Jerusalem can live according to the government of God's laws and that the sacrifices to God can be observed, goals held by every Jew. A true Ἰουδαῖος is being defined—one who lives according to the Torah and celebrates the ancestral festivals. I would suggest the same for *Bel and the Dragon* 28, where the Babylonians become angry at the king for allowing the worshiped dragon to be killed and claim that the king has become a Jew. That is, the king is accused of overturning the government of the city in allowing its god to be destroyed. The Babylonians claim, in effect, that the king wants to introduce the polity of the Jews. See also the story about the Scythian kings Anacharsis and Scylas. When Anacharsis was found sacrificing to the Mother of the Gods as he had learned at Cyzicus, he was executed. When the Scythians learned that Scylas had snuck off to take part in a Dionysiac festival, they rebelled and Scylas was beheaded (Herodotus 4.76–80). Here the kings were thought to be introducing a form of polity different from that of the ancestral Scythian way of life.

■ **7** The monthly celebration of Hellenistic kings is well documented.[63] Schwartz, however, noted that "apart from the Ptolemaic kingdom there is hardly any evidence for such celebrations elsewhere in the Hellenistic world, and there seems to be none for the Seleucid kingdom."[64] He therefore suggested that the reference to a monthly celebration of the king's birthday was supplied by the author of 2 Maccabees on the basis of what happened in the Ptolemaic kingdom. Schwartz does not take account of James C. VanderKam's argument that the evidence at present shows that inscriptions detailing a monthly celebration of the king's birthday are found in "three Hellenistic kingdoms (Egypt, Pergamum and Commagene) and from three centuries (the third, second and first centuries B.C." and evidence its widespread acceptance.[65]

References to the banquet meal (σπλαγχνισμός) and its verb occur in 6:8, 21, and in the verse that concludes the martyr narratives, 7:42. I have translated σπλαγχνισμός as "banquet meal" rather than "sacrificial meal." The σπλάγχνα were the choice parts reserved to be eaten by the sacrificers at the beginning of their banquet. Dennis Smith has shown that among the Greeks and Romans, almost every banquet was connected with a sacrifice. The sacrificial banquet was a subtype of the Greco-Roman banquet.[66] Jews were forbidden to eat of pagan sacrifices (Exod 34:15).

Dionysos's attributes included ivy wreaths and wine branches. The reference to Dionysos fits well with the author's intention. In 6:4, he began his description of the evil that encompassed the temple with a reference to

62   Shaye Cohen, "Ἰουδαῖος τὸ γένος and Related Expressions in Josephus," in Fausto Parente and Joseph Sievers, eds., *Josephus and the History of the Greco-Roman Period: Essays in Memory of Morton Smith* (SPB 41; Leiden: Brill, 1994) 23–38; idem, "Religion, Ethnicity and 'Hellenism' in the Emergence of Jewish Identity in Maccabean Palestine," in Per Bilde et al., eds., *Religion and Religious Practice in the Seleucid Kingdom* (Studies in Hellenistic Civilization 1; Aarhus: Aarhus University Press, 1990) 204–23; idem, "Ioudaios: 'Judean' and 'Jew' in Susanna, First Maccabees, and Second Maccabees," in Peter

Schäfer, ed., *Geschichte–Tradition–Reflexion: Festschrift für Martin Hengel zum 70. Geburtstag*, vol. 1: *Judentum* (Tübingen: Mohr Siebeck, 1996) 211–20.
63   Christian Habicht, *Gottmenschentum und griechische Städte* (Munich: Beck, 1956) 152 n. 60, 156. Habicht refers to *OGIS* 56, 33–34; 49, 8; 90, 47; 339, 35; 383, 132–33; 456, 21.
64   Schwartz, *2 Maccabees*, 540.
65   VanderKam, "2 Maccabees 6,7a," 67.
66   Smith, *From Symposium to Eucharist*, 85.

137

debauchery, courtesans, and sex. The stories and images of Dionysos are associated with promiscuous sexuality. In Euripides *Bacch.* 217–25, Pentheus accuses the women of engaging in wild sexual intercourse. Processions to celebrate Dionysos included the ritual presence of male sexuality. Besides these associations, however, Dionysos was one of the most important deities for the Greek cities.[67] The reference to Dionysos is therefore important to the author, as it encapsulates the wantonness of the activity celebrated on the Temple Mount and the change to Greek city cult.[68] In emphasizing the wantonness of the cult and its connection to Dionysos, is the author reflecting in some way the expulsion of Dionysos from Rome in 186 B.C.E.? Gruen has finely shown how the account in Livy (39.8.3–9.1), notwithstanding that "exaggeration, distortion, and calumny dominate the Livian picture of Dionysiac ritual and its participants," evidences a movement among Roman leaders "to promote a sense of independence from the cultural world of Greece."[69] The Dionysiac ritual was seen to epitomize this cultural, non-Roman world, and so the attempt to control it was a gesture to stress Roman cultural values. Gruen's analysis is persuasive, but it is also important to keep in mind how Livy's rhetoric emphasizes the cult's wantonness.

A connection between the God of Israel and Dionysos was discussed among Greco-Roman writers. In one of Plutarch's dinner conversations, the question of whom the God of the Jews is like is raised; the answer is Dionysos because of the drinking of wine (*Table Talk* 4.6, 671C–672C). Tacitus, however, rejected the comparison as superficial (*Hist.* 5.5).

■ **8-9a** As Grimm, Habicht, and Bringmann[70] note, the reference is to Ptolemy the governor of Coele-Syria and Phoenicia (4:45; 8:8). Whether this Ptolemy was Ptolemy son of Dorymenes or Ptolemy Makron is disputed. See the comment on 4:45, where I argue for Ptolemy son of Dorymenes. Grimm and Habicht both understand ψήφισμα as a decree ordered by Ptolemy to the Greek cities, rather than, as I have translated, a vote by the Greek cities at the suggestion or proposal of Ptolemy. However, given the desire of Antiochus IV "to infuse new vigour into city-life"[71] within his realm, it is unlikely that he would force a decree on Greek cities. Rather, I would suggest that Ptolemy proposed a decree to the Greek cities, and they voted for its acceptance.

Abel, Goldstein, and Bunge[72] prefer the plural reading, "on the proposal of the citizens of Ptolemais." Ptolemais seems opposed to Judean interests in 13:25. First Maccabees portrays the citizens of Ptolemais, Tyre, and Sidon as acting to destroy utterly the Jews in Galilee (5:15) and Ptolemais acting against Jonathan (12:48). However, the coordination of the vote in all the Greek cities suggests that a figure such as Ptolemy, the governor, was behind it.

The phrase ἐπὶ τὰ Ἑλληνικά ("toward the Hellenic lifestyle") is the same as that found in the letter of Antiochus V to Lysias, where the new king recognizes that the attempt to change the polity of the Jews has failed and that the Jews prefer their own way of life (ἀγωγὴν) (11:24). The author clearly understands the effort of the king to make the Jews adopt a Greek way of life and not some Syrian cult or "purified" Judaism. In 4:10, the author blames Jason for starting this change to the Hellenic character.

67 Fritz Graf, "Dionysia," *Brills New Pauly* (2004) 4:470; Renate Schlesier, "Dionysus," *Brills New Pauly* (2004) 4:496–508, particularly 498–502.

68 Schwartz (*2 Maccabees*, 542–43) suggests that the reference to Dionysos is simply the author's reflection of the royal cult of Dionysos in the Ptolemaic kingdom. However, the text simply does not say that this was a *royal* Dionysian cult, but that people in Jerusalem were forced to celebrate the festivals of Dionysos.

69 Erich S. Gruen, "The Bacchanalian Affair," in idem, *Studies in Greek Culture and Roman Policy* (Cincinnati Classical Studies 7; Berkeley: University of California Press, 1990) 34–78; quotations from 64 and 77, respectively.

70 Bringmann, *Hellenistische Reform*, 102.

71 Mørkholm, *Antiochus IV*, 130.

72 Jochen-Gabriel Bunge, "Die sogenannte Religionsverfolgung Antiochos IV Epiphanes und die griechischen Städte," *JSJ* 10 (1979) 155–65.

General Commentary

Before this section begins, Menelaus has been portrayed as full of evil and a traitor to his people (4:50). The author skillfully structures his narrative to engage the emotions of his audience. With Antiochus away, the author uses a traditional trait of Hellenistic historians, the premonitory sign, but he does not clarify whether it is a sign for good or bad. The attack of Jason at first seems good, as it makes Menelaus flee, but then it turns bad, as Jason is just as cruel toward his fellow citizens as Menelaus was. Then the author proleptically tells of Jason's flight and death, so the audience can relax. But then, just as Jason had listened to rumors of Antiochus's death, so too Antiochus misreads the situation in Jerusalem and attacks. From now on the city is "spear won," and Antiochus no longer is bound to follow the precedent of his father, Antiochus III, and allow the city to live according to the ancestral laws. He despoils the city and installs overseers but then goes away, and so the city thinks that the affair is at an end. The author exploits this series of relief and reversal to heighten the emotional effect on the audience.

According to the author, Antiochus, soon after he left Jerusalem, sent someone to further depopulate the city. The extent of such ethnic cleansing is overstated by the author, as the next chapter shows Jews still living in Jerusalem. Nevertheless, it does point to a reorganization of who dwelt in the city. Tcherikover and Bringmann argued that military colonists were settled there, while Bar-Kochva maintained that only a military garrison was introduced.[73] Whatever the case, the status of Jerusalem was changed profoundly.

The final event is the sending of Geron the Athenian to ensure the installation of a Greek form of government in Jerusalem and to abrogate the ancestral laws. No longer would the policy of Antiochus III be followed, which allowed Jerusalem to be governed by its ancestral laws. Jerusalem now had to follow the laws and customs found in other Greek cities of the Seleucid Empire. Jason's revolt had brought on the persecution, and the warning

of 4:16 that their models would become their enemies had been fulfilled.

Chronologies of Events
2 Maccabees

The narrative of 2 Maccabees is coherent in its outline of events. What happened to Jerusalem was a result of Antiochus IV's viewing the city as in revolt. He therefore considered the city as "spear won" and his to do with as he chose. He no longer had to allow the city to be governed by its ancestral laws and polity as his father, Antiochus III, had done (Josephus *Ant.* 12.142). The following chapter will show the consequences of this change. Changes to the status of the ancestral laws occurred also after other cites were captured. After Seleucus son of Antiochus III had taken Phocaea, the ancestral constitution must have been changed, for later the Romans restored to the Phocaeans their ancestral constitution (τὸ πάτριον πολίτευμα) (Polybius 21.6; 21.45.7; see also Livy 37.11.15). Antiochus III seems to have taken away the ancestral polity also of Apollonia on the Rhyndakos, but Eumenes II restored it.[74] Polybius relates how those cities that had been compelled (ἠναγκασομένους) to join the Aetolian League against their will were reinstated in their ancestral form of government (εἰς τὰ πάτρια πολιτεύματα) and could use their ancestral laws (νόμοις χρωμένους τοῖς πατρίοις) (4.25.7). Polybius notes also that Cleomenes replaced the Spartan constitution with a tryanny but that later Antigonos restored to the Spartans their ancestral polity (2.47.3; 2.70.1). The actions of Antiochus IV in abrogating the Jewish polity and instituting another thus follow a common pattern.

1 Maccabees

While this pattern of events is clear in 2 Maccabees, it is at odds with other accounts, particularly that in 1 Macc 1:20-64. There the author has Antiochus IV attack[75] Jerusalem in 143 s.e., that is, 170–169 b.c.e., after his first expedition into Egypt. Antiochus despoils the temple, and the author gives a detailed description of the vessels taken (1:21-23). After two years, with no mention of a

---

73   Tcherikover, *Hellenistic Civilization*, 194–95; Bring-
      mann, *Hellenistische Reform*, 87–89, 127; Bar-Kochva,
      Judas Maccabaeus, 438–44.
74   Corsten, *Die Inschriften*, 2, no. 1001.

75   In 1:20 the author uses the same phrase, ἐν ὄχλῳ
      βαρεῖ, that he used to describe Antiochus's attack
      on Egypt. It is therefore difficult to hold that the
      author speaks of a peaceful visit to Jerusalem.

second attack on Egypt by Antiochus IV and his repulse by the Romans, Antiochus again sends a large force, which deceitfully enters Jerusalem, attacks the citizens, and installs a garrison in the Akra (1:29-35). Then Antiochus orders his whole kingdom to give up their particular customs (1:41).

There are similarities between the accounts of 1 and 2 Maccabees—the deceitful entering of Jerusalem by a Seleucid general named Apollonius in 2 Maccabees, whereas the text of 1 Macc 1:29 calls him a chief collector of tribute.[76] However, the details are also quite different—the event takes place after the first expedition to Egypt in 1 Maccabees, whereas it occurs after the second attack on Egypt in 2 Maccabees. More importantly, no motivation is given in 1 Maccabees for the attack on Jerusalem—Antiochus IV is depicted as simply a powerful bully who takes what he wants—nor is any reason provided for why he sends someone to cause further slaughter. The final notice that he wanted everyone to be the same and therefore abrogated the polity of the Jews is not borne out by what we know of Antiochus IV from other sources.

Josephus

Josephus gives two accounts of these events. In the *Jewish War* 1.31–35, he does not link the events to the specific occasion of Antiochus IV's expeditions against Egypt; rather, he places the assault on Jerusalem in the time of the high priest Onias, blames the whole affair on dissension among the Jewish nobles, and portrays it as a conflict between supporters of the Ptolemies and supporters of the Seleucids. Josephus tells of only one assault on Jerusalem, in which Antiochus IV pillages the temple and then forces the Jews to abrogate their laws (καταλύσαντας τὰ πάτρια) because he was angered by what he had suffered in the siege. This language of abrogation comes close to other accounts of conquerors taking a city by force and in this is similar to the account in 2 Maccabees. However, the narration in the *Jewish War* is so different from the other accounts in chronology and

pattern that it is difficult to make any connection with them.

In the *Antiquities of the Jews* 12:239–54, the whole scenario is quite different. First, Josephus has Jason rebel against Menelaus with the help of pro-Ptolemaic supporters. Menelaus and his pro-Seleucid party go to Antiochus IV and ask for support and for permission to build a gymnasium. Then, Josephus has Antiochus IV make one assault on Egypt but be driven out by the Romans. These events are dated by Josephus to 143 s.e., the same dating as in 1 Macc 1:20, but incorrect for the second invasion of Egypt. On his way back from Egypt, Antiochus IV attacks Jerusalem to oust Jason and his supporters, and in this attack (Josephus uses the same language of assault that he did for Antiochus's attack on Egypt [*Ant.* 12.242]) Josephus has Antiochus take the town because his supporters open the gates to him, slaughter those who oppose him, and leave with a great deal of money (*Ant.* 12.246–47). In accord with 1 Maccabees, Josephus has another attack on Jerusalem two years later, but in contrast to 1 Maccabees, it is Antiochus himself who practices deceit to gain Jerusalem. He slaughters many, pillages the temple, builds a citadel, and abrogates the laws. In this account, Josephus maintains the notion of parties in Jerusalem. He gives the same date as 1 Maccabees, but incorrectly, as he places the first attack after the rebuff of Antiochus by the Romans. He also has Antiochus make two attacks on Jerusalem, not just one, as in 1 and 2 Maccabees. In contrast to the narration in 1 Maccabees, Josephus grounds the first attack on the rebellion of Jason, as in 2 Maccabees, but bases the second attack on Antiochus's greed. In this version of events, Josephus seems quite influenced by 1 Maccabees but with some variation and maintains that the whole event is dominated by competing pro-Seleucid and pro-Ptolemaic divisions.

Daniel 11:28-31a

In his schematic narration of events from the time of Alexander the Great down to his own time, Daniel

---

76 This disparity is usually taken to be the result of a mistranslation from an original Hebrew text. The original Hebrew שׂר מוסים ("chief of the Mysians"), as in 5:24, would have been read as שׂר מיסים ("chief of tribute"). However, it is interesting that the mention of tribute resonates with the description of the arrogant Alexander the Great, who collected tribute from all he conquered (1 Macc 1:4).

describes the visits of Antiochus IV to Jerusalem cryptically. He first narrates the first invasion of Egypt by Antiochus IV in 11:25-27. After this first attack, "he shall return to his own land with great wealth and his heart shall be set against the holy covenant and he shall do and he shall return to his own land" (11:28). Then Antiochus's second attack on Egypt is recounted, as is Antiochus's rebuff by the Romans (11:29-30a). "And he shall return and he will be enraged against the holy covenant and he will do and he will return and he will take heed to those who forsake the holy covenant. Forces sent by him shall occupy and profane the temple" (11:30b-31a).

In this series of clauses connected by a *waw* conversive, the use of the verb עשה in the absolute sense is unusual, as can be seen by the various attempts to translate it:

(1) NRSV: 11:28 "He shall work his will"; 11:30 "he [will] take action against the holy covenant."
(2) Jewish Study Bible: 11:28 "Having done his pleasure"; 11:30 "Having done his pleasure."
(3) John J. Collins: 11:28 "He will act"; 11:30 "he will act."[77]

Collins is the closest to a literal translation, but in his commentary on the verses makes clear that the verb "to do" refers to actions taken against Jerusalem. Little discussion has taken place on the absolute use of the verb עשה, but it has been interpreted in terms of the events described in 1 and 2 Maccabees to mean that there were two attacks on Jerusalem either by Antiochus himself[78] or under his orders.[79] The verb עשה is used absolutely in Dan 8:12, 24, where it forms a hendiadys with the following verb to mean "act successfully": 8:12, ועשתה והצליחה; 8:24, והצליח ועשה. This use is similar to the absolute use at Dan 11:7, 32, "act strongly": 11:7, ועשה בהם והחזיק; 11:32, יחזקו ועשו. The combination in Dan 11:28, 30 does

not seem to form a hendiadys, however, and seems more like the usage in 1 Kgs 8:32: "Hear in heaven and do and judge [ועשית ושפטת] your servants" and in 1 Kgs 8:39: "Hear in heaven your dwelling place and forgive and do and give [ועשית ונתת] to each person." Here the absolute use of עשה followed by a *waw* conversive seems to mean that the second verb specifies the general verb: "do, i.e., judge"; "do, i.e., give." If this is the case, Dan 11:28, 30 would be stating that Antiochus did indeed go home. Daniel 11:30 then goes on to say that, after his second return, Antiochus will listen to those who forsake the covenant and send forces against Jerusalem. This reading would hold that Antiochus IV sent forces against Jerusalem only once, after his second invasion against Egypt and his rebuff by the Romans, a reading in line with the account in 2 Maccabees 5, although it does not mention that Antiochus himself plundered the temple.

4Q248 = Acts of a Greek King

This scroll fragment has been edited and discussed by Magen Broshi and Esther Eshel.[80] They concluded that this text suggests that there were two visits of Antiochus IV to Jerusalem, one after the first invasion of Egypt and one after the second, and that the temple treasures were taken after the first invasion of Egypt. The account in 1 Maccabees would therefore be correct.[81] However, the fragmentary nature of this text requires that one supply already known historical facts to come to this reading. For example, line 8, "he shall overthrow lands of the nations," is interpreted as a reference to Antiochus IV's capture of Cyprus. The claim of line 1 that this king will rule Egypt and Greece is not discussed, but one wonders how it would apply to Antiochus IV? One therefore has to be cautious about deciding the precise historical order of events on the basis of this fragment.[82]

77 John J. Collins, *Daniel: A Commentary on the Book of Daniel* (Hermeneia; Minneapolis: Fortress, 1993).
78 Tcherikover, *Hellenistic Civilization*, 186.
79 Schürer, *History*, 1:151–52. Lester L. Grabbe, *Judaism from Cyrus to Hadrian*, vol. 1: *The Persian and Greek Periods* (Minneapolis: Fortress, 1992) 283–84.
80 Magen Broshi and Esther Eshel, "The Greek King is Antiochus IV (4QHistorical Test = 4Q248)," *JJS* 48 (1997) 120–29; see also S. J. Pfann et al., eds., *Qumran Cave 4.XXVI: Cryptic Texts. Miscellanea, Part 1* (DJD 36; Oxford: Clarendon, 2000) 192–200.
81 Broshi and Eshel, "Greek King," 128.
82 For a fuller discussion of this text, see John J. Collins, "New Light on the Book of Daniel from the Dead Sea Scrolls," in Florentino García Martínez and Ed Noort, eds., *Perspectives in the Study of the Old Testament and Early Judaism: A Symposium in Honour of Adam S. van der Woude on the Occasion of His 70th Birthday* (VTSup 73; Leiden: Brill, 1998) 191–95.

Analysis of the accounts of Antiochus's attack on the Jerusalem temple suggests the following scenario. A visit to/attack on the Jerusalem temple after the first invasion of Egypt seems unlikely. There would be no reason for the victorious Antiochus to annoy the people of Jerusalem, and he clearly had plenty of booty from the Egyptian campaign. The mention of 143 s.e. by 1 Maccabees reflects knowledge of the date of the first campaign but nothing else. Rather, sometime during the second campaign, Jason made an attack on Jerusalem and forced Menelaus to withdraw to the citadel. Antiochus, after his rebuff by the Romans in July 168 B.C.E., learned of Jason's attack, besieged Jerusalem, and forced Jason to flee. He then freed Menelaus, plundered the temple of the rebellious city, and no longer considered himself bound to allow the city to live according to its ancestral laws. He carried out a further depopulation of the city under Apollonius, quartered a garrison in the city, and, as we shall see in the following chapter, changed the polity of the city.

6

9b/ Then it was easy to see the misery at hand. 10/ For two women were brought up[a] as they had circumcised their sons. From their breasts they hung the newborn babes, publicly paraded them through the city, and hurled them headlong down from the wall. 11/ Others who assembled together nearby into the caves to celebrate clandestinely the seventh day were denounced to Philip. They were burned up because, in conformity with the glory of this most august day, they avoided helping themselves.

12/ I exhort those reading this present scroll not to be depressed because of these misfortunes, but to consider the punishments to be not for the destruction, but for the training, of our race. 13/ For indeed it is a sign of great beneficence that the ungodly not be left alone for a long time but that they immediately encounter penalties. 14/ For toward the other races the Master patiently waits until he chastises them when they attain the full measure of sins. But he was determining not to be this way toward us, 15/ so that he would not prosecute us later when our sins had reached full realization. 16/ Wherefore, he never removes mercy from us, but, training us with misfortune, he does not desert his own people. 17/ However, let these things be said by us for a reminder. After these few words, we must set out on the narrative.

18/ Eleazar was one of the leading officials, a man at that time advanced in age and, in personal appearance, most honorable.[b] He was being compelled to eat pig meat. 19/ However, he accepted death with honor rather than life with defilement, and was going[c] by free choice toward the instrument of torture, 20/ modeling[d] how those should present themselves who stand firm to guard themselves[e] from those things which it is not lawful to take because of affection for

a   The manuscripts have both $\dot{\alpha}\nu\eta\nu\epsilon\chi\vartheta\eta\sigma\alpha\nu$ (from $\dot{\alpha}\nu\alpha\phi\acute{\epsilon}\rho\omega$) and $\dot{\alpha}\nu\eta\chi\vartheta\eta\sigma\alpha\nu$ (from $\dot{\alpha}\nu\acute{\alpha}\gamma\omega$). The meaning for both is the same. One might suggest an emendation to $\dot{\alpha}\pi\eta\chi\vartheta\eta\sigma\alpha\nu$, which has the sense of "they were led away."

b   The text here can be read several ways:
(1) La[LXVP] Armenian, Hanhart, Abel, and van Henten: $\kappa\acute{\alpha}\lambda\lambda\iota\sigma\tau\sigma\varsigma\ \dot{\alpha}\nu\alpha\xi\alpha\nu\grave{\omega}\nu\ \dot{\eta}\nu\alpha\gamma\kappa\acute{\alpha}\zeta\epsilon\tau o$, "most honorable, opening his mouth he was being pressed."
(2) V La[BM] Syriac Achminic: $\kappa\acute{\alpha}\lambda\lambda\iota\sigma\tau\sigma\varsigma\ \dot{\eta}\nu\alpha\gamma\kappa\acute{\alpha}\zeta\epsilon\tau o$, "most honorable, he was being pressed."
(3) L' 46-52 58 311: $\kappa\acute{\alpha}\lambda\lambda\iota\sigma\tau\sigma\varsigma\ \tau\upsilon\gamma\xi\acute{\alpha}\nu\omega\nu\ \dot{\alpha}\nu\alpha\xi\alpha\nu\grave{\omega}\nu\ \dot{\eta}\nu\alpha\gamma\kappa\acute{\alpha}\zeta\epsilon\tau o$, "being most honorable, opening his mouth he was being pressed."
(4) Emendation by Peter Katz ("Eleazar's Martyrdom in 2 Maccabees: The Latin Evidence for a Point of the Story," *Studia Patristica* 4 [TU 79; Berlin: Akademie, 1961] 118–24) accepted by Habicht: $\kappa\acute{\alpha}\lambda\lambda\iota\sigma\tau\sigma\varsigma\ \tau\upsilon\gamma\xi\acute{\alpha}\nu\omega\nu\ \dot{\eta}\nu\alpha\gamma\kappa\acute{\alpha}\zeta\epsilon\tau o$, "being most honorable, he was being pressed."
I have chosen to follow Katz and Habicht. See commentary on the verse.

c   Whether one reads $\pi\rho\sigma\sigma\hat{\eta}\gamma\epsilon$ with Hanhart or $\pi\rho\sigma\hat{\eta}\gamma\epsilon$ with Habicht, the meaning is not substantially changed. The imperfect tense here and in v. 21 ($\pi\alpha\rho\epsilon\kappa\acute{\alpha}\lambda\sigma\upsilon\nu$, "were urging") is an imperfect of description.

d   I have followed Katz and Habicht in reading $\pi\rho\sigma\tau\upsilon\pi\acute{\omega}\sigma\alpha\varsigma$ instead of $\pi\rho\sigma\pi\tau\acute{\upsilon}\sigma\alpha\varsigma$ with Grimm, Abel, and Hanhart. See commentary on verse.

e   Katz suggests following the Syriac and reading $\mu\grave{\eta}\ \mu\iota\alpha\acute{\iota}\nu\epsilon\sigma\vartheta\alpha\iota$ ("not to defile themselves"). However, the form $\dot{\alpha}\mu\acute{\upsilon}\nu\alpha\sigma\vartheta\alpha\iota$, as Hanhart reads, is attested in the papyri. See Preisigke, *Wörterbuch*, 1:72. The accusative object of $\dot{\alpha}\mu\acute{\upsilon}\nu\alpha\sigma\vartheta\alpha\iota$ is omitted, and the relative is in the genitive case as governed by $\gamma\epsilon\acute{\upsilon}\sigma\alpha\sigma\vartheta\alpha\iota$.

life. 21/ Those in charge of the unlawful repast took him aside privately because of their long-standing acquaintance with the man. They were urging him to pretend by eating meat which he could legally use and which was supplied and prepared by him, as if he were eating what had been ordered by the king from the meats coming from the sacrifice. 22/ By eating this way, he would be released from the sentence of death and obtain friendly treatment because of his previous friendship with them. 23/ However, he took up again the high-principled position, one worthy of his time of life, the dignity of his old age,[f] his acquired and distinguished grey hair, and his honorable behavior since he was a child, one [worthy] of the holy and God-founded code of laws. Accordingly, he promptly declared that [they] should conduct him into Hades. 24/ "It is beneath the dignity of my time of life to pretend, in order both that many youths, when they think that ninety-year-old Eleazar has crossed over to foreign ways, 25/ will themselves through me be deceived by means of my pretense for the sake of this brief and fleeting life, and that I myself incur defilement and ignominy for my old age. 26/ For if for now I remove from myself punishment by humans, neither alive nor dead shall I escape the hand of the Almighty. 27/ Therefore, I will courageously leave this life. I will show myself worthy of my old age 28/ and leave for the youth a noble example to die willingly and nobly for the august and holy laws." Having said this, he straightaway was being dragged to the instrument of torture, 29/ as those leading him away changed their recent goodwill toward him to ill will because of the aforesaid words, since they thought them to be foolishness.[g] 30/ About to die under the blows, he groaned aloud and said, "To the Lord who possesses holy knowledge,

f   Niese ("Kritik," 524), followed by James Moffatt ("The Second Book of Maccabees," *APOT* 1:140), Katz, and Habicht, prefers to read γένους ("family"), rather than γήρως with the manuscripts and Hanhart. Niese provides no reason, but Moffatt and the others argue that old age is sufficiently represented by "time of life" and "grey hair." Moffatt suggests that the "two considerations of age and race are developed in the following clauses." He neglects to note, however, that both ἡλικία and γήρως are used in vv. 24 and 25. Goldstein rightly notes that, while it might not be to our taste, the author seems to like this heaping up of synonyms for old age.

g   The manuscripts here are quite confused, and Abel and Hanhart see the sentence as it stands as impossible. I have followed the reconstruction of Risberg ("Textkritische und exegetische Anmerkungen," 19–22), which makes grammatical sense and connects the genitive absolute construction of v. 29 with a main clause (v. 28b): τοσαῦτα δὲ εἰπὼν ἐπὶ τὸ τύμπανον εὐθέως εἵλκετο, τῶν δὴ ἀπαγόντων μεταβαλόντων πρὸς αὐτὸν τὴν μικρῷ πρότερον εὐμένειαν εἰς δυσμένειαν κτλ.

it is clear that, though I could have been released from death, I endure these harsh sufferings in my body, but suffer them glad in soul because of the fear of him." 31/ So in this way, he exchanged this life for another;[h] he left behind his own death as an example of nobility and a memorial of excellence not only to the youth but also to the bulk of the nation.

7:1/ Also, seven brothers along with their mother were seized. Tortured with whips and cords, they were being compelled by the king to partake of the unlawful pig meat. 2/ Their spokesperson said, "Why should you question and learn from us? For we are ready to die rather than transgress the ancestral laws." 3/ Enraged, the king ordered that frying pans and cauldrons be heated. 4/ When they were straightaway heated, he ordered that the spokesperson's tongue be cut out, that he be scalped in the Scythian manner, and that his hands and feet be cut off while the other brothers and his mother looked on. 5/ The king commanded that the completely disabled man be brought to the fire and, still breathing, be fried. As the fumes from the frying pan amply spread abroad, the brothers with their mother encouraged each other to die nobly, saying, 6/ "The Lord God looks down and truly consoles us, just as Moses made clear in the song where he confronted and witnessed against [the community], 'The Lord will console his servants.'"

7/ After the first had died in this fashion, they led the second along, mocking him. As they were tearing the skin off his head with his hairs, they were asking, "Will you eat rather than have [your] body punished limb by limb?" 8/ He used his ancestral speech to say, "No!" Thereupon he received the next torment like the first brother. 9/ At his last gasp he said, "You wretch! You remove us from

h As Katz ("Text of 2 Maccabees," 18) notes, "the best and next best groups of the Latin, LX and BM, conclude the story of Eleazar's martyrdom" at this point.

this present life, but the king of the universe will raise us up to return to eternal life since we die in defense of his laws." i

10/ After this person, the third was being mocked. When his tongue was demanded, he immediately stuck it out, courageously stretched forth his hands, 11/ and said nobly, "I acquired these from the heavenly one and I take no notice of these on account of his laws. From him, I hope to gain these again."[i] He was regarding the sufferings as naught 12/ so that the king himself and his companions were astonished at the spirit of the young man.

13/ When he was put to death, they tormented and tortured the fourth likewise. 14/ On the point of death he said, "For those about to leave humans, to await what is hoped for from God, namely, to be raised again by him, is preferable. As for you, there will be no resurrection into life."

15/ Next they brought forward the fifth and were torturing him. 16/ But he looked at the king and said, "You do what you want as you have authority among humans, although you are mortal. But do not suppose that our race has been abandoned by God. 17/ Be obstinate, and see his magnificent power as he will torment you and your seed."

18/ After this brother, they brought the sixth. About to die, he said, "Do not be falsely misled. For we are suffering these things because of our own selves as we sinned against our own God.[j] 19/ But do not think that you will get off scot-free, because you have tried to fight against God."

20/ The mother was extraordinarily marvelous and worthy to be singled out for mention. She had seen seven sons perish in one day, yet she bore it with a high courage because of her hope in the Lord. 21/ Filled with noble resolution, she was encouraging each in the ancestral language. She stirred up

i Verse 11 is missing from LBM, and so Katz ("Text of 2 Maccabees," 19–20) suggests that it be dropped, as the story would make sense if it were. Van Henten (*Maccabean Martyrs*, 113) counterargues that a purely logical approach would not do justice to this text. Most manuscripts have here the sentence: "Things worthy of marveling had happened." Some Latin witnesses omit the text, and Katz ("Text of 2 Maccabees," 20) argues that it is a marginal gloss that disrupts the contrast between we and thou, the brothers and the king. He also notes how "the wealth of variants permits a glance at the efforts devoted to assimilating this erratic bloc to the context so that it might better fit into the speech."

her womanly way of reckoning with manly ardor as she said to them, 22/ "I do not know how you came[k] into my womb: I did not bestow breath and life to you, nor did I compose the elementary structuring of each. 23/ So, the creator of the world, he who molded human production and invented the production of all things,[l] mercifully gives back[m] to you breath and life, as you now take no notice of yourselves on account of the laws."

24/ Antiochus, however, thought that he was being despised and viewed the reproachful voice suspiciously. He not only appealed to the still-surviving youngster with words, but he guaranteed on oath that, if he would change from his ancestral traditions, he would enrich him and make him envied, hold him as Friend, and entrust him with royal service. 25/ When the young man showed not the slightest interest, the king recommended to the mother that she act as advisor to the lad for his safety. 26/ As he kept on recommending, she undertook to persuade her son. 27/ Leaning toward him, she scoffed at the cruel tyrant and spoke in the ancestral language, "Son, pity me who carried you around in my womb for nine months and suckled you three years. I brought you up and led you to this age, and nurtured you.[n] 28/ I beseech you, child, to look toward heaven and earth and, on seeing all that is in them, to know that God did not make these things from what existed and the human race came into existence in the same way. 29/ Do not fear this public executioner, but be worthy of your brothers. Embrace death, so that I may get you back along with your brothers in God's mercy."

30/ As soon[o] as she stopped, the young man said, "For whom are you waiting? I do not obey the king's ordinance, but I obey the ordinance of the law given to our ancestors through Moses.

k   Katz ("Text of 2 Maccabees," 14) and Habicht, following Schulz (review of *Die beiden Makkabäerbücher übersetzt und erklärt*, by Hugo Bévenot, *TRev* 30 [1931] 498) suggested changing ἐφάνητε ("came into being, appeared") to ὑφάνθητε ("weave, construct"). However, the text as found in the manuscripts does make sense, and just after this the mother talks about the composition of the fetus in her womb, so the change would seem to be redundant.

l   The twofold repetition of γένεσιν has appeared to Katz ("Text of 2 Maccabees," 14) and Habicht as untenable, but I hold that it resonates with the text of Genesis.

m   Abel and Habicht read the future ἀποδώσει with L'·542 instead of the present ἀποδίδωσι, but the present here expresses a general truth.

n   Several witnesses omit καὶ τροφοφορήσασαν. Abel, Habicht, and Goldstein see it as duplicating the previous ἐκθρέψασαν. However, it could be seen as summing up the previous actions, as it is used in Deut 1:31 to indicate how a father rears his son.

o   Reading not ἔτι, but ἄρτι δὲ ταύτης καταληγούσης, as in 9:5.

147

31/ As for you, you are the originator of all damages to the Hebrews, but you shall certainly not escape God's grasp. 32/ For we suffer because of our own sins. 33/ If our living Lord has been angry for a little while for punishment and training, he will again also be reconciled with his own servants. 34/ As for you, unholy and most polluted of all humans, do not in insolence be falsely buoyed up with uncertain hopes because you raised your hand against the heavenly children.[p] 35/ For you have not yet escaped the judgment of the all-powerful God, the overseer. 36/ For our brothers have fallen,[q] having endured under the divine covenant brief pain for everlasting life, but you will obtain by God's sentence the proper penalties for arrogance. 37/ I, like my brothers, surrender both body and soul for the sake of the ancestral laws. I call upon God soon to deal propitiously with the nation, and so you, by means of afflictions and whippings, acknowledge that he alone is God, 38/ and the wrath of the Almighty, which rightly was applied upon our whole race, come to a halt in me and my brothers."

39/ **Enraged, the king engaged him more severely than the others, vindictive because of the taunting. 40/ So he left life undefiled, trusting completely in the Lord. 41/ After her sons, the mother died.**

42/ **Let so much be set forth concerning the meals and the excessive tortures.**

p The Lucianic recension and several minuscules read "his servants" (*τοὺς δούλους αὐτοῦ*), most probably influenced by its appearance in v. 33.

q Moffatt followed a conjecture by Hort to read *πεπώκασι* rather than the manuscript *πεπτώκασι*. They connect this verb with the genitive "eternal life," and so Moffatt translates: "have now drunk of everflowing life, in terms of God's covenant." *Πίνειν* can take the genitive with an abstract notion, as in Job 15:16: *πίνων ἀδικίας*. Here, however, the genitive is separated from the verb by the phrase *ὑπὸ διαθήκην θεοῦ*, and the genitive belongs more likely to the phrase *ὑπενέγκαντες πόνον*, where it is a genitive of price. Finally, the perfect has the sense that the brothers have already begun to enjoy eternal life, which seems contrary to the future hope expressed in 7:11, 14, and 23.

Commentary by Verse

■ **9b** The consequences of the abrogation of the Torah as the polity of Jerusalem are described.

■ **10** The same story is told in 1 Macc 1:60-61. There the author refers in general to women who circumcised their sons, whereas the author of 2 Maccabees specifies two women. The women here are said to have circumcised their sons, in contrast to the narrative in 1 Macc 1:60-61, where the women are said to have had their children circumcised. Susan Haber has demonstrated that in the text of 2 Maccabees women are held responsible for circumcising their sons. She notes that this position contrasts with later rabbinic views that argue even against the case of Zipporah in Exod 4:25.[1] The author neatly contrasts the terms "hung [κρεμάσαντες] from their breasts" with "they were hurled headlong [ἐκρήμνισαν]." In 14:43, Rhazis hurls himself down from a wall of a tower in which he is trapped. However, throughout the verse here stress is on the "city." The women are led (the same verb, περιάγειν, is used for the humiliation of Andronikos in 4:38) publicly (δημοσίᾳ) through the city (τὴν πόλιν) and thrown down from the wall, an edifice set up to protect and defend the city. Like the later charades put on by the Romans, when criminals like the Christians were displayed publicly in the amphitheater,[2] here two women are put on public display. They are childbearing women, their babies hung at their breasts, the very symbol of fertility. In 1 Macc 1:61, the babies are hung from the women's necks, a much more practical suggestion, but the author of 2 Maccabees emphasizes the women's fertility. Cities in the ancient world survived through childbearing, yet here childbearing women are presented and paraded as antithetical to the values that Antiochus IV espoused for the city.

Circumcision was the entryway into the people of the Jews: "Any uncircumcised male who is not circumcised in the flesh of his foreskin shall be cut off from his people; he has broken my covenant" (Gen 17:14). By prohibiting circumcision, the new government in Jerusalem was excluding new Jews from the city. It is important to note also that for the Greeks, circumcision was a mutilation. The prepuce was an ornament provided by nature (Galen *De usu partium corporis humani* 11.13), and circumcision was seen as arising from superstition (Strabo *Geogr.* 16.4.5). Philo, even while dismissing the notion that circumcision involved mutilation, recognized that circumcision was ridiculed by many people (*Spec. leg.* 1.1.2). To be circumcised was thus not appropriate for a member of a Greek city.[3]

■ **11** Συμφλογίζειν is an unusual verb used here instead of the more frequent συμφλέγω.

The second incident takes place away from the city. The group gathers in secret, out of public view, and in caves, not in civilized dwellings. Here the city has been symbolically abandoned. However, even secret ritual actions are destroyed. Plato argued that no one should possess shrines in private houses and that anyone who did so was to be executed (*Leg.* 10.909–910D). Plato recognized religion as a central part of city life, as did Aristotle (*Pol.* 1322b, 1328b). Private shrines suggest anti-public, anti-political activity.[4] They involve alien rites. In Jerusalem under Antiochus IV's new rules, Jewish rituals were attacked as anti-*polis*, as a threat to the state and as if they were foreign. The irony is that the audience knows that the observance of the Sabbath is part and parcel of Jewish ancestral tradition and that Philip the Phrygian (5:22) is the foreigner.

A similar incident is told in 1 Macc 2:29-38. In contrast to the brief description in 2 Macc 6:11, the group in 1 Maccabees takes all the elements of social living with them when they leave for the wilderness—sons, wives, and livestock. An effort is being made to set up an alternate society. When the group's move is reported, soldiers come out to pursue them. Given an opportunity to save their lives, the Jews refuse to budge. They do nothing to violate the Sabbath. The group of one thousand people are slaughtered. The story in 1 Maccabees is placed between the beginning of the revolt by Mattathias (2:27) and the decision by Mattathias and his followers to fight on the Sabbath (2:40-41). By placing this community-based decision after the narrative of the seekers of

---

1　Susan Haber, "Living and Dying for the Law: The Mother-martyrs of 2 Maccabees," *Women in Judaism: A Multidisciplinary Journal* 4(1), retrieved May 20, 2010 from the online periodical *Genderwatch* (http://www.library.pitt.edu/articles/database_info/gender.html, Document ID 1948694231) 2–4). Haber cites *b. ʿAbod. Zar.* 27a.

2　K. M. Coleman, "Fatal Charades: Roman Executions Staged as Mythological Enactments," *JRS* 80 (1990) 44–75.

3　On this whole question, see Frederick M. Hodges, "The Ideal Prepuce in Ancient Greece and Rome:

Male Genital Aesthetics and Their Relation to *Lipodermos*, Circumcision, Foreskin Restoration, and the *Kynodesme*," *Bulletin of the History of Medicine* 75 (2001) 375–405.

4　The rites of Dionysos were suppressed in Rome in 186 B.C.E. because they were secret/hidden rites performed at night. See Livy 30.14.8.

righteousness who were slaughtered (1 Macc 2:29-38) and before the Hasideans join Mattathias's band (2:42), the author of 1 Maccabees shows that the Maccabeans are linked to the most Torah-observant Jews, and he uses the deaths of the innocent Jews to clothe the Maccabeans as the representatives of the best traditions of the whole community. The author of 2 Maccabees, by contrast, lets the deaths stand alone to bring out the horror. Those assembling in the caves do not try to help themselves. Εὐλαβῶς ἕξειν, equivalent to εὐλαβέομαι ("to be discreet, cautious, to have a care of, beware"), and the noun, εὐλάβεια, can have the sense of avoidance (Plato *Leg.* 815A; Aristotle *Eth. Nic.* 1121b24 [4.1.38]).

In the account in 2 Maccabees, it is not known who denounced the people. The same verb (μηνύειν) is used in 14:37, when Rhazis is denounced, and in 3:7, when Apollonius spoke of the monies made known to him by the Judean Simon. It would appear that those who gathered in the caves were denounced by supporters of the Seleucid officials.

■ **12-17** The author intrudes himself again, as in 4:16-17 and 5:17-20, and provides for his audience a third reflection on the events of the narrative. The misfortunes of the people are not by chance but by design.

■ **12** The connotations of the word παιδεία include "rearing of a child," "teaching," and "education." I have chosen "discipline" to cover both the sense of "learning" and the sense of the hard work needed. God is training, disciplining, educating the people in how to behave. This motif is found in Deut 8:5 LXX: "Know then in your heart that as a parent disciplines [παιδεύσῃ] a child, so the Lord your God will discipline [παιδεύσει] you."

The author repeats the motif of learning through misfortune in 7:32-33, and it is found also in Ps 118:18. It is often combined with a comparison with what happens to the wicked (Ps 94:12-15) and to nations who oppress God's chosen people (Wis 11:9-10; 12:22; Jdt 8:27). The phrase "for destruction" is found in 13:6 in the description of those guilty of sacrilege or notorious for other crimes.

■ **13** Judas and his followers request in 10:4 that they not encounter such evils again but that if they do sin, God will discipline (παιδεύεσθαι) them himself with leniency and not hand them over to the Gentiles. Psalm 93:12-13 LXX: "Happy are those whom you discipline [παιδεύσῃς] . . . giving them respite from evil [πονερῶν] days until a pit is dug for the sinner [τῷ ἁμαρτωλῷ]." God is the one who greatly benefits his people (10:38). The sense of God quickly punishing his people is found in Isa 54:7-8. In Wis 16:11, God's quick punishment is to remind the people of his beneficence (εὐεργεσία). When speaking of the death of the righteous, Wis 3:5 states: "Having been disciplined [παιδευθέντες] a little, they will receive great beneficence [εὐεργετηθήσονται]."

■ **14-15** In Gen 15:16, God is said to wait as the iniquity of the Amorites is not yet complete (οὔπω ἀναπεπλήρωνται). In speaking of the end of the oppressions of the Jews, Dan 8:23 says: "At the end of their rule, when the transgressions have reached their full measure [πληρουμένων τῶν ἁμαρτιῶν αὐτῶν]." The motif is continued in early Christian writings (1 Thess 2:16; Matt 23:32) and also in Pseudo-Philo *L.A.B.* 26.13.

■ **16-17** The notion of God's mercy coming after punishment is developed by the author in his narrative when, after the executions of the martyrs, the forces of Judas become unstoppable as the anger of the Lord had turned to mercy (8:5). The same idea was expressed in 5:20. There the author contrasted the verbs καταλείπειν and καταλλάσσειν; here he uses two negatives to underscore God's commitment.

The word for narrative (διήγησις) is the same as in 2:32. The author uses the same kind of transitional phrase as Polybius.[5] "For a reminder" is literally "as far as reminding." The use of ἕως here is unusual. Usually it has the sense of "up to, as far as" with a temporal or locative meaning. It can also be used to describe number or degree, for example, "up to drunkenness" (ἕως μέθης). Here its use with a substantive denoting action reflects the same tendency as in Polybius for an abstract style.[6]

---

5   Polybius 1.35.10; 4.21.10–12; 4.33.11; 9.20.10; 9.37.1. See Foucault, *Recherches*, 305–6. Schwartz seems to see in ἐλευστέον a reference to the future and so sees the martyrdoms as an excursus (δι᾽ ὀλίγων) before the author returns to the main narrative. However, verbal adjectives are derived from the future stem form (Smyth, *Greek Grammar*, §471a), and in the impersonal construction they emphasize the necessity of the action.

6   See Foucault, *Recherches*, 205–20.

■ **18-31** The intent of the author to heighten the emotional effect on his audience is shown in this narrative of the martyrdom of Eleazar. The author highlights the interaction between Eleazar and his former friends (vv. 21-30) and provides a speech and a prayer by Eleazar (vv. 24-28, 30). However, the author does not make clear what exactly the occasion for the confrontation is. Eleazar is pressed to eat pig meat. When he refuses, his "friends" suggest that he prepare food that he can eat, bring that, and pretend to eat unlawful food. These elements would seem to suggest, therefore, that Eleazar and his friends are at a banquet at which pig meat is being served. When Eleazar refuses to eat it, his friends suggest that at a future banquet, Eleazar secretly bring his own food and pretend that he is eating unlawful food. He rejects that suggestion also and so is led out to death. However, the facts that the instrument of torture is nearby and that Eleazar does not want to provide a wrong example to the youth would seem to hint at a public spectacle, as is assumed by the author of *4 Maccabees*. A compromise solution would be to situate the proceedings at a dinner in the gymnasium, which was near the temple, at which the νέοι, those who had passed through the ephebate, would be present.

■ **18-20** The manuscript traditions provide two different tellings of what transpired at the beginning of the narrative of Eleazar's death. One has Eleazar being pressed to open his mouth (v. 18: ἀναξανὼν ἠναγκάζετο) to eat pig meat, which he spits out (v. 20: προπτύσας). Van Henten argues for this version of the narrative. He includes "opening his mouth" on the grounds that it "suggests that Eleazar had to open his mouth immediately or that his mouth was even wrenched open before he had a chance to make up his mind. The formulation emphasizes in any case the brute force of the Seleucids."[7] He further notes: "Προπτύω is a hapax legomenon, but it fits the context well, πτύω means 'to spit' and the prefix προ- may express that Eleazar spitted in a forward direction or that he spitted before the meat was put in his mouth, in order to get rid of it at once. . . . Προπτύω might be taken metaphorically (like the expression 'venting one's gall'), meaning that Eleazar was very angry."[8] This telling suggests the violence of the confrontation:

the Seleucid followers try to force open Eleazar's mouth, while Eleazar reacts by spitting. Van Henten points to parallels in the stories found in Diogenes Laertius of two philosophers brought before a tyrant (9.27, 59). Each story seems a variant of the other. In one, the philosopher denounces the tyrant and upbraids the audience before finally biting off his tongue and spitting it at the tyrant (ἀποτραγόντα τὴν γλῶτταν προσπτύσαι αὐτῷ). In the other, when the tyrant commands the philosopher's tongue to be cut out, the philosopher bites it off and spits it at him.[9] While the verb προσπτύω is similar to the one (προπτύω) found in the story in 2 Maccabees, the stories of Eleazar and the philosophers are quite different. Moreover, van Henten's reading seems to be at odds with the rest of the narrative, which provides no evidence of such brute force. Eleazar's former friends try to find a way to get him off, his pretending to eat other food allowed by the Torah. If Eleazar had spat out the pig meat, such an overt rejection would not seem to allow room for Eleazar's friends to attempt any subterfuge. If one accepts this telling of the story, one is tempted to see vv. 21-29 as an interpolation and to end the story in v. 31 with the best Latin manuscripts: "So in this way he exchanged this life." The use of force and Eleazar's spitting are not found in the narrative as developed in *4 Maccabees* 5–7.

The second telling has Eleazar being pressed to eat pig meat, and the participle "opening his mouth" (ἀναξανὼν) is omitted. Eleazar provides a model (v. 20: προτυπόσας) of how one should behave when under such pressure. This telling of the narrative seems to hang together better than the alternative, and so I have chosen it.

■ **18** Eleazar is described as a γραμματεύς, often translated as "scribe." Christine Schams has shown the range of meanings this term can have and how the increased demand for documentation by the Ptolemies resulted in the increased importance of scribes in the bureaucracy. She further suggests that, although no evidence of Eleazar's ability to write is given, the emphasis on his nobility and high social status as well as his reverence for the laws fits a "Near-Eastern-Jewish type of scribe/sage which is described in Ben Sira."[10]

I have translated κάλλιστος as "most honorable," as

7   Van Henten, *Maccabean Martyrs*, 96.
8   Ibid., 97 n. 34.
9   Ibid., 272–73.

10   Christine Schams, *Jewish Scribes in the Second-Temple Period* (JSOTSup 291; Sheffield: Sheffield Academic Press, 1998) 314.

I wanted to connote not only physical beauty but also dignity of presence. To be beautiful was a sign of divine bounty toward a person. Josephus described Moses as characterized by beauty ($\kappa\dot{\alpha}\lambda\lambda o\varsigma$) (*Ant.* 2.224, 231–32).[11]

The eating of pigs is forbidden in Lev 11:7 and Deut 14:8 and condemned in Isa 65:4; 66:17. Plutarch devotes a whole discussion to why Jews abstain from swine flesh (*Quaest. conv.* 4.5). In 1 Macc 1:47, Antiochus IV is said to have enjoined sacrificing pigs and other unclean animals. Scholars have gone to great pains to explain why pigs were sacrificed. Bickerman notes that "among the Greeks, as a rule, the pig was customary only for sacrifices that were considered unfit for human consumption; further, for sacrifices to Demeter and in the cult of Dionysus."[12] He goes on to state that the pig was chosen precisely because it was abominable to the Jews. However, Walter Burkert states quite categorically that the pig, though not the most expensive sacrifice, was sacrificed by the Greeks.[13] Gunnel Ekroth has shown from the epigraphical evidence that pigs were sacrificed in Athens to heroes, an act followed by a banquet.[14]

■ **19-20** In discussing the decision of Eleazar, the author uses elevated language to stress the dignity of Eleazar. The choice, long life with pollution or death with renown, is reminiscent of the choice placed before Achilles: death at Troy with immortal glory ($\kappa\lambda\acute{\epsilon}o\varsigma$ $\ddot{\alpha}\varphi\vartheta\iota\tau o\nu$) or long life without glory (Homer, *Il.* 9.410–16). On one hand, the term $\epsilon\dot{\upsilon}\kappa\lambda\epsilon\acute{\iota}\alpha$ ("honor") is used by the dramatists to indicate the good name their heroes wish to leave behind (Aeschylus *Cho.* 349; *Sept.* 683; Sophocles *Ai.* 465). On the other hand, the term $\mu\acute{\upsilon}\sigma o\varsigma$ ("defilement, pollution"), repeated in v. 25, is what Sophocles has Oedipus ironically proclaim his father's murderer to be

(*Oed. Tyr.* 1231; see also Euripides *Suppl.* 931). A polluted person must be excluded from all religious and social intercourse. Both terms are in some way linked to family: a good name for one's father and children, pollution at killing one's brother or children.[15] The author's choice of "affection, tender love" ($\varphi\iota\lambda o\sigma\tau o\rho\gamma\acute{\iota}\alpha$) to end this sentence is thus appropriate, as the term is often used of family affection (Polybius 31.25.1; Diodorus Siculus 4.44).[16] Valerius Maximus insists that desire for death is sometimes wiser than desire for life, which should not lead to shameful behavior (9.13). Emphasis is placed on the free choice of Eleazar—the term $\alpha\dot{\upsilon}\vartheta\alpha\acute{\iota}\rho\epsilon\tau o\varsigma$ is used to describe how Jocasta chose to kill herself and Oedipus to blind himself (Sophocles *Oed. Tyr.* 1231; see also Euripides *Suppl.* 931)—and on his desire to be a model of behavior, a motif that Eleazar will emphasize in his speech (v. 28) and that appears also in the conclusion of the narrative of this episode (v. 31). Polybius relates some anecdotes about Publius Scipio for the sake of the good fame of the departed and to incite their successors to achieve noble deeds (23.14.12).

"instrument of torture" ($\tau\acute{\upsilon}\mu\pi\alpha\nu o\nu$). Aristophanes used the plural to describe instruments of punishment, and the meaning seems to be that of a cudgel or a piece of wood used to beat ($\tau\acute{\upsilon}\pi\tau\omega$) someone (*Pl.* 476).[17] By the time of Lucian of Samosata, the term appears to refer to a post on which a person could be bound or stretched out and whipped, even to death (*Tyr.* 6). In v. 30, the use of "blows" to describe Eleazar's death reinforces this interpretation. The use of the article seems to refer to a specific post of punishment.

"Not lawful" ($o\dot{\upsilon}$ $\vartheta\acute{\epsilon}\mu\iota\varsigma$) resonates with the use of $\dot{\alpha}\vartheta\acute{\epsilon}\mu\iota\tau o\iota$ ("lawless") in 6:5.

---

11 See Ludwig Bieler, *ΘΕΙΟΣ ΑΝΗΡ: Das Bild des "göttlichen Menschen" in Spätantike und Frühchristentum* (1935–36; reprinted Darmstadt: Wissenschaftliche Buchgesellschaft, 1976) 51–54.

12 Bickerman, *God of the Maccabees*, 88.

13 Walter Burkert, *Greek Religion* (trans. John Raffan; Cambridge, Mass.: Harvard University Press, 1985) 13, 55.

14 Gunnel Ekroth, *The Sacrificial Rituals of Greek Hero-cults in the Archaic to the Early Hellenistic Periods* (Kernos Supplément 12; Liège: Centre international d'étude de la religion grecque antique, 2002) 150–69.

15 In the story of how Typhon killed his brother Osiris (Diodorus Siculus 1.21); Herakles after he killed his children in his fury (Euripides *Herc. fur.* 1155).

16 Polybius (16.17.8) also uses the term to describe patriotism.

17 See the scholia on this verse for the derivation from $\tau\acute{\upsilon}\pi\tau\omega$.

■ **21-22** The suggestion of those in charge of the meal seems to entail that at a later banquet where there would be sacrifices, Eleazar could bring his own food and pretend to eat from the sacrificial meat. It seems unlikely that Eleazar had food on hand to eat when he was being pressed to eat pig meat. The social prominence of Eleazar is underscored by his acquaintance with those in charge of the repast. The author connects their friendship ($\varphi\iota\lambda\acute{\iota}\alpha$) with their treatment of him ($\varphi\iota\lambda\alpha\nu\vartheta\rho\omega\pi\acute{\iota}\alpha$). Tessa Rajak refers to the Socratic quality of the interaction.[18]

■ **23** "High-principled position" is literally "refined reasoning/calculation." The use of $\grave{\alpha}\sigma\tau\epsilon\hat{\iota}o\varsigma$, whose basic meaning is urbane as opposed to rustic, can mean "beautiful" when used of persons, as of Moses in Exod 2:2. It again contrasts Eleazar with his former friends. Note how $\grave{\alpha}\sigma\tau\epsilon\hat{\iota}o\varsigma$ also links back to the first description of Eleazar as honorable ($\kappa\acute{\alpha}\lambda\lambda\iota\sigma\tauo\varsigma$), as the two words are linked in 12:43.

In stressing the age of Eleazar, the author also stresses that Eleazar had acquired his position. "The beauty of the aged may be their grey hair" (Prov 20:29), but Sirach counsels his students to choose discipline ($\pi\alpha\iota\delta\epsilon\acute{\iota}\alpha\nu$) so that when they have grey hair, they will still find wisdom (Sir 6:18; 25:3-6). "Old age is not honored for length of time, or measured by number of years; but understanding is grey hair for anyone, and a blameless life is ripe old age" (Wis 4:8-9).[19]

The adverb $\grave{\alpha}\kappao\lambdao\acute{\upsilon}\vartheta\omega\varsigma$ is elsewhere followed by the dative, not the genitive, and so it is best to see it as qualifying the verb "declare."

"conduct into Hades." The verb "conduct" ($\pi\rhoo\pi\acute{\epsilon}\mu\pi\epsilon\iota\nu$) is used to describe those who escort a corpse to the grave, as at the end of Aeschylus's *Seven against Thebes*, where the members of the chorus decide to follow the dead brothers to the grave (*Sept.* 1059: $\pi\rhoo\pi\acute{\epsilon}\mu\pi\epsilon\iota\nu$ $\grave{\epsilon}\pi\grave{\iota}$ $\tau\acute{\upsilon}\mu\beta o\nu$) as escorts (1069: $\pi\rhoo\pi o\mu\pi o\acute{\iota}$). The author of 2 Maccabees thus has Eleazar ironically invite his persecutors to be his funeral escort.

"Hades" is frequently used in the LXX as a term for the underworld, but it is interesting to see it surface in this narrative so heightened by tragic vocabulary. Of particular interest is its occurrence in Wis 16:13: "For you [Lord] have power over life and death; you lead mortals down to the gates of Hades and back again"; and Tob 13:2: "[God] leads down to Hades in the lowest regions of the earth, and he brings up from the great abyss, and there is nothing that can escape his hand."

■ **24-28a** The author has Eleazar declare his position.
■ **24** "pretend." Eleazar's behavior (6:24-25) contrasts not only with that suggested by his persecutors (6:21) but also with the behavior of Apollonius when he took control of Jerusalem through pretense (5:25). "To cross over to foreign ways" resonates with the use of $\mu\epsilon\tau\alpha\beta\alpha\acute{\iota}\nu\epsilon\iota\nu$ in 6:1, 9 and with $\grave{\alpha}\lambda\lambdao\varphi\upsilon\lambda\iota\sigma\mu\acute{o}\varsigma$ in 4:13, where the flowering of Hellenism and the growth of foreign ways are seen in the building of a gymnasium in Jerusalem.
■ **25** "Ignominy" is literally "stain, spot, defilement, dishonor." The negative is found in the Wisdom of Solomon: "Wisdom is a spotless [$\grave{\alpha}\kappa\eta\lambda\acute{\iota}\delta\omega\tauo\nu$] mirror of the working of God" (Wis 7:26), and "a blameless [$\grave{\alpha}\kappa\eta\lambda\acute{\iota}\delta\omega\tauo\varsigma$] life is ripe old age" (Wis 4:9). The tragedians liked the term to describe the stain, contagion, or infection that arose through parricide and incest. While Oedipus has a stain, Theseus does not.[20]

In this sentence, the preposition $\delta\iota\acute{\alpha}$ + the accusative is used with three different nuances: as means, "by means of my pretense"; as goal, "for the sake of this . . . life"; and as cause, "through me."
■ **26** The use of "all-powerful" ($\pi\alpha\nu\tauo\kappa\rho\acute{\alpha}\tau\omega\rho$) resonates with its use in 5:20 and looks forward to its use in 7:35, 38. Eleazar's insistence that he can escape from the Almighty neither alive nor dead suggests that the author accepted the notion of reward or punishment after death. In the Jewish tradition, this concept is strikingly portrayed in the journey of Enoch to the mountain of the dead (*1 Enoch* 22).[21] It is present also in Plato: the place of judgment and the punishment of the wicked are described in the myth of Er, and Plato also describes the realm of Tartarus (*Resp.* 10.614-21; *Phaed.* 113D-114C).

18 Rajak, *Jewish Dialogue*, 122–23.
19 The wicked elders in the story of Susanna also are shown not to have wisdom (Sus 8-12).
20 Aeschylus *Eum.* 787; Sophocles *El.* 446; *Oed. Tyr.* 1384; *Oed. Col.* 1634.
21 See the discussion in George W. E. Nickelsburg, *1 Enoch 1: A Commentary on the Book of 1 Enoch, Chapters 1–36; 81–108* (Hermeneia; Minneapolis: Fortress Press, 2001) 300–309.

■ **27-28a** The first μέν is emphatic, stressing the courage of Eleazar. The second μέν in a μὲν ... δέ construction then connects the two verses. The author neatly contrasts Eleazar's old age with the youth. When Agesilaus, king of Sparta, was asked why even when very old he wore no tunic in cold weather, he answered, "So that the youth [οἱ νέοι] may imitate, having as an example [παράδειγμα] the old men and the officials" (Plutarch *Apoph. lac.* 210B).[22] Kevin Osterloh has finely highlighted in this connection the praise Polybius makes of the Roman institutions, particularly at the funerals of celebrated men.[23] Polybius concludes that "the most important consequence of the ceremony is that it inspires young men to endure the extremes of suffering for the common good in the hope of winning the glory that waits upon the brave" (6.54.2-3).[24]

As Grimm notes, the construction διαλλάξας τὸν βίον ("leave this life") is not otherwise attested. The author contrasts the way Eleazar shows himself (v. 27: φανήσομαι; v. 23: ἐπιφανοῦς πολιᾶς; ἀπεφήνατο; v. 30: φανερός) with the pretense suggested to him. The phrase "to leave an example" is repeated and elaborated in 6:31.

Note the repetition of "noble" (γενναῖον), "nobly" (γενναίως).

The verb ἀπευθανατίζειν ("to die well") is otherwise unattested.

■ **28b-29** In v. 29, the author plays with the contrast of goodwill and ill will, εὐμένειαν ... δυσμένειαν, as he had previously done in 5:6: εὐημερίαν ... δυσημερίαν. What the persecutors think is foolishness (ἀπόνοια) is really noble reasoning or high-principled position (λογισμὸν ἀστεῖον).

■ **30** The use of "blows" supports the sense that the place of torture (τύμπανον) is a post where offenders were beaten or flogged, sometimes to death.

About to die, Eleazar makes a final statement as if he is in the dock calling on God as a witness.[25] His statement repeats the offer of his friends for his release from death (v. 22: ἀπολυθῇ), and his endurance (ὑποφέρειν) links with that of the seven brothers (v. 36).

"the Lord who possesses holy knowledge." God of knowledge is a title found in 1 Sam 2:3 ("For the Lord is a God of knowledge, and by him actions are weighed") and frequently in the Dead Sea Scrolls. For example, "because from the God of knowledge comes all [that existed for ever]" (4Q402 frg. 4, lines 12–13);[26] "consider the wonderful mysteries [of the God of awe (אל הנוראים)] ... And then you will know (the difference) between [goo]d and [evil in their] work[s,] for the God of knowledge [אל הדעות] is the foundation of truth, and through the mystery of existence he expounded its basis" (4Q417 2 i 8–9).[27] The exact phrase "holy knowledge" does not seem to occur elsewhere. "Holy knowledge" could be used simply because it is God's knowledge, and God is by definition holy. However, the author might also be contrasting this γνῶσις of God with the γνῶσις of Eleazar's former friends at v. 21, where I translated γνῶσις as "acquaintance." In v. 30, Eleazar could be appealing to God's intimate acquaintance with him, a knowledge that results in holiness, not in defilement, as with the former friends.

"because of the fear of him." The wisdom of Eleazar is shown in that he fears God. "The fear of God is the beginning of wisdom" (Prov 1:7).

What is most interesting is the distinction the author

---

22 See also the honor given to Zeno because he encouraged the youths who came to him toward virtue (ἀρετή) and set his own life as an example (παράδειγμα) (Diogenes Laertius 7.10).

23 Kevin Osterloh, "Multiple Forms of Judean Patriotism: Redefining the Martyrologies of 2 Maccabees," paper presented in a section entitled "Violence and Representations of Violence among Jews and Christians" at the Society of Biblical Literature annual meeting in New Orleans, Louisiana, in 2009.

24 The funeral ceremony is described in Polybius 6.53–54. It is also interesting how Polybius (23.14.12) relates anecdotes about Publius Scipio "for the sake of the good fame of the departed and to incite their successors to achieve noble deeds."

25 See the comment on 7:9 and n. 34 below. The classic example is Socrates, as Rajak (*Jewish Dialogue*, 120–22) and van Henten (*Maccabean Martyrs*, 208–9) among others have discussed. One might also recall the confrontational attitude of Zeno of Elea and Anaxarchus before torturing tyrants (Diogenes Laertius 9.27, 59).

26 See also 1QS 3.15; 1QH^a 9.26.

27 For a list of references where God's knowledge is called upon in the context of vindication of the righteous, see George W. E. Nickelsburg, "Apocalyptic

has Eleazar make between body and soul. Whereas earlier Eleazar had been ready to be escorted to Hades, to the shadowy underworld, the introduction of the soul–body distinction seems to reflect a worldview akin to that of Wis 3:1-4: "The souls of the righteous are in the hand of God, and no torment will ever touch them. In the eyes of the foolish they seemed to have died, and their departure was thought to be an affliction, and their going from us to be their destruction; but they are at peace. For though in the sight of men they were punished, their hope is full of immortality." Eleazar's distinction between body and soul thus looks forward to the possibility of a future life.

■ **31** The use of μεταλλάσσω ("to exchange") as a synonym for "to die" is found in 4:7, 36; 5:5; 6:31; 7:7, 13, 14, 40; 14:46. As Welles notes, the verb μεταλλάσσειν was first used of heroes like Herakles, who being immortal, "changed existence." It came to be used of Hellenistic kings, as in 4:7. Welles notes that "later, however, the euphemism became established, and was used without regard to the religious character of the person in question."[28] Here it would be most appropriate for the heroic Eleazar.

This summative verse reflects back to v. 28: τοῖς νέοις, ὑπόδειγμα, γενναῖον, γενναίως/γενναιότητος, καταλελοιπως/καταλιπών. In addition, the author says that Eleazar leaves behind a "memorial of excellence." In the LXX, the term "memorial" (μνημόσυνον) is used of God's name and of Passover (Exod 3:15; 12:14; 13:9) as well as of other events such as the stones set in the Jordan after the Israelites crossed over (Josh 4:7). Here it is a memorial of excellence (ἀρετή). The term is used in 10:28 and 15:17 in the sense of "valor," but it is found also in the description of Onias in a dream of Judas (15:12). In this last case, as also in 6:31, the term has the connotation of moral excellence.

■ **7:1** "Also, seven brothers" is literally "it happened that seven brothers. . . ." The author likes to use the formula συμβαίνω + accusative infinitive construction (3:2; 4:30; 5:2, 18; 9:2, 7; 10:5; 12:24, 34; 13:7). This verse resonates with the earlier persecution statements: "compelled" (ἀναγκάζεσθαι) as in 6:1, 7, 18; "unlawful" (ἀθέμιτος)

as in 6:5, 20 (οὐ θέμις); "pig meat" (ὕειον κρέας) as in 6:18. The verb for "torture" (αἰκίζομαι) and its noun αἰκία pepper this chapter (7:1, 13, 15, 42) and occur again in 8:28 and 30. The word for whips (μάστιξι) links back to Eleazar's torture (6:30). This narrative of the persecution is thus tightly wound together. The style in this narrative, however, is quite different from the elevated style of the preceding story. In this verse, the use of ἐφάπτεσθαι with the preposition ἀπό instead of the simple genitive is an example of the growing use of ἀπό and ἐκ to replace the partitive genitive. It is not, as Habicht asserts, "ungriechisch."[29]

In this account of the seven sons and the mother, the emphasis is, as Schwartz notes, on the seven sons rather than the mother, which comports with Eleazar as an example for the youth. A prominent position is given to Antiochus IV even though neither a change of scene nor the arrival and presence of Antiochus IV in Jerusalem have been mentioned. The presence of the king seems to reflect the traditional folktale pattern whereby a ruler is bested by a wiser subject. The number seven is a round number for completion, as in Ruth 4:15; 1 Sam 2:5; Job 1:2; and Jer 15:9.

■ **2** The question of the spokesperson ironically underscores that the interaction is not one of debate or discussion but one of brute force. The king is represented as not open to persuasion. "Ready to die" (ἕτοιμοι ἀποθνήσκειν) describes also the followers of Maccabeus before their first battle with Nikanor and after Judas's words of encouragement (8:21). "Ancestral laws" are also what the youngest brother states he is ready to die for (7:37; see also the tempting offer of the king if the youngest will abandon the ancestral ways, 7:24). Throughout the chapter, the adjective πάτριος ("ancestral") is used to describe the language the martyrs use (7:8, 21, 27). The contrast between the young men and the foreign king is highlighted.

■ **3** The anger of the king flares up again, against the youngest son in 7:39. The "brutish disposition" of the king is seen in 5:11 at his seizing of Jerusalem and when he learns that Judas and his followers have defeated Nikanor (9:4). In all this display of anger, the king shows

and Myth in 1 Enoch 6–11," *JBL* 96 (1977) 383–405, here 387 n. 16.
28   Welles, *Royal Correspondence*, 348.
29   See Doran, *Temple Propaganda*, 36–37.

a lack of the control that should characterize a good ruler.

In the LXX, τήγανον refers to a cooking instrument that would be heated (2 Kgs 13:9; Ezek 4:3), presumably by the cauldrons in which the fire would be started and over which the pan would be placed.

■ **4** "Scalping" is literally "to scalp in Scythian fashion" as described in Herodotus 4.64. In Pliny, the Scythians are classed as barbarians who eat human flesh (*Hist. nat.* 6.53; 7.9–11).[30] In the aftermath of Molon's unsuccessful revolt against Antiochus III, Hermias, the harsh commander of Antiochus, destroyed many of the people of Seleucia by such mutilation as described here, and Achaeus, who proclaimed himself king in opposition to Antiochus III, was also so mutilated (Polybius 5.54.10; 8.21.3). The torture is dehumanizing: the first brother's tongue, by which humans communicate, and extremities are cut off, so that he is like a slab of meat when fried. The pathos is heightened by the mother and brothers' watching the torture. The mother's onlooking is mentioned again before the death of her last son (7:20).

■ **5** In contrast to the former friends of Eleazar who urged and encouraged (παρεκάλουν) him to escape death (6:21), the mother and brothers encourage each other "to die nobly," as Eleazar had done (6:28).

■ **6** In 12:22 and 15:2 the author describes God as the one who sees all. God is said to see when people are in trouble: Hagar (Gen 16:13); the Israelites in Egypt (Exod 2:25); the psalmist (LXX Ps 30:7). The LXX particularly heightens this view of God as all-seeing: LXX Job 22:12; 34:21-24; Zech 9:1; Ps 112:5-6. The impious think that God does not see (Ezek 8:12; 9:9). The mention of a song about confronting and witnessing closely reflects the text of LXX Deut 31:21. The actual quotation is from Deut 32:36, found also in Ps 135:14. The song of Deut 32:1-33 recounts what God did for his people, how they turned away from him, and that he punished them. In Deut 32:34, the song foretells God's compassionate turning toward his people and his vindication of them from their enemies. The last son states that God will be reconciled with his own servants (7:33: τοῖς ἑαυτοῦ δούλοις) and this phrase is found also at the victory over Nikanor (8:29).

■ **7** "Mocking him" is literally "for the purpose of mockery" (ἐπὶ τὸν ἐμπαιγμόν). The verb for mocking is found also in 7:10 and 8:17. Ἐμπαιγμός can also refer to torture or cruel treatment.[31] However, the use of the imperfect ἐπηρώτων ("they were questioning") while the brother's skin is being torn off suggests mockery. The question is not a real question leading to discussion but is in opposition to the first son's statement to the king in v. 2. In 9:7, all the limbs of Antiochus IV's body are wrenched.

The use of εἰ to introduce a question is often seen as a Semitism, but this is not necessarily so.[32] Here πρό means "rather than."[33]

■ **8** The emphasis on the ancestral voice stresses the distance between the brother and his foreign torturers and is echoed in vv. 21 and 27. Abel suggested that the last words of the sentence, "like the first" (ὡς ὁ πρῶτος), should be seen as a gloss, as it is not clear that all the tortures that the first brother underwent were applied to the second. However, ἑξῆς ("next in order") may be used here in a general sense to mean that he is brought to death.

■ **9** While the first brother had been deprived of speech by having his tongue cut out, the remaining brothers get to give a last speech, as the author thereby increases the emotion. Heroes about to die are often given long speeches—Alexander on his deathbed discourses at length (Ps.-Callisthenes 3.32–33). See also the speeches of Jacob in Gen 49:1-27, Moses in Deuteronomy 33; and Jesus in John 14–17.[34]

The brother addresses not the torturers who questioned him but the king. "Wretch" (ἀλάστωρ) was used by the tragedians of the avenging deity (Aeschylus *Pers.* 354; *Ag.* 1501, 1508), and then of the one who suffers from such vengeance (Aeschylus *Eum.* 236; Sophocles

30 See also Euripides *El.* 241; Ulrich Kellermann, *Auferstanden in den Himmel: 2 Makkabäer 7 und die Auferstehung der Märtyrer* (SBS 95; Stuttgart: Katholisches Bibelwerk, 1979) 22.

31 See G. Bertram, "ἐμπαίζω," *TDNT* 5 (1967) 630–36.

32 See the discussion in Doran, *Temple Propaganda*, 34–35.

33 Ibid., 34.

34 Johannes Munck, "Discours d'adieu dans le Nouveau Testament et dans la littérature biblique," in *Aux sources de la tradition chrétienne: Mélanges offerts à M. Maurice Goguel à l'occasion de son soixante-dixième anniversaire* (Bibliothèque théologique; Neuchâtel: Delachaux & Niestlé, 1950) 155–70; Anthony J.

Ai. 374). By using a μὲν . . . δέ construction, the author contrasts the king and his control of this present life with the king of the cosmos who controls future life. Later, Nikanor makes the distinction between a ruler of earth and the ruler of heaven, but does not understand the power of the king of heaven (15:3-5). In the Eleazar narrative, while his friends had tried to persuade Eleazar to escape death (6:22: ἀπολυθῇ), he had preferred not to be released (6:30: ἀπολυθῆναι). Whereas there the verb ἀπολύειν referred to being released from death, here the verb means to be removed/freed from this life.

Here the hint of future reward and punishment found in 6:26 begins to be elaborated. "To return to eternal life" is literally "to an eternal reviving of life" (εἰς αἰώνιον ἀναβίωσιν ζωῆς). This is a case of the poetic figure of hypallage, whereby "a word, instead of agreeing with the case it logically qualifies, is made to agree grammatically with another case."[35] "Eternal" should qualify "life" rather than "reviving"—one is not eternally revived. The author also neatly juxtaposes two words with a similar meaning: βίος and ζωή. The phrase is similar to that in Dan 12:2: "many . . . will be raised, some to eternal life" (πολλοὶ . . . ἐξεγερθήσονται, οὗτοι εἰς ζωὴν αἰώνιον).[36] By the repetition of the first person plural pronoun ἡμᾶς and the use of the second person singular pronoun σύ, the author also highlights the contrast between the fate awaiting the king and the fate of the brothers.

■ **10-12** The third brother knows the drill. Later, Judas makes his followers courageous before their first big battle (8:21). "Heaven" is here a circumlocution for "God."[37] Katz has argued strongly for the elimination of v. 11, not only on text-critical grounds but also on literary grounds. First, while the other brothers address the king and tell the diverse fates that lie in store for them and the king, the third brother makes a statement to no one in particular. Second, the result clause of v. 12 (ὥστε . . .) would

follow directly on the brother's courageously stretching forth his hands as well as his tongue and would give the reason for the king's astonishment.[38] We thus have two tellings of the story. If one follows the telling evident in the Latin manuscript tradition and eliminates v. 11, then the narrative focuses on the astonishment at the courageousness of the brother. If one follows the longer version including v. 11, then the emphasis falls on the brother's faithfulness to God's laws and his hope for future life. The threefold repetition of "these" (ταῦτα) in v. 11 underscores that the brother hopes to regain the same limbs. Hope, in fact, becomes a major term in this narrative, positive in 7:14, 20, negative in 7:34.

The young man takes no notice (ὑπερορᾶν) of the sufferings, as the mother later is said to have instructed her sons (7:23). This disregard contrasts with God's watching (7:6: ἐφορᾶν) over them. The same theme of creation appears in both contexts: the young man acquires his limbs from the heavenly one (7:11) and the mother confesses that God is the creator who forms humans (7:23).

"Regarding the sufferings as naught" (ἐν οὐδενὶ τὰς ἀλγηδόνας ἐτίθετο) is the opposite of what is said in 4:15 about those who frequented the gymnasium: τὰς μὲν πατρῴους τιμὰς ἐν οὐδενὶ τιθέμενοι, "They held the ancestral honors of no account."

Astonishment—in this instance of the king and his attendants at the courage of the brother—is a frequent topos: the followers of Alexander the Great marveled at the fortitude of Calanus, the Indian gymnosophist, when he set himself on fire (Arrian *Anab.* 7.3.5; Diodorus Siculus 17.107.5); Hecataeus of Abdera at the willingness of the Jews to undergo any punishment rather than transgress the law (see Josephus *Ap.* 1.190-93); and God at the fortitude of Job (Aristeas the Exegete in Eusebius *Praep. ev.* 9.25.4).

■ **13-14** The account of the death of the fourth brother uses language similar to that of the second: 7:7, 13-14:

Saldarini, "Last Words and Deathbed Scenes in Rabbinic Literature," *JQR* 68 (1977) 28-45.

35 Smyth, *Greek Grammar*, §3027.

36 For a thorough discussion of the belief in resurrection in this period, see George W. E. Nickelsburg, *Resurrection, Immortality, and Eternal Life in Intertestamental Judaism* (Cambridge, Mass.: Harvard University Press, 1972).

37 See the list of such usage in Ralph Marcus, "Divine Names and Attributes in Hellenistic Jewish Literature," *American Academy for Jewish Research* 3 (1931-32) 43-129, here 96-97.

38 Katz, "Text of 2 Maccabees," 19-20.

μεταλλάσσω; 7:8, 13: βάσανος, βασανίζω; 7:9, 14: ἀνίστημι, ἀνάστασις. As discussed above on 6:31, the verb μεταλλάσσω literally means "to change, alter, or to exchange" and is frequently used figuratively in 2 Maccabees for "to die" (4:7; 5:5; 6:31; 7:7, 13, 40; 14:46). It is most often used alone or with τὸν βίον in the accusative (4:7; 5:5). Here, with the prepositional phrase "from humans" (ἀπ᾽ ἀνθρώπων), it appears to mean to leave/change from human existence. In rather tortured language, the brother seems to say that everybody hopes in some way for life after death. No previous mention had been made of the fate of the king, except perhaps an oblique allusion in the use of the term "wretch" (7:9). Here, however, the king is told he will not have a resurrection to life. The solitary μέν emphasizes the reference to the king.[39] See also Wis 3:4: "The hope [of the righteous] is full of immortality."

"What is hoped for from God" is literally "the hopes from God."

■ **15-17** The ability of a ruler to do as he wills is stated in Dan 8:4 (referring to the kings of Media and Persia) and in Dan 11:3 (referring to Alexander the Great). But the asyndetic grouping of participles ἔξων ... ὤν ("having ... being") emphasizes the transient quality of the power.

"abandoned by God." The author had previously stated in his digression that God does not abandon his own people (6:16). This passage recalls the beautiful verse of Isa 54:7-8 "For a brief moment I forsook you [ἐγκατέλιπόν σε], but with everlasting love I will have compassion on you, . . . says the Lord, your Redeemer." See also Isa 49:21-26, where Zion will say, "I was left all alone [ἐγὼ δὲ κατελείφθην μόνη]" but God promises redemption.

The verb καρτερεῖν, which I have translated "be obstinate," can also mean "be patient." In this latter sense, it would ironically contrast with the patience of the one being tortured.

"the magnificent power." Just as Heliodorus felt the effects of God's epiphany and was told to proclaim the magnificent power of God (3:34), so Antiochus IV will experience God's power. Just as the brothers were tormented so will be Antiochus.

"You and your seed." That not only the sinner but also his subsequent family would be punished is summed up in the proverb: "The fathers have eaten sour grapes, and the children's teeth are set on edge" (Jer 31:29; Ezek 18:2). In the list of blessings and curses that Moses expounds, if the people obey the Lord's commandments, blessed will be the fruit of their womb (Deut 28:4); if they do not obey, cursed will be the fruit of their womb (Deut 28:18). According to Lam 5:7: "Our fathers sinned, and are no more; and we bear their iniquities." Jeremiah and Ezekiel combat the proverb, arguing that each individual will be punished for his/her own sin. Is the author simply using a general threat, as in LXX Isa 14:21, where the king addressed there is told that his children will be slaughtered for the sins of their father, so that they will not rise again and inherit the earth and fill the land with wars? Or is he referring more specifically to the account of the death of Antiochus IV in 9:5-28 and to the fact that Antiochus IV's son Antiochus V was murdered (14:2; 1 Macc 7:2-4)? Alexander Balas, who claimed to be a son of Antiochus IV (Diodorus Siculus 31, 32a; Justin 35.1.6–7), ruled for some time but was eventually beheaded (1 Macc 11:7).

■ **18-19** By the repetition of the reflexive pronoun ἑαυτός, the brother continues the solidarity with "our race" (v. 16) and stresses the communal sense of sinning as the people stand in covenant relationship with God. He thus contrasts their God with other gods. The king must not think that he has acted on his own (5:17) but realize that he has been an instrument of God. Like Assyria, which had been God's rod of anger against the Jews but had arrogantly overreached himself (Isa 10:5-19), so too Antiochus will be punished. It was never good to fight against a god, as the giants found out, a story that was carved in stone on the Great Altar of Pergamon in the first half of the second century B.C.E. Apollo had warned Diomedes off (Homer *Il.* 5.440–43), and Pentheus had found out to his dismay what it was to fight against God (Euripides *Bacch.* 45, 325, 1255).[40]

■ **20-23** The placing of this scene interrupts the listlike quality of the deaths of the first six sons. As the mother's encouragement was directed to all her sons (v. 21), the

---

39   Smyth, *Greek Grammar*, §2897.
40   See also Euripides *Iph. Aul.* 1408; Epictetus 3.24.24; Plutarch *Superst.* 168C. See Kamerbeek, "Conception," 271–83.

scene should have been placed before their deaths, but the author has consciously placed it here in order to give greater emphasis to the death of the youngest son and also to emphasize that the mother is the teacher of all her sons.

The love of a mother for her dead children is graphically stated by Jeremiah: "Rachel is weeping for her children; she refuses to be comforted for her children, because they are not" (Jer 31:15). The weeping of Hekabe for her dead son Hektor is overpowering (Homer *Il.* 22.405-7, 430-36). When Cratesicleia was to be killed, she showed no emotion for herself but asked only one favor, that she die before her children died. However, the children were executed first and then Cratesicleia, who cried out, "Children, where have you gone?" (Plutarch *Ag. Cleom.* 38.4-5). Megistho preferred to see her son dead rather than a slave. When Aristotimus, the tyrant, was angered by the rebuke of Megistho, he ordered her son to be brought, as if to kill him in her sight. When the child could not be found immediately, Megistho called him to her and declared, "For me it is harder to look upon your undeserved slavery than upon your death" (Plutarch *Mulier. virt.* 252C–D). For the woman to see seven sons killed is astonishing. In 14:18, the forces of Judas are said to have a high courage (εὐψυξία) just as the mother bears the events "with high courage" (εὐψυχῶς). The phrase "in one day" (μιᾶς ὑπὸ καιρὸν ἡμέρας) is exactly as in *3 Macc.* 4:14.

■ **21** The woman's resolution is noble (γενναῖος), linking her not only with her sons, who die nobly (7:5, 11), but also with Eleazar (6:28) and Judas (12:42). She stirs up her womanly way of reckoning (λογισμός) just as Eleazar took up a high-principled position (6:23: λογισμός) and as Judas stirs up the emotions of his troops (15:10). The androcentric mentality is obvious, as women were considered weaker vessels in this culture, but the mother shows that she is made of sterner stuff. That a king should be bested by a weak woman is even stronger evidence of the rightness of the Jewish cause.

■ **22-23** When Rachel demands of Jacob that he give her children or she will die, Jacob responds, "Am I in the place of God, who has withheld from you the fruit of the womb?" (Gen 30:1-2). Ecclesiastes observes, ". . . you do not know the way of the wind, or how the bones [are] in the womb of a pregnant woman" (Qoh 11:5). The lack of knowledge about the formation of babies is found also in

Ps 139:13-15 and Job 10:8-12. This is not to say that the audience did not know that sexual intercourse was necessary to produce babies, but that the ultimate decider of whether a fetus appeared was, in their opinion, God.

"breath and life." The phrase, repeated in v. 23, appears to be a reference to Gen 2:7, where God breathed life into Adam, and so I have translated πνεῦμα as "breath," rather than "spirit." The two terms are linked in 14:46, where Rhazis calls on the Master of life and breath. This would seem to be an example of hendiadys, where two words are used to express a single complex idea. See, e.g., Gen 6:17 and 7:15: "all flesh in which there is the breath of life [πνεῦμα ζωῆς]"; Gen 7:22: πνοὴν ζωῆς ("breath of life"). In Wis 15:11, where there is a clear reference to Gen 2:7, the phrase πνεῦμα ζωτικόν is found.

"composing the elementary structuring." The verb used for "compose," διαρρυθμίζω, is unusual. Like ῥυθμίζω, it has the sense of "rhythm," as well as meaning "order, arrange, compose." In LXX Isa 44:13, the idol maker "shapes [ἐρύθμισεν] the wood with glue" and then makes it into the shape of a man. Even more unusual is the abstract noun στοιχείωσις, from the term στοιχεῖον. It can have the meaning of "elementary teaching" and in physics has the meaning of a component part of matter, or an elementary principle. Aristotle argues against those who think that flesh could possibly come from a simple arrangement of elements (Aristotle *Cael.* 3.8 306b22-29). The author of 2 Maccabees does not appear to be making a technical argument, but he is using terms not usually found in the LXX.

■ **22** The stress on the first person pronoun ("my [ἐμήν] womb"; "I" [ἐγώ] twice), together with the emphatic particle τοιγαροῦν, prepares for the contrast with the one who does know—God. God is called the Master of the world in 13:14. He is the creator of all (1:24; Sir 24:8; *Ep. Arist.* 16) and creator in 2 Kgdms 22:32. "Molding human production" refers back to Gen 2:7: "God molded [ἔπλασεν] the human, soil from the earth, and he breathed into his face a breath of life, and the human became [ἐγένετο] a living soul." In Gen 5:1, when the biblical narrative lists the progeny of Adam and Eve, LXX reads: "This is the book of the generation of humans [βίβλος γενέσεως ἀνθρώπων]," and this harks back to LXX Gen 2:4, the beginning of the account of the molding of Adam and Eve: "This is the book of the production of heaven and earth, when it happened [βίβλος γενέσεως οὐρανοῦ καὶ γῆς, ὅτε ἐγένετο]." God is thus described in 7:23 as involved in all aspects of the cosmos. For ἐξευρών, I have used "invented," since to translate as "discover, search out, find" would suggest that God was not involved in the process. The verb occurs in Baruch: "But the one who knows all things knows [Wisdom], he found [ἐξεῦρεν] her by his understanding. . . . This is our God; no other can be compared to him. He found [ἐξεῦρεν] the whole way to knowledge, and gave her to his servant Jacob and to Israel, whom he loved" (Bar 3:32, 35-36). The term is thus linked with God's all-knowing ability.

While the wicked say that "no one has been known to return from Hades" (Wis 2:1), the wise person knows that God has power over life and death, he can lead mortals down to the gates of Hades and back again (Wis 16:13).

"with mercy." In 6:16, the author had argued that it was good for God to punish sins immediately, as he would not keep his mercy away from them for long. The youngest brother hopes that his and his brothers' deaths will end God's anger against the race (7:38) and soon thereafter God's anger turns to mercy (8:5).

As the third brother took no notice of the tortures (7:11), so the mother asks her youngest not to do so on account of the laws, as in 7:2, 9.

■ 24 As the text now stands, the mother spoke in her ancestral language (7:21: φωνή), and Antiochus does not understand the voice (φωνή). The attributive position of the participle "reproachful" makes the sense a little unclear. Is the mother reproaching or upbraiding her sons, or is she reproaching Antiochus? One might suspect that the scene depicted in vv. 20-23 was injected into the sequence of deaths and that the reproachful voice is really that of the sixth brother. However, there is no way that the speech of the sixth brother, which is not said to have been uttered in his ancestral language, could have been understood as anything but disparaging.

The speech of vv. 22-23 had been to all the mother's sons (v. 21), so now, with the youngest still alive, Antiochus intervenes to win over one. His appeal, using the periphrastic form of the indirect middle voice, ἐποιεῖτο τὴν παράκλησιν, contrasts with the brothers' encour-

agement (v. 5: παρεκάλουν) and the mother's encouragement (v. 21: παρεκάλει), but especially with God's encouragement (7:6: παρακαλεῖται, παρακληθήσεται). The contrast between "with words" (διὰ λόγων) and "on oath" (δι᾽ ὅρκων) accentuates the guarantee of the king and also contrasts with the mother's hope in the Lord (v. 20; also v. 14). The reader already knows how untrustworthy oaths can be, as Andronikos had given oaths that Onias would not be harmed (4:34). Later, Judas would stress that Gentiles always broke their oaths (15:10).

"change." Usually the verb used is μεταβαίνω (6:1, 9, 25). The verb μετατίθημι is used in 4:46, where the mind of Antiochus is changed.

"Envied" is literally "deemed happy" (μακαριστός). The happiness promised by the king contrasts with that promised in Prov 29:18: "Happy [μακαριστός] is he who keeps the Law" and Prov 16:20: "Happy is he who trusts in the Lord."

"Friend." This was the title given to a select group entitled to the privileges of members of the king's court.[41] In the second prefixed letter, Antiochus and his friends are said to have gone to the temple of Nanaia to plunder it (1:14). The group is depicted as counseling the king (10:13; 14:11) and Nikanor is mentioned as one of the group (8:9). Such a position was said to have been offered to Mattathias (1 Macc 2:18), and Jonathan and Simon were appointed Friends by various Seleucid kings (1 Macc 10:16, 19-20, 65; 11:26-27, 57; 13:36.)

"entrust." The same verb is used in 10:13 to describe how Cyprus had been entrusted to Ptolemy Makron. Here it refers to unspecified services on behalf of the king.

■ 25-26 As the text sequence now stands, the suspicion of the king (v. 24) is overcome by his desire to win over the boy. The word σωτηρία ("safety") is used to denote the physical well-being of an individual, as in 3:29, 32; 12:25, or of the nation, as in 11:6 and 13:3. In 14:3, it means "safe return." The emphasis on the king's persistence is humorous. When the boy shows no interest (προσέχοντος), the king encourages (προσκαλεσάμενος) the mother. The only effect of the king's insistence is that, after the mother's persuasion (πείθω), the lad dies, trusting (πεποιθώς) completely in the Lord (7:40).

---

41 Bickerman, *Institutions*, 40–50.

■ **27-29** As with Polybius,[42] the author of 2 Maccabees likes to string together participles in apposition, so here, literally, "leaning . . . scoffing" (asyndeton); "carrying . . . suckling . . . bringing you up . . . leading . . . nurturing." The string of participles stresses the close connection between mother and son and his debt to her (see Xenophon *Mem.* 2.2.3–4). The phrase "cruel tyrant" is used of Menelaus in 4:25.

The mother again emphasizes that God is the creator of the cosmos, as can be seen by viewing heaven and earth.[43] The mother states that God fashioned the individual things from previously unformed matter.[44] Note that in LXX Jer 4:23, the Hebrew terms תהו ובהו (the same as in Gen 1:2) are translated by οὐθέν ("nothing"). The Lucianic manuscripts have not οὐκ ἐξ ὄντων but ἐξ οὐκ ὄντων, which could be translated as "from things which do not exist." A parallel to this phrase is found in Xenophon: "parents made [their children] to be from what did not exist [ἐκ μὲν οὐκ ὄντων)]" (*Mem.* 2.2.3).

■ **29** In 5:8, Jason is called δήμιος, a public enemy of the fatherland and citizens. The mother encourages her youngest son to embrace (ἐπιδέχεσθαι) death, just as, on the king's request, she had undertaken (ἐπιδέχεσθαι) to persuade him for his safety (7:26).

"In God's mercy" (ἐν τῷ ἐλέει) is, literally, "in the mercy," that is, the mercy of God mentioned in 7:23.

■ **30** In using the second plural verb form (μένετε), the young man does not address his mother or the king, but, presumably, the executioners. His words echo those of the eldest brother (7:2), just as the mention of Moses echoes the reaction of the mother and the remaining

sons at the first son's death (7:6). Again the emphasis on ancestors surfaces.

■ **31** Here the young man begins to address the king. He calls him by an epithet that Philo uses of the conspirators against the Jews, κακῶν εὑρεταί (originator of damages), and of Flaccus himself, ὁ καινῶν ἀδικημάτων εὑρετής ("originator of novel iniquities") (*Flacc.* 20, 73; see also Rom 1:30), and Tacitus says of Sejanus that he was thought to be the originator of all villainies (*facinorum omnium repertor*) (*Ann.* 4.11). Onias was accused of being the author of evils (4:1: τῶν κακῶν δημιουργός), while in 5:22 Antiochus had set up overseers to harm the race. Menelaus is the cause of all troubles (4:47; 13:4).

"Hebrews" is found also in 11:13 and 15:37. The reference to Moses in the previous verse may explain its presence here, as the term occurs most frequently in the early chapters of Exodus,[45] where the Hebrews are forced into slave labor by Pharaoh. It is a term that stresses the dignity of the race.[46]

"God's grasp" is literally "the hand of God." Eleazar had stated that one could not, either living or dead, flee the hand of God (6:26), and Wis 16:15 reiterates this. As Heb 10:31 says, "It is a fearful thing to fall into the hands of the living God."

■ **32** As Grimm notes, the particle γάρ shows that the reason for the deaths lies beyond Antiochus's control and that God is in charge. The same reason is given in 7:18, and the personal pronoun and the reflexive pronoun reinforce that the punishment comes because of the sins of the people.

42 Foucault, *Recherches*, 172.
43 God as creator of heaven and earth is a theme found frequently. LXX Pss 88:12; 145:6; Isa 40:26; Esth 4:17b-c; Wis 11:17; 13:5; *Ep. Arist.* 132; *2 Bar.* 54:17-22; Philo *Praem. poen.* 43.
44 For the debate over whether this phrase means that God created out of nothing, see David Winston, "The Book of Wisdom's Theory of Cosmogony," *HR* 11 (1971) 185–200; Georg Schuttermayr, "'Schöpfung aus dem Nichts' in 2 Makk 7,28?" *BZ* 17 (1973) 203–22; Gerhard May, *Schöpfung aus dem Nichts: Die Entstehung der Lehre von der creatio ex nihilo* (Arbeiten zur Kirchengeschichte 48; Berlin: de Gruyter, 1978). See the debate between Jonathan A. Goldstein ("The Origins of the Doctrine of Creation Ex Nihilo," *JJS* 35 [1984] 127–35) and David Winston ("Creation Ex Nihilo Revisited: A Reply

to Jonathan Goldstein," *JJS* 37 [1986] 88–91). Paul Copan ("Is *Creatio ex Nihilo* a Post-Biblical Invention? An Examination of Gerhard May's Proposal," *Trinity Journal* n.s.17 [1996] 75–93, here 85) maintains that *creatio ex nihilo* is present in this passage.
45 Exodus 1:15, 16, 19; 2:6, 7, 11, 13; 3:18; 5:3; 7:16; 9:1, 13; 10:3.
46 Graham Harvey, *The True Israel: Uses of the Names Jew, Hebrew and Israel in Ancient Jewish and Early Christian Literature* (AGJU 35; Leiden: Brill, 1996) 104–27; idem, "Synagogues of the Hebrews; 'Good Jews' in the Diaspora," in Sián Jones and Sarah Pearce, eds., *Jewish Local Patriotism and Self-Identification in the Graeco-Roman Period* (JSOTSup 31; Sheffield: Sheffield Academic Press, 1998) 132–47. See also David T. Runia, "Philonic Nomenclature," *Studia Philonica Annual* 6 (1994) 1–27, here

■ **33** This verse reiterates what the author had stated in his reflection in 5:17-20 (5:17 ἀπώργισται βραξέως; 5:20: καταλλαγῇ). The author may have used here ἐπώργισται to go with his use of ἐπιπλήξεως just previously. The reference to "training" links back to the reflection in 6:12-16. "Living Lord" is found also in 15:4. "Servants" echoes the quotation of Deut 32:36 in 7:6. In 8:29, after their first victory over Nikanor, Judas and his followers thank God and pray that God will be fully reconciled with his own servants.

■ **34-35** The sentence starts off with the same direct accusation against the king as in 7:31. Elsewhere, the text has the late form μιερός (4:19; 5:16; 9:13; 15:32). In this highly charged speech, the author has the youngest son use the early form μιαρός. As executioner of the brothers, Antiochus has polluted himself with blood, and the combination of ἀνόσιε . . . μιαρώτατε has the same power as Teiresias's accusation against Oedipus that he is the unholy pollutor (ἀνοσίῳ μιάστορι) of the land (Sophocles *Oed. Tyr.* 353). The sentence reflects again the author's language in 5:17, ἐμετεωρίζετο, but here the sentence has the connotation of rebellion. "To raise the hand" can be used for a sign of blessing (Sir 50:20) or prayer (Neh 8:6; LXX Ps 133:2), but it can also be used to signify rebellion (LXX 2 Kgdms 18:28; 20:21; 3 Kgdms 11:27; Ps 73:3). Here Antiochus has attacked the heavenly children. If the sentence were taken in isolation, it would resonate with rebellious attacks on the gods such as are found in Isaiah 14 and Ezek 28:6-9. The term "sons of heaven" refers to heavenly, angelic beings in *1 Enoch* 6:2; 13:8; 14:3; 106:5;[47] 1QS 4.22; 11.8; 1QHᵃ 11.22; 23.10. However, those faithful to the law are so described in *Jub.* 1:25, when God informs Moses that the people will repent of their sins and do his commandments: "And I shall be a father to them and they will be sons to me. And they will all be called 'sons of the living God.'" In *3 Macc.* 6:28, they are called "the sons of the all-powerful heavenly living God" (τοὺς υἱοὺς τοῦ παντοκράτορος ἐπουρανίου θεοῦ ζῶντος). The righteous person is seen as a "child of the Lord" (παῖδα κυρίου) and the Israelites as the children of God (θεοῦ παίδων) (Wis 2:13; 12:6). Given the context in which the sentence in 7:35 appears, and since in 7:11 "heaven" is a title for God, the phrase τοὺς οὐρανίους παῖδας ("the heavenly children") should be taken as equivalent to "children of God."

Antiochus's false hopes contrast with the hopes of the brothers and mother (7:14, 20). His own hope of escaping (ἐκπέφευγας) death (9:22) will not be realized, for just as Eleazar had stated (6:26), either living or dead one cannot escape from God, the overseer who sees all (3:39; *Ep. Arist.* 18; LXX Esth 5:1a).

■ **36** The μὲν . . . δέ construction once again contrasts the fate of the brothers with that of the king. The shortness of God's anger was noted in 7:33, and later martyrdoms would make the same contrast between the shortness of the suffering compared to what is hoped for (1 Pet 1:6; *Mart. Pol.* 2).

The translation of part of this verse has been controverted: βραχὺν ὑπενέγκαντες πόνον ἀενάου ζωῆς ὑπὸ διαθήκην θεοῦ πεπτώκασι. Is the genitive "eternal life" to be connected with the accusative "pain,"[48] or does it form with θεοῦ a second genitive to διαθήκην?[49] Is ὑπο διαθήκην θεοῦ connected to the verb, or does the verb stand alone? Hermann Bückers, Günther Stemberger, Ulrich Kellermann, and Schwartz all connect the prepositional phrase with the verb. All translate as if πίπτειν ὑπό had the meaning of "to fall into": Bückers: "haben sie jetzt die göttliche Bundesverheissung erlangt"; Stemberger: "sind sie des Bundes Gottes teilhaftig geworden";

14–17. An important article on this point is Barbara Schmitz, "Geschaffen aus dem Nichts? Die Funktion der Rede von der Schöpfung im Zweiten Makkabäerbuch," *Sacra Scripta* 9 (2009) 199–215.

47 Nickelsburg (*1 Enoch 1*, 504) sees the reading of the Ethiopic text in 101:1 as a textual corruption.

48 Hermann Bückers, "Das 'ewige Leben' in 2 Makk 7,36," *Bib* 21 (1940) 406–12; Günther Stemberger, *Der Leib der Auferstehung: Studien zur Anthropologie und Eschatologie des palästinischen Judentums im neutestamentlichen Zeitalter (ca. 170 v. Chr.–100 n.*

Chr. (AnBib 56; Rome: Biblical Institute Press, 1972) 21–22.

49 Kellermann, *Auferstanden*, 79; Schwartz, *2 Maccabees*, 316–17.

Kellermann: "(sie) sind jetzt in der Bereich der göttlichen Verheissungsgabe der Tora eingetreten"; Schwartz: "have come into God's covenant of eternal life."[50] However, while ὑπό can have the local sense of "into" as in "enter under," that is, into the cave, this locative sense would not apply with a term such as "covenant." In this context, the meaning of ὑπό would seem to be "to come under the control, dependence, subjection" as in 3:6: "these things fall under the power of the king" (ὑπὸ τὴν τοῦ βασιλέως ἐξουσίαν πεσεῖν ταῦτα). The prepositional phrase thus seems to mean that the brothers' deaths took place in the context of God's covenant and, as such, their brief pain bought them eternal life. The verb "to fall" has the meaning of "to die," as it does in 12:34 and 40. "Everlasting life" is a genitive of value, "pain that is worth everlasting life."[51] Just as Eleazar endured (6:30), so do the brothers, because they are assured that if they keep the commandments, God will redeem them. Here the reciprocal nature of the covenant is in play, just as it was enunciated in Deut 7:12: "If you keep these ordinances, by diligently observing them, the Lord your God will maintain with you the covenant and the mercy [τὴν διαθήκην καὶ τὸ ἔλεος] that he swore to your ancestors."

The combination of "sentence" (κρίσις) and "arrogance" (ὑπερηφανία) occurs in the narrative of Antiochus's death (9:4, 7-8, 11) and reflects back to 5:21.

■ 37 "body and soul." Rhazis had risked body and soul in the defense of Judaism (14:38), and Judas is the foremost champion of the citizens with both body and soul (15:30). The author has noted a difference between body and soul in 6:30, but the two are intertwined (3:16). He does not have the same viewpoint as the author of Wisdom of Solomon, for whom "the mortal body weighs down the soul" (Wis 9:15). Here the brothers surrender both for the ancestral laws.

The author had foretold in his preface that the Lord would be propitious to the Jews (2:22), and the Jews, before their battle with Timothy, pray that God will continue to be merciful (10:26). The theme of mercy runs through chaps. 7 and 8 (7:23, 29; 8:3, 5, 27) and appears also in the reflection of the author in 6:16. After Helio-

dorus had been whipped by the angels, he witnessed to all the great deeds of God (3:34-39). The Jews had been unable to acknowledge that they were Jews (6:6); now Antiochus, after being tormented, will want to be a Jew and he will acknowledge the God of the Jews (9:17) (see LXX Dan 3:45; Ep. Arist. 132).

■ 38 This has been a time of the wrath of the Lord, beginning with the desecration of the temple (5:17, 20) and through the executions of the Jews (7:33). The race (τὸ γένος) had been under attack since the appointment of overseers (5:22), but the author insists that the persecution was for its training (6:12), and the brothers insisted that the race had not been abandoned by God (7:16). As the narrative continues, the wrath of the Lord will stop (8:5), and the Jews under Judas will begin to be unstoppable.[52]

■ 39-40 The king remains enraged, as he had been at the beginning of the trial (7:3). The executioners had made fun of the second brother (7:7); now Antiochus feels he is being taunted, as he also had suspected earlier on hearing the mother's reproachful tone (7:24). Her persuasion (7:24: πείσειν) had succeeded, as the son now trusts (πεποιθώς) in the Lord. As here, the author often uses φέρειν + adverb to express emotion: + βαρέως (11:1; 14:27); + δυσφόρως (14:28). The adjective πικρός is found at the beginning of the persecutions (6:7) and will be used also of the sufferings of Antiochus IV (9:5). In these two verses, the author piles up a series of adverbs, two for the king, χειρίστως ("more severely") and πικρῶς ("vindictive"), and two for the young boy, καθαρῶς ("undefiled") and παντελῶς ("completely"). The concluding perfect participle πεποιθώς adds to the sound of words ending in -ως.

The youngest son leaves life "undefiled" (καθαρῶς). Antiochus IV had been characterized as "polluted" (μιερός: 5:16; 7:34; 9:13) and "unholy" (βέβηλος: 5:16). Jason is also polluted (4:13, 19), as is Alcimus (14:3: μεμολυμμένος). Most importantly, it is the temple that undergoes pollution (6:2: μολῦναι; 8:2 and 10:5: βεβηλόω). Judas avoids pollution (5:27: μολυσμός). So the youngest brother is linked to Judas, but the use of the

---

50 Schwartz (2 Maccabees, 317) refers to cases where πίπτειν can have the meaning of "fall into one's possession" but nowhere explores the significance of the preposition.

51 See Smyth, Greek Grammar, §1336.

52 For the motif of the deaths of martyrs ending divine anger, see As. Mos. 9:7 and Jacob Licht, "Taxo, or the Apocalyptic Doctrine of Vengeance," JJS 12 (1961) 95–100.

term καθαρῶς resonates with the purification (καθαρισμός) of the temple (2:19; 10:3, 5, 7).

■ **41** Even to the end, the mother remains part of the background such that the manner of her death is not described.

■ **42** The author uses a μὲν . . . δέ construction to link one section of his narrative to another, as he does in 3:40—4:1; 9:28—10:1; 10:9-10. The excessive tortures are the response to Jason's excessive impurity (4:13: τὴν . . . ὑπερβάλλουσαν ἀναγνείαν). The author has tied together the persecutions by his use of "meal" (σπλαγχνισμούς) and "tortures" (αἰκίας). Σπλαγχνισμός and its related verb are found in 6:7-8 and 21, while the verb "to torture" is found throughout the story of the seven brothers and their mother, in 7:1, 13, 15. The verb δηλόω ("set forth") is used also in 2:23 and 10:10.

General Commentary

The consequences of the king's abrogation of the ancestral laws that governed Jerusalem's life are seen in these events. The first two incidents (6:9b-11) focus on the life of the city: no new Jews were to be found there, as circumcision was forbidden and the ancestral festivals were not to be celebrated, even in secret. What gave the city and its citizens their particular culture and character was removed.

The author's characterization of the afflictions as παιδεία ("training") in his reflection (6:12-16) is ironic. This term has the connotations of training and education, Jason's goals when founding a gymnasium and ephebate (4:9). The author had earlier said that these innovations abrogated the polity of the Jews (4:11) and would cause them harm (4:16). He had also earlier stated that such an affliction was due to their sins but would be temporary and that God would be reconciled with his people (5:17-20). This last reflection by the author in 6:12-16 thus sums up the previous reflections. In it, the author tries in a special way to involve his readers as he uses the homiletic first person plural in 6:12, 15, and 16. By this usage, he contrasts his race (γένος) with others as God's people (λαός). Given the excessive cruelty of the tortures to follow, the author's insistence that God could have been even more severe and will be to other nations again underscores the theme of us versus them. This severe attitude toward other nations seems at odds with the view of books such as Wisdom of Solomon and Sirach, wherein God's forbearance toward other nations allows them time to repent (Wis 11:10—12:27; Sir 5:4-9; 18:10-14). The author of 2 Maccabees holds that all humans sin, but God has Israel suffer and pay for its sins now, so that it will not have to pay for their cumulative effect later. Such a view is in line with the author's stress on training and education; one should not spare the rod and spoil the child.

That the author is not providing a simple summary of Jason of Cyrene's work becomes evident in his description of the martyrdoms. Here he gives full rein to emotional rhetoric, as he had done in the initial narrative about Heliodorus, and makes these stories the centerpiece of his narrative. The martyrs' sufferings will put a stop to the persecution and change God's wrath to mercy.

These stories have all the hallmarks of stories of noble deaths found in the Greco-Roman tradition. Peter Scaer has usefully brought together the motifs about praiseworthy death as found both in the rhetorical tradition and in the influence of the story of Socrates' death.[53] He states that among the motifs are (1) virtue, especially courage and righteousness, (2) willingness to die, (3) being beneficial to others, and (4) dying victoriously (not a victim).[54] The first two are abundantly clear in the stories of Eleazar and of the brothers and their mother. Eleazar also sets an example for the young men to follow, and the seventh brother prays that the deaths will reconcile God to his people. The fourth motif is especially interesting. The connotation of a martyr is that the martyr is a victim of oppression. The story of Eleazar shows, however, that it is Eleazar who is the winner. He does not compromise his dignity by pretense but courageously leaves this life. His statement that neither alive nor dead can one escape the judgment of the Almighty hints that he will be vindicated, as do his last words, that he is glad in soul as he suffers the torments. The brothers and their

53   Peter J. Scaer, *The Lukan Passion and the Praiseworthy Death* (New Testament Monographs 10; Sheffield: Sheffield Phoenix, 2005).

54   Ibid., 93.

mother too are not victims. The trial scene is fascinating because there is no real trial. The judge is silent, and it is those on trial who speak so confidently and boldly before him, condemning him to death without resurrection. The condemned triumph. They are not losers but winners in the quest for eternal life. They reason soundly while the king falls into a rage. The story of Eleazar has frequently been compared to the death of Socrates and the deaths of non-Jewish philosophers.[55] Goldstein lists several correspondences between the two accounts, although he notes that the wordings of the two accounts have nothing in common.[56]

The martyrdoms of Eleazar and of the seven brothers and their mother are tightly connected by the author,[57] but there are also differences. While the narrative of the brothers and their mother has a trial setting—the accused are seized or arrested and brought before the king—the setting for the Eleazar narrative is quite different. As argued in the commentary by verse, the narrative appears to take place in a meal setting with Eleazar among his former friends. The author emphasizes that Eleazar is of the same social status as his dining companions, and the story is a debate among equals about how to behave. Like any well-brought-up gentleman, Eleazar rejects pretense. He chooses God as his Master and Friend (6:30: his lord knows who he is) and rejects the others' friendship. His behavior thus becomes a model for the youth. In this sense, the narrative can be seen as an example story. The confrontation is between equals, concerning how a man should behave in this society. As Sirach expressed the proverbial wisdom: "The one who fears God will accept his discipline [παιδείαν] . . . the one who seeks the law will be filled with it, but the hypocrite will be scandalized at it [ὁ ὑποκρινόμενος σκανδαλισθήσεται]"; "The wise will not hate the law, but the one who is hypocritical about it [ὁ ὑποκρινόμενος] is like a boat in a storm" (Sir 32:14-15; 33:2).

The narrative of the brothers and their mother is clearly not about equals. They are arrested and brought before the king. This narrative has puzzled scholars. When did the king come back to Jerusalem? In 6:1, the king had sent Geron to Jerusalem and so was presumably somewhere else. Did the martyrdoms therefore take place in Antioch, the Seleucid capital?[58] These questions simply are not the concern of the author of 2 Maccabees. This has led other scholars to posit a source behind the narrative or even to exclude the narrative from the work of Jason of Cyrene.[59] However, the reasons given are not probative. The presence of Semitisms is not as strong as Habicht claims: the use of μέλλω + present infinitive as in 7:2 is common in Greek, as is the use of σπέρμα for "offspring" found in 7:17; the thrice-repeated first person plural in 7:9 consciously opposes the king as a wretch and, as noted in the verse commentary, αἰώνιον ἀναβίωσιν ζωῆς is an interesting use of hypallage.[60] As the rabbinic tradition shows, a story about a mother and her seven sons[61] undergoing persecution could be told in many different situations.[62] But the author has thoroughly woven the story into his narrative, particularly in the echoing of terms used in his reflections: παιδεία at 6:12 and 7:33; βραξέως ἀ(ἐ)πώργισται at 5:17 and 7:33; μετεωρίζω at 5:17 and 7:34; ὀργή-ἔλεος at 5:20; 6:16; 7:37-38; 8:5.

55 Yehoshua Gutman, "The Story of the Mother and Her Seven Sons in the Aggadah and in II and IV Maccabees" (in Hebrew), in M. Schwabe and I. Gutman, eds., Commentationes Iudaico-Hellenisticae in Memoriam Iohannis Levy (Jerusalem: Magnes, 1949) 25–37; Kellermann, Auferstanden, 46–52.
56 Goldstein, II Maccabees, 285.
57 The opening words of the second story, συνέβη δέ, with no change of location or time, indicate the connection between the two, as does the closing verse, 7:42, which links the narratives together.
58 Among others, Kellermann (Auferstanden, 16–17) and Thomas Fischer, who dates the event to the summer of 168 B.C.E. (Seleukiden und Makkabäer: Beiträge zur Seleukidengeschichte und zu den politischen Ereignissen in Judäa während der 1. Hälfte des 2. Jahrhunderts v. Chr. [Bochum: Brockmeyer, 1980] 28).
59 Habicht, 2 Makkabäerbuch, 171, 187.
60 See further Doran, Temple Propaganda, 34–36.
61 Or a father and his seven sons: As. Mos. 9; Josephus Bell. 1.312-13; Ant. 14.429-30.
62 See Robert Doran, "The Martyr: A Synoptic View of the Mother and Her Seven Sons," in John J. Collins and George W. E. Nickelsburg, eds., Ideal Figures in Ancient Judaism: Profiles and Paradigms (SBLSCS 12; Chico, Calif.: Scholars Press, 1980) 189–221.

Whereas Eleazar is given a name and social status, the seven brothers and their mother remain anonymous. The similarly emotional tale of the death of a mother and children found in Polybius names the mother, Theoxena, and gives her social status as the wife of a victim of Philip V of Macedon. Rather than fall into the hands of the king, they all commit suicide.[63] The brothers and their mother in 2 Maccabees are quite different. They do not try to escape, nor do they commit suicide; they confront the king. Their anonymity makes them not so much individuals as representatives of the underdog before the oppressor. The role of the mother is particularly intriguing. Not only is she not named, but her death is not even developed. Even more interesting is that no mention is made of her husband, the boys' father. However, the adjective πάτριος formed from the substantive for father, πατήρ, is found throughout their story: the ancestral/fatherly voice is used (7:8, 21, 27); they do not transgress the ancestral/fatherly laws (7:2, 24, 37). This emphasis on "fatherly" and the absence of a human father leads me to suggest that the story is a contest about who is the father of the children.[64] It is a contest between Antiochus IV and God, a theomachy (7:19) wherein Antiochus IV is seen as opposing god. The mother declares that she does not know how the children came into her womb or how they were formed there (7:22). God is thus the true father of the children, who show their lineage by obeying his laws. This element of the story underpins the strong stress on God as creator and that he alone is God (7:37).[65] The emphasis on God as creator of the world in this contest about life and death explains the extraordinary emphasis in this story on the resurrection of the complete human, body and soul.

---

63 The story is found in Livy 40.4. However, Walbank ("Polybian Experiment," 61) is convinced that it comes from Polybius.

64 I have been led to this view from reading the insightful work of Gayle Rubin, in which she argues that the role of women in literature is often that of a prize from a contest between men. See Gayle Rubin, "The Traffic in Women: Notes on the 'Political Economy' of Sex," in Rayna R. Reiter, ed., *Toward an Anthropology of Women* (New York: Monthly Review Press, 1975) 157–210.

65 Barbara Schmitz has also emphasized the role of God as creator in the martyrdom stories: "daß Gott nicht nur am Anfang und Ende des Lebens präsent ist, sondern sich jeweils als Herr über die Grenzen des Lebens an ihrem Anfang und ihrem Ende erweist: Es ist Gott, der das Leben nach dem Tod ermöglicht, und es ist Gott, der seiende Dinge aus nicht seienden Dingen schafft" ("Geschaffen aus dem Nichts?" 215).

8

1/ Now Judas, also called Maccabeus, and his companions were
slipping into the villages unno-
ticed and were calling upon
their kinsfolk. They recruited
the steadfast in Judaism and
brought together around six
thousand, 2/ and they were
calling on the Lord to look
upon the people maltreated[a]
by all, to have pity also on the
temple profaned by godless
humans, 3/ to show mercy to
the despoiled city that would
soon be flattened, and to give
ear to the blood clamoring out
to him, 4/ and to remember also
the lawless destruction of the
guiltless infants and the blasphemies against his name, and
to hate evil.

5/ As Maccabeus had a corps, he
immediately could not be withstood by the Gentiles, since the
wrath of the Lord had turned to
mercy. 6/ Approaching unexpectedly, he burnt towns and
villages. By picking advantageous spots, he put to flight
quite a few of the enemy. 7/ He
especially used the nights as
accomplices for such assaults.
And word of his good-sized
force spread far and wide.

8/ When Philip detected that the
man was little by little making headway and advancing
more and more by means of his
military successes, he wrote
to Ptolemy, the governor of
Coele-Syria and Phoenicia, to
assist in royal matters of state.
9/ [Ptolemy] quickly appointed
Nikanor, son of Patroklos, one
of the First Friends, assigning
[to him] no fewer than twenty
thousand Gentiles of different races,[b] and he sent him to
remove the whole race within
Judea. He allied with him
Gorgias, a manly commander,
experienced in military engage-
ments. 10/ Now Nikanor determined in his own mind[c] to make
up for the king from the body
of Judean captives the tribute,
about two thousand talents, to
the Romans. 11/ He quickly sent
to the cities by the sea, sum-
moning [people] to the sale of
Jewish slaves. He promised to

a   V l La Sy Arm read the verb καταπατούμενον
("trodden down") rather than καταπονούμενον. The
former is found often in the LXX, whereas the latter
is found in the LXX only here and in *3 Macc.* 2:2, 13.
The verb καταπονεῖν is found in descriptions by
Hellenistic historians of the treatment of a city, e.g.,
Polybius 29.27.11, and is to be preferred as the more
difficult reading.

b   Katz ("Text of 2 Maccabees," 14) stated that παμφύλων ἔϑνη was awkward and suggested that one
emend to παμφύλων ἐϑνῶν. Hanhart (*Zum Text*, 33)
defends the present text, as does Habicht. The present text is understandable, and it keeps the stress on
"Gentiles," as in 8:5, 16.

c   The verb διίστημι usually means "to set apart, to separate," and Goldstein states that he knows of no usage
in ancient Greek that would support his translation
"resolved." Habicht suggested on the basis of the parallel passage in 8:38 that one read ἀνεδέξατο ("was
undertaking"). However, Preisigke (*Wörterbuch*, 1:378)
provides an instance from a papyrus of the first century C.E., as well as other cases where the verb has the
meaning of "to agree." One could also take the middle
voice as expressing the intention of Nikanor, that is,
"to set apart as far as he was concerned." Finally, the
use of διίστημι here avoids hiatus with the preceding
ἔχοντα. Foucault (*Recherches*, 29) has noted the same
tendency in Polybius to use a composite verb in place
of the simple form. Here the middle voice of ἵστημι
would mean "appointed himself."

deliver ninety slaves for a talent, not expecting the punishment about to overtake him from the Almighty.

12/ Word about the invasion of Nikanor came to Judas, and when he communicated the arrival of the army to his companions, 13/ the cowards who doubted the punishment of God were running away and taking themselves off. 14/ The rest[d] were selling everything and together were beseeching the Lord to deliver those sold before the event by the impious Nikanor. 15/ If not on their own account, [would he deliver them] on account of the covenants with the ancestors and because his august and majestic name was their name?

16/ Maccabeus gathered his followers, numbering about six thousand, and was encouraging them not to be panicked by the enemy nor to be in awe at the great number of Gentiles coming unjustly against them, but to contend nobly, 17/ having before their eyes the wanton violence lawlessly perpetrated against the holy place, the outrage against the disrespected city, and also the dissolution of the ancestral constitution. 18/ "For," [he said,] "they trust in weapons and daring deeds, but we rely on the almighty God who can overthrow with a single nod both those coming against us and the whole world." 19/ He also gathered together for them the instances of assistance performed in the time of their ancestors: that at the time of Sennacherib, when 185,000 were destroyed; 20/ the one in Babylonia, the battle against the Galatians, when they all came to the engagement, 8,000 with 4,000 Macedonians. While the Macedonians were in desperate condition, the 8,000[e] destroyed 120,000 through the aid that came to them from heaven, and they took much booty.[f] 21/ With these [words] he inspired them to be of good courage, prepared to die for the sake of the laws

d   The manuscripts read: "they [others] were selling all that was left over" (οἱ δὲ τὰ περιλελειμμένα πάντα ἐπώλουν). I prefer the emendation suggested by Niese (*Kritik*, 112) and adopted by Katz ("Text of 2 Maccabees," 14): οἱ δὲ περιλελειμμένοι πάντα ἐπώλουν. What would "what was left over" or "superfluous" mean? The emended text contrasts with the cowardly behavior in the previous verse.

e   The manuscripts are divided between 8,000 and 6,000. One can either leave 6,000 and suggest that the discrepancy between the first number given, 8,000, and the 6,000 is to be explained by some of the Jewish soldiers acting like the Macedonians (Goldstein); or hold, as I do, that the number 6,000 is a slip caused by assimilation to the number of Judas's forces in 8:16, 22.

f   I have followed Abel, who suggests that one should read ὠφέλειαν ἔλαβον ὑπέρ τι παμπληθῆ instead of the more generally read ὠφέλειαν πολλὴν ἔλαβον. The sense remains the same, but as for the use of ὑπέρ τι, in Abel's words, "this recherché form should be kept." The manuscript tradition evidences the scribes' misunderstanding of the phrase, reading instead of τι, τη, της την. The insertion of πολλήν appears to be an attempt to explain a more unusual phrase.

and the fatherland. He divided the army into four units. 22/ He put his brothers, Simon, Joseph, and Jonathan, 23/[g] in charge of each unit and, under each, 1,500 men. He declaimed from the holy scroll, and gave as watchword "God's Help." He himself led the first unit and pitted himself against Nikanor.

24/ With the Almighty as their ally, they slaughtered above nine thousand of the enemy, made the greater part of Nikanor's army wounded and maimed in their limbs, and forced all to flee. 25/ They took the money of those who had come along with them. After they had pursued them a considerable distance, they left off as they were hemmed in by time. 26/ For it was the day before Sabbath, and for this reason they did not prolong pursuing them. 27/ After collecting the weapons from them and stripping the arms off their enemies, they were taking part in the Sabbath, abundantly blessing and singing praises to the Lord, who preserved them to that day, and who ordained[h] [it] a beginning of mercy for them. 28/ After the Sabbath, they allotted some of the booty to the tortured and to the widows and orphans, the rest they divided among themselves and their children. 29/ After finishing this and making a communal supplication, they besought the merciful Lord to be completely reconciled to his servants.

30/ Clashing[i] with the followers of Timothy and Bacchides, they destroyed over twenty thousand of them and gained full control of fortified heights. They divided much spoil, making themselves equal partners with the tortured and widows and orphans, as well as the elders.[j] 31/ They collected their weapons and carefully consigned all of them to advantageous places, the rest they brought to Jerusalem. 32/ They destroyed the tribal leader of those followers of Timothy, a most godless man who had much troubled the

g The manuscripts here have "and moreover Eleazar." The Latin tradition has Esdras, perhaps in line with the Esdris mentioned in 12:26 or the Azariah of 1 Macc 5:18. The mention of Eleazar appears to be a gloss to bring the list of brothers in line with that of 1 Macc 2:2-5. The Syriac text separates out Eleazar and has him read from the holy scroll, rather than Judas.

h As Katz ("Text of 2 Maccabees," 15) notes, the genitive τάξαντος is an adaptation to a proximate case ἐλέους, and so there is no need to change it to τάξαντι. The Latin manuscript tradition supports the reading of Greek manuscripts 243–71 with the reading στάξαντος ("to drop, let fall"), where the meaning would be "and who let drop a beginning of mercy." Abel accepts this on the analogy of passages such as 2 Chr 12:7, where the Lord promises that his anger will not be poured out (οὐ μὴ στάξῃ ὁ θυμός μου). See also LXX Jer 49:18 and 51:6, where the verb στάζω is also used. However, the reading of τάξαντος is better, I suggest, as the reading "'ordaining a beginning" leads to the prayer in 8:29 that the Lord be completely (εἰς τέλος) reconciled to them.

i Reading with Hanhart συνερείσαντες rather than the well-attested συνερίσαντες. In Polybius 5.84.2, συνερείδω has the sense of "to meet in close conflict, to clash with," while συνερίζω, given its root, would have the sense of "quarrel with," which would not be completely appropriate here.

j The response of Hanhart (Zum Text, 34) to the reading proposed by Risberg ("Textkritische," 22) and Katz ("Text of 2 Maccabees," 15), ἰσομοίρους αὐτοῖς καὶ τοὺς ἠκισμένους καὶ ὀρφανοὺς καὶ χήρας ἔτι δὲ καὶ πρεσβυτέρους, is persuasive; that is, the fighters are putting themselves on an equal footing with the widows, orphans, and elders, rather than the other way around.

Jews. 33/ They celebrated the victory in the fatherland, and they set on fire those who had burned the holy gates, namely, Callisthenes and certain others who had fled[k] into one small dwelling. They received a fitting recompense for their ungodliness.

34/ The triply offensive Nikanor, who had brought one thousand merchants for the sale of the Jews 35/ and had been humbled through the Lord's help by those thought in his estimation to be well beneath him, took off his splendid raiment. All alone, he made himself look like a runaway slave and came across country to Antioch, having exceeded beyond all expectation[l] in the destruction of his army. 36/ He who had taken upon himself to settle finally the tribute to the Romans by the body of captives from Jerusalem, proclaimed that the Jews had a champion and that the Jews were invulnerable in consequence of this way of life, namely, their following the laws prescribed by [this champion.]

k With L′ 46–52 58 311 Syriac, I read the plural πεφευγότας rather than the singular, and also the third plural verb ἐκομίσαντο. As Katz ("Text of 2 Maccabees," 11) argued, the flight is into one small building (εἰς ἓν οἰκίδιον), and if the word for "one" is to be given its full meaning, then likely more than one person fled into it. The καί before Callisthenes I take as explicative, and this requires the Lucianic and Syriac fuller reading of καλλισθένην καὶ τινάς ἄλλους.

l I retain, with Hanhart (*Zum Text*, 39), the *lectio difficilior* of ὑπὲρ ἅπαν rather than, with Katz ("Text of 2 Maccabees," 15), the Lucianic reading of ὑπεράγαν. There is no substantial difference in meaning.

Commentary by Verse

■ **1** This verse is connected to the preceding by a μὲν οὖν . . . δέ construction, which is often used by the author as he passes to another subject (3:22-23; 9:28–10:1; 10:22-23; 10:28; 11:18, 19). Here the author takes up again the story of Judas Maccabeus, whom he had mentioned in 5:27 before the description of the measures taken by Antiochus against Jerusalem as he abrogated the ancestral laws. The use of the term "Judaism" contrasts with the Hellenism begun under Jason (4:13) and continued under Antiochus, as the author fulfills the promise made in the prologue of his work (2:21) to describe the resistance of those who fought eagerly on behalf of Judaism. In contrast also to 1 Macc 3:1-9, there is no mention of Judas's father, Mattathias, and no hymn celebrating his valor. Judas enters the villages secretly, just as earlier people had tried to celebrate the Sabbath secretly (6:11: λεληθότως) and had been executed for doing so. While Jason had no mercy on his kinsfolk (5:6), Judas calls upon them to help. Where Judas called upon (προσεκαλοῦντο) his kinsfolk, Nikanor will call upon (v. 11: προσκαλούμενος) the towns to buy Judean slaves. In 1 Macc 4:6, Judas has three thousand fighters beside him in his first battle.

■ **2-4** The prayer of Judas and his companions echoes the prayer of the seventh brother (7:37: ἐπικαλούμενος; 8:2: ἐπεκαλοῦντο). The prayer divides into three sections, as God is called upon to see, to hear, and to remember. The same triptych is found in Exod 2:24-25: "And God heard [εἰσήκουσεν] their groaning, and God remembered [ἐμνήσθη] his covenant with Abraham and Isaac and Jacob, and God saw [ἐπεῖδεν] the children of Israel, and he knew them."

■ **2-3a** God is first asked to look upon his people. In 7:6, the brothers and their mother had consoled each

170

other by noting that God looks down, and in 15:2, God is described as "the one who observes everything" (ὑπὸ τοῦ πάντα ἐφορῶντος). Here he is called to look upon the people. The term "people" has previously occurred only in 6:16, where the author, in a reflection, promised that God does not desert his people. The maltreatment of the people is further described by the two appositive infinitive phrases about the temple[1] and the city. The two verbs, "to have pity" (οἰκτεῖραι) and "to show mercy" (ἐλεῆσαι), are frequently paired in the LXX, as in the scene where God proclaims his name to Moses and continues: "I will show mercy [ἐλεήσω] on whom I show mercy, and I will have pity [οἰκτειρήσω] on whom I pity" (Exod 33:19).[2] Particularly interesting is the prayer of Sirach: "Have mercy [ἐλέησον], O Lord, on the people [λαόν] called by your name . . . Have pity [οἰκτείρησον] on the city of your sanctuary, Jerusalem, the place of your dwelling" (Sir 36:17-18).

In 5:16, Antiochus took the temple vessels with defiled hands, and in 10:5 the profaned temple is purified. In 5:14, eighty thousand people were said to be ruined during the attack of Antiochus IV on the city. Here the use of the present participle suggests that the ruination continues. In 9:14, Antiochus is said to have vowed to flatten the city. The author thus reuses phrases from earlier and later descriptions to tie the story together.

■ **3b** Abel's blood cries out (βοᾷ) to the Lord from the ground and becomes a prototype for those innocently slain. In *1 Enoch* 9:10, "the souls of those who have died cry out [βοῶσιν] and entreat, and their groan has gone up to the gates of heaven."[3] One might think of the notion of the Erinys in Greek tradition, where they represent the angry dead come back to punish the guilty.[4] In Virgil's *Aeneid*, the story is told of how the dead Polydorus speaks and condemns his slayers after Aeneas tries

to pull up branches from the soil and drops of blood appear (3.1-68).

■ **4** When Antiochus IV took Jerusalem by storm, infants were among those slaughtered (5:13), and he later threatened to throw the Jews and their infants out for the wild beasts to eat (9:15). In Ps 9:12 is found, "For [the Lord] who avenges blood is mindful [ἐμνήσθη], he does not forget the cry of the afflicted." Here in 2 Maccabees the verb μνησθῆναι is used with two constructions: with the genitive and with περί. The verb with περί is found in Tob 4:1 and Esth 10:3[b], but also in classical authors: for example, Homer *Od.* 7.191–192: περὶ πομπῆς μνησόμεθα ("we will take thought of his sending").

The enemies of the Jews are frequently accused of blasphemy in 2 Maccabees: Antiochus is a blasphemer (9:28); the Gentiles are described as blasphemous (10:4); Timothy and his men blaspheme (10:34-36), as do the men at Kaspin (12:14). In Ezek 35:12-14, the Lord promises doom to the inhabitants of Mount Seir for their blasphemy. In the narrative so far, however, no blasphemies have been uttered.

■ **5** The word for "corps," σύστημα, is found with this meaning in Polybius (1.81.11; 3.74.8; 30.25.8). In the second prefixed letter, the forces of Antiochus IV had been described as seemingly unstoppable (1:13: ἀνυπόστατος δοκοῦσα). The turning of the Lord's wrath to mercy echoes the prayer in 7:38.

■ **6-7** Verse 8 states that Judas progressed little by little. Here his tactics are described. They are hit-and-run methods: surprise burnings in the towns and villages and ambushes. The ambushes described in vv. 6b-7 are depicted using two asyndetic participial phrases: ἀπολαμβάνων . . . τροπούμενος, which gives the sense of quick and hurried action. The word ἐπικαίρους ("advantageous") is found also in 8:31; 10:15; 14:22. It is used

---

1   The author seems to make no distinction, *pace* Paul Joüon ("Les mots employés pour designer le Temple dans l'Ancien Testament, le Nouveau Testament et Josèphe," *RSR* 25 [1935] 329–43, here 342–43 n. 32), between ναός and νεώς. In 10:3-5 the two terms are used interchangeably: 10:3: τὸν νεὼ καθαρίσαντες; 10:5: τὸν καθαρισμὸν γενέσθαι τοῦ ναοῦ. Note also 8:2: τὸν ναὸν . . . βεβηλωθέντα and 10:5: ὁ νεὼς . . . ἐβεβηλώθη.

2   For further examples, see 3 Kgdms 8:50; 4 Kgdms 13:23; Ps 76:9-10. In Ps 102:14 (LXX 101:14) God is asked to have pity on Zion.

3   This is according to the Greek version found in Syncellus. Nickelsburg (*1 Enoch 1*, 205) prefers the reading found in Codex Panopolitanus, where the verb "cry out" is not found, but the souls do make suit against their killers.

4   See Sarah Iles Johnston, "Erinys," *Brill's New Pauly* (2004) 5:34–35. Note their role as outlined by Aeschylus in his *Eumenides*.

with the sense of "strategic" in Xenophon *Hier.* 10.5: "guarding the strategic positions" (τὰ ἐπίκαιρα φυλάτ-τοντες).[5] Here, however, the term seems to signify that Judas carefully chose his point of attack, rather than referring to strategic positions.[6]

"good-sized force." εὐανδρία can also mean "bravery," which is the connotation in 15:17. There clearly is a sense in which the daring bravery of Judas has infected and inspired his forces. However, Philip is worried not about Judas's bravery but about the size of Judas's force (see Plutarch *Per.* 19; Xenophon *Mem.* 3.3.12).

■ **8-9** The successes of Judas have come to the attention of Philip the Phyrgian, left in control of Jerusalem (5:22; 6:11). The author depicts the advance of Judas with two participial phrases, first stating his small (κατὰ μικρόν) achievements, and then his larger successes (πυκνότερον . . . προβαίνοντα). It is this development that attracts Philip's attention. The verb συνορῶν ("detected") is used when Onias recognizes the extent of Simon's attacks (4:4). This quick description of the initial successes of Judas contrasts with the more detailed account in 1 Macc 3:10-25. There Judas first bests Apollonius, whom Josephus identifies as the *stratēgos*, or governor, of Samaria, presumably because an Apollonius is named *meridarch* of Samaria in the letter of Antiochus IV to the Sidonians in Shechem (Josephus *Ant.* 12.261, 287).[7] Then Judas defeats Seron in an ambush at Beth Horon. In the narrative of 1 Maccabees, both these events take place in 147 s.e., probably between the summer of 166 b.c.e. and the spring of 165 b.c.e. Since the author of 2 Maccabees aims at rhetorical effect, he may have concentrated all the audience's attention on the major battle and victory against Nikanor, rather than disperse it on these skirmishes with more local officials. The author of 1 Maccabees, however, magnifies the extent of these early successes—Seron is even called "chief of the army of Syria" (1 Macc 3:13)—which therefore come to the knowledge of Antiochus IV, who determines to send a host to uproot and remove the strength of Israel and to erase the memory of the Jews from that place (1 Macc 3:34-35). It is his regent, Lysias, who sends Ptolemy, Nikanor, and Gorgias against the Jews. The movement in 1 Maccabees is from the top down and so emphasizes the importance of what Judas had achieved.

In 2 Maccabees, Philip, the *epistatēs*, or supervisor, of Jerusalem, follows the chain of command, writing to Ptolemy, the governor of Coele-Syria, who was also in charge of troops. There is debate about whether this is Ptolemy Makron (10:12) or Ptolemy son of Dorymenes. In 1 Macc 3:38, the Ptolemy identified in this action is Ptolemy son of Dorymenes, and I have argued in the comment on 4:45 that this is the person referred to here. As seen in 4:45, Ptolemy son of Dorymenes was very much on the side of Menelaus. Bar-Kochva surmises that he lost his post because of the subsequent defeat and was replaced by Ptolemy Makron (10:12).[8] On πράγματα as "matters of state," see also 4:21 (where I have translated the phrase as "empire") and 10:11 (where I have translated the phrase as "government"). Just as Seleucus had appointed Heliodorus (3:7), so too Ptolemy appointed Nikanor. Whereas in 1 Macc 3:38, Ptolemy, Nikanor, and Gorgias are listed side by side, here there is a clear hierarchy. Nikanor is one of the "First Friends" and so was a high-ranking noble official.[9] He is not, therefore, to be identified with the Nikanor in charge of Cypriot troops (12:2), nor, as Bar-Kochva argues,[10] with the recipient of the letter from Antiochus IV about the Sidonians in Shechem, as that Nikanor seems to hold a medium-rank position over finances (Josephus *Ant.* 12.261). We now know more about Ptolemy's father from the Heliodorus inscription, which shows that he was governor of Coele-Syria and Phoenicia in 178 b.c.e. Nikanor was quite a common name at this time, and one has to be cautious before identifying the name as belonging to one and the same person. For example, one of Demetrius I's friends in Rome was called Nikanor and helped Demetrius escape from Rome (Polybius 31.14.4). Is he to be identified with this Nikanor? If so, how, then, can his appearance in

5 The phrase is also found in the treatise on protecting cities against siege by the third century b.c.e.
   Philon of Byzantium; see Herman Diels and Erwin
   Schramm, *Exzerpte aus Philons Mechanik B.VII und
   VIII* (Berlin: Verlag der Akademie der Wissenschaften, 1920) 83.10 (p. 28).
6 Bar-Kochva, *Judas Maccabaeus*, 138–41.

7 See ibid., 201.
8 Bar-Kochva, *Judas Maccabaeus*, 536.
9 In 1 Macc 3:38, Nikanor is ranked only as one of the
   Friends of the King, not as one of the First Friends.
10 Bar-Kochva, *Judas Maccabaeus*, 239.

Rome be explained? That he fell out with Antiochus V and left the Seleucid kingdom and joined Demetrius? But we have no evidence for such a move on his part. More likely, the Nikanor in Rome is to be identified with the later opponent of Judas in 2 Maccabees. That the Nikanor of 2 Maccabees 8 and the later Nikanor are both called τρισαλιτήριος ("triply offensive") (8:34; 15:3) could be a literary effect to tie the two stories together. The author makes no effort to distinguish the men.

"no fewer than twenty thousand Gentiles." The author uses a double negative here, as he does so often.[11] The numbers given in 1 Macc 3:39, 41 are forty thousand infantry and seven thousand cavalry as well as auxiliary forces from Syria and the land of the Philistines. The numbers in 1 Maccabees are exaggerated, perhaps by association with the numbers of Arameans killed by David in 1 Chr 19:18. Given his view of the unreliability of the narrative in 2 Maccabees, Bar-Kochva is astonished that the number in 2 Maccabees is smaller than that in 1 Maccabees and is not an impossible figure. He therefore suggests emending the text from δισμυρίων ("twenty thousand") to μυρίων ("tens of thousands," unspecified).[12] However, this emendation seems unnecessary: the author of 2 Maccabees uses the figure of twenty thousand in 10:17 and 23, and in 10:31 twenty thousand + five hundred. The author also has combined the neuter ἔθνη with the masculine adjective ἐλάττους, where the real, not the grammatical, gender has determined the gender of the adjective, particularly in view of the genitive it governs.

"To remove the whole race within Judea" is literally "the whole race of Judea." The genitive here limits the scope of the extermination. In 5:22, Antiochus IV had left overseers to maltreat the race, and in 7:38, the youngest of the martyred brothers had confessed that the wrath of the Lord had rightly come upon the whole race. Now the threat is to remove the whole race. The verb ἐξαίρω has the basic meaning of "to lift up" and can be used either in the sense of "to raise in dignity" or, as here, "to remove." Is the author playing on this double meaning, as the author of the Gospel of John does in describing the death of Jesus as also his exaltation (John 12:32)? In 1 Macc 3:35, the same verb is used in parallelism with the verb ἐκρίπτω ("to cast out"), and so no double meaning is possible.

Gorgias, who is described literally as "a man, a commander," is later identified as the governor of Idumea (10:14; 12:32), part of the satrapy of Coele-Syria and Phoenicia. Under the command of Nikanor, he is mentioned here, although he is not present in the description of the battle in 2 Maccabees. However, in 1 Macc 4:1-22, Gorgias plays a major role in the Seleucid plan of attack on Judas.[13] His mention here in 2 Maccabees is thus appropriate.

■ 10 As Mørkholm has shown, Antiochus IV gave major and extravagant benefactions to Greek cities to "acquire prestige and influence for himself and his kingdom throughout the Greek world."[14] Such magnificent gifts would have required considerable sums of money. While the author of 1 Maccabees suggests that Antiochus IV set out to invade Persia to refill his treasury, which had been depleted by the disaster he had caused in Judea (1 Macc 3:29-31), the author of 2 Maccabees sees Antiochus IV in need of money to pay the Roman indemnity imposed on the Seleucids by the treaty of Apamea in 188 B.C.E. That treaty specified that the Seleucids had to pay an indemnity to the Romans of twelve thousand talents over twelve years (Polybius 21.42.19). The two thousand talents mentioned here would thus represent payment for two years. However, Mørkholm has argued that Antiochus IV had paid off the indemnity in 173 B.C.E.[15] He quotes Livy, who reports that Antiochus IV's ambassador apologized to the senate for paying the installment later than it was due and stated that he had brought the entire sum, *omne advexisse* (42.6.7). It is not clear, however, whether the ambassador is saying that he has brought the entire installment for that year or all the rest of the indemnity. By the terms of the treaty, the indemnity should have been paid by 176 B.C.E. at the latest. But we do not know how far in arrears the Seleucids were in their payment, and Schwartz is right to say that we should leave the question open.[16]

---

11 See Doran, *Temple Propaganda*, 42.
12 Bar-Kochva, *Judas Maccabaeus*, 41–42.
13 For a description of the plan, see ibid., 260–73.
14 Mørkholm, *Antiochus IV*, 51–63; quotation from 62.
15 Ibid., 65.
16 Schwartz, *2 Maccabees*, 544–45.

"for the king." The dative would seem to be a dative of advantage.[17]

■ **11** The cities by the sea were sometimes hostile to the Jews.[18] Merchants provided services to a Hellenistic army, and 1 Macc 3:41 also states that merchants came in the hope of purchasing slaves. As Bar-Kochva notes, according to Polybius 30.15, 150,000 people in Macedonia had been sold into slavery by the Romans in 167 B.C.E., after the Romans had defeated Perseus, and two inscriptions from Delphi of 170–157 B.C.E. record the liberation of Judean slaves.[19] Given the population of Judea, however, the number of slaves expected, 180,000, is exaggerated, and their price seems bargain-basement.[20] Schwartz, reckoning from six thousand drachmas per talent, comes to a figure of sixty-seven drachmas per slave, which is about half the normal rate.[21] The author of 2 Maccabees stresses that the initiative came from Nikanor, not from the merchants themselves as in 1 Macc 3:41. By presenting the battle as a confrontation between individuals, the author has again structured his narrative to heighten its rhetorical effect. This intent is in tension with his lessening of the audience's concern about the future, for as in 5:20, 6:12-17, and in the speeches of the brothers in chap. 7, the author gives away the outcome.

The word used for "slaves" in this verse ($\sigma\acute{\omega}\mu\alpha\tau\alpha$) is literally "bodies."

■ **12-15** The construction of $\pi\rho\sigma\pi\acute{\iota}\pi\tau\omega$ + dative is found in 5:11; 9:3; 13:1; 14:1, 28. The shift from Judas in the dative, $\tau\hat{\omega}$ Ἰούδα, to Judas in the genitive, $\mu\epsilon\tau\alpha\delta\acute{o}\nu\tau\sigma\varsigma$, reflects that the status of Judas is different from that of his followers and points toward their different reactions.

■ **13** While the author of 1 Maccabees explicitly follows the prescriptions of Deut 20:5-9 in his description of those who are sent away from his force, the author of 2 Maccabees has taken a different tack, stating that the faint-hearted ran away in flight.[22] Two participles are used in conjunction here, governed by one article: literally the text reads "the acting cowardly and the doubting."

■ **14-15** Verses 14 and 15 constitute one sentence in the Greek.

Most interestingly, the author mentions only one of the exemptions, cowardice, allowed in Deut 20:5-9 for not participating in war and rejects the others—building a new house, or planting a new vineyard, or recent marriage—by having his soldiers dispossess themselves of everything. No material thing is to cause anxiety to them. A parallel might be found in the Athenians' leaving Athens to the mercy of the Persians (Herodotus 8.41; Plutarch *Them.* 9–10).

The verb "to beseech" ($\grave{\alpha}\xi\iota\omega\hat{\nu}$) is frequent in 2 Maccabees, but here it resonates particularly with its use in 8:29, after the battle, when the victorious Jewish forces beseech the Lord to be fully reconciled with his servants. Only here in 2 Maccabees is the verb "to deliver" ($\acute{\rho}\upsilon\acute{\epsilon}\sigma\vartheta\alpha\iota$) found, and it is appropriate in the context of deliverance from slavery. The same verb is used by Herodotus (5.49; 9.90) to speak of delivering from slavery. Simon (3:11), Antiochus IV (9:9), and the second Nikanor (15:33) are all called "impious."

■ **15** The plea is based on the covenants and the name of the Lord. The plural "covenants" is rare in the LXX, appearing only in Wis 18:22; Sir 44:11, 18; 45:17. In the series of blessings and curses of the covenant in Deuteronomy 28, Israel is called by the name of the Lord (Deut 28:10). Samuel had promised that the Lord would not cast away his people, "for his great name's sake, because it has pleased the Lord to make you a people for himself" (1 Sam 12:22). The Lord is frequently called on to act for his name's sake as, for example, in Jer 14:7; Dan 9:19. Particularly relevant in this connection is the beautiful passage in Isa 43:1-7: "But now, thus says the Lord, he who created you, O Jacob, he who formed you, O Israel: Do not fear, for I have redeemed you; I have called you by your name, you are mine. . . . I will bring your offspring . . . everyone who is called by my name." The emphasis on the holiness of God's name stands in sharp

17   Smyth, *Greek Grammar*, §1481.
18   Aryeh Kasher, *Jews and Hellenistic Cities in Eretz-Israel: Relations of the Jews in Eretz-Israel with the Hellenistic Cities during the Second Temple Period (332 B.C.E.–70 C.E.)* (TSAJ 21; Tübingen: Mohr, 1990) 54–90. Tcherikover (*Hellenistic Civilization*, 91–96) lists the eleven cities.
19   Bar-Kochva, *Judas Maccabaeus*, 246; *CIJ* 709, 710.
20   Grimm; Abel; Goldstein, *II Maccabees*, 329.
21   Reinhold Scholl (*Corpus der ptolemäischen Sklaventexte* [3 vols.; Forschungen zur antiken Sklaverei, Beiheft 1; Stuttgart: Steiner, 1990] 1:213) provides prices ranging from 112 to 300 drachmas per slave.
22   See Polybius 1.74.7 for the expression $\grave{\epsilon}\kappa\tau\sigma\pi\acute{\iota}\zeta\omega$ $\grave{\epsilon}\alpha\upsilon\tau\sigma\acute{\upsilon}\varsigma$.

contrast to the blasphemies committed against it by the Gentiles (8:4). God is called majestic at Deut 33:26. Here the text reads literally, "because of the surname upon them of his august and majestic name"; the close connection between the Jews and God is emphasized in that the former have the surname of the latter.

■ **16-20** The author presents Judas as giving a pre-battle speech. This type of speech is found rarely in the Hebrew Scriptures (2 Sam 10:11-12; 1 Chr 19:12-13; 2 Chr 32:7-8). The pre-battle description in 1 Macc 3:44-60 differs from that in 2 Maccabees. In the former, the assembly, when gathered for battle, prays and asks for mercy, then sings a hymn before going to Mizpah. There they fast, open the book of the law, pray, and then Judas appoints leaders in the same way as Moses had in Exod 18:25. Only after all this ritual activity does Judas give a short speech, which echoes the language of the Hebrew Scriptures and, as in 2 Sam 10:11-12 and 2 Chr 32:7-8, emphasizes the role that God plays.

In the Greek tradition, W. Kendrick Pritchett has isolated eleven motifs in the pre-battle speeches found in Herodotus, Thucydides, Xenophon, and Polybius.[23] Among the more important are: (1) an emphasis on the previous battle experience of the soldiers; (2) a discussion of the tactics in play; (3) the goals—to win liberty, to defend the country, to repel aggressors, to take vengeance on those wishing to enslave them; (4) a comparison of forces; (5) a call for help from the gods and statements that the auspices are favorable. It is important to note that the Greeks sacrificed before battle.[24] The author of 2 Maccabees appears to combine Jewish and Greek pre-battle traditions. Judas calls on his soldiers not to fear but to remember the outrages done against them (8:16-17, motif 3); then to realize that they have God on their side (8:18, as in 2 Chr 32:7-8); finally he recalls past occasions on which God helped the Jews (8:19-20, motif 1). In contrast to the speeches in the Greek historians, the emphasis falls more on God's help than on the battle training of the soldiers.

■ **16-17** Just as Judas gathered (συνήγαγον) six thousand in 8:1, so now he gathers six thousand again. Bar-Kochva thinks the number is reasonable.[25] According to 1 Macc 4:6, there were only three thousand men. The verb εὐλαβεῖσθαι means both "to respect" and "to be afraid of, be on one's guard" (2 Macc 9:29; Sir 34:16: "Those who fear the Lord will not be timid [εὐλαβηθήσεται], or play the coward, for he is their hope"). "To contend nobly" is found also in 13:14, while nobility is a trait of Eleazar (6:28), the martyred brothers (7:5, 11), Rhazis (14:43) and Judas (15:17). In 14:31, γενναίως Judas excellently outsmarts his opponent. God's anger had come justly (δικαίως) on the Jews (7:38), but the assault of the Gentiles was unjust (8:16: ἀδίκως).

Jason had precipitated the crisis by his suddenly perpetrating (συνετελέσατο) an attack on the city (5:5) that had led to Antiochus IV's despoliation of the temple. The terms "outrage" (αἰκισμός) and "disrespect" (ἐμπαίζω) and their respective roots were terms used in the martyrdom accounts (7:1, 13, 15, 42; 7:7, 10). The "dissolution of the ancestral constitution" reflects the wording used to condemn Jason's reform in 4:11. In this speech by Judas before the first major battle in 2 Maccabees, the order of what was attacked—temple, city, legal constitution—is the same as that in the author's prologue in 2:22.

■ **18** The author breaks into direct speech for this one verse. He likes to contrast the two sides, as in 10:28; 12:14-15; and 15:25-26. The same contrast can be seen in Ps 20:8 (LXX 19:8): "These in chariots and these in horses, but we will be strengthened in the name of the Lord our God." As in the speeches of the brothers and their mother (7:9, 23), the author stresses here that God is in complete control of the world; the author will do so again in 12:15 and 13:14. "With a single nod" reflects kingly power, as at 4:10. See the comment thereon.

■ **19-20** The author returns to indirect speech, using the middle aorist of an unusual verb, προσαναλέγειν. Preisigke supplies one other example, from the papyri, where the meaning is "to gather up."[26] The composite verb has here the meaning one finds for the verb ἀναλέγω ("to gather, collect"). The general reference to earlier assistance is specified by two examples. The first is taken from Isa 37:36; 2 Kgdms 19:35; and 2 Chr 32:21,

---

23   W. Kendrick Pritchett, *Essays in Greek History* (Amsterdam: Gieben, 1994) 101–5; idem, *Ancient Greek Battle Speeches and a Palfrey* (Archaia Hellas 9; Amsterdam: Gieben, 2002).

24   Pritchett, *Greek State at War*, 1:109–15.
25   Bar-Kochva, *Judas Maccabaeus*, 47–48.
26   Preisigke, *Wörterbuch*, 2:387.

and it is cited in Sir 48:18-22 and *3 Macc.* 6:5. Judas uses the same example in his pre-battle speech before the final battle, also against a Nikanor, in the narrative in 15:22.

The second example of God's assistance has caused much discussion, as no such battle is otherwise attested. The text does not explicitly state that the 8,000 were Jews, but the examples refer to Jewish forces. Thus, 8,000 Jewish soldiers with 4,000 Macedonians fought against 120,000 Galatians. Some have seen here a reference to the victory of Antiochus I against the Galatians, the elephant victory, in 273 B.C.E.[27] However, Bar-Kochva rightly objects that this campaign took place in western Asia Minor, not near Babylonia.[28] Isidore Levy suggested emending the text from $Βαβυλωνία$ to $βαγαδαονία$ (= Bagadonia),[29] but, as Bar-Kochva notes, Bagadonia also is too far from the cities in western Asia Minor.[30] James Moffatt proposed that the reference might be to a war of Antiochus III against the revolt of Molon, satrap of Media, in 220 B.C.E., but Polybius, in his account of this revolt, mentions only Galatians as being on the side of Antiochus III.[31] Arnaldo Momigliano offered the possibility that the reference was to a battle against the Galatians in the time of Antiochus III between 197 and 190 B.C.E.[32] Bar-Kochva rightly disposes of this hypothesis.[33] Bar-Kochva himself suggests that the reference should be "connected with the second stage of the 'War of the Brothers' between the legitimate king, Seleucus II Callinicus, and his brother Antiochus Hierax (229/8 B.C.), who benefited from Galatian help."[34] This seems a very plausible suggestion, though the number of troops

involved remains a problem, as always. It seems unlikely that 120,000 Galatians were involved, as the number who invaded Asia Minor in 189 B.C.E. was, according to Livy (38.16.9), 20,000, of whom only 10,000 were armed. The inflated number of the enemy versus the small number of Jews only increases the sense of divine intervention. As Bar-Kochva further observes, this story can be another addition to reports of Babylonian Jews fighting in foreign armies.[35] It is also important to ask how the author of 2 Maccabees could have come by such information.

By emphasizing that such well-known soldiers as the Macedonians were discomfited[36] by the Gauls, known to strike terror into their opponents (Justin 25.2.10), while the Jews were victorious, the author shows that the unexpected and glorious victory could be attributed only to the help of God. While it is true that the term "Macedonians" could also describe Seleucid forces,[37] the name connotes great military prowess and so enhances the prestige of the Jews. The author insists, as he often does (3:39; 8:35; 12:11; 13:13; 15:8), that it was with the help of God that victory was won. The author will use the term for "help" ($βοήθεια$) in describing God's assistance (8:23) and again in 8:35, when describing Nikanor's discomfiture and humiliation. The term thus helps to bind the narrative together.

■ **21-23** Judas, by his words, inspired his forces ($αὐτοὺς$ $παραστήσας$ is, literally, "bringing his forces around") to be courageous, as good commanders are supposed to do with their speeches. Just as the third brother courageously ($εὐθαρσῶς$) stretched out his hands to be cut off

27   Moffatt, "Second Book," 142; Abel; Hengel, *Judaism and Hellenism*, 29. For an account of this battle, see Lucian *Zeux.* 8–11.

28   Bar-Kochva, *Judas Maccabaeus*, 501.

29   Isidore Lévy, "Notes d'histoire hellénistique sur le second Livre des Maccabées," *Mélanges Henri Grégoire* (4 vols.; Annuaire de l'institut de philologie et d'histoire orientales et slaves 9–12; Brussels: Secrétariat des Éditions de l'Institut, 1949–53) 2:681–99, here 688–89.

30   Bar-Kochva, *Judas Maccabaeus*, 501.

31   Moffatt, "Second Book," 142. The revolt is described in Polybius 5.41–55, and the Galatians are mentioned in 5.33.3.

32   Arnaldo Momigliano, "Un' ignota irruzione dei Galati in Siria al tempo di Antiocho III?" *Bollettino di Filologia Classica* 36 (1929–30) 151–56.

33   Bar-Kochva, *Judas Maccabaeus*, 502–4. See also Menahem Stern, "The Battle against the Galatians (8:20)," appendix 7 in Schwartz, *2 Maccabees*, 546–48.

34   Bar-Kochva, *Judas Maccabaeus*, 504; for the whole argument, see 504–6.

35   Ibid., 506.

36   See Xenophon *Cyrop.* 7.1.40. Goldstein's brilliant suggestion (*II Maccabees*, 334) that $ἀπορουμένων$ be read as if it were $ἀπορρουμένων$, as "in Hellenistic Greek a single *rho* in such cases was common," is therefore not necessary.

37   For example, *OGIS* 239; see Charles Edson, "Imperium Macedonicum: The Seleucid Empire and the Literary Evidence," *CP* 53 (1958) 153–70.

(7:10), so too Judas's forces are now eager and prepared ($\dot{\epsilon}\tau o\acute{\iota}\mu o\nu\varsigma$, as the first brother declared in 7:2 about his brothers and himself) to fight. While Simon (4:1) and Jason (5:8) had been against the fatherland, and Menelaus (5:15; 13:3) had been a traitor to the laws and the fatherland, Judas and his troops are prepared to die for the laws and the fatherland.[38]

In the Hebrew Scriptures, the army is often divided into three.[39] The division into four equal groups makes sense mathematically, but one wonders exactly how the army was organized. Each unit would comprise fifteen hundred men. In v. 23, the term $\sigma\pi\epsilon\hat{\iota}\rho\alpha$ must be given the general meaning of "unit," rather than the smaller group in a fully organized army, equivalent to a Roman maniple of two hundred men. The author of 2 Maccabees is not interested in tactical details, as can be seen from a comparison with 1 Macc 4:1-22, where the maneuvers of the two opposing forces are given. The author seems to think in terms of a pitched battle between opposing armies. However, as Bar-Kochva noted, the force of Nikanor probably consisted of lightly armed and semi-heavily armed forces, as was usual for ethnically diverse forces, which would suggest that the engagement was not a pitched battle.[40]

The names of the three leaders besides Judas are surprising. Simon and Jonathan are known as brothers of Judas (1 Macc 2:3-5). However, 1 Macc 2:2-5 also mentions brothers named John and Eleazar. The insertion of Eleazar into the manuscripts as a gloss in 8:23 was no doubt caused by a desire to name all five brothers, although it is interesting that in Hebrew the name is אלעזר and the Hebrew for the watchword "God's Help" is אל עזר (1QM 4.13). The difference between John and Joseph still remains. First Maccabees 5:18 and 56 name a Joseph and an Azariah, but that Joseph is the son of Zechariah. The author of 2 Maccabees seems to have a different list of names for the brothers and a different number of brothers.[41] In the Latin manuscript tradition, Eleazar was replaced by Esdra. As Katz observes, "[I]n LXP [Judas] reads *Hesdrae* (B, *Ezr(a)e* M) *sanctum librum*, that is, the Bible as reconstituted by Ezra; in the Vulgate Ezra reads the lesson, as Eleazar does in L Sy ($\check{\epsilon}\tau\alpha\xi\epsilon\nu$ . . . $\pi\alpha\rho\alpha\gamma\nu\hat{\omega}\nu\alpha\iota$) where he is made the Army chaplain or at least reader."[42] These scribes no doubt had a problem with Judas officiating as at a liturgical service, just as the author of Chronicles held that David could not build the temple because of the blood he had shed (1 Chr 22:7-9). In the instructions for war in Deuteronomy 20, a priest is to come forward and address the troops before they engage in battle (Deut 20:2-4; see 11QT [11Q19] 61.15).[43]

What exactly is meant by "the holy scroll"? What would have been its contents? How might it have looked? Would it have been made of leather hide or papyrus? The present-day Hebrew Scriptures would need several scrolls and would be rather cumbersome. Holding a scroll and fighting at the same time would have been difficult, so was someone appointed to carry the scroll(s)? Are we to imagine the scroll being carried into war as was the ark of the covenant in 1 Sam 4:3-5? Or is Judas's reading from the holy scroll a reflection of the command in Deut 17:19 that the king shall read in the law all the days of his life? Note how, in 15:9, Judas encourages his soldiers "from the law and the prophets." As Judas and his men are fighting for the sake of the laws (8:21), it is appropriate that these laws be in evidence.

In 13:15, the watchword is "God's Victory." Similar watchwords are found in Greco-Roman authors. Vegetius gives as an example, *Deus nobiscum,* "God with us" (*De re militari* 3.5), while Xenophon reports as a watchword, $Z\epsilon\grave{\upsilon}\varsigma\ \sigma\acute{\upsilon}\mu\mu\alpha\chi o\varsigma\ \kappa\alpha\grave{\iota}\ \dot{\eta}\gamma\epsilon\mu\acute{\omega}\nu$, "Zeus ally and leader" (*Cyrop.* 3.3.58).[44] See also the phrases that are to be written on the banners in 1QM 3.13—4:14.

■ **24-25a** The battle is described in one verse, which again shows that the author is not interested in tactics.

---

38 See also the use of "fatherland" in 13:10, 14; 14:18.

39 Judges 7:16; 9:43; 1 Sam 11:11; 2 Sam 18:2; 1 Macc 5:33.

40 Bar-Kochva, *Judas Maccabaeus,* 240–41.

41 Tal Ilan (*Lexicon of Jewish Names in Late Antiquity* [TSAJ 91; Tübingen: Mohr, 1995] 7) holds that Joseph should be added to the list of Judas's brothers.

42 Katz, "Text of 2 Maccabees," 15. For the acceptance of Ezra/Esdras as original, see Abel and Goldstein.

43 See also the use of battle trumpets by the priests to start an engagement in Num 10:9 and 2 Chr 13:12-14, as well as 1QM 3.1-11; 7.9–9.8.

44 See also Xenophon *Cyrop.* 7.1.10; *Anab.* 1.8.17; 6.5.26; Appian *Bell. civ.* 2.76. For further discussion, see Bar-Kochva, *Judas Maccabaeus,* 220–21; and Yvon Garlan, "Études d'histoire militaire et diplomatique, XII: $\Sigma\Upsilon N\Theta HMATA$," *BCH* 100 (1976) 299–302.

The emphasis remains on God as the ally of the Jews, and their complete victory. The term for "ally" ($\sigma\acute{\nu}\mu\mu\alpha\chi o\varsigma$) is the same as that found in the watchword of Xenophon noted above. Here the ally is the God of Israel, as also in 10:16; 11:10; 12:36. In 8:36, God is $\acute{\nu}\pi\acute{\epsilon}\rho\mu\alpha\chi o\varsigma$ ("champion"). In 1 Macc 4:15, three thousand of the enemy are said to have fallen. Here in 2 Maccabees, Judas's forces slaughter ($\kappa\alpha\tau\alpha\sigma\varphi\acute{\alpha}\zeta\epsilon\iota\nu$) about half of Nikanor's forces (8:9), as Antiochus IV (5:12), Apollonius (5:24), and the surrounding Greek cities (6:9) had slaughtered the Jews.

"for the sale of the Jews" ($\epsilon\pi\grave{\iota}\ \tau\grave{o}\nu\ \grave{\alpha}\gamma o\rho\alpha\sigma\mu o\acute{\nu}$) refers back to Nikanor's plan to sell the Jews as slaves (8:11: $\acute{\epsilon}\pi'\ \grave{\alpha}\gamma o\rho\alpha\sigma\mu o\acute{\nu}$) and gives an ironic twist to the narrative as Judas's forces take the money of those who had come to buy them.

■ **25b-27** The piety of Judas's forces is shown by their strict observance of the Sabbath. In 1 Macc 4:15, Judas's forces stop the pursuit as they are too close to the coastal cities, and there is no mention of the Sabbath. The same respect for the Sabbath is shown in 12:38, and in 15:1-4 even the Jews who followed the thrice-offensive Nikanor protested when he wished to attack Judas on the Sabbath. It is also noteworthy that in 2 Maccabees there is no mention of a communal vote by the forces of Judas to defend themselves on the Sabbath if attacked, as in 1 Macc 2:40-41.

"hemmed in by the time." Polybius uses a similar turn of phrase in 18.7.3 and 18.9.2 to describe the imminent end of the day. Whether one reads the verb as $\mu\alpha\kappa\rho o\tau o\nu\acute{\epsilon}\omega$ ("to stretch out") or as $\mu\alpha\kappa\rho o\vartheta\nu\mu\acute{\epsilon}\omega$ (in the sense of "to persevere"), the language used here is unusual. The verb "to collect weapons" ($\acute{o}\pi\lambda o\lambda o\gamma\acute{\epsilon}\omega$) in the active sense is found only here and in 8:31. To describe the participation in the Sabbath observances, the author switches from the previously used aorist tense to the imperfect and so puts the reader in the midst of the events as they were taking place. The phrase $\grave{\epsilon}\gamma\acute{\iota}\nu o\nu\tau o$ $\pi\epsilon\rho\acute{\iota}$ + accusative is found also in 12:1 and is used by Polybius (1.29.5; 1.74.8; 27.13.2). The verb $\epsilon\grave{\nu}\lambda o\gamma\epsilon\hat{\iota}\nu$ (here translated "blessing") is frequent in 2 Maccabees (3:30; 10:28; 11:9; 12:41; 15:28, 34), while "to sing

praises" ($\grave{\epsilon}\xi o\mu o\lambda o\gamma\acute{\epsilon}o\mu\alpha\iota$) reflects the usage in the LXX (e.g., Gen 29:35; Pss 6:5; 7:17).

"Beginning of mercy" refers back to 8:5, where God's anger had turned to mercy, and looks forward to 8:29, where Judas and his forces pray to the merciful God to be reconciled with them completely, literally "to the end" ($\epsilon\grave{\iota}\varsigma\ \tau\acute{\epsilon}\lambda o\varsigma$).

■ **28** The division of the booty is quite remarkable. In the Hebrew Scriptures, there had been a dispute between David and some of his followers as to who should share in the spoil, and David had decreed that "the share of the one who goes down into battle shall be the same as the share of the one who stays by the baggage; they shall all share alike. From that day forward he made it a statute and an ordinance for Israel; it continues to the present day" (1 Sam 30:24-25). In Num 31:25-30, Moses was commanded by the Lord to divide the spoil into two parts, between the warriors who went out to battle and all the congregation. The *Temple Scroll* from Qumran adjusts these two statements and admits also portions for the king and the priests and Levites (11QT [11Q19] 58.11–15). The author of 2 Maccabees, in the present arrangement of the text, makes the soldiers receive what is left over after the booty has been allotted to the tortured, the widows, and the orphans. There is no mention of the priests and Levites, nor of the whole congregation. Rather, preeminence is given to those who had suffered in the persecution—apart from 8:28 and 30, the verb $\alpha\grave{\iota}\kappa\acute{\iota}\zeta o\mu\alpha\iota$ ("to torture") and its cognates are found only in the story of the seven brothers and their mother (7:1, 13, 15, 42) and in a general description of what had befallen Jerusalem (8:17). The seventh brother had expressed the hope that the anger of God would come to an end through the deaths of his brothers (7:38). Exodus 22:22-24 had warned against abusing widows and orphans, and it became a staple command not to oppress them. The inclusion of the widows and orphans both shows the piety of Judas's forces and has them stand as an image of the oppressed Jewish community.

■ **29** "Merciful" as an adjective for God is found frequently in the Psalms[45] and is appropriate here. "To be reconciled to his servants" again echoes the prayer of the

---

45   LXX Pss 85:15; 102:8; 110:4; 111:4; 114:5; 144:8. See
      also Exod 34:6 and especially the use in Tob 6:18;
      7:12.

seventh brother (7:33). As Schwartz suggests, the phrase "to his servants" may echo the passage cited by the brothers and their mother in 7:6: "He will have compassion on his servants" (Deut 32:36).

■ **30-33** The introductory καί ("and") acts to show that these verses are a continuation of the previous section, as in 15:6. Only here and in 8:27-28 in 2 Maccabees is the taking of spoils noted. In addition to those named as receiving spoils in 8:28, the elderly are also mentioned. Here, the context demands that πρεσβύτερος "elder") is not a member of the council of elders, as in 13:13 and 14:37, but an elderly person. By the description similar to the division of the spoils in 8:28 and by the repetition of the same aorist participle "collecting the weapons" (ὁπλολογήσαντες) from 8:27, the author strongly connects these verses to the end of the preceding section.

However, there has been no previous mention of Timothy and Bacchides, and the taking control of fortified heights suggests some siege action. The taking of the booty to Jerusalem, while perhaps in compliance with the command in Num 31:28-29 to separate out from the booty tribute to the Lord and to make an offering to the Lord, does seem to presume that Judas's forces had some control over Jerusalem, a control not described fully until 10:1. Bar-Kochva has cogently argued that the snippet of information in these verses is actually a doublet of the campaign mentioned in 2 Maccabees 12, where Judas goes on the hunt for a local governor, Timothy.[46] During this campaign, he defeats a force of Arabs (12:10-12) and captures various fortified towns (12:13-23). Timothy is said to escape (12:24-25), and the Jews eventually return to Jerusalem to celebrate Pentecost (12:31). Bar-Kochva proposes,

> It thus appears that the passage in II Maccabees 8.30-3 is a summing up of Judas Maccabaeus's accomplishments in the Gilead campaign which are described in detail in ch. 12. . . . Presumably Jason of Cyrene combined these passages in order to stress that the lofty qualities of the Jewish soldiers, and their strictness in observing the precepts which led to the drastic change in events beginning with the battle of Ammaus, were discernible in other battles as well.

For that purpose he here summarized the episode of the war in Gilead described at greater length and in greater detail later in his book, emphasizing the qualities noted.[47]

For Bar-Kochva, the "epitomist" misunderstood the purpose of Jason of Cyrene. He insists that there was only one Timothy who was an opponent of the Jews, Timothy, governor of Gilead. His position is in line with the account of 1 Maccabees.

It is important, however, not to make judgments before analyzing the text as it now stands. The narrative of 2 Maccabees has two men named Timothy: one Timothy was killed in Gazara (10:37); the other Timothy was governor of Gilead and was not killed (12:25). Since we do not have the longer work of Jason of Cyrene, we cannot tell whether our author so misunderstood the intention of its author.

■ **30-31** There is no need to identify this Bacchides with the Bacchides sent by Demetrius I. That Bacchides is said to be a high-ranking official, one of the Friends of the King (1 Macc 7:8), and there is no indication of such rank for the Bacchides mentioned here. The reference to fortified heights and the storing of weapons in advantageous places shows that Judas and his forces were carefully planning tactics for future attacks. The construction of ὑπέρ + accusative to denote number is found also in 14:39; that of ἐγκρατῆ τινος γίνεσθαι ("gain control of something") is found also in 10:15, 17; 13:13 and also in Polybius 1.7.5; 3.51.11. The word for "stronghold," ὀχύρωμα, occurs also in the attacks against the Idumeans and the first Timothy (10:15, 16, 23, 32), once in the attack of Lysias against the strongholds controlled by Judas's forces (11:6); and once in the campaign against the second Timothy (12:19), and the adjective ὀχυρός is found in 12:13, 18, 27 as well as 10:18.

■ **32** Grimm held that φυλάρχην must be a proper name, Phylarches, as otherwise one should have had not the article but the indefinite pronoun τινά. However, a proper name does not usually use the article, unless it has been previously mentioned. See, for example, the way that Lysimachos and Sostratos are introduced in 4:29.[48] Rather, the article is used here as in 5:24, where

---

46 Bar-Kochva, *Judas Maccabaeus*, 510–12.
47 Ibid., 511–12.

48 The article is used in 1 Macc 7:8, when a person is introduced for the first time: ἐπέλεξεν ὁ βασιλεὺς

Antiochus IV sends the chief of the Mysians: ἔπεμψε δὲ τὸν Μυσάρχην Ἀπολλώνιον. Here the term φυλάρχην would refer to a leading figure in Timothy's forces, a tribal leader. It is often translated as cavalry commander but literally means a tribal chief and is used by Strabo to refer to the leaders of Arab tribes who allied themselves with the Romans (16.1.28).[49] The description of this tribal leader as one who had much troubled the Jews, where a perfect past participle is used, would appear to fit someone who had been in the area for a long time, rather than a cavalry commander.[50]

■ **33** If one accepts the present order of 2 Maccabees, the term ἐπινίκια would be used in a general sense of victory celebration, rather than have the specific meaning of "victory sacrifices," as the temple had not yet been restored. Judas's forces would have access to Jerusalem (8:31) but not full control of the city, a reading supported by the author's statement that the celebrations took place "in the fatherland." Elsewhere, the author clearly distinguishes temple, city, and fatherland (13:14; see also 13:11). The celebration thus seems to have taken place outside Jerusalem. The mention of fatherland also reflects back to the willingness of Judas's forces to die for the fatherland (8:21). Where Callisthenes and the gate burners died is not specified, but, given the reference to the burning of the holy gates, I suspect that this event happened in Jerusalem, where street fighting would have broken out. The author once again uses his favorite motif of just deserts, where the punishment fits the crime. The use of δυσσέβεια ("ungodliness") acts to return the story back to Nikanor, who at 8:14 had been described as "godless" (δυσσεβής).

■ **34-35** The adjective "triply offensive" (τρισαλιτήριος) is also used in 15:3, of the second Nikanor, which helps bind the narrative together. The author returns to the

motif of the punishment fitting the crime. He refers again to Nikanor's desire to sell the Jews as slaves (8:11, 25) and even depicts Nikanor acting like a runaway slave, keeping himself apart from everyone as though scared of everyone and at everyone's mercy (8:35). The topsy-turviness of the result is stressed, as Nikanor becomes the one lessened by his supposed inferiors. This inversion is particularly emphasized by Nikanor's change of clothes, as dress is an indication of social status. In 4:38, Andronikos is stripped of his purple; in 8:35, Nikanor removes his "splendid raiment." All this change happened through the Lord's help; βοήθεια ("help") refers back to the references in Judas's speech to what the Lord had done in previous generations (8:19-20) and to the watchword given before the battle (8:23).

"Across the country" is literally "through the interior" (διὰ τῆς μεσογείου) where ὁδός ("way") is understood. Grimm suggests that the phrase means the shortest route possible. Could it also mean avoiding the coastal highway?

"All alone" (ἔρημος) has the sense of defenseless, as are orphaned children or those without friends.[51]

The use of the preposition ἐπί + dative here has the sense of time, as in Herodotus 1.170: ἐπὶ διεφθαρμένοισι Ἴωσι ("after the destruction of the Ionians"). The irony is palpable, as Nikanor can barely save himself and even then only by acting like a runaway slave.[52]

■ **36** The incident closes with a reference back to Nikanor's plan to settle the tribute owed to the Romans through selling the Jewish captives. The juxtaposition of the two verbs beginning with the preposition κατά –κατορθώσασθαι κατήγγελλεν ("to settle finally he proclaimed"), where one spoke of his hope, the other of his failure—underlines the complete failure of Nikanor's attempt. "Tribute" (φόρος) and "body of captives" (αἰχμαλωσία) occur as in 8:10. Nikanor's proclama-

τὸν Βακχίδην τῶν φίλων τοῦ βασιλέως ("The king chose Bacchides, one of the Friends of the King"). However, the author seems to be distinguishing this Bacchides from others of the same name. He is the Bacchides who is one of the Friends of the King.

49 See also Bar-Kochva, *Judas Maccabaeus*, 511.

50 Goldstein's translation of τῶν περὶ Τιμοθέον, "of the two Timothies," is not supported. The passages in Polybius (4.85.1-4; 5.1.7-9) to which he refers and which were discussed by Foucault (*Recherches*, 113-15) are all cases in which the immediate context

clearly indicates that the phrase refers to the party of Aratos as opposed to the party of Apelles and Leontius. When Polybius wants to speak directly about the individuals, he distinguishes between the elder and the younger Aratos (5.1.9). The same is even more true of 8:32, where there is no mention in the immediate context of another Timothy.

51 Plato *Leg.* 927D; Sophocles *Oed. Col.* 1717; *Ant.* 919. Aeschylus (*Pers.* 734, 832-36) imagines Xerxes fleeing all alone and with his garments rent.

52 See Doran, *Temple Propaganda*, 58.

tion is similar to that of Heliodorus in 3:36. God is the champion of his people, as in 14:34. The statement of Heliodorus is supplemented here with the idea that the people are invulnerable because they follow God's laws. The alliteration of διὰ τὸν τρόπον τοῦτον ἀτρώτους highlights the connection between the obedience of the Jews to the Torah and the help of God.[53] The second διά in this section is explicative of the first preposi- tional phrase with διά. Heliodorus had been turned back because he came at a time when the laws were kept because of Onias's piety (3:1) and at that time the Lord had answered the prayers of the Jews when they called (ἐπικαλέω) upon him (3:15, 22). Now prayer has been taken up again, by the martyrs (7:37) and by Judas and his forces (8:2), who fight for the laws (8:21) and obey the laws about the Sabbath (8:26) and the distribution of booty and the care for the orphans and children (8:28, 30). Some manuscripts and translations omit the second mention of the Jews, but I have retained it as I see it as emphasizing the connection between the Jews and their ancestral laws.

General Commentary

This chapter shows the rise of the insurgency against the Seleucid forces. Judas first gathered a force together and then used the tactics of minority groups—setting fire to villages, attacks under cover of night—to gain control of key areas. When the local Seleucid official in charge of Jerusalem realized the extent of the insurgency, he wrote for reinforcements to the next higher official, who responded by sending in a force to stamp out the insurgency. The ensuing battle was won by Judas and his forces, and the Seleucid commander was forced to flee in disgrace back to his base in Antioch.

The author of the narrative has taken this bare-bones account and embellished it to show Judas and his forces to the best advantage. The account of the gathering of the forces is linked to the account of the execution of the brothers and their mother. Judas and his group call upon the Lord just as the brothers had (ἐπικαλέω in 7:37 and 8:2); the wrath of the Lord has been stayed (7:38; 8:5). In both accounts, the Lord is asked to be reconciled with his

servants (7:33; 8:29; see also 7:6). While from 8:8 on the story has the basic frame of a battle account—preparation for battle (8:8-23a); the battle (8:23b-24); the result of the battle (8:25-36)—the disproportion in the limited space given to the actual battle shows that the author's concern is not with battle tactics. There is no mention of Mattath- ias, the father of Judas, in the account of the beginning of the revolt, in contrast to 1 Maccabees 2. While the parallel account of this first attack on Judas in 1 Macc 3:38–4:25 describes the interesting surprise tactics used by one of the Seleucid commanders, Gorgias, the author of 2 Maccabees centers all the discussion of the Seleucid forces on one commander, Nikanor. The author thus sets up a more rhetorically effective, one-on-one confronta- tion between two opponents. In the account of the prep- arations for battle, the Seleucid leader is characterized from the first as evil, as he is the one who plans to sell the Jews as slaves (8:10-11), in contrast to 1 Macc 3:41, where the slave traders join the invading force on their own. Nikanor's plan backfires and the author emphasizes how the Jews got the money of the slave traders (8:25) and how Nikanor was himself forced to act like a run- away slave (8:35). The author here uses the motif of just deserts, a punishment appropriate to the crime. A simi- lar use of the motif is found in Thucydides' description of the flight of the Athenian army from Syracuse: the Athenians who had come to enslave others now feared that they might suffer enslavement (7.75.7). Judas and his forces prepare for the battle piously. They beseech the Lord (8:14), and the pre-battle speech of Judas (8:16-20) calls on the Jews to trust in the Lord, recalls God's great deeds for them in the past, and makes them ready to die for God's laws. The holy scroll is read from (8:23) and the watchword is "God's Help" (8:23). This devotion to God is further emphasized in the troops' honoring the Sabbath rather than pursuing plunder (8:25-26) and in their care for the tortured, the widows, and the orphans. At the end of the story, the humbled Nikanor confesses the power of the Lord (8:36). The irony of Nikanor's sav- ing his own skin at the cost of his whole army evidences the desire of the author to involve the audience of the story in cheering on the underdog and laughing at the humiliated oppressor.

---

53   Pindar (*Isthm.* 3.18) had stated: ἄτρωτοί γε μὰν παῖδες θεῶν.

Another rhetorical device used by the author is the insertion of 8:30-33 into the narrative. In attempting to establish the exact historical sequence of incidents in the Maccabean revolt, scholars have argued that the events described in these verses belong elsewhere.[54] However, if one reads the account as it stands, the stories describe mopping-up operations in the countryside against allies of a Seleucid officer, Timothy, and some notable examples of success against high-ranking Seleucid officers. The killing of Callisthenes even suggests some house-to-house operations in Jerusalem. All of these events are presented as prolegomena to the capture of Jerusalem, described so briefly in 10:1. More importantly, they are inserted before the description of the humiliation of Nikanor. His fate had not been included in the account of the flight of his army, but is left until the very end of the relation of this episode. Verses 30-33 serve to extend the narrative and to heighten the audience's desire to know what happened to Nikanor. It is a technique that is found later in the Gospel of Mark. When Jesus is asked to heal the daughter of Jairus, he goes along with the father toward the girl (Mark 5:21-24). Before he reaches the girl, however, another story is interpolated, that of the woman suffering from hemorrhages (Mark 5:25-35).

Only after the healing of this woman does the account return to Jairus's daughter (Mark 5:35-43), whom Jesus then raises from the dead. The audience's interest is held as they await the outcome of the episode involving Jairus's daughter. Similarly, after Jesus sends out his disciples on a preaching and healing mission (Mark 6:7-13), but before they return to tell him what they have done (Mark 6:30), the author interpolates the story of the beheading of John the Baptist (Mark 6:14-29). The fate of John the Baptist prefigures the fate of those who preach the gospel. Within a similar structure, 8:30-33 continues the description of the piety of Judas's forces and their successes, and the fate of Callisthenes, an example of just deserts, prefigures the fate of Nikanor as a runaway slave. Tobias Nicklas has acutely noted how this passage shows that the defeat of Nikanor was not a single intervention on God's part but that God continues to help his people. More importantly, the illogic of the sequence awakens the audience to the fact that this performance does not follow exactly the historical sequence of events but rather brings out other dimensions of the story.[55]

---

54 See Grimm, Abel, Bunge (*Untersuchungen*, 277–87), and especially Momigliano, *Prime linee*, 67–80.
55 Tobias Nicklas, "Aus erzählter Geschichte 'Lernen': Eine narrative Analyse von 2 Makk 8," *JSJ* 32 (2001) 25–41, here 40.

9

1/ About that time, Antiochus had unceremoniously returned from the regions around[a] Persis. 2/ For he had entered the city called Persepolis and attempted to rob the temple and secure the city. Well, on account of this, great numbers rushed to the aid of men-at-arms, and they were put to flight.[b] So it was that Antiochus, put to flight by the inhabitants, made his way home shamefaced. 3/ When he was by Ekbatana, news came to him of what had happened to Nikanor and the followers of Timothy. 4/ Enraged, he intended to fix onto the Jews the injury due to those who had driven him away. Therefore, he ordered his charioteer to drive on without a break and finish the journey, while the judgment from heaven traveled with him. For he said so arrogantly, "When I get there, I will make Jerusalem a communal burial ground for Jews." 5/ But the all-seeing Lord, the God of Israel, afflicted him with an incurable, invisible blow. As soon as he stopped speaking, an irremediable pain seized him in his innards, and sharp inner torments [seized] 6/ in a thoroughly equitable way the one who had tormented the innards of others with many strange misfortunes. 7/ However, he in no way ceased from his high-handedness, but he made his arrogance still more complete, boiling over in his fits of anger against the Jews as he commanded to quicken the journey. Moreover, he fell from his chariot as it rushed along; as he fell with an awkward fall, all the limbs of his body were wrenched. 8/ Still opining through his inordinate pretense that he could command the waves of the sea and presuming that he could place the mountain heights on a scale, he was down on the ground and carried on a litter. In himself he demonstrated to all the manifest power of God, 9/ as worms swarmed from the eyes

a I have followed AVqLa[P] in reading $\pi\epsilon\rho\acute{\iota}$ rather than $\kappa\alpha\tau\acute{\alpha}$ with L' La[BM]. While $\kappa\alpha\tau\acute{\alpha}$ specifies the region of which Persepolis in v. 2 is the capital, the fact that Antiochus's itinerary is not known suggests that he was in the several regions "around" Persis.

b Abel follows the Vulgate, taking the subject of the verb to be the citizens of the city, and connects the verb with the prepositional phrase: "The crowd, rushing out, turned to the aid of weapons." He points to the similar use of $\tau\rho\acute{\epsilon}\pi\omega$ in 12:42. However, grammatically it would be unusual to have the subject of the verb be in the genitive absolute phrase. Goldstein notes that this sentence, if the understood subject is Antiochus's army, would duplicate the following sentence. He therefore proposes that one read instead of $\acute{\epsilon}\tau\rho\acute{\alpha}\pi\eta\sigma\alpha\nu$ the l reading $\acute{\alpha}\nu\epsilon\tau\rho\acute{\alpha}\pi\eta$ and reread this as $\mathring{\alpha}\nu$ $\acute{\epsilon}\tau\rho\acute{\alpha}\pi\eta$. He thus translates "[the king] could have been routed." Ingenious as this is, the assumption that the second sentence simply duplicates the first is not necessary. The emphasis of the second sentence is on the shameful retreat of Antiochus, and a slightly different verb, $\tau\rho\sigma\pi\acute{o}\omega$, is used instead of $\tau\rho\acute{\epsilon}\pi\omega$.

of the impious one and also pieces of flesh crumbled off him while he was still living in pains and sufferings, and all the army was burdened at the decay[c] by his stench. 10/ Because of the unbearable burden of his stench, no one could carry one who, a little before, opined that he could grasp the stars of heaven. 11/ Thereupon, broken down, he began to cease his arrogance very much and to come to comprehension, racked with sufferings by the divine whip like a brand mark. 12/ Not able to endure his stench, he said, "It is right to be subject to God and not, being mortal, to be godlike minded."[d]

13/ The polluted one vowed to the Master, who would not now be merciful to him, saying 14/ that he would proclaim the holy city, which he had been eager to level and make a communal burial ground, to be free. 15/ As for the Jews, who he had determined did not merit a burial place and that they and their infants should be cast out with the animals to be eaten by birds, [he said] that all would be on a par with the Athenians. 16/ He would adorn the holy temple, which he had earlier despoiled, with the most beautiful votive offerings, restore all the holy vessels many times over, and supply the money required for the sacrifices out of his own expenses. 17/ Besides this, he would be a Jew and would travel to every inhabited region to proclaim the power of God.

18/ As the pains by no means ceased—for the just judgment of God had come against him— he despaired as far as he himself was concerned and wrote to the Jews the following letter in the form of a supplication. Its contents were as follows:

19/ "The King and Commander Antiochus to the well-deserving Jews, the citizens, much greeting, good health and prosperity.[e] 20/ [f]If you are in good health and your children and your interests are going as

c   L puts this phrase in the dative, but the accusative should be seen as an accusative of respect denoting the respect in which the verb is limited. See Smyth, *Greek Grammar*, §1600.

d   Reading, with Grimm, Abel, Habicht, and Goldstein, ἰσόθεα and not the more banal ὑπερήφανα.

e   V 347 reads διευτύχειν in place of εὖ πράττειν, while L 311 has both. There is no significant change in meaning. However, as White notes, letters of petition close with the more formal εὐτύχει ("farewell"), which reflects the subordinate position of the sender. White also states that the form διευτύχει is found in the Roman era (*Light from Ancient Letters*, 195).

f   This verse has been variously transmitted in the manuscript tradition. See Hanhart, *Maccabaeorum liber II*, 27, and Abel. Abel takes as the apodosis the short text ἔχομεν τὴν μεγίστην χάριν, κἀγὼ δὲ ἀσθενῶς διεκείμην. With 347 La he omits "as I place my hope in heaven," as does Goldstein. Goldstein however reads the apodosis as ἔχω μὲν τῷ Θεῷ τὴν μεγίστην χάριν. . . . The phrase χάριν ἔχω, χάριν ἔχομεν does occur in private correspondence, but not in the health wishes (Stanislaw Witkowski, *Epistulae privatae graecae quae in papyris aetatis Lagidarum servantur* [Leipzig: Teubner, 1906] no. 63 [*P. Lips.* no. 104]), and so I see no need to change to ἔχω. From the fact that one Latin text, La[P], has the first person plural *habemus*, and La[P] and Arm reflect a first person plural *agimus*, Victor Parker ("Letters," 394) suggested that the letter "may originally have switched between the first person plural and the singular. Genuine letters of Seleucid kings do this as well."
I have preferred to keep the longer text as found in the majority of manuscripts. The reason for the omission of "placing my hope in heaven" would appear to be either that it inappropriately uses "heaven" as a substitute for a divine name as this reflects Jewish usage, or that it contradicts what was just said in v. 18 where Antiochus despairs.

you wish, I declare the greatest thanks to God as I place my hope in heaven. 21/ Now I was feeling weak, and so I remembered affectionately your esteem and goodwill. While returning from the regions around Persia, I experienced an unpleasant weakness and thought to provide for the common security of all. 22/ I do not despair as far as I myself am concerned, but have great hope to escape the weakness. 23/ However, as I considered that even my father, each time that he marched toward the upper regions, proclaimed his successor 24/ so that, if something unexpected happened or some difficulty was reported, those throughout the country would not be troubled, as they would know who was in charge of affairs. 25/ Besides this, as I recognize that the rulers nearby and adjacent to the kingdom look out for opportunities and await what will happen, I have proclaimed as king my son Antiochus, whom, while I was often traversing the upper satrapies, I used to entrust and commend to the majority of you. I have written the appended [letter] to him. 26/ Therefore, I call on you and expect that each of you, mindful of the benefactions performed publicly and privately, maintain your present goodwill toward me and my son. 27/ For I have persuaded him to follow closely my own policy and, with mildness and benevolence, to accommodate himself to you."

28/ So the murdering blasphemer, suffering terribly just as he had treated others, ended his life with a miserable death on foreign soil in the mountains. 29/ Philip, his foster brother, escorted the body but, on his guard against the son of Antiochus, crossed over into Egypt to Ptolemy Philometor.

Commentary by Verse

■ **1-2** "About that time." The general time frame ($\pi\epsilon\rho\grave{\iota}$ $\delta\grave{\epsilon}$ $\tau\grave{o}\nu$ $\kappa\alpha\iota\rho\grave{o}\nu$ $\grave{\epsilon}\kappa\epsilon\hat{\iota}\nu o\nu$), similar to that found in 5:1 ($\pi\epsilon\rho\grave{\iota}$ $\delta\grave{\epsilon}$ $\tau\grave{o}\nu$ $\kappa\alpha\iota\rho\grave{o}\nu$ $\tauo\hat{\upsilon}\tau o\nu$, "about this time"), suggests a connection with the preceding events, and this connection will be specified in v. 3. For the use of $\tau\upsilon\gamma\chi\acute{\alpha}\nu\omega$ + participle, see 4:32.

These two verses neatly reflect each other by the use of similar phrases—$\grave{\alpha}\nu\alpha\lambda\epsilon\lambda\upsilon\kappa\grave{\omega}\varsigma$ $\grave{\alpha}\kappa\acute{o}\sigma\mu\omega\varsigma$ . . . $\grave{\alpha}\sigma\chi\acute{\eta}$-$\mu o\nu\alpha$ $\tau\grave{\eta}\nu$ $\grave{\alpha}\nu\alpha\zeta\upsilon\gamma\acute{\eta}\nu$. The use of two verbs that are variations of one another ($\grave{\epsilon}\tau\rho\acute{\alpha}\pi\eta\sigma\alpha\nu$ [$\tau\rho\acute{\epsilon}\pi\omega$] and $\tau\rho o\pi\omega\vartheta\acute{\epsilon}\nu\tau\alpha$ [$\tau\rho o\pi\acute{o}\omega$]) is also noteworthy.

In July 165 B.C.E., Antiochus IV had set out to regain control of Armenia. In October 165 B.C.E., he was at the Persian Gulf. Peter Mittag convincingly argued that Antiochus's main concern was to secure the trade routes and, therefore, the income they generated and suggested that Antiochus would have first gone to newly founded Antiocheia-Charax at the head of the Persian Gulf.[1] From there he would have moved toward the regions of Elymais and Persis. The details concerning this journey are variously reported. According to Polybius, Porphyry, Appian, and Jerome, Antiochus IV sought to plunder the temple of Artemis/Aphrodite/Diana in Elymais.[2] Josephus has Antiochus attempt to plunder the temple of Artemis in the city of Elymais in Persis, while 1 Maccabees leaves the god/goddess of the temple unnamed (1 Macc 3:31, 37; 6:1-3; Josephus *Ant.* 12.354-55. In 1:13-17, Antiochus is attacked by the priests of the temple of Nanaia in Persis when he attempts to rob her temple. The motif of the temple-plundering monarch is the stuff of negative propaganda, but Mittag sees behind the accounts an attempt by Antiochus to strengthen control over the various cities of these regions at the extremity of his kingdom. Part of this reassertion of control would be the collection of taxes and monies that these cities had neglected to pay in the previous years.[3]

The author of the abridged version gives the name of the city as Persepolis. Goldstein suggests that this is based on a misreading of an original Hebrew source that read "in Persis a city," *bprs ʿyr*.[4] It seems more likely that the author simply gave the name of the most renowned city in Persis in order to highlight the effrontery of Antiochus IV. Persepolis, the capital of the Achaemenid Empire, was a well-known city and had been looted and destroyed by Alexander the Great (Diodorus Siculus 17.20-22). One wonders if there was anything left to be looted and if the author chose the name because of the city's reputation.[5] Schwartz suggests that the author used the participle "called" because ordinarily the designation for "city of the Persians" would be two words, not the single $\Pi\epsilon\rho\sigma\acute{\epsilon}\pi o\lambda\iota\varsigma$.[6]

■ **3-10** These verses describe the affliction and sickness of Antiochus IV. The author, through his choice of words, has linked this account to those of the humiliation of Heliodorus (3:24-40) and of the torments imposed on Eleazar and the seven brothers (6:18—7:42). The author delights in the description of the torments Antiochus suffers. He first has Antiochus afflicted with an intestinal complaint (9:5) and then has him fall from his rushing chariot (9:7) before worms emerge from him and his flesh drops off him (9:9). All of these torments are seen as just deserts for his previous actions.

■ **3** The author ties the death of Antiochus IV to the events in Judea. Where Antiochus died has been much disputed. Polybius states that he died at Tabai in Persis (31.9.3), and so does Porphyry.[7] Since there is no city Tabai in Persis, W. W. Tarn, following E. Herzfeld, emended the name to Gabai near Isfahan.[8] However, this

---

1   Peter Franz Mittag, *Antiochus IV. Epiphanes: Eine politische Biographie* (Berlin: Akadamie, 2006) 302.

2   Polybius 31.9; Porphyry *FGH* 260, F 53 and 56.1; Appian *Syr.* 66; Jerome *Commentary on Daniel* 718 (*PL* 11:36).

3   Mittag, *Antiochus IV. Epiphanes*, 309–17.

4   Goldstein, *II Maccabees*, 349. See also Geert W. Lorein, "Some Aspects of the Life and Death of Antiochus IV Epiphanes: A New Presentation of Old Viewpoints," *Ancient Society* 31 (2001) 157–71, here 168 n. 55.

5   See Jacob Wackernagel, "Griechische Miszellen, 1: $\Pi\epsilon\rho\sigma\acute{\epsilon}\pi o\lambda\iota\varsigma$," *Glotta* 14 (1925) 36–44.

6   Schwartz, *2 Maccabees*, 353.

7   Porphyry, in *FGH* 260 F 56.

8   W. W. Tarn, *The Greeks in Bactria and India* (2nd ed.; Cambridge: Cambridge University Press, 1951) 214–15; E. Herzfeld, "Pasargadae: Untersuchungen zur persischen Archäologie," *Klio* 8 (1908) 1–68, here 18–19.

Gabai does not lie in Persis, and so Mittag has suggested the town Gabai in the southeast corner of Persis, near the border with Carmania.[9] Whatever the case, the author of the shortened version has Antiochus take the road back toward Antioch, going northwest from Persepolis on the major road to Ekbatana. From Ekbatana the road led over the Tigris and Euphrates to Antioch. The author's knowledge of this route is interesting, as by 141 B.C.E. this area, including Ekbatana, would have been controlled by the Parthians.[10] The author has some knowledge of the major cities in that area, even if his account of the events surrounding Antiochus's death is not reliable. His main concern is to link the death of Antiochus IV to events in Jerusalem, and his mention of the defeats of Nikanor and Timothy's men achieves that purpose. The same construction is used as in 8:30 and 8:32 to describe the contingent of Timothy's forces who were defeated.

■ **4-5a** "Enraged" is literally "lifted up in spirit." $\Theta\nu\mu\acute{o}\varsigma$ can have a wide range of meanings, including the sense of "anger," as here. Note its use in 13:4 and the similar expressions for anger in 4:38; 10:35; and 14:45. In 5:11, Antiochus IV was compared to a beast in his anger at hearing the news of the "revolt" in Jerusalem. As Tobias Nicklas notes, Antiochus IV is depicted as thinking he had been wronged, as if the defenders of the city had done him an injury in protecting their city.[11] The implied sense of psychological transference is found also in the account of Polybius, in which Philip V took the news badly ($\beta\alpha\rho\acute{\epsilon}\omega\varsigma\ \phi\acute{\epsilon}\rho\omega\nu$) that he would have to evacuate the Thracian cities and fixed his fury ($\acute{\epsilon}\nu\alpha\pi\eta\rho\epsilon\acute{\iota}\sigma\alpha\tau o\ \tau\grave{\eta}\nu\ \grave{o}\rho\gamma\acute{\eta}\nu$) on the unfortunate people of Maronea (22.13.2).

The emotion of the king is mirrored by the speed he demands for the long journey from Ekbatana to Jerusalem. The author cleverly places in a genitive absolute construction the announcement that death rides with the king. Earlier, the seventh son executed had foretold that the king would not escape the judgment of God the overseer (7:35-36). God is the one who disposes the outcome of events (15:21). The contrast between the king's inten-

tions and God's actions is continued in the next two sentences. The king's arrogance had been stated before, in 5:21, when he plundered the Jerusalem temple. Now the king threatens to go further and make Jerusalem a communal burial ground. Gog was to be given by God a communal burial ground in Israel for all his followers (Ezek 39:11-12 LXX). Aelian distinguishes between the family cemetery ($\tau\grave{\alpha}\varsigma\ \pi\alpha\tau\rho\acute{\omega}\alpha\varsigma\ \tau\alpha\phi\acute{\alpha}\varsigma$) and the less honorable mass grave ($\pi o\lambda\nu\alpha\nu\delta\rho\epsilon\hat{\iota}o\nu$) (*Var. hist.* 12.21). Goldstein suggests that the threat presupposes that Jerusalem has been restored by Judas. Given the hint in 8:33 that the Jews were already in Jerusalem, his suggestion has merit, but it is not absolutely necessary, as the threat is simply to kill all Jews in Jerusalem. There is thus no need to transpose the account of Antiochus's death to after the account of the restoration of the temple in 10:1-8.

The description of God as all-seeing resonates with the acclamation by Heliodorus in 3:39 and with the statement of the seventh son in 7:35. The term is found also in *Sib. Or.* frg. 1.4.[12] See also the description of Wisdom as $\pi\alpha\nu\epsilon\pi\acute{\iota}\sigma\kappa o\pi o\varsigma$ in Wis 7:23; the epithet is attributed to God in *Sib. Or.* 5:352. Zeus is said to be $\pi\alpha\nu\acute{o}\pi\tau\eta\varsigma$ ("all-seeing") in Aeschylus *Eum.* 1045 and Sophocles *Oed. Col.* 1086.[13]

The verb "to strike" ($\pi\alpha\tau\acute{\alpha}\sigma\sigma\omega$) is used in Deut 28:21 to describe what God will do to those who do not obey his commands. The verb is prominent in the LXX account of the plagues God inflicted on the Egyptians prior to the exodus.[14] In 2 Chr 21:18, God smote ($\acute{\epsilon}\pi\acute{\alpha}\tau\alpha\xi\epsilon\nu$) the wicked king Jehoram in his bowels with an incurable disease ($\mu\alpha\lambda\alpha\kappa\acute{\iota}\alpha\nu\ \hat{\eta}\ o\grave{\nu}\kappa\ \acute{\epsilon}\sigma\tau\iota\nu\ \iota\alpha\tau\rho\epsilon\acute{\iota}\alpha$). Eleazar had earlier been struck by blows ($\pi\lambda\eta\gamma\alpha\hat{\iota}\varsigma$) in 6:30, and Heliodorus had been whipped by the angels as they inflicted many blows (3:26). King Nabonidus was afflicted with an evil ulcer but was healed by a Judean exorcist and confessed his evil (4Q242).[15] These afflictions had been seen by the onlookers, but no one sees God inflicting his blow. The effect of God's action will soon become manifest.

9   Mittag, *Antiochus IV. Epiphanes*, 319–20.
10   Sherwin-White and Kuhrt, *From Samarkhand to Sardis*, 223–25.
11   Tobias Nicklas, "Der Historiker als Erzähler: Zur Zeichnung des Seleukidenkönigs Antiochus in 2 Makk. IX," *VT* 52 (2002) 80–92, here 83.
12   As in Theophilus *Autol.* 2.36.
13   See Arnold H. M. Jones, "Inscriptions from Jerash," *JRS* 18 (1928) 173 n. 42.
14   Exodus 3:20; 7:20, 25; 8:16-17; 9:15, 25; 12:12, 23, 27, 29.
15   See Doron Mendels, "A Note on the Tradition of Antiochus IV's Death," *IEJ* 31 (1981) 53–56.

■ **5b-6** The immediacy of God's reaction is stressed.[16] The just judgment of God against Antiochus was foretold in 7:36 by the youngest brother, who recognized that God's punishments had been inflicted on his own people justly (7:38) but requested that the punishments cease because of the brothers' deaths. The author enjoys using the motif of just deserts: the fates of Jason (5:9-10) and Menelaus (13:8); the death of Andronikos on the same spot at which he had killed Onias (4:38); the dismemberment of Nikanor (15:32-33). Such a motif is found in the Elijah cycle (3 Kgdms 21:17-19; 4 Kgdms 9:30-37), in Wis 11:5, 15-16; 18:3, and in Josephus's description of the death of Apion (*Ap.* 2.143–44). The theme is frequent in Greek literature.

■ **7-11** Antiochus remains obstinate. The verb "to cease" (λήγω) is negated in v.7 but in 9:11 is used to indicate that Antiochus had ceased his arrogance; it is thus used to structure this section.

■ **7** "High-handedness" (ἀγερωχία) is found in Wis 2:9, where the wicked threaten high-handedness against those not of their company, and in *3 Macc.* 2:3, where God is said to judge those who practice hubris and high-handedness. The term is also used by Polybius, who links high-handedness and arrogance (ἀγερώχως καὶ λίαν ὑπερηφάνως) (10.35.8; 2.8.7). The arrogance of the king becomes a leitmotif in this account of the king's punishment and conversion. The arrogance of 9:7 ceases in 9:11-12. It had earlier characterized the king in 5:21.

"Boiling over," literally "breathing fire," is similar to the phrase in 9:4, and the king also becomes enraged in 4:38 (justly, at Andronikos for killing Onias). The phrase is found again in 10:35, where Judas's men are enraged at the blasphemies of their enemies, and in 14:45, where Rhazis confronts those who seek him.

"Moreover"; δὲ καί has the sense of addition.[17] Once again, the author contrasts Antiochus's designs with the unexpected suddenness of his downfall. The images of the rushing chariot and the body of Antiochus being wrenched apart are quite striking, the headlong rush stopped dead in its tracks. The author heightens the dramatic effect by the use of unusual words: ἐποξύνειν, ῥοῖζος, ἀποστρεβλοῦσθαι.

■ **8-10** The contrasts continue as Antiochus's ambitions are set against his dire situation. First comes the frequently used image of the impossibility of commanding the waves of the sea, a task only God can do (Job 38:11; Pss 65:8; 89:10; 106:9; Isa 51:15; Nah 1:4). The term "inordinate" is literally "above human." The image is similar to that attributed to Xerxes, who hoped "to check [σχήσειν] the sacred waters of the Hellespont by chains as if it were a slave" (Aeschylus *Pers.* 745; see also Herodotus 7.35). Second comes the image of weighing the mountains (Isa 40:12). Antiochus's overweening claims had already been noted by the author, who used similar but different images in 5:21. Ἀλαζονεία ("pretense") is also used to describe Nikanor's thoughts of an easy victory (15:6, where I translated the term as "cockiness" because of the context), and his defeat is also made manifest (15:35). The power (δύναμις) of God was evident also in the case of Heliodorus (3:24, 38). Heliodorus too had been placed on a litter (3:27). The verb "to carry" (παρακομίζω) is used three times in this chapter (9:8, 10, 29) and so links the parts of the account of Antiochus's death together.

The gruesome effects of God's punishment are clearly seen in the worms and the decaying flesh and are smelled in the stench. Zechariah 14:12 portrays a similar death for those who wage war against God. Worms at the death of those who go against a god is a motif found frequently. Pheretime, queen of Cyrene, died after worms came from her body (Herodotus 4.205), as they did from Cassander (Pausanias 9.7.2-3; Justin 16.2), Herod the Great (Josephus *Ant.* 17.168-70), Herod Agrippa (Acts 12:23), and Alexander of Abonuteichos (Lucian *Alex.* 59-60).[18] The flesh of the

16 Doran, *Temple Propaganda*, 94–95.
17 See J. D. Denniston, *The Greek Particles* (2nd ed.; Oxford: Clarendon, 1970) 305.
18 See also the death of Sulla in Plutarch *Sull.* 36.3-6. For a full list, see Wilhelm Nestle, "Legenden vom Tod der Gottesverächter," *ARW* 33 (1936) 246–69. See also Thomas W. Africa, "Worms and the Death of Kings: A Cautionary Note on Disease and History," *CA* 1 (1982) 1–17. Jörg-Dieter Gauger ("Der 'Tod des Verfolgers': Überlegungen zur Historizität eines Topos," *JSJ* 33 [2002] 42–64) provides a nice summary of the various accounts of the death of Antiochus IV and then concentrates on the connection between persecution and death through worms coming out of the decaying flesh. Curiously, however, he then assumes that a combination of

godless is also said to putrefy.[19] The horrible smell of the victims is also noted. In Joel 2:20, the Lord promises: "I will remove the northerner far from you, . . . the stench [σαπρία] and foul smell of him will arise." No one could approach Herod the Great as he lay dying because of his smell (Josephus *Ant.*17.168–70).[20] George W. E. Nickelsburg also saw resonances with the fate of the king of Babylon recounted in the poem in Isa 14:4-21, particularly in the worms in 14:11.[21] The author uses a favorite term, "impious" (δυσσεβής; 3:11; 8:14; 15:33), to drive home the reason for this punishment.

Verse 10 sums up the previous description by its use of similar language: δοκέω in vv. 8, 10; ὀσμή in vv. 9, 10; φορεῖον/ἀφόρητον in vv. 9, 10; βαρύνω/βάρος in vv. 9, 10. Antiochus's assertion that he was able to touch the stars resonates with the boastful claims found in Isa 14:12-14. Horace concludes his first ode by declaring that if he is ranked among lyric bards, "I shall touch the stars with my exalted head [*sublime feriam sidera vertice*]" (*Odes* 1.1.36).

■ 11-12 The Conversion of Antiochus

The use of "cease" and "arrogance" echoes their negative use in v. 7; in addition, the end of Antiochus's arrogance was foretold in 7:36. Antiochus comes to knowledge as do Heliodorus (3:28), Nikanor (8:36), and, to a certain extent, Lysias (11:13). The image of the persecutor converting is found also in the court tales of Daniel (3:28-30; 4:25, 34-37; Bel 41) and the *Prayer of Nabonidus* (4Q242). Heliodorus was whipped (3:26) and promised that anyone sent against Jerusalem would be whipped (3:38). The martyrs are whipped (6:30; 7:1), and the youngest of the seven brothers foretells that Antiochus will be whipped into confessing God (7:38). The sufferings of Antiochus

(9:5, πληγῇ; 9:9, ἀλγηδόσι) reflect the sufferings of the martyrs (6:30, πληγαῖς; 7:12, ἀλγηδόνας).

In κατὰ στιγμήν I have taken στιγμή to mean "brand mark" as in Diodorus Siculus 34/35.2.1, as this whipping would parallel Nikanor's low status. Nikanor had been reduced to dressing like a runaway slave to escape capture (8:35). Most scholars take the term, which means "point, prick," as temporal, and so translate as "at each moment."[22]

The statement of Antiochus is a common notion. It is present in the great hymnic condemnations in Isa 14:12-21; Ezek 28:2-10; and Dan 11:36. The term "godlike" (ἰσόθεος) is a Homeric term for heroes (e.g., *Il.* 2.565; 3.310; 4.212). Aeschylus described Darius as "godlike," but the epithet as applied to Xerxes at the beginning of the play is ironic, as his attacks on temples bring his downfall (*Pers.* 80, 820, 857). The Greek tragedians had warned that humans should think mortal thoughts (θνητὰ φρονεῖν).[23] A similar thought is found in *Ep. Arist.* 263.

■ **13-17** The vow made by Antiochus is in two parts: the first (9:14-16) consists of benefits for the city, the Jews, and the temple, while the second (9:17) outlines the obligations that the king will lay upon himself.

■ **13** In 5:16, Antiochus had placed his polluted hands on the temple vessels. The word "polluted" is used appropriately here, as Antiochus's intention to make Jerusalem a cemetery would have made the city unclean. Now Antiochus makes a vow in order to gain relief. Heliodorus had made a vow in thankful response to God's mercy toward him (3:35). Here Antiochus tries to strike a bargain with God. Whereas the Lord had shown mercy to his people (8:5), he will not do so to Antiochus.

motifs can go only in either a descending or an ascending order of amplification and concludes that since the combination of persecution and worm death is found late in the second century C.E., such a combination in 2 Maccabees 9 means that this account was written at that time. However, motifs can be combined and used at the discretion of an author. There is no inflexible rule of amplification.

19 Herodotus 3.66; Diodorus Siculus 21.16.4–5; Plutarch *Sera* 548F–549A.
20 On the relationship between smell and holiness/sinfulness, see Susan Ashbrook Harvey, *Scenting Salvation: Ancient Christianity and the Olfactory Imagina-*

tion (Berkeley: University of California Press, 2006) 29–96.
21 Nickelsburg, *Resurrection*, 79. See also Daniel R. Schwartz, "Why Did Antiochus Have to Fall (II Maccabees 9:7)?" in Lynn LiDonnici and Andrea Lieber, eds., *Heavenly Tablets: Interpretation, Identity and Tradition in Ancient Judaism* (JSJSup 119; Leiden: Brill, 2007) 257–65.
22 Hanhart, *Zum Text*, 19; NRSV.
23 Sophocles *Trach.* 473; *Tereus* no. 590; Antiphanes frg. 282 in R. Kassel and C. Austin, eds., *Poetae Comici Graeci* (Berlin: de Gruyter, 1991) 2:469.

■ **14** The first benefit of the vow is the retraction of the threat of 9:4, to which the author refers using a conative imperfect. To level (ἰσόπεδον ποιῆσαι) the city is the same threat that Judas and his companions had earlier expected (8:3). Positively, Antiochus vows to bestow the gift of "freedom." This was quite an honor. Erich Gruen has shown that declarations of freedom "had a long and continuous history throughout the Hellenistic period,"[24] and, as John Ma has demonstrated, freedom was no empty benefit but represented a legal status and commitment on the part of a Hellenistic king.[25]

The verb ἀναδεικνύειν in the sense of "to proclaim" is found also in 9:23, 25; 14:12.[26]

■ **15** Jason the high priest had been excoriated for allowing many to be without a grave and had received his just deserts for such action (5:10). To be left unburied and to the wild beasts was a great dishonor in antiquity, as Sophocles' great play *Antigone* had epitomized. Goliath had threatened to leave David's body to the beasts of the field and the birds of the air (1 Sam 17:44, 46), and God promised such an end to the forces of Gog (Ezek 39:4, 17-20).

What exactly is meant by "on a par with the Athenians" (ἴσους Ἀθηναίοις) is not clear. Antiochus IV was well known for his gifts to Athens,[27] and this connection to Athens may be in play here. More likely, the author was part of the growing movement among Greek-speaking Jews that extolled the place and importance of Jewish tradition and culture alongside that of Greek culture.[28] For example, Clearchus of Soli attributed to Aristotle the statement that a Jew he had met not only spoke Greek but also had the soul of a Greek (Josephus *Ap.* 1.180). Athens, although no longer a major player on the political scene at this point, retained its prestige for learning and culture.

■ **16** Antiochus vows in effect to restore the relations between the Seleucid rulers and the temple in Jerusalem to the status described in 3:1-3. Antiochus IV was well known for his benefactions to Greek cities, part of his policy of finding support among the Greek states.[29]

■ **17** Antiochus promises to proclaim the power of God as the angels had asked Heliodorus to do (3:34, 38-39) and as the defeated Nikanor had proclaimed (8:36). But here Antiochus goes further still in vowing to "be a Jew." Where earlier Antiochus IV had not allowed Jews to profess themselves to be Jews (6:6), he himself would now become a Jew.

The Ptolemaic practice was for noncitizens to be identified by their place of origin, be it as Macedonian, Lycian, Athenian, or Jew, even if the original city-state no longer existed and those so designated had lived in Egypt for generations.[30] In a series of articles, Shaye J. D. Cohen has pointedly raised the problem of translation: should one translate Ἰουδαῖος as "Jew" or "Judean"?[31] He contends that in 2 Maccabees one can see a shift from "Judean" as an ethnic designation, for "2 Maccabees is the first work to use *Ioudaismos* and the first work to use *Ioudaios* in the sense of 'Jew.'" Cohen notes that normally the epitome uses *Ioudaios* to designate Jews in Judea, but sees the shift particularly in its use in 6:6 and 9:17. As he sums up: "In the Maccabean and early Roman periods the ways of the *Ioudaioi* loomed larger and larger in the definition of a *Ioudaios*, while ethnic and geographic factors loomed smaller and smaller."[32]

Cohen is clearly onto something in his analysis, but I would phrase it differently. Rather than talk of a change in translation whereby in 6:1, 7 *Ioudaios* would be translated "Judeans," and in 6:6 it would be translated "Jew," I suggest that one is dealing with identifying who is a real Jew. The language of 6:1 is political: τοὺς

24 Gruen, *Hellenistic World*, 132–57; quotation from 156.

25 Ma, *Antiochus III*, 150–74.

26 See Welles, *Royal Correspondence*, 311. In 2 Macc 10:11; 14:26, the verb has the sense of "appoint."

27 Mørkholm, *Antiochus IV*, 58–60.

28 Erich Gruen, in his two books *Heritage and Hellenism* and *Diaspora: Jews amidst Greeks and Romans* (Cambridge, Mass.: Harvard University Press, 2002) has marvelously displayed this creative fusion in the writings of Hellenistic Jews.

29 Mittag, *Antiochos IV. Epiphanes*, 89–91, 103–18.

30 Bickermann, "Beiträge zur antiken Urkundengeschichte," 216–39, esp. 223–25; also Préaux, "Les Étrangers," 141–93, esp. 189–93. See the commentary on 1:1.

31 Cohen, "Ἰουδαῖος τὸ γένος," 23–38; idem, "Religion, Ethnicity and 'Hellenism,'" 204–23; and idem, "Ioudaios," 211–20.

32 The citations, in order, are from Cohen, "Ioudaios," 219, 215 n. 16, 219.

Ἰουδαίους μεταβαίνειν ἀπὸ τῶν πατρίων νόμων καὶ τοῖς τοῦ θεοῦ νόμοις μὴ πολιτεύσθαι ("the Jews to change from their ancestral laws and not to conduct the government by the laws of God"). This is followed in 6:2 by a change in the name of the temple and its subsequent pollution. I thus see 6:6 as a summary of what has gone before. One can no longer live under the government given by God nor celebrate the festivals; that is, one can no longer live as a Jew should. To be a Jew is to live as a Jew. The same usage appears in 9:17: Antiochus was vowing to make Jerusalem a free city and to maintain through his own finances the sacrifices at the temple. In this context he vows to become a Jew. This step is no doubt hyperbole, even perhaps, as Gruen has suggested,[33] sly humor at Antiochus's expense. But Antiochus is promising that Jerusalem will live according to the government of God's laws and that the sacrifices to that God will be observed, a goal for which every true Jew should strive. *Ioudaios* therefore retains its ethnic character, but what is being defined is what a true *Ioudaios* is. I suggest that the same is true of the passage in Bel 28, where the Babylonians become angry at the king for allowing the worshiped dragon to be killed and claim that the king has become a Ἰουδαῖος ("Jew"); that is, the king is accused of overturning the *politeia* of the city in destroying its god. The Babylonians are in effect claiming that the king wants to introduce the polity of the Jews. A similar story is found in Herodotus about the Scythian kings Anacharsis and Scylas. When Anacharsis was found sacrificing to the Mother of the Gods as he had learned at Cyzicus, he was executed. When the Scythians discovered that Scylas had slipped away to take part in a Dionysiac festival, they rebelled, and Scylas ended up beheaded (Herodotus 4.76–80). One might also recall how Plutarch discusses the attempts of Agis and Cleomenes to return Sparta to its proper way of life. The people held that Agis was a king worthy of Sparta (*Agis* 10.1), while Agis states that Lycurgus, the famed Spartan

lawgiver, held foreigners in less displeasure than those to whom the Spartan practices and ways of living were not congenial (10.3). As for Cleomenes, it was declared that he alone was a descendant of Herakles, that is, a true king of Sparta (*Cleom.* 13.2). In all these cases an argument is being made as to whom a name rightly belongs; that is, ethnic names involve more than just the assumption of a name. They have to do with ways of behaving.[34]

As John Barclay lays out, the ethnic identity of Judaism is stressed by both Jews and non-Jews.[35] The author of the condensed version is concerned with questions of identity, with what really makes a Jew. It would thus seem that for the author, Antiochus IV is not only proclaiming the power and might of the Jewish God, as had Heliodorus and Nikanor while remaining attached to other gods, but also promising to follow Jewish customs.

■ **18** This verse is a bridge to the following letter. The author again uses the verb λήγειν ("to cease") as in 9:7, 11, as well the noun κρίσις ("judgment"; 9:4), and so ties the first part of this account of the death of Antiochus together. It is important to note that, while this verse speaks of Antiochus's despair, the following letter emphasizes his hope (9:20, 22). This discrepancy between the context and the content of the letter will continue.

■ **19-27** In the previous verse, the letter is classified as a supplication.[36] The form of the greeting formula bears this out. While royal correspondence has the form "A to B χαίρειν," here the letter has the form of a petition, "To B χαίρειν A" = "To B, greetings A."[37] The letter thus follows the conventions of one person petitioning another. We have no evidence of a Hellenistic king using such a letter style. For other arguments against the authenticity of this letter, see the individual verses. The author of the condensed version has placed this letter at the time of Antiochus IV's death, and one often finds a last will and testament from major protagonists at the time of their deaths.[38] This testamentary place underscores that the king recognizes with his dying

33   Erich S. Gruen, *Diaspora: Jews amidst Greeks and Romans* (Cambridge, Mass.: Harvard University Press, 2002) 179.

34   One might also note the story ascribed to Prodicus wherein Herakles has to choose between following the path of a true king or that of a false king (Xenophon *Mem.* 2.1.21–33).

35   Barclay, *Jews in the Mediterranean Diaspora*, 402–13.

36   See John P. Gould, "HIKETEIA," *JHS* 93 (1973) 74–103.

37   See White, *Light from Ancient Letters*, 194–96; also Exler, *Form*, 42–44, 122. See also the discussion of 1:1.

38   See Jacob's last speech in Genesis 49 and the will attributed to Alexander the Great before his death (Ps.-Callisthenes 3.32–33).

breath the loyalty of the Jews. Goldstein has observed that the letter was written according to proper rhetorical rules. The author of the letter first uses effusive expressions to gain the interest and sympathy of the listeners (vv. 19-21), then shows how agreeing to what he proposes is in the addressees' own best interests, for protection from foreign invasion and civil unrest (vv. 21b-25) and how his action is in accord with precedents (vv. 23, 25). He then reminds the addressees of previous benefactions (v. 26) and hints at further future benefactions (v. 27).[39] Such good rhetorical style does not argue for authenticity, but only that the writer, whoever he was, was versed in rhetoric.

■ **19** As mentioned above, the form of the greeting follows that of a letter of petition. Other unusual elements include the addition of the adjective "good" to describe the recipients, and the apposition "the citizens." The first emphasizes the high standing the Jews have in the king's eyes. What is meant by the appositive "the citizens" is unclear. Does it describe the "Jews," or does it distinguish those Jews who are citizens from other Jews? For Goldstein, the apposition is evidence that Antiochus IV had established an Antiochene republic and that the Hellenizing Jews were citizens of it.[40] For those who hold that Jerusalem was turned into a *polis* under Jason the high priest, the letter would be addressed to those Jews who were members of that *polis*. As Tcherikover showed, Jews en masse were not given citizen rights in other cities, even though Josephus claims that they were.[41] Victor Parker argued that such a reference to the fact that Antiochus IV had made Jerusalem a *polis* would be dramatic irony and would reinforce how the repentant Antiochus foolishly did not realize that what he had done was wrong. He then suggested that the letter writer "stood relatively close in time to the events of the 160s B.C.—and so did those for whom he wrote."[42] Throughout 2 Maccabees, however, the term πολίτης refers in a

general way to the members of the community of Judea (4:5, 50; 5:6, 8, 23; 14:8; 15:30), as it does in the LXX (Prov 11:9, 12; Jer 36:23; 38:34). One could argue that it has the same meaning here and that there is thus no need for the historical allusion Parker suggests. Rather, Antiochus would seem to be claiming co-citizenship with the Jews as he had promised to become a Jew in v. 17. As Habicht stated, the king could not be a πολίτης in a city of his own kingdom.[43] Such a claim would be another argument against the authenticity of this letter.

The greeting formula comprises three wishes—"much greeting [πολλὰ χαίρειν], good health [ὑγιαίνειν] and prosperity [εὖ πράττειν]." In the extant Greek correspondence there is no other example of three infinitives being used in a greeting formula. Normally only χαίρειν is found in letters, but the combination of χαίρειν καὶ ὑγιαίνειν is also found in 1:10. Goldstein patiently tracked down examples where χαίρειν καὶ ὑγιαίνειν are found.[44] Adverbial modifiers are found with both χαίρειν (πολλά or πλεῖστα),[45] and with ὑγιαίνειν (διὰ παντός).[46] That the two infinitives, χαίρειν and ὑγιαίνειν, could be interchanged is evident in the jest that Agesilaus is said to have made when Menecrates, also called Zeus, wrote to him "Menecrates Zeus to King Agesilaus, χαίρειν" and he responded: "King Agesilaus to Menecrates, ὑγιαίνειν," meaning by this response, be of sound mind (Plutarch *Reg. imp. apophth.* 191A). In the friendly correspondence between Archytas and Plato of which Diogenes Laertius reports, the initial greeting from Archytas to Plato is χαίρειν, while Plato replies, "Plato to Archytas εὖ πράττειν" (Diogenes Laertius 8.79-81).[47] These two greetings would thus seem also to be interchangeable. The piling up of these infinitives found in private correspondence reinforces the sense that the author has the king write in a friendly tone to the Jews.

39 Goldstein, *II Maccabees*, 359.

40 Ibid., 361.

41 Tcherikover, *Hellenistic Civilization*, 309-32. Josephus *Ant.* 12.8.11; 14.188; 16.60; 19.281; *Ap.* 2.35.

42 Parker, "Letters," 397.

43 Habicht, *2. Makkabäerbuch*, 247.

44 Goldstein, *II Maccabees*, 164-65.

45 For examples, see White, *Light from Ancient Letters*, πολλά no. 104 A and B; πλεῖστα nos. 70, 72-75,

79-80, 89, 102, 103A and B, 105, 111, 112. πολλὰ χαίρειν is also found in Witkowski, *Epistulae privatae*, no. 62 (*P. Leid.* no. 402).

46 For examples, see White, *Light from Ancient Letters*, nos. 64, 77, 81, 90, 92-93, 100-101. See also Exler, *Form*, 107-11.

47 One also finds the combination χαίρειν καὶ διὰ παντὸς εὖ ἔχειν. See White, *Light from Ancient Letters*, no. 98.

The title "commander" is not found in other royal correspondence, and Habicht saw it as another clue to the inauthenticity of the letter. Nicklas suggested that the use of the term here only reminds the audience how disastrous a commander Antiochus had shown himself in 9:2.[48]

■ **20-21a** A wish for health is found in private correspondence but is rare in royal letters. However, it is found in letters from 109 B.C.E. of a King Antiochus to Ptolemy IX Alexander and to the city of Seleucia in Pieria: *Εἰ ἔρρωσαι, εἴη ἂν ὡς βουλόμεθα καὶ αὐτοὶ δὲ ὑγιαίνομεν καὶ σοῦ ἐμνημονεύομεν φιλοστόργως* ("If you are well it would be as we wish. We ourselves are well and remember you affectionately").[49] Many of the elements of this letter are similar to those of our verses, not only the use of the verbs *ῥώννυμι* and *μνημονεύω*, with the imperfect tense anticipating the point of view of the recipient,[50] but also the use of *εἰ* and the adverb *φιλοστόργως*. The health wish could be expanded to include not only the recipient but also his affairs. The letter of Jonathan and the *gerousia* to the Spartan *ephors* hopes not only that the recipients are well but that their public and private affairs advance are as intended (*εἰ ἐρρωμένοις ὑμῖν καὶ τὰ κοινὰ καὶ τὰ ἴδια χωρεῖ κατὰ νοῦν*) (Josephus *Ant.* 13.166). One also finds in private correspondence the wish that "your other affairs go correctly" (*τἄλλα σοι κατὰ γνώμην ἐστιν*).[51] In 9:20, the phrase *τὰ ἴδια* ("your interests") seems equivalent to the phrase *τἄλλα σοι* ("whatever else concerns you") or to another phrase that occurs in private correspondence, *τὰ λοιπά σοι* ("everything else that concerns you"). Children also are sometimes included, as in the letter of Eleazar the high priest to Ptolemy Philadelphus: "You yourself be well and Queen Arsinoe, your sister, and your children, it will be well and as we wish" (*αὐτός τε ἔρρωσο καὶ ἡ βασίλισσα ἡ ἀδελφή καὶ τὰ τέκνα, καλῶς ἂν ἔχοι καὶ ὡς βουλόμεθα*) (*Ep. Arist.* 41).[52] This letter

addresses Ptolemy as an equal, and so here and in all the previous cases apart from the Spartan letter one is dealing with health wishes that are found in private correspondence. The combination of best wishes for children and for private affairs in the letter before us underlines the personal quality of the writing.

The expression of the king's wish for the well-being of the Jews is problematic, and the transmission shows this. As seen in the examples above, the wish is usually expressed with an impersonal verb + *ὡς* + first person plural. Here the verb is in the first person singular, which is not found in royal correspondence. The Latin text has the first person plural verb.[53] "As my hope is in heaven" is omitted in several manuscripts.[54] Many have been the attempts to reconstruct an original and to explain its changes and development.[55] None of them is convincing.

The verb *εὔχομαι* is found in private correspondence between a woman and her sister: "Before all else I pray for you to be well and your children" (*πρὸ μὲν πάντων εὔχομαί σε ὑγιαίνιν καὶ τὰ παιδία σου*) (*P. Tebt.* no. 414, lines 5–6). *Εὔχομαι* in the context of 2 Macc 9:20 means not "to pray" but rather "to declare, profess." The verb is found in private correspondence, but without an object and with the meaning "pray to the god/gods" (*τοῖς θεοῖς εὐχόμενος*).[56] Thanks to the gods are also present in such correspondence: "If you are well, and if the objects of your care and other concerns go correctly it will be as I wish, and much gratitude to the gods [*καὶ τοῖς θεοῖς πολλὴ χάρις*]" (*P. Hibeh* no. 79, lines 2–6). The use of the singular "god" rather than "gods" is also found in a private correspondence: *εἰ ἔρρωσαί τε καὶ τἄλλα σοι κατὰ γνώμην ἐστίν, θεῶι πλείστη χάρις* ("If you are in good health and whatever other concerns that you have are going as you wish, much thanks to God").[57] See also the use of the singular for "god" in thanksgiving in Polybius 1.36.1: "There was no extravagance of rejoicing in which [the Carthaginians] did not indulge, paying thank-offering

---

48   Nicklas, "Der Historiker," 88.
49   Welles, *Royal Correspondence*, no. 71, lines 2–4.
50   Ibid., 248.
51   Witkowski, *Epistulae privatae*, no. 19 (*P. Petr.* III 53o). See also nos. 2, 3, 26.
52   See the slightly different version in Josephus *Ant.* 12.51.
53   La^P Arm (*agimus*) where La^P has *habemus*. For a fuller discussion, see Abel.
54   347 La Arm.
55   See Goldstein, *II Maccabees*, 364–66.
56   Witkowski, *Epistulae privatae*, nos. 11 (*P. Petr.* II, 2, 3); 35 (*P. Lond.* no. 42).
57   Witkowski, *Epistulae privatae*, no. 19 (*P. Petr.* III 53o).

to the god [διά τε τῆς πρὸς τὸν θεὸν εὐχαριστίας] and giving congratulatory entertainments."

"Heaven" is used metonymically also in 2:21; 3:20, 34; 7:11; 8:20; 9:4; 15:8.[58]

The wish for the health of the recipients is followed by a statement about the sender's health, and their connection is shown by the use of the μὲν . . . δέ construction. The sender's health is mentioned in private letters[59] but would not be expected in a formal letter concerning the succession. Here the imperfect is used, as the writer places himself in the time of the recipient. Abel, followed by Goldstein, accepted the Latin manuscript tradition and omitted "your esteem and goodwill." This also required Abel to replace the connecting τέ and read δέ. The use of τέ alone here denotes the consequence of the king's ill health. What should the sick king do? He should call upon those members of his kingdom who will support him. The king thus emphasizes the reciprocal relationship between the king and his subjects—the esteem and goodwill of the latter will be answered by the affection of the former.[60] As Welles notes, the term φιλόστοργος belongs to the Koine.[61] Earlier φιλοστοργία was used, in 6:20. A close parallel to its usage here is found in a letter of Antiochus VIII to Ptolemy IX: "we ourselves were well and were remembering you affectionately" (καὶ σοῦ ἐμνημονεύομεν [φιλοστ]όργως).[62]

■ **21b-27** This is the body of the letter, in which the king is shown arguing persuasively that his son be accepted as co-regent.

■ **21b** The king first notes where he is. Whereas the surrounding narrative has the king on his way back from Ecbatana in Media, here the author is content to give only a general geographical notion that echoes the reference in 9:1. He has the king provide a very mild version of his illness, although previously worms had been coming out of his eyes and he had had to be carried on a litter (9:7-9). The language, περιπεσὼν ἀσθενείᾳ

δυσχέρειαν ἐχούσῃ ("experiencing an unpleasant weakness"), resonates with that of 9:7: "falling with an awkward fall" (δυσχερεῖ πτώματι περιπεσόντα) but here is used to suggest that the sickness is not so bad. The term δυσχερές is found also in v. 24, where I have translated it as "difficulty." The term δυσχερήν has a different nuance depending on the context, and so I have translated it differently in these three occurrences. The two references to his illness in vv. 21b and 22 surround the reason for his letter—his concern for the common security of his subjects. Here the king touches on the self-interest of the letter's recipients and why they should accept his appointment of his son.

■ **22-25** These verses form one sentence in the Greek. The king first allays fears about his health and states that he is following precedent (vv. 22-24) and then neatly distinguishes between the reactions of those inside and outside the kingdom (v. 25).

■ **22** The king expects to recover, the opposite of what he thought when he began to pen the letter, and the expectation of recovery contrasts with the despair of v. 18. The king's hope to escape (ἐκφεύγειν) contrasts with both the belief of Eleazar that neither living nor dead could he escape the hand of God (6:26) and the prediction of the seventh brother that Antiochus would not escape the judgment of God (7:35).

■ **23-24** Antiochus III designated his eldest son, Antiochus, as co-regent and heir from 210/209 to 193/192 B.C.E. On this son's death, he designated his second son, Seleucus, as co-regent and heir from 189 to 187 B.C.E.[63] Antiochus III was already in Media on his famous expedition when he designated his son Antiochus as co-regent. The campaigns of Antiochus III were designed to reassert Seleucid authority in the eastern part of his empire. He brought Commagene and Armenia under direct Seleucid control; Parthia and Bactria recognized Seleucid suzerainty; he renewed friendship with Indians; and he

58 See also *Sib. Or.* 3:591; *3 Macc.* 5:9, 50; 6:17, 33; *4 Macc.* 4:11; 6:6.

59 *P. Columbia* 10 in William Linn Westermann and Elizabeth Sayre Hasenoehrl, eds., *Zenon Papyri: Business Papers of the Third Century B.C. Dealing with Palestine and Egypt* (2 vols.; New York: Columbia University Press, 1934–40) 1:46. See also the letter from Hierokles to Artemidoros in Grete Rosenberger, "Griechische Privatbriefe," in Karl Kalbfleisch, ed.,

Papyri Iandanae (6th fascicle; Leipzig: Teubner, 1934) no. 92, pp. 221–22.

60 See Ma, *Antiochus III*, 179–242.

61 Welles, *Royal Correspondence*, 374.

62 Ibid., no. 71, 3-4.

63 Parker and Dubberstein, *Babylonian Chronology*, 22; Bickerman, *Institutions*, 21–22.

exercised some control over the Persian Gulf.[64] After the defeat by the Romans and the peace treaty of Apamea in 188 B.C.E., Antiochus III was still in control of a large empire. The tribute imposed by the Romans of one thousand talents of silver a year for ten years had the king seeking quick sources of wealth, and so he attempted to plunder the temple of Bel in Elymais. He was killed there in 187 B.C.E. So Antiochus III died not during the first co-regency but during the second. The language of "the upper regions" (εἰς τοὺς ἄνω τόπους) is the same as that used by Polybius to describe Antiochus III's expedition (11.39.14).

"if something unexpected happened." Ptolemy VIII, writing in 155 B.C.E. about what should happen on his death, uses a similarly innocuous expression, "if something of what falls to humans should happen" (ἐὰν δέ τι συμβαίνηι τῶν κατ᾽ ἄνθρωπον).[65]

To install his co-regent, the king would normally present him to an assembly with a proclamation (ἀνά-δειξις).[66] Here, however, Antiochus's co-regent is installed by means of a letter in which the author twice uses the verb ἀναδείκνυμι ("proclaim"; vv. 23 and 25).

■ **25** Antiochus mentions foreign threats to the empire but not that a major threat to his appointment of his son would most probably come from Demetrius, the surviving son of his brother, Seleucus IV. The mention of foreign threats would be most inappropriate in the letter of a king to his subjects. The Seleucids from Antiochus III to Antiochus VIII faced such challenges.

"Often" (πολλάκις). Antiochus IV made only one expedition to the upper satrapies, to Mesopotamia and Iran, and so the statement here has been seen as a mistake. To avoid this error, Goldstein suggested that the adverb πολλάκις should be seen as qualifying the verbs in "entrust and commend," which would be in the epistolary imperfect, rather than the participle "travers-

ing." The participle would seem to reflect an action subsequent to the action of the main verbs.[67] However, the epistolary imperfect is very rare,[68] and the imperfects should be seen as reflecting customary action[69] and the adverb as qualifying the participle that immediately follows. While it may be historically incorrect, the sentence suggests that Antiochus V has been on the scene for quite some time and is now able to be co-regent. There is no mention of Lysias as guardian of the king.

Again, the language used, in this instance to describe the area to which Antiochus IV is going, "the upper satrapies" (εἰς τὰς ἐπάνω σατραπείας), is similar to that used by Polybius in describing the effects of Antiochus III's campaign where he brought "the upper satraps" (τοὺς ἄνω σατράπας) to accept his control (11.39.14).

The verb συνιστάω can mean "to commend, recommend, appoint."[70] Here, as the verb parallels the verb "to entrust," the translation seems to require less a connotation of command and more one of reciprocity.

That Antiochus is entrusting and commending his son "to the majority of you" (τοῖς πλείστοις ὑμῶν) rather than to all the recipients seems strange. The use of οἱ πλεῖστοι ("the majority") is similar to that in 6:31. Does the term in both cases refer to all the people?

There is no appended letter. See also 11:17, where an attached document is mentioned but not present.

■ **26-27** The letter closes with a reminder of the benefits that can accrue to a community if it remains subject to the king. Ma has shown convincingly the connection between the εὐεργεσία ("benefactions") of the king and the εὔνοια ("goodwill") of the people.[71]

In a letter of Seleucus II to Miletus, the king remembers the benefactions his ancestors and his father had bestowed on the city and follows in their tradition.[72] The use of the word προαίρεσις ("policy") is frequent in

64 Ma, *Antiochus III*, 63–65; Sherwin-White and Kuhrt, *From Samarkhand to Sardis*, 190–202.
65 *SEG* 9 (1944) no. 7, lines 11–12. See also what Herod says as he leaves to meet Augustus (Josephus *Ant.* 15.184).
66 Elias Bickerman, "Ἀνάδειξις," *Annuaire de l'Institut de Philologie et d'Histoire Orientales et Slaves de l'Université Libre de Bruxelles* 5 (1937) 117–24; idem, *Institutions*, 23.
67 Smyth, *Greek Grammar*, §1872.
68 Ibid., §1942b.
69 Ibid., §1893.
70 Jeanne Robert and Louis Robert, "Bulletin épigraphique," *REG* 59–60 (1946–47) 298–372, here 354.
71 Ma, *Antiochus III*, 182–94.
72 Welles, *Royal Correspondence*, no. 22.

royal letters,[73] where συμπεριφέρεω in the sense of "be accommodating/indulgent" is also found.[74]

These two verses, with their use of usual chancery language, do not reflect at all the experiences of the Jews at the hands of Antiochus IV.[75]

■ **28-29** The peaceful overture by Antiochus IV contrasts sharply with the closing description of the king. The author harks back to the capture of Jerusalem, during which many were slaughtered and the king dared to enter the temple (5:12-16), as well as to the martyrdoms (6:18–7:42). The same verb is used to describe how the king suffers (παθών) as is used for the suffering of Eleazar and the brothers (6:30, πάσχω; 7:18, 32, πάσχομεν). As Jason had died in a foreign land (5:9), so does the king. While Judas's time in the mountains (5:27) had prepared him to fight against the king, the king now dies in the mountains,[76] which he had thought he could weigh on a scale (9:8). The phrase for miserable death, οἴκτιστος μόρος, is found also in Dionysius of Halicarnassus (*Ant. rom.* 2.68.4; 6.7.2) and Chariton (6.7.13).[77] The phrase "ended his life" (κατέστρεψε τὸν βίον) is used by Plutarch in *Thes.* 19.8.

Philip may be mentioned in an inscription found at Babylon, but the identification is not certain.[78]

The use of the verb παρακομίζειν ("escorted") echoes its use in 9:8, 10, where Antiochus was said to have needed to be carried along. According to the Babylonian astronomical diaries, the body was carried through Babylon in the month Tebet, between 19 December 164 B.C.E. and 16 January 163 B.C.E.[79] The use of the middle voice suggests that Philip, as Antiochus's companion, acted willingly, and the imperfect tense implies continuous action. Goldstein, followed by Gera, suggested that the imperfect implied that Philip did not carry out his mission of bringing the king's body back

to Antioch.[80] Schwartz rightly notes that if that were the case, one would expect the author of 2 Maccabees to trumpet the lack of burial. Granius Licinianus certainly does when he asserts, "While his body was being carried back to Antioch, the animals suddenly took flight and his body was tossed into the river and disappeared. This was the penalty he paid for his flagrant sacrilege" (28.6). In fact, as Mittag has noted, one should be cautious about giving too much credence to the report of Antiochus IV putting Philip in charge of affairs and replacing Lysias.[81] Philip was a courtier who had been given the title of σύντροφος ("foster brother"), which placed him above a "Friend."[82] The author states that Philip crossed over to Ptolemy Philometor, that is, to Ptolemy VI, the son of Antiochus IV's sister. Because of the infighting between Ptolemy VI Philometor and his brother Ptolemy VIII Euergetes II, Ptolemy Philometor had to leave Egypt in October 164 and did not return until May 163, when the two brothers had resolved their differences for the time being.[83] The author thus does not discuss the intervening period between the death of Antiochus IV in November/December 164 and Philip's move to Egypt. It appears that he wanted to bring the narrative of Antiochus IV's death to a close and, in doing so, brings in events that belonged to the return of the king's body to Antioch.[84] The way the narrative ends leaves unanswered what happened to the body of Antiochus IV. Did it receive a proper burial, and, if not, what did happen to it? Should not one presume that Antiochus V and Lysias would have made sure that they met the body when it arrived in Antioch around March 163 after finishing the journey of 1,065 kilometers from Babylon to Antioch and gave it a fitting burial? The author seems to resist giving any final honors to Antiochus IV.

---

73   Ibid., p. 310.

74   Ibid., no. 44,16; p. 365.

75   Nicklas, "Der Historiker," 89.

76   T. Drew-Bear suggested one should translate "in the desert" ("Recherches épigraphiques et philologiques, I: Où mourut Antiochos IV?" *REA* 2 [1980] 155–57). However, this would be a rare meaning for ὄρος and does not take account of the plural. Schwartz notes that LXX Isa 14:19 has the king of Babylon die in the mountains.

77   Note also Homer *Od.* 11.412: ὡς θάνον οἰκτίστῳ θανάτῳ ("so I died a miserable death").

78   *OGIS* 253, 7. See Mørkholm, *Antiochus IV*, 100 n. 48, 105–6.

79   Gera and Horowitz, "Antiochus IV," 240–52.

80   Gera, *Judaea*, 256.

81   Mittag, *Antiochos IV. Epiphanes*, 328–31.

82   Bickerman, *Institutions*, 42–43.

83   Will, *Histoire politique*, 2:302–3.

84   It is interesting that Polybius too seems to allow the course of events to dictate his chronological arrangement. See Paul Pédech, *La méthode historique de Polybe* (Collection d'études anciennes 119; Paris: "Les Belles Lettres," 1964) 494–95.

It is interesting too that the author makes mention only of Antiochus V, not of Lysias. Antiochus V was a child (Polybius 31.2.6; 31.11.8–11) under the control of Lysias, his guardian. The author does not stress the youth of Antiochus V but rather that he succeeded as king. No mention is made in the letter of 9:19-27 that Antiochus V was a child or that he needed a guardian. Rather, the author has deliberately structured his narrative so that the reign of Antiochus IV ends and the reign of Antiochus V begins. In his desire to provide ease of memorization (2:25), he has simplified what actually happened. It is not until 11:1 that the reader learns that Antiochus V had a guardian. The author is following the scheme he proposed in the prologue: to talk about the wars against Antiochus IV and his son Eupator (2:21). This schematic presentation of events has led to some confusion, as it is so different from what one finds in 1 Maccabees. There, Antiochus IV appoints Philip as guardian of his son, Antiochus V Eupator, and hands over the royal insignia to him (1 Macc 6:14-15). This sets up a conflict between Lysias, who had the young Antiochus in his possession, and Philip that is resolved when Lysias's forces subdue Philip (1 Macc 6:55-63).[85] Lysias in this account is a usurper, which would suit the polemic of 1 Maccabees. An alternative narrative is given in 2 Maccabees, where Philip is not installed by Antiochus IV as guardian of his son, and the reader is told only that Philip left for Egypt because he was apprehensive of Antiochus, not Lysias. Habicht has suggested that since the account of Philip's capture and death in Josephus is followed immediately by an account of Onias IV leaving for Egypt, the author of the condensed narrative has confused the two stories, which were narrated in a source that both he and Josephus used. The recourse to a common but unknown source is always suspicious. Moreover, since the account in Josephus follows the usual treatment of a rebel—capture and then death—and there seems no particular reason why the author of the condensed

narrative should insert the reference to Philip's action, I think it likely that Philip did defect to the Ptolemaic side. In the episode in 2 Maccabees that corresponds to the account in 1 Maccabees of Philip's return to Antioch, there is ambiguity as to whether this Philip is the same as the Philip who escorted the body of Antiochus IV. The text simply states that Philip, who had been left in charge of state affairs, revolted (13:23). The phrase "left in charge of affairs" seems in the context to refer to a Philip whom Antiochus V and Lysias had left in charge of affairs in Antioch while they were on the campaign against Judea. No clear link is made between the earlier Philip and this Philip. Someone who read only 2 Maccabees would not connect them.

In v. 28, one finds the particle μὲν οὖν. It is always difficult to estimate the strength of the antithesis introduced by μέν. Sometimes it is emphatic and used alone, as in 7:14; sometimes it is found in a subordinate clause and therefore a corresponding δέ is not present, as in 4:11-12, 14; 10:22. Once it is followed by καί (5:11). However, in all cases there is some antithesis present.[86] Is it responded to by the δέ in v. 29? In v. 29, however, there is no contrast to the blasphemer but a development of what happened to his corpse.[87] I would argue that the emphatic position of the subject at the beginning of v. 28, ὁ μὲν οὖν ἀνδροφόνος καὶ βλάσφημος, suggests that the appropriate correspondent is found in 10:1, Μακκαβαῖος δὲ καὶ οἱ σὺν αὐτῷ. Here the μὲν οὖν rounds off the old topic, the death of Antiochus IV, while the δέ introduces the new topic, the role of Judas in restoring the temple. The striking contrast is between the dead body of Antiochus, the rebel against God, and the actions of Judas and his forces that revitalize the city and its traditions, a description that extends over three verses.

---

85 Josephus (Ant. 12.386) has Philip killed by Antiochus V.
86 Even in 11:5, the contrast between Beth-Zur and Jerusalem is expressed by ὄντι μέν . . . Ἱεροσολύμων δὲ ἀπέχοντι. In 12:18, the contrast lies between Timothy's having fled and his leaving behind a force: Τιμόθεον μέν . . . καταλελοιπότα δέ.
87 Goldstein (II Maccabees, 346) asserts without any justification that the author "must have been thinking of the contrast between the living wicked tyrant and his dead body."

197

General Commentary

The punishment and death of Antiochus IV are portrayed as the direct involvement of God. As noted in the comment on the second prefixed letter, there are many accounts of the death of Antiochus IV. Both the author of 1 Maccabees and the author of the condensed version have Antiochus die in response to events in Judea. In this account, the author has used the traditional pattern of the Divine Warrior to persuade his audience of the power of God and the foolishness of trying to attack him. Since his return from Egypt and his attack on Jerusalem, Antiochus has been consistently depicted as an opponent of God. He had dared to enter God's holy temple, and his polluted and profane hands had touched the holy vessels (5:15-16). He is frequently said to think himself capable of superhuman feats (5:21; 9:8); he is said to fight against God (7:19, 34). The people suffered greatly, but after they turned to God for help (7:37-38; 8:2-4) God became their ally and they conquered the king's representatives. But God kept for himself the task of defeating the king. Antiochus is not only defeated but even forced to confess his defeat. The prophetic utterance of the seventh brother as he is about to be executed (7:35-37) is thus fulfilled.

The author has used extravagant language not only in the description of Antiochus's sufferings but also in his portrayal of Antiochus's repentance. In his letter, Antiochus uses the form of a suppliant, and the opening greeting is packed with fulsome phrases. The author wishes to show the utter reversal that has happened to the king. Victor Parker suggests that this extravagance is meant to stress the king's continuing incomprehension of what he has done.[88] However, I would see it as underscoring the reduced status of the king, as suppliant to God's people.

---

88 Parker, "Letters," 392 n. 22. This reading hinges on Parker's understanding of "the citizens" in 9:19 as a reference to Antiochus's changing Jerusalem to a *polis* and so to the king's incomprehension and the author's use of dramatic irony. In his character analysis of Antiochus IV in this passage, Nicklas ("Der Historiker," 89) suggested that the language of vv. 26-27 portrays Antiochus IV as not understanding that he had committed any wrong against the Jews and so his "promises" do not evidence true repentance.

10

10:1-8

1/ As for Maccabeus and his companions, with the Lord leading them on they took back the temple and the city, 2/ but they demolished the altars fabricated by the foreigners in the agora as well as the sacred areas. 3/ They purified the temple and made another altar. Making stones red hot and catching a flame from them, they offered sacrifices and incense after a two-year hiatus, and they made lamps and the showbread. 4/ After doing this, flat on the ground they prayed to the Lord that they would no longer meet with such evils but, if ever at some time they would indeed sin, that they would be disciplined with mildness by himself and not be handed over to blasphemous and barbaric Gentiles. 5/ The purification of the temple occurred on the very same day as the one on which the Temple was defiled by foreigners, the twenty-fifth of the month Kislev. 6/ For eight days they observed tent living, as they recalled how, a little time before at the festival of Tents, they had been living like wild animals in the mountains and in the caves. 7/ Therefore, holding ivy-wreathed wands and harvest branches as well as palm fronds, they offered up hymns to him who succeeded in having his own place be purified. 8/ They decreed by a communal ordinance and vote for all the nation of the Jews to observe these days each year.

Commentary by Verse

■ **1-3** These three verses form one lengthy sentence in the Greek, where a μὲν . . . δὲ . . . δέ construction is followed by three coordinate clauses. One finds a similar lengthy sentence at 5:8-10, where an opening clause with four participial phrases is followed by three coordinate clauses. The author seems to want to convey the near simultaneity of the various actions. The sentence contrasts with the complex description of the events found in 1 Macc 4:42-53.

■ **1** Here is the only time that Judas Μακκαβαῖος ("Maccabeus") is used without the article. This usage led Diego Arenhoevel to suggest that the hand of a redac-

199

tor was in evidence.[1] However, such a conclusion needs to be supported by further criteria. As Smyth noted, appellatives may omit the article.[2] I suggest that, since the prolix treatment of the death of Antiochus IV has intervened since the last mention, in 8:16, of Maccabeus, the author decided to omit the article, particularly since it allowed him to highlight the epithet by placing it in the most prominent part of the sentence. The combination of "Maccabeus and his companions" [οἱ σὺν αὐτῷ] also echoes the use in 8:1 of Judas Maccabeus and his companions, so that this section of the narrative concludes the resurgence of the Jews that began in 8:1.

"took back the temple and the city." The language echoes that of the prologue at 2:22, where Judas is said to have recovered (ἀνακομίσασθαι) the temple and to have freed the city. The use of κομίζειν here is similar to that found in Aristophanes *Birds* 548–49: "Our life is not worth living unless we find a way to take back our former kingship [εἰ μὴ κομιούμεθα παντὶ τρόπῳ τὴν ἡμετέραν βασιλείαν]." The verb contrasts and resonates with the use of περικομίζειν and διακομίζειν ("escorted" and "crossed over") in 9:29.

■ 2 The Greek term for altar is different in vv. 2 and 3. The first term (v. 2), referring to altars made by foreigners, is βωμός, a word often used negatively in the Hebrew Bible, as, for example, in Exod 34:13 and Deut 7:5, but also positively, as in Num 3:10. The usage in 2 Macc 2:19 and 13:8 is positive. The second term, used for the Jewish altar, is θυσιαστήριον. For "temple," the Attic form νεώς is used. In 2 Maccabees, as in Polybius, one finds both the Attic νεώς and the Dorian ναός.[3] Most interesting is that both forms are used in the same sentence in 10:5.[4]

The building of altars and sacred areas is described in 1 Macc 1:47, 54. Only here and in 10:5 is ἀλλοφύλοι used for foreigners, although the author coins the abstract ἀλλοφυλισμός in 4:13 and 6:24. The term

ἀλλοφύλοι is used frequently in the LXX. Anne-Emmanuelle Veïsse has shown that the term is not often found elsewhere and that the meaning of "stranger" is attested only in the confrontation between Jews and non-Jews.[5] Here the author uses the biblical term to stress once again that confrontation.

■ 3 The author is concerned to show that the fire kindled is of natural origin, not from some previous profane fire. The expression "making the stones red hot" (πυρώσαντες λίθους) is unusual, as it does not say that they drew sparks from the stones. A similar use of the active form of πυρόω is found in the *Acts of Thomas* (140), where the enraged king gave orders "to make the [iron] plates red-hot [πλάκας πυρῶσαι] and to stand [Thomas] on them barefoot." The author seems concerned to show that the fire is somehow unusual. Elsewhere, where the active verb is used, the source of the fire is given: "Wherefore we need to sprinkle the stones with vinegar, then heat them by means of the timber at hand [τὰς πέτρας καταρράναντας εἶτα πυρώσαντες διὰ τῶν παρακειμένων ξύλων] to render the passage to the people without danger."[6] At the dedication of Solomon's temple, heavenly fire is said to have descended (2 Chr 7:1), and the second prefixed letter shows how the sun's power rekindled the naphtha (1:22). These passages are different ways for describing the nonhuman formation of the fire.

The length of the two-year hiatus contrasts with a three-year period in 1 Maccabees (1:54 and 4:52) and a period lasting three-and-a-half times in Dan 12:7. For the discrepancy in time reckoning, see the Introduction.

The combination of incense, lamps, and showbread is found in Exod 40:23-27.

■ 4 "Flat on the ground" is literally "falling on their stomach." The expression is unusual. It is found in the Amarna letters: "I fall at the feet of my lord, seven times and seven times, *here and now*, both on the stomach and on the back, at the feet of the king, my lord."[7] In the

1   Arenhoevel, *Theokratie*, 108.
2   Smyth, *Greek Grammar*, §1140.
3   Attic: 4:14; 6:2; 9:16; 10:5; 13:23; 14:33; Doric: 8:3; 10:5; 14:35; 15:18, 33.
4   Doran, *Temple Propaganda*, 27.
5   Anne-Emmanuelle Veïsse, "L'expression de l'altérité dans l'Égypte des Ptolémées: Allophulos, Xénos et Barbaros," *REG* 120 (2007) 50–63. Veïsse writes: "Non seulement il est peu fréquent, mais son sens

premier d''étranger' n'est attesté avec certitude que dans des contextes de confrontation entre Juifs et non-Juifs" (p. 51).
6   Anonyma Tactica Byzantina *De re strategica* ιη, TLG 3234.001.
7   William L. Moran, *The Amarna Letters* (Baltimore: John Hopkins University Press, 1992) EA 65, p. 136; see also EA 64, p. 135.
8   *ANET,* 21a.

Story of Si-Nuhe, Si-Nuhe says: "I put myself upon my belly; I touched the ground; I scattered it upon my hair."[8] As the Amarna letters show, the description is of an attitude of extreme prostration.

The language of the prayer echoes language used earlier, in the author's reflections and in the prologue. Περιπίπτειν ("to meet with") is used in 6:13, where it is a sign of God's benevolence for his people to meet their penalties immediately for their sins. The persecutions are depicted as God's discipline or "training" (πρὸς παιδείαν) for his people (6:12; see also 6:16; 7:33). In the prologue, God is said to have acted toward his people with all mildness or fairness (2:22: μετὰ πάσης ἐπιεικείας). At the beginning of Judas's insurgency, he and his followers had prayed that God remember the blasphemies committed against his name (8:4), and Antiochus IV is described at his death as a blasphemer (9:28). Later in the narrative, the enemies are frequently portrayed as blasphemers (10:34-36; 12:14; 15:24). In the prologue, the Greek enemies had been described as barbarians (2:21; see also the description in 4:25 of Menelaus as having the passions of an untamed beast).

■ **5** The author likes to show how sinners receive their just deserts, a subsection of which topos is the coincidence of events: Andronikos, for example, is killed at the very spot at which he had murdered the high priest Onias (4:38). Such coincidence was popular also among Greco-Roman historians. For example, Tacitus records how Augustus died on the anniversary of the day on which he had achieved supreme power (*Ann.* 1.9).[9] Such a coincidence shows that, behind a favorite phrase of the author, "occurred" (συνέβη literally, "it happened"),[10] lies not chance but divine plan.

"was defiled." Antiochus IV had used defiled hands against the temple vessels (5:16), and Judas and his com-

panions, at the beginning of the insurgency, had prayed that God would have mercy on the defiled temple (8:3).

■ **6-7** As the Jews had rejoiced at the repulse of Heliodorus (3:30), so they rejoice now at the purification of the temple. They are to rejoice just as the Lord commanded for the feast of Tents. The terms κλάδος ("wands"), ὡραῖος ("harvest"), and φοῖνιξ ("palm fronds") are all found in Lev 23:40 in the command to celebrate the feast of Tents.[11] Judith and her companions carry ivy-wreathed wands as they celebrate the salvation of Jerusalem (Jdt 15:12). Plutarch states that Jews carry such ivy-wreathed wands at the feast of Tabernacles/Booths/Tents and sees a similarity with the celebration for Dionysos (*Table Talk* 4.5, 671E).[12] As the feast was set up "so that your generations may know that I made the people of Israel dwell in tents when I brought them out of the land of Egypt" (Lev 23:43), the feast of Purification commemorates the time of the people's dwelling in the mountains. The reference is to 5:27. In 6:11 people had gone to caves to celebrate the Sabbath secretly, a condition to which both Josephus (*Ant.* 14.421–22; 15:346) and Strabo (61.2.20) refer.[13]

"offered up." The verb ἀναφέρω usually connotes sacrifice, although in Prov 8:6 it has the sense of "utter": "I will utter [ἀνοίσω] right things from my lips." This sense is found also in Alexandrian poets.[14] The verb was just used in 10:3 to refer to sacrifice, and so prayer is seen here as similar to sacrifice.

■ **8** The same formula, "they decreed by a communal ordinance" (ἐδογμάτισαν μετὰ κοινοῦ . . . ψηφίσματος), is used in 15:36, and so it is a structuring element for the book. The emphasis falls on the feast being for all Jews, as the temple is the central symbol for the nation.

9   See also Josephus *Bell.* 2.457. Isaiah M. Gafni has noted the motif in rabbinic literature ("Concepts of Periodization and Causality in Talmudic Literature," *JH* 10 [1996] 28–29).

10   The same Greek verb (συμβαίνω) occurs in 3:2; 4:30; 5:2, 18; 7:1; 9:2, 7; 12:34; 13:7, but the translation of the verb differs according to context.

11   On the symbolism of φοῖνιξ, see Stephen Fine, "On the Development of a Symbol: The Date Palm in Roman Palestine and the Jews," *JSP* 4 (1989) 105–18.

12   See Hayim Lapin, "Palm Fronds and Citrons: Notes on Two Letters from Bar Kosiba's Administration," *HUCA* 64 (1993) 111–35, esp. 116–18.

13   See also *OGIS* 424.3, an inscription condemning outlaws who live in an animal-like condition (θηριώδους καταστάσεω[ς]).

14   LSJ, s.v. ἀναφέρω, I.2.

General Commentary

The use of terms that resonate with the rest of the narrative argues that this section was composed by the author. The author has used a traditional literary pattern to shape his account of the actions of Antiochus IV. Since the beginning of his assault on Jerusalem, Antiochus has been portrayed as hubristic (5:17, 21; see also 9:7-8), as one who fights against God (7:19, 34). The pattern the author has employed is that of the Divine Warrior, in which a challenge is issued to a deity, the deity responds by defeating his opponent, and, frequently, the building of a temple provides the ending.[15] Here in 2 Maccabees 9, the author has enjoyed describing the downfall of Antiochus IV and the king's confession of defeat before he turned to the restoration and purification of the temple that he had defiled. A variation of this pattern is found in chap. 3, where the assault on the temple is repulsed and the attacker, Heliodorus, is forced to capitulate and confess the power of God. The author has chosen this traditional literary form to bring home forcefully to his audience the power of God. I do not see this section as out of place. It may not replicate the sequence of 1 Maccabees, but the author has composed a rhetorically persuasive narrative of the downfall of God's opponent.

It is also significant that the author highlights the prayer of Judas and his companions by specifying its content. In the corresponding section in 1 Macc 4:36-61, Judas and his companions are said to pray, but no details are given. For the author of 2 Maccabees, prayer is an important element of Jewish life.

---

15 See Cross, "Divine Warrior," 11–30; Miller, *Divine Warrior,* 155–65.

10

10:9/ So the events at the end of Antiochus called Epiphanes were after this manner. 10/ Now, however, we will set forth the events during the time of Antiochus Eupator, son of the ungodly one, briefly describing the main points of the wars.[a] 11/ Now, when he received the kingdom, he appointed a certain Lysias in charge of the government and Protarchos as governor of Coele-Syria and Phoenicia. 12/ For Ptolemy called Makron took the initiative, vis-à-vis the Jews, to strictly observe what was just because of the injustice that had been committed against them, and he tried to settle peacefully what concerned them. 13/ Because of this, he was denounced by the Friends to Eupator. He heard himself constantly labeled a traitor because, after having been entrusted with Cyprus by Philometor, he had abandoned it and withdrawn to Antiochus Epiphanes and, a noble, had not ennobled the office.[b] Poisoning himself, he left life behind.

14/ Once Gorgias became a commander of the region, he was maintaining mercenary soldiers and in every way was keeping up hostility toward the Jews. 15/ Together with him, the Idumeans also, as they were in control of advantageous strongholds, were harassing the Jews. Enrolling those who had fled from Jerusalem, they were undertaking to keep up hostility. 16/ The followers of Maccabeus, making entreaty and praying that God would be their ally, marched against the strongholds of the Idumeans. 17/ Assaulting them vigorously, they gained control of the places; they took vengeance on those fighting on the wall, and they slaughtered those attacking them, and they destroyed no fewer than twenty thousand. 18/ No fewer than nine thousand fled into two well-secured towers that had

a   I agree with Risberg ("Textkritische und exegetische Anmerkungen," 23–24) that κακά is unnecessary here.

b   Following Risberg ("Textkritische und exegetische Anmerkungen," 24) and Katz ("Text of 2 Maccabees," 15), I read the infinitive εὐγενίσαι rather than the participle εὐγενίσας. The infinitive is coordinated with the previous two infinitives, ἐκλιπεῖν . . . ἀναχωρῆσαι.

everything needed [to withstand] a siege. 19/ Maccabeus himself parted for regions that urgently needed him but left behind Simon and Joseph as well as Zacchaeus and his companions, enough to carry on the siege. 20/ Simon's companions, however, loved money and were bribed with silver by some of those in the towers. On receiving twenty thousand drachmas, they allowed some to slip away. 21/ When what had happened was announced to Maccabeus, he gathered together the leaders of the people and denounced how, for money, they had sold their kinsmen in loosing their enemies against them. 22/ So he put to death those who had become traitors and straightaway he seized the two towers. 23/ Altogether successful in the sphere of arms, he destroyed in the two strongholds more than twenty thousand.

24/ Timothy, earlier defeated by the Jews, gathered a vast number of mercenary forces and assembled quite a few horses from Asia. He was there to take Judea at spear point. 25/ As he drew near, the forces around Maccabeus, in order to supplicate God, strewed dust on their heads and girded their loins with sackcloth. 26/ They prostrated themselves on the foundation before the altar and prayed that he would be merciful to them and be an enemy to their enemies and be opposed to their opponents, as the law clearly states. 27/ On finishing their entreaty, they took up arms and advanced farther from the city and were drawing near to the enemy by themselves. 28/ Just as sunrise overspread, both attacked: one side had their refuge in the Lord as guarantee of success and victory with valor, the other assigned passion as a guide in contests. 29/ As the strongly contested battle was taking place, from heaven there appeared to the

opponents five magnificent
warriors on horses with gold-
studded bridles, and they were
leading the Jews. 30/ Two[c] took
Maccabeus between them and
were protecting him with their
armor, keeping him unharmed,
while they were discharg-
ing arrows and thunderbolts
against the opponents. Therefore, [the opponents], thrown
into confusion by blindness and
completely disordered, scattered. 31/ Two thousand five
hundred infantry and six hundred cavalry were slaughtered.

32/ Timothy himself took refuge in
a stronghold called Gezer, well
fortified and with Chaereas
in command there. 33/ The
forces of Maccabeus, upbeat,
besieged the citadel for four
days. 34/ Those inside, trusting
in the security of the position,
were being especially blasphemous and spouting unlawful
phrases. 35/ As the fifth day
broke, twenty young men from
the Maccabean forces, inflamed
by passion because of the
blasphemies, attacked the wall
courageously and were smiting
anyone attacking them with
ferocious anger. 36/ During the
distraction, others likewise
were going up against those
inside; they were setting the
towers on fire and, kindling
funeral pyres, were burning the
blasphemers alive, and were
breaking through the gates.
They admitted the rest of the
soldiers, and occupied the city.
37/ They slaughtered Timothy,
who had hidden himself in a
cistern, as well as Chaereas
his brother and Apollophanes.
38/ Having accomplished this,
with hymns and confessions
they were praising the Lord,
who had been a benefactor
to Israel and given them the
victory.

c With Hanhart (*Zum Text*, 450) and Habicht, I have retained οἱ δύο. It is hard to see how five riders could keep Judas between them, although Grimm suggested one in front and two on either side. Grimm's concern as to whether all five or only the two were the subject of the verb ἐξερρίπτουν is answered if one accepts Habicht's suggestion that through haplography the genitive plural relative pronoun has disappeared and that the text should read τῶν Ἰουδαίων ὧν οἱ δύο.

Commentary by Verse

■ **9-10** The same $\mu\acute{\epsilon}\nu \ldots \delta\acute{\epsilon}$ is used to signal a change in topic in 3:40–4:1. In the prologue, the author had noted how Jason of Cyrene had set forth (2:23: $\delta\eta\lambda\acute{o}\omega$) the wars against Antiochus Epiphanes and his son Eupator (2:20).

I have translated $\tau\epsilon\lambda\epsilon\upsilon\tau\acute{\eta}$ by "end" rather than "death." Elsewhere in 2 Maccabees, the verb $\tau\epsilon\lambda\epsilon\upsilon\tau\acute{\alpha}\omega$ has the meaning of "to die" (6:30; 7:5, 14, 41). However, $\tau\epsilon\lambda\epsilon\upsilon\tau\acute{\eta}$ is found at the close of the book (15:39), where it has the meaning of "end of the narrative." The use of the term here thus appears to contain both nuances: Antiochus has died and the events of which he was the cause have ended. When one insists on the meaning of "death," the temptation is to assert that the verses 10:1-8 have been misplaced and that 10:9 should immediately follow 9:28-29. However, awareness of the nuance of "end" may make one less pressured to say that 10:1-8 has been misplaced. In this meaning, the purification of the temple is the proper end to the theomachy begun by Antiochus IV.

Eupator etymologically means "born of a noble father." Irony occurs in that Antiochus his father is described as ungodly and blasphemous.

As Grimm suggests, $\alpha\dot{\upsilon}\tau\acute{\alpha}$ should be seen as referring back to $\tau\grave{\alpha}\ \kappa\alpha\tau\grave{\alpha}\ \tau\grave{o}\nu\ E\dot{\upsilon}\pi\acute{\alpha}\tau o\rho\alpha$ ("the events during the time of Eupator").

"briefly describing." The sense of $\sigma\upsilon\nu\tau\acute{\epsilon}\mu\nu\omega$ as "speaking briefly" is found in Aristophanes *Thes.* 178 and Plato *Prot.* 334D. The sense of providing briefly the main points is found in the phrase $\tau\grave{\alpha}\ \dot{\epsilon}\nu\ \mu\acute{\epsilon}\sigma\omega\ \kappa\epsilon\phi\acute{\alpha}\lambda\alpha\iota\alpha\ \sigma\upsilon\nu\tau\epsilon\mu\nu\acute{\omega}\nu$ ("describing briefly the uncertain main topics").[1] Polybius (18.44.2) also uses the plural neuter participle $\tau\grave{\alpha}\ \sigma\upsilon\nu\acute{\epsilon}\chi o\nu\tau\alpha$ to mean "the main points" ($\ddot{\eta}\nu\ \delta\grave{\epsilon}\ \tau\grave{\alpha}\ \sigma\upsilon\nu\acute{\epsilon}\chi o\nu\tau\alpha\ \tau o\hat{\upsilon}\ \delta\acute{o}\gamma\mu\alpha\tau o\varsigma\ \tau\alpha\hat{\upsilon}\tau\alpha$).[2]

■ **11** The particle $\gamma\acute{\alpha}\rho$ here has a prefatory force.[3]

The use of $\pi\alpha\rho\alpha\lambda\alpha\mu\beta\acute{\alpha}\nu\omega$ in the sense of receiving office is found frequently.[4] The phrase $\pi\alpha\rho\alpha\lambda\alpha\mu\beta\acute{\alpha}\nu\epsilon\iota\nu\ \tau\grave{\eta}\nu\ \beta\alpha\sigma\iota\lambda\epsilon\acute{\iota}\alpha\nu$ ("receiving the kingdom") is found elsewhere (see Herodotus 2.120).[5] The author here refers back to 9:25, where Antiochus IV at the end of his life is said to have appointed his son as king. According to 1 Macc 3:32-33, Antiochus IV, on leaving for the eastern provinces, had left Lysias in charge of the government and as guardian of his son. It was probably at this time that he appointed his son as co-regent.[6] Most likely, coins were struck for Antiochus V in Ptolemais, while Antiochus IV was on his eastern expedition.[7] As noted in the Introduction, the author of the condensed version wished to present an easily memorable account (2:25). He therefore kept in one narrative all the events in which Antiochus IV was a major figure and then, in a separate narrative, all the events during the reign, even as co-regent, of Antiochus V. The use of the general verb $\pi\alpha\rho\alpha\lambda\alpha\mu\beta\acute{\alpha}\nu\omega$ thus helps to maintain the ambiguity in the author's construction of events.

At this time Antiochus V was only nine years old, but the author portrays him as appointing Lysias, using the same verb as he had used when stating that Antiochus IV appointed Antiochus V his co-regent (9:25) and that Antiochus III had appointed a successor (9:23). In 1 Macc 6:17, Lysias, on the news of Antiochus IV's death, is said to have appointed Antiochus V to reign in his father's place and to have named him Eupator.

As Habicht argues, $\pi\rho\acute{\omega}\tau\alpha\rho\chi o\nu$ is to be taken as a proper name. His reasons are that (1) if it were an office,

---

1   Emil Seckel and Wilhelm Schubart, *Ägyptische Urkunden aus der staatlichen Museen zu Berlin*, vol. 5: *Der Gnomon des Idios Logos* (Berlin: Weidmann, 1919) Prooemium 5. For the translation, see Woldemar Graf Uxkull-Gyllenband, *Der Gnomon des Idios Logos*, Zweiter Teil: *Der Kommentar* (Berlin: Weidmann, 1934) 9–10.

2   Goldstein also notes the phrase in Philodemus, who speaks of searching out the gods properly, being delivered of difficult evils, and acquiring the most important goods ($\tau\grave{\alpha}\ \sigma\upsilon\nu\acute{\epsilon}\chi o\nu\tau\alpha\ \dot{\alpha}\gamma\alpha\vartheta\acute{\alpha}$). See Hermann Diels, *Philodemos über die Götter: Erstes Buch* (Berlin: Georg Reimer, 1916) 25.27-28 (p. 44).

3   Smyth, *Greek Grammar*, §2808.

4   Thucydides 1.9; in Polybius 1.8.4; 3.70.7, one has the phrase $\pi\alpha\rho\alpha\lambda\alpha\mu\beta\acute{\alpha}\nu\epsilon\iota\nu\ \tau\grave{\eta}\ \dot{\alpha}\rho\chi\acute{\eta}\nu$. The verb is used in Aristotle *Pol.* 1285b to describe those who receive kingship by lineal descent: "the kings used to come to the throne with the consent of the subjects and hand it on to their successors [$\tau o\hat{\iota}\varsigma\ \pi\alpha\rho\alpha\lambda\alpha\mu\beta\acute{\alpha}\nu o\upsilon\sigma\iota$] by lineal descent."

5   *OGIS* 56.6; 90.1, 47.

6   Mittag, *Antiochos IV. Epiphanes*, 328.

7   Arthur Houghton and Georges Le Rider, "Le deuxième fils d'Antiochos IV à Ptolémaïs," *SNR* 64 (1985) 73–89.

the form should be πρωτάρχοντα; (2) the particle δέ suggests not an appositive to the role of Lysias but something new; (3) the role of chancellor in charge of the government is always distinguished from that of governor of Coele-Syria and Phoenicia.[8] Nothing more is known about this Protarchos who succeeded Ptolemy.

■ **12-38** The events in these verses are seen as occurring before the invasion of Lysias. As discussed in the Introduction, the order and timing of the events that followed the introduction of the new political order in Jerusalem are strongly debated. Here it is important to see how the author has structured the events and to what end.

■ **12-13** The author begins his account of the reign of Antiochus V in an ominous way. He tells of how a governor of Coele-Syria and Phoenicia who had been friendly to the Judean position, Ptolemy Makron, was slandered into committing suicide. Here surfaces the theme found throughout the narrative that hostility between the Jews and their Seleucid overlords was not inherent. There can be good relations between the Judean community and the larger non-Judean community. Ptolemy Makron had succeeded Ptolemy, son of Dorymenes, as governor, most likely after the defeat of Nikanor (4:44-46; 8:8; 1 Macc 3:38-40; 4:12-15). I posited in the Introduction that, before he left for his eastern campaign in spring 165 B.C.E., Antiochus IV, at the instigation of Menelaus, had changed his policy toward Judea (11:27-33). This would have led to a change in governor from one more hostile to the Jews, Ptolemy son of Dorymenes, to one more open to their position. The attack of Nikanor was unjust (8:16: ἀδίκως), and so Ptolemy Makron attempted to remedy it. Ptolemy had been loyal to Ptolemy VI Philometor in 170 B.C.E. (Polybius 27.13),[9] but, as Antiochus IV's forces are said to have arrived in Cyprus before the second invasion of Egypt in 168 B.C.E. (Livy 45.11.9–11; 45.12.7; Polybius 29.27.9–10),[10] Ptolemy Makron had left Ptolemy VI Philometor's service.

"to settle peacefully." A similar use of διεξάγω is found in Polybius 18.51.10, where Antiochus III stated that he would settle everything toward Ptolemy in a manner agreeable to the king (τὰ δὲ πρὸς Πτολεμαῖον . . . διεξάξειν εὐδοκουμένως ἐκείνῳ).

"Labeled a traitor" is literally "traitor."

"Friends." This term refers to that special group around the king. It would seem that this group pursued a more hard-line approach toward the situation in Judea. Its members did not wish to follow more diplomatic means but wished to avenge the defeat of their colleague Nikanor (8:9).

"left life behind." This phrase is used by Polybius (e.g., 31.9.3) and Lucian (e.g., *Macr.* 19). Note the paronomasia between εὐγενῆ and εὐγενίσαι.

■ **14** Gorgias had been mentioned before as a commander of much military experience (8:9), but his role in the incursion of Nikanor was not described. First Maccabees, by contrast, had given Gorgias quite a substantial role in that attack (1 Macc 4:1-22). The author of the condensed narrative likes to focus on a one-on-one confrontation in order to heighten interest. The use of the imperfect tense suggests that Gorgias kept up constant harassment of the Jews. Note the homoioteleuton between ἐξενοτρόφει ("maintaining mercenary soldiers") and ἐπολεμοτρόφει ("keeping up hostility").

Second Maccabees consistently associates Gorgias with the Idumeans, locating him at Marisa (12:32-34), whereas in 1 Macc 5:59 Gorgias is in Jamnia. Both cities are in the coastal plain, and the use of the plural στρατηγὸς τῶν τόπων (literally "commander of the places") to describe Gorgias's position might suggest that Gorgias had a wide-reaching command.

■ **15-23** While the author of 1 Maccabees describes the battle against the Idumeans in one verse (5:3), the author of the condensed version spends nine verses in describing the conflict (2 Macc 10:15-23). The author likes to hone in on and elaborate a particular example to move his audience more effectively emotionally.

■ **15** The imperfect tense gives the sense of constant hostility. Those who fled from Jerusalem must be the followers of Menelaus, as 1 Macc 4:41 notes that the citadel (ἄκρα) in Jerusalem was still garrisoned at the

8 Protarchos as a personal name is attested in *OGIS* 139, 29; *CPJ* 2, no. 149, line 1.
9 See also *OGIS* 117.
10 On the career of Ptolemy Makron, see Terence B. Mitford, "Ptolemy Macron," in *Studi in onore di Aristide Calderini e Roberto Paribeni* (3 vols.; Milan: Ceschina, 1957) 1:163–87; and W. Peremans and E. Van't Dack, "A propos d'une inscription de Gortyn (Inscr. Gret. IV 208)/ Ptolémée Makron, Nouménios et Hippatos," *Historia* 3 (1955) 338–45.

purification of the temple. The author links the actions of Gorgias in v.14 with those of the Idumeans, using the same verb for both, πολεμοτροφεῖν ("keep up hostility"). Throughout this campaign and the next, as well as in the description of the first expedition of Lysias, the author uses the term ὀχύρωμα ("strongholds") (10:15, 16, 23, 32; 11:6).[11] Its use ties together these accounts. Precisely which strongholds are intended is not clear, but presumably they would lie in the direction of Hebron and Beth-Zur. The use of the verb γυμνάζειν in the sense of "harass" recalls both the gymnasium that Jason had established (4:9) and the idea that God troubled his people for their instruction (6:12: πρὸς παιδείαν).

■ 16 The emphasis on the piety of Judas's forces continues. The same combination of the middle form of ποιέσθαι + λιτανείαν ("making entreaty") is used as in 3:20, when the whole population of Jerusalem entreated God to stop the movement of Heliodorus into the temple. God is often called the ally (8:24; 11:10; 12:36; see also 11:13).

■ 17-18 The adverb εὐρώστως ("vigorously") is found also in 12:27, 35. The Jews take control (ἐγκρατεῖς) of what the Idumeans had controlled (10:15: ἐγκρατεῖς). As happens frequently in 2 Maccabees, the numbers are exaggerated to heighten the sense of victory. It is extremely difficult to uncover the precise events of the battle. First of all, the author speaks of "strongholds," all of which are taken. However, in v. 18 the author speaks of the defenders taking refuge in two towers. Is their taking refuge in response to the attack on one of the strongholds, or on many strongholds? That nine thousand defenders could have taken refuge in two towers seems unlikely. The author intends, it seems, to give the impression of quick and effective action. The adverb εὖ μάλα ("well") is found also in 8:30 and 10:32. The difficulty of the siege for Judas's forces is shown by the fact that the towers have everything necessary to maintain a long siege.

■ 19-22 No reason is given for Judas's departure. "Regions that urgently needed him" is literally "to urging regions." The two men left in charge are two of his brothers, identified in 8:23. The tendency of 2 Maccabees is

to exalt the figure of Judas, not the whole family as in 1 Maccabees. Another of Simon's problems is mentioned in 14:17, where Simon is said to stumble briefly at the sudden appearance of the enemy. Zacchaeus is otherwise not known. Abel suggests that he be identified with Zacharias, father of Joseph, mentioned in 1 Macc 5:18, 56, inasmuch as Ζακχαῖος is an abbreviation of Ζαχαρίος. However, the two situations are different, and there is no need to identify every person in 2 Maccabees with one in 1 Maccabees.

"to slip away." The verb is found in Polybius (2.122.11; 15.28.4). The author again uses paronomasia to emphasize the dastardly nature of the crime: φιλαργυρήσαντες . . . ἀργυρίῳ ("lovers of money . . . silver/money"). Seventy thousand drachmas—where six thousand drachmas = one talent—is a large amount of money.

This section of the narrative began with a false denunciation (κατηγορέω) of Ptolemy Makron as a traitor (10:13: προδότης). In this subsequent military action of Judas, a real act of betrayal occurs (10:22: προδότας), which he denounces (10:21: κατηγορέω). His response is harsh. There is to be no compromise with the enemy and no mercy shown them for their attacks. The language used here, πεπράκασι τοὺς ἀδελφούς ("sold their kinsmen"), is very powerful. Schwartz suggests that the term ἀδελφούς here has the meaning of "brethren-in-arms," citing its use in the Bar-Kokhba revolt.[12] However, such a restricted meaning downplays the connotative force of the term. Earlier in the condensed narrative, Jews had been sold into slavery at Antiochus's attack on Jerusalem (5:14) and at the later attack by Apollonius (5:24). Nikanor had intended to sell the Jews into slavery (8:10, 14). The followers of Simon are thus portrayed as comparable to the enemy. In a world where slavery was present, selling one's kin was particularly shameful and an act that the Mosaic laws hedged with many restrictions (Exod 21:2-11; Deut 15:12-17). Nehemiah had reproached the leaders of the people for selling their kin (Neh 5:8). Judas, by the execution of those who had committed this act, uses the threat of terror to instill in his followers the need to separate themselves from their enemies. This insistence on total destruction of the enemy is similar

---

11 In 8:30, I have translated the phrase ὀχυρωμάτων ὑψηλῶν as "fortified heights."

12 Schwartz refers to the work of Baruch Lifshitz, "The

Greek Documents from Nahal Seelim and Nahal Mishmar," *IEJ* 11 (1961) 60–61.

to the story of King Ahab and the Arameans in 1 Kgs 20:26-43. A prophet announced to Ahab that the Lord had given the Arameans into his hand, but Ahab allowed Ben-hadad, the king of Aram, to survive and made a treaty with him. Another prophet appeared and declared to Ahab, "because you have let the man go whom I had devoted to destruction, therefore your life shall be for his life, and your people for his people."[13] While the technical term ḥērem ("devoted to destruction") is not found at 2 Macc 10:22, the same sense of separation from the enemy is present.

Another act of betrayal is found in 13:21. The use of amulets by some soldiers (12:40) is also a betrayal of Jewish law. The author does not paint all the Judean insurgents as motivated by complete adherence to the highest motives.

■ **23** Just as Joseph was successful because the Lord was with him (Gen 39:3: ὅσα ἐὰν ποιῇ κύριος εὐοδοῖ ἐν ταῖς χερσὶν αὐτοῦ), so too Judas is successful in all he undertakes. God had previously been called the one who succeeded) in 10:7 (τῷ εὐοδώσαντι). Often this verse is seen as the conclusion of the siege of the two towers, on the assumption that πύργος ("tower") is the same as ὀχύρωμα ("stronghold"), perhaps on the basis of 10:18: εἰς δύο πύργους ὀχυρούς ("into two well-secured towers"). However, I suggest that this verse sums up the result of Judas's campaign against the Idumeans, during which two Idumean strongholds were destroyed. In 10:17, no fewer than twenty thousand were destroyed; here more than twenty thousand are destroyed. The author seems to have matched up the exaggerated figures.

■ **24-38** The second episode recounted involves Timothy. See the Introduction (p. 10) on the relationship of this Timothy to others named Timothy in 2 Maccabees. The dire urgency of the situation is underlined by describing Timothy's intention to take Judea at spear point (10:24). Antiochus had done so (5:11), and then desecrated the temple (5:15-16) and changed the constitution and the laws (6:1-2). To underline the threat to the temple, the author has Judas's forces praying before the altar and citing the Mosaic law (10:26). It is also shown by the striking epiphany. God is always described as the ally and

helper of the Jews, but here in 10:29-30 and in 11:8 there are visible manifestations, just as in 3:24-28. The author wishes to show how now that the temple has been purified, God directly defends it against further attacks.

The battles with the Idumeans had been on the southern frontiers of Judea. Verses 24-38 describe an invasion of Timothy, and the reference to Gezer (10:32) points to an invasion from the north.

■ **24** This Timothy was mentioned in 8:30 along with a Bacchides. He is said to have a tribal chief under him (8:32). That cryptic mention has been shown to have been placed there for rhetorical purposes. News of the defeat of Timothy is said to have been one of the causes of Antiochus IV's decision to return and make Jerusalem a burial ground (9:3-4).

Here Timothy's forces are described as formidable, and the mention of Asian horses helps build that effect. As Bar-Kochva has stated, "The best war horses of the period were imported from Media, or at least were of Median stock, and all the author wants to say is that Timotheus had at his disposal real war horses."[14] Grimm and Bunge suggested that the term ἵππους meant "cavalry."[15] In 2 Maccabees, the plural ἵπποι means "horses" in 5:3 and 10:29. The singular ἵππος, as often in Greek, is used for cavalry in 11:2 and 15:20, but the more usual term for cavalry in 2 Maccabees is ἱππεῖς.[16] These Asian horses were used by the cavalry, and the author is showing how well equipped Timothy's forces were.

"spear-point." Antiochus IV had taken the city at spear point in 5:11, but here not only the city but the whole of Judea is to be considered captive territory, with which the king could do as he wanted.

■ **25-26** The piety of Judas's forces is stressed in this long sentence, where three participial phrases, καταπάσαντες, ζώσαντες, προσπεσόντες ("strewed," "girded," "prostrated") precede the verb ἀξιόω ("to pray"). The first two actions are parallel to each other while the third, joined asyndetically to the second participial phrase, is linked to the verb ἠξίουν ("they prayed"). The asyndeton underscores the interconnectedness of the ritual actions. I have given the preposition πρός in the phrase πρὸς ἱκετείαν τοῦ θεοῦ the sense

13 See also Saul's allowing Agag of the Amalekites to live, along with the choicest of his flocks, and the denouncement by Samuel in 1 Samuel 15.
14 Bar-Kochva, *Judas Maccabaeus*, 514.
15 Grimm, *Das zweite, dritte and vierte Buch*, 162; Bunge, *Untersuchungen*, 283.
16 2 Maccabees 5:2; 10:31; 11:4, 11; 12:10, 20, 33, 35; 13:2.

of purpose, literally "with a view to the supplication of God." This phrase determines the following actions of supplication. Throwing dust on one's head and girding oneself with sackcloth are ritual actions of mourning and grief.[17] A fascinating example is found in 1 Kgs 20:31 (LXX 3 Kgdms 21:31), when Ben-hadad of Aram has been defeated. His servants say to him: "Look, we have heard that the kings of the house of Israel are merciful kings; let us put sackcloth around our waists and ropes on our heads, and go out to the king of Israel; perhaps he will spare your life." Maccabeus's forces prostrate themselves in the area before the altar. Joel 2:17 orders the priests to weep between the portico and the altar (בֵּין הָאוּלָם וְלַמִּזְבֵּחַ), which the LXX translates as ἀνὰ μέσον τῆς κρηπῖδος τοῦ θυσιαστηρίου ("in the midst of the foundation of the altar"). Sophocles *Trach.* 989 speaks of the foundation of the altars (κρηπὶς βωμῶν). The emphasis is that Maccabeus's men do not touch the altar.[18] They pray for the Lord's mercy using a phrase found earlier in 2 Maccabees, ἵλεως αὐτοῖς γενόμενον ("that he would be merciful to them"; see 2:22; 7:37).

The Jews' piety is shown by following the law. The reference is to Exod 23:22, where the paronomasia is present. One might note that in the next verse, Exod 23:23, God sends his angel before the Israelites and promises to blot out their enemies.

■ **27** The distance is not specified, but the implication is that Maccabeus and his forces leave the city to go out to confront Timothy, who is marching toward the city. The phrase "by themselves" (ἐφ' ἑαυτῶν) means that they kept apart from the enemy. The asyndeton between the two participles γενόμενοι ... ἀναλαβόντες ("finishing . . . taking up arms") links the two actions. The repetition of the verb συνεγγίζειν ("to draw near") now has Judas and his forces on the offensive against the approaching Timothy, who was described in 10:25 as drawing near.

■ **28** As often before a battle, the author contrasts, using a μέν ... δέ construction, the opposing sides (8:18; 15:6-

7, 25-26). As in 15:21, victory is not through weapons but through refuge in the Lord. The term for refuge, καταφυγή, is found frequently in the Psalms.[19] The term for guarantee, ἔγγυος, is infrequent in the LXX, where proverbial wisdom warns against giving guarantees (Prov 6:1-5; 17:18; LXX 19:28; 22:26; Sir 8:13). However, Sirach advises that "a good person will be surety for his neighbor" and that one should not forget the kindness of one's guarantor (Sir 29:14-15). In Heb 7:22, Jesus is said to have become the guarantee of a better covenant.

The Attic double consonant ττ is found here in the participle ταττόμενοι ("assigned"). The word I have translated "passion," θυμός, has a wide range of meanings, including "courage" and "anger." In 7:21, the mother of the seven sons has a woman's reasoning reinforced by a male courage (ἄρσενι θυμῷ). Elsewhere in 2 Maccabees θυμός has the sense of passion and emotion, whether used of opponents or of the forces of Maccabeus (4:25, 37; 9:4, 7; 10:35; 13:4; 14:45; 15:10). The contrast here would suggest the less complimentary meaning of "passion."

■ **29-31** Here occurs the first full-blown description of an epiphany since 3:24-26. Five heavenly figures lead the Jews. The horses have golden bridles, usually a sign of divinity, although Herodotus reports that a Persian officer rode a horse with a golden bridle (9.20, 22). Just as in 3:26 the apparel of the figures was magnificent, so here too the warriors are magnificent. The number of angelic helpers, five, is unusual. Grimm tentatively suggested that this number might reflect the number of the Maccabean brothers, while Louis Ginzberg proposed Abraham, Isaac, Jacob, Moses, and Aaron.[20] In the *Iliad*, the gods often defend their heroes as, for example, when Apollo defends Aineias from Diomedes (5.436-37).[21] Note that Maccabeus is unharmed (ἄτρωτος) and Nikanor had said the Jews were invulnerable (8:36: ἀτρώτους).

The use of the term κεραυνός ("thunderbolt") is noteworthy. It is rare in the LXX, found only in Job 38:35,

---

17 See, e.g., Jer 6:26; Esth 4:1-3; Mic 1:10; also *As. Mos.* 3:4.

18 There is no need to follow Abel and change the text to ἀπέναντι τῆς κρηπῖδος τοῦ θυσιαστηρίου, which requires a significant reordering of the text.

19 Psalms 9:9; 18:2; 31:3; 32:7; 46:1; 59:16; 71:3; 90:1; 91:2, 9; 94:22; 144:2.

20 Louis Ginzberg, *Legends of the Jews* (trans. Henrietta Szold; 7 vols.; Philadelphia: Jewish Publication Society, 1925) 6:251.

21 See Chaniotis, *War*, 143-65. J. T. Milik drew attention to the numerous inscriptions to angels who were believed to have brought about the construction of all the sanctuaries of the region: "Par opposi-

where the natural phenomenon of lightning is attributed to God, and in Wis 19:13, where God sends lightning as a warning sign to the Egyptians to let his people go. In the many storm epiphanies of God in the Hebrew Bible, $\kappa\epsilon\rho\alpha\upsilon\nu\acute{o}\varsigma$ is not used. At Sinai, God thunders and peals but does not send thunderbolts, although Josephus does use the term in his telling of the event (*Ant.* 3.80). Lightning is described as God's arrows in Ps 18:14 (LXX 17:14): "And he sent out his arrows [$\beta\acute{\epsilon}\lambda\eta$] and scattered them, and he flashed forth lightnings [$\grave{\alpha}\sigma\tau\rho\alpha\pi\acute{\alpha}\varsigma$] and routed them." Rather, Zeus, who is called Zeus Keraunos, hurls thunderbolts at his enemies (Homer *Od.* 23.330; Hesiod *Theog.* 854). The gods defending Delphi also hurl thunderbolts at the Persian invaders (Herodotus 8.37; see also Pausanias 10.23.3). The author is influenced by Greek epiphanic descriptions.

"Blindness" ($\grave{\alpha}o\rho\alpha\sigma\acute{\iota}\alpha$) is the punishment sent against those attacking Lot (Gen 19:11; Wis 19:17) and against the Syrian army when it sought Elisha (2 Sam 6:18). It is threatened against those who do not obey the Lord's commandments (Deut 28:28). The adjective $\grave{\alpha}\acute{o}\rho\alpha\tau o\varsigma$ ("invisible") is used in 9:5 to describe the punishment sent on Antiochus IV.

"Completely disordered" is literally "full of disorder."

■ **32-38** Just as the author had highlighted how Nikanor had been forced to flee in disgrace after his defeat (8:34-36), so too he emphasizes the flight of Timothy and his death. As the battle against the Idumeans had ended in a flight to two towers, which Maccabeus had then besieged (10:18-23), so also this battle ends in a siege. On the number of Timothys, see the Introduction, p. 10.

■ **32** $\Gamma\alpha\zeta\alpha\rho\alpha$ is the name for Gezer, which lies northwest of Jerusalem. If one identifies this battle against Timothy with that found in 1 Macc 5:6-8, then the name is changed to $\Breve{I}\alpha\zeta\eta\rho$ (Jazer), a town east of the Jordan. The author of the condensed version, however, holds that Judas's forces left Jerusalem to go out to battle, and that Timothy is advancing on Judea.

Chaereas is later revealed to be the brother of Timothy (10:37).

■ **33** Some manuscripts read twenty-four days for the siege, some even forty. However, such a time frame would have required quite a sustained siege operation, and the author intends to emphasize the enthusiastic rashness of Judas's troops and their ability to overpower even a well-fortified stronghold. The precision of four days seems at odds with the tendency of the author to give rounded numbers. Abel suggests that the attack of the young men takes place on the fifth day, perhaps a resonance with the five angelic co-fighters of 10:29.

■ **34** In 10:4, the people had prayed that they not be handed over to blasphemous and barbarous Gentiles. Here the enemy is shown to be such, just as Antiochus IV had been (9:28). The term for "unlawful," $\grave{\alpha}\vartheta\acute{\epsilon}\mu\iota\tau o\varsigma$, is found in the LXX only in 2 Maccabees (6:5 and 7:1) and in *3 Macc.* 5:20.

■ **35-36** Attacks at dawn gave the element of surprise. Pritchett provides a table of dawn attacks and notes how Xenophon reasoned that dawn was "the hour when the night guards were retiring but before the general body had risen and gotten under arms."[22]

As Antiochus IV was rightly enraged at the way Andronikos had executed Onias (4:38), so here the young men are enraged. The same phrase ($\pi\epsilon\pi\upsilon\rho\omega$-$\mu\acute{\epsilon}\nu o\varsigma$ $\tau o\~\iota\varsigma$ $\vartheta\upsilon\mu o\~\iota\varsigma$) is used to describe the emotional state of Rhazis as he dies (14:45). The emotional response to the blasphemies causes such a distraction that the other Maccabean forces can attack almost unopposed. The concern to describe the tactics is unusual, as the author tends not to worry about the details of battles but seeks instead simply to convey that God helps the Jews win. Note how the imperfect tense is used to describe the action, while the aorist is used to say that the forces of Judas took the city.

"courageously" ($\grave{\alpha}\rho\rho\epsilon\nu\omega\delta\~\omega\varsigma$). The adverbial use is unusual, found only here. "ferocious" ($\vartheta\eta\rho\iota\acute{\omega}\delta\eta\varsigma$). The

---

tion à la vieille persuasion religieuse que le future titulaire d'un temple intervenait de façon ou d'autre, lors de l'érection de l'édifice, ici, dans la campagne de Tyr au IIIᵉ siècle avant notre ère, les simples propriétaires agricoles attribuent un rôle analogue non pas au dieu lui-même, mais à son hypostase personnel, à son Ange. . . . On priait l'Ange, on lui promettait des offrandes et on réalisait ces

promesses" (*Recherches d'epigraphie proche-orientale*, vol. 1: *Dédicaces faites par des dieux (Palmyre, Hatra, Tyr) et des thiases sémitiques à l'époque romaine* [Paris: Paul Geuthner, 1972] 427).

22   Pritchett, *Greek State at War*, 2:162; the reference is to Xenophon *Hell.* 7.1.16.

adverb is found in 12:15. It is another in the series of animal figures that the author likes to use. As Grimm noted, the combination of both terms to describe the actions of the Jews is interesting, as the root meaning of the first is "man," while the root meaning of the second is "beast."

"distraction" (περισπασμός). Here the word has a different meaning from that often found in tactical descriptions, "wheeling around" (Polybius 10.23.3; 12.18.3). Here, as Risberg showed, the meaning is "distraction."[23]

In 1 Macc 5:5, Judas's forces burn the towers of the sons of Baean (ἐνεπύρισε τοὺς πύργους). In 1 Macc 5:8, during many battles with the forces of Timothy, Judas occupied Jazer (προκατελάβετο τὴν Ἰαζηρ). The verb προκαταλαμβάνειν is found frequently in Judges, and so also often in 1 Maccabees,[24] but 10:36 is the only occurrence in 2 Maccabees.

■ **37** Waterless cisterns were good hiding places. Jonathan and Ahimaaz were hidden in one to escape Absalom (2 Sam 17:18-19). Nothing more is known about Apollophanes. The death of Timothy is not mentioned in 1 Maccabees, and he appears after the incident at Jazer (1 Macc 5:6-8). See the Introduction (p. 10) on the number of Timothys.

■ **38** The events end with language similar to that at the defeat of Nikanor in 8:29 and 10:38: ταῦτα δὲ διαπραξάμενοι ("having accomplished this"); 8:27: εὐλογοῦντες καὶ ἐξομολογούμενοι ("praising and confessing"); 10:38: μεθ᾽ ὕμνων καὶ ἐξομολογήσεων εὐλόγουν ("with hymns and confessions they were praising"). In the reflection in 6:13, the author stated that God had shown great beneficence (μεγάλης εὐεργεσίας) in his dealings with his people. That victory has been given echoes the attitude of the Jews in 10:28, as they went out to face the enemy. The author uses νῖκος ("victory"), the later form of νίκη, which reflects back to the Jews' hope of victory in 10:28.

General Commentary

The account of the reign of Antiochus V begins inauspiciously for the Jews when a Seleucid official who had wanted to redress their wrongs is dismissed. From then on the story is one of harassment of the Jews by neighboring Gentile communities. This account reflects one of the author's main emphases: the Jews do not start trouble but only defend themselves against attacks.

To retain interest, the author does not recount many battles but concentrates on two, one to the south of Judea and one to the north, and so dramatizes the account. The first battle is a defensive action against continual attacks, the second a struggle to repel an armed invasion and a conquest of Judea. In the first, the siege of a stronghold causes the defenders to flee to two towers, which are then captured. In the second, the defeated enemy flees to a stronghold, which is cleverly taken, and the enemy leader is killed. In both accounts, God's help is stressed. The author livens these accounts by relating a tale of treachery in the first episode and a wondrous epiphany in the second.

---

23   Risberg,"Textkritische und exegetische Anmerkungen," 24–25.
24   Judges 1:12-13; 3:28; 7:24; 9:50; 12:5; 1 Macc 5:8, 11, 35, 36, 44; 6:27; 9:2; 12:33.

11

11:1-38

1/ After an extremely short interval, Lysias, guardian of the king and "Cousin" as well as in charge of affairs, as he was excessively annoyed over what had happened, 2/ assembled around eighty thousand infantry and the whole cavalry and came up against the Jews. He thought he would make the city into a place for Greeks to live, 3/ the temple taxable just like the rest of the Gentile precincts, and the high priesthood up for sale every year. 4/ He thought not at all about the power of God, but was heartened by the ten thousands of infantry, the thousands of cavalry, and the eighty elephants. 5/ He entered Judea and approached Beth-Zur, a fortified position about five schoinia from Jerusalem, and he was pressing it hard. 6/ When the forces of Maccabeus received notice that he was besieging the strongholds, together with the populace with tearful laments they were supplicating the Lord to send a valiant angel for the salvation of Israel.

7/ Maccabeus was the first to take up arms and urged the others, risking all with him, to come to the aid of their brethren. Together they set out eagerly. 8/ But there, as they were still near Jerusalem, there appeared at their head a rider clothed in white, brandishing golden weapons. 9/ All together they blessed the merciful God and were strengthened in their souls, ready to destroy not only humans but also the fiercest beasts and iron walls. 10/ They advanced well prepared, as they had a heavenly ally since the Lord had mercy on them. 11/ Like lions, they hurled themselves against the enemy, and they laid low 11,000 as well as 1,600 cavalry, forcing all to flee. 12/ Most of them escaped to safety but wounded and naked. Lysias himself fled to safety shamefully. 13/ However, he was not stupid. Weighing within himself the defeat done to him, he realized that the Hebrews were unbeatable as their powerful God fought as their ally. He sent them a message, 14/ and persuasively proposed to come to an agreement on completely equitable terms, and thereupon to constrain[a] the king as well to be a friend to them. 15/ Maccabeus gave the nod to all the terms that Lysias was urging, as he considered what was in the best interests [of the Jews]. For the king granted whatever Maccabeus proposed to Lysias in writing about the Jews.

16/ For letters were written to the Jews containing the following. First, from Lysias.

"Lysias to the populace of the Jews, greetings. 17/ John and Absalom were sent by you and, when they delivered the attached document, they were requesting [an answer] about the matters indicated by it. 18/ So I made clear what needed to be addressed by the king, but I granted what was in my competence. 19/ Therefore, if you maintain goodwill toward the empire, I will strive henceforward to be to you a benefactor. 20/ I have enjoined your emissaries and my own to discuss the details with you. 21/ Be well. Year 148, the twenty-fourth of the month Dioskorinthios.[b]"

22/ In response, the king's letter contained the following:

"King Antiochus to his brother Lysias, greetings. 23/ As our father has departed to the gods, we wished the members of the kingdom to be without disturbance and to pursue their own affairs. 24/ When we heard that the Jews did not agree with the change toward the Hellenic lifestyle initiated by our father but, preferring their own way of life, they asked that their customary usages be granted to them, 25/ we preferred that this nation also be without disturbance. Therefore, we determine that the temple be restored to them and they conduct the polity according to the customs in place at the time of their forefathers. 26/ So please send

a With Hanhart (*Zum Text*, 466) and Habicht and against Katz ("Text of 2 Maccabees," 15), I agree that $\pi\epsilon\acute{\iota}\sigma\epsilon\iota\nu$ is a gloss to soften the harsh $\grave{\alpha}\nu\alpha\gamma\kappa\acute{\alpha}\zeta\epsilon\iota\nu$, where Lysias is said to constrain the king. The suggestion of Deichgräber (noted by Hanhart, "Zum Text," 44) that $\grave{\alpha}\nu\alpha\gamma\kappa\alpha\hat{\iota}o\nu$ be read following the use in Acts 10:24, where $\grave{\alpha}\nu\alpha\gamma\kappa\alpha\acute{\iota}o\upsilon\varsigma$ $\varphi\acute{\iota}\lambda o\upsilon\varsigma$ means "close friends," is intriguing and would do away with the problem of the harshness, but it is unlikely that the king would use the term to describe his relationship with all the Jews. It would seem that the term is used for close friends rather than for a whole community. Moreover, one is a friend of the king, rather than the reverse.

b The name of the month is corrupt. Besides $\Delta\iota\grave{o}\varsigma$ $Ko\rho\iota\nu\vartheta\acute{\iota}o\upsilon$, the manuscripts have Dioscori, Dioscordi, Dioscoridi(s), Deoscolori. A letter written by a Seleucid official would use the Macedonian month, as Habicht holds against Hanhart ("Text of 2 Maccabees," 473–74). As Habicht notes, the first month of the Macedonian calendar, $\Delta\acute{\iota}o\varsigma$, which began in October, is more likely than the fifth month, $\Delta\acute{\upsilon}\sigma\tau\rho o\varsigma$, or the eighth, $\Delta\alpha\iota\sigma\acute{\iota}o\varsigma$.

to them and give assurances so that, once they know our purpose, they may be content and gladly act to take in hand their own affairs."

27/ The king's letter to the nation was like this:

"King Antiochus to the council of the Jews and to the other Jews, greetings. 28/ If you are well, it will be as we wish. We ourselves are in health. 29/ Menelaus explained to us that you wish to return to your own affairs. 30/ So, to those who return home up to the thirtieth Xanthikos, there will be an assurance 31/ that the Jews use without fearᶜ their own customsᵈ and laws as formerly, and none of them will be harassed in any way over past wrongs. 32/ I am sending Menelaus to invite you. 33/ Be well, 148th year, the fifteenth Xanthikos."

34/ The Romans also sent them a letter like this:

"Quintus Mammius, Titus Manius, Roman ambassadors, to the people of the Jews, greetings. 35/ We also agree concerning what Lysias, "Cousin" of the king, has granted. 36/ As for what he decided to be addressed by the king, review them and send someone forthwith, so that we may take a position as befits your interests. For we are moving toward Antioch. 37/ Wherefore, hasten and send some people, so that we may know what your judgment is. 38/ Be in health. 148th year, fifteenth Xanthikos."

c   I have followed here the reading of Hanhart in placing no period after ἀδείας and in omitting δέ after χρῆσθαι. Habicht ("Royal Documents in Maccabees II," *HSCP* 80 [1976] 1–18, here 8 n. 15) maintains the opposite. Manuscripts Lʹ⁻⁵³⁴ 311 have the δέ, but then the accusative infinitive construction, χρῆσθαι τοὺς Ἰουδαίους, is not connected grammatically to a main verb. Habicht also connects μετὰ τῆς ἀδείας with the verb ὑπάρξει: the right hand is without fear. I read this phrase in conjunction with the infinitive χρῆσθαι, so that the Jews use without fear their own customs, and the accusative and infinitive construction specifies the content of the assurance given.

d   I follow Wilhelm ("Zu einigen Stellen," 22–25) in reading διαιτήμασι instead of the unknown δαπανήμασι. Wilhelm was followed in this by Katz ("Text of 2 Maccabees," 16). Habicht rightly shows that Hanhart's objection ("Text of 2 Maccabees," 467) that διαιτήμα is not found in the LXX does not hold for a work written originally in Greek.

Commentary by Verse

■ **1-4** This long sentence consists of five participial clauses, two before the main verb and three after. The two before the main verb are asyndetically connected, as the annoyance of Lysias is closely associated with the assembling of the army. The first two participial clauses after the main verb play off one another: 11:2: λογιζό-μενος; 11:4: ἐπιλογιζόμενος, which I have translated as "he thought." The last two participial phrases contrast what Lysias does not consider, the power of God, with his reliance on his own forces.

■ **1** The author uses an unusual word, the diminutive χρονίσκος (= (short time interval), to emphasize the extremely short time between the defeats of the previous chapter and the reaction of Lysias. Although Lysias had been mentioned in 10:11 as having been put in charge of affairs by Antiochus V, here his position is elaborated to emphasize the importance of the attack. This is no local offensive, but one by the leader of the king's forces. As was discussed in the Introduction, the author has arranged his material so that events that occurred while Antiochus IV was still alive and Antiochus V was co-regent are placed in the reign of Antiochus V. According to 1 Macc 3:32, Antiochus IV had appointed Lysias to manage affairs and also to bring up ($\tau\rho\acute{\epsilon}\varphi\epsilon\iota\nu$) his son. Lysias is again called the guardian of Antiochus V in 13:2 and 14:2. In 10:11, Antiochus V had seemed not to need a guardian but to be in control as he appointed Lysias to be in charge of affairs. Apart from these references to Lysias as Antiochus V's guardian there is no hint in the narrative that the king is only nine years old. $\Sigma\upsilon\gamma\gamma\epsilon\nu\acute{\eta}\varsigma$ ("Cousin") was a fictive relationship title bestowed on high court officials.[1]

Demetrius the king is annoyed as well when Alcimus reports what has happened in Judea (14:27). The use of $\varphi\acute{\epsilon}\rho\omega$ + adverb is found also in 7:39 and is well known in Greek.

■ **2-3** No explicit reason is given for Lysias's decision to invade Judea except for the narrative connection with the events in 2 Maccabees 11. In the corresponding place in 1 Macc 4:26, Lysias is told of what had happened to the invasion of Ptolemy, Nikanor, and Gorgias. The force assembled, particularly with the mention of elephants, is enormous, but 1 Macc 4:28 has sixty thousand infantry and five thousand cavalry. In both accounts the figures for the size of the enemy are excessive to enhance the victory of the Jews.[2] In 1 Macc 6:30, elephants are mentioned in the second invasion of Lysias with Antiochus V. Although elephants had been forbidden by the treaty of Apamea (Polybius 21.45.12), it is clear that later Seleucids did have elephants, as Gnaius Octavius had elephants destroyed just before Demetrius I became king (Polybius 31.12.11; Appian *Syr.* 239).

In describing Lysias's intentions, the author uses an unusual word, $o\grave{\iota}\kappa\eta\tau\acute{\eta}\rho\iota o\nu$ ("place to live") and a *hapax legomenon*, $\grave{\alpha}\rho\gamma\upsilon\rho o\lambda\acute{o}\gamma\eta\tau o\varsigma$ ("taxable"). These usages stress the significance of his objectives. As Goldstein observed, that tribute was levied on temples in this period is unknown.[3] However, temples were always a source of ready cash. Using a $\mu\grave{\epsilon}\nu\ldots\delta\acute{\epsilon}\ldots\delta\acute{\epsilon}$ construction, the

author first mentions the fate of the city and then that of the temple and priesthood. He also twice uses the future infinitive $\pi o\iota\acute{\eta}\sigma\epsilon\iota\nu$ to link the two elements together. Lysias intends to go even further than Antiochus IV by having Greeks inhabit Jerusalem. While Seleucids before Antiochus IV had supported the temple (3:2-3) and Antiochus at his death is reported by the author to have promised to do the same (9:16), now money is to be levied from the temple. Both Jason and Menelaus (4:8, 24) had used money to attain the high priesthood, but now an annual payment is to be made for that office.[4]

■ **4** As so often, the author contrasts dependence on God with dependence on human strength, as at 10:28. One finds the same contrast in Jdt 9:11: "For your power [$\tau\grave{o}\ \kappa\rho\acute{\alpha}\tau o\varsigma\ \sigma o\upsilon$] is not in multitude." The author of 2 Maccabees uses the term $\kappa\rho\acute{\alpha}\tau o\varsigma$ of God's power in 3:34; 7:17; 9:17; 12:28.

■ **5** Lysias uses the southeastern route through Idumea and Hebron to approach Jerusalem, as in 1 Macc 4:29. Beth-Zur is identified as "Khirbet el Tabeiqa, a tel at the northwestern edge of the village of Ḥalḥul, about a kilometer from the main road. The ancient name has been preserved in the name of the ruin of a Mameluke watchtower near the road, known as Khirbet Beit Zur."[5] Lysias could not allow such a position to lie unoccupied behind his army. As the site lay on the southern border between Judea and Idumea, Bar-Kochva states that it would have been fortified in some way in the Persian and Ptolemaic periods.[6] Archeologists have uncovered three forts, two of mixed style and the last Hellenistic.[7] Bar-Kochva argues that the first fort was constructed before the Maccabean revolt and was taken over by forces sympathetic to Judas.[8] Lysias destroyed this fort during his first invasion, but later it was again strengthened by Judas (1 Macc 4:61). During the second invasion of Lysias, the inhabitants surrendered, and Lysias took control without having to destroy the fort (1 Macc 6:49-50). Later Bac-

1   Xenophon *Cyrop.* 1.4.27; 2.2.31; Diodorus Siculus 16.50; *OGIS* 104.2; *BGU* 1741.12. See Bickermann, *Institutions*, 42.

2   Bar-Kochva, *Judas Maccabaeus*, 42.

3   Goldstein, *II Maccabees*, 404; see also Bickermann, *Institutions*, 114–15.

4   Walter Otto, "Kauf und Verkauf von Priestertümern bei den Griechen," *Hermes* 44 (1909) 594–99.

5   Bar-Kochva, *Judas Maccabaeus*, 285; see also F. M.

Abel, "Topographie des campagnes Maccabéennes (cont.)," *RB* 33 (1924) 209.

6   Bar-Kochva, *Judas Maccabaeus*, 286.

7   See Robert W. Funk, "Beth-Zur," in Ephraim Stern, ed., *The New Encyclopedia of Archeological Excavations in the Holy Land* (4 vols.; Jerusalem: Israel Exploration Society and Carta, 1993) 1:259–61.

8   Bar-Kochva, *Judas Maccabaeus*, 287.

chides made the existing fort stronger (1 Macc 9:52), and finally Simon Maccabeus strengthened it (1 Macc 14:33).

The land measure σχοῖνος was used in Egypt in particular, and was assigned various lengths. Herodotus had it as equivalent to sixty stadia, while Artemidorus as reported by Strabo (17.1.24, 41) said it could be thirty, forty, or sixty stadia. Bar-Kochva estimates that if the length of thirty stadia is taken, "the estimation of II Maccabees is surprisingly more or less accurate (28.5 km)."[9] The brilliant analysis by J. T. Nelis to explain the variants among the numbers found in the manuscripts does not persuade us to read σταδίους, a standard of length about one-eighth of a mnile, instead of σχοίνους, because Nelis assumes that the author of 2 Maccabees must be bound by LXX usage.[10]

The account in 2 Maccabees has Judas attack Lysias while he is besieging Beth-Zur, while 1 Macc 4:29 states that Lysias encamped at Beth-Zur. The plural "strongholds" suggests that Lysias was not concentrating just on Beth-Zur but was attacking all of Judea. However, sometimes the plural is used by Polybius when only one stronghold is in play (2.69.9; 5.73.1).

■ **6** Here the prayer is a communal prayer, while in 1 Macc 4:30 Judas prays alone before the engagement. "Tearful laments" is literally "with laments and tears," an example of hendiadys. The content of the two prayers is different. Here Judas's forces, like Judas in 15:23, refer to God's promise to send his angel before the face of Israel to guard them on their way (Exod 23:20: Καὶ ἰδοὺ ἐγὼ ἀποστέλλω τὸν ἄγγελόν μου πρὸ προσώπου σου ἵνα φυλάξῃ σε ἐν τῇ ὁδῷ = "And behold, I am sending my angel before your face to guard you on the way"). Here, the prayer specifies ἀγαθὸς ἄγγελος, which literally means "good angel." I have translated "valiant angel," as ἀγαθός can have that nuance. In Tob 5:22, Tobit comforts his wife when Tobias is about to leave by saying: "For the good angel [ἄγγελος γὰρ ἀγαθός] will

accompany him and his journey shall be prosperous, and he will return safe."[11] Grimm likens this construction to the usage among the Greeks of ἀγαθὸς δαίμων. When one drinks unmixed wine, one raises a toast to "good fortune" (Diodorus Siculus 4.3; Plutarch *Table Talk* 3.7.1, 655E). There is also a building sacred to "Good Fortune" before an oracle site (Pausanias 9.39.5). In 5:4, everyone hoped that the epiphany seen across the city might be ἐπ' ἀγαθῷ ("for good"), as though an epiphany could signify evil tidings. One thinks of the fascinating passage at 1 Kgs 22:19-23, where the prophet Micaiah tells of the vision of a lying spirit being put in other prophets' mouths. In the *War Scroll* from Qumran, God's angels are holy (1QM 7.7; 10.11: מלאכי קודש), while Belial is an angel of enmity (1QM 13.11: מלאך משטמה) and his angels are angels of destruction (1QM 13.12: מלאכי חבל). 1QM 17.6–8 reads: "He sends everlasting aid to the lot of his [co]venant by the power of the majestic angel [מלאך האדיר] for the sway of Michael in everlasting light, to illuminate with joy the covenant of Israel, peace and blessing to God's lot, to exalt the sway of Michael above all the gods, and the dominion of Israel over all flesh." Philo urged his audience: "Many say good δαίμονας and evil δαίμονας, and likewise [good and evil] souls. So you too will also not go wrong if you reckon as angels, not only those who are worthy of the name, who, as ambassadors from humans to God and from God to humans, are holy and inviolate because of that glorious and blameless ministry, but also those who are unholy and unworthy of the title" (*Gig.* 16).[12]

■ **7-10** Just as the author emphasized that the prayer was a communal prayer, so here the concern of Judas is for his brethren in Beth-Zur. As a good commander, Judas leads in taking up arms. The author situates Judas and his forces in Jerusalem.

Just as before the battle against Jericho Joshua had met the commander of the Lord's army (Josh 5:13-15),

9   Ibid., 276.
10   J. T. Nelis, "La distance de Beth-Sur à Jérusalem suivant 2 Mac. 11,5," *JSJ* 14 (1983) 39–42; the assumption is stated on p. 39.
11   Milik (*Dédicaces*, 199) stated that there was the phrase "*mlʾkʾ tbʾ* dans un texte araméen du livre de Tobie à Qumrân," but Joseph Fitzmyer has not seen it in his commentary on 4Q 197 frg. 4 (DJD 19, 44–45).
12   Note how in his discussion of Jacob's wrestling (Gen 32:22-32), Josephus (*Ant.* 1.332) wrote that Jacob was told he had wrestled with a divine angel (θεῖον ἄγγελον) and it would be a sign of many goods. Presumably, Jacob could have been wrestling with an evil angel.

so now an angel leads Judas and his men into battle. The closest parallels, however, are found in Greek literature. Dionysius of Halicarnassus relates how in the battle between the Latins and the Romans at Lake Regillus, the Dioscuri "charged at the head of the Roman horse, striking with their spears all the Latins they encountered and driving them headlong before them" (*Ant. Rom.* 6, 13). Theseus, at the battle of Marathon, rushed at the head of the Greeks against the barbarians (Plutarch *Thes.* 35). Plutarch tells how Athena appeared to many in Ilium "with the sweat running down her person, and showed them the robe torn in one place, telling them that she had just arrived from relieving the Cyzicians" (*Luc.* 10.3). The role of the divine heroes in Greek literature has been taken over by the angel of the Lord. The word πανοπλία ("suit of armor") is used here for the weapons carried. As noted in 3:25, gold is the color for divine figures. Here the angel is dressed in white, as are the Ancient of Days (Dan 7:9), the angel who appears in Mark 16:5, and Jesus at his transfiguration (Mark 9:3).

The effect on Judas's forces is immediate. Note how the adversaries that Judas's forces are willing to face become increasingly difficult: first men, then beast, then iron itself. The verb used, τιτρώσκειν, usually means "to wound, kill," but here the more general sense of doing damage/destroying seems appropriate. How does one wound iron walls?

The description of the forces marching in good order underscores their trust in God. Twice the author describes God as merciful, as God's mercy is necessary for success, as in 8:5. The adjective "merciful" is found in 8:29 and 13:12. On God as ally (σύμμαχος), see 8:24; 10:16; 12:36 as well as the related verb συμμαχεῖν in 11:13.

■ **11-12a** The adverb λεοντηδόν ("like lions") is a *hapax legomenon*. The author likes this way of forming adverbs: ἀγεληδόν (3:18; 14:14), κρουνηδόν (14:45). The method of adding numbers through πρός + dative is found in later Greek authors, including Polybius.[13]

The battle itself receives scant attention. The emphasis as always is on God's mercy and help. That the defeated enemies flee naked stresses the completeness of the defeat, as a soldier would never willingly throw away his

arms. Recall the saying of the Spartan to her son as he left for battle carrying his shield: "Come back with it, or on it" (Plutarch *Apoph. lac.* 241F).

■ **12b-15** Just as Nikanor had fled disgracefully and had recognized that the Jews had a super ally (8:35-36: ὑπέρμαχος), so Lysias, the chancellor of the Seleucid Empire, flees shamefully to save himself. This telling of the story fits with the emphases of the author. In 1 Macc 4:34-35 a very different picture is given. There five thousand of Lysias's men are said to have fallen, but then Lysias makes an orderly retreat to Antioch. Bar-Kochva makes a good case for the affair not being a pitched battle, but "probably a 'hit and run' raid against the Seleucid army encamped at Beth-Zur."[14] In 1 Maccabees, Lysias seeks not a settlement but to gather another army. The peace negotiations in 2 Maccabees would seem to be the result of the author's having to incorporate the four letters that follow within his narrative. The peace negotiations also make a fitting comparison with the end of the second invasion of Lysias accompanied by Antiochus V (13:23-24). The same phrase, "on completely equitable terms" (ἐπὶ πᾶσι τοῖς δικαίοις), is found in 13:23 and reinforces the correspondence.

■ **13** The author introduces the peace negotiations with a compliment to Lysias: he is not stupid, as Simon was (4:6). Lysias recognizes before a major battle that the Jews are unbeatable and cannot be harmed, earlier said of Judas's forces (8:5: ἀνυπόστατος; 8:36: ἀτρώτους), and so seeks peace. The asyndeton between the participles ὑπάρχων, and ἀντιβάλλων underlines the immediacy of the reflection, and the use of the complimentary term "Hebrews" elevates the description of the Jews. "Hebrews" is also used at 7:31, and see the comment on its use at 15:37.

■ **14** The word ἔπεισε ("persuasively proposed") must be seen here as an ingressive aorist, as the following verse shows the reaction to the proposal. A king can be said to extend friendship toward a city.[15]

■ **15** The verb ἐπινεύειν ("gave the nod") is used also in 4:10 and 14:20. The author has Lysias initiating the negotiations and Judas responding through written proposals. This fits with the wording of the first letter, where Lysias

13   See Doran, *Temple Propaganda*, 27–28.
14   Bar-Kochva, *Judas Maccabeus*, 134–35, 288–89; quotation from 288.
15   See Welles, *Royal Correspondence*, nos. 14, 9; 22, 13; 64, 9.

has Judas's intermediaries debate a written proposal. For the use of this verb in assent to proposals between a king and his subjects, see the inscription of the two letters from Eumenes II to the Phrygian community of Tyriaion. The community had asked that they be made a *polis* and Eumenes assented (ἐπινεῦσαι) to their request and granted (συνχωρῆσαι) it.[16] There the king gave the nod; here Judas does.

Often translators insert here αὐτούς so that the sentence is translated "he persuaded [them] to come to an agreement." But it would seem that the two infinitives, συλλύεσθαι ("to come to an agreement") and ἀναγκάζειν ("to constrain"), have the same subject, Lysias.

Just as Onias the high priest had acted out of consideration of the best interests of his people (4:5), so too does Judas. The verb "to grant" (συγχωρεῖν) runs throughout the letters (11:18, 24, 35) and is frequent in royal correspondence.

The γάρ ("for") that introduces v. 15b is explanatory.[17]

■ **16-38** The four letters found in these verses have been the subject of intense scholarly debate. It is now generally accepted that the letters are genuine, though some scholars have excised parts. The sequence and dating of the letters are also lively questions. See the excursus on the letters for a discussion of this debate. Where either the author of the condensed narrative or Jason of Cyrene found these letters is unknown, as is the arrangement in which they were found. Were they in some archive, or are they from some other source? We do know that, as so often in late Jewish histories,[18] the author of 2 Maccabees wanted to incorporate documents, even though his is a condensed narrative. They must have served his rhetorical purpose. I would suggest that his placing of these documents at this point and his emphasizing the date as during the reign of Antiochus V fit his purpose of showing Antiochus IV as an opponent

of God. It also demonstrates how the Jews are ready to cooperate with authorities if they are allowed to follow their own traditions.

■ **16** "letters . . . containing the following." The same introduction to letters is found in 1 Macc 11:29, when Demetrius writes to Jonathan. Note the μέν . . . δέ construction, which links the letters together: the μέν of v. 16 is responded to by the δέ in vv. 22, 27, 34.

The letter begins with the usual formula: A to B, greeting. What is interesting is that the letter is sent not to the council (γερουσία) or nation (ἔθνος) or people (δῆμος), but to the populace (πλῆθος) of the Jews. As Habicht noted, this "means an unconstitutional body, not competent for negotiations in a proper sense."[19] Goldstein suggested that after the demolition of the walls of Jerusalem by the Mysian commander (1 Macc 1:29), the Judean community was no longer considered a nation. However, the use of "council" in the address in 11:27 would seem to discount this. This letter is thus addressed to Judas's forces.

■ **17** The Hebrew names John (most likely Johanan, יוחנן) and Absalom have been seen as an indication that these were not members of the party of Menelaus, who would have adopted Greek names.[20] They are called not ambassadors but simply "the ones sent" (οἱ πεμφθέντες), as is frequent in royal letters.[21]

The term for "document," χρηματισμός, is found in the royal correspondence.[22]

The sentence contains some ambiguity. Should ἐπιδόντες be seen as the aorist participle of ἐπιδίδωμι ("give over, deliver") or as the participle of ἐπεῖδον ("look upon, behold, see")? Should ἠξίουν be given the nuance "they were requesting" or "they were inquiring"? One could translate as, "When they saw the attached document, they were inquiring about the matters indicated by it" or "When they delivered the attached

---

16 Jonnes and Rici, "New Royal Inscription," 1–29. The verbs are found in lines 14 and 18 of the inscription.

17 Smyth, *Greek Grammar*, §2808.

18 See the article by Arnaldo Momigliano, "Eastern Elements in Post-Exilic Jewish, and Greek, Historiography," in idem, *Essays in Ancient and Modern Historiography* (Middletown, Conn.: Wesleyan University Press, 1977) 25–35. Momigliano writes: "In the use of archival documents Jewish historians were certainly influenced by Persia" (p. 33).

19 Habicht, "Royal Documents," 10. This had already been noted by Niese, *Kritik der beiden Makkabäerbücher* (Berlin: Weidmann, 1900) 68.

20 Habicht, "Royal Documents," 10; Bar-Kochva, *Judas Maccabaeus*, 521; Ilan, *Lexicon*, 60–61, 134–43.

21 Welles, *Royal Correspondence*, nos. 31, 4; 32, 4; 63, 2.

22 Ibid., 375.

document, they were requesting [an answer] about the matters indicated by it." Since in the following sentence Lysias distinguishes between what he can grant and what has to be sent to the king, the second meaning is to be preferred.

The actual document is not given, as is also the case for the document referred to in 9:25.

■ **18** "What was in my competence" is literally "what was possible."

Most manuscripts have the first person singular, which is to be followed rather than the third person singular of Hanhart. Habicht refers to a letter written by Aristobulos, an official of Ptolemy I, to the city of Iasos in Caria. In this letter, Aristobulos makes the same distinction as Lysias between what he can allow and what he has sent to the king for ratification: ὑπὲρ μὲν οὖν τῶν λ[οιπῶν] συνεκεχωρήκαμεν αὐτοῖς, ὑπὲρ δὲ τῆς συντάξεως ἐδόκει μοι ἀνενέγκαι εἰς τὸν βασιλέα (= "So concerning the rest we have granted to them, but concerning the contribution it seemed to me to be referred to the king").[23] Note how in the letter of the Romans, Lysias is said to have granted (11:35: συνεχώρησεν) something to the Jews.

The Macedonian-Seleucid year 148 ran from October 165 B.C.E. to late September 164 B.C.E. Since Antiochus IV died in November/December 164 B.C.E.,[24] the letter, if the year is accepted, was written while he was still alive. The king referred to in this verse therefore would be Antiochus IV, not Antiochus V. Since Lysias was guardian of the young Antiochus V, it would seem that he would not have to make a distinction such as in this verse if Antiochus IV were dead. The narrative of 2 Maccabees, however, has not previously given a date for

Antiochus IV's death. It implies that the letter is being sent to Antiochus V.

■ **19-20** As Ma has shown, the language of reciprocity is endemic to relations between the king and his subjects.[25] This letter is to lead to a further diplomatic mission. "Empire" translates πράγματα ("affairs") and has the sense of "state affairs."

As Ma notes, "[t]he most common word in the euergetic exchange is εὔνοια, 'goodwill,' imputed or avowed by both city and king."[26] An example of a similarly conditional description of the relationship is found in the letter of Antiochus III to the Herakleians: "If in the future too, you make through your [actions] the appropriate displays of your goodwill towards our affairs [τῆς πρὸς τὰ πράγματα ἡμῶ(ν εὐνοίας)]. . . ."[27]

Hanhart omits ὑμῖν ("to you") as it is not found in all manuscripts, but Abel and Habicht rightly include it. Parallels can be found in a letter of Ptolemy II to Miletus[28] and in the letters collected by Robert Sherk.[29]

"Benefactor" is literally "to be a cause of benefits to you." Παραίτιος is found in the decree of the Chersonites that authorized a golden crown to be sent to the people of Athens because they had been the cause of all the great benefits (πάντων τῶν μεγίστων ἀγαθῶν παραίτιος) in freeing them from Philip and restoring their fatherlands, their laws, their freedom, and their sanctuaries.[30] The term occurs also in the first Teian decree for Antiochus III and Laodike III, where Antiochus is praised for being responsible for many favors (πολλῶν ἀγαθῶν πα(ρ)αίτιος).[31] It is also attested in connection with the verb πειράω ("to strive") in the letter of Scipio to the Herakleians from 190 B.C.E.: "we will strive [πειρασόμεθα] to assist you and always be

23 Giovanni Pugliese Carratelli, "Supplemento Epigrafico di Iasos," *Annuario Scuola archeologica italiana di Atene e delle missioni italiane in Oriente* 45–46 (1969) 437–86, I. B, 12–14, with the corrections suggested by Jeanne Robert and Louis Robert, "Bulletin épigraphique," *REG* 84 (1971) 397–540, here 502. Here the first person plural is found.

24 Sachs and Wiseman, "Babylonian King List," 204, 208–9.

25 Ma, *Antiochus III*, 179–242.

26 Ibid., 191.

27 As in Ma, *Antiochus III*, 340–41, no. 31A, lines 14–15. The inscription on this block cannot be read

after this point. The restoration of εὔνοια is undisputed.

28 Welles, *Royal Correspondence*, no. 14, 4–5.

29 Robert K. Sherk, *Roman Documents from the Greek East: senatus consulta and epistulae to the Age of Augustus* (Baltimore: Johns Hopkins Press, 1969) nos. 35, 9–10; 38, 22–23; 58, 80.

30 Decree cited in Demosthenes *Cor.* 92; see also Polybius 7.11.7 and *OGIS* 4, 9–10.

31 Decree as published in Ma, *Antiochus III*, 308–10, no. 17, lines 25–26.

a cause of some good [τινος ἀγαθοῦ (παραίτ)ιοι γίνεσθαι].”[32]

■ **21** The letter ends with the usual wish for well-being, ἔρρωσθε.[33]

As stated in note b on the text, the month given is problematic. Bar-Kochva refers to the statement of Josephus (*Ant.* 12.264) that Antiochus Epiphanes introduced the names of Attic months and that in the letter to the Sidonians in Shechem an Athenian month name is found.[34] He therefore concludes that the month Dios should be taken at face value and that the date refers to October 165 B.C.E. This interpretation fits with Bar-Kochva's theory that the peace negotiations began after the defeat of Nikanor. One has to ask why the Seleucid chancellor would initiate negotiations after a defeat of Seleucid forces. Would he not rather be inclined to show who is in control? It is clear that the author places all these letters in the time of Antiochus V, and he has structured his narrative to suggest that they were written after the death of Antiochus IV. This must mean that for the author, 148 S.E. indicates a time in the reign of Antiochus V, as three of the documents are dated to this period. I recommend caution in basing a theory on these dates. See the excursus on the letters.

■ **22-26** This letter, through a μὲν . . . δέ construction, responds to the letter of Lysias. It has the usual opening formula of "A to B, greeting," but has neither closing formula nor date.

■ **22** The names of the sender and the recipient are enlarged. It was not unusual for a king to address his high officials as "brother," as Alexander Balas and Demetrius both refer to Jonathan (1 Macc 10:18; 11:30).[35]

■ **23-25** These three verses form one sentence in the Greek. The verbs "wished," "heard," and "preferred" in my translation are in fact three participles. The first two participles, βουλόμενοι . . . ἀκηκοότες, are in asyndeton

as together they ground the king's decision and relay his argument.

■ **23** After a genitive absolute, the first of the three participial phrases composes v. 23. The king uses the first person plural of majesty, as in the letter of Alexander Balas to Jonathan at 1 Macc 10:18.1 Macc 10:18.

"Departed to the gods."[36] That the Seleucids had been honored with cult is seen in the decrees of the Teians that put cultic images of Antiochus III and Laodike in the temple of Dionysos to be honored alongside the main god of the city.[37] Antiochus IV went a little further, as he placed on his coins the epithets θεός ("God") and ἐπιφανής ("Manifest"). Mittag concludes that Antiochus IV was presenting himself as the connection between the earthly and the heavenly spheres.[38] Further, on some coins he had a star placed at the end of the diadem on his head or over his forehead and on others a crown with rays shooting forth.[39] These divine representations were designed, particularly for his Greek subjects, to emphasize the legitimacy of Antiochus IV's rule.[40] For the reader of 2 Maccabees, what is striking is the contrast between the description of Antiochus IV's very human death in 2 Maccabees 9 and this claim that he had gone to the gods, a contrast that was underscored by his loss in the fight against the God of the Jews.

"without disturbance" (ἀταράχους). The same word is used in the letters attributed to Artaxerxes in which he orders both the destruction of the Jews and their survival (LXX Esth 3:13g; 8:12h). However, it was the Seleucids who brought disorder and disturbance (ταραχή: 3:30), and the Lord who brought tumult and disturbance on their armies (10:30; 13:16).

"own affairs." The term for "own," ἴδιος, is repeated in 11:26, 30. The term is often found in royal correspondence. Commenting on a letter from Antiochus III to the Amyzon, Welles writes that the term means that "the

32   As found in Ma, *Antiochus III*, 367, no. 45, lines 13–14.
33   Hans-Josef Klauck, *Ancient Letters and the New Testament: A Guide to Content and Exegesis* (Waco, Tex.: Baylor University Press, 2006) 24–25; White, *Light from Ancient Letters*, 201–2.
34   Bar-Kochva, *Judas Maccabaeus*, 522–23.
35   Welles, *Royal Correspondence*, no. 71, 2; see also Bickermann, *Institutions*, 43, 193.
36   See *OGIS* 304, 4; 339, 17. A similar phrase is found in *OGIS* 56, 56.
37   Ma, *Antiochus III*, 308–11, no. 17, lines 44–52.
38   Mittag, *Antiochus IV. Epiphanes*, 130.
39   Georges Le Rider, *Antioche de Syrie sous les Séleucides. Corpus des monnaies d'or et d'argent*, vol. 1: *de Séleucos I à Antiochos V, c. 300–161* (Mémoires de l'Académie des Inscriptions et belles-lettres n.s. 19; Paris: Académie des Inscriptions et belles-lettres, 1999) 192–222.
40   For an overview of the whole question, see Mittag, *Antiochus IV. Epiphanes*, 128–39.

people of Amyzon should refrain from agitation of any sort."[41] He also refers to the usage in Polybius 2.57.3–4.

■ **24** The second of the participial phrases begins ἀκηκοότες ("After we had heard") and contains two further participial phrases in the accusative: μὴ συνευδοκοῦντας ("did not agree") and αἱρετίζοντας ("preferring").

"agree" (συνευδοκεῖν). The term is used again in the letter of the Romans at 11:35. It is also found in 1 Macc 1:57, where "if someone agrees [συνευδόκει] to the law," he is to be put to death.

The change to Greek customs had started under Jason (4:10, 15) and had been accelerated with the arrival in Jerusalem of Geron the Athenian (6:1), as well as the decisions made in surrounding cities (6:8-9). The substantive "change" (μετάθεσις) reflects back to the attempt by Antiochus IV to change (μετατίθημι) the mind of the last of the seven brothers (7:24) from his ancestral traditions. The same term is used here for "way of life," ἀγωγή, as was used in 4:16 to describe the gymnastic training that some Jews emulated.

"customary usages" (τὰ νόμιμα). The substantivized plural adjective is found frequently in the LXX to describe the laws.[42] The adjective is found in 4:11, where Jason is said to have abrogated lawful usages and introduced unlawful ones.

■ **25** Here begins the third participial phrase before the verb. The king's choice is grounded on the previous two participial phrases. Whereas in 6:1 Geron the Athenian had been sent to compel the Jews not to conduct the polity (πολιτεύσθαι) according to the laws of God, now the king determines that they may.

In v. 25 the king is said to restore the temple to the Jews. However, according to the narrative flow in 2 Maccabees, Judas's forces are already in control of the temple (10:1). The king therefore appears to be simply recognizing the de facto situation. However, if the advance of Lysias took place before Judas's forces regained the temple, as in 1 Macc 4:26-35, then the concession is real. Here is a hint that the author of the condensed narrative has rearranged his material to provide the most rhetori-

cally powerful description of the end of Antiochus IV, the god attacker.

The verb ἀποκαθίστημι is found also in 12:25, 39; 15:20 with the sense of "restore, reestablish." The verb is used by Polybius in 3.98.7, when plans to restore hostages to their kin and cities are put forward to secure the goodwill of the inhabitants.[43]

"conduct the polity" (πολιτεύεσθαι). This replaces the decree given to Geron the Athenian in 6:1. A similar use is found in the decree of the Iasians honoring Antiochus III and his family, in which the ancestral god of the Seleucids is said to have exhorted the citizens to live harmoniously in the city (παρακαλῶν μεθ᾽ ὁμονοίας πολιτεύεσθαι).[44]

"according to the customs." The word ἔθος is used in the same context in the correspondence relayed by Josephus concerning the rights of the Jews under Roman rule: *Ant.* 14.213, "as you by vote prevent them from using their own customs and sacred affairs" (τοῖς πατρίοις ἔθεσι καὶ ἱεροῖς χρῆσθαι); 14.246, "I decided not to prevent the Jews from using their own customs" (τοῖς αὐτῶν ἔθεσι χρῆσθαι); 14.260, "so that they may gather according to their accepted customs and conduct polity" (κατὰ τὰ νομιζόμενα ἔθη συνάγωνται καὶ πολιτεύεσθαι).

"at the time of their forefathers" is also found at 8:19.

■ **26** "Please" is literally "you will do well." εὖ or καλῶς + future of ποιέω is a polite form of request.

"Give assurances" (δοὺς δεξίας), literally "giving the right hand." The Greek phrase is also found in 4:34; 11:30; 12:11, 12; 13:22; 14:19, 33.

"purpose" (προαίρεσις). The same Greek noun is found elsewhere in the condensed narrative at the end of the letter ascribed to Antiochus IV (9:27), where it describes his policy. The verb is found in 6:9, where those who did not choose (προαιρουμένους) to change over to the Greek way of life are to be killed. The word is also used in the correspondence between Antiochus III and his son, on one hand, and the Magnesians, on the other.[45]

41 Welles, *Royal Correspondence*, 168, comment on ἴδιος at no. 38, 3, 7. See also Diodorus Siculus 18.18.6.

42 For example, LXX Lev 10:11; 18:3, 26, 30; 20:23; Ezek 5:6, 7, and also 1 Macc 1:14, 41, 44; 3:21, 29; 6:59.

43 See also Welles, *Royal Correspondence*, 316–17.

44 *OGIS* 237.4–6 as in Ma, *Antiochus III*, no. 28 (pp. 336–37).

45 Welles, *Royal Correspondence*, nos. 31, 21; 32, 22.

"To take in hand" is literally "toward the laying hold [ἀντιλήμψιν] of their own." Here ἀντιλήμψις has a meaning different from that in 8:19 and 15:7, where it refers to the help/support given by God.

"content." Εὔθυμοι is used in a letter of Zeuxis to the Amyzonians in conjunction with the phrases καλῶς ποιησέτε and γινόμενον πρὸς τῶι [ἐπιμελεῖσθαι . . .] τῶν ἰδίων ("direct yourselves toward . . . of your own property").[46]

No date is given at the end of this letter. In light of the reference to the death of Antiochus IV, it must be dated to after November/December 164 B.C.E., most likely in early 163 B.C.E.

■ **27-33** From the author's point of view, this letter stands in succession to the previous two letters and is that sent by Antiochus V Eupator to the Jews in formal response to them after the decision relayed to Lysias in the previous letter. However, the letter alludes to none of the negotiations carried out by Lysias; rather, it speaks of an appeal by the high priest Menelaus, which is granted by the king. Most scholars hold that this letter was written not by Antiocus V but by his father, Antiochus IV. See the excursus on the letters for a full discussion of authorship and date.

■ **27** The letter is addressed to the γερουσία, or council, of the Jews and to the other Jews. The council was last mentioned in 4:44, where three members were sent to complain about Menelaus's selling of temple treasures. Menelaus was able, through bribery, to obtain their execution. Throughout the change in constitution effected by Geron the Athenian, the council must have remained in place.

■ **28** The address is followed by well wishes, as in the king's letter in 9:20. Here the well wishes follow a formulaic pattern found in other royal correspondence.[47]

■ **29** The verb ἐμφανίζειν ("to explain") is found in royal letters.[48] The verb translated "to return," κατέρχομαι, and the similar verb in the following verse, καταπορεύομαι ("to return home"), often are used in the context of exiles returning home. Is there the sense that others have voluntarily exiled themselves as Judas Maccabeus is said to have done in 5:27, where the verb used for Judas's departure is ἀναχωρέω ("go away, withdraw")?

The word ἰδίος ("own") is used as in the second letter in 11:23, 26.[49]

■ **30-31** The king accedes to Menelaus's request, setting a timetable for the return of the Jews to their homes by the thirtieth Xanthikos. This was the sixth Macedonian month, and the thirtieth would be around the end of March, or about the time when military actions begin. The same date is set for another amnesty, in the period immediately after Alexander the Great as the Macedonian Polyperchon tried to outwit Cassander, and the Ides of March (15 March) is proposed as a deadline in the course of the Mutinensian War in 43 B.C.E. (Diodorus Siculus 18.56.5; Cicero *Phil.* 8.33). As mentioned in the text notes to these verses, Habicht and others separate 11:30 from 11:31. For Habicht, the first verse deals with the guarantee of safe passage for those who return, while the second states that the Jews can follow their own laws. However, this reading does not work grammatically, even if one reads with some manuscripts a δέ after χρῆσθαι. More importantly, the guarantee from molestation is found in v. 31b.

"without fear" (μετὰ τῆς ἀδείας). Grimm interpreted the phrase as meaning "with permission" and cited the case of the mythical queen Lamia, who when drunk "gave to all the permission/opportunity/license [ἄδειαν] to do what they pleased unobserved" (Diodorus Siculus 20.41.5).[50] However, a better parallel in a political context is provided by its use in Demosthenes, who argued that if all the Athenians had acted as he had, "all would be free and independent without any fear" (μετὰ πάσης ἀδείας, *Cor.* 305).[51]

Here Antiochus IV rescinds the decrees set out in 6:1. A similar phrase is found in the inscription of King Philip to the people of Nisyria, where Philip sends back a citizen of Nisyria who is a friend of his announcing

---

46 Welles, *Royal Correspondence*, no. 38, 6–7 and p. 337.

47 See the letter of Antiochus III to Zeuxis in Josephus *Ant.* 12.148; also Welles, *Royal Correspondence*, nos. 61, 1–2; 71, 2–3; 72, 3–4.

48 Welles, *Royal Correspondence*, nos. 6, 9; 17, 4; 57, 4.

49 See Preisigke, *Wörterbuch*, s.v., #9 (vol. 1, p. 68), and Welles, *Royal Correspondence*, no. 38, 3, 7.

50 Grimm also referred to the way that Dionysius of Halicarnassus (*Comp.* 6.19.9) speaks of prose as enjoying "complete freedom and license [ἄδειαν] to vary composition."

51 See also Preisigke, *Wörterbuch*, s.v. ἄδεια (vol. 1, p. 18).

that the king had granted them the use of their ancestral and present laws (νόμοις τοῖς πατρίοις καὶ ὑπάρχουσιν χρῆσθαι).[52] As noted in textual note d, I have read διαιτήμασι ("customs") rather than δαπανήμασι ("expenses"). Bickermann accepted the latter reading but understood it to have the unusual meaning of "foods," which would not be appropriate in a chancellory letter.[53] Bunge suggested that the expenses of the temple were meant.[54] Bar-Kochva accepts the reading of διαιτήμασι, but interprets it as referring specifically to "foods."[55] However, the parallelism with "laws" suggests the more general reading of "customs" for διαιτήμασι. Wilhelm notes in this connection how νόμοι is found coupled with ἐθισμοί.[56]

"As formerly" is literally "according to what was earlier."

"harassed." The verb παρενοχλεῖν is found in the royal correspondence with the sense of "to hinder, hamper."[57] See also in the letter of Demetrius to Jonathan in 1 Macc 10:35.

"over past wrongs." The perfect participle of ἀγνοέω literally means "concerning things done in ignorance/without knowledge." One wonders exactly what is meant here. The substantive ἀγνόημα is found in 1 Macc 13:39. Is the king providing an excuse for the actions of Judas and his followers? Or is the letter aimed mainly at followers of the former high priest Jason who had attacked Jerusalem (5:5-7)? An interesting parallel is found in Polybius, where the advice is given that "good men ought not to war to destroy and annihilate those who act amiss [ἀγνοήσασι] but rather to correct and amend them of their errors" (5.11.5). See also the decree of amnesty of Ptolemy VI Philometor of 17 August 163 B.C.E., where he

gives amnesty for infractions "intentional or involuntary" ([τῶν ἁμαρτημ]άτων καὶ τῶν ἀγνο[ημάτων).[58]

■ **32** Menelaus is still envisioned as the major intermediary between the king and the Jews. His failure to secure peace prepares the way for his execution, encouraged by Lysias, as the cause of all the troubles in Judea (13:4). The epistolary perfect is used for "send." The verb παρακαλέω is used here with the sense of "invite."[59] The future participle is used here with a sense of purpose.[60]

■ **33** The date given, the fifteenth Xanthikos, allows only fifteen days for the return home, a very short time if the date refers to the date on which the letter was written. Gera has suggested that the date may refer to when "the king's letter arrived in Jerusalem, and the latter date was appended to the end of the document by the archivist in Jerusalem."[61] He cites the end of a letter of Eumenes II to a Carian city, where one reads: "Megan delivered this on the sixth of Anthesterion."[62] Gera notes how in Ptolemaic Egypt only twenty days were allotted for someone to reach Alexandria, no matter where in Egypt the person lived. Therefore he concludes that the fifteen days would not be too short for people living in the much smaller area of Judea and Samaria.[63] Schwartz notes that fifteenth Xanthikos was the same as fifteenth Nisan,[64] that is, the first day of Passover, which, if the date is genuine, would seem to make the relocation all the more difficult.

■ **34-38** A letter from some Roman ambassadors. This letter is tied to the letter of Lysias, as the Roman ambassadors approve of Lysias's grants and ask the Jews to tell them what they think about the matters referred to the king. It thus seems to belong to a period immediately following the negotiations with Lysias but before an answer from the king has been received. The language of

52 *SIG*, 572.

53 Bickermann, *Der Gott der Makkabäer*, 180 n. 5; also Schwartz, *2 Maccabees*, appendix 8.

54 Bunge, *Untersuchungen*, 397–98.

55 Bar-Kochva, *Judas Maccabaeus*, 518 and n. 3.

56 Wilhelm, "Zu einigen Stellen," 25, where he refers to Welles, *Royal Correspondence*, no. 53 IIIB, 1.

57 Welles, *Royal Correspondence*, 353. The verb ἐνόχλειν is found there also; see ibid., nos. 38, 11; 40, 4.

58 Marie-Thérèse Lenger, *Corpus des Ordonnances des Ptolémées (C.Ord.Ptol.)* (1964; reprinted Brussels: Palais des académies, 1980) no. 34.9 (p. 84). The same phrasing is found also in no. 35.3–4 (p. 89).

59 See Welles, *Royal Correspondence*, nos. 31, 13; 60, 6–7.

60 Smyth, *Greek Grammar*, §2065.

61 Gera, *Judaea*, 244.

62 Welles, *Royal Correspondence*, no. 49, 11.

63 Gera, *Judaea*, 244. He cites *C. Ord. Ptol.* no. 29. See also the case in no. 22, where anyone who has taken a slave in any way has to declare it to the administrator of the economy of the hyparchy within twenty days.

64 For the identification of Xanthikos and Nisan, see Josephus *Ant.* 1.81.

the letter closely resembles that of the first two letters in this collection: συγχωρέω in 11:18, 35; προσενεχθῆναι in 11:18 with προσανενεχθῆναι in 11:35; συνευδοκέω in 11:24, 35.[65] Lysias is called the Cousin of the king (συγγενής) in 11:1 and 11:35.

■ **34** The names of the Roman ambassadors are problematic. The manuscript reading is Quintus Memmius and Titus Manius. After Manius, V adds Ernios, and 311 has Ernios maniou. Niese suggested that the second ambassador was thus Manius Sergius, who with Gaius Sulpicius was sent to the East in the autumn of 164 B.C.E.[66] This identification seems unlikely, as Mørkholm believes.[67] It is true, however, as Bar-Kochva notes,

> [W]e do not have information on all the delegations sent from Rome to Antioch. . . . It is highly probable that in the fifteen months between these two delegations [i.e., the delegation headed by Tiberius Gracchus at the end of summer 165 B.C.E. (Polybius 30.27) and that of Manius Sergius at the beginning of 163 B.C.E. (Polybius 31.1.6–8)], when practically speaking a new ruler in the guise of Lysias was reigning, and the developments in Antiochus's anabasis were not regularly reported, a Roman delegation was dispatched to explore the intentions of the man in Antioch.[68]

As Gruen noted, this letter of the Romans is a response to a Judean initiative, rather than a Roman initiative.[69]

■ **35-37** Who these Romans were remains unknown, but it is certainly significant that the letter is framed almost as if the Romans are asking for advice from the Jews. The ambassadors address the δῆμος ("people") of the Jews, a significant upgrade from the address of Lysias to the πλῆθος ("populace") of the Jews. The Romans do not otherwise figure in the condensed narrative, and having them play a subordinate role to the Jews would

heighten the position of the latter. Is there a conflict between "someone" (v. 36: τινα) and the plural "some people" (v. 37: τινας)?

■ **38** Habicht concurs with John Strugnell and Bernard Knox that the final wish ὑγιαίνετε instead of ἔρρωσθε is a Latinism, the equivalent of the Latin *valete*.[70]

The date given is the same as that at the end of the third letter. As Gera remarks, "it is inconceivable that Roman officials would have employed a Macedonian month and an official era of the Seleucid kingdom."[71] Here Gera is drawing on the work of earlier scholars such as Adolf von Schlatter and Victor Tcherikover.[72] It would seem that the author is trying to fit all the documents together with these dates: the first letter is placed at the first month of 148 S.E., the second is undated, and the last two are placed in the sixth month of 148 S.E. For a discussion of the possible dates, see the excursus on the letters.

General Commentary

The author, as we have seen, was determined to portray Antiochus IV as an archvillain and has him die ingloriously at the hand of God before the temple is recovered and restored. Antiochus IV was therefore not to be understood as in any way relenting in his hatred of the Jews, and no peace negotiations were to be seen as taking place while he was alive. Events that took place during his lifetime and while Antiochus V Eupator was co-regent are placed in the narrative at a time after Antiochus IV's death and when Eupator was sole ruler (10:9-10).

Particularly interesting is the way the author has crafted his story to prepare for the first incursion of Lysias. In the previous chapter, the author emphasizes that Judea is under attack from outside forces. First, the Idumeans are described as harassing (ἐγύμναζον) the Jews (10:15). It is only in response to these incursions

---

65 See Bévenot, *Die beiden Makkabäerbücher*, 233; Bunge, *Untersuchungen*, 386–87; Habicht, "Royal Documents," 11–12.

66 On the embassy of Gaius Sulpicius and Manius Sergius, see Polybius 31.1.6–8 and Niese, *Kritik*, 72–74.

67 Mørkholm, *Antiochus IV*, 163–64; see also Mittag, *Antiochos IV. Epiphanes*, 276.

68 Bar-Kochva, *Judas Maccabaeus*, 532–33.

69 Gruen, *Hellenistic World*, 2:745–47.

70 Habicht, "Royal Documents," 12 n. 24, refers to

separate conversations he had with John Strugnell and Bernard Knox.

71 Gera, *Judaea*, 243.

72 Adolf von Schlatter, *Jason von Kyrene: Ein Beitrag zu seiner Wiederherstellung* (Munich: Beck, 1891) 30; Victor Tcherikover, *The Jews in the Graeco-Roman World* (in Hebrew; Tel Aviv: Neumann, 1960–61) 191–92. See also Goldstein, *II Maccabees*, 425; and Bar-Kochva, *Judas Maccabaeus*, 531.

into their territory from the south that the Jews attack the strongholds of the Idumeans (10:16-23). Next is described an attempt to take Judea at spear point (10:24: δοριάλωτον), apparently from the north, if the manuscript tradition is taken seriously and the place to which Timothy retreated is read as Gezer (10:33); Judas reacts by setting out from Jerusalem to meet Timothy (10:27). These two episodes are described as wars of self-defense against those who disrespected the territorial integrity of Judea and wanted to overrun it. It is only in response to the failure of these local attempts at incursion into Judea that Lysias sets out toward Judea.

While some scholars have doubted that there were two expeditions under Lysias,[73] Bar-Kochva is right in showing that the main similarity is that in both expeditions Lysias invaded from the south and had to take Beth-Zur and in noting that the first expedition is concentrated around Beth-Zur while the second is around Beth-Zacharia.[74]

For the author of the condensed narrative, Lysias's first expedition comes not long after the more local attempts at disrupting the territorial integrity of Judea (11:1). In 1 Maccabees, Lysias waits till the next year, after Ptolemy son of Dorymenes, Nikanor, and Gorgias are defeated (1 Macc 3:38—4:25). Both accounts of Lysias's first expedition are extremely condensed and lack detail. According to 1 Macc 4:29-35, Lysias set up camp at Beth-Zur; Judas attacked the camp; about five thousand of Lysias's forces fell; Lysias departed in an orderly fashion to get another army ready to invade Judea.[75] In 2 Maccabees, Judas's forces appear to attack Lysias while he is still besieging Beth-Zur; Lysias is forced to flee but then begins negotiations for peace. Both descriptions aim to show that Judas's forces had some sort of engagement, but that engagement was probably a minor skirmish rather than the rout that 2 Maccabees describes. Both are determined to highlight the valor

and determination of Judas and his men. Whereas the author of 1 Maccabees ignores any attempt at peace negotiation between Lysias and Judas, the author of the condensed narrative highlights such an endeavor. It would seem that one should tone down the victory that each narrative ascribes to Judas. In the condensed narrative, when Lysias understood that Judas headed a formidable force ready to fight, he recognized that it was better to settle rather than engage in what could be a drawn-out guerrilla campaign against a foe who knew the terrain well. From this point on, Lysias has lost respect for the leadership of Menelaus, as is seen later (13:4) when he agrees that Menelaus is the cause of the whole trouble.

The author of the condensed narrative backs up his version of events with the help of four documents. For a discussion of the possible correct order of these letters, see the excursus on the letters. It is important to note that the author has not previously given any precise dates for the events narrated but has kept to general indications—"about/about this/that time" (5:1; 9:1); "after not much time" (6:1); "after an extremely short interval" (11:1). The audience thus has received no indication of the year in which the events narrated occurred. The author has clearly set out to arrange the letters in his own chronological order: the first is dated to the first month of the Macedonian calendar for the year 148 s.e. (11:21) and the second letter, undated, is the king's response to that letter of Lysias; the third letter is seen by the author of the condensed narrative as the king's letter to the Jews and is dated to the sixth month of 148 s.e. (11:33); the fourth letter is given the same date (11:38) and so is later than Lysias's letter. By including a letter of Roman ambassadors in the midst of peace negotiations between the Jews and the Seleucid king, the author shows that the forces of Judas have come into their own on the world scene.

---

73   Walther Kolbe, *Beiträge zur syrischen und jüdischen Geschichte: Kritische Untersuchungen zur Seleukidenliste und zu den beiden ersten Makkabäerbüchern* (Stuttgart: Kohlhammer, 1926) 78–81; Mørkholm, *Antiochus IV*, 152–54.

74   Bar-Kochva, *Judas Maccabaeus*, 275–76. Earlier, Tcherikover, *Jews in the Graeco-Roman World*, 195–96;

Solomon Zeitlin, *The First Book of Maccabees* (English translation by Sidney Tedesche; New York: Harper, 1954) 60; Goldstein, *I Maccabees*, 268.

75   For a strategic analysis, see Bar-Kochva, *Judas Maccabaeus*, 285–90.

The Letters in 2 Maccabees 11:16-38

These letters have been the subject of much scholarly debate. While early scholars doubted their authenticity,[1] the increase in knowledge of the chancery style of royal letters led to acceptance of their authenticity.[2] Within this general agreement, there have been exceptions for some of the documents. Both Kolbe and Mørkholm doubted the authenticity of the fourth letter.[3]

The First Letter

If the letters are regarded as authentic, then questions arise as to the order of the documents and their recipients. Tcherikover argued that the recipients of the first (11:16-21), third (11:27-33), and fourth letters (11:34-38) were members of Menelaus's party.[4] Here the mention of Menelaus in the third letter is extremely important. However, Habicht has convincingly shown that the address to the Jews as "populace" ($\pi\lambda\acute{\eta}\vartheta o\varsigma$) in 11:17 as well as the Hebrew names of those sent to Lysias both point to this first letter being written to Judas's forces.[5] From the present context in 2 Maccabees, it would appear that it was written after the first expedition of Lysias, which is usually dated to October 164.[6] However, the date at the end of the letter is 148 s.e., that is, from 2 October 165 b.c.e. to 22 September 164 b.c.e.[7] It is important to recall that the author of the condensed narrative has previously given no year dates for the narrated events. One finds, however, events of the reign of Antiochus V dated

to the years 149 s.e. (13:1) and 151 s.e. (14:4). It would seem that the author has placed the dates for the letters in the year prior to the events narrated in 2 Maccabees 13, that is, to 148 s.e. The dates given at the end of the letters should all be deemed suspect, and attempts to date these letters should be based on their contents. The confusion over the month of the first letter only confirms this misgiving. The author wanted to place this letter at the head of the documents and so chose a name for a month that looked earlier than the sixth Macedonian month, Xanthikos, mentioned in the body of the third letter. Bar-Kochva has striven mightily, mainly on the basis of the date given, to date the document to the end of October 165, immediately after the defeat of Ptolemy, Nikanor, and Gorgias.[8] Yet why would Lysias allow the defeat of a force sent by the governor of Coele-Syria to go unavenged? Given that the account of Lysias's first expedition in 1 Maccabees appears to be less a defeat of Lysias and more a skirmish, it seems more likely that Lysias, having assessed the size and determination of Judas's forces, was ready to come to an accommodation with them. The first letter, thus, is to be placed after Lysias's first expedition into Judea in October/November 164 b.c.e., before the death of Antiochus IV. Lysias therefore sends a letter to Antiochus IV outlining what he has agreed to and asking for clarification of some details.

---

1   Grimm, *Das zweite,* 172–74; Wilhelm Schubart, "Bemerkungen zum Stile hellenistischer Königsbriefe," *Archiv für Papyrusforschung und verwandte Gebiete* 6 (1920) 324–47; Hugo Willrich, *Urkundenfälschung in der hellenistisch-jüdischen Literatur* (Göttingen: Vandenhoeck & Ruprecht, 1924) 30–36; Kolbe, *Beiträge,* 74–107.

2   An excellent overview is given by Elias Bickermann, "Une question d'authenticité: Les privileges juifs," in idem, *Studies in Jewish and Christian History* (3 vols.; AGJU 9; Leiden: Brill, 1976–86) 2:24–43. See also Richard Laqueur, "Griechische Urkunden in der jüdisch-hellenistischer Literatur," *HZ* 136 (1927) 229–52; Victor Tcherikover, "The Documents in II Maccabees" (in Hebrew), *Tarbiz* 1 (1929) 31–45; Bickermann, *Der Gott der Makkabäer,* 179–81; Abel, *Les livres,* 426–31; Klaus Dietrich Schunk, *Die Quellen des I. und II. Makkabäerbuches* (Halle: Niemeyer, 1954) 103–9; Zambelli, "La composizione," 213–34;

Mørkholm, *Antiochus IV,* 162–65; Tcherikover, *Hellenistic Civilization,* 213–19; Bunge, *Untersuchungen,* 386–436; Habicht, "Royal Documents," 7–17; Goldstein, *II Maccabees,* 426–28; Fischer, *Seleukiden und Makkabäer,* 64–80; Bringmann, *Hellenistische Reform,* 40–51; Gruen, *Hellenistic World,* 2:745–47; Bar-Kochva, *Judas Maccabaeus,* 516–42; Gera, *Judaea,* 239–47.

3   Kolbe, *Beiträge,* 82–87; Mørkholm, *Antiochus IV,* 163–64.

4   Tcherikover, *Hellenistic Civilization,* 217.

5   Habicht, "Royal Documents," 9–10. In this he is followed by Bar-Kochva, *Judas Maccabaeus,* 520–21; and Gera, *Judaea,* 244–45.

6   Bar-Kochva, *Judas Maccabaeus,* 284.

7   Parker and Dubberstein, *Babylonian Chronology,* 41.

8   Bar-Kochva, *Judas Maccabaeus,* 522–23.

The Second Letter

The second letter was written soon after the death of Antiochus IV. Habicht correctly saw it as a programmatic statement at the beginning of the reign of Antiochus V that announces a new policy. "Such announcements, containing an amnesty or privileges, were customary for a new Hellenistic ruler and are known as *philanthropa*."[9] Bar-Kochva attempts to follow an earlier opinion that dated this letter after the second expedition of Lysias.[10] His argument founders first, however, on the fact that he does not take into consideration that the text speaks of the recent death of Antiochus IV, while the expedition of Lysias, on Bar-Kochva's own calculation, took place in 162 B.C.E., a year or more after Antiochus V's accession.[11] Second, the author of 1 Maccabees depicts Lysias as consistently hostile to Judas's forces, as is seen in Lysias's response to his first expedition, which involves a decision to hire numerous soldiers to go back and attack Judea (1 Macc 4:35). The author of 1 Maccabees simply ignores any peace negotiations until forced to acknowledge them by outside events (1 Macc 6:55-59). Bar-Kochva also holds that after the restoration of the temple by Judas and his forces (1 Macc 4:36), the temple was no longer something that could be returned to them, as the letter states (11:25). Therefore, Bar-Kochva argues that the king could only return the temple after he had retaken it in Lysias's second expedition (1 Macc 6:54). However, it is not clear that Antiochus V had control of the sanctuary during that second expedition of Lysias.[12] Moreover, if Lysias's first expedition took place before Judas recaptured the temple as in 1 Maccabees, then the restoration of the temple could have been one of the matters open for negotiation. The most likely dating for the second letter thus seems to place it after the first expedition of Lysias, when, once Antiochus IV had died, the new king annulled the previous policy of his father.

The *Megillat Taanith* ("The Scroll of Fasting") for the month of Adar reads: "On the twenty-eighth [of Adar] the good news reached the Judeans that (they did not) have to abandon the Torah [דלא מן אוריתא]." Such a dating to early spring would fit with a proclamation of the new king following his installation after the death of his father, Antiochus IV. Bar-Kochva uses the data from the Scroll of Fasting to argue for a date six months before Lysias's first expedition, that is, spring of 164 B.C.E.[13] See the discussion below on the third letter.

The Fourth Letter

The fourth document is connected with the first two documents. Not only is their wording similar, as noted in the commentary, but the first and the fourth documents speak of negotiations between Lysias and the Judeans and of matters referred to the king. Whereas Lysias had addressed the group as a "multitude" or "populace" ($\pi\lambda\hat{\eta}\vartheta o\varsigma$), the Romans addressed them as a recognizable political community (11:34, $\delta\hat{\eta}\mu o\varsigma$).[14] The time frame for the letter would thus seem to be between, at one end, Lysias's withdrawal from Beth-Zur and the beginning of the negotiations and, at the other end, the news of Antiochus IV's death. Mørkholm, following Kolbe, doubts the letter's authenticity.[15] First, the dates assigned at the end of letters 1 and 4 show a difference of six months, while the content proves that they belong to the same period. However, this is to place too much confidence in these dates, as argued above. Second, the names of the ambassadors prove to be a difficulty, but, as noted in the commentary, at this time one simply does not have substantial evidence about Roman embassies to the East. Third, why would the ambassadors hope to influence Antiochus IV, who was away not in Antioch but on his eastern campaign at this time? Indeed, are the Roman ambassadors on their way to see Antiochus IV, or are they hoping to influence which matters Lysias was deciding to send to the king? In his letter to the Judeans, Lysias had stated that he had made clear (11:18: $\delta\iota\epsilon\sigma\acute{\alpha}\varphi\eta\sigma\alpha$) what ought to be sent to the king. It would seem that he had made

---

9   Habicht, "Royal Documents," 15–17; quotation from 17.

10   Bar-Kochva, *Judas Maccabaeus*, 523–25. Previous scholars to hold this opinion include Mørkholm (*Antiochus IV*, 163) and Bunge (*Untersuchungen*, 437–43).

11   Bar-Kochva, *Judas Maccabaeus*, 543–51.

12   Does ὀχύρωμα in 1 Macc 6:61 necessarily mean "sanctuary" in this context? Are there still some defenders in the temple (1 Macc 6:54)?

13   Bar-Kochva, *Judas Maccabaeus*, 526–27, 533.

14   See ibid., 530–33.

15   Kolbe, *Beiträge*, 82–87; Mørkholm, *Antiochus IV*, 163–64.

it clear to the Judeans. Are the Romans hoping to meet with Lysias before he sends something to the king? Is the verb in 11:36, ἔκρινε, an aorist, or should one read it as an imperfect, reflecting a process that had begun in the past but was still continuing?

Kolbe and Mørkholm have made a strong case for inauthenticity, but, on balance, the argument from the Latinism of the final greeting (11:38: ὑγιαίνετε [valete]) is more compelling. The question remains of how to imagine what is happening. Were the withdrawal of Lysias back to Antioch and the beginning of negotiations so well known that they came to the ears of traveling Romans? Or did Judas send some kind of message to the Romans? Were the Romans only too happy to interfere in the internal affairs of the Seleucid kingdom to keep Antiochus IV in check, particularly after the impressive display of power at Daphne? The details are missing.

Chronology of the First, Second, and Fourth Letters

1. The first letter was written after Lysias's first expedition and withdrawal to Antioch, sometime in the late autumn of 164 B.C.E., but before the news of Antiochus IV's death reached Antioch.
2. The fourth letter was written during the ensuing negotiations between Lysias and Judas's forces.
3. The second letter was written soon after the death of Antiochus IV, when Antiochus V had assumed sole rulership.

The Third Letter

The third letter was addressed by Antiochus IV to the ruling party in Jerusalem at the instigation of Menelaus. A limited amnesty is offered so that all those who had left their regular way of life can return to their own affairs.

There has been much debate over the date of this letter. For a long time, scholars thought that it was the king's response to Lysias's letter, and the letter was

therefore placed after the first and fourth letters.[16] One exception was Marcello Zambelli, who recognized that this letter must be seen as the earliest of the documents.[17] Habicht argued that it was written by Antiochus IV from beyond the Euphrates, early in 164 B.C.E. if not in late 165 B.C.E.[18] As noted above, Bar-Kochva dated this letter to February 164 B.C.E., six months before Lysias's first expedition and while Antiochus IV was campaigning in the East. However, one is not told how to imagine the sequence of events. Is one to suppose that Menelaus sought out Antiochus IV while he was on campaign? More importantly, would Antiochus IV have been amenable to Menelaus's suggestion of an amnesty after the defeat of an army led by his governor of Coele-Syria, Ptolemy son of Dorymenes? Would his reaction not rather be that attributed to him in 9:3-4, where he angrily set out to destroy the Jews and Jerusalem? Admittedly, the whole account of the last days of Antiochus IV in 2 Maccabees 9 is highly sensational, yet this desire for revenge seems a more likely response by a king to the defeat of his governor's army. I would suggest, therefore, that Menelaus approached Antiochus IV much earlier than spring 164 B.C.E. My starting point for dating the letter is the date of thirtieth Xanthikos found in the middle of the third letter (11:30) and therefore more reliable than the highly problematic dates found at the end of the letters. Given this date, a more likely time for Menelaus to have approached Antiochus IV would be before the spring of 165 B.C.E. Antiochus IV had successfully showcased his army at Daphne in 166 B.C.E.[19] and was to begin his eastern campaign in spring 165 B.C.E. Between these two events would, I suggest, be the most plausible time to place Menelaus's request. Events in Judea were still confined to the tactics of insurgency mentioned in 8:6-7. As Bar-Kochva suggests, the clashes with Apollonius and Seron mentioned in 1 Macc 3:10-26 were probably of this type.[20] No major operation, such as that of Ptolemy son of Dorymenes, had yet occurred. Less than eighteen months had elapsed since the abrogation of the Jewish

16 Niese, "Kritik," 484; Kolbe, *Beiträge*, 84; Bickermann, *Der Gott der Makkabäer*, 179–81; Tcherikover, *Hellenistic Civilization*, 215; Bunge, *Untersuchungen*, 386–88.
17 Zambelli, "La composizione," 213–34.
18 Habicht, "Royal Documents," 14–15.
19 For the date, Gera and Horowitz ("Antiochus IV,"
240–52) refute the attempt of Bar-Kochva (*Judas Maccabaeus*, 467–73) to date the procession at Daphne to 165 B.C.E.
20 Bar-Kochva, *Judas Maccabaeus*, 200–201.

ancestral laws, and Menelaus may have thought that if the ancestral laws were reintroduced, the insurgency would end, a more probable scenario than that Menelaus proposed an amnesty after Judas's forces had inflicted a major blow to Seleucid forces. Antiochus IV would have been more likely to relax his harshness toward Judea and show his benevolence after he had shown his power. Judas and his forces had already committed themselves too much to take advantage of the offered amnesty. For them, the die was cast and there was no turning back, particularly to a situation where Menelaus still retained control. In response to the rejection of the amnesty, the governor of Coele-Syria felt he had to intervene. When he too failed, Lysias advanced. However, when Lysias had had a taste of the strength of Judas's forces and their knowledge of the terrain, he may have recalled the attempt of Antiochus IV to reach an accommodation by repealing the abrogation of the Jewish ancestral laws and decided to follow his example. He entered into direct negotiations with the insurgents, however, recognizing that they were the most important force in Judea, not the party of Menelaus.

12

12:1-45

1/ With these agreements in place, Lysias departed toward the king; the Jews engaged themselves with agriculture. 2/ However, some of the local commanders, Timothy, Apollonius, son of Gennaios, as well as Hieronomos and Demophon and besides these Nikanor, commander of the Cypriot troops, were not allowing [the Jews] to enjoy stability and to live at ease. 3/ The citizens of Joppa perpetrated a hugely impious act. By a communal vote of the city, they summoned the Jews living with them to embark with their wives and children onto ships docked by them nearby, as if no ill will threatened them. 4/ [The citizens of Joppa] welcomed [the Jews] as if they were wanting to be at peace and had nothing suspicious in mind, but when the Jews set sail, they threw no fewer than two hundred [Jews] into the sea. 5/ When Judas learned of the cruelty done toward his kinsfolk, he gave instructions to his fighting followers. 6/ He called upon God, the righteous judge, and went against the foul murderers of his brethren. At night he set the harbor on fire and burned the ships and slaughtered those who were there in flight. 7/ With the town closed, he withdrew with the purpose of coming again in the future to root out the entire body of Joppa citizens. 8/ However, he learned that those in Jamnia also meant to perpetrate the same behavior on the Jews dwelling among them. 9/ He fell upon the Jamnians by night and fired the harbor with its fleet so that its fiery glare could be seen in Jerusalem, 240 stadia away.

10/ After withdrawing nine stadia from [Jamnia], while they were making their way toward Timothy, no fewer than five thousand Arabs with five hundred cavalry attacked him.[a] 11/ After a strongly contested battle, Judas's forces were successful because of God's help. Defeated, the nomads asked Judas to

a The grammar of this sentence leaves much to be desired, and later scribes have tried to fix it. According to A V q La^X, a nominative plural participle referring to the Jews (ἀποσπάσαντες, "withdrawing") is followed by a plural genitive absolute construction with the Jews as its subject (ποιουμένων, "making"), while the plural main verb of the sentence (προσέβαλον) has as its subject Arabs. Having the subject of the genitive absolute identical with the object of the leading verb would "emphasize the idea contained in the genitive absolute" (Smyth, *Greek Grammar*, §2073b; see also Edwin Mayser, *Grammatik der griechischen Papyri aus der Ptolemäerzeit* [2 vols.; Berlin and Leipzig: de Gruyter, 1923–34] 2:3.68). The presence of the singular dative (αὐτῷ) is usually seen as referring to Judas and therefore anomalous, as Judas does not otherwise appear in the sentence. As in 10:17, 35, προσβάλλειν is followed by a dative of what is attacked. The presence of the nominative plural participle referring to the Jews has suggested to some commentators that we can see here the work of the abridger.

make a treaty with them and promised to send cattle and to be of service to them in the future. 12/ Judas, understanding how they could be truly useful in many ways, consented to keep peace with them. Receiving these assurances, they went back to their tents.

13/ He next attacked a certain city with bridges,[b] strong and enclosed all around with walls, peopled with a mixture of ethnic groups. It was called Kaspin. 14/ Those inside, trusting in the security of their walls and in the stock of provisions, treated the forces of Judas vulgarly, abusing and moreover blaspheming and saying things not allowed. 15/ Those following Judas, however, called upon the great Master of the universe, he who, disdaining battering rams and manufactured machines, threw down Jericho during the time of Joshua. [Judas's forces] attacked the wall ferociously. 16/ Seizing the city by God's goodwill, they slaughtered untold many, so that the adjacent harbor, two stadia wide, appeared filled and flowing with blood.

17/ When they had withdrawn 750 stadia from there, they arrived at a palisaded enclosure where there were the Jews called Toubians. 18/ They did not seize Timothy in the region; as he had been unsuccessful,[c] he had withdrawn from the region, but he had left behind in a certain place a very strong garrison. 19/ Dositheos and Sosipater, two of the commanders of Maccabeus, marched out and destroyed the forces left behind by Timothy in the stronghold, more than 10,000 fighters. 20/ Maccabeus arranged his army into companies and appointed the[d] company leaders. He started off toward Timothy, who had 120,000 infantry and 2,500 cavalry.[e] 21/ Learning of Judas's approach, Timothy sent out the women and children and the other household belongings into a place called Karnion, for

b   Hanhart bracketed the term γεφυρουν as do Abel, Habicht, and Schwartz. Abel suggests that the word is a gloss put in by a scribe to provide a name for the "certain town." Citing Polybius 5.70.12, where a town in the Transjordan region around Pella is named Γεφρôυν, identified with Ephron, Goldstein suggested that the town's name was changed to Γεφυρουν, "because the resultant spelling resembled the Greek word *gephyra*. The description of Ephron at vs. 27 is almost identical to the description of Kaspin here. An early scribe, who intended to insert into the margin at vs. 27 the alternative spelling, mistook vs.13 for vs. 27 and wrote the word into the margin here, and the scribes underlying A and q copied the word from the margin into the text" (Goldstein, *II Maccabees*, 439). However, this two-step attempt to explain away the term is not satisfactory. Manuscript 55 has the reading γεφύραις. Both Abel and Goldstein note that the noun γέφυρα means a bridge, dam, or causeway, which does not seem to be a means of fortification. However, bridges can limit the means of access to a town and hinder attack. A classic example is the defense of Rome by Horatius Cocles, as narrated in Polybius 6.55 (see also Polybius 1.75; 2.5). I can understand why someone would leave out the term but not why someone would put it in, *pace* Goldstein. Given the presence of a lake about two hundred meters wide near this city, I have kept the term γεφύραις ("with bridges"). I consider it more likely that the notion of bridges being part of a fortified town was changed in some manuscript traditions to the name of an unknown town Γεφυρουν than the other way around, and that other manuscript traditions simply excised it.

c   I have followed Grimm in reading ἄπρακτον τέ (V L′ 58 311) rather than ἄπρακτον τότε. Grimm suggested that the reading τότε came about through a reduplication of the ending of ἄπρακτον. Here τέ corresponds to the following δέ and contrasts the two decisions of Timothy.

d   As Grimm argued, followed by Abel and Habicht, one should read here τούς instead of the received αὐτούς. Judas is not speaking of the forces given to Dositheos and Sosipater but is appointing leaders of the smaller companies of about five hundred men.

e   The number of cavalry differs in various manuscripts: 3,700; 2,700; 1,700; 1,500.

the town was hard to besiege and hard to attack because of the narrowness of the spaces. 22/ When the first company of Judas appeared, dread was on the enemy and fear was on them from the appearance of the one who watches over all things. They rushed to flight at full speed, one here another there, so that often they were accosted by their own people and run through at sword point. 23/ Judas vigorously pursued. Stabbing at the offenders, he killed about 30,000 fighters. 24/ As for Timothy, when he fell into the hands of the forces of Dositheos and Sosipater, he pleaded very bewitchingly [for them] to send him away safe and sound because he held the parents of many, of others the kinsfolk, and "they will not be mistreated." 25/ As he repeatedly confirmed the commitment to restore them unharmed, they let him go for the sake of their kinsfolk's safety. 26/ Marching out against Karnion and the temple of Atargatis, [Judas] slaughtered 25,000.

27/ After their overthrow and destruction,[f] he warred against Ephron, a strongly defended city in which Lysias and a mixed populace dwelt.[g] Virile youths stood in front of the walls and fought vigorously, and a great store of war machines and missiles was there. 28/ Calling upon the Master, he who powerfully shatters the forces[h] of the enemy, they put the city under their control, and laid low about 25,000 of those inside. 29/ Moving off from there, they marched against a city of Scythians, about sixty stadia distant from Jerusalem. 30/ When the Jews who had settled there witnessed to the goodwill that the Scythopolitans had toward them and their civilized interaction during these ill-fated times, 31/ they gave thanks and exhorted them to be well disposed toward the race also in the future. They came to Jerusalem as the feast of Weeks was at hand.

f De Bruyne (*Les anciennes traductions*, xi) and Abel see καὶ ἀπώλειαν ("and destruction") as a gloss to explain the word τροπήν, as v. 26 had spoken of slaughter, not flight. However, 12:22-23 speaks of the flight of the enemy, and so this is a good summary of the events surrounding Timothy.

g The manuscript tradition has three main variants: (1) ἐν ᾗ Λυσίας (Λυσάνιας) κατῴκει ("in which Lysias dwelt"); (2) ἐν ᾗ πάμφυλα ἐν αὐτῇ πλήθη κατῴκει ("in which a mixed populace in the same place dwelt"); (3) ἐν ᾗ κατῴκει Λυσίας καὶ πάμφυλα πλήθη ("in which dwelt Lysias and a mixed populace"). Hanhart prefers reading 2 but leaves out the verb, as does Schwartz. Habicht rightly notes that the combination of ἐν ᾗ and ἐν αὐτῇ is impossible. Along with Grimm, Abel, and Goldstein, Habicht keeps the mention of Lysias and follows the Lucianic manuscript reading 3. Grimm and Goldstein hold that the reference is to the chancellor Lysias of 2 Maccabees 11 and 12:1 and so suggest that Lysias kept a residence in Ephron or had previously dwelled there. However, Lysias is a common name, and the author of 2 Maccabees often names individuals who do not turn up again in the narrative, as in 12:2. As Grimm suggested, later scribes may have wondered why the chancellor Lysias would have a home in Ephron, and so deleted the reference.

h Reading ἀλκάς for ὁλκάς ("weights"). The same confusion is found in Sir 29:13. Hanhart, Habicht, and Schwartz take ὁλκάς as the *lectio difficilior*. Grimm states that "weight" does not fit well with συντρίβειν ("to break"), whereas Schwartz holds that this verb "fits better with an object which has weight." I find this metaphorical interpretation of "weight" unconvincing, particularly since the term is in the plural ("shattering the weights of the enemies"). Ἀλκή has the meaning of "force, strength." The plural is found with the sense of "forces" in Euripides *Rhes.* 933: "when you were arming blood-loving forces [φιλαιμάτους ἀλκάς] in defense of your country." In Diodorus Siculus 2.43.1, the Scythians are said to have increased their territory because of their forces and their bravery (διὰ τὰς ἀλκὰς καὶ τὴν ἀνδρείαν). In Lucian *Anach.* 35, a trainer is reprimanded for wearing out the bodies of the young men, for "not husbanding their strength [τὰς ἀλκὰς αὐτῶν]." Ἀλκάς is also used of the strength of animals, and its use here is consistent with the author of the condensed version's liking for drawing images from the animal realm.

32/ After the so-called Pentecost, they marched against Gorgias, the commander of Idumea. 33/ He came out with 3,000 infantry and 400 cavalry. 34/ As the battle lines met,[i] a few Jews fell. 35/ Dositheos, one of the Toubians,[j] a staunch cavalryman, followed Gorgias closely and, seizing his cloak, he was vigorously leading him away. He was wanting to take the accursed one alive, but one of the Thracian cavalry bore down on him and destroyed his shoulder, and Gorgias fled to Marisa. 36/ As Esdrin's forces had been fighting for a long time and were very weary, Judas called on the Lord to appear as a cofighter and leader of the battle. 37/ In the ancestral language he started the hymnodic war cry and, charging unexpectedly at Gorgias's forces, turned them back.

38/ Judas came with his army to the city of Adullam. With the Sabbath coming on, after they had been purified according to custom, they spent the Sabbath where they were. 39/ On the following day, Judas's forces came, at the time when what was necessary fell due,[k] to recover the bodies of the fallen and to restore them with their kinsfolk into their ancestral graves. 40/ They found under the tunics of each of the dead an object consecrated to the idols at Jamnia, from which the law forces the Jews to refrain. It became clear to all why they had fallen. 41/ Accordingly, they all blessed the power of the just judge, who makes hidden things manifest, 42/ and they turned to supplication, pleading that the sin committed be completely wiped away. The noble Judas exhorted the populace to observe strictly that they be sinless as they had seen with their own eyes what had happened[l] because of the sin of the fallen. 43/ Consequently, he made a collection from each man, and he sent about 2,000 silver drachmas to Jerusalem to bring a sacrifice for sin.

i   Hanhart keeps the accusative plural παραταξαμένους. However, this does not make sense, as it would have to be attached to the nearest accusative plural, "a few of the Jews." It is better to read the genitive plural παραταξαμένων with L[1].

j   Hanhart (*Zum Text*, 469) reads "one of Bakenor's men" (τις τῶν τοῦ Βακήνορος) and views it as the *lectio difficilior*. Katz ("Text of 2 Maccabees," 16) follows Niese and Abel, as do Habicht and Schwartz, in seeing this as a corruption where "του was mistakenly considered the article." See also Bar-Kochva, *Judas Maccabaeus*, 82.

k   Abel, following LXV and the Syriac, omits this phrase as an unnecessary reflection on the need for the bodies to be buried as they were decomposing. But Schwartz rightly notes that it refers to the end of the Sabbath.

l   Wilhelm ("Zu einigen Stellen," 25–28), followed by Katz ("Text of 2 Maccabees," 16), suggested that τὰ γεγονότα should have as a substantive the noun κατασκευάσματα, which is found in some manuscripts in v. 43. Wilhelm argued that this term was originally in the margin and so was misplaced. He would have Judas point to the objects. Schwartz rightly rejects the reasoning and follows Hanhart's text.

He acted very correctly and honorably as he considered the resurrection. 44/ For if he were not expecting that the fallen would rise, [it would have been] superfluous and silly to pray on behalf of the dead. 45/ If he was looking at the most noble reciprocation placed for those who fall asleep piously, the thought was holy and pious. Wherefore, concerning the dead he made atonement to be absolved from the sin.

Commentary by Verse

■ **1-2** The author uses the term συνθήκη ("agreements") to describe what has occurred in the letters of the previous chapter. The term is not used there, and while Judas is said to agree with what Lysias proposed (11:15), the letters reflect a decision by the king rather than a covenant. However, the term carries the connotation of "treaty" and so suits the author's rhetorical purpose of elevating the position of the Jews under Judas. The term is also used to describe the agreement reached after the invasion of Antiochus V (13:25) as well as those between Nikanor and Judas (14:20, 26, 27). The term and its verb συντίθημι are found in agreements between cities and imperial powers, for example, between Cassander and Athens (Diodorus Siculus 18.74.2), Eupolemos and Theangela,[1] the Carthaginians and Nuceria (Appian *Punic Wars* 63), Rhodes and Antigonos (Diodorus Siculus 20.99.3), and the Romans and Tauromenians (Appian *Sicily* 5). The term can thus be used for an agreement between a major power and a city.

■ **2** This sentence is connected to the previous two clauses ("Lysias departed . . . Jews engaged . . .") through a μὲν . . . δέ . . . δέ construction.[2]

Just as the author has the surrounding local communities annoyed after the rededication of the temple (10:14-38), so too here after the agreement with Lysias by which the Jews were allowed to practice their own ancestral customs, the local authorities are not happy. The use of agricultural imagery to depict peaceful endeavors is found also in 1 Macc 14:8. The author emphasizes that it is local commanders,[3] not more senior officers, who initiate activities against the Jews. Through his emphasis on local commanders, the author distinguishes this Timothy from the one in 10:24-38, who was able to muster a large force to attempt to conquer Judea and who was killed. See Introduction, p. 10, on the question of the number of Timothys. The next three commanders are otherwise unknown. Nikanor the Cypriarch is a commander of Cypriot mercenaries. Cypriots are mentioned as stationed in the Jerusalem citadel in 4:29.

"not allowing to enjoy tranquility and live at ease." A similar phrase is found in the complaint of Alcimus against Judas and his followers in 14:6, where Judas does not "allow the kingdom to enjoy stability." The same complaint is made by Haman in the Greek Esther in 3:13e (= Addition B 13:5), and later the king "allows" the Jews to use their own laws (Esth 8:11). Similarly, in

1   Hatto H. Schmitt, *Die Staatsverträge des Altertums*, vol. 3: *Die Verträge der griechisch-römischen Welt von 338 bis 200 v. Chr.* (Munich: Beck, 1969) no. 429.
2   On the duplicated δέ after μέν, see the discussion in J. D. Denniston, *The Greek Particles* (2nd ed.; Oxford: Clarendon, 1970) 183–85.
3   See *P. Oxy.* 833: οἱ κατὰ τόπον σιτολόγοι ("the local collectors of provisions").

3 Macc. 3:26 and 7:4, the same accusation is made, and it is refuted in *3 Macc.* 7:6-7. The verb of "ease," ἡσυ- χάζειν, is found repeatedly in 1 Maccabees (1:3; 7:50; 9:57; 11:38, 52; 14:4), following its use in Judges, to denote a land at peace. The use of ἐᾶν ("allow") is found also in Thucydides, in the speech by the Corinthians to the Spartans describing how the Athenians "were born neither to enjoy rest [ἔχειν ἡσυχίαν] themselves, nor to allow [ἐᾶν] others enjoy it" (1.70.9).

■ **3-7** The first incident occurs in Joppa. There is no explicit connection with the purposes of the local governors mentioned in v. 2, but, as seen in 6:8, the view of a governor could have an impact on a city's decision. There had been rising tension between the Jews who lived in neighboring cities and the citizens of those cities since the uprising in Judea. Joppa was an important port, as the next major harbor was Alexandria (Diodorus Siculus 1.31.2).[4]

■ **3a** "perpetrate a hugely impious act." The verb συντελεῖν ("perpetrate") is found often in 2 Maccabees (3:32; 4:3; 5:5; 8:17; 13:8), and the unusual noun δυσ- σέβημα[5] ("impious act") reflects the author's use of the adjective δυσσεβής, which is mainly found in tragedy. Such a word usage highlights the emotional quality of the action that follows. The author uses compounds with δυσ- frequently: δυσημερία, δυσημερεῖν (5:6; 8:35); δυσμένεια (6:29; 12:3; 14:39); δυσμενῶς (14:11); δυσπο- λιόρκητος (12:21); δυσπρόσιτος (12:21); δυσσέβεια, δυσσεβεῖν (8:33; 6:13); δύσφημος (13:11; 15:32); δυσφορεῖν (4:35; 13:25); δυσφόρως (14:28); δυσχέρεια (2:24; 9:21); and δυσχερής (6:3; 9:7, 24; 14:45).

■ **3b-4** This single sentence consists of two attributive and three circumstantial participles, as well as five genitive absolutes. Such a clustering suggests much condensation and focuses the attention on the one verb, βυθίζω, which has the meaning of "to sink a ship" but here has the sense of "drown, throw into the sea," without implying that the ships were destroyed. The cryptic quality of the description does not allow one to grasp the details of

the event. The author intends to highlight the innocence of the Jews and the impiety of the citizens of Joppa. What exactly was the vote? Where did the Jews think they were going—on a voyage to Alexandria or to found a colony somewhere else? It seems highly unlikely that they would have suspected nothing, or at least not realized that they were being expelled from Joppa. Lactantius ironically describes how the "pious" Galerius gathered all the beggars together and had them dumped into the sea (*Mort.* 23.8–9).

τούτων ἐπιδεξαμένων (literally, "these welcoming"). The referent of the demonstrative is unclear, and most translators have opted for "the Jews" as the referent. However, as Grimm, who also chose "the Jews," noted, one has to supply an object for the verb and the presence of ἄν is not taken into account. Grimm suggested that one has to read τούτων ἐπιδεξαμένων [τὴν παρά- κλησιν] νομιζόντων ὅτι (οἱ Ἰοππῖται) ἂν εἰρηνεύειν θέλοιεν καὶ μηδὲν ὕποπτον ἔχοιεν, "(The Jews) welcomed (the summons) thinking that (the citizens of Joppa) wanted to be at peace and had nothing suspicious in mind." However, this proposal has the subject of the first genitive participle different from that of the second and third. I have taken all three participles as referring to the citizens of Joppa and translate the first participle "[The citizens of Joppa] welcomed [the Jews]." Deceit on the part of the opponents of the Jews was seen also in 5:25-26. This translation does require that the citizens of Joppa are the subject of the main verb ἐβύθισαν and of the attributive participle παρακαλέσαντες and also of the genitive absolute ἐπιδεξαμένων . . . ἐχόντων. As Smyth notes, "the effect of this irregular construction is to emphasize the idea contained in the genitive abso- lute."[6]

■ **5-6** This long sentence with its four introductory circumstantial participles followed by three main verbs suggests rapid action. The first two participles are in asyndeton, as are the third and fourth: to hear is to react; prayer is linked to action. The assonance between ὁμο-

4   See J. Kaplan, "The Archeology and History of Tel Aviv-Jaffa," *BA* 35 (1972) 88–90.

5   In classical literature, see only Dionysius of Halicar- nassus *Ant. rom.* 7.44.4, where one of the tribunes tries to persuade the senate by predicting the impious acts that would follow a bloody civil war if

the senate tried to curtail the prerogatives of the people.

6   Smyth, *Greek Grammar*, §2073b.

ἐθνεῖς ("kinsfolk") and ὡμότητα ("cruelty") heightens the significance of what had been perpetrated. As usual, God's help is invoked, with the emphasis being on his justice in repaying the Joppites for their inhumane deed. In 12:41, God is also described as just judge (δικαιο-κρίτης). The unjust murderer of Onias, Andronikos, is called a foul murderer (4:38: μιαιφόνος). As there, here too the theme of just deserts is present: the ships of the Joppites are destroyed, and those who flee to the ships for safety are killed; the Joppites killed the Jews on the ships, and now they themselves are killed there too.

■ **7** The alarm raised, the city of Joppa closed its gates. The future participle is used to denote purpose.[7] The later fate of Joppa is described in 1 Maccabees. At first, in 1 Macc 10:74-77, Jonathan besieged Joppa, and in fear the citizens opened the gates to him. Later, in 1 Macc 13:11, Simon sent Jonathan, son of Absalom, to drive out the occupants and gain a harbor for the Jews (1 Macc 14:5). Here πολίτευμα is used in a general sense to denote the body politic of Joppa.[8]

■ **8-9** The same participle, μεταλαβών, as in v. 5 is used here to introduce the second attack of Judas, this time on Jamnia. The city of Jabneh, or Jamnia, lay inland, and so its port was Jabneh-Yam. An inscription that has been dated to July 163 B.C.E. records the request by the citizens of Jamnia to the Seleucid government for tax relief in return for assistance given earlier. The fragmentary quality of the inscription does not allow one to decide whether the request came before or after the attack of the Jews.[9] According to 1 Macc 10:75, a Seleucid garrison was stationed in Jamnia at the time of Jonathan.

The use of the verb παροικεῖν ("dwelling") shows that the Jews are not citizens but resident aliens.

Two hundred and forty stadia is about forty-five kilometers. Bar-Kochva states that "the straight-line distance between Jerusalem and Jamnia harbour is 55 km, but the road distance was twice as long as the 240 stadia estimated by II Maccabees."[10] For Bar-Kochva this shows that Jason of Cyrene had only a vague idea of the geography of Eretz Israel. However, Schwartz notes that "it is perfectly possible that our author, or his source, could figure the distance as the crow flies." Schwartz notes that Strabo (*Geogr.* 16.2.28) and Josephus (*Bell.* 5.160) claim that one could see the coastal region from high points in Jerusalem and that Appian (*Mith.* 12.67, 278) claims that one could see a great fire at a distance of one thousand stadia.

■ **10-16** The opening phrase, ἐκεῖθεν δὲ ἀποσπά-σαντες σταδίους . . . , is repeated in 12:17, and so the author seems to have joined the two episodes in vv. 10-16 together, with first an incident with a company of Arabs and then another at Kaspin. Kaspin, when identified with the Χασφω of 1 Macc 5:26, 36, is situated in the Golan, and 1 Macc 5:25 has Judas's forces clash with Arabs after a three-day march beyond the Jordan. So, in comparison with the narrative of 1 Macc 5:9-54, the account here seems glaringly wrong. A distance of nine stadia would keep Judas's forces on the wrong side of the Jordan. Most commentators have seen this distance as a sign that this incident has been drawn from another context.[11] Schwartz argued that vv. 10-16 should come after vv. 17-19. Before moving to that drastic decision, it is important to look at the narrative as presently structured, not at how it compares to the narrative of 1 Maccabees.

By stating that the march is against Timothy, the author appears to have combined these two incidents

---

7   Ibid., §2065.
8   As, for example, in Polybius 30.7.9: "In Rhodes, in Cos, and in several other cities [πόλεσιν] there were some among those who sided with Perseus who had the courage to speak in their own cities [ἐν τοῖς ἰδίοις πολιτεύμασι] about the Macedonians, to accuse the Romans and to recommend unity of action with Perseus but who were unable to bring over their cities [τὰ πολιτεύματα] towards an alliance with the king"; 21.17.12: "embassies . . . also from Rhodes, Smyrna, and almost all peoples and cities [ἐθνῶν καὶ πολιτευμάτων] living on this side of the Taurus mountains"; see also 28.9.5. Gert Lüderitz ("What Is the Polituema?" 188 n. 15) sug-

gested that πολίτευμα here might refer only to the ruling class at Joppa. However, in 12:3 the author indicts the citizens of Joppa in general—Ἰοππῖται.
9   See Benjamin Isaac, "A Seleucid Inscription from Jamnia-on-the-Sea: Antiochus V Eupator and the Sidonians," *IEJ* 41 (1991) 132–44, with the important textual considerations made by Phillipe Gauthier, "Bulletin épigraphique," *REG* 105 (1992) 435–547, here 528–30; and Ariel Kasher, "A Second-Century B.C.E. Greek Inscription from Iamnia," *Cathedra* 63 (1992) 3–21.
10   Bar-Kochva, *Judas Maccabaeus*, 514 n. 14.
11   See, e.g., Abel, Habicht, and Bar-Kochva, *Judas Maccabaeus*, 514 n. 14.

as a prelude to the encounter with Timothy. What is fascinating is the contrast between the two incidents. While the first highlights the ability of Judas to work harmoniously with unspecified Arabs who live in tents, the second stresses how dwellers in Seleucid-controlled cities are inimical to Judas.

■ **10-13** As mentioned in the textual note on v. 10, the ungrammatical quality leads to an emphasis on Judas as the leader against Timothy. Who these Arabs were is not specified. In 1 Macc 5:25, Judas is said to have met with Nabateans, but there the Nabateans meet him peacefully. The very difference between the accounts in 1 and 2 Maccabees should give one pause before simply equating them. No reason is given for the attack, and no connection between the Arabs and Timothy is posited. The author describes the incident with language used in previous accounts: $προσβάλλειν$ ("to attack") as in 10:17, 28, 35; $γενομένης καρτερᾶς μάχης$ ("a strongly contested battle") as in 10:29. The large force of the attackers ($οὐκ ἐλάττους$) is defeated ($ἐλαττονωθέντες$), and the help of God is emphasized. The stress seems to be on the attackers' nomadic status, and their return to tents emphasizes their rural character. As such, they send livestock rather than money.

■ **11** In this verse, one again has a heaping up of participles: two genitive absolute constructions and two circumstantial participles. Two future infinitives are used in indirect discourse. The verb $εὐημερεῖν$ ("be successful") and the substantive are used frequently by the author.[12]

"make a treaty" is literally "give the right hand." The phrase is found in 11:26, 30 in the letters of the king consolidating the agreement between the Seleucids and the Jews. There the Jews are said to request ($ἀξιοῦν$) concessions from the Seleucid king (11:24). Here it is Judas who accedes to the Arabs' request.

■ **12** Schwartz has suggested that this verse, as well as 11:15, "sounds like an apology, as if there is some problem with the notion of making agreements with foreign powers."[13] However, Judas is being portrayed as a far-sighted leader, looking out for what is helpful to the common good, as Onias did in 4:5. Here again the language of reciprocity surfaces, as Judas can expect help from the Arabs. For example, Queen Laodike sends grain to the Iasians as she follows Antiochus III's lead in wanting to provide an advantage ($εὐχρηστίαν$) to the whole people.[14]

■ **13-16** Whereas the previous incident was fought in the open, this incident involves the siege of a fortified town, which the author identifies as Kaspin ($Κασπιν$). In 1 Macc 5:26, 36, a city named $Χασφω$ is mentioned among other cities in Gilead. Although most scholars have identified this site with Khisfin in the southern lower Golan,[15] the issue is not settled. Habicht, following Gustav Hölscher, suggested that the site should be located at el-Muzerib in the Auranitis.[16] Schwartz notes, however, that in antiquity el-Muzerib was located within a lake, which does not seem to be the case for the city mentioned here. More importantly, Zeev Ma'oz suggested that in the absence of Hellenistic pottery at Khisfin, one should locate Kaspin at the neighboring village of Tell Dhabab.[17] Dan Urman asserted that Hellenistic ceramics were found at the site,[18] but Moshe Hartal and Chaim ben David have disputed this claim.[19] It would seem that at present the site of Kaspin must remain unresolved.

The siege at Kaspin follows a usual pattern: the besieged city is described as well fortified (as in 10:18, 32); its inhabitants rely on the strength of their fortifications and taunt the besiegers (as in 10:34); the besiegers call on the Lord (as in 10:16), attack fiercely (as in 10:35), and capture the besieged (as in 10:22) with much slaughter.

12   The verb is found in 12:11 and 13:16; the noun in 5:6; 8:8; 10:28; 14:14; the adverb in 8:35.

13   Schwartz, *2 Maccabees*, 403.

14   See Ma, *Antiochus III*, 196.

15   Michael Avi-Yonah, *The Holy Land, from the Persian to the Arab Conquests, 536 B.C. to A.D. 640: A Historical Geography* (rev. ed.; Jerusalem: Carta, 2002) 166–67, 170; Dan Urman, "Public Structures and Jewish Communities in the Golan Heights," in Dan Urman and Paul V. M. Flesher, eds., *Ancient Synagogues: Historical Analysis and Archaeological Discovery* (2 vols.; SPB 47; Leiden: Brill, 1995) 2:556–61; Abel and Schwartz.

16   Gustav Hölscher, "Die Feldzüge des Makkabäers Judas," *ZDPV* 29 (1906) 149–50.

17   Zee U. Ma'oz, "Haspin," in *New Encyclopedia of Archeological Excavations in the Holy Land* (ed. Joseph Aviram; 4 vols.; Jerusalem: Israel Exploration Society and Carta; New York: Simon & Schuster, 1993) 2:586–88.

18   Urman and Flesher, *Ancient Synagogues*, 556 n. 5.

19   In a private communication of 30 December 2008, Moshe Hartal kindly sent me a translation from his work *Land of the Ituraeans: Archeology and History of Northern Golan in the Hellenistic, Roman and Byzan-

■ **13** The sentence is nicely structured with three adjectives filled out with three datives: "strong," "enclosed," and "peopled." The author likes a pattern of threes, as in the following verse: λοιδοροῦντες . . . βλασφεμοῦντες . . . λαλοῦντες ("abusing . . . blaspheming . . . saying").

Παμμιγέσιν ἔθνεσι ("mixture of ethnic groups"). Schwartz saw παμμιγής ("mixed of all sorts") as suggesting contempt. Depending on the context, the term could have the meaning seen in Appian *Bell. civ.* 2.120, where a speaker sees the times as corrupt in that plebeians are now mixed with foreign blood. Elsewhere, however, the term is used to praise the leader of an army composed of various groups (παμμιγὴς στρατός) in which there was never any sedition (Appian *Hisp.* 6.75). The use of the term in the present context is less suggestive of contempt than of the solidarity of many groups against the Jews. See also the use of πάμφυλος ("mixed populace") in 12:27. Contempt is shown more by the term ἀναγωγότερον in the following verse, which I have translated "vulgarly," but which at root means "uneducated."

■ **14-16** οἱ ἔνδον . . . οἱ περί ("those inside . . . those following"). The same way of formulating a contrast is found in 10:33-34. A juxtaposition of the piety of Judas's forces and the attitude of the enemies is found also in 8:18; 15:6-7, 25-26. These verses both use language similar to that of 10:34-35, ἐρυμνότης ("security"), βλασφημέω ("blaspheme"), θηριωδῶς ("ferociously"), ἀθεμίτους ("things not allowed"), and begin to reuse vocabulary from earlier in the narrative: ἐνσείω (12:15, 37: "attacked"), had been used in 3:25; δυνάστης ("Master") in 3:24 and also in 12:28; 15:3, 4, 5, 23, 29; ἀμνθήτος ("untold") in 3:6; κατακρημνίζειν ("threw down") picks up κρημνίζειν ("hurl down") from 6:10. Particularly noticeable is the alliteration in v. 14:

πεποιθότες τῇ τῶν τειχέων ἐρυμνότητι τῇ τε τῶν ("trusting in the security of their walls and in the . . .").

The reference is to Josh 6:1-21. Elsewhere examples from the past occur in the prayers of Judas (8:19-20 and 15:22). Here, however the whole company is seen as recalling God's past act. Bar-Kochva provides an excellent description of Hellenistic siege instruments.[20]

Ὥστε . . . φαίνεσθαι ("so that . . . appeared"). The same construction is found at the end of the section 12:3-9. It connects the two sections and leads on to the attack on Timothy.

■ **17-19** After the two intervening incidents, one peaceful and one hostile, the search for Timothy, first-named of the troublesome local commanders, continues. As mentioned above, the same opening phrase, ἐκεῖθεν δὲ ἀποσπάσαντες ("when they had withdrawn from there"), is used in 12:10. The incident recounted here is quite different from that in 1 Macc 5:9-13. First Maccabees recounts how the Jews in the land of Tob had been killed and their wives and children captured. It was the Jews in Gilead who had fled to the fortress of Dathema and were attacked by Timothy. Here the Toubians are safely ensconced in their palisaded enclosure and have successfully withstood Timothy, who has left the region. Common to the two accounts is that the Jews are under attack by Timothy, but which Jews are affected varies, as does the strength of the threat from Tobias.

■ **17** "palisaded enclosure." Abel and Michael Avi-Yonah hold that Χάρακα was a place-name, which is possible.[21] However, Louis Robert, Habicht, Bar-Kochva, Gera, and Schwartz all see this term as referring to a stronghold.[22] The presence of the article suggests that it is not a place-name.

tine Periods (in Hebrew; Golan Studies 2; Qazrin: Golan Research Institute and Golan Archeological Museum, 2005) 384–86. He states that, apart from the fact that there is no lake in the area, "there are no finds of the Hellenistic period" and "the site is too far from the area of the war." Chaim ben David also noted, in a private communication of 29 December 2008, that the site at Khisfin was established "not earlier than the second or third century C.E."

20 Bar-Kochva, *Judas Maccabaeus,* 19–21.
21 Avi-Yonah, *Holy Land,* 166–67, 170.
22 Louis Robert, "Review of *Samothrace. Vol. 2 part 1:*

The Inscriptions on Stone by Karl Lehmann; P. M. Fraser," *Gnomon* 35 (1963) 79; idem, "Review of *Griechische Mauerbauinschriften* by Franz Georg Maier," *Gnomon* 42 (1970) 599 n. 12; Bar-Kochva, *Judas Maccabaeus,* 510 n. 3; Dov Gera, "On the Credibility of the History of the Tobiads (Josephus, *Antiquities* 12.156–222, 228–36)," in A. Kasher, U. Rappaport, and G. Fuks, eds., *Greece and Rome in Eretz Israel: Collected Essays* (Jerusalem: Yad Ben-Zvi, 1990) 29–30.

The author evidences a sense of the distinction between the preposition εἰς (for place or state) and πρός (for persons).

"Toubians." Abel and Avi-Yonah see this term as referring to those living in the land of Tob (Judg 11:3) in northern Gilead, east of Edrei.[23] Habicht follows Niese and sees here a reference to the descendants of Jews who were Ptolemaic military settlers, as does Hengel, who refers to the military settlers mentioned in the Zenon papyri.[24] In addition, Bar-Kochva, Gera, and Schwartz connect the Toubians to the family of Joseph ben Tobias, whose son Hyrcanus had a settlement in Transjordan around ʿArak el-ʾAmir, in Ammonite territory (Josephus *Ant.* 12.229–34).[25] Timothy, according to 1 Macc 5:6, was a leader among the Ammonites.

Seven hundred and fifty stadia, about 140 kilometers. Some manuscripts (542 46–52 La[BMP] Arm) read 550 stadia, about 105 kilometers. Placing the Toubians in Ammonite territory, Bar-Kochva and Gera note that the distance between Kaspin, identified as Khisfîn, and ʿArak el-ʾAmir is about one hundred kilometers, and so the distance given in 12:17 is almost right. On the one hand, Gera holds that Judas traveled south to rescue the Jews who had not yet fled. Bar-Kochva, on the other hand, states that, since 1 Macc 5:9-13 has all the Jews in those settlements fleeing to Dathema or slain with their wives and children taken captive, the author "mistakenly interpreted it as relating to the distance between Kaspin and the place where the 'Toubian Jews' found a haven."[26] However, 1 Macc 5:13 has all the Jews in the land of Tob already killed, so why would Judas travel there? Schwartz notes that it is unlikely that the author would narrate the long trip south from Kaspin/Khisfîn to Ammon without mentioning the return north. He therefore suggests that the text is out of order and that the measurement refers to the distance from the coastal cities to the Transjordan and Dathema, the fortress to which the Gilead Jews had

fled (1 Macc 5:9). Dathema, for Schwartz, is the fortress mentioned in 12:17 and lies not far from Kaspin/Khisfîn; he therefore holds that the encounter with the Arabs and Kaspin of 12:10-16 should come after 12:17-19.[27]

As I have mentioned so often, it is important to take each narrative in its own right, before attempting to reconcile the different accounts in 1 and 2 Maccabees. Neither narrative is an exhaustive account of what took place—at times, 1 Maccabees provides simply a list of place-names, as in 5:36: "he took Chaspho, Maked, and Bosor, and the other towns of Gilead." The author of 2 Maccabees is consciously trying to make his narrative as gripping as possible and has selected the incidents he recounts with attention to how they will move the listener. He therefore focuses on the march into Transjordan as a search for Timothy. He structures this search so that it starts with a peaceful outcome with Arabs and ends with a peaceful encounter at Scythopolis. In between are battles where the enemies are characterized as blasphemous and unable to prevail against prepared Jews like the Toubians. The attempt to reconstruct "what really happened" is a different process from exploring what the narrative tells us.

■ **18** For the author, this Timothy is the local commander who is harassing the Jews in his territory. In stark contrast to 1 Macc 5:13, the author insists that Timothy has been unsuccessful but has kept the pressure on by setting up a strong garrison, which presumably was ready to take advantage of any weakness of the Jews. The juxtaposition of ἐπὶ τῶν τόπων . . . ἀπὸ τῶν τόπων ("in the region . . . from the region"), separated by only four words, seemed harsh to Grimm, who suggested that the latter phrase (ἀπὸ τῶν τόπων) had been inserted later because the intransitive form of ἐκλύω is unusual and so needed clarification. However, the intransitive form is found also in 13:16 without clarification.

The Toubians' retreat to a palisaded enclosure shows

23 Avi-Yonah, *Holy Land*, 30, 40–41.
24 Benedikt Niese, *Geschichte der griechischen und makedonischen Staaten seit der Schlacht bei Chaeronea* (3 vols.; Gotha: Perthes, 1893–1903) 3:226 n. 1; Hengel, *Judaism and Hellenism*, 1:276; 2:182 nn. 121–22. *CPJ* 1, no. 1, lines 6–8, 17, 19 (pp. 119–20); no. 2d, line16 (p.123). See the location of the cleruchy of Toubias as discussed by Tcherikover, *CPJ* 1:116–17.
25 In particular, Bar-Kochva (*Judas Maccabaeus*, 83 n.

42) sees the theophoric suffix here as distinguishing it from the land of Tob mentioned in Judg 11:3.
26 Bar-Kochva, *Judas Maccabaeus*, 83 n. 42.
27 Schwartz, *2 Maccabees*, 418, 429.

them in a different light from the citizens of Joppa, who had innocently trusted their neighbors (12:3-4). The relationship between Jews and their neighbors requires vigilance.

■ **19** Dositheos and Sosipater are well-attested Greek names for Jews, particularly Dositheos. In 12:35, a Dositheos is mentioned as a cavalryman. It seems unlikely that the same person is in view in both instances.[28] Hengel and Bar-Kochva have argued that these two men of v. 19 were from the Toubian military settlers.[29] The author stresses that Dositheos and Sosipater are leaders of Maccabeus's forces, but the ability of Timothy later, in vv. 24-26, to persuade the followers of Dositheos and Sosipater to let him go free does suggest that they might be from the region of the Toubians. The condensation of the account is shown by the repetition in vv. 18 and 19: καταλελοιπότα, ὀχυράν (v. 18); καταλειφθέντας, ὀχυρώματι (v. 19).

■ **20-26** Battle is finally joined with Timothy, whose overwhelming forces are destroyed by the help of an epiphany of God. Timothy remains at large, however, as he promises not to harass the Jews under his power. Karnion is taken.

■ **20** The impression given is that, while Dositheos and Sosipater are dealing with the garrison stationed near the Toubians, Maccabeus hurries off against Timothy. As in 8:22-23, Judas divides his company, and σπειρηδόν ("into companies") should be seen as a general term, not as a specific unit of 256 men.[30] The use of the term does emphasize the smallness of Judas's army compared with the large numbers around Timothy. It must be noted, however, that Judas too does seem to have cavalry, as recorded in 12:35. Note the paronomasia between σπειρηδόν . . . σπειρῶν, as well as the similar sounding στρατιάν ("army").

■ **21** Earlier in the text, in 12:5, 8, it had been Judas who heard news (μεταλαβών). Now it is Timothy who hears, and he takes precautions by sending the women, children, and other household belongings to safety. The term ἀποσκευή could cover, as Bar-Kochva states, armor-bearers, cooks, storekeepers, and maintenance men, as well as slaves.[31] As Schwartz notes, the attitude to women and children is very male-centered (cf. Deut 20:14; Judg 18:21; Josephus Ap. 2.157). As in other siege accounts, the strong defense of the besieged city, in this instance Karnion, is emphasized. Karnion is usually identified with the Karnain of 1 Macc 5:26, 43 and the Ashteroth-karnaim of Gen 14:5 and located at Seh-Saʿd, four kilometers northeast of Tell ʿAstara, about thirty-five kilometers east of the Sea of Galilee.[32]

Note again the paromoiosis of δυσπολιόρκητον . . . δυσπρόσιτον. It is interesting how the third-century B.C.E. writer Philo of Byzantium, in his treatise on how to make cities well protected against siege, uses compounds of δυσ, for example, δυσεκπορεύτους and δυσχρηστότεροι.[33]

■ **22** The first part of the sentence, which consists of three genitive absolutes, is intricately woven. At the appearance (ἐπιφανείσης) of Judas's first unit, dread and fear fall on the enemy. However, the formulaic pair δέος . . . φόβος[34] is split. The first member is connected with the appearance of Judas's unit and has its own aorist genitive absolute, γενομένου, while the second member deals with God's appearance (ἐπιφανείας) and has its own aorist genitive absolute (γενομένου). Such a splitting reinforces the close entwining of the actions of Judas's forces with the action of God. God as the one who watches over all things is found also in 7:6; 15:2. See also the term ἐπόπτης ("overseer") in 3:39 and 7:35.

28 See also Bar-Kochva, *Judas Maccabeus*, 82, but for different reasons.
29 Hengel, *Judaism and Hellenism*, 1:276; Bar-Kochva, *Judas Maccabeus*, 82.
30 Bar-Kochva, *Seleucid Army*, 66.
31 Bar-Kochva, *Judas Maccabeus*, 45–46. See especially Holleaux, *Études*, 3:15–26; Bickerman, *Institutions*, 91; Launey, *Recherches*, 2:785–90; Pritchett, *Greek State at War*, 5:173–74.
32 D. Kellermann, "ʿAstarot – ʿAstorot Qarnayim – Qarnayim: Historisch-geographische Erwägungen zu Orten im nördlichen Ostjordanland," *ZDPV* 97 (1981) 49–50.
33 Diels and Schramm, *Excerpte*, 79.25 (p. 18), 81.40–41 (p. 24).
34 In 3:22 and 13:16: δέος . . . ταραχή; in 15:23: δέος . . . τρόμος. The pairing τρόμος . . . φόβος is frequent in Hebrew Scriptures; see, e.g., Exod 15:16; Deut 2:15; 11:25.

The divine appearance causes confusion, as in 10:30. Such confusion often resulted in allies fighting among each other, as in the account in 2 Chr 20:22-23 (see also Polybius 11.33–34; Diodorus Siculus 16.80.2; 17.34.8).

Note the paronomasia of ἄλλος ἀλλαχῇ. I have translated the verb βλάπτεσθαι as "accosted." The verb had had the sense of "to hurt, damage" (Homer *Il.* 23.782; Thucydides 6.33). However, given that the description of the enemy running into each other is followed by a description of their deaths, the sense seems to be that their deaths were a result of these encounters.

■ **23** Judas continues the pursuit. The enemies are called ἀλιτηρίους ("offenders"). The high priest Menelaus is so described in 13:4, and the attackers of Rhazis in 14:42. Both Nikanors are deemed even more offensive–τρισα-λιτήριος–in 8:34 and 15:3.

"pursued." The author uses the periphrasis ποιέω + substantive (τὸν διωγμόν).

■ **24-25** Just as Nikanor was put to shameful flight (8:35), so Timothy flees rather than staying to fight. The narrative suggests that Dositheos and Sosipater, having destroyed the garrison left by Timothy (12:19), are now approaching the battlefield where Timothy was defeated. Perhaps Timothy was fleeing back to that garrison.

"very bewitchingly" (μετὰ πολλῆς γοητείας). As Jacqueline de Romilly has shown so well,[35] the connection between magic and rhetoric was well established among the practitioners of rhetoric. Here Timothy is portrayed as a clever speaker. In Polybius, the term γοητεία has the sense of "beguiling, bewitching" (4.20.5; 15.17.2; 33.18.11). In Diodorus Siculus, it also suggests leading people astray, before they can reflect (1.76.1; 20.8.1). But the term could be used in a less derogatory sense, "the charm of conversation" (Dionysius of Halicarnassus *Ant. rom.* 11.25.4). Here the intention seems to be to convey the persuasive character of the speech rather than that Dositheos and Sosipater were deceived.

"mistreated" (ἀλογηθῆναι). The basic meaning is "to pay no regard to." The meanings of "mistreat" or "intimidate" are found in a complaint about an assault: "drawing [his sword] and wishing to mistreat me he brought [it] down with three blows on the head and the neck and the shoulder-blade" (*P. Tebt.* 138).[36] As Grimm noted, there is a change from indirect to direct speech here, as the use of the future shows. In Timothy's own words, if he is not set free, "it will happen that [their relatives] will be mistreated." To make the meaning clearer, L′ 311 La^BM add εἰ ἀποθάνοι. Grimm sees this addition as necessary for the meaning, but the threat is present even without it.

■ **25** "Repeatedly" is literally "through many."

This verse resonates with the situation in 10:20, where Simon's troops had let enemies escape in return for money. The verb ἀπολύω ("let go") is found also in 10:21 (where because of the context I have translated it "loosing," when Judas describes how for money the enemies had been let go). In contrast to these instances, Dositheos and Sosipater act for the safety of their kinsfolk, and so no blame is attached to them. Their action also contrasts with that of Menelaus in 13:3, who does not think of the safety of the fatherland but only of his own return to power.

■ **26** The author returns to the actions of Judas. After the rout of Timothy's forces, Judas moves against the nearby city. While the author had insisted on the difficulty of besieging Karnion (12:21), here he simply ends this incident around the city and the temple of Atargatis without any discussion of either the siege or the fate of the wives and children of Timothy's followers. As mentioned above, the name is given in Gen 14:5 as Ashteroth-karnaim, so the place was dedicated to the goddess Astarte. Atargatis is the later name for Astarte.[37]

"Twenty-five thousand" is literally "twenty-five thousand bodies." In 8:11, σώματα ("bodies") had been used derogatively to speak of Judean slaves. It can also be used

---

35   Jacqueline de Romilly, *Magic and Rhetoric in Ancient Greece* (Carl Newell Jackson Lectures 1974; Cambridge, Mass.: Harvard University Press, 1975).

36   The verb is used in a similar context of hostages in Polybius 8.36.2–4: "For it is absolutely impracticable to place trust [πιστεύειν] in no one, and we cannot find fault with anyone for acting by the dictates of reason after receiving adequate pledges, such pledges being oaths, wives and children held as hostages, and above all the past life of the person in question; thus, to be betrayed [ἀλογηθῆναι] and ruined by such means carries no reproach to the sufferer but only to the author of the deed."

37   J. L. Lightfoot, *Lucian, On the Syrian Goddess* (Oxford: Oxford University Press, 2003) 11–15. See also Robert A. Oden, *Studies in Lucian's De Syria Dea* (HSM 15; Missoula, Mont.: Society of Biblical Literature, 1977).

to denote prisoners.[38] Schwartz suggests that the author uses the term here to make the slaughter as graphic as possible.

■ **27-28** Here the attack on Ephron is the next in the series of battles against fortified cities. In 1 Macc 5:45-51, the battle against the city occurs while Judas and his forces are returning from Gilead toward Jerusalem. Judas and his followers must pass through Ephron but are denied permission to do so. They therefore assault Ephron and very gruesomely march through the city over the bodies of the slain. The story mimics that of Num 21:21-24. Here the author once again portrays the difficulties facing Judas's forces in besieging a city that possessed war machines and had young men standing before the walls of the city. He heightens the problems facing Judas's men with a play on the same sound between ῥωμαλέοι ("virile") and εὐρώστως ("vigorously"). The latter term is used of Jews in 10:17 and 12:35.

Ephron is identified as et-Taiyiba. It lies north of Pella and to the northeast of Beth-Shean, across the Jordan. It is about twelve kilometers from the present-day city of Irbid. It is mentioned in Polybius 5.70.12.

■ **28** Whereas the narrative to this point was in the third person singular with Judas as the implied subject, it now changes to the plural, which it retains until v. 31. Perhaps the mention of the virile opponents led the author to change to the plural for the Jews as well.

As usual, the Lord, the Master (12:15), is called upon (12:6, 36). Here God is described as the one who shatters (συντρίβοντα). This verb, used only here in 2 Maccabees but frequently in 1 Maccabees, recalls the language of the hymn sung at the Red Sea: the Lord who shatters the enemies, the opponents (Exod 15:3, 7). "Powerfully" is literally "with power." The term κράτος ("power") is found in 3:34; 7:17; 9:17; 11:4; 12:28.

■ **29-31** After their bloody victories, the Jews are seen to act peacefully toward those who treat them properly.

The language of this encounter resonates with inscriptional language between cities and sovereigns: εὔνοια, εὐχαριστέω, εὐμενεῖς, παρακαλέω.[39] In one document, Menestratos is praised for having given testimony of the goodwill of the people (ἐγμαρτυρῶν ὑπὲρ τῆς εὐνοίας τῶν πολιτῶν).[40] The use of this language suggests that the author wanted to portray Judas and the Jews as forming reciprocal arrangements with the city of Scythopolis, which is Beth-Shean. Six hundred stadia would be around 115 kilometers, which is fairly accurate.[41]

"Ill-fated" (ἀτυχία) is found also in 14:14, where I have translated it as "misfortunes" because of the context.

"civilized interaction." Here again the language seems to be that of protocol and agreement. See Polybius 5.63.7: "making the meetings on friendly terms [φιλανθρώπως ποιούμενοι τὰς ἀπαντήσεις]." The language contrasts with the vulgar/uneducated behavior at Kaspin (12:14), and being well-disposed (εὐμενεῖς) with the ill will (δυσμένεια) in Joppa (12:3).

"festival of Weeks." For the festival, see Lev 23:15-21 and Deut 16:9-12. The name is found also in 4Q196, frg. 2 1.10: ביום חג שבו[עיא in a text from Tobit.[42]

■ **32-45** After fighting in Gilead, Judas now turns, after celebrating the festival of Weeks, to the southeastern border of Judea. The author thus picks up on the simple mention of Gorgias in 10:14. In the battle with Gorgias some Jewish casualties occurred, and the author seeks to explain why this happened. Often this incident is seen as comparable to that in 1 Macc 5:55-62. The only point in common, however, is that there are some Jewish casualties.

■ **32** The author varies the term used for the festival of Weeks.[43] In 10:14, Gorgias had been identified vaguely as στρατηγὸς τῶν τόπων ("commander of the region"). Here he is commander of Idumea. Since Gorgias is said to cover territory from Jamnia (1 Macc 5:58-59) to Marisa

---

38 Pritchett, *Greek State at War*, 5:182–85.
39 For εὔνοια, see Ma, *Antiochus III*, 179–242. On εὐχαριστέω and its substantive and adverbial forms, see the epigraphical dossier in ibid., no. 16, line 20; no.18, lines 68, 74; no. 19, line 5; no. 26, line 28; no. 27, line 8; no. 40, line 10. On παρακαλέω, see ibid., no. 11, line 6; no. 12, line 2.
40 Ma, *Antiochus III*, no. 10, line 12.
41 Gera, "Credibility," 29 n. 37.
42 See Joseph A. Fitzmyer, *Tobit* (Commentaries on

Early Jewish Literature; Berlin and New York: de Gruyter, 2003) 131–32. As Schwartz argues, the Latin reading of Passover in some manuscripts is unlikely, since why would Judas take a seven-week hiatus in the early part of the summer?
43 See André Pelletier, "La nomenclature du calendrier juif à l'époque hellénistique," *RB* 82 (1975) 224–25.

(12:35), Schwartz is right to suggest that Idumea denotes the southern part of Palestine.

■ **33** The subject of the sentence is Gorgias. In the previous sentence, a third person plural verb was used and so, even though Gorgias is not named in v. 33, he must be the subject of the sentence. The narrative here is completely different from that of 1 Macc 5:55-60, and comparison is unfruitful. In the narrative in 1 Maccabees, the attack on Jamnia is not authorized by Judas, and this is why there were Jewish casualties.

■ **34** One could read either the genitive plural, $\pi\alpha\rho\alpha\tau\alpha\xi\alpha\mu\epsilon\nu\omega\nu$ ("as the battle lines met") with some manuscripts, as do Abel and Habicht, or the accusative plural, $\pi\alpha\rho\alpha\tau\alpha\xi\alpha\mu\epsilon\nu\upsilon\varsigma$, with Hanhart. In the latter case, the accusative would be an accusative of extent. The meaning does not change.

Here, for the first time in 2 Maccabees, mention is made of Jewish casualties. Do these men fall right at the beginning of the battle?

■ **35** The mention of Jewish casualties is immediately followed by the valiant adventure of a Jew and the shameful flight of Gorgias. From this mention of a cavalryman, Bar-Kochva deduces "a drastic change in the tactical composition and armament of the Jewish force."[44] A papyrus of 259 B.C.E. had mentioned a cavalryman from the Tobiad territory.[45] Linking up with the Toubians had strengthened Judas's forces. The onrush of Dositheos, who is not to be confused with the Jewish leader of 12:19, 24, is highlighted by the use of the imperfects $\epsilon\tilde{\iota}\chi\epsilon\tau o$ and $\tilde{\eta}\gamma\epsilon\nu$. The asyndetic pairing of his desire ($\beta ou\lambda o\mu\epsilon\nu ou$) with the onrush of the Thracian cavalryman ($\epsilon\pi\epsilon\nu\epsilon\chi\vartheta\epsilon\nu\tau o\varsigma$) indicates how the two actions are intertwined.[46] As Schwartz notes, Thracian cavalrymen were reputed to be especially cruel, and Josephus (*Ant.* 13.383) reports that Alexander Jannaeus was nicknamed "Thrakidas" because of his cruelty. Set against this heroic action, the flight of Gorgias to safety is rendered more shameful, particularly as his forces are said in 12:36 to fight on. Marisa was the main city of Idumea. It is not mentioned in 1 Maccabees.[47]

■ **36-37** Esdris is otherwise unknown. "Very weary" ($\kappa\alpha\tau\acute{\alpha}\kappa o\pi o\iota$) is used in this sense also in Diodorus Siculus 13.18.

The asyndetic grouping of participles with Judas as subject—$\epsilon\pi\iota\kappa\alpha\lambda\epsilon\sigma\acute{\alpha}\mu\epsilon\nu o\varsigma, \kappa\alpha\tau\alpha\rho\xi\acute{\alpha}\mu\epsilon\nu o\varsigma, \epsilon\nu\sigma\epsilon\acute{\iota}\sigma\alpha\varsigma$—not only suggests rapid and lively action but also closely connects the activity of Judas with that of his heavenly ally. As in 8:24, 10:16, and 11:10, God is the $\sigma\acute{\upsilon}\mu\mu\alpha\chi o\varsigma$ ("ally") of the Jews.

"leader" ($\pi\rho oo\delta\eta\gamma\acute{o}\nu$). This unusual word reflects the use of $\pi\rho o\acute{\alpha}\gamma\epsilon\iota\nu$ in 10:1, where the Lord leads the Jews to retake the city, and the appearance of a heavenly leader ($\pi\rho o\eta\gamma o\acute{\upsilon}\mu\epsilon\nu o\varsigma$) in 11:8. In 15:23, God is asked to send a good angel before the Jews, as God had been requested in 11:6.

"ancestral language," as in 7:8, 21, 27; 15:29. "Tumultuous shout" is used also in 15:29, $\epsilon\nu\sigma\epsilon\acute{\iota}\epsilon\iota\nu$ ("attack") in 3:25; 12:15; 14:46, and "unexpectedly" ($\alpha\pi\rho o\sigma\delta o\kappa\acute{\eta}\tau\omega\varsigma$) in 8:6. "Hymnodic" ($\mu\epsilon\vartheta$ $\acute{\upsilon}\mu\nu\omega\nu$) is used in 10:38, when the Jews bless the Lord for their victory. Songs and shouting were usual in battles,[48] and in 15:25 Nikanor's forces are said to advance with war chants ($\mu\epsilon\tau\grave{\alpha}$ . . . $\pi\alpha\iota\acute{\alpha}\nu\omega\nu$). Schwartz rightly notes how the author, by this usage, distinguishes the pagan songs ($\pi\alpha\iota\acute{\alpha}\nu$) from those of the Jews ($\acute{\upsilon}\mu\nu o\varsigma$).

Notice how the battle is against the forces of Gorgias, as the commander had already fled. Again, the author uses the periphrasis of $\pi o\iota\acute{\epsilon}\omega$ + noun ($\tau\rho o\pi\acute{\eta}\nu$).

■ **38** The piety of Judas is stressed, as he takes the army to the nearby city of Adullam, about fifteen kilometers northeast of Marisa. According to Josh 15:35, Adullam lay within Judah. The sanctity of the Sabbath is kept, as in 8:26-28. What was the nature of this customary purification? In 1QM 14.2–3, the Sons of Light are instructed: "When they have departed from the slain in order to enter the camp, they shall all sing the hymn of return. In the morning they shall wash their clothes and cleanse themselves of the blood of the guilty corpses. They shall go back to the site of their positions, where they arranged the battle line before the slain of the enemy

---

44   Bar-Kochva, *Judas Maccabaeus*, 69.
45   *CPJ* 1, no. 1, line 8 (p. 119).
46   For a description of Thracian cavalrymen, see Bar-Kochva, *Judas Maccabaeus*, 10–11 with the illustration on p. 576.

47   See Amos Kloner, "Underground Metropolis: The Subterranean World of Maresha," *BAR* 23, no. 2 (1977) 24–35, 67.
48   Pritchett, *Greek State at War*, 1:105–8.

fell." In Num 31:19, those who had killed or touched a corpse were required to spend seven days outside the camp purifying themselves. However, since temple service is not at issue for Judas's forces in Adullam, these forces could participate in some Sabbath observance. However, would not those who lived in Adullam and who came into contact with Judas's forces also be rendered unclean? The text does not provide an answer. Goldstein referred to *b. Šabb.* 25b: "R. Nahman b. R. Zabda—others state, R. Nahman b. Raba—said in Rab's name: The kindling of the lamp for a Sabbath is a duty; the washing of the hands and feet in warm water on the eve [of the Sabbath] is voluntary. While I maintain that it is a *mitzvah.*" The author seems concerned to show that purity rules were important. Gilles Dorival has noted how the LXX, following a tendency in Greek religious terminology, distinguishes between ἁγνίζειν, purification by water, and καθαίρειν, purification by fire.[49]

■ **39** "At the time when what was necessary fell due." This phrase is missing in Syriac and La^LXV, and so Abel brackets it. Grimm suggested that one had a necessity (χρεία) to bury the bodies before they began to rot, but Goldstein finds it unlikely that the author would have expressed this idea by such obscure language and proposes a translation of "permissible," although this reading is a far move from the usual meaning of χρεία. Schwartz translates χρεία as "task," but this also retains the sense of something that had to be done. To bury the bodies of the fallen was an important task for a commander.[50] The importance of burial in ancestral graves was stressed in 5:9-10.

■ **40** "objects consecrated" (ἱερώματα). The term is used by Josephus (*Ant.* 1.322) to refer to the household gods of Laban that Rachel stole (Gen 31:19). An inscription by the citizens of Epidauros does not specify what ἱαρ[ώ]ματα were sent in procession.[51] From inscriptions set up on Delos by citizens of Jamnia to Herakles and Horon,[52] Isidore Lévy suggested that, as these were deities who provided protection, the consecrated objects were in fact amulets used to secure protection from harm in battle.[53] Goldstein states that to his knowledge, "there is no ancient context in which *hierôma* can be shown to mean 'amulet.'"[54] His main objection to Lévy's thesis is that Judas's followers would not have put faith in pagan gods, following Deut 7:25-26. He therefore sees these objects as referring to gold and silver ornaments or vessels dedicated to pagan gods that the fallen Jewish soldiers had taken as booty in the attack on Jamnia. Schwartz suggests that the objects may be pendants, as they were under the soldiers' tunics.[55] The author of the condensed narrative stresses that wearing such objects was against the law, but some followers of Judas may have wanted all the help they could get.[56] The repetition of the demonstrative—τήνδε . . . τούσδε—stresses the specificity of the cause. The author uses ὅδε frequently (6:12; 10:8; 14:33, 36, 46; 15:15, 22, 36).

■ **41** "The just judge" is one word in Greek—δικαιο-κρίτης—and is not well attested, found at present only in a petition of 133 C.E. to a Roman prefect (*P. Ryl.* 113.35). The author uses it here to resonate with the prayer of Judas as he attacked Jamnia on the Sea and called on God, τὸν δίκαιον κριτήν (12:6). The term thus helps form a fitting *inclusio* and helps frame the incidents in 2 Maccabees 12.

---

49   Gilles Dorival, "'Dire en grec les choses juives': Quelques choix lexicaux du Pentateuque de la Septante," *REG* 109 (1996) 527–47, here 542–43.

50   See Diodorus Siculus 13.61.6 coupled with 13.75.4, which shows the results of leaving the fallen on the battlefield; also 17.68.4. In general, see P. Vaughn, "The Identification and Retrieval of the Hoplite Battle-Dead," in Victor D. Hanson, ed., *Hoplites: The Classical Greek Battle Experience* (London: Routledge, 1991) 38–62.

51   *IG* 4:917.

52   See Philippe Bruneau, *Recherches sur les cultes de Delos* (Bibliothèque des écoles françaises d'Athènes et de Rome 217; Paris: E. de Boccard, 1970) 410, 475.

53   Isidore Lévy, *Recherches esséniennes et pythagoriciennes*

(Haute études du monde gréco-romain 1; Geneva: Droz, 1965) 65–71.

54   Goldstein, *II Maccabees*, 449.

55   He refers to a pendant of the Egyptian god Harpokrates from Jamnia-on-the-Sea; see M. Fischer and R. E. Jackson-Tal, "A Glass Pendant in the Shape of Harpokrates from Yavneh-Yam, Israel," *Journal of Glass Studies* 35 (2003) 35–40.

56   I would not be as ready as Schwartz to say that the phrase "from which the law prohibits the Jews" was aimed at a non-Jewish audience. While not rejecting that the God of Israel was the highest God, some Jews were amenable to accepting that other gods had some power.

It is a commonplace that God knows the hidden things.[57] Later the notion will be found in proverbial form in Mark 4:22; Matt 10:26; Luke 8:17; 12:2. Here the author has used antithesis to heighten the effect.

■ **42** The prayer here resembles that found in 8:29, after the defeat of Nikanor, when the Jews with a communal supplication (κοινὴν ἱκετείαν) beseech (ἠξίουν) that God be completely (εἰς τέλος) reconciled to them. Here God is asked to wipe away the sin. In Isa 43:24, God is the one who wipes away (ὁ ἐξαλείφων) the transgressions of his people.[58] In this sentence, the repetition of different terms formed from the root for "sin" (ἁμάρτημα, ἀναμαρτήτους, ἁμαρτίαν) focuses the audience's attention on the magnitude of what had happened. At the beginning of the insurgency, Judas had recalled the destruction of the guiltless/sinless infants (8:4: ἀναμαρτήτων νηπίων), and the author has him here call the people back to that state of sinlessness.

■ **43a** This verse is connected to the last clause of v. 42 through the particle τέ. After emphasizing the need for the community to be sinless, Judas takes up a collection from all the members (κατ᾽ ἄνδρα)[59] for a purification offering for the community, to cleanse its members of any association with sin. Here the language, προσάγειν περὶ ἁμαρτίας, is similar to the language used for purification offerings in Leviticus 4.

■ **43b-45a** This section begins another reflection by the author on the events. Just as Eleazar took up the high-principled position (6:23: ὁ δὲ λογισμὸν ἀστεῖον ἀναλαβών) to be sent into Hades rather than transgress the law, so Judas's considerations are honorable. The author uses the adverb πάνυ ("very") in 15:17, where I have translated it as "exceedingly," to describe Judas's speech. Elsewhere, in 9:6 and 13:7, it is used in the description of how God justly, that is, by means of just deserts, repays sins. The two participles πράττων . . .

διαλογιζόμενος are in asyndeton, as action is linked to thought.

Two thousand drachmas, about one-third of a talent. The amount sent by Jason for the sacrifice to Herakles was three hundred drachmas (4:19), so this is decidedly more.

This section has been the subject of much discussion. The first conditional clause is an unreal past conditional without ἄν in the apodosis.[60] For the second conditional clause, I have read εἰ τέ rather than the particle εἴτε. A disjunctive particle makes no sense in this context. With the two conditional sentences of vv. 44 and 45a, the reflection continues. Elmer O'Brien[61] and Abel see these two sentences as the result of several glosses made to an original text and follow the Latin text of La^L: "because [reading ὅτι instead of εἰ μὴ γάρ] he hoped that the fallen would rise (superfluous and silly to pray for the dead), considering that the best reward was reserved for those who die piously (a holy and pious thought)." The phrases in parenthesis would have been made by later editors, the first by a skeptical reader, the second by someone who believes in resurrection. However, I have chosen to follow the text as found in Hanhart's critical edition and see these two conditional sentences balancing one another. As in previous reflections, the author counters opposing positions, as in 5:18 and 6:12-13. Here the author first refutes the opinion that it is pointless to pray for the dead and then encourages people to live and die piously.

Throughout all this section on the fallen, the author has emphasized the communal aspect. Judas and his followers wanted to return the fallen to their ancestral graves with their kinsfolk (12:39). Each member of the force contributes to the sacrifice so that the sin might be completely taken away from the community (12:42-43). Goldstein refers to rabbinic procedures whereby

---

57   Jeremiah 16:17; Prov 16:5; Dan 2:47; Sus 42; Sir 16:17-18; 17:15-20; 39:19; 42:20.

58   See also LXX Pss 50:1, 9; 108:13-14; Sir 40:12; 41:11; 46:20.

59   I do not understand why Schwartz sees this phrase as meaning "for each of the fallen." The distributive use of κατά seems to rule this meaning out, as how can one make a collection from people who are dead? The phrase κατ᾽ ἄνδρα is found in lists

from which taxes or fines are taken. See, e.g., *P. Oxy.* 2668, 2927, 3364 among many others.

60   Smyth, *Greek Grammar*, §2313.

61   Elmer O'Brien, "The Scriptural Proof for the Existence of Purgatory from 2 Machabees 12:43-45," *Sciences ecclésiastiques* 2 (1949) 80–108.

the community had to make a special offering to pay for the sacrifice for a community purification offering and extra money would be used as a donation to the temple (*t. Šeqal.* 2:6; *b. Menaḥ.* 52a). What is interesting here is that Judas believes that the community reaches beyond the grave. Whereas later rabbinic thought would see death itself as an expiation,[62] here the author sees those dead who acted against the law as requiring purification. Grimm already pointed to the fascinating passage in 1 Cor 15:29: "What do people mean by being baptized on behalf of the dead? If the dead are not raised at all, why are people baptized on their behalf?" One could also mention the prayer of Perpetua for her dead brother. In a vision, she saw him disfigured and in pain, but after her prayer, she saw him healthy and joyful (*Martyrdom of Perpetua and Felicitas* 7–8). The idea that the dead had a disembodied existence after life was widespread in the Hebrew Bible.[63] However, *1 Enoch* 22 holds that the dead are already separated into the righteous and unrighteous, with no hope of movement from one camp to the other, as one sees also in Luke 16:26.[64] The sense of ethnic identity seems predominant for our author. Here one is reminded of the way that Vergil portrays those in the underworld as still belonging to one camp or the other—one is either on the Trojan side or on the Greek side (*Aen.* 6.644–50).[65]

Schwartz emphasizes that the author says "to pray" rather than "to sacrifice," which he sees as a sign of diasporan usage. But there does not seem to be such a huge divide between the two. Isaiah had emphasized that the temple is for prayer: "The temple shall be called a house of prayer" (Isa 56:7). Solomon asked that if the people were defeated because of their sin and turned to God and prayed in the temple, God would forgive them (3 Kgdms 8:33-34). Isaiah 60:7 reads: "All the sheep of Kedar shall be gathered and the rams of Nabioth will come, and they will be offered up on your altar, and my house of prayer will be glorified." It is true that the noun and verb used here are προσευχή, προσεύχεσθαι, but the simple εὔχεσθαι fits the rhythm of this sentence better.

The second conditional clause puts forth an exhortation to live piously, so that one will not need such an expiation. Here "fall asleep" is a euphemism for "die."[66] I have translated χαριστήριον with the rather clumsy "reciprocation." Literally it means "thanksgiving" and is normally found in the context of a thank offering to the gods,[67] even in the works of Philo and Josephus.[68]

62 David Charles Kraemer, *The Meanings of Death in Rabbinic Judaism* (London and New York: Routledge, 2001).

63 Marie-Thérèse Wacker, *Weltordnung und Gericht: Studien zu I Henoch 22* (FB 45; Würzburg: Echter, 1982) 179–80. See also the essay by Herbert C. Brichto, "Kin, Cult, Land, and Afterlife — A Biblical Complex," *HUCA* 44 (1973) 1–54, in which he argues that the condition of the dead in the afterlife was dependent on the actions of their posterity.

64 Salomon Reinach ("L'origine des priers pour les morts," *REJ* 41 [1900] 161–73, here 169) referred to Diodorus Siculus as offering an analogy to the case here. Diodorus is describing the funeral rituals among the Egyptians (1.91–94), and after the mourners have recounted the piety of the deceased, the Egyptians are said "to call upon the gods of the lower world to receive him into the company of the righteous" (1.92.5). The cases are not at all similar.

65 One should perhaps also note the way that Roman tombs were seen as "consolidating the family, constructing it as a continuity over time" (Andrew Wallace-Hadrill, "Housing the Dead: The Tomb as House in Roman Italy," in Laurie Brink and Deborah Green, eds., *Commemorating the Dead: Texts and Artifacts in Context. Studies of Roman, Jewish, and Christian Burials* [Berlin and New York: de Gruyter, 2008] 39–77, here 60). In the same volume, see also the article by Robin M. Jensen, ("Dining with the Dead: From the *Mensa* to the Altar in Christian Late Antiquity," 107–43. She writes, "Roman tombs were gathering places for the living as well as the dead. Family members and friends came to graves at regular intervals in order to honor the departed by sharing a meal with them" (p. 107).

66 Marbury B. Ogle, "The Sleep of Death," *Memoirs of the American Academy in Rome* 11 (1933) 81–117.

67 Among many examples, see Plutarch *Caes.* 57.3; *Lyc.* 11.4; *Marc.* 8.6; Polybius 21.1.2; Diodorus Siculus 11.26, 33; 20.76.6. The term is found also in the inscriptions by the Jamnites to Herakles and Horon (*I. Delos* 2308–9).

68 Philo *Deus imm.* 4; *Decal.* 160; *Spec. leg.* 2.134, 146; *Virt.* 159.3; Josephus *Ant.* 6.10; 12.25.

Goldstein was right to note that the term usually refers to a thank offering to the gods. However, it is important to recognize that this term belongs to the language of euergetism and reciprocity so well studied by Ma.[69] While cities normally gave thanks to their kings for favors granted, Ma has also noted how "a city could represent itself as the *euergetes* of the king, and speak of royal *eucharistia* instead of the (more familiar) reverse situation."[70] It is this reverse situation that is present here. God is perceived as bestowing thanks on those who have died piously. The situation is different for those who fell in the battle wearing idol images. Note the paronomasia of εὐσεβείας . . . εὐσεβής.

■ **45b** The language here is particularly close to that of Lev 4:13-35. In Lev 4:20, 26, 35, the formula used for a purification offering for the people, the priest, and an individual is ἐξιλάσεται περί, comparable to the present τὸν ἐξιλασμὸν ἐποιήσατο περί ("made atonement"), where the author again uses the periphrasis of ποιέω + noun. The author has Judas think that the efficacy of the purification offering reaches beyond the grave and reunites kinsfolk.

General Commentary

The author, as noted in the Introduction, has arranged the incidents under Antiochus V Eupator so that confrontations with local leaders hostile to the Jews (10:14-37; 12) are followed by incursions of the main Seleucid government (11:1-12; 13). While the incidents in 10:14-37 involve serious attacks on the Jews within Judea, those of chap. 12 concern the reaction of Judas and his followers to attacks on Jews outside Judea.

The locations of the incidents in 2 Maccabees 12 range from the southwest of Judea (12:1-16) to the northeast territory of Gilead (12:17-28) before returning to the southwest again (12:32-37) and then back into Judea (12:38). While there is no parallel to the incidents at Joppa and Jamnia in 1 Maccabees, scholars usually see the events in Gilead as parallel to the events in 1 Macc 5:3-51, and the setback in 2 Macc 12:34 may respond to the defeat in 1 Macc 5:55-61. The names of some towns are common to both: Κάρνιον (2 Macc 12:21, 26) and

Καρναϊν (1 Macc 5:26, 43, 44); Εφρων (2 Macc 12:27; 1 Macc 5:46). Κασπιν, the town named in 2 Macc 12:13, is often identified with the Χασφω of 1 Macc 5:36, but in 1 Maccabees the town is securely linked to other towns in Gilead, Maapha, Maked, and Bosor, while in the narrative of 2 Maccabees it lies 750 stadia away from those events and in the narrative is tied to events not far from Jamnia. There are protagonists in common, Timothy and the Toubian Jews, as well as Gorgias. What is striking, however, is how differently the stories are told. Apart from the names, almost nothing else can be reconciled.

Rather than try to decide which account is more accurate or better preserves "what really happened," it is important to note what the author of 2 Maccabees is trying to accomplish in this narrative. It is clear that, as he had said at 2:31, the author is not trying to provide a complete narrative. First, he repeatedly emphasizes that God is the ally of the Jews, but he also subtly suggests that God and Judas work hand in hand (see 12:22). The emphasis in the narrative is clearly on Judas. While the narrative of 1 Maccabees 5 has Judas divide his forces into those who remain to defend the homeland, those who move into Galilee, and those who accompany him into Gilead (1 Macc 5:17-20), in 2 Maccabees Judas is always in command. Second, the author stresses that the Jews move outside their territory only to help Jews who are being attacked. In 1 Maccabees, the trigger for the events is the rebuilding of the altar in Jerusalem (1 Macc 5:1-2); in 2 Maccabees the trigger is the peace agreement with Lysias, which the Gentiles want to break. Third, what is striking in the recounting of the events is how the Jews under Judas are portrayed as willing to make peaceful arrangements with those around about them. The dastardly deed at Joppa and the proposal at Jamnia as well as the blasphemies of Kaspin must be resisted, but these incidents surround the story where Judas, recognizing the advantage to the Jews, makes peace with Arabs. Likewise, the destruction of Ephron (12:27-28) is balanced by the treatment of the residents of Scythopolis (12:29-31). As they had been gracious toward the Jews in their midst, so too Judas is gracious toward them. This intermingling of defense of one's kinsfolk with an eye peeled for possible alliances with neighbors pervades the

69   Ma, *Antiochus III*, 179–242.
70   Ibid., 242.

narrative. "If you do well toward me, I'll do well toward you." Reciprocity is found also in the story where Timothy is set free because he promises not to harm the Jews in the future (12:25). Finally, it is present in the portrayal of God as bestowing a thankful gift on those who die piously (12:45).

This series of events, therefore, portrays Judas not only as a great fighter with God on his side but also as a leader who thinks only of the good of his people, as did Onias (4:5).

13

13:1-26

1/ In the year 149, it came to the ears of Judas's forces that Antiochus Eupator was coming with great numbers against Judea 2/ and with him was Lysias, his guardian and the one in charge of state affairs, each[a] having a Greek army of 110,000 infantry, 5,300 cavalry, 22 elephants, and 300 chariots with scythes. 3/ Menelaus talked with them and was inciting Antiochus with much dissembling, as he was thinking not about the safety of the fatherland but that he would be set over the rulership. 4/ But the King of Kings aroused the anger of Antiochus against the offender and when Lysias pointed out that he was the cause of all the troubles, he commanded them to take him to Beroea and destroy him, according to the custom of the place. 5/ There is in that place a tower fifty cubits high and full of ashes. It had a circular contraption that goes straight down on all sides into the ashes.[b] 6/ There they raise up[c] and push forward[d] to destruction whoever is guilty of temple robbery or who becomes notorious for certain other crimes. 7/ By such a doom[e] the lawless one, Menelaus, died, without reaching the earth[f] 8/ and that completely justly. For since he perpetrated many sins connected with the altar, whose fire and ashes are hallowed, he got back for himself his death in ashes.

9/ Barbarous in intent, the king was coming to show forth to the Jews worse things than those committed at the time of his father. 10/ When Judas learned of these, he gave the word to the populace to call upon the Lord day and night so that, if [he had] ever before [helped], so now he would help those about to be deprived of the law and the fatherland and the holy temple, 11/ and not allow his people, just a short time ago revived, to be under the control of abusive Gentiles. 12/ After they all did the same thing

a   Abel, Habicht, and Goldstein read ἐκτὸς ἔχοντα δύναμιν with La[LXBP], rather than ἕκαστον ἔχοντα δύναμιν, as in Hanhart's text, which is followed by Schwartz. Goldstein translates ἐκτός as "recruited abroad" while Habicht translates it as *"ferner"* ("furthermore"); Abel does not translate it. Two armies of 110,000 each would be enormous. First Maccabees 6:30 has 100,000 infantry for the whole army. Exaggerated numbers would not be unexpected in Second Maccabees, but this figure seems extreme.

b   The description of this death-dealing contraption has given translators difficulty, as Habicht remarks. NRSV has: "it has a rim running around it that on all sides inclines precipitously into the ashes"; Habicht: "eine rundherum zur Asche abschüssige Ebene"; Abel: "munie d'une machine tournante qui, de tous côtés, faisait glisser dans la cendre"; Goldstein: "with a rotating device descending steeply from every direction into the ashes." Friedrich Wilhelm König (*Die Persika des Ktesias von Knido* [Graz: Selbstverl. des Hrsg. Ernst Weidner, 1972] 85–88) suggested that it was round and funnel-like, so that those thrown into it had nothing to hold onto to stop themselves falling into the ashes.

c   Reading ἄραντες instead of ἅπαντες, as Niese ("Kritik," 527) conjectured, followed by Risberg ("Textkritische und exegetische Anmerkungen," 25 n. 1) and Katz ("Text of 2 Maccabees Reconsidered," 16).

d   Reading προωθοῦσιν instead of προσωθοῦσιν, again following Niese and Katz. The confusion between the two is frequent, as in Polybius 1.48.8 and Diodorus Siculus 20.95.1. The meaning does not change significantly.

e   Risberg ("Textkritische und exegetische Anmerkungen," 25) cleverly suggested that one read τοιούτῳ νόμῳ instead of τοιούτῳ μόρῳ. This would make a nice play on words with παράνομον and has some support in some Latin manuscripts (*tali lege praevaricatorem legis*). However, the majority of the manuscripts support μόρῳ.

f   Certain manuscripts specify the implication that Menelaus did not receive burial. L 311 reads ταφῆς instead of τῆς γῆς. La[BM] makes a doublet: *nec terrae sepulturam mereretur*, and Syr Arm are similar.

together and for three days were unceasingly bidding the merciful Lord with weeping and fasts and prostration, Judas encouraged them and ordered them to be on hand. 13/ Alone with the elders, he determined that before the king's army could enter Judea and take control of the city, [the Jews] would go out to decide matters, with God's help. 14/ Handing over the decision to the Master of the world, he encouraged his forces to fight nobly to the death for the sake of laws, temple, city, fatherland, and constitution, and encamped near Modein. 15/ He gave out to his forces the watchword "God's Victory." With excellent, picked young men, he attacked by night the royal residence[g] and killed about two thousand[h] soldiers and put out of action[i] the best of the elephants with its controller.[j] 16/ In the end they filled the camp with fear and confusion and successfully got away free 17/ as day was already beginning to break.[k] This had taken place through the protection of the Lord aiding him.

18/ Once the king had tasted the daring of the Jews, he tested the places methodically. 19/ Against Beth-Zur, a secure stronghold of the Jews, he advanced, was put to flight, was tripped up, suffered a loss. 20/ Judas sent to those inside what was necessary. 21/ However, Rhodokos, from the Jewish ranks, disclosed the secrets to the enemy. He was sought out, seized, and confined. 22/ The king spoke a second time to those in Beth-Zur, exchanged assurances, departed. 23/ He made an attack on Judas's forces, suffered loss, learned that Philip, who had been left behind in charge of state affairs in Antioch, had lost his senses, was in disarray, called upon the Jews, submitted and affirmed by oath on completely equitable terms, came to a settlement, and brought a sacrifice,

g Habicht is right to see "the camp" (τὴν παρεμβολήν) as a later addition to the text. As Schwartz suggests, it was added by someone who wanted to explain that the "royal residence" meant the enemy's camp. See Polybius 5.25.3 for the phrase τῆς τοῦ βασιλέως αὐλῆς.

h The manuscripts offer different numbers: 1,000 (V 771); 3,000 (Sy); 4,000 (L' 55 311 La Arm); 14,000 (La[X V·O]). Two thousand is the best-attested figure.

i The reading of Hanhart—συνέθηκεν ("he put together/constructed")—makes no sense. I have followed Grimm's emendation to συνεκέντησε. The verb was used already in 12:23. As Goldstein notes, "the emendation is supported by La[LXBMP], all of which have 'slew'; Sy has 'smashed and cast away.'"

j Hanhart reads σὺν τῷ κατ' οἰκίαν ὄντι, whereas Abel reasons from the ancient Latin superpositum, sessore that the Greek was originally σὺν τῷ κατοικοῦντι. The other variant, σὺν τῷ ὄχλῳ (q 58 311[c]), is to be understood with Abel as an attempt to make sense of the verb συνέθηκεν: "he put together the best of the elephants with the crowd," i.e., he killed the soldiers and the elephant together. Both Hanhart's and Abel's readings are obscure. Polybius, frg. 162b, uses the term οἰκίδιον to refer to the riding platform on top of the elephant, and this may have influenced the use of the term οἰκίαν here. If the participle is read as neuter, one would translate Hanhart's text as "with the thing being houselike," that is, the riding platform. If the participle is taken as a masculine, the translation would be "with the one being with it," that is, the elephant driver. Elephant drivers often lived with their elephants. With Abel's text, it would seem that one could take the participle only as masculine. The verb συνοικέω can have the meaning of "govern, administer" and so, if the phrase here, σὺν τῷ κατ' οἰκίαν κατοικοῦντι, is comparable to that verb, the meaning would be "with its controller." Bar-Kochva (Judas Maccabaeus, 317–18 and pls. 12–14), commenting on the wooden towers on top of the elephants in 1 Macc 6:37, provides a nice overview with illustrations.

k Katz ("Text of 2 Maccabees," 17) and Habicht follow Niese in connecting this genitive absolute with the end of the previous verse: "they successfully got away free as day was already beginning to break." He transposes δέ from its present position after ὑποφαινούσης to now read τοῦτο δὲ ἐγεγόνει. This makes for a clearer sentence structure, and the sense is not altered.

honored the temple and was benevolent toward the place, 24/ and he welcomed Judas favorably. He left Hegemonides as governor from Ptolemais to Gerar. 25/ He went to Ptolemais. The citizens of Ptolemais were horrified about the agreement—for they were very[1] angry—they wanted to annul the regulations. 26/ Lysias went up onto the platform, spoke in defense as well as he could, won them over, placated them, made them well-disposed, returned to Antioch. So turned out the events of the king's advance and return.

1   With Hanhart and Habicht, I read ὑπεράγαν. The manuscripts q 58 give the reading ὑπὲρ ὧν, which Abel follows and sees as equivalent to ὑπὲρ τούτων ὧν ("for they were angry over those things which they wanted to annul").

Commentary by Verse

■ **1-2** "the year 149." This is the first date given in the narrative. In 1 Macc 6:20, Judas's siege of the Akra, begun in 150 s.e., was the cause for Lysias's campaign. If one dates according to the Seleucid Macedonian calendar, 149 would be from September 164 to October 163 b.c.e. If one dates events connected with Jewish history according to the Seleucid Babylonian calendar, the date in 1 Macc 6:20 would fall between spring 162 and spring 161. Debate has raged between those who accepted the date of 2 Maccabees and placed the invasion in 163 b.c.e.,[1] and those who opted for 162, following 1 Maccabees[2]; Hanhart attempted to harmonize the two dates by placing the siege of the Akra and the following invasion between October 163 and April 162 b.c.e.[3] According to the Babylonian astronomical diaries, the corpse of Antiochus IV was in Babylon no later than 16 January

163. As Gera and Wayne Horowitz argue, there is no reason why Philip and his army could not have covered the 1,065 kilometers from Babylon and reached Antioch in a few months.[4] The inscription from Jamnia-on-the-Sea tells how the Sidonians in the port of Jamnia asked for, and received, the same exemption from taxes as another community.[5] The reply of the king is dated to the month of Loos 149 s.e., that is, July 163 b.c.e. Phillipe Gauthier suggests that the inscription comes from the time of peace after Antiochus V had allowed the Jews to follow their own laws (11:22-26),[6] and it could be that the Sidonians at Jamnia-on-the-Sea wanted to take advantage of the new king's benevolence and stressed their help to his father. If they wrote at the beginning of 163 b.c.e., soon after Antiochus IV's death, it would be strange for the Seleucid bureaucracy to take so long to reply.[7] Gera and Horowitz suggested that the context is the campaign of Antiochus V against the Jews: "The Sidonians of Jamnia-

1   Julius Wellhausen, "Über den geschichtlichen Wert des zweiten Makkabäerbuchs, im Verhältnis zum ersten," *Nachrichten von der Königl. Gesellschaft der Wissenschaften zu Göttingen*, Phil.-hist. Kl. (1905) 117–63, here 151–52; Mørkholm, *Antiochus IV*, 153; Bringmann, *Hellenistische Reform*, 19–20, 27 n. 50; Goldstein, *II Maccabees*, 458.

2   Tcherikover, *Hellenistic Civilization*, 224–25; Schürer, *History*, 1:167 n. 14; Bar-Kochva, *Judas Maccabaeus*, 543–51.

3   Robert Hanhart, *Zur Zeitrechnung des I. und II. Makkabäerbuches* (BZAW 88; Berlin: Töpelmann, 1964) 57–59, 67–68.

4   Gera and Horowitz, "Antiochus IV," 249–51.

5   The inscription is found in Isaac, "Seleucid Inscription," 133. I am following the suggestions of Gauthier, "Bulletin épigraphique," 528–30.

6   Gauthier, "Bulletin épigraphique," 529.

7   See Ma, *Antiochus III*, 138–47, for a description of the Seleucid Empire at work.

on-the-Sea, on hearing of the approach of the royal army, sent their delegates to the king and stressed their long-standing loyalty to his predecessors (lines 8–11)."[8] The request would have been made sometime in June, before the king turned inward toward Beth-Zur. Given the state of the inscription, it is hard to draw definite conclusions. The coincidence of the date of the inscription with the other factors mentioned above tends to support Gera and Horowitz's suggestion.

The use of προσπίπτειν + dative is found often in 2 Maccabees (5:11; 8:12; 9:3; 14:28) as it is used also in Polybius (5.101.3; 28.16.2).

The absolute use of τὸν ἐπίτροπον is interesting. The noun, in conjunction with "the one in charge of state affairs," could be translated as "overseer, administrator" just as easily as "guardian." In fact, at 9:25, Antiochus IV in his "letter" appointed Antiochus V as king with no mention of a guardian, and the text suggests that he is capable of being co-regent; in 10:11, it is said that Antiochus V appointed Lysias to be in charge of the affairs of state. Simply from the narrative one would therefore expect that ἐπίτροπος should be understood as "overseer" or "administrator." Regardless of whether one reads ἕκαστον ("each") or ἐκτός ("outside," which Goldstein sees as referring to those recruited abroad, while Habicht interprets it as a conjunction "moreover") in 13:2, the participle ἔχοντα refers to Antiochus V as being in charge. Bar-Kochva notes that "token or active participation of teenage kings and princes in military undertakings are well known in Hellenistic traditions."[9] Nevertheless, it is striking how the king is described as being in charge of the operation. However, in 11:1 Lysias is ἐπίτροπος τοῦ βασιλέως as well as kinsman and in charge of the affairs of state. Usually ἐπίτροπος + genitive of a person means "guardian," and given that, according to Josephus, Antiochus V was only nine years old at the time of his father's death, this is how it is understood. By this reckoning, Antiochus V would have been about ten years old during the invasion (Josephus *Ant.* 12.296; Appian *Syr.* 46, 66).[10]

The size of the army contrasts with the figures in 1 Macc 6:30, where the army is said to be 100,000 infantry and 20,000 cavalry as well as thirty-two elephants trained for war. The army is characterized as composed of mercenaries gathered from other kingdoms and islands (1 Macc 6:29). Josephus (*Bell.* 1.41) has 50,000 infantry and 5,000 cavalry. Bar-Kochva has argued that the estimate of Josephus is not far off, although this judgment is based on the supposition that part of Antiochus IV's army had returned from the eastern campaign and had become part of the expedition, which Bar-Kochva dates to 162 B.C.E.[11]

"twenty-two elephants." This is fewer than the eighty elephants in 11:4, the thirty-two in 1 Macc 6:30, and the eighty given by Josephus (*Bell.* 1.41). Bar-Kochva emends the text of 1 Macc 6:30 to read "eight elephants," and reconstructs how they would have been deployed by Lysias in the battle at Beth-Zacharia.[12] He also provides an excellent overview of both the advantages and disadvantages of elephants in warfare.[13] For those unused to elephants, they could cause great confusion and fear (Plutarch *Eum.* 18.2; Lucian *Zeux.* 9–11). By the presence of elephants in the procession at Daphne, Antiochus IV had violated the treaty made with the Romans by Antiochus III at Apamea (Polybius 21.42.11–12). The Romans dispatched a legate, Gnaeus Octavius, to burn decked warships and hamstring the elephants (Polybius 31.2.8–11). Walbank has carefully argued that the embassy was sent out sometime in 163 B.C.E. and the legates were murdered in Antioch in 162 B.C.E.[14] Bar-Kochva, however, insisted that this embassy would have been sent to Antioch in 162 B.C.E., rather than 163 B.C.E.[15] However, the variance does not seem to be so great, as Bar-Kochva himself notes that it is not stated that the legates are sent

8 Gera and Horowitz, "Antiochus IV," 251.
9 Bar-Kochva, *Judas Maccabaeus*, 304. See Plutarch *Pyrrh.* 9.
10 The age of twelve given by Porphyry (*FGH* 260, F32, 13) was rejected by Mørkholm (*Antiochus IV*, 48 n. 41) as it would require Antiochus IV to have married while a hostage in Rome.
11 Bar-Kochva, *Judas Maccabaeus*, 42–43, 546–47.
12 Ibid., 307, 324.
13 Ibid., 16–19; see also idem, *The Seleucid Army: Organization and Tactics in the Great Campaigns* (Cambridge: Cambridge University Press, 1976) 75–83.
14 Walbank, *Polybius*, 3:35–36.
15 Bar-Kochva, *Judas Maccabaeus*, 547–48, with references.

to Antioch as a result of the use of elephants by Lysias, and the fragmentary quality of the Polybian texts does not allow for a precise chronology of the legates' journey from Rome via the kingdom of Ariarathes (Polybius 31.8). It would seem that the legates arrived after Lysias had dealt with Philip.

"chariots with scythes." This traditional weapon was used by the Seleucids.[16] Bar-Kochva has argued that the chariots' retreat at Magnesia, which caused the collapse of the left flank "and, consequently, of the whole line (Livy 37.41.6–42, esp. 42.1), brought to a close the unhappy story of scythed chariots in the Seleucid army." He dismisses the mention of scythed chariots in 1 Macc 1:17 in connection with Antiochus IV's Egyptian campaign, as "the sandy terrain of Egypt's western frontier did not favour armaments of this kind."[17] Their presence in this campaign of Antiochus V Eupator and Lysias is unlikely, as Bar-Kochva has pointed out that the mountainous route chosen by Lysias and the lack of the even ground in the Judean plateau required if the chariots were to gather speed make it unlikely that chariots would have been used.[18] The author of 2 Maccabees wanted to heighten the frightful (see Appian *Mith.* 18) character of the invasion. Even Chariton, author of the romance *Chaereas and Callirhoe*, knew that the Persian king Cyrus had drawn up the system of mobilization of Persian forces to include infantry, chariots both ordinary and scythed, and elephants (*Chaer.* 6.8.7). The force here appears to be less a Greek force than specifically a Seleucid force that carried on the Persian traditions. The procession at Daphne had infantry, cavalry, chariots, and elephants (Polybius 33.25.1–11).

■ 3-8. The death of Menelaus

Menelaus has not been mentioned since 11:29, when, in the framework of the letters given by this author, he mediated a settlement with the king for the Jews to return to their own affairs and to use their own laws. This media-tion was unsuccessful, and Menelaus could no longer function as high priest and be in charge of the nation. He now receives his just deserts. Josephus (*Ant.* 12.383–85) has Menelaus put to death after the campaign.

■ **3** Menelaus seeks an audience with the king and Lysias. The author, by the contrast between the aorist συνέμειξε and the imperfect παρεκάλει, brings out the persistence of Menelaus's request. The verb συμμίγνυμι is used in this sense of "meet with, converse with" in 3:7.

The author shows a good sense of the different meaning of ἐπί in this sentence. He first uses it with the dative to show cause, ἐπὶ σωτηρίᾳ, and then with the genitive to show authority over, ἐπὶ τῆς ἀρχῆς.

"dissembling." The term εἰρωνεία here is used in a pejorative sense to characterize someone who conceals his intentions, as in Theophrastus *Characters I*.[19] The author spells out Menelaus's true intention, not the false intentions Menelaus gives to the king. Whereas Onias had sought what was best for the community and was not an accuser of the citizens (4:5), and Dositheos and Sosipater had let Timothy free so that their kinsfolk might be safe (12:25), Menelaus is only out for his own power, as he had shown before (4:27, 50). The verb καθίστημι ("to install") is used in 14:13, when Demetrius sends letters to Nikanor to install Alcimus as high priest.

■ **4** "King of Kings." The title is common in speaking of Persian and Egyptian rulers and is used in the Hebrew Scriptures of Nebuchadnezzar (Ezek 26:7; Dan 2:37) and Artaxerxes (Ezra 7:12). It, or the similar βασιλεὺς τῶν βασιλευόντων, is found also in *3 Macc.* 5:35; *1 Enoch* 9:4; 63:4; 84:2. In Deut 10:17, the titles "God of gods and lord of lords" (θεὸς τῶν θεῶν καὶ κύριος τῶν κυρίων) are found, as also in Ps 136:2-3 (LXX Ps 135:2-3).[20]

"aroused the anger." Just as God chose Cyrus as his instrument, as he is a God who makes peace and creates evils (Isa 45:1-7), so now he uses Antiochus V as his instrument of punishment.

---

16   Seleucus I at Ipsus (Diodorus Siculus 20.113.4; Plutarch *Demetr.* 28.3; 48.2).

17   Bar-Kochva, *Seleucid Army*, 83.

18   Ibid., 83–84; see also idem, *Judas Maccabaeus*, 19.

19   For the various meanings of the term, see G. Markantonatos, "On the Origin and Meanings of the Word ΕΙΡΩΝΕΙΑ," *Rivista di Filologia e di Istruzione Classica* 103 (1975) 16–21; Leif Bergson, "Eiron und Eironeia," *Hermes* 99 (1971) 409–22.

20   See also Philo *Decal.* 41. On the history of this title, see J. Gwyn Griffiths, "Βασιλεὺς βασιλέων: Remarks on the History of a Title," *CP* 48 (1953) 145–54.

"offender." The term ἀλιτήριος is used of the enemies in 12:23 and 14:42. By it, Menelaus is linked to non-Jews.

"the cause of all the troubles." Menelaus had been the cause of the uprising in 4:39-42, where with Menelaus's connivance, Lysimachos had committed temple robbery. That time Menelaus, the cause of all the evil (4:47: τὸν μὲν τῆς ὅλης κακίας αἴτιον), had escaped through bribery (4:45-47).

The participle ἀγαγόντας is a supplementary participle that I have translated as an infinitive. Beroea is Aleppo, which is about eighty-five kilometers east of Antioch. Seleucus I Nicator changed the name to Beroea after the city in Macedonia (Strabo *Geogr.* 16.2.7; Josephus *Ant.* 12.385).

■ **5-6** Persian kings are known to have used this method of execution.[21] A passage from Valerius Maximus as well as the description here imply that the contraption was always available. As Grimm has suggested, the offender would most likely have suffocated, rather than being burned by hot ashes.

"Notorious for certain other crimes" is literally "having procured for himself preeminence in certain other evils."

■ **7-8** As noted in text-critical note f, certain manuscripts add that Menelaus was deprived of burial. This would add another appropriate punishment to what the author wanted. He intended to emphasize how the death of Menelaus corresponded to his misbehavior at the altar, just as Aaron's sons were burned with fire from God because they had brought unholy fire before the Lord (Num 10:1-3). The author often uses the term πάνυ ("completely": 12:43; 15:17), notably in the context of appropriate punishment (9:6). As in 2:19, the term βωμός is employed to designate the altar, a usage that might be compared to LXX Num 3:10, which reads: "And you shall appoint Aaron and his sons over the tent of witness, and they will guard their priesthood and all those things around the altar [κατὰ τὸν βωμόν] and outside the veil." The verb κομίζειν ("get back for oneself") is used also for the payback to Callisthenes and those who had burned the entrances to the temple (8:33).

■ **9-17 The approach of Antiochus V and the first encounter with Judas**

While 1 Macc 6:31 has Lysias following the same route he had taken on his earlier expedition (1 Macc 4:29), through Edom to Beth-Zur, the author of 2 Maccabees has Judas make a sortie from Modein against the army while it is traveling down the coast.

■ **9** The perfect participle βεβαρβαρωμένος is used to show that the king is permanently barbarous.[22] The enemy had been described as barbarous before (2:21; 4:25; 5:22; 10:4). In 5:22-23, Philip was said to be more barbarous than Antiochus IV and Menelaus even more so (χείριστα τῶν ἄλλων). Does the phrase "worse things than those committed by his father" (χείριστα τῶν ἐπὶ τοῦ πατρὸς αὐτοῦ γεγονότων) make fun of the king's cognomen Eupator, "of noble sire"?

The verb ἔρχομαι + future participle signifies intent. The use of the imperfect stresses the continuation of the action.

■ **10-11** This long sentence shows that the author's interest is in portraying the prayerful attitude of the Jews rather than in focusing on military details. God is asked to help as he had shown himself their helper before (3:39; 8:20, 35; 12:11) and would again (15:35). "If [he had] ever before" is literally "if at some time or another" (εἴ ποτε καὶ ἄλλοτε). Note the homoioteleuton in this phrase.

It is noteworthy that in this context of prayer, Judas emphasizes the singular "law," fatherland, and holy temple, as these are what God had given to the people. The mention of "fatherland" contrasts with the description of Menelaus as not concerned about the safety of the fatherland (13:3). The prayer is similar to those in 8:29 and 10:4.

"Populace" recalls 12:42, and the singular πλήθει emphasizes the unity of the Jews as opposed to the great numbers of 13:1, where the plural σὺν πλήθεσιν is used, who come against Judea.

"Under the control" as in 14:42.

■ **12** The emphasis is on the collective action of the community and the call on God's mercy, as in 3:20-21, which had been shown in 8:5 and 11:10. As in 11:6, there

---

21 Herodotus 2.100; Ctesias *Persica* (*FGH* 688 F15 [52]); Valerius Maximus, *Facta et Dicta Memorabilia* 9.2, Externa 6; Ovid *Ibis* 315–16.   22 Smyth, *Greek Grammar*, §1872d.

is weeping and, as in 3:21, prostration. Fasting is linked with a call for mercy in LXX Dan 9:3. The encouragement (παρακαλέσας) of Judas to his people contrasts with that of Menelaus to the king in 13:3 (παρεκάλει). The use of καταξιόω in the meaning of the simple ἀξιόω ("to entreat, to pray")[23] is unusual, as Grimm notes.

■ **13** Here Judas is said to have a private consultation with the elders. Presumably this is a reference to the council (γερουσία) mentioned in 4:44 and 11:27. Later Rhazis is said to be one of the Jerusalem elders (14:37). The decision is to keep the king's army from entering Judea at all. Such a plan has little effect, as later the king's army will enter Judea at Beth-Zur (13:19). In 1 Maccabees, Antiochus V is said to have besieged Jerusalem and to have broken down the wall at Mount Zion (1 Macc 6:48-53). The author of 2 Maccabees, however, insists that at no time did Antiochus V have control of the city. Antiochus V is said to have honored the temple, not set up siege engines against the sanctuary.

The collective singular noun for "army," τὸ στρά-τευμα, is used distributively when describing it as in control (ἐγκρατεῖς) of the city.[24] Note 15:37, where the verb κράτειν is used to describe how the Hebrews "control" the city.

"to decide matters." The same phrase is found in 15:17 and also in Polybius 1.15.4; 1.87.7; 5.82.1. In Polybius the verb κρίνειν often has the sense of risking a battle (3.69.12; 3.70.1; 3.107.14; 3.117.11).

The use of the noun "help" here resonates with the verbal use in 13:10 (ἐπιβοηθεῖν).

■ **14** This sentence is marked by asyndeton. The two aorist participles—δούς, παρακαλέσας—express successive actions,[25] while also heightening the tension. The string of five nouns asyndetically creates an emotional effect. When Judas gave the word to the people in 13:10 to call on the Lord, the prayer was on behalf of the

syndetically arranged group of law (singular), fatherland, and holy temple. Now Judas arouses his soldiers' patriotism by appealing to what holds their particular society together—laws (plural), temple, city, fatherland, and constitution. A similar grouping is made by Lycurgus when he argues against readmitting someone who has not fought for the fatherland: "that he takes part in the cult, the sacrifices, the assembly, the laws, the government [ἱερῶν, θυσιῶν, ἀγορᾶς, νόμων, πολιτείας μεθέξων]" (Lycurgus 142).[26] As J. D. Denniston notes, "the number of co-ordinated words or clauses is seldom less than three."[27] This holds true for Polybius as well.[28]

"handing over the decision." As always, God is in control of the battle. See 8:18 and Josephus *Vita* 138.

"creator of the world." God is called ὁ τοῦ κόσμου κτίστης in 7:23.

"to fight nobly." The adverb γενναίως is found also in 8:16 and 15:17.

Modein lies northwest of Jerusalem, close to the Judean border. It is disputed whether it lay in Judea, as Schwartz notes. Given the plan in 13:13, the author would seem to locate Modein close to the border. In 1 Macc 2:1; 13:25, it is said to be the home of the Hasmoneans. There is no mention of such an encampment in 1 Macc 6:31.

■ **15** Again two asyndetic aorist participles stress the rapidity of the events. The first—ἀναδούς—resonates with δούς at the beginning of the previous sentence. The watchword is given, as in 8:23. The author stresses that victory comes from God, as in 10:28, 38; 15:8, 21, echoing the previous verse. Dov Gera has noted that the construction victory + personal name in the genitive is found on a sling bullet from Dor, and he connected it with similar inscriptions that Theodore Reinach had argued came from gymnasial contests.[29]

This attack by night returns to the tactics used by Judas in the early stages of the rebellion (8:7). It reflects

23 The verb ἀξιόω is found in 2 Macc 5:4; 7:28; 8:14, 29; 10:4, 16, 26; 12:42.

24 Smyth, *Greek Grammar*, §§996–98.

25 J. D. Denniston, *Greek Prose Style* (Oxford: Clarendon, 1965) 102.

26 See also Antiphon 6.4: "The law banishes him from his city, its temples, its games, and its sacrifices [πόλεως, ἱερῶν, ἀγώνων, θυσιῶν], the greatest and most ancient of human institutions."

27 Denniston, *Greek Prose Style*, 105.

28 Foucault, *Recherches*, 261.

29 Dov Gera, "Tryphon's Sling Bullet from Dor," *IEJ* 35 (1985) 154–56. Theodore Reinach, "Les Inscriptions d'Iasos," *REG* 6 (1893) 153–203, here 197–203.

the sense that the Seleucid army is too powerful to be attacked openly and appears to back away from Judas's decision to decide the events in 13:13. This sortie is of a quite different character from the description of the battle at Beth-Zacharia in 1 Macc 6:33-46, in which Eleazar killed one of the elephants during the battle.

■ **16-17** "In the end" ($\tau\grave{o}$ $\tau\acute{\epsilon}\lambda o\varsigma$), as in 5:7. The combination of fear and tumult is found in 3:30, but one of the pair could be substituted, as in 12:22 and 15:23. The verb "get away" ($\grave{\epsilon}\kappa\lambda\acute{v}\omega$) is also in 12:18. The genitive absolute for daybreak is found in 10:35, but there it signals the beginning of attack. Verbal, nominal, and adverbial uses of the root $\epsilon\grave{v}\eta\mu\epsilon\rho$- are found in 5:6; 8:8, 35; 10:28; 12:11; 14:14. Here, with the verb and participle in the plural, the action is attributed to the group. However, the protection ($\sigma\kappa\acute{\epsilon}\pi\eta$) of God is said to be for Judas, just as in 10:30.

The author notes that the whole affair took place as a night raid. As Pritchett observes, "In one of his didactic interludes, Polybius groups the night attack with fraudulent and petty operations (4.8.11) employed by the cowardly ($\grave{\alpha}\gamma\epsilon\nu\nu\epsilon\hat{\iota}\varsigma$ $\kappa\alpha\grave{\iota}$ $\pi\lambda\acute{\alpha}\gamma\iota o\iota$ $\tau\alpha\hat{\iota}\varsigma$ $\psi\nu\chi\alpha\hat{\iota}\varsigma$) Cretans."[30] Here, however, it is question of guerrilla warfare by insurgents.

■ 18-24a The siege of Beth-Zur and the eventual reconciliation with Judas

■ **18-22** In 1 Macc 6:31, 49-50, the town is forced to capitulate because of the lack of provisions due to the previous Sabbath year.[31] Second Maccabees 13:19-22 does not mention the capture of Beth-Zur but does refer to a parley intended to resolve the situation.

■ **18** The phrase $\gamma\epsilon\hat{v}\mu\alpha$ $\lambda\alpha\mu\beta\acute{\alpha}\nu\epsilon\iota\nu$ ("tasted") is used in Plato *Hipparchus* 228E in the context of acquiring a taste for wisdom.

"tested . . . methodically" ($\kappa\alpha\tau\epsilon\pi\epsilon\acute{\iota}\rho\alpha\sigma\epsilon$ $\delta\iota\grave{\alpha}$ $\mu\epsilon\vartheta\acute{o}\delta\omega\nu$). The verb $\kappa\alpha\tau\alpha\pi\epsilon\iota\rho\acute{\alpha}\zeta\omega$ is used in Polybius, most often with the genitive, with the sense of "attempted to take" (4.13.5; 4.19.3; 4.78.10; 5.97.5). However, it does seem also to have the sense of "test, sound out" (Polybius 2.54.9; 4.50.6; 4.76.3; 5.52.8; 20.7.8). $\mu\epsilon\vartheta\acute{o}\delta o\varsigma$ has been a problem. Abel and Habicht have given the meaning of "trick, stratagem," a con-

notation found in Plutarch *Reg. imp. apophth.* 176a; the author would then be showing that the king has learned to be cautious and would remind the reader how Apollonius had used trickery to catch the Jews off guard (5:25). Schwartz notes that nowhere in this episode does the king use trickery, and he suggests that one translate etymologically, "by devious routes." However, this translation does not correspond to the context either. The king follows the path followed by Lysias in 11:5. The Jews would seem to be the ones who would know all the "devious routes" in the area, and it is hard to imagine an army of 110,000 infantry, plus elephants and cavalry, being able to be inconspicuous. The king's camp had suffered a night raid by the Jews, and I suggest that in response the king tightened up his camp defenses. He made sure suitable sites were chosen for the camp, which he set up using the methods and systems that would best protect it. Polybius had noted how inferior the Greek system of camp fortification was in comparison to that of the Romans, because the Roman camp always followed the same pattern (6.42).[32] However, this does not mean that the Seleucid army on the march had developed no system of fortification. My translation therefore keeps a usual meaning of $\mu\epsilon\vartheta\acute{o}\delta o\varsigma$, "method, system," and suits the context.

■ **19** This sentence contains four verbs in the imperfect placed asyndetically. The imperfect captures the sense of continuous action, while the asyndeton stresses the unexpectedness of the events, as the huge Greek army is unsuccessful. The asyndetic grouping is similar to that found in Xenophon: $\kappa\alpha\grave{\iota}$ $o\grave{\iota}$ $\mu\grave{\epsilon}\nu$ $\psi\iota\lambda o\grave{\iota}$ $\epsilon\grave{v}\vartheta\grave{v}\varsigma$ $\grave{\epsilon}\kappa\delta\rho\alpha\mu\acute{o}\nu\tau\epsilon\varsigma$ $\grave{\eta}\kappa\acute{o}\nu\tau\iota\zeta o\nu$, $\acute{\epsilon}\beta\alpha\lambda\lambda o\nu$, $\grave{\epsilon}\tau\acute{o}\xi\epsilon\upsilon o\nu$, $\grave{\epsilon}\sigma\pi\epsilon\nu\delta\acute{o}\nu\omega\nu$ ("And the light troops, rushing forth at once, set to throwing javelins, hurling stones, shooting arrows, and discharging slings"); $\kappa\alpha\grave{\iota}$ $\sigma\upsilon\mu\beta\alpha\lambda\acute{o}\nu\tau\epsilon\varsigma$ $\tau\grave{\alpha}\varsigma$ $\grave{\alpha}\sigma\pi\acute{\iota}\delta\alpha\varsigma$ $\grave{\epsilon}\omega\vartheta o\hat{v}\nu\tau o$, $\grave{\epsilon}\mu\acute{\alpha}\chi o\nu\tau o$, $\grave{\alpha}\pi\acute{\epsilon}\kappa\tau\epsilon\iota\nu o\nu$, $\grave{\alpha}\pi\acute{\epsilon}\vartheta\nu\eta\sigma\kappa o\nu$ ("and setting shields against shields they shoved, fought, killed, and were killed") (*Hell.* 2.4.33; 4.3.19).

■ **20** This action of Judas—the aorist implies a one-time event—is not mentioned at all in the account in 1 Maccabees. Quite the contrary, in fact, as in 1 Macc 6:49, the

---

30   Pritchett, *Greek State at War*, 2:171. He also refers to Polybius 4.25.3.

31   See Bar-Kochva, *Judas Maccabaeus*, 544–45, for a discussion of this dating.

32   Polybius gives a full discussion of the Roman system in 6.27–41. For a fuller view, see Pseudo-Hyginus *De munitionibus castrorum*, particularly nos. 6–58 on the choice of site.

people of Beth-Zur had to evacuate because they had no provisions to withstand the siege.

■ **21** Goldstein argued that Rhodokos was an Iranian name. Bar-Kochva recognizes that the name itself is no indicator of whether Rhodokos was a volunteer from the Diaspora, or a Judean.[33]

"from the Jewish ranks" (ἐκ τῆς Ἰουδαϊκῆς τάξεως). Schwartz has raised the issue whether Rhodokos was a soldier in the king's army. He argues that one would expect Beth-Zur to have been taken if Rhodokos had revealed the secrets, but that the text does not say that the city fell. He suggests that Rhodokos may have been a member of the Jewish unit in the Seleucid army, "as distinguished from other national units; his treason, then, was against the Seleucids, and consisted of passing on to Judas's side the secret information which allowed them to smuggle in supplies."[34] As Schwartz himself notes, however, this reading runs against the fact that πολέμιος ("enemy"), except when used metaphorically in 15:39, is always used of the Jews' enemies.[35] The noun τάξις ("rank") is used elsewhere of Jewish forces (8:22; 10:36). In response to Schwartz's concern that Rhodokos is expressly said to be from the *Jewish* rank, one could note how Ἰουδαϊκῆς brings out the contrast between Rhodokos's action and that of Ἰούδας in the preceding verse, as well as twice-mentioned Jews in vv. 18-19. Schwartz is right to note how the condensed narrative is rather cryptic, but Rhodokos's action mirrors the wrong action of other Jews in 10:20, which is punished with death (10:22). On the analogy of παρέκλεισεν in 4:34, where the verb παρακλείω ("to shut up") is used euphemistically to mean "kill," Abel, Habicht, and Goldstein take this meaning here. However, the verb κατακλείω is used in Wis 17:2, 16 with the meaning of "shut in, confine," and it could have this meaning here—Rhodokos could have been thrown into prison. Whether he was imprisoned or killed, Rhodokos is punished for his treachery.

What were the secrets Rhodokos disclosed? Bar-Kochva showed that "the secrets" referred to neither shafts seen in the southern part of the hill nor a "secret access," through which, it had been hypothesized, the Seleucids broke.[36] His arguments are derived from the

account in 1 Macc 6:49-22, where the defenders gave up because of starvation. His suggestion is that the secrets might be "the paths and methods by which supplies were carried into the besieged hill." However, the account in 13:22 does not have the defenders capitulate but rather has the king initiate the agreement reached. There is no hint in 13:22 that Beth-Zur could not withstand the siege.

What is interesting stylistically here is how the events concerning Judas and Rhodokos in 13:20-21 are not asyndetic but are surrounded by lists of asyndetic verbs in 13:19 and 13:22 that describe the setback of the king and his initiative for a peaceful settlement. Within this rapid-fire succession of events, the pace is slowed down and the treachery of Rhodokos highlighted.

■ **22** Again we find a series of four asyndetic verbs in the aorist. Here the king is said to address those in Beth-Zur a second time. This presupposes that he had asked the town to surrender before his first attack. Now he seeks to make peace.

"Exchanged assurances" is literally "he gave the right hand, he received." For the combination of διδόναι δεξιάν and λαμβάνειν δεξιάν, see 12:11-12. The phrase "to give the right hand" is found in 4:34; 11:26, 30; 14:19. The same verb for leaving (ἀπήει) is used after Lysias made agreements with the Jews (12:1).

■ **23-26 The encounter with Judas's forces**
This narrative is completely different from that in 1 Macc 6:32-63, and the two cannot be reconciled. In 1 Maccabees, the king, after setting up a siege against Beth-Zur, moved out to fight against Judas, who had encamped at Beth-Zacharia. When the king's army moved forward, Judas's forces moved away, although one man performed a daring deed and killed one of the elephants. The king made peace with the people of Beth-Zur, who then left the town (1 Macc 6:49-50). The king then besieged the temple and was on the verge of taking it when he had to leave because Lysias heard of Philip's return from Persia and tricked the king into calling off the siege (1 Macc 6:51-60). Peace was made on terms different from those in 2 Macc 13:23. The king then broke his oath and had the wall on Mount Zion torn down (1 Macc 6:62).

33   Bar-Kochva, *Judas Maccabaeus*, 88 n. 54.
34   Schwartz, *2 Maccabees*, 457.
35   2 Maccabees 4:16; 5:6; 8:6, 16, 24, 27; 10:21, 27; 11:11; 12:22, 28; 14:22; 15:20, 26.
36   Bar-Kochva, *Judas Maccabaeus*, 309.

■ **23-24a** This section continues the string of asyndetic verbs found at the end of 13:22. There is, in fact, a string of twelve asyndetic verbal clauses in 13:22-23. I do not consider that the clauses at the end of 13:23–ὑπετάγη καὶ ὤμοσεν, συνελύθη καὶ θυσίαν προσήγαγεν, ἐτίμησε τὸν νεὼ καὶ τὸν τόπον ἐφιλανθρώπησε— break the string, as the two verbs in each section complement each other and form a unit.

Just as the king had suffered a loss before Beth-Zur (13:19: ἠλαττονοῦτο), so now he suffers a loss (ἥττων ἐγένετο) before Judas's forces. At the battle at Beth-Zacharia in 1 Macc 6:33-47, the only loss the king's forces suffered was the death of an elephant.

The story about Philip here verges dramatically from that in 1 Macc 6:55-60. According to the version in 13:22, Philip, left in charge of affairs in Antioch, had gone crazy. The root of the verb used, ἀπονενοῆσθαι, where the perfect shows that the effect of his madness remained, is found in what Eleazar's "friends" think has happened to him (6:29). The account in 13:23 has Antiochus V appointing Philip, who rebels against him. The verb for "left behind" (ἀπολείπειν) is the same as that used in 4:29; "in charge of state affairs" is the function given to Lysias in 10:11 and 13:2. Most scholars interpret this verse in terms of 1 Macc 6:55-56: this Philip is the one whom Antiochus IV had appointed in place of Lysias. This verse in 2 Maccabees, then, would be at odds with what the author had already said in 9:29, where that Philip is said to have gone over to Ptolemy Philometor. The narrative as it stands, however, argues for two Philips, one who had been with Antiochus IV and one who had been appointed by Antiochus V and Lysias when they invaded Judea. The challenges in identifying the Timothys in the narrative are replicated for Philips.

The verb συγχύω ("was in disarray") is found also in 10:30, where the enemy is confounded by the appearance of heavenly helpers around Judas, and in 14:28, where Nikanor is confused when he learns that he must arrest Judas.

"called upon." The verb παρακαλέω is found in the context of calling upon or urging a peace settlement in Diodorus Siculus 15.38.1-2; 15.50.4.

The use of the aorist passive of the verb ὑποτάσσω to describe what the king did is audacious. The verb usually has the sense of "become subject to."[37] Its use here underlines the concern of the author to show the Jews in a dominant position vis-à-vis the king's forces. The verb is connected with the taking of an oath "on completely equitable terms," the phrase used in 11:14 to describe the terms agreed between Lysias and Judas on their first encounter. Here the oath seals the agreement. Ma has noted how frequently "the local communities attempt to bind their political masters by the exchange of oaths or the publication of agreements" and provided an interesting example of an alliance between Antiochus III and Perinthos from ca. 196 B.C.E. in his epigraphical dossier.[38]

The verb συλλύω ("came to a settlement") and its substantive are frequently found in peace settlements and are connected with the forming of συνθήκας ("agreements"), a term found in 13:25.[39] Here the settlement is sealed with a sacrifice. Such a thing often happened. In the epic tradition, when Agamemnon and Priam agree to let a dispute be decided by a fight between Menelaus and Paris, a sacrifice is offered (Homer *Il* 3.264–301). Likewise, in Virgil's *Aeneid*, when Aeneas and Turnus agree to decide by single combat whether the Trojans shall remain in Rome or leave, a sacrifice seals the deal (*Aen.* 12.216–94). In Isocrates *Paneg.* 43 sacrifices and oaths accompany peace settlements. An interesting exception that proves the rule is found in Plutarch's *Life of Pyrrhus*: When Pyrrhus made peace with Lysimachus and all met to ratify the agreement with sacrificial oaths, one of the victims, a ram, fell down dead of its own accord. Pyrrhus then renounced the peace.

It is hard to see exactly what is so important a difference between "submitted and affirmed by oath" and "came to a settlement and brought a sacrifice" that the author insists on narrating both, particularly after the breathless run-through of events. The author seems to be slowing down the pace of events and leading to the

---

37   See Diodorus Siculus 12.50.7; 12.64.3; 16.46.1; 19.75.6. It can have the sense of "align oneself with," as in Diodorus Siculus 16.73.2, but still in a subordinate position.

38   Ma, *Antiochus III*, 170–71; no. 35 (pp. 351–52).

39   See Diodorus Siculus 12.4.5; 15.38.12; 15.50.4; 18.18.3–4; 29.12; 31.33.

final complementary pair, "honored the temple and was benevolent toward the place." This combination echoes the statement at the very beginning of the work, where the kings "were honoring the place and they were glorifying the temple with excellent gifts" (3:2: τιμᾶν τὸν τόπον καὶ τὸ ἱερὸν ἀποστολαῖς ταῖς κρατίσταις δοξάζειν). The use of φιλανθρωπέω in this context is interesting. Usually the verb is used to show how a general, after subduing a city, treats it with kindness or deals humanely with it (Polybius 3.76.2; Diodorus Siculus 18.18.3–4); it is used in this sense in 4:11, which records how the Seleucid kings had benevolently allowed the Jews to follow their own laws. Schwartz interprets the verb in this sense, holding that it refers to an agreement reached and that the term "the place" has the broader meaning of "city." The meaning would thus be that the Jews by their actions that appeared rebellious had caused the revocation of the previous agreement of Antiochus V to allow them to follow their own laws (11:22-26). The king now graciously restores this permission to the Jews. However, the author has said in 13:24 both that the king had submitted and that he had come to a settlement. The comparison with 3:2 suggests that the verb φιλανθρωπέω parallels the verb τιμάω and that νεώς parallels τόπος. The sense here seems to be that the king bestowed some special benefit on the temple, which would be parallel to the meaning in 3:2.

The asyndeton is broken when the king is described as receiving Judas. The verb ἀποδέχομαι is used to describe how Onias the high priest received Heliodorus (3:9) and how Heliodorus received Onias (3:35), as well as the reception given to Antiochus IV by Jason (4:22). This favorable reception of Judas is the highlight of this incursion of the king: Judas is now no longer a rebel leader but a leader accepted by the king himself.

■ **24b-26 The departure of the king**
Here begins again a series of ten asyndetic clauses, broken only by the parenthetical comment that the citizens of Ptolemais were very angry. The king's departure is thus presented exceedingly briefly.
■ **24b** Antiochus V appoints a new ruler of the region from Ptolemais to Gerar, using the same term κατα-

λείπω as found in 4:31 and 5:22. This would indicate a change in policy toward the Jews, the opposite of what is said to have happened in 10:12-13, where the favorable policy of Ptolemy Makron toward the Jews was attacked and he committed suicide. Hegemonides would have been appointed to carry out the new attitude toward the Jews. This administrative zone reaches down the coastal plain south of Gaza, and Hermann Bengtson suggests that it is a smaller unit that replaces the larger unit of Coele-Syria and Phoenicia.[40] The Greek phrase I have translated as Gerar is ἕως τῶν Γερρηνῶν, literally "up to the Gerrens." Since the normal term for Gerar in LXX is Γέραρα, Goldstein suggested that this area actually lay north of Ptolemais, near Beirut, which is mentioned in Polybius 5.46.2. However, it is hard to see what immediate relevance this geographical area would have for the Jews, though Goldstein attempts to establish its significance. Grimm pointed to the city Γέρρον (listed at Ptolemy *Geog.* 4.5.11 as a boundary point after Pelusium) or Γέρρα (Strabo 1.3.4; 1.3.13; 16.2.33) that lay between Pelusium and Rhinocolura. Grimm noted that MS 55 has Γεραρηρῶν, and he surmised that Γεραρηνοί could easily have been read as Γερρηνοί. Whatever the case, with Abel and Schwartz it seems more likely that the area should be seen as belonging to the southern coastal region of Palestine.

Hegemonides, son of Zephyros, is known from two inscriptions from the Achaean city of Dyme: in one, Hegemonides makes a dedication to Antiochus IV and his family, in the other, the honor accorded Hegemonides of Dyme by the city of Laodicea is recorded.[41]
■ **25** According to 1 Macc 5:15, Ptolemais was known for its hostility to the Jews. It could have been one of the neighboring Greek cities that followed the suggestion of Ptolemy that Jews be forced to take part in non-Jewish festivals (6:8-9).

The combination of ἐδυσφόρουν . . . ἐδείναζον ("were horrified . . . were angry") is found in 4:35, where the reaction of Greek cities to unjust behavior is described. The author moves from the aorist tense (ἦλθεν) to the imperfect (ἐδυσφόρουν) to indicate the

---

40 Bengtson, *Strategie*, 2:176–81.
41 See Christian Habicht, "Der Stratege Hege-
    monides," *Historia* 7 (1958) 376–78. See *SEG* 14.368
    (= *OGIS* 252), 369.

continuance of the emotion felt by the citizens of Ptolemais. As Grimm noted, given the rapid-fire description of events, it seems strange that the author should insist that the citizens were "very angry." It would seem that the author wished to underscore the hostility of Ptolemais toward the Jews. Does this emphasis reflect the fact that Simon Maccabeus was later appointed governor over the area in which Ptolemais lay (1 Macc 11:59)?

The combination of the verb $\dot{\alpha}\vartheta\epsilon\tau\dot{\epsilon}\omega$ and the root of $\delta\iota\alpha\sigma\tau\dot{\epsilon}\lambda\lambda\omega$ is found also in 14:28, when Nikanor is forced to change his position (13:25: $\delta\iota\dot{\alpha}\sigma\tau\alpha\lambda\sigma\iota\varsigma$; 14:28: $\delta\iota\epsilon\sigma\tau\alpha\lambda\mu\dot{\epsilon}\nu\alpha$). The verb $\delta\iota\alpha\sigma\tau\dot{\epsilon}\lambda\lambda\omega$ has the meaning of "to separate, define precisely, give orders." Here the noun is in combination with $\sigma\upsilon\nu\vartheta\dot{\eta}\kappa\eta$ and so I have chosen to translate it with the general sense of "regulations."[42]

■ **26** Lysias here addresses the crowd in place of the king, perhaps a recognition of the youth of Antiochus V. Ezra is said to get up on a wooden platform ($\beta\hat{\eta}\mu\alpha$) to address the assembly (Neh 8:4 = LXX 2 Esdr 18:4; LXX 1 Esdr 9:42). Pericles and Alexander the Great are said to have addressed the crowd from such platforms (Thucydides 2.34; Curtius 9.3.18; 10.2.30). Lysias succeeds in making the citizens of Ptolemais well disposed, as were the people of Scythopolis/Beth-Shean, toward the Jews (12:31).

The verb $\dot{\alpha}\nu\alpha\zeta\epsilon\dot{\upsilon}\gamma\nu\upsilon\mu\iota$ ("returned") is found in 5:11 to describe the withdrawal of Antiochus IV from Egypt and in 12:29 to describe Judas moving off from Gilead. In 14:16, it describes the breaking of camp to march forth.

The terms "advance and retreat" are found elsewhere in the work: "advance" in a hostile sense in 5:1; 8:12 (where I have translated it "invasion" because of the context); 14:15; 15:8; "retreat" in 9:2 to describe how Antiochus IV had to leave for home.

The verb $\chi\omega\rho\dot{\epsilon}\omega$ ("to turn out") is found also in the summary statements in 3:40 and 15:37.

General Commentary

The author of 2 Maccabees had promised in the prologue that he would try to persuade his audience and to show both the greatness of God's protection of the Jews, their temple, and their city and that one should follow God's laws or face the consequences. His intent is evident in this chapter. The narrative is about the advance and retreat of Antiochus V's army, but six of the twenty-six verses are given over to the death of the wicked Menelaus. And the night sortie of Judas, a minor event, is given the next nine verses. The siege of Beth-Zur receives four verses, the attack on Judas's forces half a verse, and the treaty between the king and the Jews one and a half verses. The emphasis is clearly on the power of God punishing Menelaus and protecting Judas and his men. The style of the narrative also signals this focus. The narrative of the death of Menelaus and of the night sortie of Judas uses the usual connecting particles, except for the emphatic use of asyndeton in 13:14, where two participles are asyndetic, and the emotionally powerful asyndetic list of what the troops are fighting for. Such asyndeton is not unusual in the narrative.[43] However, the normal coordinate is broken in 13:19, 22-23, 24b-26, where a string of verbs is found. This rapid-fire sequence is broken when events that affect the Jews are described: the treachery of Rhodokos and his punishment, the positive reception of Judas by the king. Schwartz finds in this "telegraphic, staccato style" evidence that the author "found the Beth-Zur campaign of Chapter 13 something of an embarrassment, or a puzzle, and it may be that the style in which he left it is that of notes—on Jason's original narrative—that he never wrote up properly because he did not know what to do with it."[44] However, the fact that the author distinguishes in his usage between the aorist and the imperfect tenses (13:19-21), introduces a doublet in 13:23 ($\dot{\upsilon}\pi\epsilon\tau\dot{\alpha}\gamma\eta$ . . . $\ddot{\omega}\mu\omega\sigma\epsilon\nu$, $\sigma\upsilon\nu\epsilon\lambda\dot{\upsilon}\vartheta\eta$ . . .

---

42   This would also seem to be the sense behind the verb as used in the command given by Ptolemy VI Philometor to Dionysius: "we thought it necessary to give orders to you [$\delta\iota\alpha\sigma\tau\epsilon\dot{\iota}\lambda\epsilon\sigma\vartheta\alpha[\iota]\,\dot{\upsilon}\mu\hat{\iota}\nu$] to take thought so that . . ." (Lenger, *Corpus des ordonnances*, no. 36.6 [p. 89]). Lenger translates the verb by "recommander," but this seems too soft.

43   Asyndetic participles are found, for example, in 8:11, 22, 34-35; 10:5, 27, 35; 11:1-2, 13-14; 12:5, 36-37; 14:1, 3, 5, 18, 31, 46; 15:21; asyndetic verbs in 10:5; 14:21, 25.

44   Schwartz, *2 Maccabees*, 34.

θυσίαν προσήγαγεν), and breaks the asyndeton when Judean interests are involved suggests that the author is in control of what he is doing. It would seem that he wishes to get through this part of the narrative as quickly as possible, so as to concentrate on the final act of the drama he is presenting: the treachery of Alcimus, the attack on the temple, and the defeat of Nikanor. Denniston has provided examples of narrative passages where asyndeta are piled up in masses. He noted that the longest series of asyndeta that he found was Demosthenes *Or.* 24.11–14 (*Against Timocrates*), "where, to say nothing of clauses, nine consecutive sentences, covering twenty-seven lines, open without a connecting particle."[45] It is interesting that Demosthenes introduces this asyndetic narrative by stating that he wants to briefly (ἐν βραχέσι) recount the facts from the beginning (*Or.* [*Tim.*] 24.10).

That the author is also concerned to show the power of God protecting his people is likewise evident in this narrative. In 1 Macc 6:30-63, Beth-Zur is forced to capitulate and the people leave; Judas's forces are repelled by those of the king; the temple is besieged and the people in the temple are on the point of starvation; Lysias per-suades the king to return to Antioch to fight Philip, who had been appointed to replace Lysias and comes back with the armies from the eastern campaign; the king makes peace with the Jews; the king then breaks his oath and has the wall around the citadel destroyed. Nothing like this happens in the narrative in 2 Macc 13:19-24. The people in Beth-Zur are not forced to leave—the king is rebuffed and has to make peace; the king's forces are turned back by Judas's forces; Jerusalem is not on the point of starvation; the king makes peace and does not break his oath and tear down the wall in Jerusalem. In this narrative, there is no hint of Jewish loss or of any damage to the city or the temple. In terms of both style and content, the author has constructed this narrative to downplay its importance.

The parallelism between 13:23, where the king honors the temple and is benevolent toward it, and 3:2-3, the opening verses of the narrative, where kings honor the place and supply everything necessary for the sacrifices, is noteworthy. This correspondence suggests that the *status quo ante* has been restored.

---

45 Denniston, *Greek Prose Style*, 117.

14

14:1-25
The Approach of Nikanor and His Treaty

1/ In the third year thereafter, news
came to those around Judas
that Demetrius, son of Seleucus, had sailed in through the
harbor at Tripolis with a strong
multitude and armament 2/ and
had taken control of the region,
doing away with Antiochus and
his guardian Lysias.

3/ Alcimus, who had previously
been high priest but who had
voluntarily defiled himself in
the times of chaos,[a] understanding that in no way did he
have safe return and no longer
an approach to the holy altar,
4/ came to King Demetrius in
the 151st year to offer him a
golden crown and a palm frond,
as well as some of the customary gifts of the temple. And that
day he kept quiet, 5/ as he was
taking time as co-worker of his
own folly. Invited to a meeting
by Demetrius and asked what
was the disposition and design
of the Jews, he said in reference to these, 6/ "Those of the
Jews called Hasidim, of whom
the leader is Judas Maccabeus,
maintain an inimical pose and
are in revolt, not allowing the
kingdom to gain stability, 7/ for
which reason, I, depriving
myself of the ancestral glory—
of course, I am speaking of the
high priesthood—have now
come here: 8/ first, genuinely
thinking about what pertains to
the king; second, having regard
also for my own citizens. For,
by the unreasonableness of the
aforementioned, our whole race
greatly suffers loss. 9/ But you,
O king, understanding each of
these things, provide for both
the region and the surrounding
race in accord with the courte-
ous benevolence that you have
toward all. 10/ For so long as
Judas is around, it is not possible that affairs of state obtain
peace." 11/ When this had been
said by him, quite quickly the
other Friends, who bore ill will
regarding those things concerning Judas, enflamed Demetrius.
12/ Immediately selecting
Nikanor, the former commander
of a squadron of elephants,

a   Reading ἀμιξίας rather than ἐπιμιξίας ("intercourse"), which is found in L' 58 311 La^BM Sy. The
term ἀμιξία is used again in 14:38. Goldstein (*II
Maccabees*, 484) accepts the reading ἐπιμιξίας, as he
constructs an antithesis between Alcimus, who was
defiled during the period of peace (ἐπιμίξια), and
Rhazis, who decided for Judaism in the period of war
(ἀμίξια). The contrast is stronger, however, if they are
compared at the same time period. Goldstein mainly
wishes to place the defilement of Alcimus after his
acceptance by the scribes and Hasideans, as described
in 1 Macc 7:12-15. We are dealing here, however, with
how the author of 2 Maccabees wanted to portray
Alcimus.

and appointing him governor of Judea, he dispatched [him], 13/ giving letters[b] that he was to make away with Judas, to scatter those with him, and to appoint Alcimus high priest of the greatest temple. 14/ Those in Judea[c] who had fled Judas flocked to join with Nikanor, thinking that the misfortunes and mishaps of the Jews would be their own prosperity.

15/ On hearing of the invasion of Nikanor and the attack of the Gentiles, they strewed earth on themselves and entreated the one who braces up his own people forever and always by epiphany takes the part of his own portion. 16/ On the command of the leader, [the army[d]] immediately moves off from there and engages with them at the village of Dessau. 17/ Simon, the brother of Judas, had met with Nikanor but had briefly stumbled because of the sudden appearance of the adversaries.[e] 18/ Nevertheless, Nikanor, hearing of the bravery that Judas's forces had and their high courage in contests for their fatherland, was shrinking from the decision being made through bloodshed. 19/ Wherefore, he sent Posidonius, Theodotus, and Mattathias to offer and receive a truce. 20/ After much investigation had taken place about this as the leader consulted with the populace and a common judgment[f] emerged, they assented to the agreements. 21/ They arranged a day in which each separately would come[g] to the same place, and from each side a chariot came forth; they placed chairs. 22/ Judas had posted in advantageous positions armed men at the ready, lest all of a sudden there might be villainy from the side of the enemy; they had a pertinent discussion. 23/ Nikanor was residing in Jerusalem and was doing nothing inappropriate, and he dismissed the herdlike[h] crowds that had gathered. 24/ He had Judas constantly in his presence; he was heartily

b   Habicht follows Abel in reading ἐντολάς ("commands") with V L 55 La Arm Sy. However, the well-attested reading ἐπιστολάς makes good sense.

c   As Katz ("Text of 2 Maccabees," 17) and Habicht note, the term ἔθνη does not make grammatical sense here and should be omitted as a gloss. The lack of concord between the article and its substantive is quite striking. This case is quite different from the lack of concord between a noun and an attributive participle in 8:9 (ἔθνη οὐκ ἐλάττους), which is to be explained as a construction according to sense (Smyth, *Greek Grammar*, §1013).

d   I have preferred to follow Hanhart's more difficult reading (ἀναζεύξας συμμίσγει) rather than Abel and Habicht, who read ἀνέζευξαν καὶ συμμίσγουσιν with L' La[LXVP] Sy. While the plural continues the plural of v. 15, the combination of an aorist and present tense is a little jarring, and the participle and present tense of Hanhart's reading make good sense. The singular would capture the sense of unified action.

e   I have followed the emendations by Risberg ("Text-kritische und exegetische Anmerkungen," 25–27) and read βραχέως ("briefly") instead of βραδέως ("lately"), and φαντασίαν ("appearance") rather than ἀφασίαν ("speechlessness"). The attempts by Hanhart (*Zum Text*, 40, 45–46) and van Henten (*Maccabean Martyrs*, 54) to maintain the reading βραδέως . . . ἀφασίαν run into difficulties. The genitive, ἀντιπάλων, hardly contains the sense of causation: Simon's forces were speechless (ἀφασίαν) because of their adversaries or about the enemy (τῶν ἀντιπάλων). φαντασία in the sense of an appearance striking terror is used by Polybius in 3.53.8 to speak of the terror caused by the appearance of elephants. See also Polybius 1.37.5 and Appian *Bell. civ.* 4.102, where Norbanus became alarmed (ἐθορυβήθη) on the appearance (φαντασίας) of the Roman ships. In Heb 12:21, the appearance (τὸ φανταζόμενον) of God at Mount Sinai caused fear.

f   Reading ὁμοψήφου γνώμης with Abel, Habicht following V L[381] 55 311, rather than the *hapax legomenon* ὁμοιοψήφου and συγγνώμης with Hanhart.

g   Literally "they will come in private."

h   The reading of ἀγελαίους ("herdlike") was dismissed by Risberg ("Textkritische und exegetische Anmerkungen," 27–28) as adding nothing, and he surmised that the proper term should be ἀκεραίους ("unharmed"). As Habicht notes, however, the term ἀγελαίους resonates with the term ἀγεληδόν used in 14:14 to describe the group flocking around Nikanor before his encounter with Judas.

attached to the man; 25/ he
encouraged him to marry and
have children; he married, he
enjoyed tranquility, he took
part in life.

Commentary by Verse

■ **1-2** At the end of 2 Maccabees 13, peace had been restored between the king and the Jews, and the surrounding cities had been forced to comply. Now a new factor emerges, the arrival of a new king. Would peace continue or would it be disrupted? The formula for the announcement of events used at the approach of Antiochus V and Lysias in 13:2, is used again here, which might intimate trouble.

The events of 2 Maccabees 13 had taken place in 149 s.e. (13:1), and Alcimus came to congratulate Demetrius on his accession in 151 s.e. (14:4). "In the third year thereafter" is literally "after a third-year period," that is, after the third year had begun, which would be 151 s.e., as in 14:4. The author thus has Demetrius's successful attempt at gaining control of the empire take place during 151 s.e., which ran from autumn 162 b.c.e. to autumn 161 b.c.e. The year 151 s.e. is the same date given in 1 Macc 7:1. Polybius relates how Demetrius fled Rome, where he had been held as a hostage, after the assassination of the Roman legate, Gnaeus Octavius, in Antioch. One Leptines of Laodicea had killed the Roman legate in the gymnasium at Laodicea on the sea after Gnaeus Octavius had ordered the destruction of the Seleucid fleet and the hamstringing of the elephants.[1] Lysias and Antiochus V sent envoys to apologize and claim no part in the assassination, and Demetrius took the opportunity to escape, with Polybius's help (Polybius 31.11–15).

Demetrius landed at Tripolis in late 162 b.c.e.[2] Richard Parker and Waldo Dubberstein give the last date for Antiochus V Eupator as 16 October 162 b.c.e., and Mørkholm posits 11 January 161 b.c.e. for a Greek coin of Antiochus V Eupator.[3] Tripolis was the Greek name of a seaport north of Byblos. According to Wolfgang Röllig, "The Phoenician name *tarpol*, 'virgin soil,' was folk-etymologically re-interpreted as 'triple city.'"[4] The city was said to have been founded by colonists from the three cities of Tyre, Sidon, and Arados, and the city itself was divided into three walled parts with a common constitution (Diodorus Siculus 16.41.1; Strabo 16.2.15; Pliny *Hist. nat.* 5.78). Tripolis lay over two hundred kilometers south of Antioch, and Demetrius would have had to rally supporters and march against Lysias and Antiochus V. None of the details of this event are narrated by the author, who deals with them all in one sentence. He reports the events in indirect speech using two participles and one infinitive. Again he shows that his interest lies elsewhere.

The same events are recounted in 1 Macc 7:1-3. There Demetrius arrives at an unnamed coastal city with a few men, and the account of his execution of Lysias and Antiochus V in Demetrius's presence is more detailed, with Demetrius not wanting to see their faces. Josephus (*Ant.* 12.389–90) notes that Demetrius landed at Tripolis and then gathered an army of mercenary soldiers. Schwartz rightly observes that, since the author had given a huge army to Antiochus V and Lysias in 13:2, he was obliged to have Demetrius land with a strongly armed force.

The same verb, ἐπαναιρέω ("do away with") is used in 14:13, where Nikanor is ordered by the king to do away with Judas.

---

1   Polybius 31.2.11; 31.11.1; Cicero *Phil.* 9.4; Appian *Syr.* 46. Julius Obsequens 15 places the occurrence in 162 b.c.e.

2   Bickermann, "Makkabäerbücher (I. und II.)," 14:783; Will, *Histoire politique*, 306–8.

3   Parker and Dubberstein, *Babylonian Chronology*, 23; Otto Mørkholm, "A Greek Coin Hoard from Susiana," *Acta Archaeologia* 36 (1965) 136 n. 7.

4   Wolfgang Röllig, "Tripolis," *Brill's New Pauly* (2009) 14:935.

■ 3-14 The end of the peace

As in 3:4-7, an intervention by a Jewish opponent providing false information breaks the peace. There the perpetrator was Simon, who could not conquer Onias, the high priest; here it is Alcimus, a former high priest, who informs on Judas.

■ 3-4 In a highly packed sentence where two attributive participles, προγεγονώς and μεμολυμμένος, are followed by the circumstantial participle συννοήσας, the author provides the history of Alcimus, his motivation for going to Demetrius, and evidence of his cunning. The Greek name Alcimus reflects the Hebrew name Yaqim (יָקִים or יוֹיָקִים with the variant form אֶלְיָקִים).

The author claims that Alcimus had previously been high priest.[5] When would this have been? Both 13:4-7 and Josephus *Ant.* 13.384–85 have Menelaus the high priest slain by Antiochus V. However, in 2 Maccabees this event takes place before the expedition of Lysias and Antiochus V to Judea, whereas Josephus places it after the expedition. Josephus goes on to say that Alcimus was high priest after Menelaus (*Ant.* 12.387). Since it is unlikely that Menelaus would have been acting as high priest in a Jerusalem controlled by Judas, one wonders if the rituals specific to the high priesthood would have been performed, and if so, by whom. We do not have this information. Whether one accepts the dating of 2 Maccabees for the death of Menelaus or that of Josephus, Alcimus would have been appointed by Antiochus V in 162 B.C.E. and so would have been high priest under the restored peace, with the Jews following their ancestral laws. The first mention of Alcimus in 1 Maccabees (7:5) states that Alcimus wished ἱερατεύειν. Since this verb is used in the LXX to signify succession to the high priesthood (Deut 10:6; Josh 24:33), the author has Alcimus "wish to be high priest." Does this mean that for the author of 1 Maccabees, Alcimus had not been high priest before? Not necessarily, as high priests were appointed/confirmed in their office at a change of rulers.[6] I discuss the reason why the author of 1 Maccabees does not mention Alcimus before this point in the commentary on 14:12.

"voluntarily defiled himself." The perfect participle is used with its sense of an action having an effect up to the present. The fact that Antiochus V had appointed Alcimus to replace Menelaus suggests that he saw Alcimus as able to maintain the peace agreements he had made with the Jews and that Alcimus would uphold the ancestral traditions of the Jews. However, the author of 2 Maccabees contrasts Alcimus's behavior with that of Judas (5:27: πρὸς τὸ μὴ μετασχεῖν τοῦ μολυσμοῦ) and Rhazis (14:38). The time of defilement is noted immediately after the departure of Judas from Jerusalem, when Geron the Athenian arrived to defile the temple in Jerusalem (6:2: μολῦναι . . . τὸν ἐν Ἱεροσολύμοις νεώ). Defilement is thus associated with temple worship, and Alcimus is portrayed as one who remained in Jerusalem after the activities of Geron began. The author provides no evidence either of a specific defilement by Alcimus or that Alcimus was a zealous supporter of Menelaus. He simply wishes to say that Alcimus did not join the forces of Judas. Attempts to find how specifically Alcimus defiled himself, such as that by Goldstein, miss the mark.

What, in fact, do we know of Alcimus? Tcherikover, followed by Bunge, rightly argued that the phrase "from the seed of Aaron," used to describe Alcimus in 1 Macc 7:14, did not mean that Alcimus was not an Oniad but reflected Lev 22:4, where the phrase "from the seed of Aaron" is used as a blanket term for priests.[7] This position is supported by the use of τὴν προγονικὴν δόξαν ("ancestral glory") in 14:7. Alcimus's relation to Onias

---

5   James C. VanderKam suggests that the absence of the definite article with ἀρχιερεύς "may imply that he had become a leading/chief priest, not the high priest" (*From Joshua to Caiaphas: High Priests after the Exile* [Minneapolis: Fortress, 2004] 231 n. 320). However, the names of occupations often omit the article; see Smyth, *Greek Grammar*, §1132; also §1140.

6   Wolfgang Mölleken argued that the use of the verb ἔστησεν in 1 Macc 7:9 betrays that the author knew that Alcimus had previously been high priest, since the verb ἱστάναι always means "confirm," whereas

καθιστάναι means "appoint" ("Geschichtsklitterung im I. Makkabäerbuch [Wann wurde Alkimus Hoherpriester?]" *ZAW* 65 [1953] 205–28, here 227). However, ἵστημι/ἱστάναι does have the meaning "appoint" (LSJ, s.v. ἵστημι A.III.3).

7   Tcherikover, *Hellenistic Civilization*, 228; Jochen Gabriel Bunge, "Zur Geschichte und Chronologie des Untergangs der Oniaden und des Aufstiegs der Hasmonäer," *JSJ* 6 (1975) 11–13.

III is not known. Attempts have been made by Goldstein and Benjamin Scolnic to find out more about Alcimus.[8] Goldstein argued that, according to 1 Macc 7:16, Alcimus wrote Psalm 79 and was to be identified with the Yakim of Zeroroth, the nephew of Rabbi Yose b. Yoʿezer, who is mentioned in *Genesis Rabbah* 65.22. Both of these points are highly speculative and debatable. Psalm 79 has more recently been dated to the exilic period.[9] The phrase in 1 Macc 7:16 "the discourse which he wrote it" betrays Hebrew syntax and is to be compared with the phrase in the Dead Sea Scrolls introducing scriptural quotations: כאשר אמר (1QS 8.14; 5.17; CD 7.19; etc.).[10] The death of Yakim of Zeroroth is quite different from that found in 1 Macc 9:55-56, and since Yakim is not an unusual name,[11] the same name does not mean the same person.

"In the times of chaos" is literally "in the times of unmixedness." The author continues with the description of the times as when things were mixed that should not have been.[12] The term ἀμίξια came to be used for "confusion," as when Polybius describes what happened to the Carthaginian army composed of various nationalities who could not understand one another: "As they were neither all of the same nationality nor spoke the same language, the camp was full of confusion and tumult [ἀμιξίας καὶ θορύβου]. . . . The consequence was that everything was in a state of uncertainty, mistrust, and confusion [ἀσαφείας, ἀπιστίας, ἀμιξίας]" (1.67.3, 11).[13] The term is used in papyri from the Ptolemaic period to mean "revolt."[14] One even finds the expression ἐν τοῖς ἀμείκτοις καιροῖς, where the adjective is used instead of the noun in the genitive.[15]

Scholars have argued whether this unmixedness refers to the split between Jews over following Greek ways, that is, before the edict of Antiochus IV,[16] or to the persecution under Antiochus IV (Abel), or to the split between the Hasideans and Judas over the appointment of Alcimus as high priest (Goldstein, Habicht). The author of 2 Maccabees is certainly against adopting Greek ways. In contrast to 1 Macc 7:10-13, the author of the condensed narrative does not mention any divergence between Judas and the Hasideans but has Judas depicted as leader of the Hasideans (14:6). However, his use of the root μολῦναι ("to defile") in 14:3, in 5:27, where Judas leaves Jerusalem to escape pollution, and in 6:2, where Geron is sent to pollute the temple, leads me to place these chaotic times in the period after Antiochus IV takes control of Jerusalem.

The present tense, ἔστιν, is used to reflect the thought of Alcimus. The term σωτηρία can mean

---

8   Goldstein, *II Maccabees*, 332–36; Benjamin Edidin Scolnic, *Alcimus, Enemy of the Maccabees* (Studies in Judaism; Lanham, Md.: University Press of America, 2005).

9   See, e.g., Beat Weber, "Zur Datierung der Asaph-Psalmen 74 und 79," *Bib* 81 (2000) 521–32.

10   See Joseph A. Fitzmyer, "The Use of Explicit Old Testament Quotations in Qumran Literature and in the New Testament," in idem, *Essays on the Semitic Background of the New Testament* (Sources for Biblical Study 5; Missoula, Mont.: Scholars Press, 1974) 8–10.

11   In 1 Chr 8:19, it is the name of a descendant of Benjamin; in 1 Chr 24:12, it is one of the priestly divisions.

12   Risberg ("Textkritische und exegetische Anmerkungen," 30) refers to Aeschylus *Ag.* 320–25: "Today the Achaeans are in possession of Troy. I imagine the city is marked by shouts and cries that do not blend well [βοὴν ἄμικτον]. If you pour vinegar and olive oil into the same vessel, they'll keep apart and you'll call them very unfriendly; so too one can hear separately the voices of the conquered and the conquerors."

13   David Balch noted that the author has used a term "from Hellenistic political philosophy in order to persuade its minority group to maintain internal cohesiveness and alienation from foreign imperial culture." See David L. Balch, "Attitudes toward Foreigners in 2 Maccabees, Eupolemus, Esther, Aristeas, and Luke-Acts," in Abraham J. Malherbe, Frederick W. Norris, and J. W. Thompson, eds., *The Early Church in Its Context: Essays in Honor of Everett Ferguson* (NovTSup 90; Leiden: Brill, 1998) 22–47, here 31. Balch cites Philo *Leg. Gaj.* 147 and Dionysius of Halicarnassus *Ant. rom.* 1.60.2–3.

14   Preisgke, *Wörterbuch*, 1:68; see also Goldstein, *II Maccabees*, 484.

15   Antoine-Jean Letronne, *Notices et textes des papyrus grecs (p.par.) du Musée du Louvre et de la bibliothèque impériale* (first ed. Paris: Imprimerie impériale, 1865; reprinted Milan: Cisalpino-Goliardica, 1975) no. 22.8–9 (p. 266).

16   Risberg, "Textkritische und exegetische Anmerkungen," 30.

"health, security, deliverance." However, given that it is used in parallel with Alcimus's approaching the holy altar, I have translated it as "safe return."[17]

"One hundred and fifty-first year" of the Seleucid era, that is, fall 162 to late summer 161 B.C.E. Habicht notes that the dating is given in a strange manner, literally "in the first and hundredth and fiftieth year," where the numbers are given in neither ascending nor descending order.

"to offer . . . a golden crown, and a palm frond as well as some of the customary gifts." Here ὡς + participle is used to express purpose. Crowns were regular gifts to kings, especially at their inaugurations. The gifts became obligatory, as in 1 Macc 10:29 and Josephus *Ant.* 12.142.[18] In 1 Macc 13:37, Demetrius II thanks Simon Maccabeus for his gift of a golden crown and a palm branch. Menahem Stern thought that this reference was not to a real palm branch but to a monetary payment.[19] θαλλός originally meant "a young branch, an olive branch." Polybius reports that Hannibal was met by local people who treacherously offered him "olive-branches and crowns/wreaths [θαλλοὺς ἔχοντες καὶ στεφάνους]" and notes that among the barbarians, these are used as tokens of friendship (3.52.3). However, θαλλός came to mean "gift," as I have translated it here, with Goldstein. As Grimm noted, it is hard to imagine how Alcimus, who had been ousted from Jerusalem, would be able to get fresh branches from the temple. The qualifier "customary" also suggests a payment.

"and that day he kept quiet." The author portrays Alcimus as clever in his use of silence. In proverbial wisdom, "others keep silent because they know when to speak [ἔστιν σιωπῶν εἰδὼς καιρόν], the wise remain silent until the right moment [ἄνθρωπος σοφὸς σιγήσει ἕως καιροῦ]"; "a time to keep silent [καιρὸς τοῦ σιγᾶν],

and a time to speak" (Sir 20:6–7; Qoh 3:7).[20] However, Alcimus's cleverness is actually folly, where ἄνοια reflects the behavior of Simon (4:6), Auranos (4:40), and Nikanor (15:33). The phrase "taking time as a co-worker" is similar to the phrase in 1 Macc 12:1: "When Jonathan saw that the time was working with him" (ὁ καιρὸς αὐτῷ συνεργεῖ).

■ **5-10 The speech of Alcimus.**
Whereas in 1 Macc 7:5-7 a group of people led by Alcimus blurt out their accusation against Judas, here the author focuses on the individual, Alcimus, who restrains himself until asked. The genuine interest in his subjects[21] shown by the new king and his council contrasts with the attitude of Alcimus. As one would expect in the delicate interaction between ruler and subject in the Hellenistic empires,[22] the gift by Alcimus requires reciprocation from the king.

The speech of Alcimus is well constructed. It contains two μὲν . . δέ constructions (vv. 8a and 8b-9), the use of litotes (οὐ μικρῶς)[23] and the unusual verb ἀκληρέω ("suffers loss") in v. 8, as well as the parallelism of sound between ἄπαντας εὐαπάντητον in describing Demetrius's behavior (v. 9). Alcimus immediately responds to the king's question, giving the facts of the case. He then wins the support of his audience by portraying himself as disinterestedly seeking what is best for the king and his subjects and, finally, by praising the king. The author contrasts the cleverness of Alcimus with his folly, and this contrast between understanding and ignorance runs throughout the speech. Alcimus first emphasizes his own thoughtfulness (v. 8: φρονῶν . . . στοχαζόμενος) and then contrasts, using μὲν . . . δέ, the unreasonableness (ἀλογιστία) of Judas with the knowledge and forethought (ἐπεγνωκώς, προνοήθητι) of the king.

---

17 See the meaning in Thucydides 7.70.7 and Plutarch *Apoph. lac.* 241E, though in both of these cases the noun is specified by a prepositional phrase.

18 See Bickermann, *Institutions*, 111–12. Also Welles, *Royal Correspondence*, nos. 15, 22; *OGIS* no. 227; Abraham Schalit, *König Herodes: Der Mann und sein Werk* (2nd ed.; Berlin: de Gruyter, 2001) 283–86.

19 Menahem Stern, *The Documents of the History of the Hasmonean Revolt* (in Hebrew; 2nd ed.; Tel-Aviv: Hakibbutz Hameuchad, 1972) 125.

20 One might also mention the silence of Themistocles before King Artaxerxes I. Themistocles skillfully

evaded recognition and refused to identify himself until brought before the king. After doing obeisance, he kept silent, building up suspense until asked by the king who he was. See Plutarch *Them.* 27–28.

21 "The disposition and design of the Jews" is literally "in what disposition and design stood the Jews."

22 Ma, *Antiochus III*, 179–242.

23 Litotes is found in 3:14; 2:26; 4:17; and 6:1.

■ **6** Here the author places Judas at the head of the Hasidim, a group mentioned in this verse for the first time in 2 Maccabees. Philip Davies correctly argues that the meaning of Hasidim in 2 Maccabees should in no way be constructed from its use in 1 Maccabees. For Davies, the term *ḥāsîd* in the Hebrew Scriptures and signifies "those Jews antagonistic to Hellenism at least in its encroachments on their religion, and determined to preserve the law."[24] The author then describes this group in terms used of the enemies of Judaism: they "maintain an inimical pose" (πολεμοτροφέω) just as Gorgias (10:14) and the Idumeans (10:15) had kept up hostility. The term στασιά-ζειν ("are in revolt") is used earlier, of the cities in revolt against Antiochus IV (4:30). After Lysias's first visit to Judea, the regional governors would not allow the Jews to have stability (12:2: οὐκ εἴων αὐτους εὐσταθεῖν). The language used here is similar to the accusations made against the Jews in other Hellenistic Jewish apologetic works.[25]

■ **7-8a** Alcimus first underlines his disinterestedness, as he acts only in the best interests of the kingdom and of his people. By using the middle aorist participle, ἀφελό-μενος, Alcimus gives the impression that it was his own decision to deprive himself of the high priesthood.[26] The use of "ancestral glory" argues for Alcimus being an Oniad.[27]

Using a μὲν . . . δέ construction, Alcimus first stresses that he is thinking only of what is best for the king. The preposition ὑπέρ is used in the sense of περί, which one finds in Hellenistic Greek. In 14:26, Alcimus will accuse Nikanor of disloyalty, the inverse of this behavior. Here he puts what is good for the king first and his concern for his fellow-citizens second. In this he contrasts with Onias (4:5) and Judas (11:15).

■ **8b-9** Alcimus uses a second μὲν . . . δέ construction, this time to contrast the unreasonableness of the Hasidim with the understanding (ἐπεγνωκώς) of the king. Polybius uses ἀλογιστία ("unreasonableness") of people who do not foresee the consequences of their actions, do not plan appropriately, or are overcome by passion (28.9.4; 29.9.12; 5.15.3; 21.26.16).

"suffers loss." The root meaning of ἀκληρεῖν is "to be without lot or portion." However, it came to have the more general meaning of "to be in misfortune, to suffer loss."[28]

The perfect participle is used here with the sense that the king, now having knowledge, will act on it. "Provide" translates προνοεῖν, and the providence of the king for his subjects was part of the ideal picture of the Hellenistic king.[29] Providence was already referred to in 4:6, where Onias recognized that the king's provision was necessary to settle the unrest in Judea. Benevolence (φιλανθρωπία) was also a recognized quality of the good Hellenistic king,[30] and one that kings had shown to the Jews before, as recorded in the royal privileges (φιλάνθρωπα βασιλικά) granted to the Jews in 4:11 and 13:23.

■ **10** The language here is the same as the language in 4:6, where Onias states that Simon's unrest cannot be stopped except by the providence of the king. Here Alcimus acts in a manner contrary to that of Onias, as Alcimus wishes to end the peace present in Judea after the events in 13:23.

■ **11** Alcimus is here linked to the other advisors, or "Friends," of the king who were with him in council. In 10:13 also, the advisors of the king had been against a more accommodating attitude toward the Jews. Ill will (δυσμενῶς) is frequently ascribed to opponents (6:29; 12:3; 14:39).

---

24 Philip R. Davies, "*Hasidim* in the Maccabean period," *JJS* 28 (1977) 127–40, here 139; see also John Kampen, *The Hasideans and the Origin of Pharisaism: A Study in 1 and 2 Maccabees* (SBLSCS 24; Atlanta: Scholars Press, 1988).

25 For example, in the letter of Artaxerxes in Greek Esth 3:13; *3 Macc.* 3:26; 6:28; 7:4-7. See the discussion in Doran, *Temple Propaganda*, 69–70, 107–8.

26 For this sense of the middle of ἀφαιρέω, see Polybius 3.29.7.

27 The same phrase is found in Polybius 13.63, when speaking of citizens illustrious for their ancestral glory. A more general sense is found in its usage in Polybius 20.5.4.

28 Polybius 30.20.4; 38.3.6, 9; 9.30.3; Diodorus Siculus 27.16.2.

29 Schubart, "Königsideal," 18–19. See Welles, *Royal Correspondence*, nos. 52, 10; 54, 11.

30 Schubart, "Königsideal," 9–11. See Welles, *Royal Correspondence*, nos. 25, 8; 32; 31, 17; 32, 17; 22, 17; 48A6; 64, 13; 66, 17; 67, 15.

■ **12-13** The author uses language for selecting and appointing ("select" = προχειρίζω: 3:7; 8:9; "appoint" = ἀναδείκνυμι: 10:11) similar to the language he had used for the selection of Heliodorus and Nikanor, and for the appointment by Antiochus V of Lysias. He uses δοὺς ἐπιστολάς ("giving letters") instead of δοὺς ἐντολάς ("giving orders") as in 3:7 (although some manuscript traditions read the latter) and ἐξαπέστειλε ("dispatch") instead of the simpler ἀπέστειλε ("sent") as in 3:7 and 8:9. Among the friends of Demetrius who assisted him in leaving Rome was one named Nikanor (Polybius 31.14.4; Josephus *Ant.* 12.402). Since the elephants had been destroyed by a Roman embassy in 162 B.C.E., just before Demetrius gained power,[31] the title of "elephant commander" (ἐλεφαντάρχης) would have been honorific, unless it refers to a former command, before Nikanor was sent to Rome.[32] No mention is made of elephants in the first attack involving a Nikanor (1 Macc 3:39; 2 Maccabees 8). They are hinted at in the first campaign of Lysias (1 Macc 3:34; 2 Macc 11:30) and are present in the second campaign of Lysias (1 Macc 6:30-46; 2 Macc 13:2, 15). In fact, is the Nikanor mentioned here to be identified with the friend of Demetrius mentioned in Polybius? Habicht thinks so, and Schwartz notes that Stern held the same opinion; this is the view also of John Grainger.[33] Demetrius was a hostage in Rome beginning in 178 B.C.E.; was this friend Nikanor always with him or did he arrive in Rome only some time later? Bar-Kochva stresses that the present Nikanor was in charge of the Seleucid elephant force that had just been destroyed, and so "he was free to take over a new job. . . . For that reason, he

cannot be identified either with the Nikanor who was Demetrius's friend and helped him flee Rome (Polybius 31.14.4)."[34] Going further, is the Nikanor here to be identified with the leader of the first attack against Judas described in 2 Maccabees 8 and with the royal agent Nikanor mentioned in the letters concerning the Sidonians in Shechem? (Josephus *Ant.* 12.261-64). Habicht makes these connections, but the frequency of the name Nikanor calls for caution, as Goldstein maintains. Trying to tie all the names together in one individual requires a great deal of speculation. Schwartz probably goes too far in stating that, for the author of 2 Maccabees, "the two Nicanors are one and the same,"[35] but he is right that the author wants to achieve a rhetorical balance between the two invasions. The title "governor of Judea" is found only here. Presumably it was an ad hoc title created to deal with the situation at hand. Goldstein suggests that one see it as "commander of operations in Judea."

Nikanor's commission is to do away with Judas as Demetrius had done away with Antiochus V (14:2) and to appoint Alcimus as high priest.[36] The contrast between Judas and Alcimus has led some scholars to suggest that the author intimates that Judas was serving as high priest.[37] However, the text here has nothing to say about Judas being high priest and speaks of him simply as a troublemaker who had to be removed. The same verb, καθιστάναι ("appoint"), is used of Menelaus's desire to be reinstalled as high priest by Antiochus V (13:3).

Alcimus was to be high priest of "the greatest temple." The same phrase is used of the temple in 2:19 and 14:31.

---

31 As Bar-Kochva (*Judas Maccabeus*, 308) notes, after the slaughter of the elephants by Octavius "for subsequent years only a few elephants are reported in the Seleucid army, primarily in connection with breaching walls and fortifications."

32 Translating τὸν γενόμενον ἐλεφαντάρχην as "the former elephant commander," as in 15:12, where τὸν γενόμενον ἀρχιερέα must mean "the former high priest Onias."

33 Habicht, *2. Makkabäerbuch*, 239 n. 9a; Schwartz, *2 Maccabees*, 473, citing Menahem Stern, *The Documents of the History of the Hasmonean Revolt* (in Hebrew; 2nd ed.; Tel-Aviv: Hakibbutz Hameuchad, 1972) 65; John D. Grainger, *A Seleukid Prosopography and Gazetteer* (Mnemosyne Supplements 172; Leiden: Brill, 1997) 107-8.

34 Bar-Kochva, *Judas Maccabeus*, 352-53.

35 Schwartz, *2 Maccabees*, 473.

36 Note the similar phrasing in *OGIS* 56.73-74: ὁ δὲ ἐν ἑκάστωι τῶν ἱερῶν καθεστηκὼς ἐπιστάτης καὶ ἀρχιερεύς.

37 See the balanced discussion in James C. VanderKam, "People and High Priesthood in Early Maccabean Times," in W. H. Propp, Baruch Halpern, and David Noel Freedman, eds., *The Hebrew Bible and Its Interpreters* (Winona Lake, Ind.: Eisenbrauns, 1990) 205-25; and idem, *From Joshua to Caiaphas*, 241-44. More recently, the issue has been raised by Michael O. Wise, "4Q245 (psDanᶜ ar) and the High Priesthood of Judas Maccabaeus," *DSD* 12 (2005) 313-62.

Here the author has put into Demetrius's mouth his own view of the temple.

■ **14** The verb φυγαδεύω used transitively usually has the sense of "make to flee, to drive away," as in 9:4. Intransitively it can mean "flee," as in LXX Ps 54:7; 1 Macc 2:43; 2 Macc 5:5; 10:15,[38] or "live in banishment," as in Polybius 5.54.10; 10.22.1. Its transitive use here with the meaning "flee" is unusual.

"Flocked to join" (συνέμισγον ἀγεληδόν) is literally "joined up in flocks." The adverb ἀγεληδόν ("in flocks") is the same as that used in 3:18. Just as Menelaus had tried to join up with Antiochus V and Lysias (13:3: συνέμειξε), so too those who flee Judas join up (συνέμισγον) with Nikanor. Their wrongful hope reflects the attitude of Jason in 5:6 and contrasts with the friendly attitude of the citizens of Scythopolis, who stood by the Jews in the time of misfortune (12:30). They should know that the mishaps of the Jews are in fact the discipline of the Lord (6:12, 16), and that the Jews' prosperity is their reliance on the Lord (10:28).

As mentioned in text-critical note c, I follow Habicht and Katz in seeing the noun ἔθνη ("nations, Gentiles") as an intrusion. It could perhaps be in apposition. Without this designation of those who fled Judas, it is not clear whether the reference is to Gentile or Jewish opponents of Judas, as was also the case in 10:15. The Jews who are in Nikanor's forces in 15:2 are said to have been forced to follow him, and the rest of the narrative of Nikanor emphasizes that the Gentiles were the opponents of the Jews (14:15; 15:8, 10).

■ **15** The author switches to a description of the Jews, without any warning and without specifying that he is talking about them. No subject is given to the main verb of the sentence, ἐλιτάνευον ("entreated"). However, the content makes clear who is intended. Previously, when describing the reception of notice of an invasion, it was usually specified that Judas or those with Judas heard the news.[39] Here the lack of specification may indicate that all the community was involved.

"the invasion of Nikanor." The same phrase is used in 8:12. The term ἐπίθεσις in the sense of "attack" is used also in 4:41 and 5:5. Is the distinction between the advance of Nikanor and the attack of the Gentiles simply another case of the author's use of doubling up, or does it reflect a distance between the behavior of Nikanor and those who seek to destroy the Jews, as the subsequent narrative shows?

"strewed earth." Here an asyndetic participle is used, as though the move toward entreaty is intimately bound up with hearing the news. The same action is found in 10:25, though there, as Abel notes, the author follows the more usual Greek order, where what one strews is placed in the dative while where one strews the earth is in the accusative. Here the author uses syntax similar to that found in Esth 4:1; Job 1:20; 2:12; Mic 1:10.

"his own people . . . his own portion." The parallelism of people and portion (λαός, μερίς) is found in the prayer of Moses in Deut 9:26 and 32:9. God chose his people (Deut 28:9; 20:13; 2 Sam 7:24; LXX Pss 32:12; 46:4). Sirach 37:25 holds that "the days of Israel are without number." In the second prefixed letter (1:26), God is asked to accept the sacrifice on behalf of all the people (ὑπὲρ παντὸς τοῦ λαοῦ σου) and to guard his portion (τὴν μερίδα σου). The verb ἀντιλαμβάνειν ("take the part") is found particularly in the Psalms (Ps 3:5; LXX Pss 17:35; 39:11; 62:8; 117:13). "Forever" is literally "as long as an aeon." "By epiphany" is literally "with epiphany."

■ **16** The community has a leader, ὁ ἡγούμενος (also 14:20). This term was used earlier of the leaders of the people (10:21), but Judas is not so designated before this point. The title is used in 1 Maccabees: for Jonathan in 9:30 and for Simon in 13:8, 42; 14:35, 41. Besides being a term for leaders in the Hebrew Scriptures (e.g., 1 Chr 27:4, 8, 16), the word is used also in Jacob's prophecy about Judah (Gen 19:10; 1 Chr 5:2) and of David (1 Sam 22:2; 25:30; 2 Sam 6:21; 7:8). Here, however, the anonymity and the lack of specificity suggest that the whole community is involved, and this involvement is reinforced by placing the leader in the genitive absolute. The sense of immediacy is conveyed by the present tense.

"the village of Dessau." Attempts have been made to

---

38   Possibly also *P. Oxy.* 1477, 15: εἰ φυγαδεύσομαι ("shall I flee?").

39   The author uses μεταλαμβάνειν in 11:6 and 13:10; προσπίπτειν in 8:12; 13:1; and 14:1.

identify this site. Abel suggested that Dessau was Adasa of 1 Macc 7:40, where the final clash with Nikanor took place.[40] Bar-Kochva places Adasa "at the junction of the Beitunyia-Biddu and Gibeon-Ar Ram roads, close to the end of the Beth Horon Ascent,"[41] just north of Jerusalem, but rejects the identification of Dessau as Adasa, although he admits that he does not know the exact location of the former.[42] He reconstructs the events as follows: "the clash at Kafar Dessau which took place shortly after Nicanor's arrival preceded the negotiations, and when these failed, the opposing sides clashed at Kafar Salama."[43] Given the very different narratives of 1 and 2 Maccabees at this point, the temptation is to combine both accounts, as Bar-Kochva has done, but one should be very cautious.

The phraseology "moves off from there" is similar to that in 12:29 ($\dot{\alpha}\nu\alpha\zeta\epsilon\dot{\nu}\xi\alpha\nu\tau\epsilon\varsigma$ $\delta\dot{\epsilon}$ $\dot{\epsilon}\kappa\epsilon\hat{\iota}\theta\epsilon\nu$). The verb $\sigma\nu\mu$-$\mu\dot{\iota}\sigma\gamma\omega$ is used here, as is the verb $\sigma\nu\mu\mu\iota\gamma\nu\dot{\nu}\nu\alpha\iota$ in 15:20, 26, to signify a clash with the enemy. The meaning of the verb here in 14:16 contrasts with the positive joining of those who had fled Judas to attach themselves to the army of Nikanor (14:14).

■ **17-18** The verb in the perfect in v. 17 prepares the way for Nikanor's decision to start peace negotiations. The author emphasizes that what happens to Simon is a minor setback, giving no indication that he does not like Simon. Simon's forces had been bribed by the Idumeans to allow them to escape (10:20), but no blame was attached to Simon there.

"met with Nikanor." The phrase $\sigma\nu\mu\beta\dot{\alpha}\lambda\lambda\epsilon\iota\nu$ $\tau\hat{\omega}$ $N\iota\kappa\dot{\alpha}\nu\rho\rho\iota$ is also used of the first encounter of Judas with Nikanor in 8:23. A similar incident occurred in the Roman civil wars: Cassius and Brutus had sent Tillius Cimber to sail along the coast and "on the appearance [$\varphi\alpha\nu\tau\alpha\sigma\dot{\iota}\alpha\varsigma$] of the ships, Norbanus became alarmed [$\dot{\epsilon}\theta\rho\rho\nu\beta\dot{\eta}\theta\eta$]" and had troops abandon one pass with the result that the forces of Brutus and Cassius were able to move forward (Appian *Bell. civ.* 4.102).

Even though Nikanor had surprised Simon's forces,

he does not press home the advantage. The phrase "through bloodshed" is literally "through bloods." Just as the Jews had heard of Nikanor's approach (v. 15: $\dot{\alpha}\kappa\rho\dot{\nu}$-$\sigma\alpha\nu\tau\epsilon\varsigma$), so Nikanor hears ($\dot{\alpha}\kappa\rho\dot{\nu}\omega\nu$) of the Jews' bravery. Word of the good-sized force ($\epsilon\dot{\nu}\alpha\nu\delta\rho\dot{\iota}\alpha$) of Judas had spread abroad before the arrival of the first Nikanor (8:7), and both Eleazar and Rhazis die courageously (6:27: $\dot{\alpha}\nu\delta\rho\epsilon\dot{\iota}\omega\varsigma$; 14:43: $\dot{\alpha}\nu\delta\rho\omega\delta\hat{\omega}\varsigma$). The term used here, $\dot{\alpha}\nu\delta\rho\alpha\gamma\alpha\theta\dot{\iota}\alpha$, is more frequently found in 1 Maccabees (5:56; 8:2; 9:22; 10:15; 16:23). Here the situation is the reverse of that in 11:11-14, where Lysias suffers a defeat and then asks for peace. In both cases, however, the bravery of the Jews is highlighted.

"contests for their fatherland." In 15:9, Judas reminds his troops of their success in previous contests ($\dot{\alpha}\gamma\hat{\omega}\nu\alpha\varsigma$), just as he had previously exhorted them to contend ($\dot{\alpha}\gamma\omega\nu\dot{\iota}\sigma\alpha\sigma\theta\alpha\iota$) for the laws, temple, city, fatherland, and constitution (13:14). In the clash with the first Nikanor, Judas had prepared his forces to be ready to die for the fatherland (8:21). Polybius speaks of the high courage ($\epsilon\dot{\nu}\psi\nu\chi\dot{\iota}\alpha$) of the Acarnians in defense of their fatherland, who, when the Aetolians advanced, placed a curse on anyone who survived the battle.[44] The high courage of the mother of the seven sons is praised in 7:20 ($\epsilon\dot{\nu}\psi\dot{\nu}\chi\omega\varsigma$). The imperfect is used to offer reasons for Nikanor's action.[45]

■ **19** Mattathias is a Jewish name, and Theodotus is also well attested as a Jewish name. Both names mean "given by God," but Abel rightly argues against the suggestion that only one person is meant; if that were the case, one would expect $\theta\epsilon\dot{\rho}\delta\rho\tau\rho\nu$ $\tau\dot{\rho}\nu$ $\kappa\alpha\dot{\iota}$ $M\alpha\tau\tau\alpha\theta\dot{\iota}\alpha\nu$. Presumably Mattathias is a follower of Alcimus, perhaps one of those who had fled Judas (14:14).

"to offer and receive a truce" is literally "to give and receive the right hand." Similar formulas are found in 4:34; 11:26, 30; 12:11, 12; 13:22. Note that a parley is completely counter to the orders given by Demetrius in 14:13.

---

40   Abel, p. 461: "$\Delta E\Sigma\Sigma AO\Upsilon$ se présente comme une alteration orale ou manuscrite de $A\Delta A\Sigma\Sigma A$."

41   Bar-Kochva, *Judas Maccabaeus*, 364.

42   Ibid., 349.

43   Ibid., 354.

44   The term $\epsilon\dot{\nu}\psi\nu\chi\dot{\iota}\alpha$ is found in Polybius 16.32.1. The description of the Acarnians' defense of their father-land is given in Livy 26.25, fragmentarily in Polybius 9.40.

45   Smyth, *Greek Grammar*, §§1898–99.

■ **20** The author emphasizes that the whole community was involved in assenting to the peace terms. In 14:16, the anonymity and lack of specific names, where Judas is not mentioned specifically but only called "the leader," underline the unity of the whole community. As the Romans suggested in their letter to the Jews (11:34-38), the people were to investigate the agreements the king proposed (11:36: ἐπισκεψάμενοι; 14:20: ἐπίσκεψις) and come to a judgment (11:37: γνώμη; 14:20: συγγνώμη).

The general description περὶ τούτων ("about this") does not lay out what exactly the envoys were proposing. Only later in the verse are agreements mentioned, but no details are given. Noticeable in all this terminology is the emphasis on community: the root κοινός ("common, shared in common") in the verb ἀνακοινόω, the prefix ὅμο- ("one and the same, joint") in ὁμόψηφος, where ψῆφος also refers to the round pebble used in voting (see Curtius 6.11.8; 7.2.7; 9.3.16); the prefix σύν ("with") in συγγνώμη ("judgment"). Given this emphasis on community, I have translated the term πλῆθος as "populace," in line with its meaning in 4:5; 11:16; 13:10, rather than restricting its meaning to simply the troops under Judas's control.

Once again, the subject of the verb "assented" is unnamed, but, given the procedure of consultation and judgment in the accompanying participles, the subject would be the populace of the Jews. While in 11:15 it was Judas who assented to the proposals, here it is the entire community. The term συνθήκη was used earlier to describe the agreements with Lysias (12:1) and Antiochus V (13:25). As noted in the comment on 12:1, the term can be used for agreements not only between equal states but also between a major power and a city.

■ **21-22** "arranged a day."The same phrase is found in 3:14. The definiteness of the time is indicated by the use of the future indicative in the relative temporal clause.[46] The two leaders are to meet in private, and so Alcimus is excluded from the discussion. "Each separately" is literally "they will come in private."

Beginning in v. 21b is a series of five asyndetic clauses: προῆλθε ("came forth") . . . ἔθεσαν ("place")

. . . διέτακεν ("posted") . . . ἐποιήσαντο ("had") . . . διέτριβεν ("was residing"). As I noted in the Introduction, the author concentrates on confrontation between the Seleucids and the Jews, and he uses speeches to delineate the character of opponents. Here, where no hostility takes place he quickly runs through the events.

"chariot . . . chairs." The author uses two similar sounding words with similar meanings: δίφραξ . . . δίφρους. With Goldstein, I have kept the translation of "chariot" to try to emulate the wordplay. Since δίφραξ usually means "chair" and δίφρος can mean "chariot," it is not at all clear what to envision here. Schwartz prefers to translate δίφραξ as "litter," but, as he notes, it is not clear whether the chairs came with the chariots/litters or were there separately. Is the author indulging in wordplay? And if so, why in such a highly condensed section of the narrative? Schwartz suggests that the clause "they placed chairs" is a gloss and looks kindly on the Lucianic text διαφράξεις ἔθεσαν διαφόρους ("they placed different enclosures"). Such a reading maintains the wordplay, but the term διαφράξις is found with the meaning "midriff,"[47] but not "enclosure." It is probably best to assume with Abel that Nikanor and Judas each arrived by chariot, alighted, and used chairs that had been brought for them.

Since Simon had been overcome by the sudden appearance (αἰφνίδιον . . . φαντασίαν) of Nikanor's forces (14:17), Judas takes precautions lest the enemies suddenly (αἰφνιδίως) make an assault. Earlier, in 3:32, the high priest Onias had worried that the attack on Heliodorus might be attributed to villainy (κακουργία).

Risberg pointed to the usages parallel to ἁρμόζω in Polybius, where the verb has the sense of "suitable, appropriate, pertinent."[48] The use of the prefix κοινός ("shared, in common") emphasizes the equal footing of both participants in the discussion, as does the similar approach to the meeting point.

■ **23** The imperfect suggests that Nikanor was spending some time in Jerusalem. As Schwartz notes, the use of the term ἄτοπος, which I have translated as "inappropriate," is peculiarly apt, given the author's use of τόπος ("place") to denote Jerusalem (3:2; 5:19; 13:23). The use

---

46 Smyth, *Greek Grammar*, §2398.

47 The verb διαφράσσω does have the meaning of "to partition."

48 Risberg, "Textkritische und exegetische Anmerkungen," 27; Polybius 1.15.13; 1.29.1; 1.44.1; 1.45.5.

of the adjective "herdlike" ($\mathring{\alpha}\gamma\epsilon\lambda\alpha\hat{\iota}o\varsigma$) to describe the crowds around Nikanor suggests that Nikanor dismissed those opponents of Judas who had earlier flocked to him $\mathring{\alpha}\gamma\epsilon\lambda\eta\delta\acute{o}\nu$ ("in flocks," 14:14).

■ **24-25** Once again one has a string of three asyndetic clauses ($\epsilon\hat{\iota}\chi\epsilon \ldots \pi\rho o\sigma\epsilon\kappa\acute{\epsilon}\kappa\lambda\iota\tau o \ldots \pi\alpha\rho\epsilon\kappa\acute{\alpha}\lambda\epsilon\sigma\epsilon\nu$), which are then shortly followed by three asyndetic verbs. The asyndeta underscore the rapid succession of events and that these events are tightly conjoined. The two imperfects used to describe Nikanor show the continuance of the action, while the pluperfect gives the sense of a permanent fixed state. The adjective $\psi\nu\chi\iota\kappa\hat{\omega}\varsigma$ (here translated "heartily") was used in 4:37 to describe the reaction of Antiochus IV to news of the murder of the high priest Onias. The advice of Nikanor also is given in the imperfect, to stress the persistence of Nikanor's encouragement. Marriage and children are the basis of social life. Genesis 2:18 states, "It is not good for man to be alone," and the command was given to increase and multiply (Gen 1:28). The Deuteronomic rules on those who should not engage in war include someone who is engaged but not yet married (Deut 20:7). Marriage and children imply stability, which is why Jeremiah's advice to the Babylonian exiles to take wives and have children in Babylon is so shocking (Jer 29:5-6). In antiquity a city depended for its continued existence on the birth rate. As Peter Brown expressed so trenchantly, "Unexacting in so many ways in sexual matters, the ancient city expected its citizens to expend a requisite proportion of their energy begetting and rearing legitimate children to replace the dead."[49]

Judas follows Nikanor's advice. The author does not mention whom he married, but presumably it was a politically advantageous marriage to one of the leading priestly families. A proper betrothal or wedding ritual is not reported. Whether he had children is not known. According to 1 Macc 9:3, Judas died within a year, but there is no hint of his imminent death in these verses. The asyndeta underscore Judas's rapid assent to Nikanor's desire for the resumption of normal social life.

The verb $\epsilon\mathring{\nu}\sigma\tau\alpha\vartheta\acute{\epsilon}\omega$ ("enjoy stability") counters the claim of Alcimus that Judas and his faction do not allow the kingdom to enjoy stability (14:6). The verb $\kappa o\iota\nu\omega\nu\acute{\epsilon}\omega$ ("take part in") resonates with the forms with $\kappa o\iota\nu\acute{o}\varsigma$ found in 14:20, 22. Judas is not part of a faction, but he is willing to participate in public life.

General Commentary

After the peace arrangements under Antiochus V, this section begins events under Demetrius I and is the lead-in to the climactic defeat of Nikanor. Its narrative provides a cogent argument against the view that the Jews are not good citizens but troublemakers. The section opens with a powerful accusation by Alcimus, the former leader and high priest of Judea, against Judas. Alcimus accuses Judas of being the head of a faction determined to cause instability and unrest in the Seleucid kingdom. The rest of the narrative refutes this argument. The anonymity of the response to Nikanor's approach, in which no mention is made of Judas's name, the involvement of all the community in the discussion about Nikanor's proposals, and the rapid settlement of Judas into normal social life all argue for Judas's leading not a faction but the whole people and for his being only too ready to settle down. This section thus reiterates the theme found earlier in the book—the Jews are good citizens if allowed to live according to their own laws. Further, just as Onias the high priest was slandered as a troublemaker (4:1-2), so too is Judas.

This section has given rise to much debate, for it is radically different from the account in 1 Maccabees 7. There Demetrius I sends Bacchides to install Alcimus and punish the Jews (1 Macc 7:8-9). Bacchides does so with brutal efficiency, as Alcimus has sixty Hasideans executed (1 Macc 7:12-18). Bacchides leaves Alcimus in charge with a force to help him, but Judas keeps up the insurgency (1 Macc 7:20-24). Alcimus returns to the king, who then sends Nikanor (1 Macc 7:25-26). Nikanor, described as a hater of Israel, tries treachery to capture Judas, but Judas escapes (1 Macc 7:27-32). After Nikanor's defeat, the king sends Bacchides back to Judea, and Judas is killed in a battle with Bacchides (1 Macc 9:1-22). Why is this role of Bacchides missing from the

---

49   Peter Brown, *The Body and Society: Men, Women, and Sexual Renunciation in Early Christianity* (New York: Columbia University Press, 1988) 6.

account in 2 Maccabees? In his attempt to show that 2 Maccabees had it right in having Alcimus be a former high priest (14:3), Wolfgang Mölleken rearranged the text of 1 Maccabees 7 and 9, so that the events of 1 Macc 7:(12)13-18, 20-24 took place during the time of the peace agreements between Antiochus V and Judas, and 1 Macc 7:8-11, 19 was set during the assault of Bacchides narrated in 1 Maccabees 9.[50] Bar-Kochva rightly notes that such a major rearrangement of the text does "not correspond to what we know about the quality of the book."[51] Mölleken explains the omission of the execution of the sixty Hasideans from 2 Maccabees as a result of the tendency of the author of 2 Maccabees to portray the peace agreements between Antiochus V and Judas as a complete success of the Jews. The installation of Alcimus and the execution of the sixty Hasideans would have thwarted this endeavor.[52]

If one takes seriously the author's professed intention to use rhetoric to involve the readers emotionally and to help them memorize the events (2:25), the absence of Bacchides may be explained. First, the author sets out to highlight how the Jews drove out the enemy. He therefore stresses the victories of the Jews rather than their setbacks, while at the same time noting their desire to live in peace as good citizens. He has structured the narrative to highlight the two feasts of Hanukkah and Nikanor's Day and ends it on a high point of victory. To mention Bacchides would complicate matters. Not only is his first invasion a setback for Judas and his forces, but Bacchides later defeats and kills Judas. The author thus has no desire to introduce this character. Second, the feast of Hanukkah follows on from the defeat of a Nikanor, as does the feast of Nikanor's Day. The two thus parallel each other nicely, providing an easily memorized account.

The other main difference between the two accounts is the behavior of Nikanor. In 1 Maccabees, he is treacherous from the start; in 2 Maccabees, he initiates negotiations. On one hand, the characterization of Nikanor in 1 Maccabees is in line with the author's stress that one should not trust the Gentiles, as they speak treacherously with peaceable words and break their word.[53] The author of 2 Maccabees, on the other hand, mentions Gentiles who are friendly toward the Jews,[54] has Lysias and Antiochus V make peace agreements with the Jews (11:13-15; 13:23-25),[55] and even has Antiochus IV upset over the execution of Onias the high priest (4:37-38). Thus, the characterization of Nikanor in 14:18-25 is consistent with the author's positive portrayal of some Gentiles and furthers his aim of showing the Jews as good citizens.

50 Mölleken, "Geschichtsklitterung," 205–28.

51 Bar-Kochva, *Judas Maccabaeus*, 345 n. 91.

52 Mölleken, "Geschichtsklitterung," 218. Bunge ("Zur Geschichte und Chronologie," 1–46) follows Mölleken in seeking sources, but is no more convincing, as VanderKam (*From Joshua to Caiaphas*, 235–37) shows.

53 See 1 Macc 1:30; 7:10, 15, 27; 11:2; on breaking one's oath, see 1 Macc 6:62.

54 The Tyrians in 4:49; Ptolemy Makron in 10:12; the people of Scythopolis in 12:29-31.

55 Note, in particular, how the author of 2 Maccabees insists that Antiochus V made terms with the Jews, while the author of 1 Maccabees insists that Antiochus V broke his oath.

14

26/ But Alcimus, noticing the reciprocal goodwill, took the agreements made and went to Demetrius and said that Nikanor was thinking what was hostile to state affairs. "For he appointed that plotter against his kingdom, Judas, as successor." 27/ The king, enraged and provoked by the accusation of the thoroughly evil person, wrote to Nikanor, first, asserting about the agreements that he took it ill and, second, commanding [him] to quickly dispatch Maccabeus in bonds to Antioch. 28/ When these [commands] came to Nikanor, he was confused and was taking it badly if he should set at naught the regulations when the man had done nothing wrong. 29/ But since to oppose the king was not possible, he was watching for a good opportunity[a] to accomplish this by a maneuver. 30/ But Maccabeus, noticing that Nikanor was treating those things concerning Judas more severely and held the usual meeting more rudely, thought that this severity was not from the best and gathered quite a few of his forces and was hiding himself from Nikanor. 31/ But the other, recognizing that he had been excellently outmaneuvered by the man, went up to the greatest and holy temple as the priests were presenting the proper sacrifices and commanded that they hand over the man. 32/ When they asserted with oaths that they did not know wherever the one sought was, 33/ he stretched out his right hand toward the temple and he swore these things, "If you do not hand over to me Judas in bonds, I will make this precinct of God into a plain and the altar I will raze to the ground and I will raise up a prominent temple there to Dionysos."
34/ After saying such things he left, but the priests stretched out their hands toward heaven and called upon the constant champion of our nation, saying these things, 35/ "You, O Lord, although you need nothing,

a   There is no parallel to the phrase εὔκαιρον ἐτήρει, whereas the phrase καιρὸν τηρέω is common. Wilhelm ("Zu einigen Stellen," 28) followed by Katz ("Text of 2 Maccabees," 17) suggested a haplography: ἀντιπράττειν οὐκ ἦν εὐ<χερές>, καιρὸν ἐτήρει ("since to oppose the king was not easy, he was watching for an opportunity"). While this suggestion is attractive, the author's fondness for unusual turns of phrase argues against it. The author also uses ἦν + infinitive in 3:21; 6:6. Hanhart (*Zum Text*, 32) refers to the phrase in Luke 22:6: ἐζήτει εὐκαιρίαν.

were pleased that a temple for your dwelling be among us. 36/ Now, holy Lord of all holiness, forever preserve undefiled this, the house freshly purified."

37/ Rhazis, one of the elders from Jerusalem, was informed against to Nikanor as a man who loved his fellow citizens, who was exceedingly well spoken of and called on account of his goodwill a father of the Jews. 38/ For, during the former periods of separation, he had pronounced judgment for Judaism, and had risked body and soul in defense of Judaism with all zeal. 39/ As Nikanor wished to show plainly the ill will that he felt toward the Jews, he sent over five hundred[b] soldiers to seize him. 40/ For he thought that, by seizing him, he would bring misfortune to the Jews. 41/ With the mob about to lay hold of the tower, breaking through the outer door and ordering to bring forward fire and set the doors on fire, Rhazis was hemmed in on all sides. He enjoined on himself the sword, 42/ willing to die nobly rather than be under the control of offenders and maltreated in a manner unworthy of his own nobility. 43/ Not hitting the right spot with the thrust because of the haste of the action and with the crowds coming through the doorways, he nobly ran onto the wall and courageously threw himself headlong into the crowd. 44/ As the crowd quickly stepped back and a space opened up, he landed in the middle of the empty space. 45/ Still breathing and emotionally at fever pitch, he stood up. With blood gushing forth and his injuries hard to endure, he went through the crowd at a run and, standing on a steep rock, 46/ completely drained of blood, he exposed his entrails, took them in both his hands and hurled them into the crowd. Calling on him who is Master of life and breath to give them back to him again, he left life in this way.

b   Some manuscripts give five thousand: 534 Sy II La[L].

Commentary by Verse

■ **26** After a series of asyndetic verbs, the author changes subject and style. He uses a chiasm to start his account of Alcimus's response to the arrangements between Nikanor and Judas: συνιδὼν . . . εὔνοιαν, συνθήκας . . . λαβών. Here the relationship between Judas and Nikanor is described using terms well known from the reciprocal interaction between cities and their sovereigns.[1] As Abel and Habicht note, the assumption is that Alcimus was in Jerusalem and was able to take a copy of the agreements with him to the king. Presumably, Alcimus had taken up the office of high priest, as ordered by the king (14:13). The author uses the same language as in 14:4 to describe Alcimus's approach to the king, and the imperfect of continuance[2] to describe his speech. The author begins to report Alcimus's words using indirect speech but then moves into direct speech.

"hostile to state affairs." The same language is used of Ptolemy Philometor's attitude to Antiochus IV (4:21). The verb φρονεῖν ("to think") was used by Alcimus in 14:8 to describe how he was "genuinely thinking" about what was best for the king.

"plotter" (ἐπίβουλος). Onias is slandered by Simon as a plotter against the government (4:2), while in 4:50 the term is used to describe the relationship of Menelaus to his fellow citizens, and so I have translated it there as "betrayer."

"his kingdom." Abel is right to attach the genitive αὐτοῦ to βασιλείας rather than to διάδοχον. In speaking to the king, Alcimus stresses the danger to the king's realm. The displacement of the possessive pronoun to after Ἰουδαν rather than before (V 46-52 106 311) or after ἀνέδειξεν (L¹) and the reading ἑαυτοῦ (L) after ἀνέδειξεν are best explained as attempts to answer the question, to whom is Judas "successor"? To Alcimus as high priest? To Nikanor? Abel suggested, following Adolf Deissmann,[3] that the term "successor" referred to those

who belonged to the lowest grade of court officials and who were next in line for a vacancy.[4] However, Bunge noted that such a title seems to be attested only for the Ptolemaic court, not for the Seleucid.[5] Bunge's argument rests on the assumption that this speech put in Alcimus's mouth by the author accurately reflects knowledge of the Seleucid titular system that the hearers of the narrative would also have had. Schwartz argues that there is no indication that Nikanor needs a deputy[6] and so holds that Nikanor appointed Judas as successor to Alcimus.[7]

I would suggest that one should look first at the rhetorical strategy of Alcimus. Here, regardless of whom Judas is to succeed, Alcimus is attacking Nikanor as hostile to state affairs. His proof is that Nikanor had appointed a plotter against the kingdom to an official position. Elsewhere in 2 Maccabees, the verb ἀναδείκνυμι ("to appoint") was used of the action of kings (9:14, 23, 25; 10:11; 14:12). Its use here suggests that the author is depicting Alcimus as claiming that Nikanor is overstepping his authority in making such an appointment. It is this abuse of authority that arouses the king's anger, particularly given that the narrative holds that Demetrius had recently succeeded in securing his own position.

■ **27** As before in the narrative, the king is shown to get angry quickly (7:3, 39). Just as Simon accused (3:11: διαβάλλων) Onias, so Alcimus uses an accusation (ταῖς . . . διαβολαῖς) to disturb the peace.

Given that Demetrius has been told that Nikanor has become hostile to the state, the king's response—he writes to Nikanor—appears less than forceful. The command reflects the two-part description of why Alcimus went to the king: to annul the agreements and to end the goodwill by arresting Judas. Just as Lysias took it ill that Timothy had been killed (11:1), so too did Demetrius react to the agreements between Nikanor and Judas. See also 7:39, where Antiochus IV becomes vindictive

---

1 For εὔνοια, see 9:21, 26; 11:19; 12:30; and Ma, *Antiochus III*, 191–92. For συνθήκη, see 12:1 and 13:25.

2 Smyth, *Greek Grammar*, §1891.

3 Adolf Deissmann, *Bible Studies: Contributions, Chiefly from Papyri and Inscriptions, to the Language, the Literature, and the Religion of Hellenistic Judaism and Primitive Christianity* (Edinburgh: T&T Clark, 1901) 115.

4 H. Kornbeutel, "Diadochos," *PW Supplement* (1940) 7:124–26.

5 Bunge, *Untersuchungen*, 199–200.

6 In 4:29, when Menelaus and Lysimachos were leaving Jerusalem to travel to the king, they left behind deputies. However, there is no indication that Nikanor, as governor of Judea (14:12), is about to leave.

7 Schwartz, *2 Maccabees*, 551–52.

(πικρῶς φέρων). The goodwill between Nikanor and Judas is to be broken by Nikanor's securing Judas. The verb ἐξαποστέλλειν ("to dispatch") is the same as that used when Demetrius dispatched Nikanor to Judea (14:12).

■ **28-29** The verb (προσπίπτω) used to describe Nikanor's receiving the news is often found in 2 Maccabees (5:11; 8:12; 9:3; 13:1; 14:1). The depth of the dismay and confusion (συγχεῖν: 10:30; 13:23) is emphasized by the use of the pluperfect, while the imperfect ἔφερεν expresses the sense of continued inner debate over what to do.

"taking it badly." The verb δυσφορεῖν ("to take it ill/badly") was used in 4:35 and 13:25. The author likes to use φέρειν + adverb (7:20, 39; 11:1; 14:27). The construction underlines the emotional hesitation of Nikanor at the injustice. It is similar to the emotions felt at the execution of Onias (4:35: ἐδυσφόρουν ἐπὶ τῷ τοῦ ἀνδρὸς ἀδίκῳ φόνῳ, "were angry over the unjust murder of the man"). Here the verb of emotion states "the cause more delicately with εἰ (ἐάν) *if* as a mere supposition than by ὅτι."[8]

"set at naught the regulations." The phrase is the same as in 13:25, except that here the perfect participle of διαστέλλειν is used instead of the noun διάσταλσις.

Nikanor, though conflicted, decides he cannot disobey the king. At this point, the description of Nikanor rejoins that of 1 Macc 7:27-29. The verb ἐπιτελεῖν ("to accomplish") is used to describe Heliodorus's attempt to carry out the king's orders (3:8, 23), the desire of the Jamnians to perpetrate the same behavior and destroy the Jews (12:8), and Nikanor's attempt to do what the king commands (15:5).

■ **30-34a Nikanor threatens the temple**

■ **31** The author uses the same participle, συνιδών ("noticing"), to describe Judas's observation as he had for Alcimus's (14:26). This sentence contains three asyndetic participles: συνιδών . . . νοήσας . . . συστρέψας. This asyndetic grouping stresses the immediacy of the reaction of Judas when he notices the change in Nikanor.

The first participial group is balanced nicely, as the beginning αὐστηρότερον διεξαγαγόντα ("treating . . . more severely) resonates with the end ἀγροικότερον ἐσχηκότα ("held . . . more rudely"), while the middle sets τὰ πρὸς αὐτόν ("those things concerning him") alongside τὴν εἰθισμένην ἀπάντησιν ("the usual meeting"). The rudeness, where the root meaning of ἄγροικος is "of the country," resonates with the description of the Seleucids as barbarians (2:21). The second group uses αὐστηρίαν ("severity") to repeat the charge of Nikanor being αὐστηρότερον ("more severely").

"was hiding himself." The imperfect continues the imperfects of description in vv. 28 (ἔφερεν, "was taking") and 29 (ἐτήρει, "was watching").

■ **31** The sentence begins with two asyndetic participles, συγγνούς . . . παραγενόμενος, and the author links these two actions as simultaneous: Nikanor recognizes and immediately moves toward the temple. Through the use of the verb στρατηγεῖν ("outmaneuvered"), the author recalls the attempt by Nikanor to catch Judas by a στρατήγημα ("maneuver," 14:29). This is just one of many such wordplays that will occur throughout the rest of the narrative. This wordplay emphasizes the superiority of Judas, as does the use of the term γενναίως ("excellently"), whose root means "noble, highborn."[9] By this wordplay, the author appears to explain the sudden shift from the Nikanor who did not want to try the issue by bloodshed (14:18) to the Nikanor who threatens the temple. No explanation is given of why Nikanor now threatens the temple. Did he understand that the fate of Judas was intimately bound to the fate of the temple? That Judas's core concern was the temple and that he would give himself up rather than see it harmed? Where is Alcimus in all this? Had not the king wanted Alcimus to be high priest of the temple? Is Alcimus still in Antioch with the king? Did Nikanor perceive that the priests were more sympathetic to Judas than to Alcimus? None of these questions is answered by the text, as the author portrays Nikanor as changing from sympathetic to antagonistic. A parallel unexplained reversal in attitude can be seen earlier in the narrative, where Antiochus IV is shown as emotionally upset over the

---

8   Smyth, *Greek Grammar*, §2247.
9   This adverb is found with various nuances in 6:28; 7:5, 11; 8:16; 13:14; 14:43; 15:17.

murder of Onias (4:37-38) but then unsparingly attacking Jerusalem and despoiling the temple (5:11-16).

The temple had been described as the greatest in the introduction, in 2:19, and in 14:13, and as holy in 13:10. The verb καθήκω ("be proper") is found also in 6:4 and 6:21 (where, because of the context, I have translated it as "legally") in the context of the persecution of the temple, where what was not appropriate was done in the temple and required of Eleazar. Jason the high priest, too, had wanted a sacrifice offered to Herakles, but his envoys deemed this not proper (4:19). Its use here underlines that temple services are being performed correctly. The author of 1 Maccabees states that the priests showed Nikanor the burnt offering that was being offered for the king (1 Macc 7:33), a detail that shows how Nikanor was set on capturing Judas at all costs. The reliability of the priests is evident in their willingness to make a statement on oath; the Gentiles are shown to be breakers of oaths (15:10). The present tense has been maintained in the response of the priests at v. 32: literally, "where the one sought is."

The phrase "to stretch out the hand" is usually used by the author to refer to an attitude of prayer (3:20; 14:34; 15:12).[10] Here this bodily movement is immediately countered by the priests' stretching out their hands in prayer in 14:34. Whereas Nikanor uses the form νεώς for temple, the priests use the form ναός in 14:35. The more vivid conditional future is followed in reporting Nikanor's oath.

The term σηκός ("sacred enclosure") occurs only here in the LXX. The threat recalls that of Antiochus IV in 9:4, 14 to level Jerusalem and make it into a cemetery (9:14: ἰσόπεδον ποιῆσαι).

"the altar I will raze." Elijah is said to have erected another altar in place of the one thrown down (3 Kgdms 18:32: τὸ θυσιαστήριον τὸ κατεσκαμμένον), and he accused the Israelites of throwing down God's altars (3 Kgdms 19:10: τὰ θυσιαστήριά σου κατέσκαψαν). In 10:3, the Jews purified the temple (νεώ) and made another altar. During the persecution, the Jews had been forced to wear wreaths of ivy at the festivals of Dionysos. The connections made by Greek authors between Jewish festivals and Dionysos are well known, and the author seems to be referring to these in the threat attributed to Nikanor. The word for "prominent," ἐπιφανές, is picked up again in 15:34 when, after the defeat of Nikanor, all praise the appearing Lord (τὸν ἐπιφανῆ κύριον).[11] The term also resonates with the epiphanies that God performs on behalf of his people and that dot the narrative (3:24; 5:4; 12:22).[12]

■ 34b-36 The response of the priests

While Nikanor had sworn these things (v. 33: ταῦτα) and had said such things (v. 34a: τοσαῦτα), the priests in response repeat Nikanor's gesture and stretch out their hands to heaven and say these things (v. 34b: ταῦτα). After the battle with the first Nikanor, Nikanor had been forced to confess that the Jews had a champion (8:36: ὑπέρμαχος). The champion is called into action again. With the mention of "our" nation, the author inserts himself at an emotional moment, as in the reflection in 6:12-17.

The prayer of the priests begins with an immediate use of the personal pronoun, as in the prayer in 15:22. That God is "in need of nothing" (τῶν ὅλων ἀπροσδεής) is found also in 3 Macc. 2:9 (τῶν ἀπάντων ἀπροσδεής) and in Josephus Ant. 8.111 (ἀπροσδεὲς . . . τὸ θεῖον ἀπάντων, "the divinity is in need of nothing"), where Josephus is restating what Solomon said at the dedication of the temple.[13] In addition, in Ep. Arist. 211 God is described as ἀπροσδεής ("without want"). In 8:18,

---

10   The phrase is used also in 7:10, where the third son courageously stretches forth his hands to be cut off. Schwartz sees the action of Nikanor as an echo of Isa 10:32, but the LXX is completely different from the MT at this verse and has no reference to Sennacherib stretching out his hand against the holy mount.

11   For a similar use of the term, see the letter of Antiochus III to Zeuxis in Ma, Antiochus III, no. 4, lines 49–50 (p. 290).

12   Also in 10:29 where the verb φαίνω ("to appear") is used.

13   3 Kingdoms 8:27: "But will God indeed dwell on the earth? Even heaven and the highest heaven cannot contain you, much less this house that I have built." Compare also Ps 50:12: "If I were hungry, I would not tell you, for the world and all that is in it is mine."

God is said to be able to overthrow the whole world (τὸν ὅλον κόσμον) with a single nod. Aristobulos stated that God had fashioned the whole world (ὁ θεὸς τὸν ὅλον κόσμον κατεσκεύακε) (Eusebius *Praep. ev.* 13.12.9).

The verb "pleased" (εὐδοκεῖν) is found associated with God's choice of Zion in Ps 68:16 ("Why do you look with envy, O many-peaked mountain, at the mount that God desired [εὐδόκησεν] for his abode, where the Lord will reside forever?") and his pleasure in the land (Ps 85:1) and the people (Ps 149:4).

"your dwelling among us" (τῆς σῆς σκηνώσεως ἐν ἡμῖν) is literally "of your tenting among us." Although this particular noun is found only here in the LXX, tenting has deep resonances in the Hebrew Scriptures, from Exod 25:9, where Israel is told to make a tabernacle/tent (σκηνή) according to the pattern shown to Moses. The prophet Joel promised that, at the day of judgment, "you will know that I, the Lord your God, am the one who dwells [ὁ κατασκηνῶν] on Zion, my holy mountain" (Joel 3:17). Zechariah 2:10 has God promise the Jews that, after the exile, he will come and dwell (κατασκηνώσω) in their midst. In Ezekiel's ideal temple, the name of the Lord will "dwell (κατασκηνώσει) in the midst of Israel forever" (Ezek 43:7). In Sir 24:8-10 we read: "Then the Creator of all things gave me a command, and my Creator chose the place for my tent [τὴν σκηνήν μου]. He said, 'Make your dwelling [κατασκήνωσον] in Jacob. . . . In the holy tent [ἐν σκηνῇ ἁγίᾳ] I ministered before him.'" In Ps 27:5-6, the psalmist proclaims that God will hide him in his tent (ἐν σκηνῇ) in the day of trouble, conceal him under the cover of his tent (τῆς σκηνῆς αὐτοῦ) and then the psalmist will offer sacrifices in his tent (ἐν τῇ σκηνῇ αὐτοῦ).

"Now" (καὶ νῦν) is literally "and now." This marks the transition, as in 15:23, from the statement of God's past benefits to the present request.[14]

God is the source of all holiness, and the author neatly balances the term for holiness, ἁγιασμός, with the term for undefiled, ἀμίαντος. The author will also repeat the phrase "preserve undefiled" in 15:34, after the defeat of Nikanor. The repetition ties the whole episode of Nikanor together and shows God as answering the priests' prayer. The use of the demonstrative ὅδε to qualify "house" both points to the object in the immediate vicinity of the speaker and also responds to its use by Nikanor in 14:33 (τόνδε τὸν . . . σηκόν), when he points to the precinct he will level. While "house" (οἶκος) is commonly used of the temple, in the narrative of 2 Maccabees it is found only here and in 15:32, another example of how this section of the narrative is tied together. Solomon had been warned by God that if he sinned, the temple he had built would become a heap of ruins (3 Kgdms 9:6-9). The narrative has made no mention of any sins, nor does the prayer of the priests ask for forgiveness of sins committed. Does this suggest that the temple will be saved?

■ **37-46 The death of Rhazis**

This name, not attested elsewhere for a Jew,[15] has several variations: Ραξις (-ξεις A; -ζης V^C 74 46-52 106 347) La^{VM}; Ραξης L'-62 (-ξις 19-542; -ξεις 93) 311 La^{L(B)P} Arm. Abel notes that the Latin manuscripts have Raxis, Radias, Razias, and Raxius, while only M has Razis. Goldstein and Ran Zadok posit that the name is of Iranian origin.[16] The Syriac is ܪܟܝܣ, and Katz accepts the suggestion of Friedrich Schulthess that the spelling Ραξις should be accepted instead of Ραζις, "due to the frequent confusion of ζ and ξ."[17] Grimm surmised that the name reflected רזי ("leanness, wasting, destruction") and so would be a nickname based on his fate. Goldstein also speculates that the name derives from רזי and links it to the rare usage in Isa 24:16.

---

14   See Num 14:7; 1 Chr 17:23; 29:13; Neh 9:32; also
     Pieter W. van der Horst, "Hellenistic Parallels to
     Acts (Chapters 3 and 4)," *JSNT* 35 (1989) 37–46,
     here 44.

15   See Ilan, *Lexicon*, 354.

16   Ran Zadok, "On the Post-Biblical Jewish Onomas-
     ticon and Its Background," in Aryeh Kasher and
     Aharon Oppenheimer, eds., *Dor Le-Dor: From the End
     of Biblical Times Up to the Redaction of the Talmud:
     Studies in Honor of Joshua Efron* (Jerusalem: Bialik

     Institute, 1995) v–xxviii, esp. v. This article is in
     English in a volume comprised mainly of articles in
     Hebrew.

17   Friedrich Schulthess, "Zur Sprache der Evangelien,"
     ZNW 21 (1922) 241–58, here 244 n. 2; the quotation
     is from Katz, "Text of 2 Maccabees," 17.

The desecration of the temple under Antiochus IV was followed by a description of the sufferings of those who resisted the king's decrees (6:9–7:42), and here too the threat by Nikanor against the temple is followed by a narrative of suffering.

■ **37** Just as those who had assembled in caves to keep the Sabbath were informed against (6:11), so too was Rhazis.[18] Rhazis may have been one of those elders with whom Judas had consulted before the attack of Antiochus V (13:13). "Elder" as a title is found in papyri from Egypt.[19]

I have translated the noun $\varphi\iota\lambda o\pi o\lambda i\tau\eta\varsigma$ ("lover of his fellow citizens") as a relative clause, "a man who loved his fellow citizens." Dio Chrysostom (1.28) argues that a king should be so; Titus Flaminius, the Roman general, was so called, and Lycurgus told a foreigner who claimed that his fellow citizens called him a "lover of Sparta" ($\varphi\iota\lambda o\lambda\acute{a}\kappa\omega\nu$) that he should rather aim to be called a $\varphi\iota\lambda o\pi o\lambda i\tau\eta\varsigma$ (Plutarch *Flam.* 13.8; *Lyc.* 20.4). Here Rhazis is shown to be like Onias the high priest, who "was keeping in mind the public and private interests of the whole group" (4:5). He is the opposite of Menelaus, who had "become a great betrayer of the citizens" (4:50). Alcimus had claimed to be concerned only for his fellow citizens (14:8), but was not.

"goodwill" ($\epsilon\check{v}\nu o\iota\alpha$). As noted earlier in the comment on 9:21a, this was the word for the reciprocal relationship between leaders and subjects (9:21, 26; 11:19), but also among those who dwell in a city. It is used to describe the attitude of the Scythopolitans toward the Jews living in their city (12:30). The presence of goodwill between Nikanor and Judas had been resented by Alcimus (14:26). The word also denotes the patriotism felt toward one's fatherland. Judas always had $\epsilon\check{v}\nu o\iota\alpha$ toward kinsfolk, where the term for "kinsfolk" ($\acute{o}\mu o\epsilon\vartheta\nu\epsilon\hat{\iota}\varsigma$) is in parallelism with the term for "citizens" (15:30). Aeschy-

lus has the messenger proclaim that Eteocles, who had died defending Thebes, is to be buried in the city $\dot{\epsilon}\pi'$ $\epsilon\dot{v}\nu o\iota\alpha$ ("because of his goodwill/loyalty") (*Sept.* 1007). Lycurgus argued that a man should have an unsurpassable $\epsilon\check{v}\nu o\iota\alpha$ for his fatherland ($\dot{a}\nu\upsilon\pi\acute{\epsilon}\rho\beta\lambda\eta\tau o\nu$ $\tau\iota\nu\alpha$ $\delta\epsilon\hat{\iota}$ $\tau\grave{\eta}\nu$ $\epsilon\check{v}\nu o\iota\alpha\nu$ $\dot{v}\pi\grave{\epsilon}\rho$ $\tau\hat{\eta}\varsigma$ $\pi\alpha\tau\rho\acute{\iota}\delta o\varsigma$ $\check{\epsilon}\chi\epsilon\iota\nu$), while Pseudo-Lucian has Philip proclaim that Demosthenes acted as a citizen on the basis of his goodwill toward his fatherland ($\tau\hat{\eta}$ $\mu\grave{\epsilon}\nu$ $\tau\hat{\eta}\varsigma$ $\pi\alpha\tau\rho\acute{\iota}\delta o\varsigma$ $\epsilon\dot{v}\nu o\iota\alpha$ $\pi o\lambda\iota\tau\epsilon\upsilon\acute{o}\mu\epsilon\nu o\varsigma$) (Lycurgus *Leoc.* 102; Lucian *Encom. Demosth.* 41).

"father of the Jews." As Van Henten has noted, this epithet can be understood in the light of Roman titles such as *parens* or *pater patriae, parens plebis Romanae, parens omnium civium,* and *parens rei publicae.*[20] In a Jewish inscription from Mantinea, Aurelius Elpides is called "father of the people" ($\pi\alpha\tau\grave{\eta}\rho$ $\lambda\alpha o\hat{v}$).[21] Later inscriptions speak of someone being $\pi\alpha\tau\grave{\eta}\rho$ $\kappa\alpha\grave{\iota}$ $\pi\acute{a}\tau\rho\omega\nu$ $\tau\hat{\eta}\varsigma$ $\pi\acute{o}\lambda\epsilon\omega\varsigma$ ("father and patron of the city") or simply $\pi\acute{a}\tau\rho\omega\nu$ $\tau\hat{\eta}\varsigma$ $\pi\acute{o}\lambda\epsilon\omega\varsigma$ ("patron of the city").[22]

■ **38** The contrast between Rhazis and Alcimus, who had voluntarily defiled himself (14:3), is again marked. The construction $\kappa\rho\acute{\iota}\sigma\iota\nu$ $\epsilon\dot{\iota}\sigma\epsilon\nu\eta\nu\epsilon\gamma\mu\acute{\epsilon}\nu o\varsigma$ $\text{᾽}Io\upsilon\delta\alpha\ddot{\iota}\sigma\mu o\varsigma$ has been interpreted in two ways. Either one takes the participle as passive (as do Abel, Habicht, and Goldstein among others) and so read the clause as "he had been accused of Judaism" (NRSV), or one takes the participle as a middle as Grimm, Risberg, Schwartz and I have done. Grimm provides analogies from Polybius for the middle use of $\epsilon\dot{\iota}\sigma\phi\acute{\epsilon}\rho\epsilon\sigma\vartheta\alpha\iota$ with the meaning "to bring forward publicly" (5.74.9; 11.10.2, 5; 21.29.12), (and so I have translated the verb as "pronounce") although Risberg rightly corrects Grimm for translating $\kappa\rho\acute{\iota}\sigma\iota\nu$ as "defence."[23] The participle would thus be parallel to the next participle, $\pi\alpha\rho\alpha\beta\epsilon\beta\lambda\eta\mu\acute{\epsilon}\nu o\varsigma$, not in contrast to it.

The phrase "body and soul" recalls the speech of the seventh brother as he offered himself for the salvation

---

18 The verb $\mu\eta\nu\upsilon\epsilon\hat{\iota}\nu$ is found also in 3:7, concerning the monies allegedly secretly kept in the Jerusalem temple.

19 Ursula Hagedorn et al., *Griechische Urkundenpapyri der Bayerischen Staatsbibliothek München,* vol. 1 (Stuttgart: Teubner, 1986) no. 49.

20 Van Henten, *Maccabean Martyrs,* 206–7. Van Henten draws on the work of Andreas Alföldi, *Der Vater des Vaterlandes im römischen Denken* (Libelli 261; Darmstadt: Wissenschaftliche Buchgesellschaft, 1971).

21 *CIJ,* no. 720.

22 David Noy, *Jewish Inscriptions of Western Europe* (2 vols.; Cambridge: Cambridge University Press, 1993) 1, nos. 115–16, 114.

23 Risberg, "Textkritische und exegetische Anmerkungen," 30–31.

of the people (7:37). Eleazar also speaks of his body and soul (6:30), and Judas is described as struggling with body and soul on behalf of the citizens (15:30). The repetition of the term "Judaism" recalls its presence at the very beginning of the narrative (2:21) and, more importantly, at the beginning of the struggle led by Judas Maccabeus against the decrees of Antiochus IV (8:1). The parallelism between the two participial clauses, "pronounced judgment" and "risked body and soul," emphasizes that one has to act on one's decisions.

■ **39-40** While the martyrs who had suffered earlier had been arrested for refusing to stop practicing Judaism (6:10-11), Rhazis is arrested in order to make an example of him. Is he taken as a substitute for Judas? "Ill will" is what was shown to Eleazar (6:29) when his friends turned on him, just as Nikanor's goodwill toward Judas (14:26) has changed. The citizens of Joppa had hidden their ill will toward their Jewish neighbors (12:3). Now Nikanor has joined with the Friends of Demetrius who had ill will ($\delta\upsilon\sigma\mu\epsilon\nu\tilde{\omega}\varsigma$ $\check{\epsilon}\chi\upsilon\nu\tau\epsilon\varsigma$) toward the Jews and had stirred Demetrius to anger (14:11). Just as the seven brothers and their mother had been seized (7:1), so now Rhazis is seized, by soldiers sent by Nikanor. Schwartz suggests that such a large number of soldiers was necessary to make a public display. The number still seems exaggerated, even for this purpose. Both Abel and Goldstein accept the variant reading, which includes the verb $\dot{\alpha}\lambda\upsilon\gamma\epsilon\tilde{\iota}\nu$ ("to pay no regard to"), also found in 12:24, where I have translated it as "mistreat." Goldstein sees this use of $\dot{\alpha}\lambda\upsilon\gamma\epsilon\tilde{\iota}\nu$ as Nikanor wanting to disrespect the high status of Rhazis. However, that so many soldiers are sent would seem to heighten the importance of Rhazis. The size of the soldiery does stress the overwhelming superiority of the force against Rhazis.

The author had argued in 6:12, 16 that God sent misfortune ($\sigma\upsilon\mu\varphi\upsilon\rho\dot{\alpha}$) to train and educate his people. The term also picks up on what those who had fled Judas hoped to inflict on the Jews (14:14).

■ **41-46** The scene shifts to where Rhazis can be found. Abel is probably right in imagining Rhazis as cornered in his house, which is described as having a tower and an

outer door (to the atrium?). When fire is brought to the doors of the dwelling, Rhazis goes upstairs, from where he flings himself down into the atrium.

The author describes Nikanor's forces derogatively, as a mob ($\tau\tilde{\omega}\nu$ . . . $\pi\lambda\eta\vartheta\tilde{\omega}\nu$). Grimm rightly asked why fire was necessary as the superior numbers had succeeded in breaking through the outer door, and how much resistance could be left if Rhazis had been caught unprepared. The fire appears to have been added to heighten the desperate straits in which Rhazis found himself, with no chance of escape. Earlier, Callisthenes and others are described as having been burnt to death when they fled into a small dwelling (8:33).

Ptolemy Makron had taken his own life rather than have his nobility questioned (10:13: "he . . . a noble, had not ennobled the office"), and Eleazar and the brothers are described as acting worthily (6:23, 24, 27; 7:18, 20, 29). Eleazar had made the decision to die nobly (6:28: $\gamma\epsilon\nu\nu\alpha\dot{\iota}\omega\varsigma$) and leave behind a noble example (6:28: $\dot{\upsilon}\pi\dot{\upsilon}\delta\epsilon\iota\gamma\mu\alpha$ $\gamma\epsilon\nu\nu\alpha\tilde{\iota}\upsilon\nu$) for the youth, and the brothers encourage one another to die nobly (7:5: $\gamma\epsilon\nu\nu\alpha\dot{\iota}\omega\varsigma$ $\tau\epsilon\lambda\epsilon\upsilon\tau\tilde{\alpha}\nu$). In a funeral epigram from Boetia dated to 293 B.C.E., Eugnotos is described fighting invading forces: alone and surrounded, rather than live defeated he decided to kill himself by throwing himself on his sword, "as is the custom of noble commanders" ($\gamma\epsilon\nu\nu\alpha\dot{\iota}\omega\nu$ $\dot{\omega}\varsigma$ $\check{\epsilon}\vartheta\upsilon\varsigma$ $\dot{\alpha}\gamma\epsilon\mu\dot{\upsilon}\nu\omega\nu$).[24]

At the approach of Antiochus V and Lysias, Judas had encouraged the populace to pray to the Lord that he would not put the people under the control of ($\dot{\upsilon}\pi\upsilon$-$\chi\epsilon\iota\rho\dot{\iota}\upsilon\upsilon\varsigma$) the abusive Gentiles (13:11). In v. 43, two asyndetic participles, $\kappa\alpha\tau\epsilon\upsilon\vartheta\iota\kappa\tau\dot{\eta}\sigma\alpha\varsigma$ . . . $\dot{\alpha}\nu\alpha\delta\rho\alpha\mu\dot{\omega}\nu$, keep the actions of his first unsuccessful attempt and his running to the wall closely conjoined.

Just as the description of Antiochus IV's death has the king suffer and die from three injuries and illnesses (9:5-11), so here Rhazis makes three attempts to die and finally succeeds. The author draws out the death scene for the fullest emotional effect, even if Rhazis's inability to give himself a proper sword stroke suggests that he is not too experienced a warrior and is a bit

---

24   The epigram is found in Luigi Moretti, *Iscrizioni storiche ellenistiche: Testo traduzione e commento*, vol. 1 (Biblioteca di studi superiori 53; Florence: La nuova Italia, 1967) no. 69 (pp. 173–75).

flustered. Rhazis's final actions, standing on a steep rock and throwing his entrails, are made for theater. It is interesting how the events of vv. 45-46 are placed in one sentence. After two opening participles, ὑπάρχων καὶ πεπυρωμένος ("breathing and emotionally at fever pitch"), the author then has an asyndetic participle, ἐξαναστάς ("stood up"), followed by two genitive absolute participles, then another asyndetic participle, διελθών ("went through"). This participle (διελθών) is connected to another participle, στάς ("standing"), which is followed by two asyndetic participles, γινόμενος προβαλών ("drained of blood . . . exposed"). Then there is another participial phrase before the author finally comes to the main verb, ἐνέσεισε ("hurled"), which is followed by another participial phrase. This heaping up of participles fuses the whole event together into one continuous action.

The author also seems to have employed language appropriate for a battle. In Greek literature, the compound verb κατευθικτεῖν ("to hit the right spot") is found only here, while the verb εὐθικτεῖν is used in a military sense to describe how one wants the missiles to hit the target in a siege.[25] In 15:38, the adverb εὐθίκτως has the more usual literary meaning. The term ἀγών, which I here translate as "action," has the connotation of battle here, as in 14:28; 15:9; 10:28. The phrase τὸν πύργον καταλαμβάνειν ("lay hold of the tower") is found also in 10:22, where it describes a military assault; the same association seems present in this passage. The adverb ἀνδρωδῶς ("courageously") resonates not only with the courageous action of Eleazar (6:27: ἀνδρείως) but also with other words based on the same root that are used in the face of battle: 14:28: ἀνδραγαθία; 15:17: ἐπανδροῦν; 8:7; 15:17: εὐανδρία. The verb ἐνσείειν ("to hurl") also has the sense of hurling oneself at the enemy, attacking, as in 3:25; 12:15, 37. The language thus evokes a battle scene, not just a police action.

Van Henten has rightly drawn attention to the analogy with non-Jewish stories about noble death to save a city.[26] Some defenders threw themselves off walls or drowned themselves.[27] Van Henten pays particular attention to the description of the death of Menoeceos, son of Creon, to save Thebes.[28] In Euripides' *Phoenician Women* 1090–92, Menoeceos stood on a tower (πύργων ἐπ᾽ ἄκρων στάς) and thrust a sword (ξίφος) into his neck. This story is elaborated in the *Thebaid* by Statius. There Menoeceos is described as standing on a wall. He first plunged his blade and, with one wound, rent life. Having purified the towers and walls of Thebes with his sprinkled blood, he then hurled himself, sword still in hand, into the battle lines (Statius *Thebaid* 10.756–82). The manifold action of killing oneself with a sword on a wall, throwing blood, and then hurling oneself against the enemy is similar to that of Rhazis. However, there are significant differences in the descriptions of the deaths. Menoeceos acts this way in response to an oracle that predicts that only by his death can Thebes be saved and purged of the crime of Cadmus, who killed the dragon. He shows himself to be a willing victim to save his city. Menoeceos kills himself with one blow, while Rhazis is flustered and misses the mark. Rhazis tries a second time to kill himself, by jumping off the wall, while Menoeceos jumps down to attack the enemy. Menoeceos sprinkles his blood on the walls of Thebes, and in this way his blood purifies the walls and the city from the guilt of Cadmus's crime. In contrast, Rhazis hurls his entrails on his enemies. This is a very different ritual action. Rhazis puts his innermost piece of himself on his enemies. Van Henten tries strongly to maintain that "the hurling of his entrails at Nicanor's soldiers can be interpreted easily as gestures of dedication. One may assume, on the basis of the analogy with Menoiceus's death and the Roman *devotio*, that with these acts Razis dedicates himself and Nicanor's soldiers to the Lord and initiates Nicanor's defeat in this way."[29] While I do think that the story initiates Nikanor's defeat, it does not seem to me to be an act of *devotio*.

---

25 Apollodorus Mechanicus *Poliorcetica* 144.11: the siege engines have not to be too far away, "lest the missiles miss the mark" (ἵνα μὴ εὐθικτῇ τὰ ἐπιβαλλόμενα).

26 Van Henten, *Maccabean Martyrs*, 144–50.

27 For example, Agraulos, the daughter of Cecrops, threw herself off a wall (*FGH* 328, frg. 105). See Friedrich Schwenn, *Die Menschenopfer bei den Griechen und Römern* (Giessen: Töpelmann, 1915). Theoxena and her sister's children throw themselves into the sea rather than be captured by Philip V of Macedon (see the reconstruction of the narrative in Polybius by Walbank, "Polybian Experiment" 61–62).

28 Van Henten, *Maccabean Martyrs*, 145–47.

29 Ibid., 150.

Throughout the story, Rhazis's motivation is shown to be his desire not to fall into the hands of his enemies but to die like a soldier. His last prayer, in contrast to that of the seventh brother (7:37-38), does not plead that his death bring God's mercy and save the nation. Rather, he prays that he receive his life back again. His throwing his entrails on his enemies symbolizes not that the nation will be purified, but that his enemies have no control over any part of him. The individual bravery of Rhazis is to the fore, not that his action is a self-sacrifice to save the city. In this way, his death conforms with the reasons for taking one's life put forward by Plato (*Leg.* 9.873C).

"on him who is Master" (δεσπόζοντα). Here the participial form is used rather than the noun as in the reflections in 5:20 and 6:14, in 9:13, and in the prayer in 15:22. The combination of give back life and breath is found in 7:23.

"He left life in this way" echoes the account of the end of Eleazar's life in 6:31.

General Commentary

In this section the author follows the pattern of the first section of his narrative from chap. 3 through chap. 7. At first the city is at peace, as in 14:23 after the agreements of 14:20, and this peace is similar to the description of peace in 3:1-3. In both cases peace is shattered by the connivance of a Jewish official (3:4-6; 14:26-27) and an attack on the city ensues. Later in this first section, Antiochus IV is initally depicted sympathetically in his reaction to Onias's murder (4:37-38), but this attitude changes when he thinks that the city of Jerusalem is in revolt (5:11-16). Jews such as Eleazar and the mother and her seven sons die courageously rather than deny ancestral laws (6:18—7:42). This pattern is repeated in 14:26-46. The peace of the city is disrupted by the slander of Alcimus (14:26); the king becomes annoyed and orders Nikanor to break the peace and arrest Judas (14:27). Nikanor, who up to this point had been friendly toward the Jews (14:18-25), now becomes their ferocious enemy and threatens to destroy the temple. As part of this attack on the Jews, he brings about the death of the innocent Rhazis.

The rapid change in Nikanor would involve the author's audience emotionally. The author has deliberately chosen to replicate the narrative structure he used earlier, no doubt as a help to his audience to easily retain the story in their memory (2:25). He has streamlined his account to fit his overall concern, which is God's defense of his temple. His plan is to end his narrative on a high note—the protection of the temple, the defeat of Nikanor, and the inauguration of the festival of the Day of Nikanor. He thus has omitted incidents that are irrelevant to this purpose, such as the invasion of Bacchides known from 1 Macc 7:8-20 as well as Bacchides' return and the death of Judas (1 Macc 9:1-22). As in the first major invasion against Judea, the contrast between the accounts of 1 and 2 Maccabees is significant. First Maccabees 3:38—4:25 emphasizes the role of Gorgias; 2 Maccabees stresses the role of Nikanor and so forms a parallel between the first major invasion and his last battle. The author of 2 Maccabees has also heightened the emotional element of his narrative by including before the first invasion accounts of the deaths of Eleazar and the mother and her seven sons and before the last battle the account of the death of Rhazis. As can be seen in the detailed notes in the commentary, the death of Rhazis echoes the earlier deaths.

With the earlier pattern in mind, where God will defend his people and their temple when an earlier Nikanor had invaded Judea and been defeated (2 Maccabees 8), the audience knows how the narrative will end: even though persecuted, the Jews with the help of their God will triumph. The question is: How will the author make the narrative interesting?

15

1/ Nikanor, receiving information that Judas's forces were in the region toward Samaria, resolved to set upon them in all safety on the day of rest. 2/ The Jews who forcibly accompanied him said, "May you by no means destroy [them] so in such an uncivilized and barbaric manner, but impart honor to the day especially honored with holiness by the one who observes everything." 3/ But the triply offensive one asked whether the[a] master who enjoined to celebrate the Sabbath is in heaven. 4/ When they declared clearly, "The living Lord himself is Master in heaven, he who commands to practice the Sabbath." 5/ But the other said, "But I am master upon the earth who enjoins [you] to take up weapons and to discharge the royal service." Nevertheless, he did not prevail to discharge his shocking purpose.

6/ So Nikanor, strutting with utter cockiness, had decided to erect a trophy in plain view over Judas's forces. 7/ Maccabeus, on the other hand, had continuously trusted with complete hope that he would obtain support from the Lord. 8/ He was exhorting those with him not to fear the invasion of the Gentiles, but to keep in mind the helps done for them previously from heaven, and, as for the present, to expect that victory would be theirs from the Almighty. 9/ Encouraging them from the law and the prophets, and reminding them also of the contests which they had accomplished, he made them even more eager. 10/ Rousing their spirits, he cheered [them] on, pointing out at the same time the faithlessness of the Gentiles and their transgression of oaths. 11/ He armed each one of them not so much with the security of shields and lances as with the encouragement of good arguments. He also related [to them] a trustworthy dream seen in

a   With Hanhart and in contrast to Habicht, Goldstein, and Schwartz, I have retained the article. This article particularizes and refers back to the mention in the previous sentence of the one who observes all things. The antithesis the author is setting up is between the master *in heaven*, and Nikanor as master *on earth*.

an awake state[b] and heartened them all. 12/ The spectacle of the dream was as follows. Onias, the former high priest, of noble character, modest when met and gentle in manner, one who spoke gracefully and had practiced since boyhood everything related to virtue, he it was who was stretching out his hands to pray for the whole community of Jews. 13/ Then likewise appeared a man distinguished by his grey hair and his splendor, and the majesty surrounding him was to marvel at and most magnificent. 14/ In response, Onias said, "This kin-loving person is one who prays greatly for the people and the holy city, Jeremiah the prophet of God." 15/ Jeremiah, stretching out his right hand, handed over to Judas a golden sword. As he gave it, he pronounced the following, 16/ "Take this holy sword as a gift from God. Through it you will break down your opponents."

17/ Encouraged by Judas's exceedingly fine arguments, which were strong enough to stimulate them to valor and to make the souls of young men courageous, they determined, because the city, the holy things, and the temple were in danger, not to delay[c] but nobly to begin and, engaged with all courage, to decide the business. 18/ For the fear over wives and children, over family and kin came, for them, in second place; the fear over the dedicated temple was greatest and prime. 19/ For those left behind in the city, their anguish was not trifling as they were troubled at the attack in the open air. 20/ As all now awaited the imminent decision, as the opponents were already joining together, the army stretched out in battle order with the beasts settled into a well-situated section and the cavalry stationed on the wings, 21/ Maccabeus looked at the multitude present and the intricate arrangement of arms and armor as

b   Reading ὕπαρ τι with L 311, rather than ὑπέρ τι ("beyond measure, beyond anything else") with Hanhart. Grimm notes both readings and that ὑπέρ can signal the comparative degree in later Greek (e.g., Polybius 3.79.8). Goldstein, followed by Schwartz, also reads ὑπέρ τι and refers to the reading of some manuscripts in 8:20, where ὑπέρ τι is found with the meaning "beyond measure, exceedingly." However Abel, followed by Habicht, observes that there had always been discussion about the validity of dreams and notes Homer *Od.* 19.547, where the distinction between a dream (ὄναρ) and a true vision (ὕπαρ ἐσθλόν) is found. The same distinction between ὄναρ ("dream") and ὕπαρ ("vision") is found in *Od.* 20.90. For a full discussion of dreams in antiquity, see Robin Lane Fox, *Pagans and Christians* (New York: Knopf, 1987) 149–66. On this particular phrase, Lane Fox notes: "It does not contrast a dream with a vision experienced in waking hours. It applies to features within a dream itself, features which are either so realistic that they seem to occur or else of significance, a 'happy reality' which will come to pass" (p. 151).

c   I have kept στρατεύεσθαι, which can have the meaning of στραγγεύομαι (*BGU* 1127.28; 1131.20; see also LXX Judg 19:8). See A. Vaccari, "Note critiche ed esegetiche," *Bib* 28 (1947) 404–6.

well as the savageness of the beasts. He stretched out his hands to heaven and implored the wonder-working Lord, as he knew that it is not by arms, but he gains the victory for the worthy when[d] it is determined by him. 22/ He imploringly was speaking as follows, "You, ruler, sent forth your angel at the time of Hezekiah, king of Judea, and he destroyed up to 185,000 from the camp of Sennacherib. 23/ So now, Master of the heavens, send a valiant angel before us [to inspire] fear and trembling. 24/ Let those who blasphemously come against your holy people be struck down by your arm's might." So [Maccabeus] ceased with these words.

25/ Nikanor's forces were moving forward with trumpet blasts and war chants, 26/ but Judas's forces met their opponents with prayerful invocations. 27/ Fighting with hands and praying to God with their minds, they laid low no fewer than thirty-five thousand, as they had been greatly heartened by God's appearance. 28/ As they joyfully returned after the battle, they recognized the one who had fallen first was Nikanor with all his armor. 29/ With a tumultuous shout, they praised the Master in their ancestral language. 30/ Now he who was absolutely the chief struggler by body and soul on behalf of the citizens and who had maintained during each stage of his life goodwill toward kinsfolk enjoined that, after cutting off the head and the hand and shoulder of Nikanor, they should carry them to Jerusalem. 31/ When he arrived there, he convened his kinsfolk and made the priests stand before the altar and summoned those in the citadel. 32/ Pointing to the head of the polluted Nikanor and the hand of the abuser which he had stretched out and boasted against the holy house of the Almighty, 33/ he cut off the tongue[e] of the godless Nikanor and said to share it among the birds,

d Reading $\kappa\alpha\vartheta\grave{\omega}\varsigma$ $\mathring{\alpha}\nu$ as in V L' 347 311. After a repeated or customary or general truth, "a temporal clause takes the subjunctive with $\mathring{\alpha}\nu$ after primary tenses" (Smyth, *Greek Grammar*, §2409). If $\kappa\alpha\vartheta\grave{\omega}\varsigma$ $\grave{\epsilon}\acute{\alpha}\nu$ is read, the sentence would be a general conditional clause (§2337).

e In his review of Hanhart's edition, G. D. Kilpatrick (*Göttingische gelehrte Anzeigen* 215 [1963] 18) suggested that the phrase "out of his head" ($\grave{\epsilon}\kappa$ $\tau\hat{\eta}\varsigma$ $\kappa\epsilon\varphi\alpha\lambda\acute{\eta}\varsigma$) found in L¹ 58 La^P Sy might have been omitted through homoioteleuton.

but to hang the wages of his
folly over against the temple.
34/ All [looking] toward heaven
blessed the appearing Lord,
saying, "Blessed be he who
preserved his own place undefiled." 35/ He hung the head
of Nikanor from the citadel, a
clear and manifest sign to all of
the Lord's aid. 36/ All decreed
by common vote never to allow
that very day to go unmarked,
but to mark the thirteenth day
of the twelfth month—called
Adar in Aramaic—one day prior
to the Day of Mordechai.

Commentary by Verse

■ 1-5 Nikanor's second challenge to the deity

In his first challenge, he had threatened to destroy God's temple (14:32). Here he attacks the notion that God has any power on earth. Throughout this section and the rest of the narrative, the contrast between Nikanor and God is heightened by the use of the same words to describe what they accomplish.

■ **1** According to 1 Macc 7:30-32, Nikanor had first tried to capture Maccabeus, but he had failed and five hundred of his men had fallen and the rest had fled into the city of David. As Bar-Kochva notes, the impression given in the account in 1 Maccabees is that Judas had "the area north of Jerusalem . . . under his exclusive supervision" and numerical superiority over Nikanor's forces, and that Nikanor was awaiting reinforcements from Antioch (1 Macc 7:39).[1] According to 13:14, Judas had earlier prepared to meet Seleucid forces around Modein, near the Gophna hills in the southern part of Samaria. Bar-Kochva locates the battle of Adasa (1 Macc 7:39-47) "at the junction of the Beitunyia-Biddu and Gibeon-Ar Ram roads, close to the end of the Beth Horon Ascent."[2]

The author will state that the resolution of Nikanor (ἐβουλεύσατο) did not prevail (15:5: οὐ κατέσχεν . . . βούλημα).

"in all safety." The Jewish custom of rest on the Sabbath was well known in antiquity, and the author of 2 Maccabees already narrated how Apollonius had treacherously used this custom to kill Jews (5:25). The author has also stressed how those who had hidden in caves to celebrate the Sabbath did not defend themselves on the Sabbath, in accordance with the honor of the most august day (6:11) and how Judas's forces had observed the Sabbath by breaking off their pursuit of Nikanor's forces (8:25-26). The Sabbath therefore was prized by the author of 2 Maccabees. Bar-Kochva, followed by Martin Goodman and A. J. Holladay, has convincingly shown that there was no total ban on self-defense on the Sabbath before Hasmonean times.[3] The term for "safety," ἀσφάλεια, is found in 15:11, where Judas does not arm his men with the security (ἀσφάλειαν) of shields and lances.

"on the day of rest." See Exod 34:21 and 35:2 for the expression.

■ **2** "who forcibly accompanied him." The phrase κατ' ἀνάγκην resonates with the description of Jews under bitter constraint (μετὰ πικρᾶς ἀνάγκης) who were forced (ἠναγκάζοντο) to wear wreaths to celebrate the festival of Dionysos (6:7). Schwartz is therefore right to suggest that the reference here is to Jews conscripted into Nikanor's forces, rather than to Jews who supported the Seleucids and Alcimus. One does not need to posit that even such renegade Jews were horrified at Nikanor's proposal.[4]

---

1   Bar-Kochva, *Judas Maccabaeus*, 359–60, 362–63; quotation from 359.
2   Ibid., 364.
3   Ibid., 474–93; Goodman and Holladay, "Religious Scruples," 151–71, esp. 165–71.
4   Bar-Kochva, *Judas Maccabaeus*, 489.

I have taken the subjunctive as a hortatory subjunctive and the following imperative as a request. The Jews could not indeed have prevented Nikanor from doing anything.

"uncivilized and barbaric manner." Nikanor had behaved rudely (14:30: ἀγροικότερον) toward Judas, and the Seleucid forces are frequently described as barbarous (2:21).[5]

"honor." Those who had hidden in caves to celebrate the Sabbath did not defend themselves according to the honor (κατὰ δόξαν) of the most august day (6:11).

"especially honored with holiness." Grimm prefers to interpret the verb προτιμᾶν as "honored before," that is, at the time of creation (Gen 2:3; Exod 20:11; 31:16-17). However, Exod 20:11 insists that God had sanctified (ἡγίασεν) the Sabbath, and so the prepositional phrase "with holiness" refers to the way God has especially honored that day. The author has insisted that kings give honor to the temple (3:2, 12; 13:10).

"the one who observes everything." This description of God is found earlier, in 7:6 and 12:22. The verb is used in LXX Job 34:23 ("for the Lord observes all things" [ὁ γὰρ κύριος πάντας ἐφορᾷ]) and in Ezek 9:9, in an accusation against those who say that God has forsaken the land, the Lord does not see (οὐκ ἐφορᾷ ὁ κύριος). Most interestingly, it is used in Exod 2:25, where God observes the suffering of his people in Egypt (καὶ ἔπιδεν ὁ θεὸς τοὺς υἱοὺς Ἰσραήλ). In 8:2, the people implore the Lord to look upon them (ἐπιδεῖν τὸν . . . λαόν).

■ **3** "Triply offensive" is a term used in 8:34, at the first invasion by a Nikanor.

"Master" (δυνάστης) is used of God in 3:24; 12:15, 28. The term is repeatedly emphasized in the next two verses, then found in a prayer before the battle (15:23) and in praise of the Lord after the victory (15:29). The reader already knows, from 3:24 and 12:28, that God is the Master of the universe, not just the heavens.

"enjoined." The verb προστάσσειν is picked up again in v. 5, where Nikanor enjoins the Jews to take up arms, and in v. 30, where Judas enjoins the forces to cut off Nikanor's head and hand. It also is used by the first Nikanor when he confesses that the Jews are invulner-

able because they follow the laws enjoined (προστεταγμένοις) by the Lord (8:36).

■ **4** The expression "living" is found also in 7:33 in the prayer of the seventh son just before he predicts a wicked end for Antiochus IV. The epithet is used of God's name in LXX Num 14:21: ζῶ ἐγὼ καὶ ζῶν τὸ ὄνομά μου. The command to honor the Sabbath is found in Exod 20:8 and Deut 5:12.

The verb used for "to practice," ἀσκεῖν, is unusual. Pindar does use it in the sense of giving honor to a divinity (Pindar *Pyth.* 3.109; *Olymp.* 8.22), but this does not seem appropriate in this case. The verb normally means "to practice, exercise, train" or "to work raw materials." Does it possibly reflect the way the author insisted that God disciplines (6:12: πρὸς παιδείαν; 6:16: παιδεύων) his people, or is the author enjoying the oxymoron?

As in 6:11 and 12:38, the author uses "the seventh day" (ἑβδομάς) to refer to the Sabbath.

■ **5** The initial sentence repeats words from Nikanor's question in v. 3, in a direct challenge to God's power.[6] The verb "to discharge" (ἐπιτελεῖν) is repeated in the author's statement that Nikanor will fail. It is the verb used when Heliodorus tries to carry out his commission (3:8, 23), when the Jamnites wanted to attack their Jewish neighbors (12:8), and when Nikanor tries to capture Judas by stealth (14:29). The next sentence suggests that the attempt to capture Judas on the Sabbath failed. There is no more mention of the Sabbath in the battle account.

■ 6-16 Judas encourages his soldiers with a pre-battle speech

■ **6** The author transitions to this section with a μὲν . . . δέ construction, as he does often (3:40—4:1; 10:8-9). "Strutting" is literally "to carry the neck high." The term ἀλαζονεία refers to the character of a braggart, and so I have translated it here as "cockiness." The term is used to describe Antiochus IV just as he is about to fall (9:8), and there, because of the context, I have translated it as "pretense." The verb "to resolve" (διαγινώσκειν) is picked up in 15:17, after Judas's speech, when the Jews resolve to commence battle and "decide the business."

---

5   See also 5:22, describing Philip the Phrygian; 10:4 speaks of "the barbarous Gentiles," and the king is described as barbarous in 13:9.

6   Schwartz refers to Holofernes' question, "Who is God but Nebuchodonosor?" (Jdt 6:2) and to *Ps. Sol.* 22:29-30.

"trophy in plain view" (κοινὸν . . . τρόπαιον). After a victory in land battle, the Greeks used to set up a suit of armor captured from the enemy so that it looked like an enemy soldier. Later, larger structures might be set up to commemorate the victory.[7] Grimm suggested that the verb συστήσασθαι (literally, "to compose, organize") was used to signify that it was not one single piece of the spoils that was set up. Goldstein objected to the translation of κοινός as "public," as if the trophy were put up by a commonwealth or a democracy. Rather, the term seems to suggest "open to the general populace," which is why I have translated it as "in plain view." A literal translation would be "trophy of the forces around Judas," where the genitive is an objective genitive.

■ 7 Here continues the contrast of Judas with Nikanor, as v. 7 contains the second part of the μὲν . . . δέ construction. The periphrastic perfect ἦν . . . πεποιθώς expresses the state of trust that Judas is in, and the placing of the adverb ἀδιαλείπτως ("continuously") before the participle with its sound reinforcement stresses the constancy of the state. The prepositional phrase μετὰ πάσης ἐλπίδος ("with complete hope") contrasts with the description of Nikanor's arrogance in the previous verse, μετὰ πάσης ἀλαζονείας ("with utter cockiness").

"support" (ἀντιλήμψις). In 8:19, Judas had reminded his forces of the instances of support their ancestors had received from the Lord. The verb ἀντιλαμβάνειν ("to take the part of, to support") was used in 14:15 when the Jews, on learning of the invasion of Nikanor, had prayed that the Lord might take their part.

■ 8 The imperfect describes Judas's continuous action in exhorting his troops. The same term for "invasion," ἔφοδος, was used to describe Nikanor's first approach in 14:15.[8] While in 8:19 Judas had encouraged his forces by recalling how God had helped their ancestors, here he recalls how God had helped them in previous battles. The term for "help," βοήθημα, recalls how God was described as "helper" (Βοηθός) in 3:39 by Heliodorus,

and how the first invasion by Nikanor was turned back by divine help–τῇ τοῦ κυρίου βοηθείᾳ (8:35). This help is mentioned also in 12:11, and it is relied upon in 13:13. The defeat of Nikanor is a clear sign of God's help (15:35: φανερὸν τῆς τοῦ κυρίου βοηθείας σημεῖον).

God is frequently termed "Almighty" (παντοκράτωρ) (3:30; 5:20; 6:26; 7:35, 38; 8:11, 18, 24).[9] In this section of the narrative, the term occurs again in 15:32, where the humiliation of Nikanor is said to have been caused because he had boasted against the "house of the Almighty."

The verb for "expect" (προσδοκᾶν) is picked up again in 15:20, as the armies are about to engage. The term for "victory" (νίκη) is found in 15:21, where Judas is said to know that victory is from God, not from arms.[10]

■ 9 The author uses sound-alike participles and an adjective–παραμυθούμενος ("encouraging"), προσυπομνήσας ("reminding"), προθυμοτέρους ("more eager")–to signal how Judas rouses his troops. First the author mentions the law and the prophets. Prior to this point there had been no mention of the prophets in the condensed narrative. However, as the author intends to relate now the vision Judas had of Jeremiah the prophet (15:13-16), he mentions the prophets here. Abel is right to point out that this encouragement from the law and the prophets is different from 8:23, where Eleazar reads from the sacred scroll. In 8:19, Judas had exhorted his forces with the example of what had happened to Sennacherib, a story found in the prophets in Isa 37:36 and 4 Kgdms 19:35. In 15:22-24, Judas calls on God to save his people as he had done at the invasion of Sennacherib. This story of the victory over Sennacherib is frequently cited, as in 1 Macc 7:41-42 and *3 Macc.* 6:5, and is mentioned in Sir 48:20-21.

Second, the author has Judas remind the troops of their past performances. This is standard in pre-battle speeches as a means of instilling confidence.[11]

7 Friedrich Lammert, "Tropaion," *PW* series 2 (1948) 7 663–73.

8 See also its use in 5:1; 8:12; 12:21; 13:26, to describe Seleucid invasions.

9 In 3:22 the adjective παγκρατής is used, which I have translated as "all-powerful." In 7:35, because of the context, I have translated the noun as an adjective, "all-powerful."

10 The term is used also in 10:28 and 13:15 to signify that victory comes from God.

11 W. Kendrick Pritchett provides a list of topoi found in pre-battle exhortations: military instructions; rewards to victors, punishment to laggards; comparison of forces; achievements of the past (ancestry, former battles); consequences of defeat; gods on our side; recent battles lost by mismanagement; death

■ **10** With the use of ἀθεσία ("faithlessness"), Judas here refers back to the action of Nikanor in deciding to set at naught (ἀθετεῖν) the regulations (14:28). Polybius uses the same term when referring to the faithlessness of the barbarians (3.49.2: τῶν βαρβάρων ἀθεσία). Earlier in the narrative, the Gentiles round about had not kept the agreements made by Lysias and Antiochus V (12:2). Judas rouses his forces' spirits just as the mother had her sons' in 7:21.

■ **11** The contrast between the enemies' trust in arms and the Jews' trust in God was found earlier (8:18; 10:28; 12:14-15, 27-28). As Grimm noted, the contrast οὐ . . . ὡς is equal to οὐχ οὕτως . . . ὡς ("not too much . . . as"). The weapons with which one arms oneself are usually in the dative, but here the accusative of respect is used. Throughout this section, Judas is seen exhorting his forces (15:8, 17). To encourage his soldiers as they set out to attack New Carthage, Scipio is said to have related to them a dream wherein Neptune had promised to aid the Romans. Scipio's use of this motif was quite cynical, but it worked (Polybius 10.11). Judas's dream heartened the soldiers, as they will be later heartened by God's appearance (15:27).

■ **12-16** The dream of Judas consists of two parts. He sees first the former high priest Onias and then the prophet Jeremiah.

■ **12** Onias is described in the most fulsome terms as noble, a good Greek gentleman, as Eleazar was (6:18, 23). He greets and treats people properly, as had the citizens of Scythopolis the Jews (12:30), whereas Nikanor had changed the way he behaved toward Judas (14:30).[12] Onias speaks gracefully, in contrast to the men in Gazara, who speak unlawful phrases 10:34: λόγους ἀθεμίτους προίεντο). In contrast to Nikanor, who stretched out his hand to threaten the temple (14:33), Onias stretches out his hands to pray.

"community" (σύστημα). This term is used in 8:5 to refer to Judas's organization of his forces (γενόμενος . . .

ἐν συστήματι, having a corps), and so Schwartz prefers to see this meaning of military organization here. However, Onias was earlier described as the protector of his kindred (4:2: κηδεμόνα τῶν ὁμοεθνῶν), and σύστημα can have the broader meaning of community (*3 Macc.* 3:9; 7:3; Josephus *Ap.* 1.32).[13] The immediate context is exhortation to a battle, but Jeremiah is said to pray for the people (15:14), and the battle itself is for the city and the temple. I have therefore taken the broader meaning, community, as appropriate here.

■ **13** The term "likewise" (οὕτως) suggests that this figure also is praying with outstretched hands. The verb "to appear" is ἐπιφαίνειν, which is the root for the term for God's miraculous appearances, ἐπιφάνεια.[14] The verb is used in 12:22 to signify the appearance of Judas's forces, and the adjective ἐπιφανής is used to describe Eleazar's noble appearance (6:23) and the noble temple to Dionysos that Nikanor threatened to raise in place of the temple (14:33), as well as God (15:34). Its use here would seem not just to imply a simple appearance as in 12:22 but also to bring with it the connotation of a divine action.

The terms πολιά ("grey hair") and ὑπεροχή ("majesty") are used in 6:23 in the description of Eleazar.

■ **14** Onias is depicted as responding to an unspoken question from Judas.

"Kin-loving" (φιλάδελφος) recalls the description of Rhazis as φιλοπολίτης (14:37, "lover of his fellow citizens") and of Onias himself as protector of his kindred (4:2). It also looks forward to the description of Judas in 15:30. The term was also used of Hellenistic kings.[15]

In Jer 7:16; 11:14; 14:11, Jeremiah had been told by God not to pray for the people. Once his predictions of destruction had been fulfilled, he was asked by all the people to pray for them. He does and receives from God the answer that, if the people stay in Judah, God will build them up and not pull them down (Jeremiah 42).

The opening words of the narrative in 3:1 are "the

as glorious to the brave; evils of the enemy; not too much overconfidence ("The General's Exhortations in Greek Warfare," in idem, *Essays in Greek History* [Amsterdam: Gieben, 1994] 102-5).

12   Compare also Polybius's description of Scipio: προσφιλὴς κατὰ τὴν ἀπάντησιν (10.5.6: "friendly when meeting").

13   It is also used for "guild" or "corporation." See T.

Drew-Bear, "An Act of Foundation at Hypaipa," *Chiron* 10 (1980) 509-36, here 521; and Aryeh Kasher, *The Jews in Hellenistic and Roman Egypt: The Struggle for Equal Rights* (rev. ed.; TSAJ 7; Tübingen: Mohr Siebeck, 1988) 229-30.

14   The noun is found in 2:21; 3:24; 5:4; 12:22; 14:15.

15   See *OGIS* 302-4.

holy city." Their use here suggests that the narrative is coming to a climax.

■ **15-16** Jeremiah gives a sword to Judas. As a divine weapon, it is golden, as the cavalier in 3:25 wore golden armor, and the rider in 11:8 brandished golden weapons. The motif of a special weapon being given to a hero is well known in traditional literature.[16] In the *Enuma Elish*, the Babylonian creation epic, Marduk is given an irresistible weapon to fight Tiamat (tablet IV.30). In *Il.* 18.127–19.23, Achilles is given arms fashioned by the god Hephaistos to fight Hektor. In Egyptian accounts, a god often gives a sword to Pharaoh to defeat his enemy.[17] The Lord is said to have a sword, most famously in Ezek 21:9-17; Zech 13:7; and Isa 66:16. Note also that in Isa 31:8 Assyria is predicted to fall by the sword not of a human being. In the allegorical vision of the history of the world (*1 Enoch* 90:19, 34), at the end of history a sword is given to the sheep to destroy the beasts who had attacked them. After their victory, the sheep bring the sword back to the temple.

"break down your opponents" ($\vartheta\rho\alpha\dot{\upsilon}\sigma\epsilon\iota\varsigma$ $\tau o\dot{\upsilon}\varsigma$ $\dot{\upsilon}\pi\epsilon\nu\alpha\nu\tau\dot{\iota}o\upsilon\varsigma$). The same language is used of God in Exod 15:6-7: "Your right hand, O Lord, broke down [$\dot{\epsilon}\vartheta\rho\alpha\upsilon\sigma\epsilon\nu$] the enemy. In the greatness of your majesty you overthrew your opponents [$\tau o\dot{\upsilon}\varsigma$ $\dot{\upsilon}\pi\epsilon\nu\alpha\nu\tau\dot{\iota}o\upsilon\varsigma$]." Antiochus IV had been broken down ($\tau\epsilon\vartheta\rho\alpha\upsilon\sigma\mu\dot{\epsilon}\nu o\varsigma$) by God (9:11).

■ **17** The verb "to encourage, exhort" ($\pi\alpha\rho\alpha\kappa\alpha\lambda\epsilon\hat{\iota}\nu$) picks up the usage of the noun in v. 11. There Judas armed his forces with the encouragement of good arguments ($\dot{\epsilon}\nu$ $\tau o\hat{\iota}\varsigma$ $\dot{\alpha}\gamma\alpha\vartheta o\hat{\iota}\varsigma$ $\lambda\dot{o}\gamma o\iota\varsigma$); here he encourages with exceedingly fine arguments ($\lambda\dot{o}\gamma o\iota\varsigma$ $\pi\dot{\alpha}\nu\upsilon$ $\kappa\alpha\lambda o\hat{\iota}\varsigma$). The troops had shown valor ($\dot{\alpha}\rho\epsilon\tau\dot{\eta}$) before (10:28), and the use of $\dot{\alpha}\rho\epsilon\tau\dot{\eta}$ here so soon after the term was used to describe Onias's virtue (15:12) suggests an emulation of the high priest.

"To make courageous" ($\dot{\epsilon}\pi\alpha\nu\delta\rho\hat{\omega}\sigma\alpha\iota$) is literally "to make manly." This unusual word continues the emphasis on courage in this section of the narrative: $\dot{\alpha}\nu\delta\rho\alpha\gamma\alpha\vartheta\dot{\iota}\alpha$ ("bravery") is used of Judas's forces in 14:18; Rhazis acts courageously ($\dot{\alpha}\nu\delta\rho\omega\delta\hat{\omega}\varsigma$) in 14:43. Judas is successful in his exhortation, for the troops resolve to engage "with all courage" ($\mu\epsilon\tau\dot{\alpha}$ $\pi\dot{\alpha}\sigma\eta\varsigma$ $\epsilon\dot{\upsilon}\alpha\nu\delta\rho\dot{\iota}\alpha\varsigma$).

"Nobly" ($\gamma\epsilon\nu\nu\alpha\dot{\iota}\omega\varsigma$) is found frequently (6:28; 7:5, 11; 8:16; 13:14; 14:31, 43). Especially noteworthy is its presence in Judas's exhortation in the first encounter with Nikanor (8:16). "To begin" ($\dot{\epsilon}\mu\varphi\dot{\epsilon}\rho\epsilon\sigma\vartheta\alpha\iota$) is literally "to enter in."

"To decide the business" ($\kappa\rho\hat{\iota}\nu\alpha\iota$ $\tau\dot{\alpha}$ $\pi\rho\dot{\alpha}\gamma\mu\alpha\tau\alpha$) is found in 13:13. Nikanor had declined to engage in battle and so decide through bloodshed (14:18: $\tau\dot{\eta}\nu$ $\kappa\rho\dot{\iota}\sigma\iota\nu$ $\delta\iota$' $\alpha\dot{\iota}\mu\dot{\alpha}\tau\omega\nu$ $\pi o\iota\dot{\eta}\sigma\alpha\sigma\vartheta\alpha\iota$).

"the holy things and the temple" ($\tau\dot{\alpha}$ $\dot{\alpha}\gamma\iota\alpha$ $\kappa\alpha\dot{\iota}$ $\tau\dot{o}$ $\dot{\iota}\epsilon\rho\dot{o}\nu$). Goldstein sees these two terms as equivalent, since in 1 Maccabees $\tau\dot{\alpha}$ $\dot{\alpha}\gamma\iota\alpha$ refers to the sanctuary;[18] he therefore omits the second term as an explanatory gloss. However, even in 1 Maccabees, $\tau\dot{\alpha}$ $\dot{\alpha}\gamma\iota\alpha$ has a connotation that encompasses more than just the temple. See also 4:48, where the concern is for the city and the holy vessels, as well as the list of concerns in 13:14.

■ **18-19** These two verses both begin with the imperfect $\hat{\eta}\nu$ to describe the continuous concern, which serves to link the concerns of those fighting and those left behind, that is, all the people. The same sense of anguish was felt by all the citizens when Heliodorus attempted to enter the temple (3:14-21). The anguish is not trifling ($o\dot{\upsilon}$ $\pi\dot{\alpha}\rho\epsilon\rho o\varsigma$), another example of the author's use of a double negative to intensify the feeling.[19] In v. 17, the author had used the term $\dot{\iota}\epsilon\rho\dot{o}\nu$ for temple; here in v. 18 he uses $\nu\alpha\dot{o}\varsigma$. "Troubled at the attack" is literally "troubled of the attack," where the genitive is an objective genitive.

---

16   Thompson, *Motif-Index*, D 812, esp. D 812.8: "Magic object received in a dream"; D 812.12.1: "Magic sword received from dwarf in dream"; D 813.1.1: "Magic sword received from Lady of Lake."

17   See Walter Otto and Hermann Bengtson, *Zur Geschichte des Niederganges des Ptolemäerreiches. Ein Beitrag zur Regierungszeit des 8. und 9. Ptolemäers* (Munich: Bayerischen Akademie der Wissenschaften, 1938) 151. See particularly Jan Willem van Henten, "Judas the Maccabee's Dream (2 Macc.

15:11-16) and the Egyptian King's Sickle Sword," *Zutot: Perspectives on Jewish Culture* 4 (2004) 8–15.

18   1 Maccabees 2:12; 3:43, 51, 59; 4:36, 41, 43, 48; 6:18, 54; 7:33, 43; 9:54; 10:39; 13:3, 6; 14:15, 29, 31, 36, 42, 48; 15:7.

19   See Introduction.

■ **20-21** This long sentence begins with five genitive absolutes followed by two asyndetic participial phrases before the main verb, which is then followed by another long participial phrase.

The term "decision" (κρίσις) picks up the verb κρῖναι ("to decide") used in v. 17. The verb for "joining together," συμμιγνύναι, is used with a hostile sense in 14:16;[20] 15:26. However, it is also employed by the author in a positive sense of "coming together, joining," as in 14:14, where the opponents of Judas flock to join with Nikanor.[21] Since the armies clash in 15:26, where the verb συμμιγνύναι is used in a hostile sense, Grimm is right to see its meaning here as that the different parts of Nikanor's army assemble and arrange themselves. The description is of Nikanor's army, not of Judas's. As Bar-Kochva noted, the placement of the cavalry on the wings with the elephants was standard formation for Hellenistic armies.[22]

The "beasts" mentioned here are elephants. Yet the presence of elephants is problematic, as the Seleucid elephants had been slaughtered by the Roman legate Gnaeus Octavius prior to the arrival of Demetrius (Polybius 31.2.11; Appian *Syr.* 46). Bar-Kochva concludes that the description is "based on a general knowledge of the practice in Hellenistic armies, but not on acquaintance with the course of this particular battle."[23] Perhaps the presence of the elephants was deduced from Nikanor's being the former commander of a squadron of elephants (14:12). There are no elephants in the battle description in 1 Macc 7:39-43.

"looked at." The participle συνιδών recalls the way Alcimus had noticed the friendly relations between Nikanor and Judas (14:26) and how Judas had noticed the change in attitude toward him by Nikanor (14:30). The savageness (ἀγριότης) of the animals also recalls Nikanor's changed attitude toward Judas (14:30: ἀγροικότερον) and his design to attack the Jews on the Sabbath (15:2: ἀγρίως). The two participles placed in asyndeton, συνιδών . . . ἀνατείνας, capture the immediate recourse to prayer on seeing the elephants. The author seems to have used for the second participle the prefix ἀνα- rather than προ- to accord with the previous word, which begins with α. See also 15:32, where the author uses ἐκτείνας because of the following ἐπί.

"wonder-working" (τερατοποιός). This unusual adjective is found elsewhere in the LXX only in *3 Macc.* 6:32. However, in the Song of Moses, the question is posed: "Who is like you, O Lord, among the gods? Who is like you, majestic in holiness, awesome in splendor, doing wonders [ποιῶν τέρατα]?" (Exod 15:11). Jeremiah had said, "You did signs and wonders [ἐποίσας σημεῖα καὶ τέρατα] in the land of Egypt, and to this day in Israel and among all humankind, and have made yourself a name that continues to this very day" (Jer 32:20 [LXX 39:20]).[24]

That God, rather than the size of the opponent, determines the outcome of a battle was a staple in Israelite thought, most dramatically shown in Gideon's victory over the Midianites, where God reduces Gideon's army from thirty-two thousand to three hundred lest the Israelites say that their own hand had delivered them (Judg 7:2-8). The Deuteronomic rules of warfare open with the command not to be afraid when going out to war against an enemy larger than they are, for God is with the Jews (Deut 20:1). Earlier in 2 Maccabees, the judgement (κρίσις) of God had been pronounced against Antiochus IV by the seventh brother (7:35-36), and it was carried out (9:4, 18). Judas had also stated in his first pre-battle speech (8:18) that victory was the work of the Lord.

In 3:35, Heliodorus had offered prayers to the one who had preserved (περιποιήσαντι) life for him.

■ **22-24 The prayer of Judas**

Judas had referred to the invasion of Sennacherib also in his prayer in 8:19. The author of 1 Maccabees also has Judas mention this invasion in his prayer before the battle with Nikanor (1 Macc 7:41), and reference is made to it in the *War Scroll* from Qumran: "From of old [you] foretold [us the appoin]ted time of the power of your

---

20   In 14:16 the form συμμίσγειν is used.

21   The context of its use in 3:7 and 13:3 prompted me to translate it as "in conversation with," "speaking with."

22   Bar-Kochva, *Judas Maccabaeus*, 366. Schwartz (p. 505) refers to his debate with Bar-Kochva over whether all the elephants were destroyed.

23   Bar-Kochva, *Judas Maccabaeus*, 366.

24   For this combination of ποιεῖν and τέρας, see also Ezek 12:11; Addition F to Esther, Esth 10:9; Sir 45:19; Dan Th 6:27; Dan LXX 4:34.

hand against the Kittim saying: 'Ashur will fall by the sword not of a man, the sword not of a human being will devour it'" (Isa 31:8; 1QM 11.11–12). The reference is particularly apt, as Sennacherib's spokesperson had questioned the power of God to save Jerusalem (Isa 36:13-20).

God is frequently called "ruler" ($\delta\epsilon\sigma\pi\acute{o}\tau\eta\varsigma$: 5:17, 20; 6:14; 9:13) and "Master" ($\delta\upsilon\nu\acute{a}\sigma\tau\eta\varsigma$: 3:24; 12:15, 28; 15:3, 4, 29). God's angel strikes Sennacherib's camp in Isa 37:36: "And the angel of the Lord went forth, and he destroyed from the camp [$\grave{\alpha}\nu\epsilon\hat{\iota}\lambda\epsilon\nu$ $\grave{\epsilon}\kappa$ $\tau\hat{\eta}\varsigma$ $\pi\alpha\rho\epsilon\mu$-$\beta o\lambda\hat{\eta}\varsigma$] of the Assyrians a hundred and eighty-five thousand." The author has the same words as are found in LXX Isa 37:36, whereas the author of 1 Maccabees uses the verb $\grave{\epsilon}\pi\acute{\alpha}\tau\alpha\xi\epsilon\nu$ ("struck down"), found in 4 Kgdms 19:35.

As in the prayer of the priests in 14:36, the turn to direct appeal after a historical reference is made by the phrase $\kappa\alpha\grave{\iota}$ $\nu\hat{\upsilon}\nu$ (literally, "and now").

Elsewhere the author had used the pairings $\delta\acute{\epsilon}o\varsigma$ . . . $\tau\alpha\rho\alpha\chi\acute{\eta}$ (3:30; 13:16) and $\delta\acute{\epsilon}o\varsigma$ . . . $\varphi\acute{o}\beta o\varsigma$ (12:22). Here he uses the pair "for fear and trembling," $\epsilon\grave{\iota}\varsigma$ $\delta\acute{\epsilon}o\varsigma$ $\kappa\alpha\grave{\iota}$ $\tau\rho\acute{o}\mu o\nu$. The term $\delta\acute{\epsilon}o\varsigma$ can have the sense of inspiring fear (Thucydides 3.45).

"valiant angel." The same request for a good angel is found in 11:6. On the use of the term, see the discussion on 11:6.

"by your arm's might" ($\mu\epsilon\gamma\acute{\epsilon}\vartheta\epsilon\iota$ $\beta\rho\alpha\chi\acute{\iota}o\nu\acute{o}\varsigma$ $\sigma o\upsilon$). The same phrase is found in Moses' hymn in Exod 15:16, whereas most other references to God's arm, such as Dan 9:15 and Bar 2:11, use the phrase $\grave{\epsilon}\nu$ $\beta\rho\alpha\chi\acute{\iota}o\nu\iota$ $\upsilon\psi\eta\lambda\hat{\omega}$ ("with an upraised arm") from Exod 6:1.[25]

"be struck down." The verb $\kappa\alpha\tau\alpha\pi\lambda\acute{\eta}\sigma\sigma\epsilon\iota\nu$ is used earlier, when Judas exhorts his followers not to be struck down by the size of their enemies (8:16) and where the author describes how the Lord of spirits struck down Heliodorus and his followers were changed to weak-kneed cowards (3:24). References to blasphemies and blasphemer are found in 8:4; 9:28; 10:34-35; 12:14.

The author connects the end of the verse with the following verse through a $\mu\grave{\epsilon}\nu$ . . . $\delta\acute{\epsilon}$ construction, as he has done frequently (3:40-41; 10:9-10; 15:6-7).

■ **25-29 The battle**

The account stresses the difference between the two sides. Trumpets and war cries were intended to frighten the enemy as well as bolster the soldiers' confidence (see Polybius 2.29.6; Diodorus Siculus 19.30.1; 19.41.3).[26] Trumpets were used in Hellenistic armies both in organizing battle formations and as a means by which officers could transmit orders in the battle itself, which would otherwise have been difficult because of the noise.[27] In 12:37, the Jews unexpectedly charged Gorgias's forces with a war cry and hymns. Schwartz notes how the author of 2 Maccabees has the Jews singing hymns ($\mu\epsilon\vartheta$' $\acute{\upsilon}\mu\nu\omega\nu$), whereas he uses the term $\pi\alpha\iota\acute{\alpha}\nu$ for the battle cries of the Gentiles, whose war chants were often addressed to Ares or Apollo. The term $\grave{\epsilon}\pi\acute{\iota}\kappa\lambda\eta\sigma\iota\varsigma$ ("prayer") recalls the repeated use of the associated verb $\grave{\epsilon}\pi\iota\kappa\alpha\lambda\epsilon\hat{\iota}\nu$ ("to implore") in 15:21, 22. The author employs a hendiadys, "with prayers and invocations." The $\mu\grave{\epsilon}\nu$ . . . $\delta\acute{\epsilon}$ construction in v. 27 tightly connects the physical and the mental attitude of the Jews. "With their minds" ($\tau\alpha\hat{\iota}\varsigma$ . . . $\kappa\alpha\rho\delta\acute{\iota}\alpha\iota\varsigma$) is literally "with hearts." A similar connection is found in Ps 149:6: "The high praises of God in their throats, and two-edged swords in their hands." Just as Judas's forces had been heartened by the vision of Onias and Jeremiah (15:11), so now they are heartened by the epiphany of God.

As in 12:22, there is no detailed depiction of how God appeared to the forces, in contrast to 10:29-30 and 11:8.

Bar-Kochva views the number thirty-five thousand as very exaggerated and prefers to follow Josephus (*Ant.* 12.411), who gives nine thousand Seleucid soldiers. Bar-Kochva notes that 1 Macc 7:39 speaks of reinforcements coming from Syria and argues that they could not have been numerous as at that time the rebellion by Timarchus was still ongoing.[28]

"battle." The term $\chi\rho\epsilon\acute{\iota}\alpha$ has this meaning in Polybius 1.84.7 and also in 2 Macc 8:20.

---

25   Enermalm-Ogawa (*Un langage de prière*, 136–38) discusses the use of the hymn of Exodus 15 in Jewish liturgy.

26   See Pritchett, *Greek State at War*, 1:105–8.

27   Bar-Kochva cites Asclepiodotus 12.10 to show how "the various tones and trills of the trumpet provided a satisfactory solution" for transmitting orders (*Judas Maccabaeus*, 394).

28   Bar-Kochva, *Judas Maccabaeus*, 362–63.

Nikanor was probably recognized by his armor as commander.[29]

Nikanor had claimed to be master on earth (15:5), but now the true master is known. The use of the ancestral language stresses, as in 7:8, 21, 27; 12:37, the distinction from the Gentiles. "With a tumultuous shout" is a hendiadys, "with a shout and tumult." Schwartz rightly notes that the terms for shout and tumult usually have negative connotations and asks why such words were used here at a moment of triumph. He suggested that "for religious people, a demonstration of God's active providence, even on one's own behalf, may first of all awaken fear, reverence, and only thereafter joy; see 12:40-41, also Exod 14:30—15:1."[30] When Achior saw the head of Holofernes, he fell down on his face and his spirit failed. When the people of Bethulia raised him up, he immediately did obeisance to Judith and blessed her (Jdt 14:6-7). One might also note how, by means of rhetoric, the author quickly turns negative emotions positive.

■ **30-35 The fate of Nikanor**

■ **30** Nikanor had enjoined that the Jews forced to accompany him take up arms (15:5) against the one who had enjoined the reverence of the Sabbath (15:3); now Judas enjoins what is to be done to the defeated body of Nikanor. It is noteworthy that after the first defeat of Nikanor, the enemy commander had stated that the Jews were unbeatable because they followed the laws prescribed by their God (8:36).

Judas is described in two long appositive phrases. He is the chief struggler ($\pi\rho\omega\tau\alpha\gamma\omega\nu\iota\sigma\tau\eta\varsigma$), a term that is often used of the chief actor in the theater but is also employed in 1 Macc 9:11 to describe the chief warriors of Bacchides' forces. The term reflects the use of the verb $\dot{\alpha}\gamma\omega\nu\dot{\iota}\zeta\epsilon\sigma\vartheta\alpha\iota$ ("fighting") in 15:27, as well as the use of $\dot{\alpha}\gamma\dot{\omega}\nu$ ("contest") in 14:18 and 15:9. The phrase "body and soul" resonates with how the martyrs had behaved—the youngest brother had "surrendered body and soul" (7:37); Rhazis had "risked body and soul" (14:38)—and Judas's concern for the citizens reflects attitudes ascribed to Onias (4:2) and Rhazis (14:37).

"maintained" ($\delta\iota\alpha\phi\upsilon\lambda\alpha\sigma\sigma\epsilon\iota\nu$). This verb was earlier used in reference to maintaining Torah laws by preserving the funds deposited in the temple (3:15), in describing how the Jews were not allowed to maintain their ancestral laws (6:6), and in depicting the preservation of Judas by angelic helpers (10:30). Used here, it enhances Judas's position.

"goodwill" ($\epsilon\ddot{\upsilon}\nu\omega\iota\alpha$). Here Judas's goodwill toward his kinsfolk is the same as that ascribed to Rhazis, who, because of his goodwill, was called a father of the Jews (14:37).

"during each stage of his life." As there is little evidence that $\dot{\eta}\lambda\iota\kappa\dot{\iota}\alpha$ has the meaning of "youth," the genitive $\tau\hat{\eta}\varsigma\ \dot{\eta}\lambda\iota\kappa\dot{\iota}\alpha\varsigma$ here would seem to suggest that Judas had observed his goodwill during each stage of his life, that is, during childhood, as a youth, and in manhood.

Josephus, in his account of the battle (*Ant.* 12.411–12), omits this dismemberment, possibly so as not to give a wrong image of Jews to his audience, as it was customary to allow enemies to gather up their dead from the battlefield.[31] From Achilles' treatment of Hektor (*Il.* 24.14–22) on, bodies of defeated enemies had been outraged.[32] Heads of defeated enemies are cut off (Judg 7:24); David brings the head of Goliath to Jerusalem (1 Sam 17:54); Saul's body was fastened to the wall of Beth-Shean (1 Sam 31:9); Judith cuts off the head of Holofernes and has it hung on the wall of the city (Jdt 13:8; 14:1, 11); Euphorbos hopes to carry the head of Menelaus back to his people (*Il.* 17.38–39); and Polybius reports that the head of a Spartan commander was taken back by his victors to show the Achaeans that he had been killed (11.18.4–8).[33]

■ **31-33** Just as the priests had witnessed Nikanor's threat against the temple and had prayed for its protection

---

29   Everett L. Wheeler, "The General as Hoplite," in Victor Davis Hanson, ed., *Hoplites: The Classical Greek Battle Experience* (London and New York: Routledge, 1991) 140–41.

30   Schwartz, *2 Maccabees*, 508.

31   Bar-Kochva, *Judas Maccabaeus*, 369.

32   Bar-Kochva (*Judas Maccabaeus*, 369 nn. 14–15) provides a long list: Xenophon *Anab.* 3.4.5; Plutarch *Nic.* 27–28, *Cleom.* 38, *Mor.* 849a, *Ant.* 20, *Cic.*

48–49; Polybius 2.59–60; 5.54.5–7; 8.21.3–4; Arrian *Anab.* 4.7.3–4; Pausanias 9.33.9; Diodorus Siculus 20.103.6; Curtius Rufus 4.6.26–29; Hegesias, *FGH* 142 F5; Dionysius of Halicarnassus *Comp.* 18; Dio Cassius 33.109.4; 47.3.2; 47.8.3–4; 48.14.3–4; 49.20.4; 51.5.5; 67.11.3; 73.13.6; 74.10.2; 76.7.3.

33   See Charles Segal, *The Theme of the Mutilation of the Corpse in the Iliad* (Mnemosyne Supplements 17; Leiden: Brill, 1971) 20–21.

(14:33-36), so now they witness his defeat and the deliverance of the temple.

"the citadel" (ἄκρα). This term, so prominent in 1 Maccabees, is mentioned in 2 Maccabees only here and four lines later in 15:35. In 4:28, Sostratos is said to be commander of the citadel (ἀκρόπολις). The role of the enemy forces in the citadel is not elaborated. In 8:31, it appears as though Judas and his forces had complete access to Jerusalem, even though the citadel was occupied by Seleucid forces. Here in 15:31 the enemy forces in the citadel appear powerless to prevent the outrage against the Seleucid commander. In 1 Macc 7:47, the head and right hand of Nikanor are displayed outside Jerusalem (παρὰ τῇ Ἱερουσαλήμ), and the citadel is controlled by the Maccabeans only under Simon (1 Macc 13:49-51). Here those in the citadel are summoned to see proof of Nikanor's death.

Three terms are used to describe Nikanor: polluted (μιαρός), abusive (δυσφήμος), and godless (δυσσεβής). The first was used earlier of Jason (4:19), as well as of Antiochus IV (5:16; 7:34; 9:13). The second is used to denote the Gentiles in general (13:11). The third term had previously been used at the first defeat of a Nikanor (8:14).

"boasted" (μεγαλαυχεῖν). This verb is used by Sir 48:18 to describe the actions of Sennacherib.

The cutting off of Nikanor's hand refers back to Nikanor's threat, where he had stretched out his right hand against the temple (14:33). Judas had exhorted his troops to look for victory from the Almighty in 15:8, and the epithet "Almighty" (παντοκράτωρ) was also used in the account of the first episode against a Nikanor (8:11, 18, 24).

Further, the cutting off of Nikanor's tongue is an appropriate punishment for Nikanor's speaking against the temple. In 9:15, Antiochus IV is said to have wanted to have the Jews "eaten by birds" (οἰωνοβρώτους), but the term used here, ὄρνεον ("bird"), is reminiscent of its use in Ezek 39:4, 17. The author made a play on words when he chose τὰ ἐπίχειρα as the term for "wages." In the singular, as in LXX Jer 31:25 (MT 48:25) and 34:5 (MT 27:5), this word can mean "hand, arm" and as used

here plays on the term for "hand" (χείρ). The wages (ἐπίχειρα) Nikanor received were to have his head and hand (χείρ)/arm (ἐπίχειρον) hung up. Polybius uses the phrase "wages of ignorance" (ἐπίχειρα ἀγνοίας) (4.63.1). As Schwartz notes, the etymology, as well as the emphasis on Nikanor's hand, goes against Habicht's suggestion that the rest of the body is being hung here. However, Schwartz's translation of ἐπίχειρα as "arms" appears too literalistic.

The whole episode of Nikanor had been started by the folly (ἄνοια) of Alcimus (14:5). Here Nikanor receives the wages of folly (ἄνοια).

In 1 Macc 7:47 the head and the right hand of Nikanor are hung up toward Jerusalem. Bar-Kochva refers to the Palestinian Talmud and the Babylonian Talmud, which have similar stories where parts of Nikanor's body are hung on a stake facing Jerusalem or at the gates of Jerusalem.[34] To show the head and the arm to the people and the priests near the altar and to hang them opposite the temple is quite dramatic but raises questions about corpse contamination. However, the Parma manuscript of the scholion on *Megillat Ta'anit* similarly has "and they hanged them opposite the Temple."[35]

■ 34 The adjective "appearing" (ἐπιφανής) recalls the epiphanies mentioned in the prayer before the invasion of Nikanor (14:15) and the appearance of God mentioned at 15:27, as well as the constant use of the word throughout the narrative since its first appearance in the prologue in 2:21. Where Nikanor had threatened to build a splendid (ἐπιφανές) temple to Dionysos (14:33), the appearing Lord (ἐπιφανὴς κύριος) had preserved his temple.

The verb "bless" (εὐλογεῖν) and the adjective "blessed" (εὐλογητός) recall the first reaction of Judas's forces on seeing the dead Nikanor (15:29), and the prayer repeats the prayer of the priests immediately after Nikanor's threat to the temple (14:36).

■ 35 The adjective "clear" (φανερός) and its adverb are used in 9:8 and 3:28 to indicate God's power. Nikanor had wanted to make manifest (14:39: πρόδηλος) his enmity toward the Jews, but now his head is a clear (ἐπίδηλος) sign of God's help. As Judas had reminded his

34   Bar-Kochva, *Judas Maccabaeus*, 369–70. He cites *y. Meg.* 1.6 (70c); *y. Ta'an.* 2.13 (66a); *b. Ta'an.* 18b, as well as *Megillat Ta'anit* on 13 Adar.

35   The arguments of Bar-Kochva (*Judas Maccabaeus*, 371 n. 22) against the reliability of this statement of the scholion are not convincing.

forces of the helps God had performed for them in the past (15:8), so now God had aided them again. On the term "help," see the comment on 15:8. Presumably, the forces in the citadel were impotent to prevent this display of Nikanor's body.

The word I have translated as "head," προτομή, most often means the head and face of a decapitated animal. Later it would describe the bust of a Roman emperor on a standard (Josephus *Ant.* 18.55). Here the connotation of animal head resonates with the description of the Seleucids as "barbarians" (2:21) and of Nikanor's behavior as barbaric (15:2). The body of King Saul was fastened to the wall of Beth-Shean to declare the Philistines' triumph (1 Sam 31:10). According to 1 Chr 10:10, the head of Saul was fastened in the temple of Dagon. The head of Holofernes was hung from the wall of Bethulia (Jdt 14:11). Herodotus (5.114) recounts how the head of Onesilus was hung above the gates of Amathous.

■ **36** That the opening words here echo those of 10:8, which inaugurated the feast of Hanukkah, shows how these two feasts dominate the structure of the entire composition. The terms "unmarked" (ἀπαρασήμαντον) and "to mark" (ἔχειν . . . ἐπίσημον) resonate with the term for "sign," σημεῖον, in v. 35. One should also note that the Syracusans set up a festival to commemorate their defeat of the Athenians (Plutarch *Nic.* 28).

"In Aramaic" (τῇ συριακῇ φωνῇ) is literally "in the Syriac language." The term συριακή refers to the Aramaic language. The term συριστεί is used where the Jewish envoys request that the Assyrian commander not use Hebrew but Aramaic in LXX 4 Kgdms 18:26// Isa 36:11. In LXX Dan 2:4, the term signifies the switch from Hebrew to Aramaic and, in LXX 2 Esdr 4:7 (MT Ezra 4:7), the language in which the letter to Artaxerxes was written. In the colophon to Job (LXX Job 42:17b), information about Job is said to have been taken ἐκ τῆς συριακῆς βίβλου ("from a scroll in Aramaic").[36] Throughout the narrative, the author has indicated when characters use their ancestral language (7:8, 21, 27; 12:37; 15:29). Is the author aware that Adar is not the Hebrew name of the twelfth month, but comes from the Babylonian exile, and from the book of Esther in particular,[37] in which the festival of the Day of Mordechai was inaugurated (Esth 9:17-19)?

General Commentary

This last section of the Nikanor narrative continues the pattern whereby a challenge is issued against the deity, battle ensues, and the deity's followers then celebrate the victory. Here Nikanor claims that he is master upon earth (15:5), the two sides are clearly demarcated, and victory is won through the help of the deity (15:27), including the gift of a heavenly weapon (15:15-16). The defeat of the enemy is clearly proclaimed, as Nikanor's blasphemous hand and head are displayed (15:33-35), and the triumph of the deity is celebrated with a festival (15:36). The author's aim of moving his audience by means of rhetoric is achieved by using such a well-known pattern. Throughout the narrative, he has not been particularly interested in the details of battle tactics, and the same is true here. He is most concerned to distinguish the two sides, one as pious, the other as impious.

The author also connects Judas back to the former pious leader Onias, the high priest. Onias was the benefactor of the city and the protector of his kindred (4:2), and his piety had kept the city at peace (3:1). Judas is described as one who had maintained goodwill toward his kinsfolk (15:30), and he ensures that the temple and the city are not disturbed (15:37). In some ways, Judas now takes up the part of the pious Onias. They also differ, however. Onias is described as "gentle" (πραΰς) in 15:12, and when the city was threatened, he had gone to the king for help (4:4-6). Judas, by contrast, is described as "chief struggler" (πρωταγωνιστής) for his people (15:30).[38] The dynamic has changed. The new leaders of the people will have to be fighters in defense of Judaism.

The author's concern for the temple, mentioned in the opening sentence of his prologue (2:19), is shown dramatically in that he ends this part of the narrative

36 On this colophon, see Annette Yoshiko Reed, "Job as Jobab: The Interpretation of Job in LXX Job 42:17 b-e," *JBL* 120 (2001) 31–55. In her translation, Reed does not take into account the initial μὲν . . . δέ construction.

37 Ezra 6:15; Esth 2:16; 3:7, 13; 8:12; 9:1, 15, 16, 19, 21.

38 I owe this insight to Kevin Osterloh, in private conversation.

in the same way as he ended the contest against Antiochus IV (10:8). The inauguration of these two festivals, Hanukkah and Nikanor's Day, structure the whole narrative. This does not mean that the narrative is a festal legend, as Momigliano held.[39] For example, the discussion of feasts in the *Atthides* is concerned with etiological explanations of why a feast is celebrated and performed in a certain way.[40] However, just as festivals were set up to celebrate deliverances from danger,[41] so here festivals are instituted to how the deity defended his temple.

---

39 Momigliano, "Second Book of Maccabees," 81–88.
40 The question of festal legend is discussed in Doran, *Temple Propaganda*, 105–8.
41 The repulse of the Gauls from Delphi by Apollo and other gods was celebrated, almost immediately after the victory, with Soteria at Athens, Cos, Chios, Teos, Tenos, and Eritrea. The epigraphical and literary accounts are discussed fully in Nachtergael, *Les Galates en Grèce et les Sôtéria de Delphes: Recherches d'histoire et d'épigraphie hellénestique* (Mémoires de l'Académie royale de Belgique 63; Brussels: Palais des Académies, 1977).

15

15:37-39

37/ As the actions at the time of Nikanor turned out this way and after these critical times the city was controlled by the Hebrews, I myself will rest the narrative at this point. 38/ If it is well [written] and hits the mark by its composition, this is what I myself wanted. If it is below par and mediocre, this is what I could do. 39/ For to drink wine by itself and again to drink water by itself is harmful, but as wine already[a] blended with water produces pleasurable delight, so the construction of the narrative pleasures the ears of those who encounter the composition. Here let the end be.

a   Reading ἤδη ("already") with Hanhart and Goldstein rather than ἡδύς ("pleasant, pleasing") with L¹⁻⁵³⁴ Laᴮ and Abel and Habicht. Goldstein makes the strong argument that to read ἡδύς would spoil "the balanced rhetoric: in the 'so' clause, which ends our sentence, there is nothing to correspond with what 'is sweet'" (*II Maccabees*, 505).

Commentary by Verse

■ **37** The verb "to turn out" (χωρεῖν) was used in 3:40 and 13:26 to signify the change from one section of the narrative to another.

"critical times." The term καιρός has this sense.[1]

Scholars have been much perturbed by the aorist participle in the genitive absolute construction κρατηθείσης τῆς πόλεως, which I have translated "the city was controlled." Since the city was quickly retaken by Bacchides a few months later and Judas was killed (1 Maccabees 9), scholars have either considered it a lie (Grimm, Momigliano,[2] Habicht) or have attempted to explain it as referring to the sanctuary (Abel,[3] Goldstein[4]). Schwartz[5] concentrated on the fact that the aorist participle has the sense of simple occurrence and suggested that one translate the verb as "to take over," that is, "the city was taken over," as κρατεῖν has this meaning in 4:10, 27; 5:7; 14:2.[6] He then posited that the present participle of εἶναι had been omitted and so translated: "ever since the city was taken over by the Hebrews it has

been in their hands." The concern of scholars might be alleviated if one considered how the two aorist participles χωρησάντων and κρατηθείσης in these genitive absolute constructions complement each other. In 3:40 and 13:26, the verb χωρεῖν marks the end of one section of the narrative and is then followed by the beginning of a new section. So too here: Nikanor is dead; now begins a new period, which the author declines to write about. He ends with the Hebrews on top, just as Dionysius of Halicarnassus recommended (*Pomp.* 3).[7] The critical times when the temple was under threat are now over, and that is where he decides to end his narrative.

"Hebrews." This term is used by the seventh brother as he is about to undergo torture (7:31) and when Lysias recognizes that the Hebrews cannot be defeated while God fights with them (11:13). Its use suggests that the "Hebrews" are the faithful followers of Judaism, a connotation that Graham Harvey has found.[8]

Here, as in the prologue, the reflection at 6:12-17 and in 14:34, the author speaks in the first person. The verb καταπαύσω picks up the beginning of the last threat of

---

1   Gerhard Delling, "Καιρός," *TDNT* 3 (1965) 455–59.
2   Momigliano, *Prime linee*, 99–100.
3   Abel: "la ville sainte considérée sous son aspect religieux pouvait être dite aux mains des Hébreux."
4   Goldstein, *II Maccabees*, 504: "Our writer does not claim that an independent Jewish state held Jerusalem from that time on, but only that the city was in possession of pious Jews rather than apostates and foreigners."
5   Schwartz, *2 Maccabees*, appendix 11, pp. 556–57.
6   In 4:50 the participle has the sense of "ruling."
7   See also Cicero *Ad Lucceium* (*Fam.* 5.12.2–4, 6), and the Introduction, pp. 8–10.
8   Graham Harvey, *The True Israel: Uses of the Names Jew, Hebrew and Israel in Ancient Jewish and Early Christian Literature* (AGJU 35; Leiden: Brill, 2001) 104–27; idem, "Synagogues of the Hebrews; 'Good Jews' in the Diaspora," in Siân Jones and Sarah

Nikanor against the Jewish day of rest (τῇ τῆς καταπαύ-σεως ἡμέρᾳ), the Sabbath (15:1). Note also the paronomasia of αὐτος αὐτόθι.

■ **38** Goldstein notes that this verse is very similar to Aeschines 3.260, the end of one of the orations. Schwartz observes that such professions of humility are common (see, e.g., Josephus *Bell.* 7.455; Aelius Aristides *To Rome* 109). The adverbs καλῶς, εὐθίκτως, εὐτελῶς, μετρίως are used instead of adjectives[9] to qualify the understood "narrative" (λόγος). The adverb εὐθίκτως ("hits the right mark") has a sound similar to ἐφικτόν ("what I could do"). The term "below par" (εὐτελῶς) is used in Polybius (32.11.6) and Lucian (*Hist. conscr.* 22) to describe a badly written work. The term for "composition," σύνταξις, refers back to the prologue, where the author had planned to shorten the five books of Jason into one composition (2:23: δι᾿ ἑνὸς συντάγματος ἐπιτεμεῖν).

■ **39** Wines were so potent in the ancient world that they were normally mixed with water (Athenaeus *Deipn.* 10.426–27).[10] Schwartz notes that those who did not do so were "Scythian" (Herodotus 6.84; Athenaeus *Deipn.* 10.427a-c). The LXX rendition of Jer 25:15 makes the cup of wrath into a cup of unmixed wine (LXX 32:15: τοῦ οἴνου τοῦ ἀκράτου) and the cup of "foaming wine, well-mixed" prepared for sinners in Ps 75:8 becomes in LXX Ps 74:8 a cup "full of unmixed wine (οἴνου ἀκρά-του πλῆρες). In *Ps. Sol.* 8:14, God is said to have mingled for the sinners of Jerusalem a spirit of wandering, to have given them a cup of unmixed wine (οἴνου ἀκράτου) that they might become drunk. Schwartz also observes that later rabbinic passages hold that "only wine that has been mixed with water deserves to be blessed as 'wine,'" and "if one drinks unmixed wine at the Passover meal he has fulfilled his obligation but not in the respectable way of a free man."[11]

"the construction of the narrative" (τὸ τῆς κατασκευῆς τοῦ λόγου). In the prologue, the author had compared himself to one who prepares (τῷ παρα-σκευάζοντι) a banquet (2:27). Just as in the prologue the author used terms known from Hellenistic historiography, so too here he uses the adjective "pleasure-able" (ἐπιτερπής) and the verb "pleasures" (τέρπειν), reflecting the term τὸ τερπνόν, so favored by Polybius to describe one of the aims of history.[12]

"the ears of those who encounter the composition" (τὰς ἀκοὰς τῶν ἐντυγχανόντων τῇ συντάξει). The author had promised usefulness to those who read his work (2:25: τοῖς ἐντυγχάνουσιν ὠφέλειαν), and he had warned those who encountered his work (τοὺς ἐντυγχάνοντας τῆδε τῇ βίβλῳ) not to be dismayed by the misfortunes of the Jews (6:12). The use of "ears" here reminds us that in antiquity works were often read aloud, rather than silently. As Polybius criticizes Timaeus, he says: "Knowledge derived from hearing [διὰ τῆς ἀκοῆς] being of two sorts, Timaeus diligently pursued the one, the reading of books, . . . but was very remiss in his use of the other, the interrogation of living witnesses" (12.27.3).

To end his prologue, the author had started off his last sentence with ἐντεῦθεν (2:32, which, because of the context, I have translated "consequently," but literally it means "hence"), so now he starts his last sentence of the epilogue with ἐνταῦθα ("here").

General Commentary

Whereas the author uses the first person plural in describing his project in the prologue, here he emphatically claims the work as his own through the use of the first person singular. He echoes the drinking party analogy he had used in the prologue (2:27). Although based on the work of Jason of Cyrene, the work is his, and he is proud of it.

Pearce, eds., *Jewish Local Patriotism and Self-Identification in the Graeco-Roman Period* (JSNTSup 31; Sheffield: Sheffield Academic Press, 1998) 132–47. See also Runia, "Philonic Nomenclature," 14–17.

9   See Smyth, *Greek Grammar*, §1097.

10   Charles Seltman, *Wine in the Ancient World* (London: Routledge & Paul, 1957) 91.

11   Schwartz, *2 Maccabees*, 514, referring to Philo *Flacc.* 136; *t. Ber.* 4.3; *b. Pesaḥ.* 104b.

12   See Frank W. Walbank, "Profit or Amusement: Some Thoughts on the Motives of Hellenistic Historians," in Verdin, Schepens, and De Keyser, eds., *Purposes of History,* 253–66; and, in the same volume, V. D'Huys, "*ΧΡΗΣΙΜΟΝ ΚΑΙ ΤΕΡΠΝΟΝ* in Polybios' Schlachtschilderungen. Einige literarische Topoi in seiner Darstellung der Schlacht bei Zama (XV 9–16)," 267–88.

1. Commentaries

Abel, Felix-Marie
Les livres des Maccabées (EtB; Paris: Gabalda, 1949).
Bartlett, John R.
The First and Second Books of the Maccabees (Cambridge: Cambridge University Press, 1973).
Bévenot, Hugo
Die beiden Makkabäerbücher (Die Heilige Schrift des Alten Testamentes; Bonn: Peter Hanstein, 1931).
Dommerhausen, Werner
1 Makkabäer. 2 Makkabäer (NEchtB 12; Würzburg: Echter Verlag, 1985).
Goldstein, Jonathan A.
I Maccabees: A New Translation with Introduction and Commentary (AB 41; Garden City, N.Y.: Doubleday, 1976).
Idem
II Maccabees: A New Translation with Introduction and Commentary (AB 41A; Garden City, N.Y.: Doubleday, 1983).
Grimm, Carl L. W.
Das zweite, dritte und vierte Buch der Makkabäer (Leipzig: Hirzel, 1857).
Habicht, Christian
2. Makkabäerbuch (JSHRZ 1, Historische und legendarische Erzählungen 3; Gütersloh: G. Mohn, 1976).
Schwartz, Daniel R.
2 Maccabees (Commentaries on Early Jewish Literature; Berlin and New York: de Gruyter, 2008).

2. Studies

Abel, Felix-Marie
"Eclaircissement de quelques passages des Maccabées," *RB* 55 (1948) 184–94.
Idem
"Les letters preliminaries du second livre des Maccabées," *RB* 53 (1946) 513–33.
Idem
"Topographie des campagnes Maccabéennes," *RB* 32 (1923) 495–521; 33 (1924) 201–17, 371–87; 34 (1925) 194–216; 35 (1926) 206–22, 510–33.
Adinolfi, Marco
"Le apparizioni di 2 Macc 5,2-4 e 10,29-30," *RivB* 11 (1963) 166–85.
Idem
"Eloquenza e patetismo nel secondo libro dei Maccabei," *RivB* 10 (1962) 18–31.
Idem
Questioni bibliche di storia e storiografia (Brescia: Paideia, 1969).

Aejmelaeus, Anneli
Parataxis in the Septuagint: A Study of the Renderings of the Hebrew Coordinate Clauses in the Greek Pentateuch (Annales Academiae Scientiarum Fennicae: Dissertationes humanarum litterarum 31; Helsinki: Suomalainen Tiedeakatemia, 1982).
Africa, Thomas
"Worms and the Death of Kings: A Cautionary Note on Disease and History," *CA* 1 (1982) 1–17.
Alföldi, Andreas
Der Vater des Vaterlandes im römischen Denken (Libelli 261; Darmstadt: Wissenschaftliche Buchgesellschaft, 1971).
Alon, Gedalia
Jews, Judaism and the Classical World (Jerusalem: Magnes, 1977).
Ameling, Walter
"Jerusalem als hellenistische Polis: 2 Makk 4, 9-12 und eine neue Inschrift," *BZ* n.F. 47 (2003) 105–11.
Amir, Yehoshua
"The Term Ἰουδαισμός (IOUDAISMOS), a Study in Jewish-Hellenistic Self-Definition," *Immanuel* 14 (1982) 34–41.
Aneziri, Sophia, and Dimitris Damakos
"Städtische Kulte im hellenistischen Gymnasion," in Daniel Kah and Peter Scholz, eds., *Das hellenistische Gymnasion* (Wissenskultur und gesellschaftlicher Wandel 8; Berlin: Akademie, 2004) 247–71.
Apcrghis, Gerassimos G.
The Seleukid Royal Economy: The Finances and Financial Administration of the Seleukid Empire (Cambridge: Cambridge University Press, 2004).
Applebaum, Shimon
Jews and Greeks in Ancient Cyrene (SJLA 28; Leiden: Brill, 1979).
Arenhoevel, Diego
Die Theokratie nach dem 1. und 2. Makkabäerbuch (Walberger Studien der Albertus-Magnus-Akademie, Theologische Reihe 3; Mainz: Matthias Grünewald, 1967).
Arnim, H. von
Stoicorum veterum fragmenta (4 vols.; Leipzig: Teubner, 1903–24).
Avenarius, Gert
Lukians Schrift zur Geschichtsschreibung (Meisenheim am Glan: Hain, 1956).
Avigad, Nahman
"Jerusalem: The Second Temple Period," in Ephraim Stern, ed., *The New Encyclopedia of Archeological Excavations in the Holy Land* (4 vols.; Jerusalem: Israel Exploration Society & Carta, 1993) 2:717–25.

Avi-Yonah, Michael
The Holy Land: A Historical Geography from the Persian to the Arab Conquest (536 B.C. to A.D. 640) (Jerusalem: Carta, 2002).

Azarpay, G.
"Nanâ, the Sumero-Akkadian Goddess of Transoxiana," *JAOS* 96 (1976) 536–42.

Babelon, Ernest
Les rois de Syrie, d'Arménie et de Commagène: Catalogue des Monnaies Grecques de la Bibliothèque Nationale (Paris: C. Rollin & Feuardent, 1890).

Bailey, D. R. Shackleton
Cicero's Letters to His Friends (Classical Resources Series 1; Atlanta: Scholars Press, 1996).

Baker, David W.
"Further Examples of the *WAW EXPLICATIVUM*," *VT* 30 (1980) 129–36.

Balch, David L.
"Attidudes toward Foreigners in 2 Maccabees, Eupolemus, Esther, Aristeas, and Luke-Acts," in Abraham J. Malherbe, Frederick W. Norris, J. W. Thompson, eds., *The Early Church in Its Context: Essays in Honor of Everett Ferguson* (NovTSup 90; Leiden: Brill, 1998) 22–47.

Ballou, Ralph B., Jr.
"The Role of the Jewish Priesthood in the Expansion of Greek Games in Jerusalem," *Canadian Journal of History and Physical Education* 1 (1970) 70–81.

Barag, Dan
"The Mint of Antiochus IV in Jerusalem: Numismatic Evidence on the Prelude to the Maccabean Revolt," *Israel Numismatic Journal* 14 (2000/2002) 59–77.

Barclay, John M. G.
Jews in the Mediterranean Diaspora: From Alexander to Trajan (323 BCE–117 CE) (Edinburgh: T&T Clark, 1996).

Bar-Kochva, Bezalel
Judas Maccabaeus: The Jewish Struggle against the Seleucids (Cambridge: Cambridge University Press, 1989).

Idem
Pseudo-Hecataeus, On the Jews: Legitimizing the Jewish Diaspora (Hellenistic Culture and Society 21; Berkeley: University of California Press, 1996).

Idem
The Seleucid Army: Organization and Tactics in the Great Campaigns (Cambridge: Cambridge University Press, 1976).

Baslez, Marie-Françoise
"The Origin of the Martyrdom Images: From the Book of Maccabees to the First Christians," in Géza G. Xeravits and József Zsengellér, eds., *The Books of the Maccabees: History, Theology, Ideology* (JSJSup 118; Leiden: Brill, 2007) 113–30.

Baumgarten, Joseph M.
Studies in Qumran Law (SJLA 24; Leiden: Brill, 1977).

Beckwith, Roger T.
The Old Testament Canon of the New Testament Church and Its Background in Early Judaism (London: SPCK, 1985).

Bedard, Stephen J.
"Hellenistic Influence on the Idea of Resurrection in Jewish Apocalyptic Literature," *Journal of Greco-Roman Christianity and Judaism* 5 (2008) 174–89.

Bell, Henry I.
"Philanthropia in the Papyri of the Roman Period," *Hommages à Joseph Bidez et à Franz Cumont* (Collection Latomus 2; Brussels: Latomus, 1949) 31–37.

Ben-Dor, S.
"Some New Seleucid Coins," *PEQ* 78 (1946) 43–48.

Bengtson, Hermann
Die Strategie in der hellenistischen Zeit: Ein Beitrag zum antiken Staatsrecht (3 vols.; Munich: Beck, 1964–67).

Benoit, P., J. T. Milik, and R. de Vaux
Les grottes de Murabba'at (2 vols.; DJD 2; Oxford: Clarendon, 1961).

Bergren, Theodore A.
"Nehemiah in 2 Maccabees 1:10–2:18," *JSJ* 28 (1997) 249–70.

Bergson, Leif
"*Eiron* und *Eironeia*," *Hermes* 99 (1971) 409–22.

Berthelot, Katell
"The Biblical Conquest of the Promised Land and the Hasmonaean Wars according to 1 and 2 Maccabees," in Géza G. Xeravits and József Zsengellér, eds., *The Books of the Maccabees: History, Theology, Ideology* (JSJSup 118; Leiden: Brill, 2007) 45–60.

Bertram, G.
"ἐμπαίζω," *TDNT* 5 (1967) 630–36.

Bevan, E. R.
"A Note on Antiochus Epiphanes," *JHS* 20 (1900) 26–30.

Bickerman [Bickermann], Elias J.
"Ἀνάδειξις," *Annuaire de l'Institut Philologie et d'Histoire Orientales et Slaves de l'Université libre de Bruxelles* 5 (1937) 117–24.

Idem
"Beiträge zur antiken Urkundengeschichte, I: Der Heimatsvermerk und die staatsrechtliche Stellung der Hellenen im ptolemäischen Ägypten," *Archiv für Papyrusforschung und verwandte Gebiete* 8 (1927) 216–39.

Idem
"Un document relatif à la persécution d'Antiochos IV Épiphane," in idem, *Studies in Jewish and Christian History* (3 vols.; AGJU 9; Leiden: Brill, 1976–86) 2:105–35.

Idem
Der Gott der Makkabäer: Untersuchung über Sinn und Ursprung der makkabäischen Erhebung (Berlin:

Schocken, 1937). English translation, *The God of the Maccabees: Studies in the Meaning and Origin of the Maccabean Revolt* (SJLA 32; Leiden: Brill, 1979).

Idem

"Héliodore au Temple de Jérusalem," *Annuaire de l'Institut de Philologie et d'Histoire Orientales et Slaves de l'Université libre de Bruxelles* 7 (1939–44) 5–40. Reprinted in idem, *Studies in Jewish and Christian History* (2 vols.; AGJU 9; Leiden: Brill, 1980) 2:159–91.

Idem

Institutions des Séleucides (Bibliothèque archéologique et historique 26; Paris: Geuthner, 1938).

Idem

"Ein jüdischer Festbrief vom Jahre 124 v. Chr. (2 Makk. 1:1-9)," *ZNW* 32 (1933) 233–54.

Idem

"Makkabäerbücher (I. und II.)," *PW* 14:779–97.

Idem

"Une question d'authenticité: Les privileges juifs," in idem, *Studies in Jewish and Christian History* (3 vols.; AGJU 9; Leiden: Brill, 1976–86) 2:24–43.

Idem

Studies in Jewish and Christian History (3 vols.; AGJU 9; Leiden: Brill, 1976–86).

Idem

Studies in Jewish and Christian History: A New Edition in English including The God of the Maccabees (ed. Amram D. Tropper; AGJU 68; Leiden: Brill, 2007).

Idem

"Sur une inscription grecque de Sidon," in *Mélanges syriens offerts à Monsieur René Dussaud* (2 vols.; Paris: Geuthner, 1939) 1:91–99.

Bieler, Ludwig

ΘΕΙΟΣ ΑΝΗΡ: *Das Bild des "göttlichen Menschen" in Spätantike und Frühchristentum* (1935–36; reprinted, Darmstadt: Wissenschaftliche Buchgesellschaft, 1976).

Bilde, Per, et al.

Religion and Religious Practice in the Seleucid Kingdom (Aarhus: Aarhus University, 1990).

Bilde, Per, Troels Engberg-Pedersen, et al., eds.

Ethnicity in Hellenistic Egypt (Aarhus: Aarhuis University Press, 1992).

Blinkenberg, Christian

"Die lindische Tempelchronik," *Kleine Texte für Vorlesungen und Übungen* 31 (Bonn: A. Marcus & E. Weber, 1915).

Blinkenberg, Christian, and Karl F. Kinch

Lindos: Fouilles et recherches (1902–1914 et 1952) (Berlin: de Gruyter, 1931–60).

Blosser, Don

"The Sabbath Year Cycle in Josephus," *HUCA* 52 (1981) 129–39.

Bölte, F.

"Tyros," *PW* (1948) 7A:1896.

Bolyki, János

"'As Soon as the Signal was Given' (2 Macc 4:14): Gymnasia in the Service of Hellenism," in Géza G. Xeravits and József Zsengellér, eds., *The Books of the Maccabees: History, Theology, Ideology* (JSJSup 118; Leiden: Brill, 2007) 131–39.

Bonnet, Corinne

Melqart: Cultes et mythes de l'Héraclès tyrien en Méditerranée (Studia Phoenicia 8; Leuven: Peeters, 1988).

Borgen, Peder

"'Yes,' 'No,' 'How Far': The Participation of Jews and Christians in Pagan Cults," in idem, *Early Christianity and Hellenistic Judaism* (Edinburgh: T&T Clark, 1996) 15–43.

Bott, Heinrich

De epitomis antiquis (Marpurgi Chattorum: J. Hamel, 1920).

Bowersock, Glen W.

Martyrdom and Rome (Cambridge: Cambridge University Press, 1995).

Brady, Thomas A.

"The Gymnasium in Ptolemaic Egypt," in R. P. Robinson, ed., *Philological Studies in Honour of Walter Miller* (Columbia: University of Missouri Press, 1936) 9–20.

Brélaz, Cédric

"Les bienfaiteurs, 'sauveurs' et 'fossoyeurs' de la cite hellénistique? Une approche historiographique de l'évergétisme," in Olivier Curty, ed., *L'huile et l'argent: Gymnasiarchie et évergétisme dans la Grèce hellénistique. Actes du colloque tenu à Fribourg du 13 au 15 octobre 2005, publiés en l'honneur du Professeur Marcel Piérart à l'occasion de son 60ème anniversaire* (Paris: Boccard, 2009) 37–56.

Idem

La sécurité publique en Asie Mineure sous le Principat (Ier–IIIème s. ap. J.-C.). Institutions municipals et institutions imperials dans l'Orient romain (Basel: Schwabe, 2005).

Bremmer Jan N.

"Close Encounters of the Third Kind: Heliodorus in the Temple and Paul on the Road to Damascus," in Alberdina Houtman, Albert de Jong, and Magda Misset-van de Weg, eds., *Empsychoi Logoi— Religious Innovations in Antiquity* (Leiden: Brill, 2008) 367–84.

Brichto, Herbert Chanan

"Kin, Cult, Land and Afterlife—A Biblical Complex," *HUCA* 44 (1973) 1–54.

Brief, Siegmund

Die Conjunctionen bei Polybius (Vienna: Verlag des k.k. Staatsgymnasium im XVII Bezirke von Wien [Hernals], 1891–94).

Idem

"Wie beeinflusst die Vermeidung des Hiatus den Stil des Polybius?" in *Dreiundfünfzigster Jahresbericht*

*des k.k. deutschen Staats-Obergymnasium in Un.-
Hradisch für das Schuljahr 1906–1907* (Ungarisch-
Hradisch: Verlag des k.k. deutschen Staats-
Oberymnasium, 1907) 3–20.

Bringmann, Klaus
"Gymnasion und griechische Bildung im Nahen
Osten," in Daniel Kah and Peter Scholz, eds.,
Das hellenistische Gymnasion (Wissenskultur und
gesellschaftlicher Wandel 8; Berlin: Akademie,
2004) 323–33.

Idem
*Hellenistische Reform und Religionsverfolgung in
Judäa: Eine Untersuchung zur jüdisch-hellenistischen
Geschichte (175–163 v.Chr.)* (Abhandlungen der
Akademie der Wissenschaften in Göttingen,
Philologisch-Historische Klasse 3/132; Göttingen:
Vandenhoeck & Ruprecht, 1983).

Idem
*Schenkungen hellenistischer Herrscher an griechische
Städte und Heiligtümer,* part 2: *Historische und
archäologische Auswertung,* vol. 1: *Geben und Nehmen:
Monarchische Wohltätigkeit und Selbstdarstellung im
Zeitalter des Hellenismus* (Berlin: Akademie, 2000).

Idem
"Die Verfolgung der jüdischen Religion durch
Antiochos IV: Ein Konflikt zwischen Judentum
und Hellenismus?" *Antike und Abendland* 26 (1980)
176–90.

Bringmann, Klaus, Hans von Steuben, Walter
Ameling, and Barbara Schmidt-Dounas
*Schenkungen hellenistischer Herrscher an griechische
Städte und Heiligtümer,* part 1: *Zeugnisse und
Kommentare* (Berlin: Akademie, 1995).

Brooke, George J.
"The Explicit Presentation of Scripture in
4QMMT," in Moshe Bernstein et al., eds., *Legal
Texts and Legal Issues: Proceedings of the Second
Meeting of the International Organization for Qumran
Studies, Cambridge, 1995: Published in Honour of
Joseph M. Baumgarten* (STDJ 23; Leiden: Brill,
1997) 67–88.

Broshi, Magen, and Esther Eshel
"The Greek King Is Antiochus IV (4QHistorical
Text = 4Q248)," *JJS* 48 (1997) 120–29.

Brown, Peter
*The Body and Society: Men, Women, and Sexual
Renunciation in Early Christianity* (New York:
Columbia University Press, 1988).

Bruneau, Philippe
Recherches sur les cultes de Delos (Bibliothèque des
écoles françaises d'Athènes et de Rome 217; Paris:
E. de Boccard, 1970).

Brunet de Presle, Wladimir. *See* Letronne, Antoine-
Jean.

Bruston, Charles
"Trois lettres des Juifs de Palestine," *ZAW* 10
(1890) 115.

Bruyne, Donatien de
Les anciennes traductions latines des Machabées

(Anecdota Maredsolana 4; Maredsous: Abbaye de
Maredsous, 1932).

Idem
"Mélanges. II. Argarizim (II Mach. 5,23; 6,2); III.
Εκ των ομματων (II Mch. 9,9); IV. Εγκλειειν,
κατακλειειν, παρακλειειν (II Mach. 5,8; 4,34;
13,21)," *RB* 18 (1921) 405–9.

Idem
"Le texte grec des deux premiers livres des
Machabées," *RB* 19 (1922) 31–54.

Idem
"Le texte grec du deuxième livre des Machabées,"
RB 39 (1930) 503–19.

Büchler, Adolf
*Die Tobiaden und die Oniaden im II. Makkabäerbuch
und in der verwandten jüdisch-hellenistischen Literatur*
(Vienna: Verlag der Israel.-theol. Lehranstalt,
1899).

Bückers, Hermann
"Das 'ewige Leben' in 2 Makk 7,36," *Bib* 21 (1940)
406–12.

Buckler, William H.
"Labour Disputes in the Province of Asia," in
William H. Buckler and William M. Calder, eds.,
*Anatolian Studies Presented to Sir William Mitchell
Ramsay* (Manchester: Manchester Press, 1923)
27–50.

Bunge, Jochen Gabriel
"Hasmonäer," *JSJ* 6 (1975) 1–46.

Idem
"Die sogenannte Religionsverfolgung Antiochos
IV Epiphanes und die griechischen Städte," *JSJ* 10
(1979) 155–65.

Idem
"'Theos Epiphanes': Zu den ersten fünf
Regierungsjahren Antiochos IV. Epiphanes,"
Historia 23 (1974) 57–85.

Idem
*Untersuchungen zum zweiten Makkabäerbuch:
Quellenkritische, literarische, chronologische
und historische Untersuchungen zum zweiten
Makkabäerbuch als Quelle syrisch-palästinenischer
Geschichte im 2. Jh.v.Chr.* (Bonn: Rheinische
Friedrich-Wilhelms-Universität, 1971).

Idem
"Zur Geschichte und Chronologie des Untergangs
der Oniaden und des Aufstiegs der Hasmonäer,"
JSJ 6 (1975) 1–46.

Burkert, Walter
Greek Religion (trans. John Raffan; Cambridge,
Mass.: Harvard University Press, 1985).

Cancik, Hubert, and Helmuth Schneider, eds.
Brill's New Pauly: Encyclopedia of the Ancient World
(16 vols.; Leiden: Brill, 2002–10).

Carlsson, Susanne
*Hellenistic Democracies: Freedom, Independence, and
Political Procedure in Some East Greek City-states*
(Historia, Einzelschriften 206; Stuttgart: Franz
Steiner, 2010).

Chaniotis, Angelos, and Joannis Mylonopoulos
"Epigraphic Bulletin for Greek Religion 2001,"
Kernos 17 (2004) 187–249.
Idem
War in the Hellenistic World: A Social and Cultural History (Oxford: Blackwell, 2005).
Chankowskii, Andrzej S.
"Date et circonstances de l'institution de l'éphébie à Érétrie," *Dialogues d'histoire ancienne* 19 (1993) 17–44.
Idem
"L'entraînement militaire des éphèbes dans les cités grecques d'Asie Mineure à l'époque hellénistique: nécessité pratique ou tradition atrophée?" in Jean-Christophe Couvenhes, Henri-Louis Fernoux, eds., *Les cités grecques et la guerre en Asie Mineure à l'époque hellénistique* (Tours: Presses Universitaires François-Rabelais, 2004) 55–76.
Idem
"L'éphébie, une institution d'éducation civique," in Jean-Marie Pailler and Pascal Payen, eds., *Que reste-t-il de l'éducation classique? Relire "le Marrou," Histoire de l'éducation dans l'Antiquité* (Toulouse: Presses Universitaires de Mirail, 2004) 271–79.
Idem
"Processions et ceremonies d'accueil: une image de la cité de la basse époque hellénistique?" in P. Fröhlich and C. Müller, eds., *Citoyenneté et Participation à la basse époque hellénistique* (Geneva: Droz, 2005) 185–206.
Idem
"Les souverains hellénistiques et l'institution du gymnase: politiques royales et modèles culturels," in Olivier Curty, ed., *L'huile et l'argent: Gymnasiarchie et évergétisme dans la Grèce hellénistique. Actes du colloque tenu à Fribourg du 13 au 15 octobre 2005, publiés en l'honneur du Professeur Marcel Piérart à l'occasion de son 60ème anniversaire* (Paris: Boccard, 2009) 95–114.
Chantraine, Pierre
Histoire du Parfait grec (Paris: H. Champion, 1927).
Chazon, Esther G.
"'Gather the Dispersed of Judah': Seeking a Return to the Land as a Factor in Jewish Identity of Late Antiquity," in Lynn LiDonnici and Andrea Lieber, eds., *Heavenly Tablets: Interpretation, Identity and Tradition in Ancient Judaism* (JSJSup 119; Leiden: Brill, 2007) 159–75.
Chiricat, Édouard
"Funérailles publiques et enterrement au gymnase à l'époque hellénistique," in P. Fröhlich and C. Müller, eds., *Citoyenneté et Participation à la basse époque hellénistique* (Geneva: Droz, 2005) 207–23.
Cohen, Getzel M.
The Seleucid Colonies: Studies in Founding, Administration and Organization (Historia, Einzelschriften 30; Wiesbaden: Steiner, 1978).

Cohen, Shaye J. D.
The Beginnings of Jewishness: Boundaries, Varieties, Uncertainties (Hellenistic Culture and Society 31; Berkeley: University of California Press, 1999).
Idem
"Ἰουδαῖος τὸ γένος and Related Expressions in Josephus," in Fausto Parente and Joseph Sievers, eds., *Josephus and the History of the Greco-Roman Period: Essays in Memory of Morton Smith* (SPB 41; Leiden: Brill, 1994) 23–38.
Idem
"Ioudaios: 'Judaean' and 'Jew' in Susanna, First Maccabees, and Second Maccabees," in Peter Schäfer, ed., *Geschichte–Traditon–Reflexion: Festschrift für Martin Hengel zum 70. Geburtstag*, vol. 1: *Judentum* (Tübingen: Mohr, 1996) 211–20.
Idem
"Religion, Ethnicity and 'Hellenism' in the Emergence of Jewish Identity in Maccabean Palestine," in Per Bilde et al., eds., *Religion and Religious Practice in the Seleucid Kingdom* (Studies in Hellenistic Civilization 1; Aarhus: Aarhus University Press, 1990) 204–23.
Coleman, K. M.
"Fatal Charades: Roman Executions Staged as Mythological Enactments," *JRS* 80 (1990) 44–75.
Collins, John J.
Daniel: A Commentary on the Book of Daniel (Hermeneia; Minneapolis: Fortress Press, 1993).
Idem
"New Light on the Book of Daniel from the Dead Sea Scrolls," in Florentino García Martínez and Ed Noort, eds., *Perspectives in the Study of the Old Testament and Early Judaism: A Symposium in Honour of Adam S. van der Woude on the Occasion of His 70th Birthday* (VTSup 73; Leiden: Brill, 1998) 180–96.
Idem
The Scepter and the Star: The Messiahs of the Dead Sea Scrolls and Other Ancient Literature (ABRL; New York: Doubleday, 1995).
Collins, John J., and Gregory E. Sterling,
Hellenism in the Land of Israel (Notre Dame, Ind.: University of Notre Dame Press, 2001).
Connor, Walter R.
Theopompus and Fifth-Century Athens (Washington, D.C.: Center for Hellenic Studies, 1968).
Copan, Paul
"Is *Creatio ex Nihilo* a Post-Biblical Invention? An Examination of Gerhard May's Proposal," *Trinity Journal* n.s. 17 (1996) 75–93.
Corsten, Thomas
Die Inschriften von Prusa ad Olympum (2 vols.; Inschriften griechischer Städte aus Kleinasien 39, 40; Bonn: Habelt, 1991, 1993).
Cotton, Hannah M.
"The Guardianship of Jesus Son of Babatha: Roman and Local Law in the Province of Arabia," *JRS* 83 (1993) 94–108.

Eadem

"The Law of Succession in the Documents from the Judaean Desert Again," *SCI* 17 (1998) 115–23.

Cotton, Hannah M., and Michael Wörrle

"Seleukos IV to Heliodoros: A New Dossier of Royal Correspondence from Israel," *ZPE* 159 (2007) 191–205.

Couvenhes, Jean-Christophe, and Henri-Louis Fernoux, eds.

Les cités grecques et la guerre en Asie Mineure à l'époque hellénistique (Tours: Universitaires François-Rabelais, 2004).

Cowey, James M. S.

Urkunden des Politeuma der Juden von Herakleopolis (144/3–133/2 v. Chr) (P. Polit. Jud.) (Abhandlungen der Nordrhein-Westfälischen Akademie der Wissenschaften, Papyrologica Coloniensia 29; Wiesbaden: Westdeutscher Verlag, 2001).

Cowley, Arthur E.

Aramaic Papyri of the Fifth Century B.C. (Osnabrück: Zeller, 1967).

Crönert, Wilhelm

"Die beiden ältesten griechischen Briefe," *Rheinisches Museum* 65 (1910) 157.

Cross, Frank Moore

"The Divine Warrior in Israel's Early Cult," in Alexander Altman, ed., *Biblical Motifs: Origins and Transformations* (Philip W. Lown Institute of Advanced Judaic Studies, Brandeis University, Studies and Texts 3; Cambridge, Mass.: Harvard University Press, 1966) 11–30.

Cumont, Franz

Fouilles de Doura-Europos (1922–1923) (Paris: Geuthner, 1926).

Curty, Olivier, ed.

L'huile et l'argent: Gymnasiarchie et évergétisme dans la Grèce hellénistique. Actes du colloque tenu à Fribourg du 13 au 15 octobre 2005, publiés en l'honneur du Professeur Marcel Piérart à l'occasion de son 60ème anniversaire (Paris: Boccard, 2009).

Daniel, Suzanne

Recherches sur le vocabulaire du culte dans le Septante (Paris: Klincksieck, 1966).

Danker, Frederick W.

Benefactor: Epigraphic Study of a Graeco-Roman and New Testament Semantic Field (St. Louis: Clayton, 1982).

Daux, Georges

Delphes au IIe et au Ier siècle depuis l'abaissement de l'Etolie jusqu'à la paix romaine 191–31 av. J.-C. (Bibliothèque des écoles françaises d'Athènes et de Rome 140; Paris: Boccard, 1936).

Davies, Philip R.

"*Hasidim* in the Maccabean Period," *JJS* 28 (1977) 127–40.

Deissmann, Adolf

Bible Studies: Contributions, Chiefly from Papyri and Inscriptions, to the History of the Language, the Literature, and the Religion of Hellenistic Judaism and Primitive Christianity (trans. Alexander Grieve; Edinburgh: T&T Clark, 1901).

Delcor, Mathias

"Le temple d'Onias en Egypte," *RB* 75 (1968) 188–205.

Delia, Diana

Alexandrian Citizenship during the Roman Principate (American Classical Studies 23; Atlanta: Scholars Press, 1991).

Delling, Gerhard

"Καιρός," *TDNT* 3 (1965) 455–59.

Delorme, Jean

Gymnasion: Étude sur les monuments consacrés à l'éducation en Grèce (des origines à l'Empire romain) (Bibliothèque des écoles françaises d'Athènes et de Rome 196; Paris: Boccard, 1960).

Denniston, J. D.

The Greek Particles (2nd ed.; Oxford: Clarendon, 1970).

Idem

Greek Prose Style (Oxford: Clarendon, 1965).

Dexinger, Ferdinand

"Der Ursprung der Samaritaner im Spiegel der frühen Quellen," in Ferdinand Dexinger and Reinhard Pummer, eds., *Die Samaritaner* (Darmstadt: Wissenschaftliche Buchgesellschaft, 1992) 67–140.

D'Huys, V.

"*ΧΡΗΣΙΜΟΝ ΚΑΙ ΤΕΡΠΝΟΝ* in Polybios' Schlachtschilderungen: Einige literarische Topoi in seiner Darstellung der Schlacht bei Zama (XV 9-16)," in Herman Verdin, Guido Schepens, and Els de Keyser, eds., *Purposes of History: Studies in Greek Historiography from the 4th to the 2nd Centuries B.C. Proceedings of the International Colloquium, Leuven, 24–26 May 1988* (Studia Hellenistica 30; Louvain: n.p., 1990) 267–88.

Diels, Hermann

Die Fragmente der Vorsokratiker: Griechisch und Deutsch (3 vols.; Berlin: Weidmann, 1922).

Idem

Philodemos über die Götter: Erstes Buch (Berlin: Georg Reimer, 1916).

Diels, Hermann, and Erwin Schramm

Exzerpte aus Philons Mechanik B.VII und VIII (Berlin: Akademie der Wissenschaften, 1920).

Dimant, Devorah

"An Apocryphon of Jeremiah from Cave 4 (4Q385[B] = 4Q385 16)," in George J. Brooke, ed., *New Qumran Texts and Studies: Proceedings of the First Meeting of the International Organization for Qumran Studies, Paris, 1992* (STDJ 15; Leiden: Brill, 1994) 11–30.

Eadem

"4Q127—An Unknown Jewish Apocryphal Work?" in David P. Wright, David Noel Freedman, and Avi Hurwitz, eds., *Pomegranates and Golden Bells: Studies in Biblical, Jewish, and Near Eastern Ritual, Law and Literature in Honor of Jacob Milgrom* (Winona Lake, Ind.: Eisenbrauns, 1995) 805–13.

Eadem, ed.

Qumran Cave 4.XXI: Parabiblical Texts, Part 4: Pseudo-Prophetic Texts (DJD 30; Oxford: Clarendon 2001).

Dimitrova, Nora M.

Theoroi and Initiates in Samothrace: The Epigraphical Evidence (Princeton: American School of Classical Studies at Athens, 2008).

Dobbeler, Stephanie von

Die Bücher 1/2 Makkabäer (Neue Stuttgarter Kommentar: Altes Testament 11; Stuttgart: Katholisches Bibelwerk, 1997).

Doran, Robert

"2 Maccabees 6:2 and the Samaritan Question," *HTR* 76 (1983) 481–85.

Idem

"The High Cost of a Good Education," in John J. Collins and Gregory E. Sterling, eds., *Hellenism in the Land of Israel* (Christianity and Judaism in Antiquity 13; Notre Dame, Ind.: University of Notre Dame Press, 2001) 94–115.

Idem

"Jason's Gymnasion," in Harold W. Attridge, John J. Collins, Thomas H. Tobin, eds., *Of Scribes and Scrolls: Studies on the Hebrew Bible, Intertestamental Judaism, and Christian Origins Presented to John Strugnell on the Occasion of His Sixtieth Birthday* (College Theology Society Resources in Religion 5; Lanham, Md.: University Press of America, 1990) 99–109.

Idem

The Lives of Simeon Stylites (Cistercian Studies Series 112; Kalamazoo, Mich.: Cistercian, 1992).

Idem

"The Martyr: A Synoptic View of the Mother and Her Seven Sons," in John J. Collins and George W. E. Nickelsburg, eds., *Ideal Figures in Ancient Judaism: Profiles and Paradigms* (SBLSCS 12; Chico, Calif.: Scholars Press, 1980) 189–221.

Idem

"The Persecution of Judeans by Antiochus IV: The Significance of 'Ancestral Laws,'" in Daniel C. Harlow et al., eds., *The "Other" in Second Temple Judaism: Essays in Honor of John J. Collins* (Grand Rapids: Eerdmans, 2011), 423–33.

Idem

"The First Book of Maccabees and the Second Book of Maccabees," *The New Interpreter's Bible* (13 vols.; Nashville: Abingdon, 1994–2004) 4:1–299.

Idem

Temple Propaganda: The Purpose and Character of 2 Maccabees (CBQMS 12; Washington, D.C.: Catholic Biblical Association, 1981).

Dorival, Gilles

"'Dire en grec les choses juives': Quelques choix lexicaux du pentateuque de la septante," *REG* 109 (1996) 527–47.

Dormeyer, Detlev

"Pragmatische und pathetische Geschichtsschreibung in der griechischen Historiographie, im Frühjudentum und im Neuen Testament," in Thomas Schmeller, ed., *Historiographie und Biographie im Neuen Testament und seiner Umwelt* (NTOA 69; Göttingen: Vandenhoeck & Ruprecht, 2009) 1–33.

Drew-Bear, T.

"Recherches épigraphiques et philologiques, I: Où mourut Antiochos IV?" *REA* 2 (1980) 155–57.

Idem

"An Act of Foundation at Hypaipa," *Chiron* 10 (1980) 509–36.

Dürrbach, Félix

Choix d'inscriptions de Délos (Paris: E. Leroux, 1921–22).

Eddy, Samuel K.

The King Is Dead: Studies in the Near Eastern Resistance to Hellenism, 334–31 B.C. (Lincoln: Univerity of Nebraska Press, 1961).

Edson, Charles

"Imperium Macedonicum: The Seleucid Empire and the Literary Evidence," *CP* 53 (1958) 153–70.

Efron, Joshua

Studies in the Hasmonean Period (SJLA 39; Leiden: Brill, 1987).

Ego, Beato

"God's Justice: The 'Measure for Measure' Principle in 2 Maccabees," in Géza G. Xeravits and József Zsengellér, eds., *The Books of the Maccabees: History, Theology, Ideology* (JSJSup 118; Leiden: Brill, 2007) 141–54.

Ekroth, Gunnel

The Sacrificial Rituals of Greek Hero-Cults in the Archaic to the Early Hellenistic Periods (Kernos Supplément 12; Liège: Centre international d'étude de la religion grecque antique, 2002).

Enermalm-Ogawa, Agneta

Un langage de prière juif en grec: Le témoinage des deux premiers livres des Maccabées (ConBNT 17; Stockholm: Almqvist & Wiksell, 1987).

Exler, Francis Xavier J.

The Form of the Ancient Greek Letter: A Study in Greek Epistolography (Washington, D.C.: Catholic University of America Press, 1923).

Fallon, Francis

"Eupolemus," *OTP* 2:861–72.

Fiensy, David A.

Prayers Alleged to be Jewish: An Examination of the Constitutiones Apostolorum (BJS 65; Chico, Calif.: Scholars Press, 1985).

Fine, Stephen
"On the Development of a Symbol: The Date Palm in Roman Palestine and the Jews," *JSP* 4 (1989) 105–18.

Fischer, M., and R. E. Jackson-Tal
"A Glass Pendant in the Shape of Harpokrates from Yavneh-Yam, Israel," *Journal of Glass Studies* 35 (2003) 35–40.

Fischer, Thomas
"Heliodor im Tempel zu Jerusalem: Ein 'hellenistischer' Aspekt der 'frommen Legende,'" in Rüdiger Liwak and Siegfried Wagner, eds., *Prophetie und geschichtliche Wirklichkeit im alten Israel: Festschrift für Siegfried Herrmann zum 65. Geburtstag* (Stuttgart: Kohlhammer, 1991) 122–33.

Idem
Seleukiden und Makkabäer: Beiträge zur Seleukidengeschichte und zu den politischen Ereignissen in Judäa während der 1. Hälfte des 2. Jahrhunderts v. Chr. (Bochum: Brockmeyer, 1980).

Fitzmyer, Joseph A.
"Some Notes on Aramaic Epistolography," *JBL* 93 (1974) 201–25.

Idem
Tobit (Commentaries on Early Jewish Literature; Berlin and New York: de Gruyter, 2003).

Idem
"The Use of Explicit Old Testament Quotations in Qumran Literature and in the New Testament," *Essays on the Semitic Background of the New Testament* (Sources for Biblical Study 5; Missoula, Mont.: Scholars Press, 1974) 3–58.

Forbes, Clarence A.
"Expanded Uses of the Greek Gymnasium," *CP* 40 (1945) 32–42.

Idem
Greek Physical Education (New York: Century, 1929).

Forbes, Robert J.
Studies in Ancient Technology (9 vols.; Leiden: Brill, 1964).

Foucault, Jules A. de
Recherches sur la langue et le style de Polybe (Collection d'études anciennes; Paris: Belles Lettres, 1972).

Fox, Robin Lane
Pagans and Christians (New York: Knopf, 1987).

Frederiksen, Paula
"Mandatory Retirement: Ideas in the Study of Christian Origins Whose Time to Go Has Come," *SR* 35 (2006) 231–46.

Fritz, Kurt von
"Die Bedeutung des Aristotles für die Geschichtsschreibung," in *Histoire et historiens dans l'antiquité: Sept exposés et discussions par Kurt Latte et al., Vandoeuvres-Genève, 2–8 août 1956* (Fondation Hardt, Entretiens sur l'Antiquitéclassique 4; Geneva: n.p., 1958) 85–128.

Fröhlich, Pierre
"Les activités évergétiques des gymnasiarques à l'époque hellénistique tardive: la fourniture de l'huile," in Olivier Curty, ed., *L'huile et l'argent: Gymnasiarchie et évergétisme dans la Grèce hellénistique. Actes du colloque tenu à Fribourg du 13 au 15 octobre 2005, publiés en l'honneur du Professeur Marcel Piérart à l'occasion de son 60ème anniversaire* (Paris: Boccard, 2009) 57–94.

Idem
"Dépenses publiques et évergétisme des citoyens dans l'exercice des charges publiques à Priène à la basse époque hellénistique," in P. Fröhlich and C. Müller, eds., *Citoyenneté et Participation à la basse époque hellénistique* (Geneva: Droz, 2005) 225–56.

Fröhlich, Pierre, and Christel Müller, eds.
Citoyenneté et Participation à la basse époque hellénistique (Geneva: Droz, 2005).

Frye, Richard N.
The History of Ancient Iran (HA 3.7; Munich: Beck, 1983).

Fuchs, Leo
Die Juden Ägyptens in ptolemäischer und römischer Zeit (Vienna: Rath, 1924).

Fujita, Shozo
"The Metaphor of Plant in Jewish Literature of the Intertestamental Period," *JSJ* 7 (1976) 30–45.

Fuks, Alexander
The Ancestral Constitution: Four Studies in Athenian Party Politics at the End of the Fifth Century B.C. (London: Routledge & Kegan Paul, 1953).

Funk, Robert W.
"Beth-Zur," in Ephraim Stern, ed., *The New Encyclopedia of Archeological Excavations in the Holy Land* (4 vols.; Jerusalem: Israel Exploration Society and Carta, 1993) 1:259–61.

Gafni, Isaiah M.
"Concepts of Periodization and Causality in Talmudic Literature," *JH* 10 (1996) 28–29.

Galdi, Marco
L'epitome nella letteratura Latina (Naples: P. Frederico & G. Ardia, 1922).

Garlan, Yvon
"Études d'histoire militaire et diplomatique, XII: ΣΥΝΘΗΜΑΤΑ," *BCH* 100 (1976) 299–302.

Gauger, Jörg-Dieter
"Der 'Tod des Verfolgers': Überlegungen zur Historizität eines Topos," *JSJ* 33 (2002) 42–64.

Gauthier, Philippe
"Bulletin épigraphique," *REG* 105 (1992) 435–47

Gera, Dov
Judaea and Mediterranean Politics 219 to 161 B.C.E. (Jewish Studies 8; Leiden: Brill, 1998).

Idem
"Olympiodoros, Heliodoros and the Temples of Koilê Syria and Phoinikê," *ZPE* 169 (2009) 125–55.

Idem

"On the Credibility of the History of the Tobiads (Josephus, *Antiquities* 12, 156–222, 228–236)," in A. Kasher, U. Rappaport and G. Fuks, eds., *Greece and Rome in Eretz Israel: Collected Essays* (Jerusalem: Yad Ben-Zvi, 1990) 29–30.

Idem

"Philonides the Epicurean at Court: Early Connections," *ZPE* 125 (1999) 77–83.

Idem

"Tryphon's Sling Bullet from Dor," *IEJ* 35 (1985) 153–63.

Gera, Dov, and Wayne Horowitz

"Antiochus IV in Life and Death: Evidence from the Babylonian Astronomical Diaries," *JAOS* 117 (1997) 240–52.

Gil, Luis

"Sobre el estilo de libro 2 de los Macabeos," *Emérita* 26 (1958) 11–32.

Ginzberg, Louis

Legends of the Jews (trans. Henrietta Szold; 7 vols.; Philadelphia: Jewish Publication Society, 1925).

Giovannini, G.

"The Connection between Tragedy and History in Ancient Criticism," *Philological Quarterly* 22 (1943) 308–14.

Goldstein, Jonathan A.

"The Origins of the Doctrine of Creation ex Nihilo," *JJS* 35 (1984) 127–35.

Goodman, Martin

"Explaining Change in Judaism in Late Antiquity," in Alberdina Houtman, Albert de Jong, Magda Misset-van de Weg, eds., *Empsychoi Logoi—Religious Innovations in Antiquity* (Leiden: Brill, 2008) 19–27.

Idem, ed.

Jews in a Greco-Roman World (Oxford: Clarendon, 1998).

Idem

"Kosher Olive Oil in Antiquity," in Philip R. Davies and Richard T. White, eds., *A Tribute to Geza Vermes: Essays on Jewish and Christian Literature and History* (JSOTSup 100; Sheffield: JSOT Press, 1990) 227–45.

Goodman, Martin, and A. J. Holladay

"Religious Scruples in Ancient Warfare," *Classical Quarterly* 36 (1986) 151–71.

Goudriaan, Koen

Ethnicity in Ptolemaic Egypt (Dutch Monographs on Ancient History and Archaeology 5; Amsterdam: Gieben, 1988).

Gould, John P.

"HIKETEIA," *JHS* 93 (1973) 74–103.

Grabbe, Lester L.

"The Hellenistic City of Jerusalem," in John R. Bartlett, ed., *Jews in the Hellenistic and Roman Cities* (London/New York: Routledge, 2002) 6–21.

Idem

Judaism from Cyrus to Hadrian (2 vols.; Minneapolis: Fortress Press, 1992).

Idem

"Maccabean Chronology: 167–164 or 168–165 BCE?" *JBL* 110 (1991) 59–74.

Graf, Fritz

"Dionysia," *Brills New Pauly* 4:470.

Grainger, John D.

A Seleukid Prosopography and Gazetteer (Mnemosyne Supplement 172; Leiden: Brill, 1997).

Grätz, Heinrich

"Die Sendschreiben der Palästinenser an die ägyptisch-judäischen Gemeinden wegen der Feier der Tempelweihe," *Monatschrift für Geschichte und Wissenschaft des Judentums* 26 (1877) 1–16, 49–72.

Green, Peter

From Alexander to Actium: The Historical Evolution of the Hellenistic Age (Hellenistic Culture and Society 1; Berkeley: University of California Press, 1990).

Greenfield, Jonas C., and Michael E. Stone

"The Aramaic and Greek Fragments of a Levi Document," in Harm W. Hollander and Marinus de Jonge, *The Testaments of the Twelve Patriarchs: A Commentary* (SVTP 8; Leiden: Brill, 1985) 457–69.

Greenfield, Jonas C., Michael E. Stone, and Esther Eshel

The Aramaic Levi Document: Edition, Translation, Commentary (SVTP 19; Leiden: Brill, 2004).

Griffiths, J. Gwyn

"Βασιλεὺς βασιλέων: Remarks on the History of a Title," *CP* 48 (1953) 145–54.

Grimm, Carl L.W.

Das erste Buch der Maccabäer (Leipzig: Hirzel, 1853).

Gruen, Erich S.

"The Bacchanalian Affair," in idem, *Studies in Greek Culture and Roman Policy* (Cincinnati Classical Studies 7; Berkeley: University of California Press, 1990) 34–78.

Idem

Diaspora: Jews amidst Greeks and Romans (Cambridge, Mass.: Harvard University Press, 2002).

Idem

"Fact and Fiction: Jewish Legends in a Hellenistic Context," in Paul Cartledge, Peter Garnsey, and Erich Gruen, eds., *Hellenistic Constructs: Essays in Culture, History, and Historiography* (Berkeley: University of California Press, 1997) 72–88.

Idem

"Hellenism and Persecution: Antiochus IV and the Jews," in Peter Green, ed., *Hellenistic History and Culture* (Hellenistic Culture and Society 9; Berkeley: University of California Press, 1993) 238–74.

Idem

The Hellenistic World and the Coming of Rome (2 vols.; Berkeley: University of California Press, 1984).

Idem

Heritage and Hellenism: The Reinvention of Jewish Tradition (Hellenistic Culture and Society 30; Berkeley: University of California Press, 1998).

Idem

"The Origins and Objectives of Onias' Temple," *SCI* 16 (1997) 47–70.

Idem

"The Purported Jewish-Spartan Affiliation," in Robert W. Wallace and Edward M. Harris, eds., *Transitions to Empire: Essays in Greco-Roman History, 360–146 B.C., in Honor of E. Badian* (Norman: University of Oklahoma Press, 1996) 254–69.

Guéraud, Octave

ΕΝΤΕΥΞΕΙΣ: Requêtes et plaints adressées au roi d'Égypte au IIIe siècle avant J.-C. (Cairo: Institut français d'archéologie orientale, 1931).

Gundlach, Rolf

"Temples," in Donald B. Redford, ed., *The Oxford Encyclopedia of Egypt* (3 vols.; Oxford: Oxford University Press, 2001) 3:363–79.

Gutman, Yehoshua

"The Story of the Mother and her Seven Sons in the Aggadah and in II and IV Maccabees" (in Hebrew), in M. Schwabe and I. Gutman, eds., *Commentationes Iudaico-Hellenisticae in Memoriam I. Levy* (Jerusalem: Magnes, 1949) 25–37.

Haber, Susan

"Living and Dying for the Law: The Mother-martyrs of 2 Maccabees," *Women in Judaism: A Multidisciplinary Journal* 4/1 (2006) 1–14. Retrieved May 20, 2010, from Genderwatch (Document ID: 1948694281), http://www.library.pitt.edu/articles/database_info/gender.html.

Habicht, Christian

Gottmenschentum und griechische Städte (2nd ed.; Munich: Beck, 1970).

Idem

"Hellenismus und Judentum in der Zeit des Judas Makkabäus," *Jahrbuch der Heidelberger Akademie der Wissenschaften für das Jahr 1974* (Heidelberg: Akademie der Wissenschaften, 1975) 97–110.

Idem

"Royal Documents in Maccabees II," *HSCP* 80 (1976) 1–18.

Idem

"Der Stratege Hegemonides," *Historia* 7 (1958) 376–78.

Habicht, Christian, and Christopher P. Jones

"A Hellenistic Inscription from Arsinoe in Cilicia," *Phoenix* 43 (1989) 317–46.

Hagedorn, Ursula, et al.

Griechische Urkundenpapyri der Bayerischen Staatsbibliothek München, vol. 1 (Stuttgart: Teubner, 1986).

Hanhart, Robert

"Die Heiligen des Höchsten," in B. Hartmann et al., eds., *Hebräische Wortforschung: Festschrift zum 80. Geburtstag von Walter Baumgartner* (Leiden: Brill, 1967) 90–101.

Idem, ed.

Maccabaeorum liber II, copiis usus quas reliquit Werner Kappler (Septuaginta 9.2; 2nd ed.; Göttingen: Vandenhoeck & Ruprecht, 1976).

Idem

Zum Text des 2. und 3. Makkabäerbuches: Probleme der Überlieferung, der Auslegung und der Ausgabe (Nachrichten der Akademie der Wissenschaften in Göttingen, Philologisch-historische Klasse, 1961, 13; Göttingen: Vandenhoeck & Ruprecht, 1961).

Idem

Zur Zeitrechnung des I. und II. Maccabäerbuches (BZAW 88.2; Berlin: Töpelmann, 1964).

Hanson, Paul D.

The Dawn of Apocalyptic: The Historical and Sociological Roots of Jewish Apocalyptic Eschatology (rev. ed.; Philadelphia: Fortress Press, 1979).

Idem

"Jewish Apocalyptic against Its Near Eastern Environment," *RB* 78 (1971) 31–58.

Hanson, Victor D., ed.

Hoplites: The Classical Greek Battle Experience (London: Routledge, 1991).

Haran, Menahem

"Archives, Libraries, and the Order of the Biblical Books," *JANESCU* 22 (1993) 51–61.

Harland, Philip A.

"Familial Dimensions of Group Identity: 'Brothers' (Ἀδελφοί) in Associations of the Greek East," *JBL* 124 (2005) 491–513.

Harris, Harold A.

Greek Athletics and the Jews (Cardiff: University of Wales, 1976).

Hartal, Moshe

Land of the Ituraeans: Archeology and History of Northern Golan in the Hellenistic, Roman and Byzantine Periods (in Hebrew; Golan Studies 2; Qazrin: Golan Research Institute and Golan Archeological Museum, 2005).

Harvey, Graham

"Synagogues of the Hebrews: 'Good Jews' in the Diaspora," in Sián Jones and Sarah Pearce, eds., *Jewish Local Patriotism and Self-Identification in the Graeco-Roman Period* (JSNTSup 31; Sheffield: Sheffield Academic Press, 1998) 132–47.

Idem

The True Israel: Uses of the Names Jew, Hebrew and Israel in Ancient Jewish and Early Christian Literature (AGJU 35; Leiden: Brill, 1996).

Harvey, Susan Ashbrook

Scenting Salvation: Ancient Christianity and the Olfactory Imagination (Transformation of the Classical Heritage 42; Berkeley: University of California Press, 2006).

Hatzopoulos, Miltiades B.

"La formation militaire dans les gymnases

hellénistiques," in Daniel Kah and Peter Scholz, eds., *Das hellenistische Gymnasion* (Wissenskultur und gesellschaftlicher Wandel 8; Berlin: Akademie, 2004) 91–96.

Haussolier, Bernard
"Inscriptions grecques de Babylone," *Klio* 9 (1909) 352–63.

Hayes, Christine E.
Gentile Impurities and Jewish Identities (Oxford: Oxford University Press, 2002).

Heinemann, Isaac
"Wer veranlasste den Glaubenszwang der Makkabäerzeit?" *Monatsschrift für Geschichte und Wissenschaft des Judentums* 82 (1938) 145–72.

Hengel, Martin
Judaism and Hellenism: Studies in Their Encounter in Palestine during the Early Hellenistic Period (2 vols.; London: SCM, 1974).

Henten, Jan Willem van
"2 Maccabees as a History of Liberation," in Menahem Mor et al., eds., *Jews and Gentiles in the Holy Land in the Days of the Second Temple, the Mishnah and the Talmud* (Jerusalem: Yad Ben-Zvi, 2004) 63–86.

Idem
"The Ancestral Language of the Jews in II Maccabees," in William Horbury, ed., *Hebrew Study from Ezra to Ben-Yehuda* (Edinburgh: T&T Clark, 1999) 53–68.

Idem
Die Entstehung der jüdischen Martyrologie (SPB 38; Leiden: Brill, 1989).

Idem
"Judas the Maccabee's Dream (2 Macc. 15:11-16) and the Egyptian King's Sickle Sword," *Zutot: Perspectives on Jewish Culture* 4 (2004) 8–15.

Idem
The Maccabean Martyrs as Saviours of the Jewish People: A Study of 2 and 4 Maccabees (JSJSup 57; Leiden: Brill, 1997).

Idem
"*ΠΑΝΤΟΚΡΑΤΩΡ ΘΕΟΣ* in 2 Maccabees," in Karl A. Deurloo and Bernd J. Diebner, eds., *YHWH-Kyrios: Antitheism or the Power of the Word–Festschrift für Rochus Zuurmond* (Heidelberg: Selbstverlag der Dielheimer Blätter zum Alten Testament, 1996) 117–26.

Idem
"Zum Einfluß jüdischer Martyrien auf die Literatur des frühen Christentums, II: Die Apostolischen Väter," *ANRW* 2.27.1 (1993) 700–723.

Hermann, Peter
"Epigraphische Notizen, 10: πολιτεία–πολιτεύεσθαι," *EA* 21 (1993) 70–72.

Herr, Bertram
"Der Standpunkt des Epitomators: Perspektivenwechsel in der Forschung am Zweiten Makkabäerbuch," *Bib* 90 (2009) 1–31.

Herzfeld, E.
"Parargadae: Untersuchungen zur persischen Archäologie," *Klio* 8 (1908) 1–68.

Himmelfarb, Martha
"Judaism and Hellenism in 2 Maccabees," *Poetics Today* 19 (1998) 19–40.

Hodge, A. Trevor
The Woodwork of Greek Roofs (Cambridge Classical Studies; Cambridge: Cambridge University Press, 1960).

Hodges, Frederick M.
"The Ideal Prepuce in Ancient Greece and Rome: Male Genital Aesthetics and Their Relation to *Lipodermos*, Circumcision, Foreskin Restoration, and the *Kynodesme*," *Bulletin of the History of Medicine* 75 (2001) 375–405.

Holladay, Carl R.
Fragments from Hellenistic Jewish Authors (4 vols.; SBLTT 20, 30, 39, 40; Chico, Calif., and Atlanta: Scholars Press, 1983–96).

Holleaux, Maurice
Études d'épigraphie et d'histoire grecques (ed. Louis Robert; 6 vols.; Paris: E. de Boccard, 1952–68).

Idem
"Inscription trouvée à Brousse," *BCH* 48 (1924) 1–57.

Hölscher, Gustav
"Die Feldzüge des Makkabäers Judas," *ZDPV* 29 (1906) 149–50.

Honigman, Sylvie
"The Jewish Politeuma at Heracleopolis," *SCI* 21 (2002) 251–66.

Eadem
"*Politeumata* and Ethnicity in Ptolemaic and Roman Egypt," *Ancient Society* 33 (2003) 61–102.

Horst, Pieter W. van der
Ancient Jewish Epitaphs (Kampen: Kok, 1991).

Idem
"Anti-Samaritan Propaganda in Early Judaism," in Pieter W. van der Horst, Maarten J. J. Menken, Joop F. M. Smit, Geert van Oyen, eds., *Persuasion and Dissuasion in Early Christianity, Ancient Judaism, and Hellenism* (Louvain: Peeters, 2003) 25–44.

Idem
Hellenism—Judaism—Christianity: Essays on Their Interaction (Kampen: Kok Pharos, 1994).

Idem
"Hellenistic Parallels to Acts (Chapters 3 and 4)," *JSNT* 35 (1989) 37–46.

Idem
Jews and Christians in Their Graeco-Roman Context: Selected Essays on Early Judaism, Samaritanism, Hellenism, and Christianity (Tübingen: Mohr Siebeck, 2006).

Houghton, Arthur

"The Seleucid Mint of Mallus and the Cult Figure of Athena Magarsia," in Leo Mildenberg and Arthur Houghton, eds., *Festschrift für Leo Mildenberg: Numismatik, Kunstgeschichte, Archäologie — Studies in Honor of Leo Mildenberg: Numismatics, Art History, Archeology* (Wetteren: Editions NR, 1984) 97–102.

Houghton, Arthur, and Georges Le Rider

"Le deuxième fils d'Antiochos IV à Ptolémaïs," *SNR* 64 (1985) 73–89.

Houtman, Alberdina, Albert de Jong, Magda Misset-van de Weg, eds.

Empsychoi Logoi—Religious Innovations in Antiquity (Leiden: Brill, 2008).

Hyldahl, Niels,

"The Maccabean Rebellion and the Question of 'Hellenization,'" in Per Bilde et al. eds., *Religion and Religious Practice in the Seleucid Kingdom* (Studies in Hellenistic Civilization 1; Aarhus: Aarhus University Press, 1990) 188–203.

Ilan, Tal

Jewish Women in Greco-Roman Palestine: An Inquiry into Image and Status (TSAJ 44; Tübingen: Mohr, 1995).

Eadem

Lexicon of Jewish Names in Late Antiquity (Tübingen: Mohr, 1995), vol. 1 of Tal Ilan, Thomas Ziem, and Kerstin Hünefeld, *Lexicon of Jewish Names in Late Antiquity* (4 vols.; TSAJ 91; Tübingen: Mohr Siebeck, 2002–).

Isaac, Benjamin

"A Seleucid Inscription from Jamnia-on-the-Sea: Antiochus V Eupator and the Sidonians,"*IEJ* 41 (1991) 132–44.

Jackson, A. H.

"Hoplites and the Gods: The Dedication of Captured Arms and Armour," in Victor D. Hanson, ed., *Hoplites: The Classical Greek Battle Experience* (London: Routledge, 1991) 228–49.

Jacoby, Felix

"*Patrios Nomos*: State Burial in Athens and the Public Cemetery in the Kerameikos," *JHS* 64 (1944) 37–66.

Jastrow, Marcus

A Dictionary of the Targumim, the Talmud Babli and Yerushalmi, and the Midrashic Literature (2nd ed.; New York: Pardes, 1903).

Jensen, Robin Margaret

"Dining with the Dead: From the *Mensa* to the Altar in Christian Late Antiquity," in Laurie Brink and Deborah Green, eds., *Commemorating the Dead: Texts and Artifacts in Context. Studies of Roman, Jewish, and Christian Burials* (Berlin and New York: de Gruyter, 2008) 107–43.

Eadem

Understanding Early Christian Art (New York: Routledge, 2000).

Johnston, Sarah Iles

"Erinys," *Brill's New Pauly* 5:34–35.

Jones, A. H. M.

The Greek City from Alexander to Justinian (Oxford: Clarendon, 1940).

Idem

"Inscriptions from Jerash," *JRS* 18 (1928) 144–78.

Jones, Christopher P.

"The Inscription from Tel Maresha for Olympiodoros," *ZPE* 171 (2009) 100–104.

Idem

Kinship Diplomacy in the Ancient World (Revealing Antiquity 12; Cambridge, Mass.: Harvard University Press, 1999).

Idem

"A Letter of Hadrian to Naryka (Eastern Locris)," *JRA* 19 (2006) 151–62.

Jones, Sián, and Sarah Pearce, eds.

Jewish Local Patriotism and Self-Identification in the Graeco-Roman Period (JSNTSup 31; Sheffield: Sheffield Academic Press, 1998).

Jonnes, Lloyd, and Marijana Rici

"A New Royal Inscription from Phrygia Paroreios: Eumenes II Grants Tyriaion the Status of a *Polis*," *Epigraphica Anatolica* 29 (1997) 1–30.

Joslyn-Siemiatkoski, Daniel

Christian Memories of the Maccabean Martyrs (New York: Palgrave-Macmillan, 2009).

Jouguet, Pierre

"Une nouvelle requête de Magdola," in *Raccolta di Scritti in onore di Felice Ramerino* (Milan: Vita e Pensiero, 1927) 381–90.

Joüon, Paul

A Grammar of Biblical Hebrew (trans. and rev. Takamitsu Muraoka; Rome: Pontificio Istituto Biblico, 1996).

Idem

"Les mots employés pour designer le Temple dans l'ancien Testament, le Nouveau Testament et Josèphe," *RSR* 25 (1935) 329–43.

Juhel, Pierre

"Ὁ ἐπι + substantif au génitif, titre des fonctionnaires de l'administration hellénistique en general et des hauts fonctionnaires royaux de la Macédoine antigonide en particulier," *Tyche. Beiträge zur alten Geschichte, Papyrologie und Epigraphik* 24 (2009) 59–76.

Kah, Daniel

"Militärische Ausbildung im hellenistischen Gymnasion," in Daniel Kah and Peter Scholz, eds., *Das hellenistische Gymnasion* (Wissenskultur und gesellschaftlicher Wandel 8; Berlin: Akademie, 2004) 47–90.

Kah, Daniel, and Peter Scholz, eds.

Das hellenistische Gymnasion (Wissenskultur und gesellschaftlicher Wandel 8; Berlin: Akademie, 2004).

314

Kamerbeek, Jan Coenraad
"On the Conception of *ΘΕΟΜΑΧΟΣ* in Relation with Greek Tragedy," *Mnemosyne*, 4th series, 1 (1948) 271–83.

Kampen, John
"The Books of the Maccabees and Sectarianism in Second Temple Judaism," in Géza G. Xeravits and József Zsengellér, eds., *The Books of the Maccabees: History, Theology, Ideology* (JSJSup 118; Leiden: Brill, 2007) 11–30.

Idem
The Hasideans and the Origins of Pharisaism: A Study in 1 and 2 Maccabees (SBLSCS 24; Atlanta: Scholars Press, 1988).

Kaplan, J.
"The Archeology and History of Tel Aviv-Jaffa," *BA* 35 (1972) 88–90.

Kappler, Werner
"De memoria alterius libri Maccabaeorum" (Diss., Göttingen, 1929).

Kasher, Aryeh
Jews and Hellenistic Cities in Eretz-Israel: Relations of the Jews in Eretz-Israel with the Hellenistic Cities during the Second Temple Period (332 BCE–70 CE) (TSAJ 21; Tübingen: Mohr, 1990).

Idem
Jews, Idumaeans, and Ancient Arabs: Relations of the Jews in Eretz-Israel with the Nations of the Frontier and the Desert during the Hellenistic and Roman Era (332 BCE–70 CE) (TSAJ 18; Tübingen: Mohr, 1988).

Idem
The Jews in Hellenistic and Roman Egypt: The Struggle for Equal Rights (rev. ed.; TSAJ 7; Tübingen: Mohr Siebeck, 1985).

Idem
"Review Essay," *JQR* 93 (2002) 257–68.

Idem
"A Second-Century BCE Greek Inscription from Iamnia," *Cathedra* 63 (1992) 3–21.

Kassel, R., and C. Austin, eds.
Poetae Comici Graeci (Berlin: de Gruyter, 1991).

Katz, Peter
"Eleazar's Martyrdom in 2 Maccabees: The Latin Evidence for a Point of the Story," *Studia Patristica IV* (Texte und Untersuchungen der altchristlichen Literatur 79; Berlin: Akademie, 1961) 118–24.

Idem
"The Text of 2 Maccabees Reconsidered," *ZNW* 51 (1960) 10–30.

Keel, Othmar
"Die kultischen Massnahmen Antiochus' IV," in idem and Urs Staub, *Hellenismus und Judentum: Vier Studien zu Daniel 7 und zur Religionsnot unter Antiochus IV* (OBO 178; Freiburg: Universitäts-verlag, 2000) 87–121.

Keel, Othmar, and Urs Staub
Hellenismus und Judentum: Vier Studien zu Daniel 7 und zur Religionsnot unter Antiochus IV (OBO 178; Freiburg: Universitätsverlag, 2000).

Keil, Bruno
"Zur Tempelchronik von Lindos," *Hermes* 51 (1916) 491–98.

Kellermann, D.
"'Astarot–'Astorot Qarnayim–Qarnayim: Historisch-geographische Erwägungen zu Orten im nördlichen Ostjordanland," *ZDPV* 97 (1981) 49–50.

Kellermann, Ulrich
Auferstanden in den Himmel: 2 Makkabäer 7 und die Auferstehung der Märtyrer (SBS 95; Stuttgart: Katholisches Bibelwerk, 1979).

Idem
"Zum traditionsgeschichtlichen Problem des stellvertretenden Sühnetods in 2 Makk 7,37f," *BN* 13 (1980) 63–83.

Kennell, Nigel M.
Ephebeia: A Register of Greek Cities with Citizen Training Systems in the Hellenistic and Roman Periods (Nicephoros Beihefte 12; Hildesheim: Weidmann, 2006).

Idem
"New Light on 2 Maccabees 4:7-15," *JJS* 56 (2005) 10–24.

Kern, Otto
Die Inschriften von Magnesia am Maeander (Berlin: W. Spemann, 1910).

Kilpatrick, George Dunbar
Review of Hanhart, *2 Maccabees;* and Hanhart, *Text,* in *Göttingische gelehrte Anzeigen* 215 (1963) 10–27.

Klauck, Hans-Josef
Ancient Letters and the New Testament: A Guide to Content and Exegesis (Waco, Tex.: Baylor University Press, 2006).

Kloner, Amos
"Underground Metropolis: The Subterranean World of Maresha," *BAR* 23, no. 2 (March/April 1977) 24–35, 67.

Knox, Bernard M. W.
"Silent Reading in Antiquity," *GRBS* 9 (1968) 421–35.

Koet, Bart J.
"Trustworthy Dreams? About Dreams and Reference to Scripture in 2 Maccabees 14–15, Josephus' *Antiquitates Judaicae* 11.302–347, and in the New Testament," in Pieter W. van der Horst, Maarten J. J. Menken, Joop F. M. Smit, Geert van Oyen, eds., *Persuasion and Dissuasion in Early Christianity, Ancient Judaism, and Hellenism* (Louvain: Peeters, 2003) 87–107.

Kolbe, Walther
Beiträge zur syrischen und jüdischen Geschichte: Kritische Untersuchungen zur Seleukidenliste und zu den beiden ersten Makkabäerbüchern (Stuttgart: Kohlhammer, 1926).

König, Friedrich Wilhelm
   Die Persika des Ktesias von Knidos (Graz: Selbstverl. des Hrsg. Ernst Weidner, 1972).
Kooij, Arie van der
   Die alten Textzeugen des Jesajabuches: Ein Beitrag zur Textgeschichte des Alten Testaments (OBO 35; Freiburg: Universitätsverlag; Göttingen: Vandenhoeck & Ruprecht, 1981).
Idem
   "The Canonization of Ancient Books Kept in the Library of Jerusalem," in Arie van der Kooij and Karel van der Torn, eds., *Canonization and Decanonization: Papers Presented to the International Conference of the Leiden Institute for the Study of Religions, Held at Leiden 9–10 January 1997* (SHR 82; Leiden: Brill, 1998) 17–40.
Idem
   "Canonization of Ancient Hebrew Books and Hasmonean Politics," in Jean-Marie Auwers and Henk Jan de Jonge, eds., *The Biblical Canons* (BEThL 163: Leuven: Leuven University Press, 2003) 27–38.
Idem
   "The Use of the Greek Bible in II Maccabees," *JNSL* 25 (1999) 127–38.
Kornbeutel, H.
   "Diadochos," *PW Supplement* 7:124–26.
Kraabel, A. Thomas
   "*Hypsistos* and the Synagogue at Sardis," *GRBS* 10 (1969) 87–93.
Kraemer, David Charles
   The Meanings of Death in Rabbinic Judaism (London and New York: Routledge, 2001).
Kraemer, Ross Shepard
   Her Share of the Blessings: Women's Religions among Pagans, Jews, and Christians in the Greco-Roman World (New York: Oxford University Press, 1992).
Eadem
   Maenads, Martyrs, Matrons, Monastics: A Sourcebook on Women's Religions in the Greco-Roman World (Philadelphia: Fortress Press, 1988).
Kramer, Samuel N.
   The Sacred Marriage Rite: Aspects of Faith, Myth and Ritual in Ancient Sumer (Bloomington, Ind.: Indiana University Press, 1969).
La'da, Csaba A.
   "Ethnicity, Occupation and Tax-status in Ptolemaic Egypt," in *Acta demotica: Acts of the Fifth International Conference for Demotists, Pisa, 4th–8th September 1993* (Pisa: Giardini, 1994) 183–89.
Lammert, Friedrich
   "Tropaion," *PW* series 2 (1948) 7.663–73.
Lange, Armin
   "2 Maccabees 2:13-15: Library or Canon?" in Géza G. Xeravits and József Zsengellér, eds., *The Books of the Maccabees: History, Theology, Ideology* (JSJSup 118; Leiden: Brill, 2007) 155–67.

Lapin, Hayim
   "Palm Fronds and Citrons: Notes on Two Letters from Bar Kosiba's Administration," *HUCA* 64 (1993) 111–35.
Laqueur, Richard
   "Griechische Urkunden in der jüdisch-hellenistischen Literatur," *Historische Zeitschrift* 136 (1927) 229–52.
Idem
   Kritische Untersuchungen zum zweiten Makkabäerbuch (Strassburg: Trübner, 1904).
Launey, Marcel
   "Études d'histoire hellénistique, I," *REA* 46 (1944) 217–36.
Idem
   Recherches sur les armées héllenistiques (2 vols.; Paris: Boccard, 1949, 1950).
Laurentin, André
   "*We‛attáh – Kai nun:* Formule caractéristique des textes juridiques et liturgiques (à propos de Jean 17,5)," *Bib* 45 (1964) 168–95.
Lebram, Jürgen-Christian
   "Purimfest und Estherbuch," *VT* 22 (1972) 208–22.
Lefkowitz, Mary R., and Maureen B. Fant
   Women's Life in Greece and Rome (Baltimore: Johns Hopkins University Press, 1982).
Legras, Bernard
   "Entre Grécité et Égyptianité: la fonction culturelle de l'éducation grecque dans l'Égypte hellénistique," in Jean-Marie Pailler and Pascal Payen, eds., *Que reste-t-il de l'éducation classique? Relire "le Marrou," Histoire de l'éducation dans l'Antiquité* (Toulouse: Presses Universitaires de Mirail, 2004) 133–41.
Leiman, Shnayer Z.
   The Canonization of Hebrew Scripture: The Talmudic and Midrashic Evidence (Transactions 47; Hamden, Conn.: Archon Books, 1976).
Lenger, Marie-Thérèse
   Corpus des ordonnances des Ptolémées (C. Ord. Ptol.) (Réimpression de l'édition princeps (1964) corrigée et mise à jour. Bruxelles: Palais des académies, 1980).
Eadem
   Corpus des ordonnances des Ptolémées (C. Ord. Ptol.): bilan des additions et corrections (1964–1988), compléments à la bibliographie (Bruxelles: Fondation égyptologique Reine Elisabeth: E. van Balberghe, 1990).
Le Rider, Georges
   Antioche de Syrie sous les Séleucides: Corpus des monnaies d'or et d'argent, vol.1, *de Séleucos I à Antiochos V, c. 300–161* (Mémoires de l'Académie des Inscriptions et belles-lettres n.s. 19; Paris: Académie des Inscriptions et belles-lettres, 1999).
Idem
   "Les resources financiers de Séleucos IV (187–175) et le paiement de l'indemnité aux Romains," in

M. Price, A. Burnett, and R. Bland, eds., *Essays in Honour of Robert Carson and Kenneth Jenkins* (London: Spink, 1993) 49–67.

Idem

Suse sous les Séleucides et les Parthes: Les trouvailles monétaires et l'histoire de la ville (Mémoires de la Mission archéologique en Iran 38; Paris: Geuthner, 1965).

Letronne, Antoine-Jean

Notices et textes des papyrus grecs (p.par.) du Musée du Louvre et de la bibliothèque impériale (Paris: Imprimerie impériale, 1865; reprinted, Milan: Cisalpino-Goliardica, 1975).

Levine, Lee I.

Judaism & Hellenism in Antiquity: Conflict or Confluence? (Seattle: University of Washington Press, 1998).

Lévy, Isidore

"Notes d'histoire héllenistique sur le second livre des Maccabées," in *Mélanges Henri Grégoire* (4 vols.; Annuaire de l'institut de philologie et d'histoire orientales et slaves 9–12 (Brussels: Secrétariat des Éditions de l'Institute, 1949–53) 2:681–99.

Idem

Recherches esséniennes et pythagoriciennes (Haute études du monde gréco-romain 1; Geneva: Droz, 1965).

Licht, Jacob

"Taxo, or the Apocalyptic Doctrine of Vengeance," *JJS* 12 (1961) 95–100.

Lichtenberger, Hermann

"Gottes Nähe in einer Zeit ohne Gebet: Zum Geschichtsbild des 2. Makkabäerbuches," in Gönke Eberhardt and Kathrin Liess, eds., *Gottes Nähe im Alten Testament* (SBS 202; Stuttgart: Katholisches Bibelwerk, 2004) 135–49.

Idem

"History-Writing and History-Telling in First and Second Maccabees," in Stephen C. Barton, Loren T. Stuckenbruck, and Benjamin G. Wold, eds., *Memory in the Bible and Antiquity: The Fifth Durham-Tübingen Research Symposium (Durham, September, 2004)* (WUNT 212; Tübingen: Mohr Siebeck, 2007) 95–110.

Idem

"The Untold End: 2 Maccabees and Acts," in Alberdina Houtman, Albert de Jong, and Magda Misset-van de Weg, eds., *Empsychoi Logoi–Religious Innovations in Antiquity* (Leiden: Brill, 2008) 385–401.

Lichtenstein, Hans

"Die Fastenrolle: Eine Untersuchung zur jüdisch-hellenistischen Geschichte," *HUCA* 8–9 (1932) 257–351.

Liebmann-Frankfort, Thérèse

"Rome et le conflit judéo-syrien (164–161 avant notre ère)," *L'antiquité classique* 38 (1969) 101–20.

Lieu, Judith

"Not Hellenes but Philistines? The Maccabees and Josephus Defining the 'Other,'" *JJS* 53 (2002) 246–63.

Lifshitz, Baruch

"The Greek Documents from Nahal Seelim and Nahal Mishmar," *IEJ* 11 (1961) 60–61.

Idem

"Sur le culte dynastique des Séleucides," *RB* 70 (1963) 75–81.

Lightfoot, J. L.

Lucian, On the Syrian Goddess (Oxford: Oxford University Press, 2003).

Lim, Timothy H.

"The Alleged Reference to the Tripartite Division of the Hebrew Bible," *RQ* 20 (2001–2) 23–37.

Lindenberger, James M.

Ancient Aramaic and Hebrew Letters (ed. Kent Harold Richards; 2nd ed.; WAW 14; Atlanta: Society of Biblical Literature, 2003).

Linderski, Jerzy

"Sacrilegium," *Brill's New Pauly*, 10:1202.

Longo, Vicenzo

Aretalogie nel Mondo Greco I: Epigrafi e Papiri (Genoa: Istituto di Filologia Classica e Medioevale, 1969).

Lorein, Geert W.

"Some Aspects of the Life and Death of Antiochus IV Epiphanes: A New Presentation of Old Viewpoints," *Ancient Society* 31 (2001) 157–71.

Lüderitz, Gert

Corpus jüdischer Zeugnisse aus der Cyrenaika (Wiesbaden: L. Reichert, 1983).

Idem

"What Is the 'Politeuma'?" in Jan Willem van Henten, Pieter Willem van der Horst, eds., *Studies in Early Jewish Epigraphy* (AGJU 21; Leiden: Brill, 1994) 183–225.

Lührmann, Dieter

"Epiphaneia: Zur Bedeutungsgeschichte eines griechischen Wortes," in Gert Jeremias, Heinz-Wolfgang Kuhn, and Hartmut Stegemann, eds., *Tradition und Glaube: Das frühe Christentum in seiner Umwelt. Festgabe für Karl Georg Kuhn zum 65. Geburtstag* (Göttingen: Vandenhoeck & Ruprecht, 1971) 185–99.

Luni, Mario

"Documenti per la storia della istituzione ginnasiale e dell' attività atletica in Cirenaica, in rapporto a quelle della Grecia," in Pietro Romanelli, Sandro Stucchi, eds., *Cirene e la Grecia* (Quaderni di archeologia della Libia 8; Rome: Bretschneider, 1976) 223–84.

Ma, John

Antiochus III and the Cities of Western Asia Minor (Oxford: Oxford University Press, 1999).

Idem

"Une culture militaire en Asie Mineure hellénistique?" in Jean-Christophe Couvenhes, Henri-Louis Fernoux, eds., *Les cités grecques et la guerre en Asie Mineure à l'époque hellénistique* (Tours: Presses Universitaires François-Rabelais, 2004) 199–220.

Maas, Paul

Epidaurische Hymnen (Halle: Max Niemeyer, 1933).

Maehler, Herwig

"Die Griechische Schule im Ptolemäischen Ägypten," in E. van't Dack, P. van Dessel, W. van Gucht, eds., *Egypt and the Hellenistic World* (Louvain: Orientaliste, 1983) 191–203.

Mango, Elena

"Bankette im hellenistischen Gymnasion," in Daniel Kah and Peter Scholz, eds., *Das hellenistische Gymnasion* (Wissenskultur und gesellschaftlicher Wandel 8; Berlin: Akademie, 2004) 273–311.

Ma'oz, Zeev U.

"Haspin," in Ephraim Stern, ed., *The New Encyclopedia of Archaeological Excavations in the Holy Land* (4 vols.; Jerusalem: Israel Exploration Society and Carta, 1993) 586–88.

Marciak, Michal

"Antiochus IV Epiphanes and the Jews," *Polish Journal of Biblical Research* 5 (2006) 61–74.

Marcus, Ralph

"Divine Names and Attributes in Hellenistic Jewish Literature," *American Academy for Jewish Research* 3 (1931–32) 43–120.

Maresch, Klaus, and James M. S. Cowey

"'A Recurrent Inclination to Isolate the Jews from Their Ptolemaic Environment?' Eine Antwort auf Sylvie Honigman," *SCI* 22 (2003) 307–10.

Markantonatos, G.

"On the Origin and Meanings of the Word *EIPΩNEIA*," *Rivista di Filologia e di Istruzione Classica* 103 (1975) 16–21.

Marrou, H.-I.

A History of Education in Antiquity (New York: Sheed & Ward, 1956).

Martola, Nils

Capture and Liberation: A Study in the Composition of the First Book of Maccabees (Acta Academiae Aboensis: Humaniora 63.1; Åbo: Åbo Akademie, 1984).

Marzullo, Benedetto

"Vetus Latina II Macc. 1,33-35 (Rec. P)," *Quaderni dell'Istituto di filologia greca* 3 (1968) 62–67.

Mason, Steve

"Jews, Judaeans, Judaizing, Judaism: Problems of Categorization in Ancient History," *JSJ* 38 (2007) 457–512.

Mayser, Edwin

Grammatik der griechischen Papyri aus der Ptolemäerzeit (2 vols.; Berlin and Leipzig: de Gruyter, 1923–34).

May, Gerhard

Schöpfung aus dem Nichts: Die Entstehung der Lehre von der creatio ex nihilo (Arbeiten zur Kirchengeschichte 48; Berlin: de Gruyter, 1978).

Mazar, Benjamin, and Hanan Eshel

"Who Built the First Wall of Jerusalem?" *IEJ* 48 (1998) 265–68.

McDonald, A. H.

"The Peace of Apamea (186 B.C.)," *JRS* 57 (1967) 1–8.

Meister, Karl

Historische Kritik bei Polybios (Wiesbaden: Steiner, 1975).

Mélèze-Modrzejewski, Joseph

"How to Be a Jew in Hellenistic Egypt?," in Shaye J. D. Cohen and Ernest S. Frerichs, eds., *Diasporas in Antiquity* (BJS 288; Atlanta: Scholars Press, 1993) 65–92.

Mendels, Doron

"Hecataeus of Abdera and a Jewish 'Patrios Politeia' of the Persian Period," *ZAW* 95 (1983) 96–110.

Idem

"A Note on the Tradition of Antiochus IV's Death," *IEJ* 31 (1981) 53–56.

Meyer, Eduard

Ursprung und Anfänge des Christentums (2 vols.; Stuttgart: J. G. Cotta, 1925).

Michel, Charles

Recueil d'inscriptions grecques (Brussels: H. Lamertin, 1900).

Milik, Jozef T.

"Dédicaces faites par des dieux (Palmyre, Hatra, Tyr) et des thiases sémitiques à l'époque romaine," in *Recherches d'Épigraphie Proche-Oriental*, vol. 1 (Paris: Geuthner, 1972).

Millar, Fergus

"The Background to the Maccabean Revolution: Reflections on Martin Hengel's 'Judaism and Hellenism,'" *JJS* 29 (1978) 10–21.

Miller, Patrick D.

The Divine Warrior in Early Israel (HSM 5; Cambridge, Mass.: Harvard University Press, 1973).

Mitford, Terence B.

"Ptolemy Macron," in *Studi in onore di Aristide Calderini e Roberto Paribeni* (3 vols.; Milan: Ceschina, 1957) 163–87.

Mittag, Peter Franz

Antiochos IV. Epiphanes: Eine politische Biographie (Klio: Beiträge zur Alten Geschichte n.F. 11; Berlin: Akademie, 2006).

Mittmann-Richert, Ulrike

Historische und legendarische Erzählungen (JSHRZ 6; Gütersloh: Gütersloher Verlagshaus, 2000).

Moffatt, James

"The Second Book of Maccabees," in R. H. Charles, *Apocrypha and Pseudepigrapha of the Old*

Testament (2 vols.; Oxford: Clarendon, 1913) 1:125–54.

Mölleken, Wolfgang
"Geschichtsklitterung im I Makkabäerbuch (Wann wurde Alkimus Hoherpriester?)," *ZAW* 65 (1953) 205–28.

Momigliano, Arnaldo
Alien Wisdom: The Limits of Hellenization (Cambridge: Cambridge University Press, 1975).

Idem
"Eastern Elements in Post-Exilic Jewish, and Greek, Historiography," in idem, *Essays in Ancient and Modern Historiography* (Middleton, Conn.: Wesleyan University Press, 1977) 25–35.

Idem
Essays in Ancient and Modern Historiography (Middletown, Conn.: Wesleyan University Press, 1977).

Idem
"Greek Historiography," *History and Theory* 17 (1978) 1–28.

Idem
"Un' ignota irruzione dei Galati in Siria al tempo di Antiocho III?" *Bollettino di Filologia Classica* 36 (1929–30) 151–56.

Idem
Prime linee di storia della maccabaica (Turin, 1931; reprinted, Amsterdam: Hakkert, 1968).

Idem
"The Romans and the Maccabees," in *Nono contributo alla storia degli studi classici e del mondo antico* (Rome: Edizioni di Storia e Letteratura, 1992) 747–61.

Idem
"The Second Book of Maccabees," *CP* 70 (1975) 81–88.

Moran, William L.
The Armarna Letters (Baltimore: John Hopkins University Press, 1987).

Moretti, Luigi
Iscrizioni storiche ellenistiche: Testo traduzione e commento, I (Biblioteca di studi superiori 53; Florence: La nuova Italia, 1967–).

Mørkholm, Otto
"The Accession of Antiochus IV of Syria: A Numismatic Comment," *The American Numismatic Society Museum Notes* 11 (1964) 63–76.

Idem
Antiochus IV of Syria (Classica et mediaevalia, dissertationes 8; Copenhagen: Gyldendal, 1966).

Idem
"A Greek Coin Hoard from Susiana," *Acta Archaeologica* 36 (1965) 127–56.

Idem
"The Municipal Coinages with Portrait of Antiochus IV of Syria," in *Congresso Internazionale di Numismatica, Roma, 11–16 Settembre 1961,* vol. 2: *Atti* (Rome: Istituto Italiano di Numismatica, 1965) 63–67.

Idem
Studies in the Coinage of Antiochus IV of Syria (Copenhagen: Munksgaard, 1963).

Morrison, Gary
"The Composition of II Maccabees: Insights Provided by a Literary *topos,*" *Bib* 90 (2009) 564–72.

Moulton, James H., and Nigel Turner
A Grammar of New Testament Greek (4 vols.; Edinburgh: T&T Clark, 1901–76).

Muffs, Yochanan
Studies in the Aramaic Legal Papyri from Elephantine (Handbook of Oriental Studies, Section 1: The Near and Middle East 66; Leiden: Brill, 2003).

Mugler, Charles
"Remarques sur le second livre des Macchabées: La statistique des mots et la question de l'auteur," *RHPhR* 11 (1931) 419–23.

Müller, Holger
"Reparationszahlungen an Rom zur Zeit der römischen Republik," *Tyche. Beiträge zur alten Geschichte, Papyrologie und Epigraphik* 24 (2009) 77–96.

Munck, Johannes
"Discours d'adieu dans le Nouveau Testament et dans la littérature biblique," in *Aux sources de la traditon chrétienne: Mélanges offerts à Maurice Goguel à l'occasion de son soixante-dixième anniversaire* (Bibliothèque theologique; Neuchâtel: Delachaux & Niestlé, 1950) 155–70.

Nachtergael, Georges
Les Galates en Grèce et les Sôtéria de Delphes: Recherches d'histoire et d'épigraphie hellénistique (Mémoires de l'Académie royale de Belgique 63; Brussels: Palais des Académies, 1977).

Negev, Abraham
"The Nabateans and the Provincia Arabia," *ANRW* 2.8 (1977) 520–686.
"La distance de Beth-Sur à Jérusalem suivant 2 Mac. 11,5," *JSJ* 14 (1983) 39–42.

Nestle, Eberhard
"Einiges zum Text des zweiten Makkabäerbuchs," *Septuagintastudien, IV* (Stuttgart: Stuttgarter Vereins-Buchdruckerei, 1903) 19–22.

Nestle, Wilhelm
"Legenden vom Tod der Gottesverächter," *ARW* 33 (1936) 246–69.

Nickelsburg, George W. E.
1 Enoch 1: A Commentary on the Book of 1 Enoch, Chapters 1–36; 81–108 (Hermeneia; Minneapolis: Fortress Press, 2001).

Idem
"Apocalyptic and Myth in 1 Enoch 6-11," *JBL* 96 (1977) 383–405.

Idem
Jewish Literature between the Bible and the Mishnah (Philadelphia: Fortress Press, 1981).

Idem

"1 and 2 Maccabees—Same Story, Different Meaning," *Concordia Theological Monthly* 42 (1971) 515–26.

Idem

"Narrative Traditions in the Paralipomena of Jeremiah and 2 Baruch," *CBQ* 35 (1973) 60–68.

Idem

Resurrection, Immortality, and Eternal Life in Intertestamental Judaism (Cambridge, Mass.: Harvard University Press, 1972).

Nicklas, Tobias

"Aus erzählter Geschichte 'Lernen': Eine narrative Analyse von 2 Makk 8," *JSJ* 32 (2001) 25–41.

Idem

"Der Historiker als Erzähler: Zur Zeichnung des Seleukidenkönigs Antiochus in 2 Makk. IX," *VT* 52 (2002) 80–92.

Idem

"Irony in 2 Maccabees?" in Géza G. Xeravits and József Zsengellér, eds., *The Books of the Maccabees: History, Theology, Ideology* (JSJSup 118; Leiden: Brill, 2007) 101–11.

Niditch, Susan

"Father–Son Folktale Patterns and Tyrant Typologies in Josephus' *Ant.* 12:160–222," *JJS* 32 (1981) 47–55.

Niehr, Herbert

Der höchste Gott: Alttestamentlicher JHWH-Glaube im Kontext syrisch-kanaanäischer Religion des 1. Jahrtausends v.Chr. (BZAW 190; Berlin: de Gruyter, 1990).

Niese, Benedikt

Geschichte der griechischen und makedonischen Staaten seit der Schlacht bei Chaeronea (3 vols.; Gotha: Perthes, 1893–1903).

Idem

"Kritik der beiden Makkabäerbücher nebst Beiträgen zur Geschichte der makkabäischen Erhebung," *Hermes* 35 (1900) 268–307, 453–527 = *Kritik der beiden Makkabäerbücher* (Berlin: Weidmann, 1900).

Nilsson, Martin P.

Geschichte der griechischen Religion (HA 5.2; Munich: Beck, 1950).

Nock, Arthur Darby

"The Guild of Zeus Hypsistos," in idem *Essays on Religion and the Ancient World* (ed. Zeph Stewart; 2 vols.; Cambridge, Mass.: Harvard University Press, 1972) 1:414–43.

Nodet, Étienne

"La dédicace, les Maccabées et le Messie," *RB* 93 (1986) 321–75.

North, Robert

"Maccabean Sabbath Years," *Bib* 34 (1953) 501–15.

Noy, David

Jewish Inscriptions of Western Europe (2 vols.; Cambridge: Cambridge University Press, 1993, 1995).

O'Brien, Elmer

"The Scriptural Proof for the Existence of Purgatory from 2 Machabees 12:43-45," *Sciences ecclésiastiques* 2 (1949) 80–108.

Oden, Robert A.

Studies in Lucian's De Syria Dea (HSM 15; Missoula, Mont.: Society of Biblical Literature, 1977).

Ogle, Marbury

"The Sleep of Death," *Memoirs of the American Academy of Rome* 11 (1933) 81–117.

Osterloh, Kevin

"Multiple Forms of Judean Patriotism: Redefining the Martyrologies of 2 Maccabees," Paper delivered in the Section on Violence at the Society of Biblical Literature annual meeting in New Orleans, Louisiana, in 2009.

Otto, Walter

"Kauf und Verkauf von Priestertümern bei den Griechen," *Hermes* 44 (1909) 594–99.

Idem

Priester und Tempel im hellenistischen Ägypten (2 vols.; Leipzig: Teubner, 1908).

Idem

Zur Geschichte der Zeit des 6. Ptolemäers: Ein Beitrag zur Politik und zum Staatsrecht des Hellenismus (Munich: Bayerischen Akademie der Wissenschaften, 1934).

Otto, Walter, and Hermann Bengtson

Zur Geschichte des Niederganges des Ptolemäerreiches: Ein Beitrag zur Regierungszeit des 8. und 9. Ptolemäers (Munich: Bayerischen Akademie der Wissenschaften, 1938).

Papillon, Terry L.

Isocrates II (Austin: University of Texas Press, 2004).

Pardee, Denis

"An Overview of Ancient Hebrew Epistolography," *JBL* 97 (1978) 321–46.

Parente, Fausto

"Onias III's Death and the Founding of the Temple of Leontopolis," in Fausto Parente and Joseph Sievers, eds., *Josephus and the History of the Greco-Roman Period: Essays in Memory of Morton Smith* (SPB 41; Leiden: Brill, 1994) 69–98.

Idem

"*ΤΟΥΣ ΕΝ ΙΕΡΟΣΟΛΥΜΟΙΣ ΑΝΤΙΟΧΕΙΣ ΑΝΑΓΡΑΨΑΙ* (II Macc. IV,9): Gerusalemme è mai stata una *ΠΟΛΙΣ*?," *Rivista di storia e letteratura religiosa* 30 (1994) 3–38.

Parker, Richard A., and Waldo H. Dubberstein

Babylonian Chronology 626 B.C.–A.D. 75 (Brown University Studies 19; Providence, R.I.: Brown University Press, 1956).

Parker, Victor L.

"Judas Maccabaeus' Campaigns against Timothy," *ZAW* 119 (2007) 386–402.

Idem
"The Letters in II Maccabees: Reflections on the Book's Composition," *ZAW* 119 (2007) 386–402.

Pax, Elpidius
Epiphaneia: Ein religionsgeschichtlicher Beitrag zur biblischen Theologie (Munich: K. Zink, 1955).

Idem
"Epiphanie," in Theodor Klauser, ed., *Reallexikon für Antike und Christentum: Sachwörterbuch zur Auseinandersetzung des Christentums mit der antiken Welt* (23 vols.; Stuttgart: Hiersemann, 1950–) 5:834–35.

Pédech, Paul
La méthode historique de Polybe (Collection d'études anciennes 119; Paris: "Les Belles Lettres," 1964).

Idem
Trois historiens méconnus: Théopompe – Duris – Phylarque (Paris: Belles Lettres, 1989).

Pélékidis, Chrysis
Histoire de l'éphébie attique: Des origines àvant Jèsus-Christ (Paris: Boccard, 1962).

Pelletier, André
"La nomenclature du calendrier juif à l'époque hellénistique," *RB* 82 (1975) 224–25.

Peremans, W., and E. van't Dack
"A propos d'une inscription de Gortyn (Inscr. Cret. IV 208)/Ptolémée Makron, Nouménios et Hippatos," *Historia* 3 (1955) 338–45.

Pestman, Pieter Willem
"L'agoranomie: un avant-poste de l'administration grccquc cnlcvé par les Égyptiens?" in H. Maehler and V. M. Strocka, eds., *Das ptolemäische Ägypten* (Mainz: Philipp von Zabern, 1978) 203–10.

Petei, Hermann
Wahrheit und Kunst: Geschichtsschreibung und Plagiat im klassischen Altertum (Leipzig: Teubner, 1911).

Pfister, R.
"Epiphanie," *PW Supplement* 4:277–323.

Piatkowska, Marta
La ΣΚΕΠΗ dans l'Égypte Ptolémaïque (Wroclaw: Zaklad Narodowy, 1975).

Plöger, Otto
"Die Feldzüge der Seleukiden gegen den Makkabäer Judas," *ZDPV* 74 (1958) 158–88.

Plümacher, Eckhard
"Cicero und Lukas: Bemerkungen zu Stil und Zweck der historischen Monographie," in Jens Schröter and Ralph Brucker, eds., *Geschichte und Geschichten: Aufsätze zur Apostelgeschichte und zu den Johannesakten* (WUNT 170; Tübingen: Mohr Siebeck, 2004) 15–32.

Pomeroy, Sarah B.
Goddesses, Whores, Wives, and Slaves: Women in Classical Antiquity (New York: Schocken, 1975).

Eadem
Women in Hellenistic Egypt: From Alexander to Cleopatra (New York: Schocken, 1984).

Porter, Stanley E.
Καταλλάσσω in Ancient Greek Literature, with Reference to the Pauline Writings (Estudios de filología Neotestamentaria 5; Cordoba: Ediciones el Almendro, 1994).

Préaux, Claire
"Les Étrangers à l'époque hellénistique (Egypte-Delos-Rhodes)," *L'Étranger/Foreigner* (Recueils de la Société Jean Bodin pour l'histoire comparative des institutions 9; Paris: Dessain et Tolra, 1984) 141–93.

Preisigke, Friedrich
Sammelbuch Griechischer Urkunden aus Ägypten I (Strassburg: Karl Trübner, 1915).

Idem
Wörterbuch der griechischen Papyrusurkunden mit Einschluss der griechischen Inschriften, Aufschriften, Ostraka, Mummienschilder usw. aus Ägypten (ed. E. Kiessling; 4 vols.; Berlin: Selbstverlag der Erben; Wiesbaden: Harrassowitz, 1925).

Pritchard, James B.
The Ancient Near East, vol.1: *An Anthology of Texts and Pictures* (Princeton: Princeton University Press, 1958).

Pritchett, William Kendrick
Ancient Greek Battle Speeches and a Palfrey (Amsterdam: Gieben, 2002).

Idem
The Greek State at War (4 vols.; Berkeley: University of California Press, 1971–91).

Idem
Essays in Greek History (Amsterdam: Gieben, 1994).

Pugliese Carratelli, Giovanni
"Supplemento Epigrafico di Iasos," *Annuario della Scuola archeologica di Atene e delle missioni italiane in Oriente* 45–46 (1969) 437–86.

Rajak, Tessa
"Dying for the Law: The Martyr's Portrait in Jewish-Greek Literature," in M. J. Edwards and Simon Swain, eds., *Portraits: Biographical Representation in the Greek and Latin Literature of the Roman Empire* (Oxford: Clarendon, 1997) 39–67.

Eadem
The Jewish Dialogue with Greece and Rome: Studies in Cultural and Social Interaction (AGJU 48; Leiden: Brill, 2001).

Rappaport, Uriel
"The Extradition Clause in 1 Maccabees, XV, 21," in Karel van Lerberghe and Antoon Schoors, eds., *Immigration and Emigration within the Ancient Near East: Festschrift E. Lipiński* (OLA 65; Leuven: Peeters, 1995) 271–83.

Idem
"The Samaritans in the Hellenistic Period," in Alan D. Crown and Lucy A. Davey, eds., *Essays in Honour of G. D. Sixdenier: New Samaritan Studies of the Société d'Études Samaritaines, III & IV:*

Proceedings of the Congresses of Oxford 1990, Yarnton Manor and Paris 1992, Collège de France: With lectures given at Hong Kong 1993 as participation in the ICANAS Congress (Studies in Judaica 5; Sydney: Mandelbaum, 1995) 281–88.

Ray, John D.
The Archive of Ḥor (Excavations at North Saqqâra Documentary Series 1; London: Egypt Exploration Society, 1976).

Reed, Annette Yoshiko
"Job as Jobab: The Interpretation of Job in LXX Job 42:17 b-e," *JBL* 120 (2001) 31–55.

Reinach, Salomon
"L'origine des priers pour les morts," *REJ* 41 (1900) 161–73.

Reinach, Theodore
"Les inscriptions d'Iasos," *REG* 6 (1893) 153–203.

Reinhold, Meyer
History of Purple as a Status Symbol in Antiquity (Collection Latomus 116; Brussels: Latomus, 1970).

Renaud, Bernard
"La loi et les lois dans les livres des Maccabées," *RB* 68 (1961) 39–67.

Reynolds, Joyce M.
"New Letters from Hadrian to Aphrodisias: Trials, Taxes, Gladiators, and an Aqueduct," *JRA* 13 (2000) 5–20.

Rhodes, Peter
"Epistatai," *Brill's New Pauly* 4:1131.

Richnow, Wolfgang
"Untersuchung zu Sprache und Stil des 2. Makkabäerbuches: Ein Beitrag zur hellenistischen Historiographie" (Diss., Göttingen, 1967).

Rigsby, Kent J.
Asylia: Territorial Inviolability in the Hellenistic World (Hellenistic Culture and Society 22; Berkeley: University of California Press, 1996).

Risberg, Bernhard
"Konjekturer till några ställen i de apokryfiska böckerna," *Eranos* 15 (1915) 25–38.

Idem
"Textkritische und exegetische Anmerkungen zu den Makkabäerbüchern," *Beiträge zur Religionswissenschaft* 27 (1918) 6–31.

Robert, Jeanne, and Louis Robert
"Bulletin épigraphique," *REG* 59–60 (1946–47) 298–372.

Eidem
"Bulletin épigraphique," *REG* 84 (1971) 397–540.

Robert, Louis
"Un corpus des inscriptions juives," *REJ* 101 (1937) 73–86.

Idem
Études anatoliennes: Recherches sur les inscriptions grecques de l'Asie mineure (Études orientales 5; Paris: Boccard, 1937).

Idem
Hellenica: recueil d'épigraphie de numismatique et d'antiquités grecques II–III (Paris: Maisonneuve, 1947).

Idem
Hellenica: recueil d'épigraphie de numismatique et d'antiquités grecques XI–XII (Paris: Maisonneuve, 1960).

Idem
"Notes d'épigraphie hellénistique," *BCH* 54 (1930) 322–51.

Idem
"Sur des inscriptions d'Éphèse; fêtes, athletes, empereurs, épigrammes," *Revue de philologie* 41 (1967) 7–84.

Roesch, Paul
"Une loi fédérale béotienne sur la preparation militaire," *Acta of the Fifth International Congress of Greek and Latin Epigraphy, Cambridge, 1967* (Oxford: Blackwell, 1971) 81–88.

Röllig, Wolfgang
"Tripolis," *Brill's New Pauly* 14:934–35.

Romeo, Antonino
"Il termine ΛΕΙΤΟΥΡΓΙΑ nella grecità biblica," in *Miscellanea Liturgica in Honorem L. Cuniberti Mohlberg, II* (Rome: Edizioni Liturgiche, 1949) 467–519.

Romilly, Jacqueline de
Magic and Rhetoric in Ancient Greece (Carl Newell Jackson Lectures 1974; Cambridge, Mass.: Harvard University Press, 1975).

Rosenberger, Grete
"Griechische Privatbriefe," in Karl Kalbfleisch, ed.; *Papyri Iandanae* (6th fascicle; Leipzig: Teubner, 1934) 218–58 + 4 tables.

Rostowzew, Michael,
"Ἐπιφάνειαι," *Klio* 16 (1919–20) 203–6.

Rothschild, Clare K.
Luke-Acts and the Rhetoric of History: An Investigation of Early Christian Historiography (WUNT 175; Tübingen: Mohr Siebeck, 2004).

Roueché, Charlotte, and Susan Sherwin-White
"Some Aspects of the Seleucid Empire: The Greek Inscriptions from Failaka, in the Arabian Gulf," *Chiron* 15 (1985) 1–39.

Roussel, Pierre
"Le miracle de Zeus Panamaros," *BCH* 55 (1931) 70–116.

Idem
"Un reglement militaire de l'époque macédonienne," *Revue archéoloique* series 6, vol. 3 (1934) 39–47.

Rubin, Gayle
"The Traffic in Women: Notes on the 'Political Economy' of Sex," in Rayna R. Reiter, ed., *Toward an Anthropology of Women* (New York: Monthly Review Press, 1975) 157–210.

Runia, David T.
"Philonic Nomenclature," *Studia Philonica Annual*
6 (1994) 1-27.

Idem
"Worshipping the Visible Gods: Conflict and
Accommodation in Hellenism, Hellenistic Judaism
and Early Christianity," in Alberdina Houtman,
Albert de Jong, and Magda Misset-van de Weg,
eds., *Empsychoi Logoi—Religious Innovations in
Antiquity* (Leiden: Brill, 2008) 47-61.

Ruppert, Lothar
*Der leidende Gerrechte: Eine motivgeschichtliche
Untersuchung zum Alten Testament und
zwischentestamentlichen Judentum* (Würzburg:
Katholisches Bibelwerk, 1972).

Rutherford, W. Gunion
*The New Phrynichus, Being a Revised Text of the
Ecloga of the Grammarian Phrynichus* (London:
Macmillan, 1881).

Sachs, Abraham J., and Donald J. Wiseman
"A Babylonian King List of the Hellenistic Period,"
Iraq 16 (1954) 202-12.

Saldarini, Anthony J.
"Last Words and Deathbed Scenes in Rabbinic
Literature," *JQR* 68 (1977) 28-45.

Sanctis, Gaetano de
"Epigraphica II: Eumene II e le città greche
d'Asia," *Rivista di Filologia e di Istruzione classica* 3
n.s. (1925) 68-78.

Savalli-Lestrade, Ivana
"Devenir une cité: *Poleis* nouvelles et aspirations
civiques en Asie Mineure à la basse époque
hellénistique," in P. Fröhlich and C. Müller,
eds., *Citoyenneté et Participation à la basse époque
hellénistique* (Geneva: Droz, 2005) 9-37.

Scaer, Peter J.
The Lukan Passion and the Praiseworthy Death (New
Testament Monographs 10; Sheffield: Sheffield
Poenix, 2005).

Schade, Ludwig
"Zu 2 Makk 1,19," *BZ* 8 (1910) 228-35.

Schalit, Abraham
König Herodes: Der Mann und sein Werk (2nd ed.;
Berlin: de Gruyter, 2001).

Schams, Christine
Jewish Scribes in the Second-Temple Period (JSOTSup
291; Sheffield: Sheffield Academic Press, 1998).

Schaumberger, Johannes
"Die neue Seleukiden-Liste BM 35603 und die
makkabäische Chronologie," *Bib* 36 (1955) 423-35.

Scheller, Paul
De hellenistica historiae conscribendae arte (Leipzig:
R. Noske, 1911).

Schlatter, Adolf von
*Jason von Kyrene: Ein Beitrag zu seiner
Wiederherstellung* (Munich: Beck, 1891).

Schlesier, Renate
"Dionysus," *Brills New Pauly*, 4:496-508.

Schmidt, Francis
*How the Temple Thinks: Identity and Social Cohesion
in Ancient Judaism* (trans. J. Edward Crowley;
Biblical Seminar 78; Sheffield: Sheffield Academic
Press, 2001).

Schmitt, Hatto H.
Die Staatsverträge des Altertums, vol. 3: *Die Verträge
der griechisch- römischen Welt von 338 bis 200 v. Chr.*
(Munich: Beck, 1969).

Schmitz, Barbara
"Geschaffen aus dem Nichts? Die Funktion
der Rede von der Schöpfung im Zweiten
Makkabäerbuch," *Sacra Scripta* 9 (2009) 199-215.

Scholl, Reinhold
Corpus der ptolemäischen Sklaventexte (3 vols.;
Forschungen zur antiken Sklaverei, Beiheft 1;
Stuttgart: Steiner, 1990).

Scholz, Peter
"Elementarunterricht und intellektuelle Bildung
im hellenistische Gymnasion," in Daniel Kah and
Peter Scholz, eds., *Das hellenistische Gymnasion*
(Wissenskultur und gesellschaftlicher Wandel 8;
Berlin: Akademie, 2004) 103-28.

Schorch, Stefan
"The Libraries in 2 Macc 2:13-15, and the Torah as
a Public Document in Second Century Judaism,"
in Géza G. Xeravits and József Zsengellér, eds.,
The Books of the Maccabees: History, Theology, Ideology
(JSJSup 118; Leiden: Brill, 2007) 169-80.

Schrenk, G.
"ἐκλεκτός," *TDNT* 4 (1967) 181-92.

Schubart, Wilhelm
"I. Aufsäze: Das hellenistische Königsideal nach
Inschriften und Papyri," *Archiv für Papyrusforschung
und verwandte Gebiete* 12 (1937) 1-26.

Idem
"Bemerkungen zum Stile hellenistischer
Königsbriefe," *Archiv für Papyrusforschung und
verwandte Gebiete* 6 (1920) 324-47.

Idem
"Παρακατατίθεσθαι in der hellenistischen
Amtssprache," *Philologische Wochenschrift* 52:1077-
84.

Schulthess, Fr.
"Zur Sprache des Evangelien," *ZNW* 21 (1922)
241-58.

Schulthess, Otto
"Mysarches," *PW* 16:1187.

Schunk, Klaus Dietrich
Die Quellen des I. und II. Makkabäerbuches (Halle:
Niemeyer, 1954).

Schürer, Emil
*The History of the Jewish People in the Age of Jesus
Christ (175 B.C. - A.D. 135)* (rev. and ed. Geza
Vermes and Fergus Millar; 3 vols.; Edinburgh:
T&T Clark, 1973-87).

Idem
"Zu II Mcc 6,7 (monatliche Geburtstagfeier)," *ZNW* 2 (1901) 48–52.

Schuppe, E.
"Petasos," *PW* 19:1119–24.

Schuttermayr, Georg
"'Schöpfung aus dem Nichts' in 2 Makk 7,28?" *BZ* 17 (1973) 203–22.

Schwabl, Hans
"Zeus I. Epiklesen. Olympios," *PW* 19:254–376.

Schwartz, Daniel R.
"Antiochus IV Epiphanes in Jerusalem," in David Goodblatt, Avital Pinnick, and Daniel R. Schwartz, eds., *Historical Perspectives: From the Hasmoneans to Bar Kokhba in Light of the Dead Sea Scrolls. Proceedings of the Fourth International Symposium of the Orion Center for the Study of the Dead Sea Scrolls and Associated Literature, 27–31 January, 1999* (STDJ 37; Leiden: Brill, 2001) 45–56.

Idem
"Foils or Heroes? On Martyrdom in First and Second Maccabees," *AJS Perspectives* (Spring 2009) 10–11.

Idem
"From the Maccabees to Masada: On Diasporan Historiography of the Second Temple Period," in A. Oppenheimer, ed., *Jüdische Geschichte in hellenistisch-römischer Zeit: Wege der Forschung—Vom alten zum neuen Schürer* (Munich: Oldenbourg, 1999) 29–40.

Idem
"How at Home Were the Jews of the Hellenistic Diaspora?" *CP* 95 (2000) 349–57.

Idem
"'Judean' or 'Jew'? How Should We Translate Ἰουδαῖος in Josephus?" in Jörg Frey, Daniel R. Schwartz, S. Gripentrog, eds., *Jewish Identity in the Greco-Roman World/Jüdische Identität in der griechisch-römischen Welt* (Ancient Judaism and Early Christianity 71; Leiden: Brill, 2007) 3–27.

Idem
"On Something Biblical about 2 Maccabees," in Michael E. Stone and Esther G. Chazon, eds., *Biblical Perspectives: Early Use and Interpretation of the Bible in Light of the Dead Sea Scrolls. Proceedings of the First International Symposium of the Orion Center for the Study of the Dead Sea Scrolls and Associated Literature, 12–14 May 1996* (STDJ 28; Leiden: Brill, 1998) 223–32.

Idem
"The Other in 1 and 2 Maccabees," in Graham N. Stanton, Gedalyahu G. Stroumsa, eds., *Tolerance and Intolerance in Early Judaism and Christianity* (Cambridge: Cambridge University Press, 1998) 30–37.

Idem
"Temple or City? What Did Hellenistic Jews See in Jerusalem?" in M. Poorthuis and C. Safrai, eds.,

The Centrality of Jerusalem: Historical Perspectives (Kampen: Kok Pharos, 1996) 114–27.

Idem
"Why Did Antiochus Have to Fall (II Maccabees 9:7)?" in Lynn LiDonnici and Andrea Lieber, eds., *Heavenly Tablets: Interpretation, Identity and Tradition in Ancient Judaism* (JSJSup 119; Leiden, Brill, 2007) 257–65.

Idem
"Wo wohnt Gott?—Die Juden und ihr Gott zwischen Judenstaat, Diaspora und Himmel," in S. J. Lederhilger, ed., *Gottesstaat oder Staat ohne Gott: Politische Theologie in Judentum, Christentum und Islam* (Linzer philosophisch-theologische Beiträge 8; Frankfurt am Main: Lang, 2002) 58–73.

Schwartz, Seth
"The Hellenization of Jerusalem and Schechem," in Martin Goodman, ed., *Jews in a Greco-Roman World* (Oxford: Clarendon, 1998) 37–45.

Idem
"John Hyrcanus I's Destruction of the Gerizim Temple and Judaean–Samaritan Relations," *JH* 7 (1993) 9–25.

Schwenn, Friedrich
Die Menschenopfer bei den Griechen und Römern (Religionsgeschichtliche Versuche und Vorarbeiten 15.3; Giessen: Töpelmann, 1915).

Scolnic, Benjamin Edidin
Alcimus, Enemy of the Maccabees (Studies in Judaism; Lanham, Md.; University Press of America, 2005).

Scurlock, Joann
"167 BCE: Hellenism or Reform?" *JSJ* 31 (2000) 125–61.

Seckel, Emil, and Wilhelm Schubart
Der Gnomon des Idios Logos (Berlin: Weidmann, 1919) = Band V, *Ägyptische Urkunden aus der staatlichen Museen zu Berlin*.

Segal, Charles
The Theme of the Mutilation of the Corpse in the Iliad (Mnemosyne Supplement 17; Leiden: Brill, 1971).

Seltman, Charles
Wine in the Ancient World (London: Routledge & Kegan Paul, 1957).

Seyrig, Henri
"Antiquités syriennes. 24: Les rois séleucides et la concession de l'asylie," *Syria* 20 (1939) 35–39.

Idem
Notes on Syrian Coins (Numismatic Notes and Monographs 119; New York: American Numismatic Society, 1950).

Shavit, Jaacov
"The 'Qumran Library' in the Light of the Attidtude towards Books and Libraries in the Second Temple Period," *Annals of the New York Academy of Sciences* 722 (1994) 299–317.

Sherk, Robert K.
Roman Documents from the Greek East; Senatus Consulta and Epistulae to the Age of Augustus (Baltimore: Johns Hopkins Press, 1969).

Sherwin-White, Susan
"Aristeas Ardibeltaios: Some Aspects of the Use of Double Names in Seleucid Babylonia," *ZPE* 50 (1983) 209–21.

Eadem
"Babylonian Chronicle Fragments," *JNES* 42 (1983) 265–70.

Eadem
"Shami, the Seleucids and Dynastic Cult: A Note," *Iran* 22 (1984) 160–61.

Sherwin-White, Susan, and Amélie Kuhrt
From Samarkhand to Sardis: A New Approach to the Seleucid Empire (Hellenistic Culture and Society 13; Berkeley: University of California, 1993).

Eaedem
Hellenism in the East: The Interaction of Greek and Non-Greek Civilizations from Syria to Central Asia after Alexander (Berkeley: University of California Press, 1987).

Shrenk, G.
"ἐκλεκτός," *TDNT* 4:181–92.

Sievers, Joseph
The Hasmoneans and Their Supporters: From Mattathias to the Death of John Hyrcanus (South Florida Studies in the History of Judaism 6; Atlanta: Scholars Press, 1990).

Idem
"Jerusalem, the Akra, and Josephus," in Fausto Parente and Joseph Sievers, eds., *Josephus and the History of the Greco-Roman Period: Essays in Memory of Morton Smith* (SPB 41; Leiden: Brill, 1994) 195–209.

Idem
Synopsis of the Greek Sources for the Hasmonean Period: 1–2 Maccabees and Josephus, War 1 and Antiquitates 12–14 (Subsidia Biblica 20; Rome: Biblical Institute Press, 2001).

Sluys, David M.
De Maccabaeorum libris I et II [i.e. primo et secundo] quaestiones (Amsterdam: J. Clausen, 1904).

Smith, Dennis Edwin
From Symposium to Eucharist: The Banquet in the Early Christian World (Minneapolis: Fortress Press, 2003).

Smith, Mark S.
"The Near Eastern Background of Solar Language for Yahweh," *JBL* 109 (1990) 29–39.

Smith, Morton
"Helios in Palestine," *Eretz Israel* 16 (1982) 199–214.

Idem
Palestinian Parties and Politics That Shaped the Old Testament (2nd ed; London: SCM, 1987).

Smyth, Herbert Weir
Greek Grammar (Cambridge, Mass.: Harvard University Press, 1920).

Sokolowski, Franciszek
Lois sacrées des cités grecques (Travaux et mémoires 18; Paris: Boccard, 1969).

Sowers, Sidney G.
"On the Reinterpretation of Biblical History in Hellenistic Judaism," in F. Christ, ed., *Oikonomia: Heilsgeschichte als Thema der Theologie* (Hamburg-Bergstedt: Reich, 1967) 18–25.

Spek, Roger van der
"The Babylonian City," in Susan Sherwin-White and Amelie Kuhrt, eds., *Hellenism in the East: The Interaction of Greek and Non-Greek Civilizations from Syria to Central Asia after Alexander* (Berkeley: University of California Press, 1987) 57–74.

Sperber, Daniel
"On the Office of the Agoranomos in Roman Palestine," *ZDMG* 127 (1977) 227–43.

Steen, Henry A.
"Les cliché épistolaires dans les letters sur papyrus grecques," *Classica et Mediaevalia* 1 (1938) 119–76.

Stemberger, Günter
Der Leib der Auferstehung. Studien zur Anthropologie und Eschatologie des palästinischen Judentums im neutestamentlichen Zeitalter (ca. 170 v. Chr.–100 n. Chr.) (AnBib 56; Rome: Biblical Institute Press, 1972).

Stendebach, Franz Josef
"Das Schweinopfer im alten Orient," *BZ* 18 (1974) 263–71.

Stern, Menahem
"The Battle against the Galatians (8:20)," appendix 7 in Daniel R. Schwartz, *2 Maccabees* (Commentaries on Early Jewish Literature; Berlin and New York: de Gruyter, 2008).

Idem
The Documents of the History of the Hasmonean Revolt (in Hebrew) (2nd ed.; Tel-Aviv: Hakibbutz Hameuchad, 1972).

Idem
Greek and Latin Authors on Jews and Judaism (3 vols.; Fontes ad res Judaicas spectantes; Jerusalem: Israel Academy of Arts and Sciences, 1974–84).

Stewart, Selina
"Emending Aratus' Insomnia: Callimachus Epigr. 27," *Mnemosyne* 61 (2008) 586–600.

Stokholm, Niels
"Zur Überlieferung von Heliodor, Kuturnahhunte und anderen missglückten Tempelräubern," *StTh* 22 (1968) 1–28.

Talmon, Shemaryahu
"The 'Desert Motif' in the Bible and in Qumran Literature," in Alexander Altmann, ed., *Biblical Motifs: Origins and Transformations* (Philip W. Lown Institute of Advanced Judaic Studies, Brandeis University, Studies and Texts 3; Cambridge, Mass.: Harvard University Press, 1966) 31–63.

Tarn, W.W.
  The Greeks in Bactria and India (2nd ed.;
  Cambridge: Cambridge University Press, 1951).
Tcherikover, Victor A.
  "The Documents in 2 Maccabees" (in Hebrew),
  Tarbiz 1, no. 1 (1929) 31–45; reprinted in idem,
  The Jews in the Greco-Roman World (Tel Aviv:
  Neumann, 1960–61).
Idem
  Hellenistic Civilization and the Jews (Philadelphia:
  Jewish Publication Society, 1959).
Idem
  *Die hellenistischen Städtegründungen von Alexander
  dem Grossen bis auf die Römerzeit* (Philologus
  Supplementband 19.1; Leipzig: Dieterich, 1927;
  reprinted, New York: Arno Press, 1973).
Idem
  The Jews in the Greco-Roman World (in Hebrew; Tel
  Aviv: Neumann, 1960–61).
Thompson, Stith
  Motif-Index of Folk Literature (rev. ed.; 6 vols.;
  Bloomington: Indiana University Press, 1955–58).
Tiller, Patrick A.
  "The 'Eternal Planting' in the Dead Sea Scrolls,"
  DSD 4 (1997) 312–35.
Toorn, Karel van der
  "Sun," *ABD* 6:237–39.
Torrey, Charles C.
  "Die Briefe 2 Makk. 1,1–2,18," *ZAW* 20 (1900)
  225–42.
Idem
  "The Letters Prefixed to Second Maccabees," *JAOS*
  60 (1940) 119–50.
Tracy, Stephen V.
  "Greek Inscriptions from the Athenian Agora:
  Third to First Centuries BC," *Hesperia* 51 (1982)
  57–64.
Treves, Piero
  "Les documents apocryphes du 'Pro Corona,'" *Les
  études classiques* 9 (1940) 138–74.
Tsafrir, Y.
  "The Location of the Seleucid Akra in Jerusalem,"
  RB 82 (1975) 501–21.
Ulrich, Eugene
  "The Non-attestation of a Tripartite Canon in
  4QMMT," *CBQ* 65 (2003) 202–14.
Urbach, Ephraim E.
  The Sages: Their Concepts and Beliefs (2 vols.;
  Jerusalem: Magnes, 1979).
Urman, Dan
  "Public Structures and Jewish Communities in the
  Golan Heights," in Dan Urman and Paul V. M.
  Flesher, eds., *Ancient Synagogues: Historical Analysis
  and Archeological Discovery* (2 vols.; SPB 47; Leiden:
  Brill, 1995) 2:556–61.
Urman, Dan, and Paul V. M. Flesher
  *Ancient Synagogues: Historical Analysis and
  Archeological Discovery* (2 vols.; SPB 47; Leiden:
  Brill, 1995).

Uxkull-Gyllenband, Woldemar Graf
  Der Gnomon des Idios Logos, Zweiter Teil: *Der
  Kommentar* (Berlin: Weidmann, 1934).
Vaccari, A.
  "Note critiche ed esegetiche," *Bib* 28 (1947) 404–6.
Vanderhooft, David
  "Dwelling Beneath the Sacred Place: A Proposal
  for Reading 2 Samuel 7:10," *JBL* 118 (1999)
  628–30.
VanderKam, James C.
  "2 Maccabees 6,7a and Calendrical Change in
  Jerusalem," *JSJ* 12 (1981) 52–74.
Idem
  From Joshua to Caiaphas: High Priests after the Exile
  (Minneapolis: Fortress Press, 2004).
Idem
  "People and High Priesthood in Early Maccabean
  Times," in W. H. Propp, Baruch Halpern, David
  Noel Freedman, eds., *The Hebrew Bible and Its
  Interpreters* (Winona Lake, Ind.: Eisenbrauns, 1990)
  205–25.
Van Hook, Larue
  *The Metaphorical Terminology of Greek Rhetoric and
  Literary Criticism* (Chicago: University of Chicago
  Press, 1905).
Vaughn, P.
  "The Identification and Retrieval of the Hoplite
  Battle-Dead," in Victor D. Hanson, ed., *Hoplites:
  The Classical Greek Battle Experience* (London:
  Routledge, 1991) 38–62.
Veïsse, Anne-Emmanuelle
  "L'expression de l'altérité dans l'Égypte des
  Ptolémées: Allophulos, Xénos et Barbaros," *REG*
  120 (2007) 50–63.
Verdin, Herman, Guido Schepens, and Els de Keyser,
  eds.
  *Purposes of History: Studies in Greek Historiography
  from the 4th to the 2nd Centuries B.C. Proceedings of
  the International Colloquium, Leuven, 24–26 May
  1988* (Studia Hellenistica 30; Louvain: n.p.,
  1990).
Vlastos, Gregory
  Plato's Universe (Seattle: University of Washington
  Press, 1976).
Wacholder, Ben-Zion
  "The Calendar of Sabbatical Cycles during the
  Second Temple and the Early Rabbinic Period,"
  HUCA 44 (1973) 153–96.
Idem
  Eupolemus: A Study of Judaeo-Greek Literature
  (Monographs of the Hebrew Union College
  3; Cincinnati: Hebrew Union College–Jewish
  Institute of Religion, 1975)
Idem
  "The Letter from Judah Maccabee to Aristobulus:
  Is 2 Maccabees 1:10b–2:18 Authentic?" *HUCA* 49
  (1978) 89–133.

Wacker, Christian
"Die bauhistorische Entwicklung der Gymnasien: Von der Parkanlage zum 'Idealgymnasion' des Vitruv," in Daniel Kah and Peter Scholz, eds., *Das hellenistische Gymnasion* (Wissenskultur und gesellschaftlicher Wandel 8; Berlin: Akademie, 2004) 349–51.

Wacker, Marie-Therèse
Weltordnung und Gericht: Studien zu I Henoch 22 (FB 45; Würzburg: Echter Verlag, 1982).

Wackernagel, Jacob
"Griechische Miszellen, I: Περσέπολις," *Glotta* 14 (1925) 36–44.

Walbank, Frank W.
A Historical Commentary on Polybius (3 vols.; Oxford: Clarendon, 1957–79).

Idem
"History and Tragedy," *Historia* 9 (1960) 216–234.

Idem
"ΦΙΛΙΠΠΟΣ ΤΡΑΓΩΙΔΟΥΜΕΝΟΣ: A Polybian Experiment," *JHS* 58 (1938) 55–68.

Idem
"Profit or Amusement: Some Thoughts on the Motives of Hellenistic Historians," in Herman Verdin, Guido Schepens, and Els de Keyser, eds., *Purposes of History: Studies in Greek Historiography from the 4th to the 2nd Centuries B.C. Proceedings of the International Colloquium, Leuven, 24–26 May 1988* (Studia Hellenistica 30; Louvain: n.p., 1990) 253–66.

Idem
Speeches in Greek Historians (Oxford: Blackwell, 1965).

Idem
"Tragic History," *Bulletin of the Institute of Classical Studies of the University of London* 2 (1955) 4–14.

Wallace-Hadrill, Andrew
"Housing the Dead: The Tomb as House in Roman Italy," in Laurie Brink and Deborah Green, eds., *Commemorating the Dead: Texts and Artifacts in Context. Studies of Roman, Jewish, and Christian Burials* (Berlin and New York: de Gruyter, 2008) 39–77.

Walter, Nikolaus
Der Thoraausleger Aristobulos: Untersuchungen zu seinen Fragmenten und zu pseudepigraphischen Resten der jüdisch-hellenistischen Literatur (Berlin: Akademie, 1964) 27–28.

Weber, Beat
"Zur Datierung der Asaph-Psalmen 74 und 79," *Bib* 81 (2000) 521–32.

Welles, C. Bradford
"Hellenistic Tarsus," *Mélanges offerts au Père René Moutard II. Mélanges de l'Université Saint Joseph* 38 (1962) 41–75.

Idem
Royal Correspondence in the Hellenistic Period: A Study in Greek Epigraphy (New Haven: Yale University Press, 1934).

Wellhausen, Julius
"Über den geschichtlichen Wert des zweiten Makkabäerbuchs, im Verhältnis zum ersten," *Nachrichten von der Königl. Gesellschaft der Wissenschaften zu Göttingen,* Phil.-hist. Kl. (1905) 117–63.

Wenning, Robert
"Eine neuerstellte Liste der nabatäischen Dynastie," *Boreas* 16 (1993) 25–38.

Westermann, William Linn, and Elizabeth Sayre Hasenoehrl
Zenon Papyri: Business Papers of the Third Century B.C. Dealing with Palestine and Egypt (2 vols.; New York: Columbia University Press, 1934, 1940).

Wet, Chris L. de
"Between Power and Priestcraft: The Politics of Prayer in 2 Maccabees," *Religion and Theology* 16 (2009) 150–61.

Wheeler, Everett L.
"The General as Hoplite," in Victor D. Hanson, ed., *Hoplites: The Classical Greek Battle Experience* (London and New York: Routledge, 1991).

White, John L.
Light from Ancient Letters (FF; Philadelphia: Fortress, 1986).

Whitters, Mark F.
"Some New Observations about Jewish Festal Letters," *JSJ* 32 (2001) 272–88.

Wiedemann, Thomas
"Rhetoric in Polybius," in Herman Verdin, Guido Schepens, and Els de Keyser, eds., *Purposes of History: Studies in Greek Historiography from the 4th to the 2nd Centuries B.C. Proceedings of the International Colloquium, Leuven, 24–26 May 1988* (Studia Hellenistica 30; Louvain: n.p., 1990) 288–300.

Wiesehöfer, Josef
"Elymais," *Brill's New Pauly.*

Wilcken, Ulrich
Griechische Ostraka aus Ägypten und Nubien: Ein Beitrag zur antike Wirtschaftsgeschichte (2 vols.; Leipzig and Berlin: Gieseke & Devrient, 1899).

Wilcken, Ulrich, and Ludwig Mitteis
Grundzüge und Chrestomathie der Papyrusurkunde (2 vols.; Leipzig: Teubner, 1912).

Wilhelm, Adolf
Beiträge zur griechischen Inschriftenkunde (Sonderschriften des österreichischen archäologischen Institutes in Wien 7; Vienna: Hölder, 1909).

Idem
"Ἐν χειρῶν νομαῖς und ἐν χειρῶν (χειρός) νομῷ," *Glotta* 24 (1936) 133–44.

Idem
Neue Beiträge zur griechischen Inschriftenkunde. Fünfter Teil (Sitzungsberichte der Akademie der Wissenschafteen in Wien, philosophisch-historische Klasse 214; Vienna and Leipzig: Hölder-Pichler-Tempsky, 1932).

Idem

"Zu einigen Stellen der Bücher der Makkabäer," *Akademie der Wissenschaften in Wien, Philosophisch-historische Klasse: Anzeiger* 74 (1937) 15–30.

Will, Edouard

Histoire politique du monde hellénistique: 323–30 av. J.-C. (2 vols.; Annales de l'Est. Mémoire 30, 32; Nancy: Presses universitaires de Nancy, 1979).

Will, Edouard, and Claude Orrieux

Ioudaïsmos-hellènismos: essai sur le judaïsme judéen à l'époque hellénistique (Nancy: Presses universitaires de Nancy, 1986).

Williams, David S.

"Recent Research in 2 Maccabees," *Currents in Biblical Research* 2, no. 1 (2003) 69–83.

Idem

The Structure of 1 Maccabees (CBQMS 31; Washington, D.C.: Catholic Biblical Association, 1999).

Williams, Margaret H.

"The Meaning and Function of Ιουδαιος in Graeco-Roman Inscriptions," *ZPE* 116 (1997) 249–62.

Winston, David

"The Book of Wisdom's Theory of Cosmogony," *History of Religions* 11 (1971) 185–200.

Idem

"Creatio ex Nihilo Revisited: A Reply to J. Goldstein," *JJS* 37 (1986) 88–91.

Wise, Michael O.

"4Q245 (psDanᶜ ar) and the High Priesthood of Judas Maccabaeus," *DSD* 12 (2005) 313–62.

Witkowski, Stanislaw

Epistulae privatae graecae quae in papyris aetatis Lagidarum servantur (Leipzig: Teubner, 1906).

Wojciechowski, Michal

"Moral Teaching of 1 and 2 Maccabees," *Polish Journal of Biblical Research* 6 (2007) 65–75.

Wolff, Hans Julius

Das Recht der griechischen Papyri Ägyptens in der Zeit der Ptolemäer und des Prinzipats (2 vols.; HA 10.5; Munich: Beck, 1978).

Wörrle, Michael

"Inschriften von Herakleia am Latmos I: Antiochus III, Zeuxis and Herakleia," *Chiron* 18 (1988) 421–76.

Idem

"Zu Rang und Bedeutung von Gymnasion und Gymnasiarchie im hellenistischen Pergamon," *Chiron* 37 (2007) 501–16.

Xeravits, Géza G., and József Zsengellér, eds.

The Books of the Maccabees: History, Theology, Ideology (JSJSup 118; Leiden: Brill, 2007).

Young, Robin Darling

"The 'Woman with the Soul of Abraham': Traditions about the Mother of the Maccabean Martyrs," in Amy-Jill Levine, ed., *Women Like This: New Perspectives on Jewish Women in the Greco-Roman World* (Early Judaism and Its Literature 1; Atlanta: Scholars Press, 1991) 67–81.

Zambelli, Marcello

"La composizione del secondo libro dei Maccabei e la nuova cronologia di Antioco IV Epifane," in *Miscellanea Greca e Romana* (Studi pubblicati dall'Istituto per la Storia Antica 16; Rome: n.p., 1965) 195–299.

Zegers, Norbert

Wesen und Ursprung der griechischen Geschichtsschreibung (Cologne: Üniversität zu Köln, 1959).

Zeitlin, Solomon

The First Book of Maccabees: An English Translation (Eng. trans. Sidney Tedesche; New York: Harper, 1950).

Idem

The Second Book of Maccabees (Eng. trans. Sidney Tedesche; New York: Harper, 1954).

Ziadé, Raphaélle

Les martyrs Maccabées: de l'histoire juive au culte chrétienne. Les homélies de Grégoire de Nazianze et de Jean Chrysostome (VCSup 80; Leiden: Brill, 2007).

Ziebarth, Erich

Aus dem griechischen Schulwesen (Leipzig: Teubner, 1914).

Ziemann, Ferdinand

De epistularum graecarum formulis sollemnibus quaestiones selectae (Halis Saxonum: Ehrhardt Karras, 1910).

Zollschan, Linda T.

"The Earliest Jewish Embassy to the Romans: 2 Macc 4:11?" *JJS* 55 (2004) 37–44.

Zsengellér, József

"Maccabees and Temple Propaganda," in Géza G. Xeravits and József Zsengellér, eds., *The Books of the Maccabees: History, Theology, Ideology* (JSJSup 118; Leiden: Brill, 2007) 181–95.

Zuckerman, Constantine

"Hellenistic *politeumata* and the Jews. A Reconsideration," *SCI* 8–9 (1985–88) 171–85.

Zwick, Reinhold

"Unterhaltung und Nutzen: Zum literarischen Profil des 2. Buches der Makkabäer," in Johannes Frühwald-König, Ferdinand R. Prostmeier, and Reinhold Zwick, eds., *Steht nicht geschrieben? Studien zur Bibel und ihrer Wirkungsgeschichte: Festschrift für Georg Schmuttermayr* (Regensburg: Pustet, 2001) 125–49.

1. Passages

a. Hebrew Bible
b. Apocrypha and Septuagint
c. Old Testament Pseudepigrapha
**   and Other Jewish Literature**
d. New Testament
e. Early Christian Literature and the
**   Ancient Church**
f. Greek and Latin Authors

a / Hebrew Bible

Genesis

1:2	161
1:28	274
2–3	57
2:3	290
2:4	159
2:7	159
2:18	274
5:1	159
6:17	159
7:15	159
7:22	159
11:1-11	57
12	48
12:1-2	50
14:5	241, 242
14:18-20	135
14:18-19	88 n. 57
15:16	150
16:13	156
17:14	149
18	50
19:10	271
19:11	211
29:34	25
29:35	178
30:1-2	139
31:5	25
31:19	245
32:22-32	217 n. 12
35:7	67
37:34	85
49	191 n. 38
49:1-27	156
49:24	87
50:16-17	33

Exodus

1:11	132
2:2	153
2:24-25	170
2:24	26
2:25	51, 89, 156, 290
3:1	132
3:15	155
3:20	187 n. 14
4:25	149
6:1	295
6:5-8	26
7:20	187 n. 14
7:25	187 n. 14
8:16-17	187 n. 14
8:22	87
9:4	87
9:15	187 n. 14
9:25	187 n. 14
11:7	87
12:10	58
12:12	187 n. 14
12:14	155
12:23	187 n. 14
12:27	187 n. 14
12:29	187 n. 14
13:9	155
13:21	57
14:30—15:1	296
15	44
15:3	243
15:6-7	293
15:7	243
15:11	294
15:16	241 n. 34, 295
15:17	51
18:16	27
18:20	27
18:25	175
19:6	61
19:7	56

20:3	109
20:8	290
20:11	290
21:2-11	208
21:24	126
22:22-24	82, 178
22:28a	109
23:8	116
23:20	217
23:22	4, 61, 210
23:23	210
24:12	56
25:9	281
25:17-22	56
25:30	32
27:20-21	32
29:22	59
29:26	59
29:33-34	59
29:38-42	32
30:1-8	56
30:3	56
30:7-8	32
30:10	56
31:16-17	290
32:10-14	88
32:12	88
34:6	49, 178 n. 45
34:13	200
34:15	137
34:21	289
35:2	289
35:22	26
40:23-27	200
40:34	57

Leviticus

1	88
1:9	32
1:13	32
1:17	32
2:1	32
2:2	32
2:4	32
2:5	32
2:7	32

Leviticus (continued)	
4:3	43
4:5	43
4:7	33, 56
4:13-35	248
4:16	43
4:18	33
5:5	32
6:1-17	88
6:15	43
6:22	43
6:30	58
7:12-14	88
8–9	58
8:12	43
8:16-17	58
8:31-33	58
9:3	59
9:23-24	58
9:24	58
10:1	33
10:11	222 n. 42
10:16-20	58
10:16-17	59
10:16	59
11	136
11:7	152
15:18	136
16:12-13	33
16:13	56
16:22	133
18:3	222 n. 42
18:26	222 n. 42
18:30	222 n. 42
20:23	222 n. 42
20:26	50
22:4	266
22:20-25	136
22:29	88
23:15-21	243
23:33	136
23:36	58
23:40	201
23:43	201
24:1-9	33
24:1-4	32
24:5-9	32
26:42	25

Numbers	
1:21	84
3:10	200, 255
5:5-10	88
5:8	88
10:1-3	255
10:9	177 n. 43
11:2	58
12:7	26
12:10	31
14:7	281 n. 14
14:21	290
14:26-34	56
15:30-31	88
16:22	87
16:27	31
17:15	32
21:7	58
21:21-24	243
24:16	88 n. 57
27:16	87
28	136
28:3-8	32
31:19	245
31:25-30	178
31:28-29	179
34:2	56
36:2	61

Deuteronomy	
1:8-9	61
1:31	147 n. n
2:15	241 n. 34
3:26	30 n. 43
4:8	56
4:29-31	27
4:31	25
5:12	290
6:5	26
6:7	30 n. 43
7:5	200
7:6-7	50
7:6	50
7:12	163
7:17-18	68
7:25-26	245
8:5	150
9:26	58, 271
10:6	266
10:17	254
10:18	82
11:25	241 n. 34

12:9-10	56
14:8	152
14:29	82 n. 29
15:12-17	208
16:9-12	243
16:19	116
17:6	119
17:19	177
19:15	119
19:16-19	120
20:2-4	177
20:5-9	174
20:7	274
20:13	271
20:14	241
24:17	82 n. 29
25:1-3	86
27:1	40
27:12	57
27:19	82 n. 30
27:25	116
28:4	158
28:9	271
28:10	174
28:18	158
28:21	187
28:28	211
28:59	87
29:17-19	56
30:1-5	51, 61
30:3-5	51 n. 16
30:3	54 n. c
31:9	54
31:21	156
32:1-33	156
32:8	88 n. 57
32:9	51, 271
32:10	133
32:34	156
32:36	156, 162, 179
33	156
33:26	175
34:1-5	56

Joshua	
4:7	155
5:13-15	217
6:1-21	239
8:15-16	31
15:8	25

15:35	244
24:25	56
24:33	266

Judges

1:12-13	212 n. 24
1:14	92
3:28	212 n. 24
7	68
7:2-8	294
7:16	177 n. 39
7:24	212 n. 24, 296
8:1	40 n. 8
9:43	177 n. 39
9:45	40 n. 8
9:50	212 n. 24
10:10-16	27
10:16	103
11:3	240
11:9	40 n. 8
11:27	40 n. 8
12:3	40 n. 8
12:5	212 n. 24
17:7	114 n. g
18:21	241
19:8	287 n. c

Ruth

3:4	25
3:7	25
3:8	25
3:14	25
4:15	155

1 Samuel

2:3	154
2:5	155
4:3-5	177
8:3	116
9:6	33
9:13	33
11:11	177 n. 39
12:22	174
15	209 n. 13
15:10-11	56
17:44	190
17:46	190
17:54	296
19:10	31
19:13	25

22:2	271
23:14	133
25:30	271
26:7	25
30:24-25	178
31:9	296
31:10	298

2 Samuel

6:18	211
6:21	271
7:8	271
7:24	271
10:11-12	275
17:18-19	212
18:2	177 n. 39
20:25	43 n. 27

1 Kings

1:32-45	43 n. 27
8	58
8:29-30	32
8:32	141
8:44-52	27
9:1-9	78
13:22	129
18:34-35	49
18:36-39	51
19:1-9	133
19:4-8	133
20:26-43	209
20:31	210
22:19-23	217

2 Kings

5:1-19	87
13:9	156
17:18	31
18–19	44
18:4-8	34
18:17—19:36	90
19:19	51
21:16	32
22:13	30 n. 43
23:21-23	34
23:27	31
24:3	31
24:4	32

1 Chronicles

5:2	271

8:13	40
8:19	267 n. 11
10:10	298
12:16	40
13:12-14	177 n. 43
17:14	26
17:23	281 n. 14
19:12-13	175
19:18	173
21:1	92
21:5	84
23:34	84
24:10	104
24:12	267 n. 11
24:14	79
27:4	271
27:8	271
27:16	271
28:9	26
29:13	281 n. 14
29:19	26

2 Chronicles

1:7-12	58
5:1	119
5:5	56
6:37	54 n. b
7:1	58, 200
7:5	66, 58
7:9	58, 66
7:11	58
7:12-22	131
8:12-16	58
9:29	30 n. 43
12:7	169 n. h
13:11	32
15:2	27
15:8	66
16:9	89 n. 60
17:6	26
20:22-23	242
21:18	187
22:7-9	177
24:11	79
24:20	27
29:3—31:21	34
29:31	26
30:1-9	33
30:1	34, 35
30:6	26

2 Chronicles (*continued*)

30:10-12	34
31–32	117
31:21	27
32:1-22	90
32:7-8	175
32:21	175
35:1-19	34
35:19	31
36:3	54 n. b
36:5	32
36:18	56

Ezra

2:2	48
2:61-63	104
3:2-11	63
3:2-6	48 n. 1
3:7-11	48
4:7	298
5:7	25
5:16	48, 63
6:9-10	79
6:16	66
7:12	254
7:20-24	79
8:6	49
10:15	49

Nehemiah

1:1	48
1:9	51 n. 16
2:1-11	48
2:17—7:3	48
3:16	48
4:8	40 n. 8
4:13	114 n. g
5:8	208
7:7	48
8:4	261
8:6	162
9:6	49
9:7	50
9:8	26
9:13	56
9:26-27	27
9:32	281 n. 14
12:5	79
12:11	49 n. 8
12:14	49 n. 8

12:18	49 n. 8
12:22	49 n. 8
12:27-45	66
12:27-43	48
13:28	40

Esther

2:16	298 n. 37
2:20 LXX	107
3:7	298 n. 37
3:13	298 n. 37
3:13g LXX	221
4:1-3	210 n. 17
4:1	84, 85, 271
4:17b-c	161 n. 43
4:17g LXX	50
5:1 LXX	88 n. 59
5:1a LXX	162
8:8	30 n. 43
8:11	235
8:12	298 n. 37
8:12h LXX	221
9:1	298 n. 37
9:15	298 n. 37
9:16	298 n. 37
9:17-19	298
9:19	298 n. 37
9:20-32	33
9:20-21	34
9:21	298 n. 37
9:23	34
9:24-26	34
9:27	34
9:29	34
10:3b	171
13:9 LXX	49

Job

1:2	155
1:20	271
2:12	271
10:8-12	159
15:16	148 n. q
15:24	30
22:12	156
24:3	82
31:22	31
34:21-24	156
34:21	89 n. 60
34:23	290

36:22	87
38:11	188
38:35	210
42:17b	298

Psalms

Common Numbering

3:5	271
6:5	178
7:17	88 n. 57, 178
149:4	281
149:6	295

Masoretic Numbering

9:9	210 n. 19
9:10	27
9:12	171
14:2	89 n. 60
18:2	210 n. 19
18:14	211
20:8	175
27:5-6	281
29:3-10	135
31:3	210 n. 19
32:7	210 n. 19
46:1	210 n. 19
50:12	280 n. 13
59:16	210 n. 19
65:8	188
66:7	89 n. 60
68:5	82
68:19	281
71:3	210 n. 19
73:3	162
74:7	130
75:8	301
76:9-10	171 n. 2
78	133
79	267
84:12	49
85:1	281
89:10	188
90:1	210 n. 19
91:2	210 n. 19
91:9	210 n. 19
94:6	82 n. 30
94:12-15	150
94:12-14	27
94:22	210 n. 19

332

102:2	27
102:14	171 n. 2
105:6	50
105:8-10	25
106:5	50
106:9	188
106:38	32
118:18	150
135:14	156
136:2-3	254
139:13-15	159
144:2	210 n. 19

Proverbs

1:7	154
6:1-5	210
6:17	32
8:6	201
8:28	61
11:9	192
11:12	192
15:3	89 n. 60
16:5	246 n. 57
16:20	160
17:8	116
17:18	210
17:23	116
18:16	116
19:26	40
19:28 LXX	210
20:29	153
21:14	116
22:26	210
26:3	85–86
29:18	160

Qoheleth

3:7	268
9:7	26
9:12	27
11:5	159

Isaiah

1:17	82 n. 30
1:23	82 n. 30
10:5-32	44
10:5-19	158
10:5	131
10:12	131
10:32	280 n. 10
14	162
14:4-21	189
14:12-21	189
14:12-14	189
14:14	88 n. 57
14:19	196 n. 76
14:21	158
15:3	85
19:19	36-37 n. 67
19:23	37 n. 67
24:5	27
31:8	293, 295
34:14	133
36:11	298
36:13-20	295
37:20	51
37:36	175, 291, 295
40:12	188
40:26	161 n. 43
41:8	50
43:1-7	174
43:24	246
44:1	50
44:13	159
45:1-7	254
45:1	32
51:15	188
52:11-12	133
54:7-8	150, 158
54:10	103
56:7	247
57:11	131
59:7	32
60:7	247
65:4	152
66:3	26
66:16	293
66:17	152

Jeremiah

2:2-3	133
2:6	133
4:23 LXX	161
6:26	210 n. 17
7:4	131
7:6	82 n. 30
7:16	292
7:32	82 n. 30
9:17-22	85
11:14	292
14:7	174
14:11	292
15:9	155
16:17	246 n. 57
17:27	32
22:3	32, 82 n. 30
22:17	32
25:15	301
27:5	297
27:33 LXX	51
29:5-6	274
31:15	159
31:25 LXX	297
31:29	158
31:31-34	26 n. 17, 57
31:33	56
32:15 LXX	301
32:20	294
34:5 LXX	297
36:20	32
36:23 LXX	192
38:31-34 LXX	26 n. 17
38:33 LXX	56
38:34 LXX	192
39:20 LXX	294
41:11	115 n. 2
41:15	115 n. 2
42	292
43:20 LXX	32
44	56
48:25	297
49:18 LXX	169 n. h
50:33	51
51:6 LXX	169 n. h
52:17-23	56

Lamentations

1:10	130 n. 25
5:7	158

Ezekiel

4:3	155
5:6	222 n. 42
5:7	222 n. 42
8:12	156
9:9	156, 290
11:19-20	26
12:11	294 n. 24
18:2	158
20	133

Ezekiel (*continued*)

21:9-17	293
22:7	82 n. 30
25:1-5	115
26:7	254
28:2-10	189
28:6-9	162
33:8a	31
35:12-14	171
35:15	51
36:26-27	26 n. 17
36:38	51
39:4	190
39:11-12	187
39:17-20	190
40:46	43 n. 27
43:7	281
43:19	43 n. 27
44:15	43 n. 27
48:11	43 n. 27

Daniel

2:4 LXX	298
2:5	42
2:21 LXX	103
2:37	254
2:47	87, 246 n. 57
3:26 LXX	88 n. 57
3:28-30	189
3:28-29	87
3:29	42
3:45 LXX	163
4:1	25
4:12	133
4:14 LXX	88 n. 57
4:15	31
4:24–25	133
4:25	189
4:34-37	189
4:34 LXX	294 n. 24
4:37	87
5:18 LXX	88 n. 57
5:21	133
5:29 LXX	88 n. 57
6:25-27	87
6:26	25
6:27 Th	294 n. 24
7:9	218
8:4	158
8:12	141

8:23	150
8:24	141
9:3 LXX	256
9:15	295
9:19	174
10:21	55
11:3	158
11:7	141
11:28-31a	140-41
11:29-30	129
11:31	103, 135
11:32	141
11:36	189
11:44	129 n. 20
12:2	157
12:7	200

Hosea

2:14-15	133

Joel

1:8	85 n. 44
2:16-17	84 n. 41
2:17	210
2:20	189
3:17	281

Amos

1:13-15	115
2:4	27

Obadiah

4	130

Jonah

3:6	85

Micah

1:10	210 n. 17, 271
2:3	27

Nahum

1:4	188

Zephaniah

1:15	30
2:11	67
2:13	133

Haggai

1:1-15	48 n. 1

Zechariah

2:10	281
2:16	31
4:9	48 n. 1
4:10	89 n. 60
6:11-13	48 n. 1
7:10	82 n. 30
9:1	89 n. 60, 156
13:7	293
14:3	40 n. 8
14:12	188

b / Apocrypha and Septuagint

1 Kingdoms

2:35	26
3	58
6:29-34	58
7:51	119
8:4	56
8:10-11	57
8:27	280 n. 13
8:54	58
8:63	58
9:1	58
18–19	60
20:35-43	60
21:17-19	121
26:19	92

2 Kingdoms

1:9	87
7:23	67
9:1-3	60
9:30-37	121
18:15-16	116
18:28	162
19:35	175
20:21	162
22:14	88 n. 57
22:32	49, 159
24:1	92
25:13-17	56
25:15	56

3 Kingdoms

8:33-34	247
8:47-48	54 n. b
8:50	171 n. 2
8:63	66

9:6-9   281
11:27   162
11:29   31
21:31   210

4 Kingdoms
9:30-37   188
13:23   171 n. 2
17:23   103
18:26   298
19:35   291, 295
23:33   103

Psalms
Greek (LXX) Numbering
11:6 LXX   52 n. 21
12:6 LXX   88 n. 57
17:14 LXX   211
17:35 LXX   271
19:8 LXX   175
30:7 LXX   156
32:12 LXX   271
36:19 LXX   27
39:11 LXX   271
46:4 LXX   271
50:1 LXX   246 n. 58
50 9 LXX   246 n. 58
54:7 LXX   271
62:8 LXX   271
73:7 LXX   130
74:8 LXX   301
85:15 LXX   178 n. 45
88:12 LXX   161 n. 43
93:12-14 LXX   27
93:12-13 LXX   150
101:3 LXX   27
101:14 LXX   171 n. 2
102:7 LXX   26
102:8 LXX   178 n. 45
105:38 LXX   32
105:47 LXX   61
106:6 LXX   30
106:13 LXX   30
106:19 LXX   30
106:28 LXX   30
108:13-14 LXX   246 n. 58
110:4 LXX   178 n. 45
111:4 LXX   178 n. 45
112:5-6 LXX   156
114:5 LXX   178 n. 45

117:13 LXX   271
133:2 LXX   162
135:2-3 LXX   254
144:8 LXX   178 n. 45
145:6 LXX   161 n. 43
146:2 LXX   51 n. 16

Baruch
2:11   295
3:32   160
3:35-36   160
4:1   27
5:3   61

Bel and the Dragon
28   137, 191
41-42   87
41   189

Susanna
8-12   153 n. 19
42   246 n. 57

1 Esdras
1:28   31
1:54   56
2:3   88 n. 57
5:8   48
5:38-40   104
5:49–6:2   48 n. 1
6:20   48
7:17   66
9:8-9   136
9:42   261
9:51   79
9:54   79

2 Esdras
4:7   298
5:7   25
18:4   261

Additions to Esther
3:13 (Addition B)   14, 269 n. 25
3:13e (= Addition B 13:5)   235
10:9 (Addition F)   294 n. 24
8:13   88

Judith
4:8   40, 114 n. g
5:18   31
6:2   290 n. 6
8:7   82
8:27   150
9:8   130
9:11   216
11:14   40
13:8   296
13:18   88 n. 57
14:1   296
14:6-7   296
14:11   296, 298
15:8   40
15:12   201
15:14   49
18:32   280
19:10   280
21:17-19   188

1 Maccabees
1:3   236
1:4   140 n. 76
1:14   16, 222 n. 42
1:17   254
1:20-64   139-41
1:20-23   125
1:21-23   130
1:29-49   32
1:29   132, 219
1:30   132, 275 n. 53
1:31   31
1:33   105
1:38   31-32
1:41-54   133
1:41   222 n. 42
1:44   222 n. 42
1:47   136, 152, 200
1:54   135, 200
1:56   60
1:57   222
1:60-61   148
1:61   149
2:1   133, 256
2:3-5   177
2:12   293 n. 18
2:18   79, 160
2:20   25
2:26-27   92

1 Maccabees (*continued*)

2:29-38	132, 149–50
2:40-41	178
2:43	127, 271
2:50	25
3:1-9	170
3:10-26	229
3:10-25	172
3:13	172
3:21	222 n. 42
3:25	66
3:29-31	173
3:29	222 n. 42
3:31	186
3:32-33	206
3:32	216
3:34-35	172
3:34	270
3:35	173
3:37	186
3:38—4:25	181, 226, 285
3:38–40	207
3:38	120, 172, 80
3:39	173, 270
3:41	174
3:42	66
3:43	293 n. 18
3:44-60	175
3:49	173
3:51	293 n. 18
3:59	293 n. 18
4:1-25	44
4:1-22	173, 177, 207
4:6	170, 175
4:10	25
4:12-15, 207	
4:15	178
4:26-35	44, 222
4:26	216
4:28	216
4:29-35	226
4:29	216, 217, 255
4:30	217
4:34-35	218
4:35	228
4:36-61	202
4:36	66, 228, 293 n. 18
4:41-60	44
4:41	207, 293 n. 18
4:42-53	199

4:43	293 n. 18
4:48	293 n. 18
4:50-53	32
4:52	33 n. 56, 200
4:59	66
4:61	216
5:1-2	248
5:3-51	248
5:3	207
5:4	212
5:6-8	211, 212
5:6	10, 240
5:8	212
5:9-54	237
5:9-13	239, 240
5:10	66
5:11	10, 212 n. 24
5:15	125 n. l, 138, 260
5:18	165, 177
5:25	237, 238
5:26	237, 238, 241
5:33	177 n. 39
5:34	10
5:35	212 n. 24
5:36	212 n. 24, 237, 238, 240
5:37	10
5:39	97
5:40	10
5:43	241
5:44	212 n. 24
5:45-51	243
5:54	16 n. 83
5:55-62	243
5:55-61	248
5:55-60	244
5:56	177, 272
5:58-59	243
5:59	207
5:60-62	16 n. 83
5:61	67
5:67	67
6:1-16	44
6:1-4	41
6:1-3	186
6:5-17	42
6:14-15	197
6:14	10
6:17	206
6:18	293 n. 18

6:20	10
6:27	212 n. 24
6:28-54	29
6:29	253
6:30-63	262
6:30-46	270
6:30	216, 250 n. a, 253
6:31	255, 257
6:32-63	258-59
6:33-46	257
6:37	251 n. j
6:48-53	256
6:49-50	216, 257
6:49-22	258
6:49	29, 257
6:54	228, 293 n. 18
6:55-63	197
6:55-59	228
6:55-56	10
6:59	222 n. 42
6:61	228 n. 12
6:62	275 n. 53
6:63	10
7	274–75
7:1-3	265
7:2-4	158
7:5-7	268
7:5	266
7:8-20	285
7:8	11, 179
7:9	266 n. 6
7:10-13	267
7:10	275 n. 53
7:12-15	263 n. a
7:14	266
7:15	275 n. 53
7:16	267
7:27-29	279
7:27	275 n. 53
7:30-32	289
7:33	280, 293 n. 18
7:39-47	289
7:39-43	294
7:39	289, 295
7:40	272
7:41-42	291
7:41	294
7:43	293 n. 18
7:47	297
7:50	236

8:2	272	12:39	30	8:13	210
8:6	79	12:48	138	10:13	87
8:13	103	13:3	293 n. 18	11:7	57
8:17	15, 104	13:5	28	13:15-23	79
8:19	104 n. 71	13:6	293 n. 18	13:26	26
9:1-22	274–75, 285	13:8	271	16:11	87
9:2	212 n. 24	13:11	63, 237	16:17-18	246 n. 57
9:3	274	13:20-22	29	17:15-20	246 n. 57
9:11	296	13:22	29	17:17	50
9:22	272	13:23	29	18:10-14	164
9:30	271	13:25	256	20:6-7	268
9:52	217	13:31-32	30	22:4	82
9:54	293 n. 18	13:31	29	24:8-10	281
9:55-56	267	13:33	29, 37	24:8	49, 159
9:57	236	13:34	29	24:12	51
9:68	126	13:36	160	25:3-6	153
9:69	107	13:37	268	29:13	233
10:15	272	13:39	224	29:14-15	210
10:16	160	13:40	27	32:1-2	71
10:18	221	13:41-42	29, 37, 63	32:15	165
10:19-20	160	13:41	30	33:2	165
10:21	18 n. 90	13:42	31, 271	34:16	175
10:29	268	13:43-48	63	36:17-18	171
10:35	224	13:48	63	37:25	271
10:39	293 n. 18	13:49-51	297	39:19	246 n. 57
10:62-63	118	14:4	236	39:33	50
10:65	160	14:5	237	40:12	246 n. 58
10:74-77	237	14:8	235	41:7	57
10:75	237	14:15	293 n. 18	41:11	246 n. 58
11:2	275 n. 53	14:20-23	128	42:20	246 n. 57
11:7	158	14:21	126	44:11	174
11:13	37	14:29	293 n. 18	44:18	174
11:19	28–29	14:31	293 n. 18	44:20	26
11:26-27	160	14:33	217	45:5	56
11:24-27	96	14:35	271	45:17	174
11:29	219	14:36	293 n. 18	45:19	294 n. 24
11:30	221	14:41	271	46:5-6	87
11:38	236	14:42	293 n. 18	46:16	87
11:43	60	14:48	293 n. 18	46:20	246 n. 58
11:44	126	15:7	293 n. 18	47:12-19	58
11:52	236	16:23	67, 272	47:24	31
11:57-58	96	16:24	35	48:18-22	176
11:57	160			48:18	297
11:59	261	Sirach		48:20-21	291
12:1	104 n. 71, 268	1:10	50	49:11-12	48 n. 1
12:5-23	108	1:26	50	49:13	48
12:6-23	128	3:30	79	50:1	43, 78 n. 1
12:6	37, 40	4:10	88 n. 57	50:12-14	66
12:33	212 n. 24	5:4-9	164	50:20	162
12:39-48	29	6:18	153	51:10-12	27

Tobit
1:4   31
1:8   82 n. 29
4:1   171
5:22   217
6:18   178 n. 45
7:12   178 n. 45
13:2   153
14:9 AB   27

Wisdom of Solomon
2:1   160
2:9   188
2:13   162
3:1-4   155
3:4   158
3:5   150
4:8-9   153
4:9   153
5:2   87
5:15   88
6:3   88
7:23   187
7:26   87, 153
9:15   163
11:5   121, 188
11:9-10   150
11:9   51 n. 17
11:10—12:27   164
11:15-16   121, 188
11:17   161 n. 43
12:3   31
12:6   162
12:22   150
12:23   51 n. 17
13:5   161 n. 43
15:11   159
15:14   51 n. 17
16:1   51 n. 17
16:4   51 n. 17
16:11   150
16:13   153, 160
16:15   161
17:2   51 n. 17, 258
17:16   258
18:3-4   121
18:3   67, 188
18:22   174
19:5   87
19:13   211
19:17   211

c / Old Testament Pseudepigrapha and Other Jewish Literature

i.   **Pseudepigrapha**
ii.   **Josephus**
iii.   **Philo**
iv.   **Dead Sea Scrolls**
v.   **Rabbinic**

i. Pseudepigrapha

Epistle of Aristeas
16   88 n. 59, 159
18   162
19   88
29–31   60
37   88
41   193
92   136
132   161 n. 43, 163
187–294   43
211   280
259   50
263   189

Assumption of Moses
3:4   210 n. 17
9   165 n. 61
9:7   163

2 Baruch
6:7-9   56
10:1-5   55
54:17-22   161 n. 43
63:10   31

Paralipomena Jeremiou
3:9-11   56
3:15   55
3:18-19   56
4:4   56
7:29-31a   56

1 Enoch
1–11   79
1:5   50
6:2   162
9:4   254
9:10   171
13:8   162

14:3   162
22   153, 247
33:2   42 n. 20
34:2-3   42 n. 20
35:1   42 n. 20
36:1-2   42 n. 20
37:2-4   87
38:4   87
39:2   87
39:7   87
41:9   87
61:10   87
63:4   254
72:2-3   42 n. 20
83–91   79
84:2   254
90:19   293
90:34   293
101:2   42 n. 20
104:2   42 n. 20
106:5   162

4 Ezra
13:48   31
19:22   56
144:37-48   60

Jubilees
1:25   162
14:2   49
14:8   49
32:1-3   43

Ps.-Philo
Liber antiquitatum biblicarum
19:10   31
26:13   150

3 Maccabees
1:5   130
1:9   93
1:16—2:24   130
2:2   49, 167 n. a
2:3   87, 188
2:9   280
2:13   167 n. a
2:21   88 n. 59
3:9   292
3:11   88
3:26   14, 269 n. 25, 236

4:14	159	*Testament of Job*		12.186–222	82
5:9	194 n. 58	33:5	31	12.222	115 n. 2
5:20	211			12.223–25	78 n. 1
5:25	88	**ii. Josephus**		12.228–36	82, 83
5:35	254			12.229–34	240
5:50	194 n. 58	*Antiquitates judaicae*		12.229	115 n. 2
5:51	87	1.81	224 n. 64	12.237	117
6:2	88	1.239–41	108	12.238–41	96
6:5	176, 291	1.240–41	129	12.238	96, 114
6:17	194 n. 58	1.322	245	12.239–54	140
6:28	14, 162, 269 n. 25	1.332	217 n. 12	12.249–50	107
6:32	294	3.80	211	12.251	129
6:33	194 n. 58	4.238	86	12.258–64	132
6:59	87	4.285	82	12.258–61	124 n. k, 134
7:3	292	5.138	2	12.260–61	135
7:4-7	269 n. 25	6.10	247 n. 68	12.261–64	270
7:4	14, 236	6.143	2	12.261	172
7:6-7	236	6.353	2	12.263	134 n. 51
7:9	88	7.184	2	12.264	221
		7.196	2	12.287	172
4 Maccabees		8.42-49	58	12.296	253
4:5	93 n. 8	8.111	280	12.354–59	44
4:11	194 n. 58	9.223	66	12.354–55	186
4:17	96	9.256	134 n. 51	12.354	41
5–7	151	10.4	117	12.383–85	254
5:13	88	11.114–15	134 n. 51	12.385	255
6:6	194 n. 58	11.195	2	12.386	197 n. 85
6:20	25	11.297	49 n. 8	12.387	266
11:5	49	11.326	85	12.389–90	265
		12.5–6	132	12.402	270
Martyrdom of Isaiah		12.8.11	192 n. 41	12.411–12	296
2:8	133	12.25	247 n. 68	12.411	295
		12.50	79	13.63	36 n. 67
Psalms of Solomon		12.51	193 n. 52	13.64	36 n. 67
2:30-31	129	12.58	79	13.65–66	36 n. 67
8:12	136 n. 59	12.120	17, 106	13.74–79	60
8:14	301	12.134–44	59	13.77	68 n. 14
8:34	51 n. 16	12.137	68	13.78	79
22:29-30	290 n. 6	12.138–44	14, 79, 103, 104	13.166	193
		12.138	105, 115, 119	13.187	29
Sibylline Oracles		12.142	13, 100, 139, 268	13.218	29
frg. 1.4	187	12.145–46	136	13.242–44	10
3:286-94	37 n. 68	12.146	80	13.254–58	36, 63
3:564-67	37 n. 68	12.148	223 n. 47	13.267	36
3:591	194 n. 58	12.150	103	13.270–74	36
3:652-56	37 n. 67	12.154–222	83	13.275–81	63
3:657-731	37 n. 68	12.154	107 n. 97	13.284–87	36
3:719	87	12.156–57	78 n. 1	13.311	40
3:767-80	37 n. 68	12.156	134 n. 51	13.352–55	37
5:352	187	12.172	92	13.353–54	36

Antiquitates judaicae (continued)

13.383	244
13.384–85	266
13.395–97	63
13.397	63
14.188	192 n. 41
14.213	222
14.246	222
14.260	222
14.278	2
14.421–22	201
14.429–30	165 n. 61
15.184	195 n. 65
15.241	69
15.254	63
15.346	201
16.60	192 n. 41
16.163	88
17.168–70	188, 189
18.28	101
18.55	298
18.86–87	57
18.273	93n. 8
19.281	192 n. 41
20.35	114
20.236–37	78 n. 1
20.240	40

Bellum judaicum

1.18	73
1.31–35	140
1.31–33	83
1.33	117
1.41	253
1.78	40
1.312–13	165 n. 61
2.344	102
2.457	201
2.591	106
3.42	126
3.427	41 n. 9
5.160	237
5.379–81	48
6.288	126
6.298	126
7.44	117
7.423–25	36 n. 67
7.423	117
7.431	36 n. 67
7.432	36 n. 67
7.455	301

Contra Apionem

1.32	292
1.118	108 n. 103
1.180	190
1.190–93	157
1.197	129
1.208–12	17
1.209–11	132
1.215–16	108 n. 104
2.35	192 n. 41
2.48	79
2.49–56	36
2.79	74
2.80–81	130 n. 27
2.82	130
2.84	74
2.92–96	130 n. 27
2.143–44	121, 188
2.157	241

Vita

74	106
138	256

iii. Philo

De Abrahamo

82	50
83	50
121	50

De cherubim

7	50

De decalogo

41	254 n. 20
52	78
160	247 n. 68

In Flaccum

20	161
43	36
73	161

De gigantibus

16	217
64	50

Legatio ad Gajum

43	83

191	68 n. 14
198	68 n. 14
223–44	84

De mutatione nominum

66	50
69	50
71	50

De praemiis et poenis

43	161 n. 43
166	2

Quod Deus sit immutabilis

4	247 n. 68

De specialibus legibus

1.1.2	148
2.134	247 n. 68
2.146	247 n. 68
3.169–77	85
4.30–32	82

De virtutibus

159.3	247 n. 68

De vita Mosis

1.212	88
2.27	68

iv. Dead Sea Scrolls

1QapGen

20.10-18	85

1QH

6.26-27	26
13.32-33	26
18.31	26
22 [frg.4].12	26

1QH[a]

8.15	26
8.25	26
9.26	154 n. 26
11.22	162
23.10	162

1QM

3.1-11	177 n. 43

3.13–4:14   177
4.13   177
7.7   217
7.9–9.8   177 n. 43
10:5   26
10.11   217
11.11-12   295
13.11   217
13.12   217
14.2-3   244
17.6-8   217

1QS
3.15   154 n. 26
4.22   162
5.17   267
8.14   267
9.19–20   133
11.8   162
11.15-16   26

CD
1   79
1.10   26
7.19   167
8.20   55
12.1-2   136
15.9-10   26

4Q 177 frg. 2 line 3
                 30 n. 43

4Q 196 frg. 2 line 10
                 243

4Q 213 [4QLevi^a^ar]
                 43
4Q 213^A^ [4QLevi^c^ar]
                 43

4Q 242   187, 189

4Q 248   141

4Q 302 3 ii 5   26

4Q 383   55

4Q 384 [?]   55

4Q385 (4QpsEzek^a)^) frg. 5 line 2
                 26
4Q 385   55-56
4Q 385^B^   55
4Q 385^B^ i 8   56

4Q 387^B^   55

4Q 389^A^   55

4Q397 (4QMMT 95-96)
frgs. 7 and 8, lines 10–11
                 60 n. 9

4Q 402 frg. 4, lines 12–13
                 154

4Q 417 2 i 8–9   154

11Q13 frg. 2, line 23
                 30 n. 43

11QPs^a^   59

11QT
45.7-12   136
47.7-18   80
[11Q19] 61.15   177
[11Q19] 58.11-15
                 178

v. Rabbinic

b. Berakot
17a   26

b. Menaḥot
52a   247

b. Šabbat
25b   245

b. Sanhedrin
11a-b   33
11b   34
38a   48

m. Pesaḥim
7:9   58

m. Roš Haššanah
2:7   35

m. Šabbat
2:2   51

m. Yoma
2:2   106

Genesis Rabbah
40.2   85

Pesiqta Rabbati
131b   55–56

t. Sanhedrin
2:5-6   33
2:15   35

t. Šeqalim
2:6   247

y. Pesaḥim
7:9   58

d / New Testament

Matthew
10:26   246
23:32   150

Mark
2:27   131
4:22   246
5:21-43   182
6:7-30   182
9:3   218
16:5   218

Luke
8:17   246
9:53   134 n. 51
10:33-37   134 n. 51
12:2   246
16:26   247
22:6   276 n. a
24:44   60
24:45   26

John
12:32   173
14–17   156

Acts
10:24   214 n. a
12:23   188
16:14   26
21:20   92
28:6   87

Romans
1:30   161

1 Corinthians
15:24   87
15:29   247

Ephesians
1:21   87

Colossians
1:16   87
2:10   87
2:15   87

1 Thessalonians
2:16   150

1 Timothy
2:8   85
6:15   87

Hebrews
7:22   210
8:8   57
10:31   161
11:35-38   3
12:9   87
12:21   264 n. e

1 Peter
1:6   162
3:22   87

Revelation
1:6   61

e / Early Christian Literature and the Ancient Church

Acts of Thomas
140   200

Apostolic Constitutions
8.6.5   26-27
8.6.15   26

Clement of Alexandria *Stromata*
1.22.150.1–3   43
1.23.153.4   60
1.141.4   104 n. 69
5.14.97.7   1

Eusebius *Historia ecclesiastica*
5.28.12   85

Eusebius *Praeparatio evangelica*
8.9.38   1 n. 1
8.10.4   43
8.10.12   87
9.17.2–9   134 n. 51, 135
9.24   88
9.25.4   157
9.26.1   104 n. 69
9.29.14   88
9.30.1–9.34.20   104 n. 69
9.30.1   60
9.31.1–34.3   60
9.31   88
9.34.18   108
9.34.19   108
9.39.1–5   60
9.39.2–5   104 n. 69
9.39.5   55, 56
13.12.1   43
13.12.9   281

Jerome *Commentary on Daniel*
718 (*PL* 11:36)   186

Justin Martyr
Apologia
5   136
Dialogus cum Tryphone
10   136

Martyrdom of Perpetua and Felicitas
7–8   247

Martyrdom of Polycarp
2   162

f / Greek and Latin Authors

Aelian *Varia Historia*
12.21   187
12.40   57

Aelius Aristides *To Rome*
109   301

Aeschylus
Agamemnon
61–62   134 n. 46
320–25   267 n. 12
374   134 n. 46
1501   156
1508   156
Choephori
349   152
Eumenides
236   156
787   153 n. 20
1045   187
Persae
80   189
354   156
734   180 n. 51
744–51   131
745   188
820   189
832–36   180 n. 51
857   189
Septem contra Thebas
683   152
1007   282
1059   153
1069   153

Antiphanes
frg. 282 in R. Kassel and C. Austin, eds., *Poetae Comici Graeci*
189 n. 23

Antiphon
6.4   256 n. 26

Apollodorus Mechanicus *Poliorcetica*
144.11 284

Appian
Bella civilia
2.120 239
4.102 264 n. e, 272
Hispanica
6.75 239
Mithridatia
12.67 237
12.278 237
18 254
Punic Wars
63 235
Sicily
5 235
Syriaca
5 107 n. 97
27 109
45 82, 89, 95
46 253, 265 n. 1, 294
66 41, 44, 186 n. 2,
253
67 29 n. 38
239 216

Aristophanes
Acharnenses
723 86
Birds
548–49 200
Lysistrata
27 71 n. 26
Plutus
476 152

Aristotle
Constitution of Athens
51.1 80
De caelo
3.8 306b22–29 159

Ethica Nicomachea
1119b22–1124b9
111
1121b24 (4.1.38) 150
1138a2-3 68 n. 16

De generatione animalium
743b24 72 n. 27

De mundo
7.401a 134 n. 46
400b24 105 n. 75

Oeconomica
1348b9 27 n. 21

Poetica
6.17 [1450a33] 70
7.10 [1451a] 70
6.28 70 n. 23

Politica
1270b24 42
1272b37 42
1285b 206 n. 4
1301a22 103 n. 63
1322b 149
1328b 149

Rhetorica
1361a37–b2 111

Arrian *Anabasis*
2.24.5 107
2.24.6 107
3.6.1 107
7.3.5 157

Artemidorus *Oneirocritica*
1.54 97 n. 17

Asclepiodotus
12.10 295 n. 27

Athenagoras *Supplicatio
pro Christianis*
32–35 136

Athenaeus *Deipnosophistae*
10.426–27 301

Caesar *Civil War*
2.76 177 n. 44
3.105 126 n. 4

Callimachus *Epigrammata*
27 71 n. 26

Ps.-Callisthenes
3.32–33 156, 191 n. 38

Chariton *De Chaerea et Callirhoe*
6.7.13 196
6.8.7 254

Cicero
De divinatione
2.56.115–16 127 n. 5
Epistulae ad familiares
5.12 70
5.12.2–8 300 n. 7
De oratore
2.5.21 106
2.5.58 no. 150 120
2.9.36 70
Orationes Philippicae
8.33 223
9.4 265 n. 1
In Pisonem
8 no. 18 120
In Verrem
2.3.76 116

Curtius
4.2.10 107
6.11.8 273
7.2.7 273
9.3.16 273
9.3.18 261
10.2.30 261

Demosthenes
De corona
18.220 132
92 220 n. 30
181–87 129
305 223

Orationes
24.10 262
24.11–14 262

Dio Cassius
37.16.2–4 132 n. 33

Dio Chrysostom *Orations*
1.28 282
12.34 50

Diodorus Siculus
1.21 152 n. 15
1.3.1 68

Diodorus Siculus (*continued*)

1.3.5	70
1.4.1	68, 71
1.31.2	236
1.36.4	70, 71
1.76.1	242
1.91–94	247 n. 64
2.43.1	244
3.17.1	70
4.3	217
4.44	152
11.26	247 n. 67
11.33	247 n. 67
12.4.5	259 n. 39
12.50.7	259 n. 37
12.64.3	259 n. 37
13.18	234
13.44.6	105 n. 82
13.61.6	245 n. 50
13.75.4	245 n. 50
14.68.7	40 n. 9
15.38.1–2	259
15.38.12	259 n. 39
15.50.4	259
16.1.1	70
16.41.1	265
16.46.1	259 n. 37
16.50	216 n. 1
16.55.3	71
16.73.2	259 n. 37
16.80.2	242
17.20–22	186
17.34.8	242
17.46.6	107
17.54.6	71
17.68.4	245 n. 50
17.107.5	157
17.415–6	127 n. 5
18.18.3–4	259 n. 39, 260
18.18.6	222 n. 41
18.56.5	223
18.74.2	235
19.30.1	295
19.41.3	295
19.75.6	259 n. 37
20.8.1	242
20.15	44
20.30.1	107
20.41.5	223
20.76.6	247 n. 67
20.95.1	250 n. d
20.102.2–3	100
20.113.4	254 n. 16
21.16.3	40–41 n. 9
21.16.4–5	189 n. 19
22.9	89–90
24.9.1–3	6 n. 35
28.3	40, 41 n. 12, 44
29.12	259 n. 39
30.7.2–3	118
31	158
31.19.7	116
31.33	259 n. 39
31.35	44
31.45	44
32a	158
34.1.1–5	74 n. 33
34.1.3–4	130
34/35.2.1	189
40.3.4–5	43
52.1	105 n. 82

Diogenes Laertius

7:10	155 n. 22
8.79–81	192
9.27	151, 154 n. 25
9.59	151, 154 n. 25

Dionysius of Halicarnassus
Antiquitates Romanae

1.1.1	73
1.1.2	73
1.3.5	68
2.68.1–2	88
2.68.4	196
6*	217-18
6.7.2	196
6.13	85
7.44.4	236 n. 5
11.1.4	69
11.25.4	242
13*	217-18

De compositione verborum

6.19.9	223 n. 50

Epistula ad Pompeium

3	8, 300
6	69

De Thucydide

45	73

Dioscorides *De materia medica*

1.73.2	49

Epictetus

3.24.24	158 n. 40

Euripides
Bacchae

20–22	50
45	158
217–25	138
325	158
1255	158

Electra

241	156 n. 39

Hercules furens

1155	152 n. 15

Iphigenia Aulidensis

1157	27 n. 21
1408	158 n. 40

Phoenissae

570–77	127
1090–92	284
1453	87

Rhesus

933	233

Supplices

931	152

Frontinus
Strategemata

2.1.17	132 n. 33

Galen *De usu partium corporis humani*

11.13	149

Granius Licinianus

28	41
28.6	196

Herodotus *Histories*

1.4	73
1.53	127 n. 5
1.61.2	27 n. 21
1.74	127 n. 5
1.170	180
1.213	134 n. 52
2.44	108 n. 103
2.98.1	116
2.100	255 n. 21
2.120	206

3.66 — 189 n. 19
4.64–73 — 120
4.64 — 156
4.76–80 — 137, 191
4.205 — 188
5.22 — 108
5.29.1 — 27 n. 21
5.49 — 174
5.114 — 298
6.84 — 301
6.108.5 — 27 n. 21
7.22–24 — 131
7.34–37 — 131
7.35 — 188
7.145.1 — 27 n. 21
7.188 — 40 n. 9
7.190 — 40 n. 9
8.35–39 — 6, 89
8.36–38 — 87
8.36 — 45, 68
8.37 — 73, 211
8.41 — 174
8.89 — 130
9.48 — 130
9.82 — 71
9.90 — 174

Hesiod *Theogonia*
854 — 211

Homer
Iliad
1.339 — 25
2.565 — 189
3.264–301 — 259
3.310 — 189
4.212 — 189
5.436–37 — 210
5.440–43 — 158
9.410–16 — 152
13.625 — 134 n. 46
17.38–39 — 296
18.127–19.23 — 293
22.405–7 — 159
22.430–36 — 159
23.782 — 242
24.14–22 — 296

Odyssey
7.191–92 — 171
11.412 — 196 n. 77

16.17 — 65 n. b
19.547 — 287 n. b
20.90 — 287 n. b
23.330 — 211

Horace *Odes*
1.1.36 — 189

Isocrates
Epistula ad Demosthenem
30 — 84 n. 40
Ad Nicoclem
22 — 105 n. 75
48–49 — 71
Panegyricus
43. 259
Philippus
5.85 — 72

Julius Obsequens
15 — 265 n. 1

Justin
2.10.24 — 131
16.2 — 188
20.3.8 — 85
24.8 — 6
24.8.3 — 89
25.2.10 — 176
35.1.6–7 — 158
36.1.7 — 29 n. 38

Pseudo-Hyginus
De munitionibus castrorum
nos. 6–58 — 257 n. 32

Lactantius *De mortibus persecutorum*
23.8–9 — 236

Livy
5.21.8–9 — 69
26.25 — 272 n. 44
35.48.6 — 109
37.11.15 — 139
37.13.9–10 — 116
37.30.9 — 109
37.41.6–42 — 254
37.45.16 — 128
38.11.8 — 83
39.8.3–9.1 — 138

39.51 — 128
40.4 — 166 n. 63
41.20.8 — 134
42.6.6 — 92
42.6.7 — 173
42.6.10–12 — 110
42.63.10–11 — 129
43.6.6 — 110
44.19.9 — 109 n. 115
45.11.9–11 — 207
45.11.9 — 109 n. 115
45.12.1–2 — 127
45.12.3–8 — 127
45.12.7 — 109 n. 115, 207
Periocha 55 — 29 n. 38

Longinus *On the Sublime*
12.4 — 69

Lucan *De bello civili*
1.525 — 126 n. 4

Lucian
Alexander
6–17 — 88
8–22 — 42
59–60 — 188
Anacharsis
35 — 233
Macrobii
19 — 207
Nigrinus
18 — 69
Piscator
33 — 86 n. 52
In Praise of Demosthenes
41 — 282
Quomodo historia conscribenda sit
22 — 301
23 — 73
53-54 — 73
Tyrannicida
6 — 152
Zeuxis
9–11 — 253

Lycurgus
102 — 282
142 — 256

Ovid *Ibis*
315–16   255 n. 21

PAPYRI

P. Columbia
10   194 n. 59

P. Hibeh
no. 79, lines 2–6   193

P. Oxyrhyncus
41.13   92
41.26   92
104.25–27   27 n. 21
833   235 n. 3
1477   15, 271 n. 38
2668   246 n. 59
2927   246 n. 59
3364   246 n. 59

P. Polit. Jud.=Urkunden des Politeuma der Juden von Herakleopolis
8.11–15   24

P. Rylands
113.35   245

P. Tebtunis
138   242
414, lines 5–6   193
703.40–411   82 n. 26
730.1   82 n. 26
781   80
788.15   82 n. 26

Pausanias
1.16.1   49 n. 7
1.18.6   134
2.29.8   135
5.12.4   134
6.2.2   86
7.25.5   102
7.26.9   118
9.7.2–3   188
9.39.5   217
10.4   101
10.23.1–12   6
10.23.2   89
10.23.3   211

26.1.10   134
30.25.13–15   134

Philodemus, Diels, *Philodemos über die Götter*
25.27–28   206 n. 2

Pindar
Isthmian Odes
3.18   181 n. 53
Nemean Odes
5.12   135
11.8   134 n. 46
Olympian Odes
8.21   134 n. 46
8.22   290
Pythian Odes
3.109   290

Plato
Alcibiades
123b-c   116 n. 9
1.122c   118 n. 17
Leges
6.764B   80
9.873C   285
653D–E   50
665A   50
815A   150
927D   180 n. 51
932B   86 n. 51
10.909–910D   149
12.953E   134 n. 46
Phaedo
113D–114C   153
Phaedrus
261A   69
271C   69
Protagoras
326D   72
334D   206
Respublica
8.548D   72
10.614–21   153
553C   103 n. 63
Timaeus
45B–D   48
58C–D   48

Pliny *Naturalis historia*
2.148   126

5.78   265
6.53   156
7.9–11   156
35   72
122–24   72
149   72

Plutarch
Aemilius Paulus
17   126
Agis et Cleomenes
10.1   191
10.3   191
38.4–5   159
Alexander
35.6   49
Amatorius
20   134 n. 46
An seni respublica gerenda sit
789E   64
Apophthegmata laconica
208D–F   131
210B   154
241E   168 n. 17, 218
Cato Major
19.3   73
Comparatio Agidis et Cleomenis cum Tiberio et Gaio Graccho
3.1   127
On Controlling Anger
456C   40
Eumenes
18.2   253
De gloria Atheniensium
346F–347A   72-73
Life of Cicero
40.2   73
Life of Cleomenes
13.2   191
Life of Demetrius
23–24   41
28.3   254 n. 16
48.2   254 n. 16
53   84 n. 43
Life of Demosthenes
8.2   73
Life of Flamininus
13.8   282
Life of Julius Caesar
57.3   247 n. 66

Life of Lucullus
10.3   218
Life of Lycurgus
11.4   247 n. 67
20.4   282
Life of Marcellus
8.6   247
Life of Nicias
1.1.5   73
28   298
Life of Pericles
6.5   106
15.4   69
19   172
Life of Philopoemen
16.5–6   16, 105, 107
Life of Pompey
36   41
Life of Pyrrhus
24.4   105 n. 82
Life of Themistocles
9–10   174
27–28   268 n. 20
Moralia
169C   132 n. 33
De mulierum virtutibus
252C–D   159
Praecepta gerendae reipublicue
789E   43
Quaestiones convivales
1.4 (620A–622B) 71
4.5   152
Quaestiones graecae
294F   41 n. 9
Regum et imperatorum apophthegmata
191A   192
De sera numinis vindicta
548F–549A   189 n. 19
Sulla
36.3–6   188 n. 18
De superstitione
168C   158 n. 40
Table Talk
4.5, 671E   201
4.6, 671C–672C   138
3.7.1   655E, 217
Theseus
19.8   196

35   218
178   206

Polybius
1.1.4   73
1.3.1   73
1.3.10   70
1.4.1   70
1.4.2   70
1.4.11   69
1.7.5   179
1.8.4   206 n. 4
1.13.12   105
1.15.4   256
1.15.13   273 n. 48
1.17.11   105
1.29.5   178
1.29.13   273 n. 48
1.35.10   150 n. 5
1.36.1   193
1.37.5   264 n. e
1.44.13   273 n. 48
1.45.53   273 n. 48
1.48.8   250 n. d
1.67.3   267
1.67.11   267
1.74.7   174
1.74.8   178
1.75   232
1.81.11   171
1.84.7   295
1.87.7   256
2.5   232
2.8.7   188
2.16.14   69
2.25^{e}.1   69
2.29.6   295
2.37–71   74
2.47.3   103 n. 63, 139
2.54.9   257
2.56.3   73
2.56.7   84
2.57.3-4   222
2.59.6   115
2.60.7   118 n. 19
2.69.9   217
2.70.1   139
2.122.11   208
3.29.7   269 n. 26
3.49.2   292

3.51.11   179
3.52.3   268
3.53.8   264 n. e
3.69.12   256
3.70.1   130, 256
3.70.7   206 n. 4
3.74.8   171
3.76.2   260
3.79.8   287 n. b
3.98.7   222
3.107.14   256
3.117.11   256
4–5   74
4.8.11   257
4.13.5   257
4.19.3   257
4.21.10–12   150 n. 5
4.25.3   257 n. 30
4.25.7   139
4.33.11   150 n. 5
4.50.6   257
4.63.1   297
4.76.3   257
4.78.10   257
4.85.1–4   180 n. 50
5.1.7–9   180 n. 50
5.1.9   180 n. 50
5.4.8   126
5.11.5   224
5.11.6   115 n. 1
5.15.3   269
5.25.3   251 n. g
5.33.8   73
5.39.3   117 n. 15
5.46.2   260
5.52.8   257
5.54.10   156, 271
5.63.7   243
5.65.3   80
5.70.12   232, 243
5.73.1   217
5.74.9   282
5.82.1   256
5.84.2   169 n. i
5.97.5   257
5.101.3   253
6.9.10   103 n. 63
6.10   63
6.10.6   42
6.11.12   43, 63

Polybius (*continued*)
6.27–41 257 n. 32
6.35.9–36 82 n. 26
6.53–54 154 n. 24
6.54.2–3 154
6.55 232
7.7.8 69
7.11.7 220 n. 30
8.11.1 73
8.21.3 156
8.36.2-4 242 n. 36
9.20.10 150 n. 5
9.30.3 269 n. 28
9.34.11 120
9.37.1 150 n. 5
9.40 272 n. 44
10.5.6 292 n. 12
10.11 292
10.22.1 271
10.23.3 212
10.35.8 188
11.10.2 282
11.10.5 282
11.18.4–8 296
11.23.1 126
11.33–34 242
11.39.14 195
12.18.3 212
12.25^b.2 69
12.25^e.7 73
12.25^h.2–3 73
12.25^i.2 73
12.26^e.3 73
12.27.4–6 73
12.27.4–5 71
12.28^a.3–4 73
13.63 269 n. 27
15.28.1 86
15.28.4 208
15.36 70 n. 22
15.36.1–9 69
15.36.3 69
16.17.8 152 n. 16
16.32.1 272 n. 44
18.7.3 178
18.9.2 178
18.44.2 106
18.51.10 207
20.5.4 269 n. 27
20.7.8 257

21.1.2 247 n. 67
21.6 139
21.17.12 100 n. 39, 237 n. 8
21.26.16 269
21.29.12 282
21.42.4–6 116
21.42.9 83
21.42.11–12 253
21.42.19 131, 173
21.43.13 109
21.45.7 139
21.45.12 216
22.8–9 111
22.13.2 187
23.14.12 152, 154 n. 24
25.3.4 130
26.1.11 134
27.13 207
27.13.2 178
27.19 119
28.1 119
28.9.4 269
28.9.5 237 n. 8
28.16.2 253
28.20.9 107 n. 97
29.9.12 269
29.27.1–10 127
29.27.9–10 207
29.27.11 167 n. a
30.7.9 237 n. 8
30.15 174
30.20.4 269 n. 28
30.25–26 117
30.25 126
30.25.8 171
30.25.13 126
31.1.6-8 225 n. 66
31.2.6 197
31.2.8–11 253
31.2.11 109, 265 n. 1, 294
31.11–15 265
31.11.1 265 n. 1
31.11.8–11 197
31.12.11 216
31.13.2 93
31.13.3 92–93, 110, 120 n. 28
31.14.4 172, 270
31.25.1 152
31.25.6–9 118

31.30.1–3 69
31.31.1 69
31.7.2–3 116
31.9 41, 44
31.9.3 186, 207
32.11.6 301
33.25.1–11 254
38.3.6 269 n. 28
38.3.9 269 n. 28
38.5–6 107

Polybios
frg. 162b 251 n. j

Ptolemy *Geographia*
4.5.11 260

Seneca the Elder *Suasoriae*
1.6 41

Sextus Empiricus
Adversus grammaticos
1.13 103

Sophocles
Ajax
374 156-57
465 152
744 27
Antigone
919 180 n. 51
960 87
Electra
446 153 n. 20
Oedipus Coloneus
1086 187
1634 153 n. 20
1717 180 n. 51
Oedipus Tyrannus
353 162
1231 152
1384 153 n. 20
Trachiniae
473 189 n. 23
989 210

Statius *Thebaid*
10.756–82 284

Strabo *Geography*
1.1.10 69

1.3.4   260
1.3.13   260
5.4.7   101
13.1.25   72
13.4.12   71
16.1.15   49
16.1.18   41
16.1.28   180
16.2.6   117
16.2.7   255
16.2.15   265
16.2.28   237
16.2.33   260
16.4.5   149
16.4.7   40 n. 6
17.1.24   217
17.1.41   217
61.2.20   201

Suetonius *Life of Vespasian*
4.5   127 n. 5

Tacitus
Annals
1.9   201
4.11   161
6.7   69
6.44   41
History
5.5   138
5.13   126 n. 3

Theophilus *Ad Autolycum*
2.36   187 n. 12

Thucydides
1.9   206 n. 4
1.22.4   71
1.70.9   236
1.138.5   116
2.34   261
3.45   295
4.59.4   27 n. 21
6.33   242
7.70.7   268 n. 17
7.75.7   181

Valerius Maximus
9:13   152
Facta et Dicta Memorabilia 9.2
Externa 6   255 n. 21

Vegetius *De re militari*
3.5

Virgil
Aeneid
3.1–68   171
6.644–50   247
12.216–94   259
Georgics
1.467–88   126 n. 4

Vitruvius
3.2.8   42

Xenophon
Anabasis
1.4.9   116

1.6.1   27 n. 21
1.8.17   177 n. 44
3.4.41   126
6.5.26   177 n. 44
Cyropaedia
1.4.27   216 n. 1
1.6.26   67
2.2.31   216 n. 1
3.3.58   177
7.1.10   177 n. 44
7.1.40   175
7.5.30   117
De equitandi ratione
11.8   85
Hellenica
2.4.33   257
4.3.19   257
7.1.16   211 n. 22
Hiero
10.5   172
Historia Graeca
4.8.27   103 n. 63
5.4.64   103 n. 63
Memorabilia
2.1.21-33   191 n. 34
2.2.3–4   161
3.3.12   172
Symposium
8:18   84 n. 40

2. Names

Abel, F.-M.
  14, 31, 33, 41, 52, 60,
  61, 66, 72, 96, 97, 125,
  138, 156, 194, 211, 210
  n. 18, 220, 239, 240,
  244, 245, 246, 257, 258,
  260, 267, 271, 272, 273,
  278, 281, 283, 291, 300
Aperghis, G. G.
  80
Arenhoevel, D.
  5, 15, 199–200
Avigad, N.
  130
Avi-Yonah, M.
  239, 240

Balch, D. L.
  267 n. 13
Barclay, J. M. G.
  15, 17, 191
Bar-Kochva, B.
  10, 105, 116, 119, 129–
  30, 139, 172, 173, 174,
  175, 176, 177, 179, 209,
  216, 217, 218, 221, 224,
  225, 226, 227, 228, 229,
  237, 239, 240, 241, 244,
  253–54, 258, 270, 272,
  275, 289, 294, 295, 297
Bartlett, J. R.
  12, 14
Baumgarten, J. M.
  106
ben David, C.
  238
Bengtson, H.
  260
Bergren, T. A.
  48, 52, 63
Bevan, E. R.
  134
Bévenot, H.
  15
Bickermann [Bickerman],
  E.
  1, 14–15, 18 n. 90, 24,
  28, 29, 31, 33, 39–40,

  62, 81, 85, 86, 96, 98,
  132, 134 n. 48, 135, 136,
  152, 224
Bringmann, K.
  17 n. 90, 29–30, 111,
  132, 138,
  139
Broshi, M.
  141
Brown, P.
  274
Büchler, A.
  5
Bückers, H.
  162
Bunge, J. G.
  1, 5, 53 n. 24, 62, 96,
  110, 138, 209, 224, 265,
  278
Burkert, Walter
  152

Chaniotis, A.
  109
Cohen, S. J. D.
  137, 190
Collins, J. J.
  61, 141
Cotton, H. M.
  90, 120
Cross, F. M.
  7

Davies, P. R.
  269
Delorme, J.
  103
Dexinger, F.
  134 n. 51
Dimant, D.
  26, 55, 56
Dommerhausen, W.
  15
von Dobbeler, Stephanie
  14 n. 68
Doran, R.
  2 n. 8, 16, 17, 134
Dorival, G.
  245
Drew-Bear, T.
  196 n. 76

Ekroth, G.
  152
Enermalm-Ogawa, A.
  50 n. 12
Eshel, E.
  141

Gauger, J.-D.
  188–89 n. 18
Gauthier, P.
  252
Gera, D.
  80–81, 90, 120, 125–26,
  132, 196, 224, 225, 239,
  240, 252–53
Geva, H.
  256
Ginzberg, L.
  210
Goldstein, J. A.
  1, 9, 24–25, 29, 31, 32,
  33, 40, 48, 51–52, 59,
  61, 62, 66, 67, 69, 72,
  81, 83, 86, 92, 93, 96,
  98, 106, 119, 128, 129,
  138, 165, 180 n. 50, 186,
  187, 192, 194, 195, 196,
  197 n. 87, 216, 219, 245,
  246–47, 248, 253, 258,
  260, 266, 267, 268, 270,
  273, 281, 283, 291, 293,
  300, 301
Goodman, M.
  289
Grabbe, L. L.
  18 n. 90, 29 n. 41
Grainger, J. D.
  270
Grimm, C. L. W.
  25, 26, 40, 42, 59, 60,
  71, 72, 97, 119, 128,
  130, 138, 154, 161, 179,
  206–7, 209, 210, 212,
  223, 236, 240, 242, 245,
  247, 255, 256, 260, 261,
  268, 281, 282, 283, 291,
  292, 294, 300
Gruen, E. S.
  13, 68, 110, 138, 190,
  191, 225

Haber, S.
  148–49
Habicht, C.
  1, 14, 24, 30, 31, 66, 72,
  96, 97, 104, 108, 110,
  117, 120, 128, 133, 138,
  165, 192, 193, 197, 206,
  219, 220, 223, 225, 227,
  228, 229, 238, 239, 240,
  244, 253, 257, 258, 267,
  268, 270, 271, 278, 297,
  300
Hanhart, R.
  19, 110, 220, 244, 252
Hanson, P. D.
  7
Haran, M.
  52, 63
Hartal, M.
  238
Harvey, G.
  300
Hayes, C. E.
  130
Heinemann, I.
  31
Hengel, M.
  240, 241
Herr, B.
  2
Herzfeld, E.
  186
Hodge, A. T.
  42
Holladay, C. R.
  43
Holladay, A. J.
  289
Hölscher, G.
  238
Honigman, S.
  24, 98
Horowitz, W.
  252–53

Jones, C. P.
  90
Jonnes, L.
  101, 102–3

Katz, P.
19, 86, 157, 271, 281
Kellermann, U.
162–63
Kennell, N. M.
97, 99, 105
Knox, B. M. W.
225
Kolbe, W.
227, 228–29

La'da, C. A.
24
Lange, A.
59 n. 6
Launey, M.
116
Laurentin, A.
28
Levine, L. I.
15–16
Lévy, I.
176, 245
Lichtenberger, H.
9
Lindenberger, J. M.
28 n. 29
Lüderitz, G.
237 n. 8

Ma, J.
93, 111, 116, 190, 195,
220, 248, 259
Ma'oz, Z. U.
238
Miller, P. D.
7
Mittag, P. F.
186, 187, 196, 221
Mittermann-Richert, U.
12
Moffat, J.
176
Mölleken, W.
266 n. 6, 275
Momigliano, A.
1, 10, 14, 62, 104, 176,
299, 300
Morgan, G.
127

Mørkholm, O.
93, 96, 98 n. 23, 102,
110, 129 n. 21, 134, 173,
227, 228–29, 253 n. 10,
265
Morrison, G.
118 n. 16, 120
Mugler, C, 6 n. 31

Nelis, J. T.
217
Nestle, E.
128
Nickelsburg, G. W. E.
11–12, 171 n. 3, 189
Nicklas, T.
4, 182, 187, 193
Niese, B, 1, 3, 240

O'Brien E.
246
Osterloh, K.
154
Otto, W.
36, 110

Parker, V. L.
192, 198
Porter, S. E.
27
Préaux, C.
24
Pritchett, W. K.
175, 211, 257

Rajak, T.
153
Richnow, W.
6
Rici, M.
101, 102–3
Rigsby, K. J.
83–84
Risberg, B.
212, 273, 282
Robert, L.
239
Röllig, W.
265
Rothschild, C. K.
70

Rubin, G.
166 n. 64
Rutherford, I.
99 n. 35

Scaer, P. J.
164
Schams, C.
151
Schmitz, B.
166 n. 65
Scholz, P.
102
Schorch, S.
59 n. 6
Schulthess, F.
281
Schwartz, D. R.
2, 3, 9, 10–11, 14, 16,
24, 26, 28 n. 29, 30 n.
43, 33, 40, 92, 116, 127,
128, 135 n. 54, 137, 138
n. 68, 150 n. 5, 155,
162–63, 174, 179, 186,
196, 208, 224, 237, 238,
239, 240, 241, 243 n. 42,
244, 245, 246 n. 59, 247,
256, 257, 258, 260, 261,
265, 270, 273, 278, 280
n. 10, 283, 289, 295,
296, 297, 300, 301
Scolnic, B. E.
267
Seyrig, H.
29
Sievers, J.
110–11
Sluys, D. M.
31, 40
Smith, D. E.
137
Stemberger, G.
162–63
Stern, M.
268, 270
Stewart, S.
71 n. 26
Strugnell, J.
225

Tarn, W. W.
186
Tcherikover, V. A.
99, 100, 117, 127, 135,
139, 192, 227, 265
Torrey, C. C.
26, 44 n. 29, 66
Turner, N.
33

Urman, D.
238

van der Spek, R.
100
van der Toorn, K.
49
van Henten, J. W.
2, 12, 15, 49, 134 n. 52,
151, 282, 284
Van Hook, L.
69
VanderKam, J. C.
137, 266 n. 5
Veïsse, A.-E.
200

Wacholder, B.-Z.
62
Walbank, F. W.
3, 80, 118–19, 253
Welles, C. B.
84, 155, 194. 221–22
White, J. L.
39–40
Wiedemann, T.
3
Wilhelm, A.
133, 224
Will, E.
82
Williams, D. S.
12
Wörrle, M.
120

Zambelli, M.
11, 229
Zeitlin, S.
15

Zollschan, L.T.
104
Zwick, R.
5–6, 12, 74

3. Greek Words

ἀβοήθητος
89
ἀγαθός
217
ἀγελαῖος
274
ἀγεληδόν
4, 89, 271, 274
ἀγερωχία
188
ἀγιασμός
281
ἅγιος
293
ἁγνίζω
51
ἀγνόημα
224
ἀγορανομία
80
ἀγορανόμος
80, 81
ἀγορασμός
178
ἀγριότης
294
ἀγροικότερος
290
ἀγυρολόγητος
216
ἀγωγή
105, 107, 138
ἀγών
272, 295
ἀγωνίζω
295
ἀγωνία
84, 85
ἀδεία
223
ἀδιαλείπτως
291

ἀενάου
4
ἀθέμιτος
152, 155. 211, 239
ἀθεσία
292
ἀθετέω
261
αἰκία
155, 164
αἰκίζομαι
155
αἰκισμός
175
αἴτιος
255
αἰχμαλωσία
180
ἀκληρέω
268, 269
ἀκμή
30
ἀκοή
301
ἀκολούθως
153
ἄκρα
296
ἄκρατος
301
ἀλαζονεία
188, 290
ἀλάστωρ
156
ἀλιτήριος
255
ἀλκή
223
ἀλλοφυλισμός
106
ἀλλόφυλος
103, 106
ἀλογέω
242, 283
ἀλογιστία
268, 269
ἀμίαντος
281
ἀμιξια
266

ἀναβίωσις
157, 165
ἀναγκάζω
133, 155, 219
ἀνάγκη
289
ἀναγνεία
164
ἀναγράφω
99
ἀναδείκνυμι
190, 195, 270
ἀναζεύγνυμι
261
ἀνακοινόω
273
ἀνακομίζω
200
ἀναστροφή
128
ἀνδραγαθέω
67
ἀνδραγαθία
272, 284, 293
ἀνδρωδῶς
284
ἄνοια
17, 297
ἀντιλαμβάνω
271
ἀντιλήμψις
223, 291
Ἀτιοχεύς
98, 108
ἀξιόω
174
ἀορασία
211
ἀπευθανατίζω
154
ἁπλῶς
136
ἀπογραφή
55
ἀποδέχομαι
88, 260
ἀποκαθίστημι
222
ἀπολείπω
116

ἀπολύω
154, 157, 242
ἀπονοέω
259
ἀπόνοια
154
ἀποσκευή
231
ἀπροσδεής
280
ἀπροσδοκήτως
244
ἀρετή
155
ἁρμόζω
273
ἀρρενωδῶς
211
ἀρχή
127
ἀρχηγέτης
73
ἀρχιτέκτων
73
ἀσεβέω
107
ἀσκέω
290
ἀτάραχος
221
ἄτοπος
273
ἄτρωτος
210
αὐθαίρετος
152
αὐστηρία
279
αὐτός
97
ἀφαιρέω
269
ἀφειδῶς
129
ἀφίστημι
31
ἄφνω
87

βάρβαρος
68, 115

βαρβαρόω
255

βασανίζω
51

βασιλεία
278

βασίλειον
51

βασιλικόν
84

βεβηλόω
130

βέβηλος
163

βῆμα
261

βιβρώσκω
58

βλάπτω
242

βλασφημέω
239

βοάω
171

βοήθεια
176, 180, 291

βοήθημα
291

βοηθός
89, 291

βραχίων
295

βυθίζω
236

βωμός
66, 255

γάρ
60

γενναῖος
154, 256, 279, 283, 293

γένος
43, 134, 163

γερουσία
219, 223, 256

Γερρηνοί
260

γέρων
133

γεῦμα
257

γνῶσις
154

γοητεία
242

γραμματεύς
151

γυμνάζω
208

δαίμων
217

δεινάζω
260

δεξιά
222, 258

δέος
241, 295

δεσπόζω
285

δεσπότης
295

δημιουργός
91, 161

δήμιος
161

δῆμος
108, 219, 225, 228

δημόσιος
149

διαβάλλω
278

διαγινώσκω
290

διαθήκη
162

διαίτημα
224

διακομίζω
93, 200

διαλάσσω
154

διαρρυθμίζω
159

διαστέλλω
261, 279

διάφορον
81, 115

διαφύλασσω
295

διεξάγω
207

διήγησις
149

δίφραξ
273

δίφρος
273

διωγμός
242

δοξα
266, 290

δοριάλωτος
129, 226

δύναμις
188

δυνάστης
87, 239, 290, 295

δυσπέτημα
4

δυσπολιόρκητος
241

δυσσέβεια
180

δυσσέβημα
236

δυσσεβής
83, 180, 189, 236, 296

δυσφορέω
260, 279

δυσχερής
135, 194

δυσχέρεια
71

ἐάω
236

ἑβδομάς
290

ἐγκαλέω
128

ἐθισμός
105

ἔθνος
61, 219, 271

ἔθος
222

εἰρήνη
24, 25

εἰσκυκλέω
69

εἰσφέρω
282

ἐκβράζω
40, 128

ἐκλεκτός
50

ἐκλύω
257

ἐκπηδάω
84

ἐκρίπτω
173

ἐκφεύγω
194

ἐλεέω
171

ἔλεος
161

ἐλεφαντάρχης
270

Ἑλληνικός
67, 138

Ἑλληνισμός
67

ἐμπαιγμός
156

ἐμπαίζω
175

ἐμφανίζω
223

ἔμφασις
82

ἐμφανισμός
82

ἐμφέρω
293

ἐνέργεια
87

ἐνσείω
92, 239, 284

ἐντυγχάνω
70

ἐξαιρέω
62

ἐξαίρω
173

ἐξαποστέλλω
279

ἐξευρίσκω
160

ἑξῆς
156

ἐξιλασμός
248

ἐξομολογέομαι
178

ἐξοπλισία
132

ἐξουσία
87

ἐπαναιρέω
265

ἐπανδρόω
293

ἐπανορθόω
131

ἐπίβουλος
120, 278

ἐπιδέχομαι
236

ἐπιδίδωμι
219

ἐπιείκεια
68

ἐπίκαιρος
171

ἐπικάλω
88

ἐπικαλέω
295

ἐπίκλησις
295

ἐπινεύω
102, 218

ἐπινίκια
180

ἐπισείω
91, 92

ἐπιστάτης
81

ἐπίσκεψις
84

ἐπιστάτης
132

ἐπιτελέω
290

ἐπιτέμνω
73

ἐπιτερπής
301

ἐπιτομή
73

ἐπίτροπος
244, 253

ἐπιχορηγέω
106

ἐπιφαίνω
292

ἐπιφάνεια
66, 67, 87, 241, 292

ἐπιφανής
67, 280, 297

ἐπίχειρος
297

ἐπόπτης
88, 241

ἔρημος
180

ἐρρῶσθαι
39, 221

ἐρυμνότης
239

ἐφάπτω
155

ἐφοράω
157

ἔτοιμος
155

εὐανδρία
172

εὐδοκέω
281

εὐεργεσία
149, 195, 212

εὐεργέτης
92

εὐημερηκώς
4

εὐημερία
127

εὐθίκτος
301

εὐλογέω
178, 297

εὐκλεία
152

εὐκοπία
70

εὐλαβέομαι
150, 175

εὐλαβῶς
150

εὐμένεια
154

εὔνοια
195, 220, 243, 282 295

εὐρώστως
208

εὐσέβεια
78, 83

εὐσταθέω
273

εὔχομαι
193

εὐψυχία
159, 272

ἐφοδεύω
82

ἔφοδος
126

ἐφοράω
51, 290

εὐχρηστία
238

ἕως
150

Ζεὺς Ἑλληνίος
134

ζηλόω
92

ζωγραφέω
72

ζωή
157

ἡγέομαι
271

ἡλικία
295

ἡσυχάζω
236

ἥττων
259

θαλλός
268

θέμις
136, 152

Θεόδοτος
272

θεομαχέω
6

θεός
50

θεωρός
108

θηριώδης
211, 239

θλίψις
27, 28

θραύω
293

θυμός
115, 187. 210

θυσία ἐγκαινισμοῦ
58

ἴδιος
221, 223

ἱεράτευμα
61

ἱερατεύω
266

ἱερόν
84, 293

ἱερός
41, 66

ἱεροσύλημα
119

ἱέρωμα
245

ἱκετεία
246

ἱλασμός
88

ἵλεως
68

Ἰουδαισμός
67

Ἰουδαῖος
24, 137, 190, 191

ἵππος
209

ἰσόθεος
189

ἴσος
190

καθιάζω
51

καθαρισμός
52

καθήκω
136, 280
καιρός
268, 300
κακία
4
κακολογέω
88, 91
κακοπάθεια
71
κακός
91
κακουργία
88, 91
καρδία
295
καρτερέω
158
καταβολή
72
κατάκοπος
244
κατακρημνίζω
239
καταλαμβάνω
284
καταλλάσσω
2
καταπειράζω
257
καταπλήσσω
295
καταπορεύομαι
223
κατατολμάω
130
κατέρχομαι
223
κατευθικτέω
284
κατηγορέω
208
κεραυνός
210
κηδεμών
92
κληρονομέω
61
κληρονομία
61

κοινός
291
κοινωνέω
273
κομίζω
255
κρατέω
115, 256, 300
κρατός
216, 243
κρεμάζω
149
κρίνω
256, 293, 294
κρίσις
163, 191
κτίστης
49, 256
κύριος
50

λαός
61, 271
λεηλατέω
68
λειτουργία
106
λεοντηδόν
4, 218
λήγω
188, 191
λιτανεία
208
λογισμός
159
λυσιτέλεια
71

μακαριστός
160
Μακκαβαῖος
199
μακροθυμέω
178
μακροτονέω
178
Ματταθίας
272
μεγαλαυχέω
297

μέγιστος
66, 88
μεθίστημι
104
μέθοδος
257
μέλλω
165
μέμφομαι
57
μέρις
50, 271
μεταβαίνω
153
μετάθεσις
222
μεταλαμβάνω
237, 241
μεταλλάσσω
155, 158
μετατίθημι
160, 222
μετάφρασις
73
μετεωρίζω
130, 161
μετεωρισμός
131
μιαρός
161, 296
μιερός
107, 161, 163
μιμνήσκω
171
μισοπονηρέω
120
μισοπονηρία
78
μνημόνυσον
155
μολύνω
267
μολυσμός
133, 266
μόνος
50
μόρος
196
μυσάρχης
132

μύσος
152

ναός
293
νεώς
133, 260
νομή
130
νόμιμος
104, 222
νομός
130
νόμος
130
νομοφύλαξ
109

ξενίζω
135
ξυστός
102, 105

ὁδός
180
οἰκητήριον
216
οἶκος
281
οἰκτείρω
171
οἰωνόβρωτος
4, 297
ὁμοεθνής
236, 282
ὁμοφῦλος
103
ὁμόψηφος
273
ὅμως
71
ὁπλολογέω
178, 179
ὄπνεον
297
οὐρανός
61, 66
ὀχύρωμα
208, 209

ὄψις
88

παγκρατής
87

παιάν
244

παιδεία
150, 153, 164, 208, 290

παιδεύομαι
150

παμμιγής
239

πάμφυλος
239

πάνδημον
85

πανεπόπτης
88

παντοκράτωρ
49, 87, 131, 153, 291
297

πάνυ
255

παραδοξάζω
87

παραίτιος
220

παρακαλέω
156, 224, 256, 259, 293

παρακλείω
117, 258

παρακομίζω
188, 196

παραλαμβάνω
206

παροικέω
237

παράνομος
104

παρατάσσω
40, 244

παρενοχλέω
224

πάρερος
293

παροράω
131

παρόω
103

πάσχω
196

πατάσσω
187

πατήρ
282

πάτριος
155, 166

πείθω
160, 218

πέρας
128

περιάγω
118

περίβολος
41

περικομίζω
200

περίπατος
73

περιποιέω
294

περισπασμός
212

πέτασος
105

πίπτω
162

πλῆθος
219, 225, 228, 255

πνεῦμα
159

πολεμοτροφέω
208, 269

πολιά
292

πολιτεία
105

πολίτευμα
237

πολιτεύομαι
133, 137, 222

πολίτης
192

πολλάκις
195

πολυπραγμονέω
73

πρᾶγμα
172, 220, 293

πραγματεία
73

πρεσβεία
104

πρεσβύτερος
179

πρό
156

προαίρεσις
195, 222

πρόδηλος
297

προδότης
208

προκαταλαμβάνω
212

προνοέω
269

πρόνοια
93

προοδηγός
244

προπέμπω
153

προπτύω
151

προσαγγελία
81

προσαναλέγω
175

προσβάλλω
238

προσδοκάω
291

προσευχή
247

προσεύχομαι
58, 247

προσπίπτω
174, 253, 279

προστάτης
79, 80

προτάσσω
290

προτομή
298

προχειρίζω
270

πρωταγονιστής
295, 298

Πρώταρχος
206

πρωτοκλισία
110

πύργος
209, 284

πυρόω
118

Ῥαξις
281

ῥύομαι
174

ῥωμαλέοι
4

σηκός
280, 281

σκέπη
129

σκηνῶσις
281

σπειρηδόν
126

σπέρμα
165

σπλαγχνισμός
137

στασιάζω
269

στιγμή
189

στοιχεῖον
159

στοιχείωσις
159

στράτευμα
256

στρατηγέω
279

στρατήγημα
279

στρατηγός
207, 243

στρατιά
241

συγγένεια
129

συγγενής
216

συγγνώμη
273
συγκεραυνόω
44
συγχύω
259
συγχωρέω
219, 225
συλλύω
219, 259
συμβαίνω
79, 155
συμβάλλω
272
συμμαχία
15
σύμμαχος
178, 218
συμμίγνυμι
254, 294
συμμίσγω
272
συμμισοπονηρέω
4, 118
συμπεριφερέω
196
συμποσίαρχος
71
συμφλογίζω
149
συνάγω
175
συνακολουθέω
57
συνεγγίζω
210
συνευδοκέω
222
συνθήκη
235, 259, 261, 273
συνιστάω
195, 291
συνοράω
68, 92, 172, 279, 294
σύνταξις
301
συντελέω
236
συντέμνω
206
συντηρέω
91

συντρίβω
243
σύντροφος
196
συριακός
298
σύστημα
171, 292
σχοῖνος
217
σῶμα
174, 242
σωτηρία
160, 254, 267

ταξις
47, 258
ταραχή
221, 295
τελείωσις
58, 59
τελευτή
206
τέλος
257
τέμενος
41
τερατοποιός
294
τήγανον
156
τηρέω
89
τιμάω
84
τιτρώσκω
218
τοιγαροῦν
159
τόπος
79, 84, 195, 240, 260
τρισαλιτήριος
173
τρόπαιον
291
τύμπανον
152, 154

ὑγιαίνω
39, 192, 225, 229

ὕλη
69
ὕμνος
244, 295
ὑπενάντιος
293
ὑπεραίρω
132
ὑπερηφανία
131, 163
ὑπεροχή
292
ὑπογραμμός
72
ὑπογράφω
72
ὑποκρίνομαι
132
ὑπονοθεύω
96, 115
ὑποτάσσω
105
ὑποφέρω
154
ὕψιστος
88

φαίνω
89, 239
φανερός
297
φαντασία
272, 273
φέρω
163
φυγαδεύω
271
φεύγω
128
φιλάδελφος
292
φιλανθρωπέω
260
φιλανθρωπία
153, 269
φιλάνθρωπος
103
φιλία
15, 152
φιλοπολίτης
282, 292

φιλοστοργία
152, 194
φιλόστοργος
194
φιλοτίμως
67
φόβος
241, 295
φόρος
180
φρικασμός
89
φρονέω
278
φροντίζω
69
φυγαδεύω
127
φυλάρχης
179
φυλή
79

χαίρω
24, 25, 39, 191, 192
χαρακτήρ
103
χάραξ
239
χάρις
193
χαριστήριον
247
χειρόω
117
χορηγός
49
χορηγέω
50
χορηγία
106
χρεία
245, 295
χρῆμα
115
χρηματισμός
219
χωρέω
261, 300

ψήφισμα
138
ψυχαγωγία
69, 70, 89

ὠότης
237
ὡς ἄν
40
ὠφέλεια
69

4. Subjects

Abraham, 50
altar
    behavior at, 210, 255
    fire on, 51
    of incense, 56, 63
    language of, 66, 200,
        255
angel, 85, 190, 210, 217–
    18, 195
anger, of God 68, 130–31,
    150, 160, 162–64,
    175, 178, 181, 254

blasphemy, 68, 118, 171,
    175, 201, 211, 240,
    248, 295
burial, 196, 245, 255

circumcision, 148–49, 164
covenant
    author's emphasis on,
        56, 57
    breaking of, 141
    and circumcision, 149,
        158
    and death of seven
        brothers, 163
    depiction of, 103
    language of, 174
    as theme of letter,
        25–26, 27, 37

David, 63, 177, 178
Dionysus, 50, 137–38, 149
    n. 4, 201, 280
    temple to, 10, 67, 221,
        292

Divine Warrior, 12, 44,
    198, 202

elephant, 216, 253–54,
    257, 259, 265, 270,
    294
epiphany
    of Artemis, 34
    first, 85–87
    implications of, 217,
        241, 295
    language of, 271, 280
    second, 210–11
    as theme, 66–67, 212
exile, 48, 51, 53, 56, 117,
    127, 223

festival
    Booths, 33
    Hanukkah, 2, 14, 275,
        298–99
    Nikanor, 10, 12, 275,
        285
    Purim, 34, 35
    Sukkoth, 35, 46 n. a, 52,
        58, 62
    Weeks, 243
fire
    of altar, 48–53, 56, 63
    as holy, 200, 255
    in Jerusalem, 31–32
    and purification, 245
    and Rhazis, 283
    in worship, 58–60
Friends of the King, 116,
    120, 160, 172, 179,
    196, 207, 269

gender, 85, 241
gymnasium
    in Jerusalem, 96–97,
        101–3, 105–7, 110–
        11
    as location, 151
    as non-Jewish, 13,
        16–17, 153, 157, 122

high priest
    anointment, 43
    language for, 81, 106,
        266

role of, 5, 49, 116–17
    significance of, 78,
        88–89
humor, 64, 89, 90, 137,
    160, 191
hymn, 212, 244, 175, 295

ingathering, 50–51, 52, 54
    n. d, 57, 61–62

Jason of Cyrene, 5–6, 9,
    11, 74, 164, 165, 219
Jerusalem
    Akra in, 105
    "Antiochenes in Jerusa-
        lem," 96–101, 108
    factionalism in, 114
    gates of, 31–32
    gymnasium in, 96–97,
        101–3, 105–7, 110–
        11
    library in, 60
    market in, 80
    as place of composition,
        15–16
    as polis, 99–102, 110–11
    population of, 129–30,
        139
    See also temple
Jesus, 92, 173, 182, 210,
    218

magic, 242
martyrdom
    language of, 131
    portrayal of, 151, 155,
        162, 164–66, 175
    reasons for, 136, 283
    role within narrative, 3,
        150 n. 5
    as theme of letters, 2,
        296
Master, 131, 159, 243, 285,
    286 n. a, 290, 295,
    296
mercy (of God)
    absence of, 189
    call for, 256
    in covenant relation-
        ship, 27

language of, 210
results of, 63, 218, 171,
    178
and seven brothers,
    160–64
after wrath, 68, 130,
    150
Moses, 53, 56–58, 63, 161
mourning, 85, 118, 210

noble death, 156, 159,
    164–65, 283, 284–85

oath, 160, 259, 280

polis
    creation of, 218–19
    and gymnasium, 97
    Jerusalem as, 99–102,
        110–11
    membership of, 192
    nature of, 98, 105
pollution
    of enemy, 107–8, 130,
        162, 163, 198, 297
    of individuals, 152
    Jerusalem, 189
    as theme, 133
    time of, 133–34
    See also purification;
        temple
portent, 126–27
prayer
    for aid, 32, 170–71, 217,
        294–95
    for the dead, 246–47
    and fire, 58
    form, 280
    language for, 28, 88,
        193, 201, 247, 256,
        295
    within narrative struc-
        ture, 37, 49–53, 181
    portrayal of, 202, 209,
        236, 255
    by Rhazis, 285
    by seventh brother, 85,
        280, 292
    after victory, 162, 297
prophet, 55, 59–60, 209,
    291

prostitution, 135
providence, 269
punishment
    as appropriate, 68, 121, 128, 180–81, 188, 255, 297
    of curiosity, 57, 63
    after death, 153, 157, 158
    discipline as, 150
    effects of, 188
    in epiphany, 85–86
    flight as, 133
    language of, 42
    as narrative focus, 7, 12, 44, 57, 117, 261
    nature of, 211
    reasons for, 161, 189, 198.
Purification
    celebration of, 52, 62, 66
    effect of, 248
    language of, 51–52, 246
    process, 244–46
    reasons for, 130
    and Rhazis, 284–85
    and seven brothers, 163–64
    of temple, 61, 136, 201

resurrection, 1, 4, 11, 156, 165–66, 246
rhetoric
    in letters, 35, 37, 53, 191–92
    and magic, 242
    and purpose of author, 69–71, 275, 296, 298

and shaping of narrative, 3–4, 10, 164, 181–82
Ritual
    author's attitude to, 63
    before battle, 175
    Dionysiac, 138
    forms, 32–33
    language and, 209
    of mourning, 210
    Rhazis's actions as, 284
    secret, 149
    as subject matter, 34
    utensils of, 56
    and worship, 58–59

Sabbath
    celebration of, 201, 244–45
    as identity marker, 136, 149
    Jesus on, 131 n. 28
    status of, 17, 178, 289, 290
sacrifice
    communal, 246
    at games, 108
    language for, 201
    pagan, 137
    payment for, 81, 136
    and peace settlement, 259
    performance of, 32, 58–59, 88, 152
    significance of, 50–51
salvation, 12, 282
slavery
    cost, 174
    after defeat, 129

enslavement, 181, 208
and Jewish identity, 68
language for, 174, 242
and portrayal of Nikanor, 180, 189
Solomon, 27, 56, 58, 63, 108
song, 156, 244
suffering
    language for, 196, 198
    within narrative structure, 189, 282
    in present, 154, 162, 164
    of Samaritans, 134
    of seven brothers, 157

temple
    architecture, 41–42
    to Artemis, 34
    building of, 48
    commemoration of, 34, 299
    contents, 56–57, 63, 116, 119
    continuity of, 49, 52–53, 56, 63
    defense of, 85–87, 89–90, 92, 131, 262
    defilement, 135–36, 163, 189, 266
    of Dionysos, 10, 67, 221, 292
    at Elymais, 41, 44
    at Heliopolis, 36 n. 67, 41
    honoring of, 60, 79, 260, 290
    language of, 66, 88, 134

200, 270–71, 280, 281, 293
    at Leontopolis, 36–37
    as location, 44–45, 297
    of Nanaia, 41, 45
    at Persepolis 41
    personnel, 81
    plundering of, 119, 121, 130, 186
    purity of, 61, 66, 107, 131, 133, 164, 177, 198–202
    role in narrative, 2, 9, 74, 209
    in structure of work, 7, 9–10, 12, 262, 285, 298, 300
    threat to, 67, 279–80
    treasury, 81–83, 131
    of Zeus, 108, 134
traitor. See treachery
treachery
    of Jason, 13, 28
    of Menelaus, 13, 117, 139
    as nature of attack, 119
    of Nikanor, 274, 275
    of Rhodokos, 258
    term, 106, 127, 207
    as theme, 212
    of Tryphon, 30

wilderness, 57, 132–33, 149
wine, 71, 301

Zeus, 6, 44, 90, 108, 134–35, 177, 187, 211

359

Designer's Notes

In the design of the visual aspects of *Hermeneia,* consideration has been given to relating the form to the content by symbolic means.

The letters of the logotype *Hermeneia* are a fusion of forms alluding simultaneously to Hebrew (dotted vowel markings) and Greek (geometric round shapes) letter forms. In their modern treatment they remind us of the electronic age as well, the vantage point from which this investigation of the past begins.

The Lion of Judah used as visual identification for the series is based on the Seal of Shema. The version for *Hermeneia* is again a fusion of Hebrew calligraphic forms, especially the legs of the lion, and Greek elements characterized by the geometric. In the sequence of arcs, which can be understood as scroll-like images, the first is the lion's mouth. It is reasserted and accelerated in the whorl and returns in the aggressively arched tail: tradition is passed from one age to the next, rediscovered and re-formed.

"Who is worthy to open the scroll and break its seals. . . ."

Then one of the elders said to me
"weep not; lo, the Lion of the tribe of David,
the Root of David, has conquered,
so that he can open the scroll and
its seven seals."

Rev. 5:2, 5

To celebrate the signal achievement in biblical scholarship which *Hermeneia* represents, the entire series will by its color constitute a signal on the theologian's bookshelf: the Old Testament will be bound in yellow and the New Testament in red, traceable to a commonly used color coding for synagogue and church in medieval painting; in pure color terms, varying degrees of intensity of the warm segment of the color spectrum. The colors interpenetrate when the binding color for the Old Testament is used to imprint volumes from the New and vice versa.

Wherever possible, a photograph of the oldest extant manuscript, or a historically significant document pertaining to the biblical sources, will be displayed on the end papers of each volume to give a feel for the tangible reality and beauty of the source material.

The title-page motifs are expressive derivations from the Hermeneia logotype, repeated seven times to form a matrix and debossed on the cover of each volume. These sifted-out elements will be seen to be in their exact positions within the parent matrix.

Horizontal markings at gradated levels on the spine will assist in grouping the volumes according to these conventional categories.

The type has been set with unjustified right margins so as to preserve the internal consistency of word spacing. This is a major factor in both legibility and aesthetic quality; the resultant uneven line endings are only slight impairments to legibility by comparison. In this respect the type resembles the handwritten manuscripts where the quality of the calligraphic writing is dependent on establishing and holding to integral spacing patterns.

All of the type faces in common use today have been designed between AD 1500 and the present. For the biblical text a face was chosen which does not arbitrarily date the text, but rather one which is uncompromisingly modern and unembellished so that its feel is of the universal. The type style is Univers 65 by Adrian Frutiger.

The expository texts and footnotes are set in Baskerville, chosen for its compatibility with the many brief Greek and Hebrew insertions. The double-column format and the shorter line length facilitate speed reading and the wide margins to the left of footnotes provide for the scholar's own notations.

Kenneth Hiebert

Category of biblical writing,
key symbolic characteristic,
and volumes so identified.

1
Law
(boundaries described)
  Genesis
  Exodus
  Leviticus
  Numbers
  Deuteronomy

2
History
(trek through time and space)
  Joshua
  Judges
  Ruth
  1 Samuel
  2 Samuel
  1 Kings
  2 Kings
  1 Chronicles
  2 Chronicles
  Ezra
  Nehemiah
  Esther

3
Poetry
(lyric emotional expression)
  Job
  Psalms
  Proverbs
  Ecclesiastes
  Song of Songs

4
Prophets
(inspired seers)
  Isaiah
  Jeremiah
  Lamentations
  Ezekiel
  Daniel
  Hosea
  Joel
  Amos
  Obadiah
  Jonah
  Micah
  Nahum
  Habakkuk
  Zephaniah
  Haggai
  Zechariah
  Malachi

5
New Testament Narrative
(focus on One)
  Matthew
  Mark
  Luke
  John
  Acts

6
Epistles
(directed instruction)
  Romans
  1 Corinthians
  2 Corinthians
  Galatians
  Ephesians
  Philippians
  Colossians
  1 Thessalonians
  2 Thessalonians
  1 Timothy
  2 Timothy
  Titus
  Philemon
  Hebrews
  James
  1 Peter
  2 Peter
  1 John
  2 John
  3 John
  Jude

7
Apocalypse
(vision of the future)
  Revelation

8
Extracanonical Writings
(peripheral records)

ΡΑΙΟ ΕΚΙΖΟΜΕΝΟΥΟ ΕΙΟ ΕΑΥΤω
ΓΕΝΟΜΕΝΟΟ ΠΡΗΓΟΡΟΟ ΕΙΠΕ
ΜΕΛΛΕΙΟ ΕΡΩΤΑΝ ΚΑΙ ΚΙΑ ΠΟΛΗ·
ΗΛΙΚΩΝ ΕΤΟΙΜΟΙ ΓΑΡ ΑΠΟ ΘΝΗ
ΟΚΕΙΝ ΕΟΜΕΝ Η ΠΑΤΡΩΟΥΟ
ΝΟΜΟΥΟ ΠΑΡΑΒΑΙΝΕΙΝ·
Ο ΚΟΥΜΟΟ ΔΕ ΓΕΝΟΜΕΝΟΟ Ο
ΒΑΟΙΛΕΥΟ ΠΡΟΟΕΤΑΞΕΝ ΤΗ ΓΛΑΝ
ΚΑΙ ΔΕΙΝ ΤΑΟ ΕΚΠΥΡΟΥΝ ΤΩΝ ΤΕ
ΠΑΡΑΧΡΗΜΑ ΕΚΠΥΡΩΘΕΝ ΤΩΝ
ΤΟ ΓΕΝΟΜΕΝΟΝ ΑΥΤΩΝ ΠΡΩΝ
ΓΟΡΟΝ ΠΡΟΟΕΤΑΞΕΝ ΓΛΩΟΟΟΠ
ΜΕΙΝ ΚΑΙ ΠΕΡΙΟΚΥΘΟΙΟΑΝΤΑΟ
ΑΚΡΩΤΗΡΙΑΖΕΙΝ ΤΩΝ ΛΟΙΠΩΝ
ΑΔΕΛΦΩΝ ΚΑΙ ΤΗΟ ΜΡΟΟ ΥΝΟΡΩΝ
ΤΩΝ· ΑΧΡΗΟΤΟΝ ΑΒΑΥΤΟΝ ΤΟΙΟ
ΛΟΙΠΟΙΟ ΓΕΝΟΜΕΝΟΝ· ΕΚΕΛΕΥ
ΟΕΝ ΤΗ ΠΥΡΑ ΠΡΟΟΑΓΕΙΜΕΝΟ ΙΤΤΗ
ΚΑΙ ΤΗΓΑΝΙΖΕΙΝ·
ΗΟ ΔΕ ΑΤΜΙΔΟΟ ΦΙΚΑΜΟΝ ΔΙΑΔΥ
ΟΗΟ ΤΟΥ ΤΗΓΑΝΟΥ· ΑΛΛΗΛΟΥΟ
ΠΑΡΕΚΑΛΟΥΝ ΟΥΝ ΤΗ ΜΗΤΡΙ
ΓΕΝΝΑΙΩΟ ΤΕΛΕΥΤΑΝ ΛΕΓΟΝΤΕΟ
ΟΥΤΩΟ Ο ΚΟΟ ΟΟ ΕΦΟΡΑ ΚΑΙ ΤΑΙΟ
ΛΛΗΘΕΙΑΙΟ ΟΦΗ ΑΓΕΠΙ ΠΑΡΑΚΑΛΕΙ
ΤΑΙ ΚΑΘΑΠΕΡ ΔΙΑ ΤΗΟ ΚΑΤΑ ΠΡΟ
ΟΩΠΟΝ ΑΝΤΙ ΜΑΡΤΥΡΟΥΟΗΟ ΩΛΗ
ΛΕΟΑΦΗΟΕΝ ΛΦΘΗΟΛΕΟΤΩΝ·
ΚΑΙ ΟΙ ΠΟΙΟΥΛΟΥΛΟΙΟ ΑΥΤΟΥ ΠΑΡΑ
ΚΑΗΟΕΤΑΙ ΜΕΤΑΛΛΑΞΑΝ
ΠΡΟΟ ΑΟΤΟΥ ΠΡΩΤΟΥ ΤΟΝ ΤΡΟΠΟΝ
ΤΟΥΤΟΝ· ΤΟΝ ΑΕΥΤΕΡΟΝ ΗΓΟ·
ΕΠΙ ΤΟΝ ΕΑΙΟΜΟΝ· ΚΑΙ ΤΟΥ ΗΟ
ΚΕΦΑΛΗΟ ΔΑΟΡΜΑΟΥΝ ΤΑΙΟ ΘΡΙΞΙ
ΠΕΡΙΟΥΡΟΝΤΕΟ ΕΠΗΡΩΤΟΥΝ
ΕΙ ΦΑΓΕΟΑΙ ΠΡΟ ΤΟΥ ΤΙΜΩΡΗ
ΘΗΝΑΙ ΚΑΤΑ ΜΕΛΟΟ ΤΟ ΟΩΜΑ·
Ο ΔΕ ΑΠΟΚΡΙΘΕΙΟ ΤΗ ΠΑΤΡΙΩ ΦΩ
ΝΗ ΠΡΟΟΕΙΠΕΝ· ΟΥΧΙ ΕΛΕΓΕΡ
ΚΑΙ ΟΥΤΟΟ ΤΗΝ ΕΞΗΟ ΕΛΑΒΕΝ ΒΑ
ΟΑΝΟΝ ΩΟ Ο ΠΡΩΤΟΟ·
ΕΝ ΕΟΧΑΤΗ ΔΕ ΟΠΝΟΗ ΓΕΝΟΜΕΝΟΟ
ΕΙΠΕΝ· ΟΥ ΜΟΝΟΝ ΛΑΟΤΩΡΕΚ ΤΟΥ
ΠΑΡΟΝΤΟΟ ΗΜΑΟ ΖΗΝΑΠΟΛΥΕΙΟ
Ο ΔΕ ΤΟΥ ΚΟΟΜΟΥ ΒΑΟΙΛΕΥΟ ΑΠΟ
ΘΑΝΟΝΤΑΟ ΗΜΑΟ ΥΠΕΡ ΤΩΝ ΑΥ
ΤΟΥ ΝΟΜΙΩΝ ΕΙΟ ΑΙΩΝΙΟΝ ΗΜΑΟ
ΑΝΑΒΙΩΟΙΝ ΖΩΗΟ ΗΜΑΟ ΑΝΛΟΤΗ·

ΜΕΤΑ ΔΕ ΤΟΥΤΟΝ Ο ΤΡΙΤΟΟ ΕΝΕ
ΠΕΖΕΤΟ· ΚΑΙ ΤΗΝ ΓΛΩΟΟΑΝ
ΑΙΤΗΘΕΙΟ ΤΑΧΕΩΟ ΠΡΟΕΒΑ
ΛΕΝ· ΚΑΙ ΤΑΟ ΧΕΙΡΑΟ ΕΥΘΥ ΑΡΕ ΦΕ
ΠΡΟΟΤΕΙΝΕΝ ΚΑΙ ΓΕΝΝΑΙΩΟ ΕΙΠΕ
ΕΞ ΟΥΡΑΝΟΥ ΤΑΥΤΑ ΚΕ ΚΑΗΤΑΙ
ΚΑΙ ΔΙΑ ΤΟΥΟ ΑΥΤΟΥ ΝΟΜΟΥΟ ΥΠΕΡ
ΟΡΩ ΤΑΥΤΑ· ΚΑΙ ΠΑΡ ΑΥΤΟΥ ΤΑΥΤΑ
ΠΑΛΙΝ ΕΛΠΙΖΩ ΚΟΜΙΖΕΟΟΑΙ·
ΩΟΤΕ ΛΑΥΤΟΝ ΤΟΝ ΒΑΟΙΛΕΑ ΚΑΙ ΤΟΥ
ΟΥΝ ΑΥΤΩ ΕΚΠΛΗΟΟΕΟΘΕ ΤΗΝ ΤΟΥ
ΝΕΑΝΙΟΚΟΥ ΨΥΧΗΝ· ΩΟ ΕΝ ΟΥ
ΔΕΝΙ ΤΑΟ ΑΛΓΗΔΟΝΑΟ ΕΤΙΘΕΤΟ·
ΚΑΙ ΤΟΥΤΟΥ ΔΕ ΜΕΤΑΛΛΑΞΑΝΤΟΟ ΤΟΥ
ΤΕΤΑΡΤΟΝ ΩΟΑΥΤΩΟ ΕΒΑΟΑΝΙ
ΖΟΝ ΑΙΚΙΖΟΛΙΕΝΟΙ· ΚΑΙ ΓΕΝΟΛΙΕ
ΝΟΟ ΠΡΟΟ ΤΟΝ ΘΑΝΑΤΟΝ ΟΥΤΩΟ
ΕΦΗ· ΑΙΡΕΤΟΝ ΜΕΤΑΛΛΑΟΟΟΜ
ΤΑΧΑ ΠΟΛΛΩΝ ΤΑΟ ΥΠΟ ΤΟΥ ΟΥ
ΠΡΟΟΔΟΚΩΜΕΝ ΕΛΠΙΔΑΟ· ΠΑΛΙΝ ΑΝΑ
ΟΤΗΟΕΟΟΛΙΠ ΑΥΤΟΥ· ΟΟΙ ΜΕΝ ΓΑΡ
ΑΝΑΟΤΑΟΙΟ ΕΙΟ ΖΩΗΝ ΟΥΚ ΕΟΤΑΙ·
ΕΧΟΛΙΕΝΟΟ ΑΕΤΟ ΝΗΠΕΙΤΟΝ
ΠΡΟΟΑΓΟΝΤΩΟ ΕΠΗΚΙΖΟΝΤΟ·
Ο ΛΟΙΠΟΟ ΑΥΤΟΝ ΟΙΑΔΩΝ ΕΙΠΕΝ·
ΟΧΟΥΟΙΑ ΤΟΙΟ ΑΝΟΙΟ ΕΧΩΝ· ΟΘΕΝΑ
ΠΟΙΕΙΟ ΦΘΑΡΤΟΟ ΩΝ· ΛΙΠΑ ΟΚΕΙ
ΛΟΟ ΤΟ ΓΕΝΟΟ ΗΜΩΝ ΥΠΟ ΤΟΥ ΟΥ
ΚΑΤΑΛΕΑΟ ΙΟ ΘΟΛΙ· ΟΥ ΔΕ ΚΑΡΤΕΡΕΙ
ΚΑΙ Ο ΘΩ ΦΕΡΟΝ ΤΟΟ ΜΕΤΑ ΛΙ ΟΝ ΛΥΙΟΥ
ΚΡΑΤΟΟ· ΩΟ ΕΟΕ ΚΑΙ ΤΟΟ ΗΕΡΜΑΛΟΟ
ΚΑ ΟΑΠ ΛΕΙ· ΜΕΤΑ ΔΕ ΤΟΥΤΩ·
Η ΤΟΝ ΤΟΝ ΟΚ ΤΟΝ ΚΑΙ ΜΕ ΛΑΩΝ
ΑΗΔΩΟ ΗΝΟΚΙΤΕΦΗ ΜΗ ΠΑΛΗΝ
ΜΑΛΛΟΝ ΗΜΕΙΟ ΓΑΡ ΑΙ ΕΑΥΤΟΥΟ
ΤΑΥΤΑ ΠΑΟΧΟΜΕΝ ΑΜΑΡΤΟΝΤΕΟ
ΕΙΟ ΤΟΝ ΕΑΥΤΩΝ ΟΝ· ΑΞΙΑ ΘΑΥ
ΜΑΟΜΟΥ ΓΕΓΟΝΕΝ· ΕΙ ΔΕ ΜΗ ΝΟ
ΜΙΟΗΟ ΗΜΑΟ ΟΟ ΕΚ ΤΟΝ ΑΟΕΒΟΟΟΝ ΘΕΟΟΜ
ΧΕΙΝ ΕΝ ΧΕΙΡ ΗΕΛΘΙ·
ΥΠΕΡΑΓΟΝΤΟΟ ΔΕ ΛΕΠΙ ΜΗΤΤΙ ΓΑΡΧΟΝ
ΚΑΙ ΜΝΗΜΙΕ ΝΑ ΤΑΟ ΗΟΑΧΑΤΙΤΕ
ΑΠΟΛΛΥΜΕΝΟΥΟ ΥΙΟΥΟ ΕΝ ΤΑΟΗ
ΟΡΩΟΑΝ ΑΕΓ ΠΟΚΑΙΡΟΝ ΗΗΕΡΑΟ
ΕΥΨΥΧΩΟ ΟΟ ΦΕΡΕΝ ΔΙΑΤΑΟΤΟΝ
ΕΛΠΙΔΑΟ ΟΕ ΚΙΟ ΤΟΝ ΛΕΤΩΝ ΑΝΑΩΝ
ΠΑΡΕΚΑΛΕΙ ΤΗΝ ΠΑΤΡΙΩ ΕΙΟ ΦΩΝΗΙ
ΓΕΝΝΕΟ ΠΙΓΛΑΙΓΙΡΙΟ ΝΕ ΦΩΡΟΝΙ
ΛΙΛΑΤΙ· ΚΑΙ ΤΟΝ ΟΝ ΛΑΥΛΟΓΙΟΜΟΝΑΡΧΗ